The Last Stand of
CHINESE CONSERVATISM

THE LAST STAND OF
CHINESE CONSERVATISM

The T'ung-Chih Restoration, 1862–1874

Mary Clabaugh Wright

STANFORD UNIVERSITY PRESS • STANFORD, CALIFORNIA

Stanford Studies in History, Economics,
and Political Science, XIII

Stanford University Press, Stanford, California.
© 1957 by the Board of Trustees of the Leland
Stanford Junior University. Printed in the United
States of America by Stanford University Press.

Library of Congress Catalog Card Number: 57-5946

For Arthur Frederick Wright

ACKNOWLEDGMENTS

This whole book is a quite inadequate acknowledgment of my debt of gratitude to John King Fairbank, professor of history at Harvard University. First as a superb teacher and later as the most esteemed of colleagues, he has been unsparing of his time and energy in encouraging this study.

Many others have helped enormously in diverse ways. Arthur F. Wright and Chaoying Fang read the final manuscript with great care and offered valuable suggestions both on major points and on innumerable details; I am honored that the characters on the title page are in Mr. Fang's hand. Jesse G. Bell, Jr., of the Stanford University Press, not only edited the manuscript with rare thoroughness and perception but also helped clarify a dozen basic questions of substance.

As this work has proceeded over many years, I have benefited from discussions with scholars both here and abroad, a number of whom were kind enough to read and to comment with care on earlier versions of the manuscript. Among these were Masataka Banno, Knight Biggerstaff, Lienche Tu Fang, Chūzō Ichiko, Joseph Levenson, Marinius J. Meijer, Franz Michael, Benjamin Schwartz, Hellmut Wilhelm, and Lien-sheng Yang. I am especially indebted to Motonosuke Amano, Alexander Eckstein, and Bert F. Hoselitz for advice on the problems of economic history raised in Chapter VIII. I should also like to thank my colleagues on the staffs of the Chinese and Japanese Collections of the Hoover Library for their cheerful help whenever I have needed it, and in particular to express my appreciation to Marianna Olmstead for her patient assistance in the long and tiresome business of preparing the manuscript for the press.

For the time to do the research for this book, I am indebted to Radcliffe College, to the Board on Overseas Training and Research of the Ford Foundation, and to the Hoover Institute and Library. For financial assistance toward publication, I am indebted to the Stanford faculty committees on Supplementary Research Grants and on Publications, and to Charles Frederick Wright.

CONTENTS

CHAPTER   PAGE

I   INTRODUCTION   I

II   THE NEW ERA   11

The Crisis of 1859–61 · Ratification of the Tientsin Treaties · The Rise to Power of Prince Kung · The Suppression of the Tsai-yüan Conspiracy and the Consolidation of Prince Kung's Position · Foreign Reactions to the New Order

III   THE CO-OPERATIVE POLICY   21

The Relation of World Politics to Developments Within China · The Role of Great Britain · Policies of the Other Great Powers · The Sinicization of Foreign Diplomats in China · Chinese Reactions to the Co-operative Policy · Conclusion

IV   THE IDEA OF A RESTORATION   43

The Restoration Phase of the Dynastic Cycle · Earlier Restorations in Chinese History · The Application of the Term "Restoration" to the T'ung-chih Period · The Imperial Role · Manchu Interests and Chinese Interests · Regionalism and Centralism · The Philosophic Bases of Restoration Thought · The Concept of Social Stability · The Concept of Social Change · The General Program of the Restoration

V   THE RESTORATION OF CIVIL GOVERNMENT   68

The Use of Men · The General Character of the Restoration Bureaucracy · Leading Metropolitan Officials of the Restoration · Leading Provincial Officials of the Restoration · The Search for Talent · The Revival of the Examination System · Limitation of the Sale of Rank · Disciplining the Bureaucracy · The Attack on Corruption · The Rule of Avoidance · Specialization vs. Omnicompetence · The Yamen Clerks · Conclusion

VI   THE SUPPRESSION OF REBELLION   96

The General Problem · The Suppression of the Taiping Rebellion · The Suppression of the Nien-fei Rebellion · The Suppression of the Northwestern Moslem Rebellion · The Pacification of Yunnan · The Pacification of Local Revolt · First Steps Toward Reconstruction

VII   THE RE-ESTABLISHMENT OF LOCAL CONTROL   125

Sources of the Traditional Equilibrium · The Effort to Restore the Gentry's Function · The Revival of Scholarship and Learning · The Appeal to the People: Social Welfare Policies · The Web of Collective Responsibility · The Role of Law · Keystone of the System of Local Control: The Local Official · The Western Impact on Local Control

CHAPTER   PAGE

VIII   THE REHABILITATION OF THE CHINESE ECONOMY   148
       The Traditional Political Economy · Economic Collapse During the
       Hsien-feng Period, 1851–61 · The General Economic Program of the
       Restoration · Agrarian Policies · Restoration Attitudes Toward Tra-
       ditional Commerce · Policies Toward Economic Development · The
       Machinery of Public Finance · The Problem of Economic Stagnation

  IX   THE SELF-STRENGTHENING MOVEMENT   196
       Dimensions of the Problem · The Ch'ing Military System Before the
       Restoration · The Nationalization of the New Regional Armies ·
       The New Military Leadership · The Shortage of Competent Middle-
       Grade Officers · Troop Morale and Popular Support · The Abortive
       Effort to Reinvigorate the Regular Army · The Militia · Central
       Military Administration · Reduction in the Size of the Army · Mod-
       ernization of Armament · The Chinese Attitude Toward Foreign Mili-
       tary Aid · Conclusion

   X   THE MODERNIZATION OF CHINA'S SYSTEM
       OF FOREIGN RELATIONS   222
       The Traditional Chinese View of Foreign Policy · The Tsungli-
       yamen · Restoration Specialists in International Affairs · China's
       Acceptance of the Treaty System · The Inadequacy of Treaties in Rela-
       tions with Russia · The Introduction of International Law · The
       Advancement of Western Learning · The T'ung-wen kuan and the
       Modernization of Chinese Education · Conclusion

  XI   NEAR VICTORY AND DISASTER   251
       The First Effort at an Equal Treaty · The Three Interested Parties ·
       The Issues as the Foreigners Saw Them · Foreign Advice on the "Re-
       generation of China": The Wade-Hart Proposals · British Preparations
       for Treaty Revision · Chinese Preparations for Treaty Revision ·
       The Issues as the Chinese Saw Them · The Burlingame Mission ·
       The Negotiations for Treaty Revision · Terms of the Alcock Conven-
       tion · The Rejection of the Alcock Convention · The Tientsin Mas-
       sacre · The End of the Restoration

 XII   THE HERITAGE OF THE RESTORATION   300

       TABLE OF ABBREVIATIONS   313

       NOTES   315

       GLOSSARY OF CHARACTERS   397

       BIBLIOGRAPHY   401

       INDEX   415

The Last Stand of
CHINESE CONSERVATISM

CHAPTER I

INTRODUCTION

No one doubts that China was for millennia a remarkably stable and conservative country, and casual references to "Chinese conservatism" crop up in most discussions of recent and current Chinese affairs. One hears it said that this or that reform came to nothing because of the strength of "conservative forces"; that foreign powers, by supporting "conservative elements" with the aim of preserving order, have hindered progress and precipitated disorder; that superficial signs to the contrary, there remains in China a "latent conservatism" which could re-emerge with proper encouragement; and so forth.

"Chinese conservatism" is important not only to the study of modern China but also to the comparative study of politics, but the label is apt to be misleading. If "to conserve" means "to keep in safety from harm, decay or loss,"[1] then the series of stands taken by the officials and literati of the Chinese Empire to preserve the Confucian order in the nineteenth and twentieth centuries is certainly conservatism. But it is instructively different from the conservatism of the modern West.

Our political term "conservative" was coined in the wake of the French Revolution by Burke's admirers, men who sought to preserve the Christian, antirationalist, aristocratic, and feudal strains of pre-Enlightenment European society. Chinese conservatism, on the other hand, which took shape quite independently a few decades later in the wake of the Taiping Rebellion, aimed at the preservation of the Confucian, rationalist, gentry, and nonfeudal strains of pre-Taiping and pre-Opium War Chinese society. Chinese conservatives, unlike Chinese radicals, have not been interested in Western political and philosophic ideas.[a] When they have been interested in the West at all, their interest has been solely in terms of the famous formula: "Chinese learning as the basis; Western learning for practical use."[b] They did not read Burke.

The hallmarks of Western conservatism in the nineteenth and twentieth centuries are belief in a divine intent that governs history; a sense of sin; distrust

---

[1] Numbers refer to Notes (pp. 315–96), primarily citations of sources and relevant collateral material. Footnotes are designated by letters.

[a] It is true that since 1912 Chinese conservatives, under extreme pressure, have occasionally searched for Western authorities to prove that Confucius was right. This pathetic and absurd device is quite different, however, from an interest in Western conservatism itself.

[b] This formula was first given wide currency in the 1890's in Chang Chih-tung's "Exhortation to Learning," and much of the twentieth-century Chinese debate on China's future has centered upon it. On the origin and significance of the idea, see Hellmut Wilhelm, "The Problem of Within and Without, a Confucian Attempt in Syncretism," *Journal of the History of Ideas*, XII, 1 (1951), 48–60.

of reason and faith in "prescription and sound prejudice"; belief in the sacredness of private property; affection for parochial ways and distrust of cosmopolitanism.[2] By contrast, Chinese conservatism is the defense of a rational, cosmopolitan order, and to a great extent of the very "radical illusions"[3] that are anathema to Western conservatives: the belief that human history is part of a harmonious and rational natural order; willingness to subordinate private property to group interests; belief in man's innate goodness and his perfectibility through moral training; the honoring of custom not as a brake on reason but as the embodiment of reason; and the persistent ideal of the universal state.

The great common ground between European and Chinese conservatism is thus only the intent to conserve. Both systems honor established ways of doing things; both discourage sweeping innovation and recommend making small improvements slowly, with due weight to custom and habit. To the Chinese conservative the Confucian social order, the Confucian political system, and the Confucian ethic are of enduring value, true and right for all men in all ages.[c] They are basic principles, capable of slight adjustment to meet new circumstances but never to be weakened or altered.[4]

Modern Chinese conservatism begins with the mid-nineteenth century. Confucianism, in one form or another, had dominated earlier Ch'ing political thought as it had most of Chinese history, but its supporters became what may properly be called conservatives only after they had to defend their position against the Taiping Rebellion and against Western influence. For the first time their fundamental propositions concerning the nature of human life and society were no longer accepted as self-evident. Increasingly they had to argue their theoretical case and to search for new ways to prove its merits in the practical affairs of government. In time there developed a cleavage between the true Confucian conservatives, who cherished the Confucian order for its inherent qualities, and a series of opportunists who used the Confucian heritage either as a spur to Chinese nationalism or as a veil for fascism. In opportunist hands Confucianism was a dull spur, a thin veil, and became a laughing stock. The true Confucian conservative position is quite different.[d]

Modern Confucianism rests on the Doctrine of the Rites—the *li*, the "principles of social usage."[e] The *li* provide both canonical and customary sanction for proper behavior in the Confucian scheme of things, a stable yet flexible hierarchy

---

[c] Historically, Confucianism includes a number of different and sometimes opposing strains. In this book, by Confucianism I mean the Confucianism of the eclectic Neo-Sung revival, which has been dominant since the mid-nineteenth century.

[d] Discussion of modern Chinese political thought has been confused by the indiscriminate lumping together of all the opponents of Western liberalism and Marxism, from Tseng Kuo-fan to Ch'en Li-fu. The differences among the Chinese opponents of modernization are as important as those among its proponents.

[e] See Chapter IV.

in which ideally every human being understands his duties and his privileges and accepts them as a part of a rational and universal natural order. For three generations the primary aim of Chinese conservatism has been to preserve the *li,* the primary aim of Chinese radicalism to destroy them. Throughout his life Ch'en Tu-hsiu recognized this doctrine as the first enemy: from his early years as an Enlightenment liberal, through his leadership of the Chinese Communist Party, to the last decade of his life after his split with the Comintern, he never wavered in his opposition to the *li.[1]*

A Confucian society is of necessity an agrarian society: trade, industry, economic development in any form, are its enemies.[9] History is viewed as a cyclical sequence of constant renewals and adjustments within a fundamentally stable order where basic conflicts cannot develop. The goal of perfect harmony is to be reached by settling minor conflicts through compromise and concession. The elite are the literati, who guide social life and help it maintain its own natural course; they do not force, create, or innovate. They are neither fanatic propagandists, political organizers, aristocrats, priests, men of wealth, nor specialists in any line. They are the *chün-tzu*—men of superior moral and intellectual capacity and training, humanists and conservatives. As a leading Chinese anthropologist puts it:

> A man who sees the world only through human relations is inclined to be conservative, because in human relations the end is always mutual adjustment. And an adjusted equilibrium can only be founded on a stable and unchanging relation between man and nature. On the other hand, from the purely technical point of view, there are hardly any limits to man's control of nature. In emphasizing technical progress, one plunges into a struggle in which man's control over nature becomes ever changing, ever more efficient. Yet these technical changes may lead to conflict between man and man. The Chinese intelligentsia viewed the world humanistically. Lacking technical knowledge, they could not appreciate technical progress. And they saw no reason to wish to change man's relation to man.[5]

The peasant had a considerably more important place in the society of Chinese conservatives than in the society of European conservatives. In the first place, Chinese conservative leaders knew what it meant to say that agriculture was the

---

[1] In the year before his death, Ch'en wrote that his opposition to the line of the Third International was comparable to his opposition to the line of Sung Confucianism: both were dogmatic, unscientific, superstitious (letter of Jan. 19, 1941, *Ch'en Tu-hsiu ti tsui-hou chien-chieh,* Hongkong, 1950, pp. 30–31). A word of caution is needed here. Although in China both Confucianism and Communism have opposed and been opposed by liberal individualism, it would be as misleading to press the comparison as it would be to group Coleridge and Marx together on the ground that they both despised the utilitarians. Confucianism is authoritarianism sanctioned by the laws of history, and its elite avowedly acts on behalf of the people, but comparisons with Marxism should stop there. Confucianism's laws of history were of a totally different type, its autocracy differently constituted, its elite of a different character and different means of operation; and its people, with their different values, had different interests.

[9] See Chapter VIII.

basis of the state. The substantive problems of agriculture—both economic and technical—were a main concern of all statesmen. Moreover, although these men were landlords attending to their own interests, they were trained to consider the peasant's affairs a part of those interests. Confucian statesmen could not, like so many of their Western counterparts, content themselves with sentimental platitudes about the bliss of agrarian life and the peasant's immemorial wisdom while occupying themselves with commerce, industry, urban life, and international affairs. In the second place, according to Chinese conservative doctrine, the peasant was a rational and perfectible human being. The precepts that guided his conduct along accepted lines were rational precepts, and the privileges of his superiors were grounded on rational propositions. His expressions of disapproval were felt—officers were perennially cautioned to watch their conduct lest they give the peasant soldiers an excuse to jeer and gossip; local officials were regularly ordered to stop the people's tongue-wagging by correcting this or that malpractice.

The Chinese peasant was held to be innately good, not originally sinful.[h] Perhaps for this reason, there is in Chinese conservatism little of the fear of mass education that has obsessed Western conservatism. The Confucian limitation on education was economic; the sons of peasants could seldom be spared from the fields. It was not imagined that if the peasant learned to read he would be led astray, but rather that he would understand the Confucian teaching better and help to propagate it. If he had superior ability, it was confidently expected that he would become an official and not an iconoclast. In theory, the second highest office on earth was always open to him if by chance he had the necessary individual capacity, and the throne itself was open if the reigning Emperor forfeited his right to rule by violating the rational moral principles on which that right was based.[i]

Chinese conservative ideas about private property show no trace of the cardinal principle of Western conservatives, the idea that property is somehow sacred and inviolable. The Chinese gentry certainly had vested interests in land and found wealth agreeable; and as in Europe private property and the decentralization of authority that goes with it were regarded as important checks on the whims of an imperial autocrat, who might be tempted to abuse his power if it were greater. But in the Chinese conservative view, private wealth was, like everything else, part of the web of social responsibility. It did not confer "inherent

[h] He was not, however, the peasant of European romanticism, untainted by corrupting civilization, and hence the wellspring of a folk revival. He was good as all men are good, potentially capable of contributing to universal Confucian thought, to the universal Confucian arts and learning. If fundamentally he was no worse than other men, he was no better either.

[i] See Chapter IV.

rights"; it was properly subject to confiscation the moment it threatened social stability by contributing to unemployment, a price rise, a food shortage, or popular disapproval.

The character of Chinese conservatism has not, of course, remained constant during the tumultuous century in which it has striven to preserve, adjust, and restore the essentials of the Confucian way of life. Conservatives of the first generation were serene; they were certain that Confucianism was universal truth, that it would survive and flourish not only in China but by degrees throughout the world. Domestic rebellion and foreign aggression compelled them to examine and restate their case with a sharpness seldom to be found in pre-Taiping writings, but it did not cause them to doubt themselves. Although they differed over the best method of reaching the goals they held in common, there was not one who was not animated by the traditional values of the universal Confucian society; not one who did not see in Confucianism both the common heritage and the common future of mankind.

Conservatives of the second generation, as Joseph Levenson has so admirably shown,[6] had no such serenity. Haunted by doubts and buffeted by circumstances, they sought long and hard for a way to reconcile the Confucian principles to which they were emotionally committed with fundamentally hostile European ideas whose efficacy they now had to recognize. In the third generation the ranks split wide open, and as certainty had earlier given way to doubt, doubt now gave way to panic as China's continued decline foreshadowed her extinction. What was the proper path to a strong new China? The radicals—few in number—were for jettisoning the whole Confucian system; the conservatives clung to their hope of a Confucian revival.[7]

Chinese conservatives of the first generation were more self-confident than European conservatives have ever been, and they were able to test their principles more fully than has ever been possible in the Western world. Chinese conservatives of the third generation have been more frightened and demoralized than European conservatives have ever been, and with reason. No other group has ever been compelled within a single lifetime to face the loss not only of livelihood and self-respect but of every moral and social value. For the Confucian principles that they had thought universal were not religious principles, to which the believer might cling in his heart, but social principles, which could be preserved only in social use. They withered beyond recognition when they were harbored in secret or cherished in exile.

In these circumstances it is scarcely surprising that the conservative cries of protest in our time have been shrill and foolish; that a great and complicated political and social heritage has been reduced to an anticommunist slogan. In the twentieth-century West, creative vitality in the arts has been associated with social and political conservatism rather than with liberalism.[8] In China, by contrast, outstanding artists and writers have followed the liberal and radical political theorists in rejecting the mockery that has been made of Confucianism. And yet the break has not been complete; what has been so emphatically abjured is not wholly dead.

In all the social studies there is need for perennial vigilance in two directions: vigilance on the one hand against the "brick-by-brick" approach, against that default of the imagination which leads us to suppose that *all* phenomena are worth our attention, that sound research on *any* topic is a contribution to knowledge; that when the bricks are all assembled (some centuries hence), they will of themselves take the shape of a well-designed construction and not a rubble heap; and vigilance on the other hand against the "magic method" approach, against the conceit that we can concern ourselves solely with the formulation of general propositions and with debate over abstractions, that the specific phenomena are too numerous and tiresome for us to labor over, that the handling of specific data is something that is farmed out to helots, that our tentative sketch of the structure will suddenly take on substance when we blow it up by our special method.

This vigilance is particularly needed where studies of China are concerned. On the one hand, the field is so difficult, so fascinating, and so little known that any fragment we stumble across seems worth our attention. On the other hand, the field is so vast and the questions it raises are of such great theoretical and practical importance that it seems necessary to plunge quickly into the heart of the matter and to discuss *the* Chinese peasant, *the* Chinese mind, *the* Chinese business class, Chinese conservatism in general, the Chinese revolution in general, the modernization of China in general, Chinese society in general.

Academic works on China have generally gone to one or the other extreme. There are the proleptical remarks on one tiny facet of the history of one period, and there are the glittering one-package explanations of what makes China tick. Neither of these approaches can with safety be neglected, but for a great range of the most interesting problems, neither is practicable. Modern Chinese conservatism cannot be profitably discussed in purely general terms, for there is no escaping the tiresome necessity of finding out who the conservative leaders were, who supported them, what kind of society was their goal, what measures they took or advocated in every field of government, and with what result. Yet while these questions may seem limited and concrete, the answers to them, for any moment in time, ramify into a cross-section of the whole of Chinese society at that moment. The difficulties in getting at the character of Chinese conservatism at any moment are compounded when we come to the interpretation of modern Chinese conservatism as a whole. For these reasons I have chosen the T'ung-chih

Restoration of the 1860's[j] as a case study of more or less manageable proportions and yet one broad enough to illumine the general problem.

In 1860 the Chinese Empire and the traditional Chinese order seemed to be on the verge of collapse. The Imperial government appeared hopeless and demoralized in the face of domestic revolution and foreign invasion. For a decade the great Taiping Rebellion had disorganized the life of the richest and most populous provinces; in 1860, in a late renewal of vigor, it had swept up across the north China plain to threaten the capital itself. Simultaneously the British and French navies had brushed past the vaunted Taku defenses, and small foreign forces had defeated the Empire's finest troops under its most famed general, the Mongol Prince Seng-ko-lin-ch'in. Barbarian soldiers were roaming the streets of the capital, and the magnificent summer palace, the Yüan-ming yüan, lay in ruins. In an open confession of utter despair the Emperor and his court had fled to Jehol. He died there the following year, bringing to a fitting end one of the most melancholy decades in Chinese history.

There was a widespread feeling that the dynasty was toppling and that an age of anarchy was at hand. From a Chinese point of view this fate was not only inevitable but just, unless the Manchu ruling house and the Chinese governing class could between them perform a miracle: suppress revolution, check foreign aggression, and re-establish domestic order. What was required was not merely the restoration at the eleventh hour of effective government along traditional lines but the creation of new policies that could ward off *modern* domestic and foreign threats and yet preserve the Confucian society and its ideology.

In the 1860's the miracle seemed very nearly accomplished. The contrast between the Hsien-feng collapse of the 1850's and the T'ung-chih Restoration of the 1860's was striking. The upper classes, Chinese and Manchu, rallied around the lately discredited throne with virtually unanimous loyalty. Men of outstanding ability assumed the chief government posts. The recovery of the Taiping capital, Nanking, in 1864 marked the end of the only rebellion that threatened the existence of the state. By degrees the Nien-fei, Moslem, and other less serious rebellions were also suppressed. The size of the army was progressively reduced, and its efficiency increased. The rate of the land tax was reduced but total govern-

---

[j] The T'ung-chih reign (1862–74) was officially classified as a restoration (*chung-hsing*). I have accepted the traditional term but not the exact traditional dates. The dates of the accession and death of the T'ung-chih Emperor do not precisely delimit the restoration phase of the historic process. The Restoration was marked in the beginning by the signature of the Conventions of Peking in 1860, by the rise to power of Prince Kung and the founding of the Tsungli-yamen in 1861; by the turn of the tide against the Taiping Rebellion with the fall of Anking later the same year; and by the emergence of new civil and military leaders in both the capital and the provinces. The end of the Restoration was marked by the Tientsin Massacre and the rejection of the Alcock Convention in 1870, and successively in the course of the next few years by the deaths of Tseng Kuo-fan and Wen-hsiang, the first losses of territory to Japan, and the growing power of the Empress Dowager Tz'u-hsi.

ment revenues were increased. New lands were opened to cultivation and vigorous efforts were made to rehabilitate the devastated areas. The standards of the civil service were re-established, and once again learning and scholarship flourished. Chinese merchants gained on foreign merchants in the competition to handle China's increasing foreign trade and outstripped them in the coastal trade. Foreign troops were withdrawn, and foreign pressure and interference were less than during any other period in the whole history of China's modern international relations. The statesmen of the Restoration succeeded in grafting a modern foreign office, the Tsungli-yamen, onto the ancient bureaucracy, and in a matter of months its members became accomplished diplomats, maneuvering successfully with treaty terms and international law to gain advantages for China. They recognized that henceforth China could neither remain isolated from modern Western countries nor absorb them into a tributary system based on the universal moral dominion of the Middle Kingdom. They began to read foreign books and world news and to establish schools for teaching Western languages and Western sciences. And, as it happened, the decade of restoration in China coincided with the high tide of anti-imperialism in the West. Western governments, sick of China incidents, were now ready to support and defend the Chinese government in its great effort at conservative reconstruction.

There are three main reasons[k] for making a case study of the T'ung-chih Restoration:

(1) Its importance to the general interpretation of modern Chinese history. This last of the great restorations of Chinese history was at the same time the first, and the most nearly successful, of a series of efforts to modify the Chinese state to a point where it could function effectively in the modern world without revolutionary changes in traditional Chinese values or in the institutions that embodied them. Yet in China the treatment of the period has been largely polemical, and in the West the subject is virtually unknown.

(2) The potential interest of the period for comparative political and social studies. The Restoration was perhaps the most elaborate, the most consistent, and the most fully documented conservative program in history; it suggests at every point useful comparisons with European conservative movements and ideologies.

(3) The light that understanding of the period may shed on twentieth-century problems. History does not repeat itself, and this book is not intended as a briefing document for policymakers. Yet as Ralph Linton once remarked, "The stream of history runs between banks"; it may shift its channel but it cannot

---

[k] There is in addition the still perfectly sound aim of traditional historical scholarship: to examine the records of a little-known era, in order to provide a fuller and more accurate account of what happened and why, and a more balanced appraisal of the place in history of a group of men who have been alternately pilloried and worshiped.

wander at will.[9] All cultures show a constant disintegration and reintegration as new elements are introduced, but in most instances they have adopted from abroad what seemed familiar and not what seemed alien, and have continued to develop further along the lines of their own long-established interests.[10] While it is nonsense to suppose that China is immune to new elements, it is an error to suppose that the new elements have a *tabula rasa* on which to develop.

Considerable American attention has lately been focused on the new elements on the Chinese scene; until lately, however, there has been little serious attention to the configuration of the banks between which the stream of Chinese history has flowed in the recent past and to established patterns of political behavior. This book offers no program for the solution of the East-West crisis, in which the role of Communist China looms ever larger. Yet if its findings are correct, they would seem to form the basis for some highly relevant and hitherto unasked questions.

Let me illustrate with an example. It is often said that Chinese society is fundamentally sound; that its apparent bankruptcy is the result of China's failure in the nineteenth century to meet the Western challenge at the diplomatic, military, and commercial levels; that this failure in turn was the result of Manchu and imperialist domination which prevented China from developing in these respects. If this interpretation of Chinese nineteenth-century history is valid, then the way to correct the error and create a strong, stable, independent China is to focus attention on a better equipped Chinese Nationalist army, on encouragement of the Westernized Chinese merchant class, and on friendly support of a conservative Chinese government by foreign powers. By this interpretation, although Chinese nationalism is important, social revolution is not only not essential to modernization and "self-strengthening" but a positive obstacle.

But will this interpretation of nineteenth-century history stand up? The present case study suggests a series of generalizations that are exactly contrary.

(1) That China was at the outset relatively successful in dealing with modern diplomatic, military, and commercial problems. These were the three fields in which Chinese of the T'ung-chih period were the *most* and not the *least* successful.[1]

(2) That the Restoration failed because the requirements of modernization ran counter to the requirements of Confucian stability.

(3) That conservatism has been tried in modern China under extraordinarily favorable conditions; that the performance was brilliant but the final result dismal failure; that the obstacles to successful adaptation to the modern world were not imperialist aggression, Manchu rule, mandarin stupidity, or the acci-

---

[1] See Chapters VIII–XI.

dents of history, but nothing less than the constituent elements of the Confucian system itself.

In the 1860's the Western powers were by no means certain that the Restoration conservatism they supported would be successful, for they recognized that when the Taiping Rebellion was suppressed, "China was arrested in that course of renovation and mutation which nations can often only effect by civil war and revolution."[11] The attempt was worth every effort, for the alternative to a successful restoration was either a revolution of unparalleled proportions or gradual weakening, decay, and submission to foreign conquest. The issue at stake was not only the future of China but the future security of the powers having interests in China. The British minister reported:

> To this question of change and the introduction of sweeping and large reforms, both the hopes and fears of Western Powers are attached. To it also is undoubtedly linked the future destiny of the Empire, and a third of the human race which constitutes its population. . . . It has now to be decided whether the political system, clogged with such worn out materials, and decrepit with age, is susceptible of a regeneration, and a new life of adaptation to modern exigencies and foreign civilization; or whether it is to be dissolved by a process of decomposition and degradation, more or less progressive and complete with all their consequences within and without the Empire.[12]

The following pages are concerned with the decision of this issue between 1860 and 1870.

CHAPTER II

THE NEW ERA

THE CRISIS OF 1859–61

From the end of the eighteenth century the government of China had grown steadily weaker, more ineffective, and more corrupt. The history of the late Ch'ing is mainly the history of domestic rebellion and foreign war, and there were few hopeful signs even before 1850. In the 1850's disintegration proceeded at an accelerated rate, and the end of the old order appeared at hand.

The Taiping Rebellion[a] broke out in Kwangsi a few months after the Hsien-feng Emperor ascended the throne in 1850, and the government was too weak to take effective measures to check it. By 1853 the Taiping armies had conquered much of south and central China and had taken the key city of Nanking, which they were to hold for eleven years. Few competent Imperial commanders could be found, and unpaid, demoralized government troops deserted and often joined the rebels. The seriousness of the Ch'ing collapse can hardly be exaggerated.[1]

By the years 1859–61, the already tottering government had met with disaster in both domestic and foreign affairs, and there seemed little possibility of its survival. These were the critical years in the Taiping rebels' bid for power. A leading Ch'ing commander, Hu Lin-i, was deadlocked with the rebel general Ch'en Yü-ch'eng in western Anhwei; Tseng Kuo-fan was hard pressed at Kimen in Anhwei by the greatest of the Taiping strategists, Li Hsiu-ch'eng, and was relieved only at the eleventh hour by Tso Tsung-t'ang.[2] A sense of doom permeated virtually all Chinese and foreign commentaries on the times; a *North China Herald* editorial published at Shanghai in January 1860 was typical of the general view:

> The Great Rebellion, like an old fungus of proud flesh, does not heal up; on the contrary, if popular rumors may be taken as an index of the matter, it continues to go from bad to worse. . . . Lord Elgin's language, when he spoke of the Chinese, "the rags and rottenness of their waning civilization," was by some good people regarded as harsh and intemperate. It may have been so; nevertheless it was quite true. The old foundations of government are thoroughly rotten; its ranks and orders are broken; and its gorgeous decorations are in tatters. It is no mere ghoul that is devouring the body politic. The evils are legion; year by year they multiply; and no mortal can tell when or what will be the end of these things.[3]

These were also the critical years in the expansion of foreign power in China. The Arrow War, begun in 1856, had been concluded by the Treaties of Tientsin

---

[a] See Chapter VI.

of 1858, which greatly increased the privileges of foreigners in China. The court had refused ratification the following year, and in a self-confidence born of ignorance and arrogance had staked the existence of the state on a battle with England. In spite of their resulting ambush and defeat at Taku in 1859, the British were prepared to overlook this incident and to negotiate with what they regarded as the less intransigent wing of the Chinese government.[4] But Chinese policy was at this moment controlled by the so-called "war party," led by the Hsien-feng Emperor himself and composed of the die-hard Manchu princes Tsai-yüan, Tuan-hua, Su-shun, and others, who in the late summer of 1860 again precipitated a showdown by force with England, in which China lost. In 1859 Seng-ko-lin-ch'in had succeeded in routing the small British and French forces that appeared at Taku to insure the ratification of the 1858 treaties, but he could not stand up against the enlarged Anglo-French expeditionary force of 1860. The port of Tientsin fell and he retreated to Tungchow on the outskirts of Peking.[5]

The Manchu statesman Wen-hsiang's account of the resulting demoralization of the government is of particular interest because he soon became a leading proponent of the new foreign policy of the Restoration. Martial law had been proclaimed in Peking two years earlier at the time of the allied attack on Taku in 1858. But the panic of 1860 far exceeded the alarm of 1858, which had subsided with the withdrawal of foreign forces.[6] In a famous description, in which the factional maneuvers within the court were scarcely veiled, Wen-hsiang wrote:

> Again there was martial law in the capital, and men's hearts trembled. Those who held metropolitan office fled in droves. It was worse than 1853.[b] . . . There were some who begged the Emperor to make an Imperial Progress to Jehol. I feared that this would disturb men's minds and affect our general position. Moreover, beyond the frontier there were no strong points to be held. If we could go there, so could the other side. Risking my life, I insisted on remaining [in Peking], and the Emperor seemed convinced; but subsequently he was again influenced by those close to him. In haste I asked for an audience and was granted a private interview. I told him bluntly the reasons for not taking precipitate action. The Emperor seemed to understand. I withdrew and with my colleagues again presented a memorial, explaining in detail where our interests lay, in order to reinforce the Emperor's view. Then we received an edict urging the army to exterminate the enemy. This was proclaimed in the capital and in the provinces, and court and countryside rejoiced equally. Soon the enemy forces approached nearer. Those who reported this hastily and in agitation received an audience and alarmed the Emperor. Subsequently, on September 22, 1860, I begged that when the Emperor departed I be left at my post as General Commandant of the Gendarmerie and that a prince and ministers be appointed to handle the defense of the city.

An edict ordered me to assist Prince Kung in handling the peace negotiations

_b_ The reference is to the panic following the loss of Nanking to the Taiping rebels in 1853.

and said that there was no need for me to remain in the city. But at this time public feeling was alarmed. Since other officers had left with the court, I had to assume their responsibilities. I could not but enter the city to calm the public.

After I had bade farewell to the Emperor, Prince Kung and I made the necessary arrangements. Between five and seven o'clock in the evening, I entered the city and climbed to the top of the Ch'ao-yang gate. Then I discovered that for several days the garrison troops had not received their rice rations and that their weapons were entirely inadequate. Our general position was about to collapse. Matters were so urgent that there was no time to memorialize. The only thing I could do was to open up the storehouses and distribute money and rice, leaving the memorial until later.[7]

By midnight the rioting and looting in the side streets had subsided, and the people, now calmer, went home.[8] The accuracy of Wen-hsiang's account was confirmed by Tung Hsün, later a Grand Secretary, a Grand Councillor, and a leader in the Tsungli-yamen, and one of the group that had attempted to prevent the Emperor's flight to Jehol.[9]

According to the American envoy, John Elliot Ward, Peking had been on the verge of a revolution, with 86,000 unpaid, undisciplined troops roaming the city. The situation was so unstable, in Ward's opinion, that general chaos would almost certainly follow in the wake of a foreign armed force.

There is but one hope of satisfactorily adjusting the present difficulties—which is, that after the fall of the Takoo forts, the Chinese may come to terms. I am satisfied that an advance of the allied forces into the country must result most disastrously to all interests.[10]

The Chinese did not yield, and the allied expeditionary force moved on to Peking. The presence of foreign troops and the flight of the court deeply disturbed civilian life in the Chihli coastal area,[11] but the total collapse that had been feared did not follow. The withdrawal to Jehol of the effete court and the die-hard "war party" marked a turning point in China's conduct of her foreign relations. The officials who had earlier urged a policy of moderation and co-operation now emerged into prominence and, under the leadership of Prince Kung as the *de facto* head of state, attempted to formulate a new national policy.

In traditional Chinese political theory any calamity, whether a defeat in war or a drought, was taken as a sign that the natural harmony had been destroyed by erroneous governmental policies. When a calamity occurred, the Emperor and all the officials were considered, and considered themselves, obliged to search out their own error and correct it. The new men who replaced those lately discredited always had a mandate to restore tranquillity by changing faulty policies. A catastrophe like the occupation of Peking in October 1860 therefore provided a great stimulus to fresh thinking about foreign affairs. In this instance, the response was both dramatic and soberly constructive.

In 1858 and 1859 Prince Kung had seen no need for any change in policy toward the West. The events of 1860 taught him and his chief assistant Wen-hsiang two important lessons: that the foreigners were too strong to defeat, and that they observed the provisions of formal treaties. Prince Kung and Wen-hsiang in the capital and Tseng Kuo-fan, Tso Tsung-t'ang, and Li Hung-chang in the provinces were the five who led China's first effort to adjust to modern conditions through diplomacy and, more fundamentally, by "self-strengthening."[12]

RATIFICATION OF THE TIENTSIN TREATIES

On September 21, 1860, the day of the decisive defeat of Seng-ko-lin-ch'in's forces, Prince Kung was ordered to replace the discredited negotiators Tsai-yüan and Mu-yin. In notes to Ambassador-extraordinary Lord Elgin on September 23 and 27, he met many of the British demands, and his language was reported as courteous and conciliatory.[13]

On September 26, Heng-ch'i, one of the new negotiators appointed by Prince Kung, visited Harry S. Parkes, who had acted as Elgin's aide and interpreter and was one of the allied prisoners still held hostage by the Chinese. According to Parkes, Heng-ch'i told him that in the past the Grand Council had always considered negotiation with foreigners useless because it invariably led to additional foreign demands, and that the attack on Peking had played into the hands of the extreme faction. But Prince Kung, Heng-ch'i said, was anxious to try a new policy.[c]

On September 28, Prince Kung sent word to Parkes that the policies of the "war party"[d] had been abandoned and that in future the treatment of for-

---

[c] Parkes to Elgin, in *Correspondence Respecting Affairs in China. 1859–1860*, p. 236. While Prince Kung advocated a change in the direction of moderation, others urged a change in the direction of greater belligerency: transfer to the north of the southern forces of Tseng Kuo-fan and Hu Lin-i, transfer of the capital to the west, etc. (Liu Fa-tseng, *Ch'ing-shih tsuan-yao*, Shanghai, 1914, p. 116. On the importance of the fact that Prince Kung did not accompany the court in flight, see Cordier, *Relations*, I, 43.

[d] Recent Japanese research has shown that Western diplomats were in error in associating Seng-ko-lin-ch'in with this "war party." According to Professor Masataka Banno of Tokyo Metropolitan University, who has prepared a monograph on Chinese diplomacy of these years, Seng-ko-lin-ch'in was not one of the die-hard opponents of negotiation in this period. Although he was not associated with Prince Kung's "peace party," his outlook was quite different from that of the Tsai-yüan clique; he is best described as a strictly military figure, aggressive from the Western point of view but realistically aware of the strength of the Western forces and the weakness of the Ch'ing forces. Professor Ichisada Miyazaki has presented a similar interpretation in "Shinagawa shiryō yori mitaru Ei-Futsu rengōgun no Pekin shinnyū jiken, tokuni shusenron to waheiron," in *Tōa kenkyū shohō*, No. 24 (Oct. 1943), pp. 852–54 (*FB* 2.3.14).

eigners would be courteous and just. The inevitable basket of fruit followed on September 30.[14]

On October 24, the Sino-British Treaty of Tientsin was finally ratified, and the supplementary Convention of Peking signed.[15] The French envoy, Baron Gros, has left a vivid description of the signing of the French Convention of Peking the following day, along with the exchange of ratifications of the Sino-French Treaty of Tientsin of 1858. The French, determined to avoid what they quite wrongly considered Elgin's coldness and rudeness, were effusively cordial. A triumphal procession was watched by crowds of curious Chinese, and all parties delivered elevating speeches at the Board of Rites, where the signing took place.[16]

On November 5, the foreign troops withdrew from Peking to Tientsin and not long thereafter they left China.

THE RISE TO POWER OF PRINCE KUNG

As the *de facto* head of state during what was considered the most serious crisis any Chinese government had ever encountered and survived, Prince Kung occupied a strong political position. In order to consolidate this position, he had first to demonstrate that his solution of the barbarian problem was effective, and second to outmaneuver the powerful domestic opposition to his program. He dealt with the foreign problem first because of the immediacy of the danger, the absence of his opposition in Jehol, and the necessity of proving the practicability of his policies before proceeding to a showdown within the court. For the moment, basic domestic reconstruction had to wait.

Fortunately for the Restoration, Prince Kung easily won the full co-operation of the Western powers; France, England, the United States, and Russia competed with each other in displays of cordiality. Owing to British preeminence in the Far East, however, it was British co-operation that proved really decisive. In British support Prince Kung had what he needed most if he was to secure his controlling domestic political position.

From the outset Prince Kung was high in British favor. The British had erroneously made Seng-ko-lin-ch'in a whipping boy and had equally wrongly been disposed to believe in the basically pacific intentions of all high civilian officials, even of Mu-yin and Tsai-yüan.[17] Fortunately their estimates of Prince Kung proved correct. As the brother of the Emperor, he enjoyed great prestige, and in every contact with foreigners he displayed perfect manners, a quick intelligence, and a realistic acceptance of China's obligations under the new treaties. (Before 1860 Prince Kung had not shown himself remarkable in any way; his able performance in the decades after 1860 has entitled him to a permanent place in Chinese history. This metamorphosis of a conventional Manchu prince into an outstanding Chinese statesman is a striking example of the emergence of latent energies and talents in time of crisis.)

Elgin was reassured by the straightforward and effective manner in which Prince Kung handled the promulgation of the new treaty; its full text was published not only in the *Peking Gazette* but in placards posted conspicuously about the city, where crowds gathered to read it. He was hopeful that good relations would continue as long as Prince Kung remained in office.[18] Gros, on behalf of France, had equal confidence in Prince Kung and considered the rapid change in the tone of Sino-Western negotiations as "without precedent in the diplomatic annals."[19] Even the "old China hands" of the treaty ports were affected by the new and optimistic atmosphere.[e]

THE SUPPRESSION OF THE TSAI-YÜAN CONSPIRACY AND THE
CONSOLIDATION OF PRINCE KUNG'S POSITION

The first test of the new policies came with the death of the Hsien-feng Emperor, who was still in Jehol, on August 22, 1861. The necessity for choosing regents for the child who was to become the T'ung-chih Emperor precipitated a dramatic struggle for power between the two Empresses Dowager and Prince Kung on the one hand, and the most powerful of the groups opposing him, led by Tsai-yüan, Tuan-hua, Mu-yin, and Su-shun, on the other.[20]

The Tsai-yüan faction succeeded in producing an alleged valedictory edict of the Hsien-feng Emperor, establishing a regency composed of members of the Tsai-yüan group.[21] The Ministers of the Presence Tsai-yüan, Tuan-hua, Ching-shou, and Su-shun and the Grand Councillors Mu-yin, K'uang Yüan, Tu Han, and Chiao Yu-ying were summoned to the Imperial deathbed and were made advisers on state affairs; the Emperor died on the following day. On August 23 both the Empress-consort Tz'u-an and the Empress-mother T'zu-hsi were named Empresses Dowager.[22]

---

[e] For a few days after the inauguration of the "new era," the *North China Herald*, which reflected the views of foreigners resident in China in a private capacity, continued as before to announce the impending doom of the Chinese government: "The idea of the destruction of the Tartar Dynasty is no figure of speech. The allies are working its ruin as fast as possible, it may be much against the will of the high officers in command. . . . Look at the Empire from one end to the other, and try and discover one bright spot in its government or morals, one single spot that is not black and utterly decayed. . . . But the change is coming. . . . No treaties or patching up can do it any good—its fall is merely a question of time—sooner or later it must come." (*NCH*, Nov. 3, 1860. See also issue of Oct. 6, 1860.)

On December 1, 1860, less than a month later, even the *North China Herald* conceded that the change which had come was very different from the one so long predicted by the foreign community: "Political affairs at Peking had taken a favorable turn, the Prince of Kung had shaken off the sulkiness that his countenance expressed during the ceremony of exchanging and signing the ratification on the 24th of October, and appeared to be desirous of maintaining friendly relations with us. . . . [Prince Kung had exchanged visits with the foreign ambassadors and the whole atmosphere of international relations had changed.]"

Meanwhile, in court politics a complicated struggle for power was taking place in Jehol and Peking. The mother of the new Emperor, the young Empress Dowager Tz'u-hsi, had succeeded in gaining possession of the Imperial Seal, without which the new regency could not issue valid edicts. With the support of the opposition to Tsai-yüan, she and the Empress Dowager Tz'u-an rushed to Peking, outdistancing the new regents, who were compelled by dynastic law to follow the slow progress of the Imperial coffin.

The supporters of Prince Kung and the two Empresses Dowager took quick action, and memorials poured in begging the Empresses to act as regents with the advice of Prince Kung. The Grand Secretaries Chia Chen and Chou Tsu-p'ei, the censor Tung Yüan-shun, and the commander of the Honan-Anhwei armies, Sheng-pao, were among the high officials who urged this course.[23] Decisive action was now possible, and on November 2, 1861, by edict of the two Empresses to the Grand Secretariat, the Tsai-yüan faction was expunged from the political scene. Su-shun, Tsai-yüan, and Tuan-hua were stripped of office, five of their supporters were removed from the Grand Council, and further investigation of the conspiracy was ordered.[24]

Su-shun was decapitated on November 8, and Tuan-hua and Tsai-yüan, as Imperial princes, were allowed to commit suicide.[25] The hereditary rank of their descendants was subsequently greatly reduced.[26] The crime was defined as "subversion of the state" (*ta-ni*), and the edict that pronounced sentence included a verdict of guilty of mishandling foreign affairs.[27] Under the Ch'ing code "subversion" was one of the "ten abominations," second only to "rebellion" as a crime against the family, the sovereign, social relationships, and virtue— abominable in the eyes of Heaven and Earth, unpardonable and irredeemable.[28]

Edicts of November 9 stripped half a dozen more high officials of office, but ordered the cessation of further impeachments for participating in the conspiracy. The witch hunt was to be stopped short and bygones investigated no further.[29] This decision in favor of moderation was of considerable political importance, since the success of the Restoration was subsequently to depend on the submergence of factional differences in the general common interest of the whole Manchu-Chinese bureaucracy. Once the leaders had been punished, their followers could be re-educated.

Meanwhile, new men had at once replaced the conspirators, and on November 2 leading officials proposed a regency of the Empresses aided by one of the Imperial princes. Prince Kung was shortly appointed "Adviser in the Administration of Government" (*i-cheng-wang*), and he and four other new members were appointed to the Grand Council. The name of the new era, originally announced as the conventionally felicitous "Ch'i-hsiang," was changed to "T'ung-chih" ("Coeval Rule")[f] effective the following year. The various branches of the administration were ordered to assume their duties, and the Restoration was officially inaugurated with the enthronement of the T'ung-chih Emperor in the Hall of Grand Harmony and the proclamation of a general amnesty.[30]

General opinion does not swing from despondency to confidence overnight, and in traditional China its shifts were perhaps unusually slow. Yet by 1862, as the central and regional governments achieved striking success in both domestic and foreign affairs, the general temper of the times was very different from what it had been in 1860.[g] Foreign relations seemed stabilized with the withdrawal of foreign troops and the founding of the Tsungli-yamen in January 1861;[31] the recapture of Anking in September 1861 marked the turn in the tide of the Taiping Rebellion; and in November 1861 a new government with new policies and considerable prestige replaced the remnants of a discredited administration. Shrewd provincial officials, when they heard of the shift in power, recognized at once what this meant in terms of policy. Robert Hart noted an immediate change in the attitude of Kuan-wen, then governor-general of Hupeh and Hunan, when Hart told him that Prince Kung's party had replaced Su-shun's party in Peking.[32]

In every sphere of public life, the new government acted in accordance with the well-known pattern of a "restoration"—a period in which the decline of a dynasty is arrested and for a time reversed.[h] The signs of the times, both political and astronomical,[i] gave grounds for believing that a restored Confucian state, ruled by the Ch'ing, might once again fulfill the responsibilities of government.

FOREIGN REACTIONS TO THE NEW ORDER

Even before the establishment of the regency of the Empresses, most foreigners in China had gradually and reluctantly come to the view that their

---

[f] Inquiries addressed to a number of specialists in the United States and abroad have failed to elicit substantial evidence on the meaning of the reign title T'ung-chih. Professor Lien-shang Yang of Harvard believes that it may refer either to the joint rule of the two Empresses Dowager or to Sino-Manchu rule. Mr. Chaoying Fang of the University of California suggests that it may just possibly mean "like Shun-chih," referring to a young emperor under a regency. For a contemporary translation from the *North China Herald*, see footnote *j*. The translation I have adopted is that of Professor Edward Schafer of the University of California. There is some evidence for the meaning Sino-Manchu coeval rule in the fact that the phrase *t'ung-chih*—without reference to the era—was so used in late-nineteenth-century essays.

[g] The shift in sentiment and tone is marked in both edicts and memorials, in letters and diaries as well as in public documents.

[h] See Chapter IV.

[i] Since Chinese society was based on a belief in the harmony of the universe and on the intimate causal connection between natural and social phenomena, the formal recording of auspicious natural phenomena in the autumn of 1861 (*WHTK*, p. 10489) meant recognition of political achievement. For an illustration of the relation between nature and politics in the 1860's, see the discussion of the T'ung-wen kuan in Chapter X.

interests lay with the much-maligned central government. As the *North China Herald* expressed it:

> The Tartar dynasty is not a perfect one, it is true, but it is the best administrative power we have at present, and until a better takes its place, it is the wisdom of foreign nations to bear with its shortcomings, and to help it to correct its faults.[33]

With the suppression of the Tsai-yüan conspiracy and the inauguration of the new era of T'ung-chih, this grudging tolerance quickly shifted to enthusiastic support of what appeared to be a new order. The Empress Dowager Tz'u-an was acclaimed as beautiful, courageous, able, and proforeign, and Prince Kung rose even higher than before in foreign estimation.[j] China's past became praiseworthy,[k] and her future bright. By May of 1862 the *North China Herald* could write:

> China at the present time is undergoing the throes of a transition state in her domestic and foreign affairs, which in all probability, may be the turning point in her destiny for future generations. . . . With such elements of material prosperity, and such an industrious population, what a magnificent country might not this become, under a rule that would be equally powerful to protect the peaceful as it would be to chastise the unruly.[34]

Even in these Sinophile moments, when they were caught up in the general enthusiasm for the Restoration, foreigners resident in China generally assumed

---

[j] The salutations of Shanghai strain the credulity of those who are acquainted with the views of that community in later decades: "Under the guidance of such a Prince and Princess, may the reign of the young Emperor approach what it is entitled, 'Union in the cause of Law and Order,' for these are much wanted in this troubled land." (*NCH*, Nov. 30, 1861.)

Those who had formerly found little to choose between government and rebels, since both were Chinese, now picked the winner, a regency which they described as "powerful and vigorous"; and they urged that "foreigners therefore eschew these indolent dogs [the Taiping rebels] and support the regent. . . ." (*Ibid.*, Dec. 7, 1861). They argued that "at this particular juncture we are more than at any other period of our connection with China, bound to support the existing government of the Empire. A revolution in the state, as sudden, sharp, and decisive as that at Paris, which astounded Europe in 1848, has just happened at Peking, which has done more to reassure foreigners and impress them with a belief in the sincerity of the Chinese Government towards their interests, than any previous demonstration since our admission to her territory. . . ." (*Ibid.*, Dec. 21, 1861. See also Dec. 28, 1861).

In their review of events in 1861, the editors of the *North China Herald* emphasized the tremendous changes that had taken place during the year. The year had opened with the Emperor dying in Jehol, where reactionary plotters were trying to seize the throne. The Treaty of Tientsin "Like all its predecessors . . . was felt to be a hollow truce until the enemy regained strength so as to drive the 'foreign barbarians' from their ancient capital and principal seaports. It is true that confidence was placed in the Prince of Kung, but he was overruled in his pacific policy by the war party. . . . Happily the year closes with the most favorable prospects of peace and amity." (*Ibid.*, Jan. 4, 1862. See also March 22, 1862.)

[k] For example: "Although the former [the Imperial government] have materially changed the ancient conservative policy of the state, yet they have done nothing so as to destroy the existing institutions of the people; and though their exaction on the industry of the inhabitants is, in a European sense, unconstitutional and in many instances unjust, with an obnoxious mode of levying the same, still the welfare of the people is cared for, the arts encouraged, agriculture fostered, commerce promoted, and, above all, there is a fair amount of security to persons and property amongst those who recognize their legitimate rule." (*NCH*, Jan. 4, 1862.)

that the regeneration of the Chinese government would be in proportion to its acceptance of foreign guidance and its acquiescence in principles of nineteenth-century liberalism.[1] However, evidence soon appeared to show that a restored Confucian state would not encourage the growth of Western political and economic institutions; that, on the contrary, it was bound by its own essential aims to suppress any incipient tendencies in that direction. It became equally clear that no amount of gentle foreign guidance could lead a Confucian state along the road of peaceful metamorphosis into a sovereign modern state, because there was no such road. A Chinese revolution might have provided the transition from the Confucian world to the modern world, but there was no revolutionary bid for power for half a century after the Taiping Rebellion; and although a foreign power could further a revolution, it could not make one.

After the first flush of enthusiasm died down and the picture became clearer, many foreign merchants and missionaries concluded that if after all the Chinese Restoration failed to meet Western specifications, the Western powers would eventually have to conquer and govern China. The important point is that foreign governments in the 1860's took a very different view: revolution and conquest were both abhorrent; both were to be avoided at all costs. They could only hope that the Restoration would be successful, and that from a revived Chinese conservatism policies acceptable to the Western world would gradually develop. Even in their most pessimistic moments, they had to base their policy on the possibility that in the long, long run the recuperative powers of Chinese society would reassert themselves; for this possibility, however remote, was the only alternative to conquest or revolution.

The policies of the Western powers in China during the 1860's are not, of course, part of the T'ung-chih Restoration. But because of these policies, the Chinese government was free in the 1860's to settle its own destiny without foreign coercion. For a decade the foreign powers held the ring and left the issue of Chinese history to be settled in China. In this external capacity the Western "Co-operative Policy" is essential to our story, and for this reason we will examine it more closely before discussing the various aspects of the Restoration itself.

---

[1] For example: "Foreign influence is slowly but steadily working its way among the people and government of China. . . . It is evident on every side that Eastern prejudice and exclusiveness have given way to Western civilization, and that the seeds of a better order have been planted by the present administration through foreign influence." (*NCH*, March 1, 1862.)

CHAPTER III

THE CO-OPERATIVE POLICY

THE RELATION OF WORLD POLITICS TO DEVELOPMENTS WITHIN CHINA

Twentieth-century Chinese scholars of varying political views have tended to consider Western imperialism responsible for China's failure to adjust to the modern world. The true conservatives among them have held that China's ancient civilization, which could have provided a solid basis for a traditionalist modern China, was ruthlessly destroyed by foreigners who hated what they could not understand. The nationalists of the new business and professional classes and the Marxists have held the West responsible on a different ground; they have argued that a nascent Chinese capitalism, which was emerging from within the traditional society, was smashed by imperialist powers determined at all costs to prevent China from becoming powerful enough economically to compete as an equal with the commercial and industrial West.

Any effort to whitewash the whole sorry record of Western special privilege in China would be nonsense. Certainly a weak and docile China has been the aim of some governments in some periods, and of some private groups in all periods. However, in the critical formative period of the 1860's, it can be shown that the British government adopted for itself and held the other powers to a basic policy of nonintervention and moderate co-operation; and that at the same time, foreign private groups were effectively prevented from unduly exploiting the unstable situation.

The record of this restoration decade calls into question the polemics of both Right and Left concerning the role of imperialism in China's domestic development. During this decade, as the following chapters will show, the old China proved incapable of even the minimum adaptation necessary to its survival; and no modern capitalist class showed signs of emerging with enough strength to transform the old order from within. If the bogey of imperialism can be reduced to its proper proportions, it should then be possible to direct attention to the actual causes of the failure of the attempted conservative reform and of modernization within the traditional framework.

The term "Co-operative Policy" was originally used in two senses: first, co-operation among the Western powers having interests in China; and second, their co-operation with the Chinese government. By 1864 the term had a single accepted meaning: co-operation on the part of Great Britain, the United States, France, Russia, *and* China to secure the peaceful settlement of disputes and the gradual modernization of China. The American minister, Anson Burlingame, outlined the policy in his instructions to United States consuls in China on June 5, 1864, which laid down four principles: (1) co-operation among Western powers, (2) co-operation with Chinese officials, (3) recognition of China's legitimate interests, and (4) just enforcement of treaty stipulations. "You will perceive that we are making an effort to substitute fair diplomatic action in China for force."[1] This policy received the avowed support of the foreign representatives in China and of their home governments.[2]

At the end of 1867 the Co-operative Policy seemed to have succeeded. In reviewing its history, the *North China Herald* wrote that the various foreign interests not only had proved identical but could demonstrably be promoted best "by argument and persuasion rather than force and violence. The latter cannot but perpetuate the fear and hatred with which foreigners were at first regarded. The former is slowly undermining those prejudices. . . ."[3]

While the attitude of treaty port residents fluctuated and was in the end reversed, the British government, with the general support of the other Western powers, followed a consistent policy of co-operation with the Chinese government. It should be noted that at this period agreement among the Western powers did not mean, as it did later, that China was a colony to them all. On the contrary, the Co-operative Policy of the 1860's provided China with a substantial international guarantee against aggression or undue pressure, and with international aid to restore and strengthen the central power.

The broad identity of British and French interests had been established during the Crimean War, and the chief collaborators in securing ratification of the Treaties of Tientsin had been Great Britain and France. Although the United States and Russia had pursued separate courses, there was from the beginning some general understanding and agreement among the four powers.[4] There had been some Anglo-French rivalry during the 1860 negotiations,[5] but the two countries' common interests had been reaffirmed by their joint action against the Taiping rebels in the early 1860's. While the British government remained the mainstay of the Co-operative Policy, the United States gradually replaced France as the second supporting power, and it was the United States that formally enunciated the doctrine.

The Co-operative Policy was based on the assumption that the common interest of foreign governments and the Chinese government lay in furthering China's dignity, independence, peace, stability, and prosperity. In the sixties this Open Door approach seemed to offer genuine possibilities for the conservative regeneration of China. A decade earlier, the British had been searching for a policy,[6] but as long as the Ch'ing government appeared hopelessly weak and inept, British counsels were divided; some favored negotiations with the Taiping authorities; others preferred negotiation backed by force with whatever provincial leaders were immediately in control of a given area. Sir Rutherford Alcock, who as British minister to China in the 1860's became the chief guardian of the Co-operative Policy, refused to countenance either of these views.[7] An alternative policy congenial both to Alcock and to the British government became feasible when the direction of domestic events in China was reversed and a new Chinese government embarked on a program of restoration and limited modernization.

The Co-operative Policy did not always work, but British policy remained firm. As Alcock put it in a particularly difficult season in 1867:

> Although the general aspect of affairs is very unsatisfactory and unpromising, I believe there is a leaven at work among the ruling classes, and more especially in the Foreign Board here, if not in the palace itself, which forbids despondency. If only means can be found of keeping from them all foreign meddling and attempts at dictation, there is yet ground of hope. But these rouse strong instincts of resistance and national pride, giving fresh force to the retrograde and anti-foreign party; while at the same time it paralyzes all hopeful effort in those more favourable to progress, from the fear of its being made a new pretext for action on the part of one or more foreign Powers, and a degree of interference with their internal affairs which affects their sovereign rights as an independent nation. . . . Great changes might be looked for at no distant period, I am satisfied, but for this ever-recurring obstacle—a veritable bête-noire to the Chinese . . . No nation likes the interference of a foreign Power in its internal affairs, however well-intentioned it may be, and China is no exception to the rule. On the contrary their pride of race, and what they conceive to be a real superiority in civilization to all outside nations, renders them peculiarly impatient and restive under the goad of foreign impulsion. I am thoroughly convinced they would go much faster and better if left alone.[8]

THE ROLE OF GREAT BRITAIN

The China Policy of the Home Government. The policy of the British government toward China has been subject to so many facile misinterpretations that its bases in British politics are worth reviewing here. In the view of the British government of the 1860's, the China trade was not of sufficient importance to England to justify costly wars and the risk of empire in China.[a] By

---

[a] The basic and enduring difference between the British government's China policy and the wishes of British merchants and missionaries is admirably described in Nathan A. Pelcovits, *Old China Hands and the Foreign Office,* New York, 1948, Introduction and Part I. For the 1860's, however, two modifications of Pelcovits' general picture are indicated. (1) He states that both sides agreed that British interests in China were purely commercial but disagreed on the importance of those interests. Admittedly, Foreign Office policy in the sixties reflected considerable disillusion with the prospects of the China trade and a resulting unwillingness to engage in a costly forward policy. However, it was also shaped by the excellent *political* analyses received from British representatives, in consequence of which British statesmen were fascinated by the tremendous historic significance of a possible gradual modernization of China from the top and within the Restoration framework. (2) During the sixties, the old China hands too were occasionally affected by the prevailing general optimism concerning the recuperative powers of the old order in China.

the time of the Restoration, therefore, England was prepared to support the central government of China against all its enemies: rebels, provincial malcontents, and foreign merchants and missionaries in China. This policy was the result both of special conditions in China, which British officials had studied attentively, and of general trends in British political thought.

The period between 1850 and 1870 marked the height of the separatist movement, dedicated to gaining autonomy for the British colonies. More and more concessions were made to this concept, and "About the years 1869–70 there was . . . a very widespread belief that the Gladstone government was about to cut the colonies adrift."[9] Although the separatists were a small radical group, centered around the Manchester school, they were supported by a much larger group which, until the turning point in the development of imperialism around 1870, regarded the emancipation of the colonies as inevitable. Gladstone himself was not a separatist, but he did advocate retrenchment.

The men who held that British imperialism had overreached itself in areas far less hazardous politically than China preferred any alternative, however weak, to the prospect of further costly, "paternalistic" responsibilities overseas. Clarendon, who was British Foreign Secretary in 1865–70, had a long record of opposition to expanding imperial commitments, and was accordingly most sympathetic to field reports from Britain's Sinophile envoys condemning the stand of the staunch imperialists of the treaty ports.[10]

This was no new view in English politics. There had been opposition to the "forward policy" from the time of the Opium War. In 1847 Grey and Wellington had agreed that no force should ever be used in China without the express authority of the Queen, and had reduced the size of the forces available in an effort to make future independent expeditions impossible.[11] In 1857 the opposition to Palmerston's forward policy in China had been strong enough to unseat the government. To the government argument that the Arrow War of 1856–57 was essential to defense of the national honor, since Chinese had boarded a vessel of British registry and hauled down the British flag, the successful opposition replied that war on such grounds was rather an insult to the national honor, more disgraceful than the conquest of India.[12]

It is important to note that the Earl of Derby, leader of the Tories and later Prime Minister (1866–68), was one of the strongest opponents of the forward policy that had led to the Arrow War. Karl Marx, writing as a journalist who knew little of China but a great deal about England, was astounded at the phenomenon of

the chief of the hereditary aristocracy of England, . . . the descendant of the conquerors . . . , a Derby branding the acts of the British Navy [in China] as "miserable proceedings" and "inglorious operations." . . . The whole parliamentary history of England has, perhaps, never exhibited such an intellectual victory of the aristocrat over the parvenu.[13]

Similarly, following the expedition of 1860, Grey reviewed the evils of a policy which, he declared, had impoverished China and led to nothing but wars and rebellions.[14]

Opponents of the Co-operative Policy have claimed that it was a passing innovation of Clarendon's; that a wise policy of force had been yielding good results until Burlingame discredited British representatives in China to Clarendon and persuaded him to change basic British strategy.[15] In point of fact, the policy had deep roots in British political thinking, and its precise application in the 1860's in China was primarily the work, not of Americans, who were given to sweeping statements of principle, but of Englishmen: Frederick Bruce, Rutherford Alcock, and Robert Hart.

As the missionary issue reached a crisis in the late sixties and came to be the focus of debates on China, the political views of the anti-imperialists were reinforced by their anticlericalism.[16] In Clarendon's view "missionaries require to be protected against themselves"; more to the point, they were a constant menace to British interests.[17] The Duke of Somerset, recently retired as First Lord of the Admiralty, pointed to alleged missionary abuses of the Chinese population and asked rhetorically, "What right have we to be trying to convert the Chinese in the middle of their country?"[18] Grey, observing that force could not help any religion, supported Clarendon's reduction of the number of gunboats on duty in China waters on these grounds:

> such is the pressure of British influence that if a strong naval force is at hand, it is extremely likely to be used; while on the other hand, if we have not enough gunboats to bully the Chinese, both merchants and missionaries will show greater prudence, discretion, and fairness than if they saw themselves supported by a powerful force.[19]

The Foreign Office spokesman in the House of Commons summarized the general considerations behind the government position. The weakness of the Chinese government, he declared, was in part the result of foreign wars; British interest lay in strengthening the Chinese government by abstaining from the use of force, rather than in further weakening it by attacking it. Clarendon's policy had always been to treat China as a civilized nation, and since China was already modernizing her defense, Britain would soon have to cease using force in any case. On the question of opening the interior, he argued that the Chinese Empire would be disorganized if foreigners, with their extraterritorial rights, were allowed further freedom of action; it was quite enough that they could reside wherever they liked, provided they waived extraterritoriality and observed

Chinese laws and customs. The Chinese, in the Foreign Office view, were correct in insisting that economic modernization, especially the introduction of railways, be undertaken very slowly because of its effect on the complex Chinese economy. And the British government refused to attach any importance to whatever phraseology the Chinese cared to use in regard to foreigners.[20]

Support for the Foreign Office position was not limited to high places. Popular sentiment at home was in agreement with government policy and hostile to the expansionism of the China hands. Even in the treaty ports it was recognized that British home public opinion was a factor to be reckoned with. In reviewing the year 1860, the *North China Herald* wrote:

> He who next plunges the country into a Chinese war without first making every admissible effort to avert it will find it easier to face a Tartar army than an indignant British public. England will not long endure the perpetual recurrence of these China wars; and it will, in every point of view, be a wise policy, on the part of those who have the management of British interests in China, to concede something at the same time to public opinion at home, and to Chinese feeling here, by trying the effect of an equally firm, though more conciliatory policy than that heretofore pursued.[21]

Eight years later the paper recognized that home public opinion strongly and increasingly favored a conciliatory policy in China:

> Whether we like it or not, public opinion in Europe is a power shaping our destinies without asking our leave; and it must be clear to the least observant that, within the last few years the political feeling against foreign conquest, foreign possession and intermeddling in the affairs of foreign nations has been on the increase. . . . In the present temper of public feeling in England, we conceive that there would be a strong dislike to war and perfect horror of any policy that might lead to annexation. . . . So that our Ministers and Consuls will probably be instructed to adopt a more and more cautious policy.[22]

In the circumstances of the time, there was only one policy that could possibly achieve this British aim: support of the Chinese attempt at restoration.

The Decision to Support the Chinese Central Government. As early as 1860 the British minister in China, Bruce, had insisted that Britain deal only with the Chinese central government. He pointed out that local pressure could be effective only in the degree to which it encouraged local revolt, and that a breakdown of government in China would be disastrous to Britain's nonterritorial interests. Bruce had analyzed the relation between central and provincial government in China and had concluded that local action and local negotiation were at best temporary expedients; that British interests were dependent on the existence of a central government whose jurisdiction would be accepted throughout China, and which could therefore assume responsibility for foreign affairs.

Local action would undercut the central authority whose strengthening was essential.[23]

Even prior to the "new era" the British government had been aware that forcing the ratification of the Treaty of Tientsin might weaken the central government and thus endanger British long-term interests in China.[b] Lord Elgin and Baron Gros were dispatched to China by the British and French governments in 1860 in the hope that they could obtain their minimum demands without causing the overthrow of the Chinese government. In his instructions Foreign Secretary Russell wrote:

> In carrying on operations in the North of China, there is a danger to which Her Majesty's Government are very sensible. . . . [The Chinese Emperor might refuse to accept peace terms and flee.] Abandoning his capital upon the advance of European troops, condemned to admit the superiority of powers whom the court of China, in its fatuity, has hitherto treated with contempt, the Emperor would suffer greatly in reputation.
>
> The rebels would take heart; the great officers of the Empire might find it difficult to maintain the central authority; the Governors of Provinces might hardly be able to quell insurrection. In short the whole Empire might run the risk of dissolution.
>
> Her Majesty would see with great concern such a state of things. It might even portend a great catastrophe; and the bonds of allegiance, once loosened, might never again be firmly united.[24]

The British and French envoys shared Russell's apprehension, and Baron Gros reported to his government:

> Only one eventuality appears to me to be dreaded, I speak of the flight of the Emperor to Tartary. We think, therefore, Lord Elgin and I, that we ought to stop at Tientsin, if, as I hope, we can reach it, and from thence, rather threaten Peking than attack it.[25]

The Emperor did flee, but the dread consequences did not ensue. Instead a new court, with a new policy, returned to inaugurate a new era.

Before 1860 the Western powers had been prepared to use force in China to assert what they considered to be their rights. After 1860 there was a nearly complete reversal: foreign governments were prepared to use force on behalf of, and at the request of, the Chinese government,[c] but they now became extremely reluctant to use force on their own behalf.

Merchant vs. Diplomat. For a brief time the prospects of the Restoration were so bright that British merchants and missionaries followed their govern-

---

[b] British policy was described as "trying to perform the delicate operation of snuffing without extinguishing" the Chinese government (*NCH*, Mar. 3, 1860), and as attempting to deliver "a blow to be aimed at the head in such a way as not to injure the body" (*ibid.*, Feb. 16, 1861).

[c] On foreign military aid to China, see Chapter IX.

ment's lead. But they were looking for quick results to serve their immediate interests; when these results did not follow, they angrily urged a reversion to strong-arm methods, and made demands ill-calculated to serve England's broader national interests or even their own long-term interests.[d] By the time of the Restoration's years of crisis and final failure, most of Britain's merchants in China and many British missionaries were once again committed to the old view that the Chinese government was essentially an enemy, ever ready to perpetrate outrages of all kinds and responsive only to the deterrent of brute force.[26] British diplomats, however, held to a policy of patient conciliation, and on the rare occasions when they were so exasperated by the China scene that they thought of gunboats, their tempers were held in check by the British home government. At the height of the wave of antiforeign outbreaks in the late sixties, when even Alcock despaired of negotiation, Clarendon, the foreign secretary, insisted that force be used only to protect life and property immediately exposed, never punitively or in reprisal. Any issues that could not be settled amicably in China were to be referred to the British home government.[27]

The new British policy was illustrated in the peaceful, almost routine, settlement of a case in which a British soldier was murdered by a Chinese in 1864. As the *North China Herald* pointed out:

> A few short years ago, such an occurrence, whether explained or not, would have produced a storm of indignation. The inquiries set on foot would have been looked on as blinds to draw attention from the real perpetrators of the outrage. The explanations offered would have been rejected disdainfully, and a war might finally have been cooked from the materials thus supplied.[28]

An early illustration of the curious role of the British government as defender of the Chinese government against British residents in China[e] was the revision of regulations for trade on the Yangtze River. When merchants protested that Bruce was "acceding to the restrictive policy of the Chinese Government,"[29] the Foreign Office sternly advised the Shanghai Chamber of Commerce as follows: the revised Yangtze regulations represented a further Chinese concession; the rights that the merchants felt had been withdrawn had never been granted by China; and it was the policy of the British government to support the Chinese government in resisting encroachment on its authority.[30] Earlier

---

[d] It could even be argued that the merchants had proved poor judges even of their most immediate interests, owing to their ignorance of China. See the astute analysis in an unsigned letter to the editor, *NCH,* June 19, 1868.

[e] There was a precedent for this set by Alcock himself, who as consul in Shanghai in the early 1850's had fined British merchants for failure to declare cargo, and had attempted to collect the Imperial customs revenues for China from British merchants when China could not do so herself. Stanley F. Wright, *Hart and the Chinese Customs,* pp. 81, 93; John K. Fairbank, *Trade and Diplomacy on the China Coast,* Cambridge, Mass., 1953, I, 432.

still, Bruce had ignored local indignation to uphold the Chinese government's right to tax Chinese subjects in the foreign concessions at Shanghai.[31]

The British merchants' acceptance of this policy[32] was short-lived. When by the end of 1865 the millennium had failed to arrive, the opposition became more bitter and more aggressive. The exacerbated China hand view was forcefully expressed in many quarters. As an angry reader of the *North China Herald* wrote the editor:

> it is now the custom to believe the Chinese incapable of any act of hostility toward foreigners, or of anything bad. Like the King of England, a Chinaman can do no wrong. Had we been caught and decapitated, or otherwise murdered, your paper, Mr. Editor, would not have been wanting in letters defending the long suffering people of this happy land, and the tacit verdict of the world would have been "serve us right" . . .[33]

The editors too reviewed the events of 1865 less cheerfully than they had those of 1864.

> At the opening of the year we had ceased to form those sanguine anticipations of the ultimate regeneration of the Chinese government, which during the Taiping campaign and for some time after its close were entertained. . . . Whatever tendency to yield has been displayed . . . by the foreign representatives, who were evidently most anxious to impress the native government of the purity of the motives which actuate Western powers.[34]

More and more outraged letters to the *North China Herald* complained that British authorities were not protecting British interests from Chinese encroachment.

> To enforce seems, nowadays, past the power of a British minister. . . . It is well that the perpetual laxity which now exists in the preservation of British interests should be duly chronicled.[35]

The editors agreed:

> So violent a reaction has set in from the extreme coercive policy which once prevailed toward China, that we are in danger of falling back on a policy of extreme weakness.[36]

The uproar did not alter British policy. The Foreign Office continued to instruct the British minister to make every concession to Chinese views and to use persuasion rather than force,[37] and Alcock followed his instructions to the letter. While the merchants saw Chinese weakness as a reason for pressing foreign demands, officials saw it as a reason for *limiting* demands, feeling in "sympathy . . . with the difficulties which Chinese statesmen . . . have to encounter in the introduction of alterations which the conservative feeling of the most exclusive nation in the world stigmatizes. . . ."[38] In his notes to Prince Kung,

Alcock gave his views on some of the problems facing China but emphasized that China must take the initiative and in her own time.[*f*]

The Effort to End Gunboat Diplomacy.[39] In the years 1868 and 1869, which saw a whole series of antiforeign demonstrations, British policy scarcely wavered. The merchants' and missionaries' incessant demands for gunboats received support only occasionally from consuls, very rarely from Alcock,[40] and never from the Foreign Office or Admiralty.[*g*]

The first outbreaks occurred in the lower Yangtze valley, at Kiukiang,[41] Yangchow,[42] and Chinkiang.[43] When negotiation failed, on-the-spot use of force produced temporary settlements. The advocates of a "strong policy" pointed out with satisfaction that they had

> predicted the height to which Mandarin insolence and obstructiveness would rise under the late placid regime; and predicted also that a display of vigor would at once bring the officials to their senses. Events in the North and South have amply verified their judgment.[44]

In fact, events did not verify their judgment. In so far as the "placid regime" of the British government (which was certainly not at an end) encouraged the Chinese Restoration, it tended not to provoke but to prevent such outbreaks by giving the Chinese time to work out considered solutions of new problems, solutions that in turn promised to reduce the incidence of sporadic, blind outbreaks of local resentment. British official policy, therefore, continued to bank on the eventual success of the Restoration. Clarendon officially reprimanded Alcock and Consul W. H. Medhurst for countenancing the use of force at Yangchow and stated his admiration for Prince Kung's statesmanlike attitude.[45]

The varying components of British policy were clearly represented in the Formosa incident of 1868–69.[46] Both the Catholic and Protestant churches near Tainan had been destroyed by mobs, following circulation of a rumor that mysterious drugs were being used to convert Chinese to Christianity. Acting Consul John Gibson and a subordinate naval officer applied force on the spot, to the applause of merchants and missionaries.[47] Alcock, more moderate, appealed to the Tsungli-yamen to remove the offending taotai. Clarendon took an even

---

[*f*] A comparison between the English original and the Chinese translation of one of these notes underlines the difficulty, even in the most favorable circumstances, of creating any real common understanding between the two parties. The English text gives, as Alcock clearly intended, the impression that England is truly anxious to help the Chinese government strengthen itself in its own way. In the Chinese version, which was the one that concerned Chinese officials, Alcock's elaborate disclaimers of any intent to interfere in Chinese affairs appear rather as veiled suggestions of the ease with which foreign powers could interfere if they wished. English text, *China. No. 5. (1871)*, pp. 93–100; Chinese text, *IWSM–TC*, Ch. 63, pp. 10–22.

[*g*] This gradation within British policy was nicely illustrated during an incident at Hankow. Consul G. W. Caine wanted a gunboat permanently stationed at Hankow; Alcock was willing to agree to two gunboats for the whole Yangtze; the Admiralty was opposed to having any gunboats on the Yangtze except as a very temporary measure (*China. No. 8. (1869)*, pp. 1, 3).

stronger stand. On February 23, 1869, he ordered Gibson's demotion, the return of the indemnity extracted, and official disavowal of the action taken, on the ground that

> There was clearly no occasion for these two subordinate authorities [the local British consular and naval authorities involved] to commit any acts of hostility whatever; any danger to life and property was, for the time at least, at an end, and had been so for many weeks; and any remissness on the part of the authorities to afford adequate reparation was matter for discussion between Her Majesty's Minister and the Chinese Government at Peking. . . .[48]

The same points were illustrated near Foochow in January 1869, where the British consul enlisted naval aid to support a claim by missionaries. Clarendon again stated British policy:

> The Consul's measures had a direct tendency to provoke, without sufficient cause, collision with the Chinese authorities and people; and I have to instruct you strongly to censure Mr. Sinclair for what he did.[49]

The *Cockchafer* incident near Swatow in January and February, 1869, made perfectly plain the British intent to intervene in China only with the sanction of the Chinese central authority. In this affair Vice Admiral Sir Henry Keppel had arranged with the governor-general of Kwangtung and Kwangsi, Jui-lin, to lend British naval support to an official Chinese mission to obtain redress for anti-foreign activities near Swatow. But the consul on the spot and the commander of the *Cockchafer* took direct action *before* the governor-general's commissioner arrived. Admiral Keppel understood very well that the commissioner had been appointed "to give countenance to our action on Chinese territory." In the prevailing atmosphere the matter was readily cleared up in an interview between Jui-lin and Keppel:

> The Viceroy remarked that officers would occasionally make mistakes; he found it so with his own; but with entire confidence between superiors, such as existed between Sir Henry Keppel and himself, and with a liberal construction placed on acts as well as motives, such occurrences were easy of settlement, and would even strengthen the ties of mutual regard and esteem.[50]

At home, however, the Admiralty agreed with the Foreign Office view that by this unilateral British action

> The character of the whole transaction was thus changed; instead of being a measure of redress spontaneously afforded by the Chinese authorities, it became one in which the action of the British force was independent of them. . . .[51]

These various incidents clearly resulted from the Chinese central government's inability to assert full control. Even Alcock, under pressure, felt that foreign powers might occasionally have to use force locally, "in default of a central government with adequate power,"[52] although he hoped that an overwhelming show of force would be effective without fighting. The British home government, however, remained determined to assume that the Chinese central government would be able to maintain its authority if the foreign powers exercised sufficient self-restraint.

The news of the China incidents set off a series of debates in Parliament in which the government's position was made plain. On April 5, 1869, the Duke of Somerset referred with pained surprise to the report that force had been used on Formosa in violation of the orders of the British government. Clarendon replied that "the operations ought not to have been undertaken at all," and that the action had been repudiated. He hoped the entire consular body in China would take notice.[53]

A week later the opposition to the government's China policy put forward H. N. Lay's[h] views on the need for force. The Foreign Office spokesman in the House of Commons replied that the various antiforeign outbreaks had occurred *in spite of* Britain's conciliatory policy, not because of it. In future incidents, he declared, the British minister was to appeal to the Chinese central government; remedy would be sought only at Peking; if any consul used force on the spot, the action would be disavowed.[54]

The following year the opposition criticized Alcock's restraint in handling another antimissionary outbreak, which had occurred at Anking in April 1869. The Foreign Office spokesman replied that the missionaries had no right to be in Anking and praised the helpful attitude of the Chinese authorities.[55] As Clarendon summarized the issue:

> The injudicious proceedings of missionaries in China, the violence engendered by them on the part of the Chinese authorities and people, and the excessive and unauthorized acts of retaliation to which British Consular and, at their requisition, the naval authorities had resorted, were indeed sufficient to cause Her Majesty's Government to look forward with apprehension to the intelligence which each succeeding mail might bring. . . . It is the intention of this country that intercourse with China should be maintained by friendly means, and should not be subject to interruption by injudicious and rash proceedings on the part of British subjects.[56]

The British government held to its policy even after the Tientsin Massacre of 1870.[i] On March 24, 1871, Somerset and Grey repeated that outbreaks against missionaries resulted from the missionaries' violation of Chinese sentiment, and that rashness on the part of British naval officers must be checked.[57]

The British Conception of Chinese Sovereignty. In 1857, during the Parlia-

[h] See Chapter IX.
[i] See Chapter XI.

mentary uproar over the Arrow War, the Palmerston government, finding it impossible to defend the legality of its action in international law, had denied that China was a sovereign state with legal rights.[58] This position was no longer tenable, if it had ever been, after the ratification of the Treaties of Tientsin. By insisting on their right to send envoys, the foreign powers had deliberately recognized China as a sovereign state.

By treating the Chinese government as if China were a modern, sovereign state, Britain gave China the most favorable opportunity in her modern history to become just that. Without this full legal sovereignty in the eyes of the West, the Chinese government could never have made the progress it did in its effort to eliminate the abuses of extraterritoriality.[j]

The way the British applied Western legal theory to protect China's sovereign interests was strikingly illustrated in 1865 in the case of *Regina* v. *Reynolds and Holt,* concerning the ownership of alluvial lands. To the indignation of the Shanghai foreign community, the British Crown proceeded to prosecute British subjects on behalf of the Chinese Throne. To the merchants' contention that the British Crown was not an interested party and hence had no right to intervene, the British judge in the Shanghai Supreme Court replied:

> Now, to my mind, it is perfectly clear that Her Majesty, in obtaining by treaty from the Emperor of China the right to retain on Chinese soil an exclusive jurisdiction over her own subjects, has implicitly undertaken that she will compel Her subjects to respect the *laws of China* as well as the laws of their own country, and by such a procedure also as will not subject the sovereign power [China] to the indignity of appearing on its own soil [the British concession in Shanghai] in the character of a suitor in a foreign court to compel the respect due to such laws.[59]

POLICIES OF THE OTHER GREAT POWERS

British power and prestige so dominated the Far East in the sixties that forceful and unequivocal support of the Co-operative Policy by the other countries was scarcely essential to its success. All that was required was formal adherence to the doctrine and a measure of good will. It was quite sufficient that these were provided lavishly by the United States, cautiously by France, and deviously by Russia.

France. Throughout the period when China was open to the West, there were two main lines of thinking behind French policy. The dominant policy-makers in most periods distrusted both the Chinese government and the other Western powers with interests in China; they consequently urged exclusive concessions, the delegation of supreme colonial powers to consuls, and vigorous support of Catholic missions and the rights of French citizens. There were also, how-

---

j See Chapter XI.

ever, tendencies toward a policy of self-restraint and co-operation with the other powers and with China, and these were particularly noticeable during the Restoration period. French supporters of the Co-operative Policy argued that France's limited interests in the Far East were identical with those of Britain, that her excessive commitments should be reduced, that the Catholic Church already enjoyed under the French Treaty of Tientsin ample rights and required no further special support, and that consular powers should be checked.[60] Opponents of the Co-operative Policy argued that the opportunity for a peaceful adjustment of Chinese and European civilization had disappeared with the age of Voltaire, and that there were no longer grounds for anticipating a pro-European policy in Peking. They therefore urged vigorous support of Catholic mission work and a "firm policy" directed toward the cultural conversion of China.[61]

Although this division in French policy persisted even at the height of the Restoration, the French government and its representatives on the whole supported the Co-operative Policy during the sixties. In 1860 the French had been even more fearful than the British of the consequences of upsetting the *status quo* in China.[62] By 1867 the French government considered that the new policy toward China was succeeding, and "that for time-honored prejudice there is gradually being substituted a more exact appreciation of common interest. . . ."[63] Up to the time when the Tientsin Massacre and the rejection of the Alcock Convention marked the end of general optimism about the Co-operative Policy, the French government, while emphasizing its treaty rights, ordered its representatives to restrain their language and to make allowance for the exceptional situation in China.[64]

During the sixties French policy also moved in the direction of closer co-operation with the other Western powers. While the French concession at Shanghai remained apart from the International Settlement, Paris declared its opposition to "seeking triumphs of exclusive influence," and insisted that the French consul co-operate with the other foreign consuls in the reorganization of the French concession. Unilateral action in the China area was abjured.[65]

Russia.[66] It is not easy to characterize Russian policy in the Restoration period briefly and judiciously. The legations established by the other Western powers in Peking after 1860 supplanted or subordinated earlier institutions for the implementation of policy toward China; the appointment of a Russian minister merely provided an additional channel for the conduct of Sino-Russian relations. The Russian military, commercial, and religious institutions that had grown up during the long period of extensive Chinese-Russian land contact[67] remained in some measure independent of the minister. Thus, whereas during the 1860's the Russian minister at Peking appears generally to have concurred in the Co-operative Policy of his diplomatic colleagues and to have acted in some measure as a check on aggression from Siberia, Russian territory and exclusive privilege continued to be extended at China's expense, through force and fraud seemingly beyond the resident minister's control.[k]

While Count Nikolai Muraviev, governor-general of Eastern Siberia, and his men were seizing vast reaches of Manchuria, culminating in the Treaty of Aigun (1858),[68] the Russian envoy, Admiral Count Efimii Putiatin, was taking advantage of Sino-Western hostilities to establish Russia as the friend of both sides, with the idea of "mediating" between them to Russia's advantage. In 1857 Putiatin offered to "assist" China in her difficulties at Canton, but the offer was declined. During the negotiation of the Treaties of Tientsin, Putiatin continued to play the friend of all parties; and although he was distrusted by both the allied powers and the Chinese,[69] he contrived to make himself appear indispensable to both.

During the campaigns and negotiations for the ratification of the Treaties of Tientsin in 1859–60, the new Russian envoy, General Nikolai Ignatiev, followed Putiatin's policy and with even greater success.[l] He moved constantly between the belligerent parties, offering his good offices to each against the other, and, in spite of their doubts, gaining concessions from both. Capitalizing on each side's ignorance of the other's intentions, he often claimed credit for actions that he had in no way influenced.[m] His crowning achievement was persuading China to cede Russia the trans-Ussuri territory, as a reward for having allegedly persuaded the British to withdraw following the signing of the Convention of Peking. He then made "a veritable triumphal march" through a number of provinces, where he was reportedly received with "transports of joy."[70] Prince Kung apparently distrusted Ignatiev but tried to use him, since he had no way of knowing that the British had already decided to withdraw as soon as the Chinese announced the signature of the convention in the provinces.

Certain other aspects of Russian policy are also worth noting. Well before 1860, Russia had clearly reached the conclusion that she could further her interests better by supporting the existing Chinese government than by supporting the Taiping rebels, and during the 1860's Russian diplomats accordingly backed the

---

[k] *See* Chapter X.

[l] Ignatiev's duplicity has since been a favorite theme for Chinese scholars and statesmen. Dr. T. F. Tsiang referred to the case at some length in the Security Council of the United Nations, emphasizing what Ignatiev had gained by pretending to be China's protector against Anglo-American imperialism (Security Council session of Aug. 17, 1950, Verbatim Record, in *New York Times,* Aug. 18, 1950, p. 8).

[m] For example, one observer reported that in the summer of 1860, Ignatiev had expressed to the French his fears for the safety of their operation in view of the strength of the Chinese defenses (Mutrécy, *Journal de la campagne de Chine,* I, 320). After the Chinese defeat, he was assiduous in helping the French solve certain complicated questions of Church property. He claimed that he alone had been able to persuade Prince Kung to negotiate (*ibid.,* II, 46–47).

Ch'ing. Russian policy also operated to clear the way for normal, modern trade and diplomatic relations between China and the West.[71] Throughout the 1860's, however, as indicated above, the civil and military officials of Russia's Far Eastern territories bypassed the new diplomatic channels to gain Chinese territory and concessions for Russia.

The United States. Secretary of State William Henry Seward and American Minister Burlingame were from the outset convinced that the Restoration government was "friendly to progress," and that the powers must be careful to avoid any action that might enable the "antiforeign" party to discredit the Ch'ing government.[72] For this reason the American government, like the British government, disavowed "gunboat diplomacy." When, for example, Consul Sandford at Chefoo arranged a naval demonstration in retaliation for Chinese desecration of a cemetery in 1866, he was immediately censured by Seward for failing to ask the Legation in Peking to seek redress through the Chinese central government.[73]

Washington was less sanguine about co-operating with Britain than about co-operating with China. To judge from Seward's instructions, he regarded the government of old China as less suspicious than the government of old England.[74] In a speech of greeting to the Burlingame Mission sent abroad by the Chinese government,[n] President Johnson named, as deserving of special credit in the implementation of the Co-operative Policy, Prince Kung, Wen-hsiang, Burlingame, Bruce, Berthemy, Balliuzek, and Vlangali.[75] The inclusion of the Russian envoys is interesting, as is the omission of Alcock, Thomas Wade, and Hart.

On the Peking scene, however, Burlingame himself enjoyed the most cordial relations with his colleagues in the diplomatic corps, and Washington agreed that those particular envoys were "enlightened." The significance for China policy of the slightly acid references to England in American documents of that period should not be overestimated. Nowhere in the record is there evidence of on-the-spot conflict in policy between the United States and Great Britain. On the contrary, the Co-operative Policy was as much in evidence in the handling of specific problems, such as the administration of the foreign concessions in the treaty ports,[76] as in general policy statements. Burlingame made concessions that were considered naïve and injudicious even by some of the staunchest supporters of the Co-operative Policy, yet in *policy terms* there was little difference between the cautious and occasionally despairing European support of the Chinese government on the ground that no more hopeful alternative offered, and the fervent American faith that by yielding everything to China the West would gain everything from China.

The appointment of J. Ross Browne to succeed Burlingame in 1868 changed the picture somewhat.[77] Browne went to the other extreme, and although he

[n] See Chapter XI.

continued to talk of China's stability and independence, it seems clear that he was thinking of foreign tutelage. At the same time, the State Department continued to abjure the use of force or pressure and apparently remained satisfied that the Chinese government, if given sufficient time and freedom of action, would of itself formulate and implement policies favorable to all the legitimate interests of the Western powers.[o]

THE SINICIZATION OF FOREIGN DIPLOMATS IN CHINA

The success of the Co-operative Policy depended in large measure upon the sympathetic interest in Chinese civilization displayed by the representatives of the great powers. According to a contemporary missionary, diplomat, and historian, "The good fortune of having men of the kindness and honor of Bruce, Vlangali, Berthemy, and Burlingame as heads of the four chief Legations can hardly be exaggerated."[78] The Co-operative Policy was grounded in national interests as they were conceived at the time, but it could not have been formulated without the insight the envoys supplied, or carried out without their support.

For several centuries before the nineteenth, European visitors to the Middle Kingdom had been as awed and respectful as any tributary mission. To them too China's material culture, social institutions, political system, and intellectual and artistic heritage had been worthy of study and emulation. The Industrial Revolution, the emergence of the strange, new Europe of the nineteenth century, and the crumbling of Asian societies before the Western onslaught changed the general Western view.[p] In the eyes of most Western merchants and missionaries, who made up the overwhelming majority of foreign residents in the nineteenth century, China was a heathen, backward, primitive country of whose institutions no serious account need be taken.[q]

Even the *North China Herald*, which usually spoke for the Shanghai merchant rather than the Peking diplomat, was shocked at the sight of merchants trying to ride roughshod "into the heart of this living antiquity," with "laws and

[o] As Clarendon's support of the Co-operative Policy with regard to China was firmly grounded in his general belief in imperial retrenchment and colonial separatism, so the similar China policy of President Grant's secretary of state, Hamilton Fish, was based on his general acceptance of the principles of free trade and the division of labor among the various areas of the world (e.g., Fish to Burlingame, Dec. 24, 1869, *U.S. Arch. China. Notes to,* pp. 9–11).

[p] Contemporaries were aware of the change that had taken place in Western estimations of China, noting that while the eighteenth-century historian Du Halde and the other Jesuit scholars had admired China, residents of the 1860's were critical of China's backwardness, owing to progress in Europe during the nineteenth century (*NCH*, Aug. 11, 1866).

[q] In the words of one of their leading apologists, the political attitudes of British merchants were based on three considerations: ". . . the fact that the Chinese . . . are a semi-barbarous people, to whose laws and judicial administration the lives and property of foreigners cannot be entrusted; the historical experience of the unreliability of the Chinese government, and the mendacity and treacherous habits even of its highest officials; and the peculiar constitution of the Chinese Empire." (Johannes von Gumpach, *The Burlingame Mission,* Shanghai, etc., 1872, p. 303.)

customs more ancient than any other on earth." "Only men who are familiar with both Eastern and Western modes of thought" could remove the misunderstandings that had grown out of the inability of either side "to understand the different aspect in which any question presents itself to the mind of the other."[79]

> The least enthusiastic of explorers in this field must confess the advantage which will accrue to us when we become more fully acquainted with Chinese forms of thought. For it is through the investigation of the forms in which a nation thinks, that we arrive at the general principles which guide its actions.[80]

It was the good fortune of the Restoration government that the chief foreign envoys to China in the 1860's were men steeped in Western tradition and at the same time eager and admiring students of "Chinese forms of thought." As early as 1855 Alcock had written:

> How a man thinks; from what point of view subjects are habitually noticed by him; what are the usual and therefore the governing principles of his action—these are the things most essential to be known in our intercourse with our fellow men if we seek to exercise any influence over them. If we have not these, we are navigating without chart or compass, and know not how to shape our course, or upon what hidden rocks and shoals we may be driving with fatal certainty and force. Great is the influence of such knowledge on the progress of affairs in China, more especially where from certain broad divergencies it is not safe to go upon the general analogy which in Europe we presume to exist between our habits of thought and action, and those of our neighbors.[81]

During the Restoration period, the absorption of the diplomatic corps in the study of China was widely reflected in official despatches. The assumptions with which Alcock, for example, began the analysis of a problem were precisely opposite to those of the Chambers of Commerce:

> After all is said against the Government of China, its institutions, and people— and foreigners are naturally led to dwell more on the defects from which they suffer, than the virtues which do not immediately affect them—it has answered the end of all Government in a very wonderful degree. It has bound together, under one ruler, nearly a third of the human race; and under its successive dynasties they have been trained to be a peace-loving, orderly, and industrious race. The Empire has, under such institutions, endured longer than any other in the history of the world, and at this moment dwarfs all others by the extent of its population and the vastness of its territories; and if there be any touch of exaggeration in the dictum that "for the rulers of all other nations the Chinese Empire constitutes a great practical lesson of 4,000 years standing," it is impossible to deny that they have attained a high state of civilization, and one peculiarly their own . . . They have much to be proud of; much they may well be excused if they are loath to part with, at the sudden requisition of foreign powers they have not yet learned to regard as other than barbarian and inferior.[82]

The diplomats studied the Chinese scene, were fascinated by it, and identified themselves with it, both personally and officially. Foreign interests in China appeared to foreign governments to be tied to the fate of the central government, and, as a consequence, foreign diplomats functioned almost in the role of Chinese representatives. Burlingame's appointment as Chinese minister to the Western powers[r] was no anomaly: foreign diplomats in China considered themselves as representing the common interests of their own *and* the Chinese government. To their critics, Wade, S. Wells Williams, Hart, and Burlingame were a "tough quadrilateral which defends more effectively than have done the Taku forts, Chinese arrogance, pride, and exclusiveness against the inroads of Western civilization."[83]

British residents had considered that Elgin and Bruce were insufficiently vigorous in pressing British claims against the Chinese government.[84] Alcock annoyed them even more; they accused him of actually representing Chinese interests,[85] and of systematically taking the Chinese side in every dispute between British merchants and the Chinese authorities.[86] His support of Prince Kung's objections to railways and river steamers was considered more forceful than Prince Kung's own remarks.[87]

> . . . the Chinese Foreign Board and Sir Rutherford Alcock are exhausting logic to rebut the arguments of foreign merchants in favour of railways, telegraphs, and free communication with the interior.[88]

> The most able member of the Tsungli Yamen, admirable casuists as the Chinese are, could not have produced a more able defence of the position of his government [than Alcock's statement of the Chinese case].[89]

> The case is referred to Peking, and—need we say it—Sir Rutherford Alcock decides adversely to the foreign claimant.[90]

The diplomats' identification of the interests of the Chinese and British governments was not accidental. Alcock, who frankly admitted the identification, labeled the demands of British residents "the case of the merchants versus their own and the Chinese government."[91]

Although consuls in the treaty ports were, by the very nature of their work, more sympathetic to the merchants than the Peking diplomats were, they too often appeared to side with the Chinese against foreign commerce. Consul P. J. Hughes's ruling that certain commodity taxes at Kiukiang were quite legal brought him under virulent attack from the British merchants, who claimed that some countermeasure was "absolutely necessary, to prevent their having to suffer further humiliation at the hands of the local mandarins in the person of Her

[r] See Chapter XI.

Majesty's representative."[92] Consul Charles A. Winchester at Shanghai announced that he intended to discourage anything "presumably offensive to the Chinese authorities," down to the closing hours of foreign theaters and the use of signboards with the words "English" and "American." When the foreign community mentioned "squeeze," Winchester replied that he refused to be the "channel through which general imputations are made against the Chinese authorities."[93]

For the diplomats, isolated as they were from the treaty ports, it was even easier to support the Chinese case on general policy grounds. As the Shanghai General Chamber of Commerce explained to the Chambers of Commerce in England: "Removed from any contact with foreign merchants, and the influence of public opinion, the Foreign Ministers become in a measure advocates of Chinese exclusiveness, rather than of the extension of foreign trade."[94]

Moreover, residence in Peking made the diplomats more susceptible than the consuls to the age-old attractive power of the Middle Kingdom. In the view of one observer: "Peking has exercised upon foreign representatives a sort of unholy glamour. They have been bewitched. Some have fallen down and worshipped before its scholastic and historical traditions; others have treated the great city as a sort of gigantic 'curio'; optimism has been the bane of all."[95]

Shanghai took the view that "a long residence in China, in intimate intercourse with the people, has absolutely the effect of rendering Europeans bad imitations of the Chinese." Alcock was "like every foreigner who ventures within the magic influence of the Peking Cabinet. He becomes gradually convinced that the Chinese are the most upright, well-meaning, and cultivated people on the face of the earth."[96]

Thomas Wade, "with his ultra-celestial views and tendencies,"[97] was perhaps the greatest diplomatic Sinophile of all. He said himself that he began his career in the Customs Service mainly in order to pursue his Chinese studies.[98] A shrewd British commentator described the effect of Wade's scholarship on his politics:

> Seen through the luminous haze of its classic history, China presents to the contemplative mind an object of reverence unlike any other existing state. . . . The burden of such vast homogeneous antiquity may well oppress the mere man of politics; he needs a certain alloy of Philistinism and a limitation of view to enable him to concentrate his attention on the exigencies of the passing hour.[99]

Less erudite criticism was presented in a Hongkong caricature that depicted Wade and Prince Kung conversing amiably while Tseng Kuo-fan danced a hornpipe on the British flag.[100]

This Sinophilism of the diplomats was something more than the normal cordiality between envoys of friendly governments, more than the customary camaraderie between professional diplomats. It reinforced policy considerations and provided the Chinese government with additional protection against undue foreign interference.

Chinese officials of the Restoration period were never quite certain what was behind the Co-operative Policy. They appear to have trusted Hart, Alcock, Wade, and Burlingame up to a point, and they were quick to grasp the opportunities for maneuver that the new diplomatic atmosphere provided.[s] Yet the latent distrust of the foreigner's ultimate intentions remained and quickly returned to the surface in times of crisis.

Well-intentioned British advice on domestic reform met with a mixed reception. Among the Chinese scholars who had begun to study the West and to re-examine China, Wade's and Hart's bold memoranda[t] to the Chinese government, for example, were earnestly discussed.[101] High officials also studied them but thought some portions impertinent. A few considered that the advice was offered not in good faith, but in an effort to weaken China by causing dissension.[102]

CONCLUSION

The importance of the Co-operative Policy to the T'ung-chih Restoration was negative: it provided a period of international peace and safety during which the success or failure of the Restoration depended almost entirely upon Chinese domestic considerations.

There is an interesting divergence of interpretation of the Co-operative Policy among Communist scholars. According to Fan Wen-lan, the Western powers never really intended to strengthen the central government and treated Prince Kung coldly as soon as the "provincial puppets" Li Hung-chang and Tseng Kuo-fan offered their services to the foreigners.[103]

Hu Sheng, on the contrary, is sharply critical of the view, "often the result of pure nationalist emotion," that the Ch'ing government led a pitiable existence, subject to constant abuse by the imperialist powers. He describes at some length the effort of the powers to assist the Chinese government in self-strengthening during the sixties, and concludes that foreign support of the Ch'ing was genuine because it amounted to self-interest. He insists, however, that the West's ultimate aim was political control.[104]

The evidence is otherwise. A succession of British foreign secretaries—Russell, Stanley, and Clarendon—and a succession of envoys to China—Elgin, Bruce, Alcock, and Wade—may sometimes have doubted the Chinese govern-

[s] See Chapters X and XI.
[t] See Chapter XI.

ment's ability to survive and flourish, but they never wavered in their conviction that the Chinese government must be allowed the fullest freedom, not only from foreign military force but from the excessive pressure of foreign advice, foreign commercial requirements, and foreign missionary activity. The British government was prepared to sacrifice immediate interests in the hope, and even the expectation, that the Chinese government would make the necessary adjustments to modern problems at its own pace and on its own terms.

The record as a whole confirms Alcock's statement of British policy during the Restoration.

> [There was] neither a desire nor intention to apply unfriendly pressure to China to induce her Government to advance more rapidly in her intercourse with foreign nations than was consistent with safety and with due and reasonable regard for the feelings of her subjects. . . . By relieving the government of Peking of all anxiety as to the desire of foreign powers either to interfere or dictate what shall or shall not be done for the introduction of great innovations, or to press them in the path of progress beyond what they deem either safe or practicable, they may be induced to listen more willingly to arguments in favour of a beginning.[105]

CHAPTER IV

THE IDEA OF A RESTORATION

THE RESTORATION PHASE OF THE DYNASTIC CYCLE

Chinese civilization has been unique in its resistance to institutional change. The wars, rebellions, and successions of dynasty that have marked its vast recorded history have appeared to be cyclical fluctuations within an enduring society rather than milestones in a progression of changing societies. From this millennial accumulation of evidence, Chinese historians and statesmen have concluded that there is in the affairs of men a natural cycle of flourishing and decay, the governing force in which is human ability (*jen-ts'ai*). In its philosophical aspect this doctrine was a part of the Sung Neo-Confucianism that dominated Chinese nineteenth-century thinking. In a collection of essays selected and presented to the throne by Wo-jen, a leading philosopher-official of the mid-century, the cycle of human affairs was compared to the alternation of *yin* and *yang*. Each phase carried within it the genesis of the other; as one reached its highest point, the other was already developing to replace it. In this process, "as the mind dominates nature, so the quality of the officials decides the fate of the Empire."[1]

In less metaphysical terms, this concept of an inevitable cycle of prosperity and decline, resulting from human talent and subject to modification by human effort, permeated all nineteenth-century Chinese thinking on political and social affairs, irrespective of scholastic affiliations. Mei Tseng-liang (d. 1856) wrote that an era of calamity occurred not when events went awry, nor when the country was bankrupt, but when officials did not attend to public affairs.[2] The administrator Tso Tsung-t'ang wrote that whereas there were cycles of order and rebellion, of security and danger, the control of rebellion and the assurance of security depended on human action.[3]

It was men imbued with this view of the universe who formulated the theory of the dynastic cycle.[a] In brief, the theory was this: A new dynasty at first ex-

---

[a] The best-known formulation is the opening line of one of the most widely read books in world history, *The Romance of the Three Kingdoms*: "When the Empire has long been divided, it must be united; when it has long been united, it must be divided." Ssu-ma Ch'ien (145–86 B.C.) is often credited with the first statement of the theory. However, Ssu-ma merely narrated the early glory of the Han and the subsequent revolt of other clans as increasing favors were granted to the Imperial clan. (Cf. Edouard Chavannes (trans.), *Les Mémoires historiques de Se-ma Ts'ien*, Paris, 1897–1905, II, 509–10.)

Of more interest here is the cyclical theory expounded by Chung-ch'ang T'ung in the third century A.D. Even as he eulogized the new dynasty of Ts'ao Ts'ao, he predicted its inevitable fall on the basis of the bitter experience of the later Han. (Cf. Etienne Balázs, "La Crise sociale et la philoso-

periences a period of great energy, and vigorous and able new officials put in order the civil and military affairs of the Empire. In the course of generations the new period of vigor is followed by a golden age. Territories acquired earlier are held, but no new territories are conquered. Learning and the arts flourish in an atmosphere of elegance. Agricultural production and the people's welfare are supported by the maintenance of peace, attention to public works, and limitation of taxes. This golden age, however, carries within it the seeds of its own decay. The governing class loses first the will and then the ability to meet the high standards of Confucian government. Its increasing luxury places a strain on the exchequer. Funds intended for irrigation, flood control, maintenance of public grain reserves, communications, and payment of the army are diverted by graft to private pockets. As morale is undermined, corruption becomes flagrant.

This process of decline may be retarded by the vigorous training of officials and people in the Confucian social philosophy, but the basic direction of events cannot be altered. Sooner or later, the governing class, blind to those reforms which alone can save it, taxes the peasants beyond endurance and fails to attend to the public welfare. Sporadic local rebellions result, necessitating additional taxes and the recruiting of troops from an increasingly disaffected population. Their stake in the existing order gone, the people express their disaffection in a great rebellion.[b] If the rebellion is successful, the "swarming bandits" become in the eyes of history the "righteous forces."

The great rebellion is usually successful. One of its leaders slowly consolidates his power by securing (1) military superiority; (2) support from the literati, to whom he offers a revived Confucian state that they will administer; and (3) support, at least tacit, from the peasantry, to whom he offers peace, land, reduced taxes, and a program of public works to protect the agricultural economy. The new dynasty thus begins where its predecessor began, and its destiny will follow the same pattern.

In the exceptional case, however, the great rebellion fails in its mission and is suppressed, and the old dynasty recovers its position for a limited time. This variation on the theme results from two concurrent circumstances: (1) the failure of any rebel leader to take the three steps essential to a successful rebellion;

---

phie politique à la fin des Han," *T'oung-pao*, XXXIX (1949), 83–131; Li Kao, "Chung-ch'ang T'ung ti cheng-chih ssu-hsiang," *She-hui k'o-hsüeh chi-k'an*, IV, 3/4 (1924), 22 pp.)

For an illuminating review of the cyclical idea as the means through which the literati could control the crises of Chinese history, see Hsü Ping-ch'ang, "Wo kuo ti hsün-hua-lun che-hsüeh," *Che-hsüeh p'ing-lun*, VIII, 2 (1943), 72–79. See also Lien-sheng Yang, "Toward a Study of Dynastic Configurations in Chinese History," *HJAS*, XVII, 3/4 (1954), 329–45.

[b] This "domestic catastrophe" (*nei-luan*) is often accompanied by "foreign calamity" (*wai-huan*), but the foreign menace is always seen as a symptom of the Chinese state's failure to maintain universal harmony by performing its proper functions, never as the cause of the domestic failure. Until well into the twentieth century, no Chinese conservative, however xenophobic, attempted to lay the responsibility for China's domestic disasters at the door of foreigners.

(2) a resurgence of vigor in the incumbent government, which backs its bid for a temporary renewal of the Mandate of Heaven by displaying military superiority, winning back the support of the literati, and stabilizing the agrarian economy.

This exceptional case of a renewed lease on life is called a Restoration (*chung-hsing*).[c] It is not a *coup d'état* or a revolution or a new age, but an Indian summer[d] in which the historically inevitable process of decline is arrested for a time by the ability and effort of the whole gentry-bureaucracy. The harmony of the natural and social order is temporarily re-established, not through basic changes but through emergency injections of the crucial element in that harmony: the devotion to duty of the indoctrinated Confucian official.

Since this is precisely what happened in the years after 1860, the T'ung-chih reign was considered by contemporaries to be an example of the rare phenomenon of restoration. Hsüeh Fu-ch'eng, in his "Narrative of the Restoration," pointed to its essence: "Within a few years, the Empire was consolidated as of old. Is this not [the result of] human effort [*jen-shih*]? Tradition says: 'To obtain men of talent is to flourish.' How can we not believe this?"[4]

It should be emphasized that the concept of *chung-hsing* was a concept of late flowering. In Chinese eyes it was a period of temporary stabilization following a period of "domestic catastrophe and foreign calamity." Officials of the T'ung-chih period, of course, stated conventionally that the Restoration would be everlasting and that a myriad years of peace and glory were assured. This was no more than a formality, however; loyal scholar-officials obviously would not state in their memorials, and perhaps not even to themselves, that the dynasty was doomed. What is important is that in describing their era as a restoration, they were unmistakably classifying it not with the great creative periods of Chinese history, but with periods between a successfully surmounted crisis and a final catastrophe.

The social and political orientation of Chinese thought has been responsible for a striking recurrence of similar ideas under comparable conditions throughout Chinese history.[5] The scholar-officials of the T'ung-chih period were devoted to the study of history, and they were certainly aware of the implications when

[c] The concept of *chung-hsing* differs considerably from *wei-hsin* and a dozen other phrases, which are also often translated as restoration. *Wei-hsin* (Japanese *isshin*) is the term for the Meiji Restoration in Japan; in the *Historical Record* it meant a new form of government under Ch'in Shih-huang-ti (221–210 B.C.). To recent Chinese writers, the phrase denotes general reform and modernization on the Meiji pattern. The term is extremely rare in Chinese sources of the T'ung-chih period. It appears to have connotations of spiritual spring cleaning and freshening up. (*WHTK*, 1862 (TC-1), p. 9874.)

All these terms can properly be applied to various specific policies and measures of the T'ung-chih period, but none of them describes that peculiar and total phase of the historic process which is meant by *chung-hsing*.

[d] In Toynbee's cycle of Far Eastern civilization, the K'ang-hsi and Ch'ien-lung periods form the Indian summer; in the Chinese view, where each dynasty passes through the complete cycle, these constitute the golden age; the Indian summer is the T'ung-chih Restoration.

they compared their own era to the reigns of Chou Hsüan-wang, Han Kuang-wu, and T'ang Su-tsung. A look at these earlier restorations, therefore, should help us comprehend the aims and estimate the efforts of the statesmen of the T'ung-chih Restoration.

EARLIER RESTORATIONS IN CHINESE HISTORY

The Restoration of Chou Hsüan-wang, 827–782 B.C. The term *chung-hsing* was apparently first used in the *Book of Poetry* with reference to the reign of Chou Hsüan-wang,[6] the first of the three great restorations to which nineteenth-century scholars compared the T'ung-chih era.[7] The decline of the Western Chou began with rebellions in the northwest during the reign of Mu-wang (traditional dates, 1001–947 B.C.), and the decay of the house continued during the misgovernment of successive rulers. Hsüan-wang, however, was an able ruler; he checked foreign calamity by expelling the hostile Jung barbarians from China, and improved internal conditions by studying the mistakes of his predecessors and allowing himself to be guided by experienced officials. There was a degree of economic development, and the Empire was extended as far south as the Yangtze. By the end of Hsüan-wang's reign, however, the Jung were again plundering Shensi and Shansi, and the Western Chou collapsed soon after his death.[8]

In characterizing the reign of Chou Hsüan-wang, Otto Franke characterized all restorations: "The new triumph of the Chou house was of short duration; Hsüan-wang left his son and successor a kingdom whose decline could not be checked, and which was never again to be equal to the external and internal dangers that threatened it."[9]

The Restoration of Han Kuang-wu, A.D. 25–57. The Restoration of Kuang-wu ti, founder of the Eastern Han, was perhaps the most impressive of the four great Chinese restorations. In its course the Han state was rebuilt from the ruin that had followed the Wang Mang usurpation,[10] and this late flowering continued until the Yellow Turban revolt in A.D. 184.

Kuang-wu ti established his capital at Loyang in A.D. 24 while rebel emperors of the Red Eyebrows and other sects were still on the throne in Changan and other parts of the Empire. As Kuang-wu ti by stages defeated the Red Eyebrows, he was able to enroll the most able and energetic of them in his own forces. He subsequently proceeded to retire many of them on liberal allowances and to undertake a program of rehabilitation. Within three years he was able to reduce taxes by two-thirds. This was and has remained the classic pattern for the liquidation of a Chinese rebellion.

Suppression and liquidation of domestic rebellion was followed by a reassertion of Chinese power over outlying dependencies. The revolt of Annam was suppressed by Ma Yüan in A.D. 42. The Hsingan area was brought back under control and the Orkhon area into alliance. By the end of the reign of Kuang-wu ti, China's hegemony in the Far East had been restored and lost territories had been not only reconquered but Sinicized.

The most important aspect of the Han Restoration was the consolidation of Confucian institutions and ideology. The political vigor of the dynasty itself, which had appeared so striking in the years immediately after A.D. 25, declined rapidly. But as the central power was weakened by luxury, eunuchs, and ineffective princes, the literati's power grew; they firmly established the Confucian political orthodoxy and used it to delay the inevitable collapse. This orthodoxy remained China's great reserve of conservative strength until the twentieth century.

The Eastern Han ended with the revolt of the Yellow Turbans, more properly the T'ai-p'ing rebels, in A.D. 184. The Yellow Turbans offered a promise of equality based on a formidable military organization, a communal life, and discipline through the public confession of sins. The rebellion itself was suppressed, but too late, by an alliance between the aristocracy and the literati. The enormous destruction it had caused favored the rise of militarists rather than the resurgence of Confucian government.[11]

The restoration of Han Kuang-wu was conspicuously successful in reviving military power, bureaucratic government, and the arts; but it was nonetheless an Indian summer, a period of retarded decline rather than a great new age. Wang Fu (ca. A.D. 90–165), in his "Deserted Village" lament for the passing of the later Han, wrote a classic description of the weakness born of strength and the poverty born of riches, the eternal fate of restorations in the dynastic cycle. He decried the display of luxury and the increasing use of exotic products. As middlemen rose, agriculture declined; the slowness and chicanery of the courts proved the inadequacy of government by virtue and the need for stern legal controls.[12]

The era was officially classified as a restoration by the compilers of the *History of the Later Han*,[13] and it has remained for later Chinese an example of what can and cannot be restored in the brief time between an unsuccessful rebellion and a subsequent successful one.

The Restoration of T'ang Su-tsung, A.D. 756–762. The Restoration of T'ang Su-tsung is the most relevant of the earlier restorations to the nineteenth-century effort. Rebellion had been widespread in the lean years preceding the An Lushan Rebellion (A.D. 755–763). Taxes, the corvée, and military service had become more oppressive, and more and more peasant lands were being sold for debt. Frontier garrisons were frequently manned by non-Chinese, and separatist feeling in the northeastern provinces (then Chihli and Shansi) mounted.

With the revolt of An Lu-shan, the already weakened T'ang financial organization collapsed. The public treasury was exhausted at the very moment when the general upheaval required increased military expenditure. As taxes rose, more than one-third of the population secured exemption through official connections, by purchasing titles, or by entering monasteries. The burden on the rest became intolerable.

Most of the cities that had been lost to the rebels were recovered during the lifetime of Su-tsung, and the rebellion was finally crushed in the year after his death. However, the Empire's military success was caused by dissension among the rebels and the use of foreign (Uighur) troops by the T'ang, rather than by fundamental recovery. Externally, China lost all her territories except Annam and Tonkin. Internally, land rents remained exorbitant—at least one-half of the harvest—nor did the land-owning peasants' status improve. Wealth and population declined, and the free peasant virtually disappeared. In a generation of civil war, prices rose threefold, and years of drought and bad harvests culminated in catastrophe in 785–786.

By the end of the eighth century only 5 per cent of the population were peasant proprietors. The government read the ominous signs, and candidates for office were asked in the palace examination of 806 to suggest how the decline might be arrested and the Empire restored to its former prosperity. In language that was to echo through the late nineteenth century, the great poet Po Chü-i replied:

> The distress of the people is due to heavy taxation, heavy taxation is due to the increase in the armed forces, the increase in the armed forces is due to the number of rebellions and the rebellions are due to defects in government.[14]

The more original reply of another poet-candidate presaged the views of the great reformers of the nineteenth century from Feng Kuei-fen to K'ang Yu-wei: Yüan Chen proposed modifying the examination system so as to recruit men of greater practical governing ability from all social classes.[15] But the decline could not be arrested. The peasant landowners, bedrock of the traditional state, had become an agricultural proletariat, and in 874 the T'ang was destroyed by a successful rebellion.[16]

THE APPLICATION OF THE TERM "RESTORATION" TO THE T'UNG-CHIH PERIOD

To the statesmen of the 1860's the suppression of the Taiping and Nien-fei rebellions appeared readily comparable to the suppression of the Wang Mang Rebellion by the Han and of the An Lu-shan Rebellion by the T'ang. The Ch'ing used European aid as the T'ang used Uighur aid, and the precedent was cited. Tso Tsung-t'ang's suppression of the Moslem Rebellion in the northwest brought to mind Chou Hsüan-wang's campaigns against the Jung. Hu Lin-i's achievements were also compared to those of the Chou Restoration.[17] Tseng Kuo-fan pointed out that the authority of the T'ang during its restoration did not extend north of the Yellow River; that the authority of the Sung during its restoration (1127–61) did not extend north of the Yangtze; but that the whole Empire was included in the T'ung-chih Restoration.[18]

As the T'ung-chih reign drew to its end, the verdict was recorded: the T'ung-chih reign was one of the four great restorations of all Chinese history. "Restoration" was not a term to be bandied about in the day-to-day business of government, and its use with reference to the era was at first cautious. But by 1869 the governor-general of Kiangsu, Kiangsi, and Anhwei, Ma Hsin-i, could refer to the "Spirit of the Restoration"; his triple elevation of the characters for *chung-hsing* indicates the august aura of the term.[19] In 1872 Li Tsung-hsi, who had succeeded to Ma's post, wrote of "Restoration" as a still imperfectly realized ideal, again elevating the term.[20] The governor of Kiangsu wrote that as the disorders of the T'ung-chih period had exceeded those of the T'ang and Sung, so was their control a greater achievement.[21] Collected memorials of the period were issued as memorials of the Restoration, collected biographies as biographies of Restoration statesmen;[22] and one of the compilers, Ch'en T'ao, in 1875 compared the T'ung-chih period to the reign of Chou Hsüan-wang.[23]

From the vantage point of 1921, the compiler of the last of the great series of Imperial encyclopedias looked back complacently on the T'ung-chih period as a time in which "domestic catastrophe and foreign calamity had been gradually eliminated." In perspective, Mu-tsung, the T'ung-chih Emperor, appeared to have followed in the footsteps of Shih-tsu, the founder of the Ch'ing, much as the Han Restoration Emperor Kuang-wu's "penetration and capacity corresponded to those of Kao-tsu," the founder of the Han; for in both the Han and Ch'ing dynasties, "one era was the Creation, the other the Restoration."[24]

The chapters which follow deal with the various aspects of the T'ung-chih reign that to contemporaries were reminiscent of the earlier restorations. In two fields, the arts and literature, no comparisons were made, for there was nothing in the T'ung-chih period to suggest the revival of the arts that marked the Eastern Han Restoration, or the superb prose and poetry of the T'ang Restoration.[e] The

---

[e] Hu Shih has pointed out that the poetry of the T'ung-chih period seldom refers to sufferings in the Taiping period; that the old forms and subjects were scarcely affected by the holocaust. ("Wu-shih nien lai Chung-kuo chih wen-hsüeh," Shen-pao kuan Fiftieth Anniversary Publication, Vol. II, *Wu-shih nien lai chih Chung-kuo*, Shanghai, 1922, pp. 3–5.) See also Wang Pi-chiang, "Chin-tai shih-p'ai yü ti-yü hsiao-ch'ien," *Chung-kuo hsüeh-pao* (Chungking), I, 1 (1943), 45–54. However, there was still creditable writing in the traditional manner. See Jen Nai, "T'ung-Kuang shih-jen Li Yü-hsien," *I-ching*, No. 8 (1936), pp. 26–31.

accomplishments of the T'ung-chih reign were primarily political and social; they were accompanied, as in the Han Restoration, by a revival of the traditional learning on which society was based, but not by a revival of its creative gifts.

The ethos of the T'ung-chih period is suggested by the fact that the gifted and versatile Kuo Sung-tao stopped writing poetry about 1854. As he himself explained in 1862, poets were now making playthings of no benefit to the individual or to society; the superior man could take no part in such activities.[25]

THE IMPERIAL ROLE

In theory, a restoration was the work of a strong, able, and virtuous ruler; and in fact the Chinese political system had always required for its proper working an effective central executive power. At first glance, therefore, it appears absurd to call the T'ung-chih period a restoration; the Emperor was a child and a weakling, and the young Empress Dowager Tz'u-hsi was more distinguished for political maneuvering than for the true statesmanship of reconstruction. It should be remembered, however, that the Chinese Emperor was always more important as a function than as a personality. The concurrence of a ritually acceptable Emperor and a group of capable officials was enough. With the formal amenities preserved, the officials could perform the Imperial function of harmonizing the social order,[26] taking care to attribute their achievements to the Throne. The combination would be, for all practical purposes, the equivalent of a strong, able, and virtuous ruler.

This synthetic substitute was less stable, of course, than the genuine product; more reform could doubtless have been risked with a K'ang-hsi on the throne. But there was in fact a restoration without a K'ang-hsi or a Han Kuang-wu, and the explanation, as far as the Imperial role is concerned, lies in the prestige and ability of Prince Kung.[f] Prince Kung provided the channel through which the ideas of Restoration statesmen could be sanctioned and implemented, and that was the essence of the Imperial role.

The Empress Dowager Tz'u-hsi's gradual rise to supreme power did not begin until 1865, and she did not achieve the position of autocrat until a decade later.[27] The real makers of the Restoration were the high civil and military officials. The bureaucracy of the Eastern Han preserved the fruits of restoration long after the rulers grew feeble; the bureaucracy of the late Ch'ing did more: it created a restoration under a feeble ruler.[g]

[f] See Chapter II.

[g] A Japanese historian of the Ch'ing has pushed this point further and argued that the absence of a strong ruler was a positive asset in the T'ung-chih Restoration. In his view, the T'ang Restoration, which was based on the Emperor's ability, could not survive the Emperor's mistakes; the T'ung-chih Restoration was more firmly grounded in the ability of high officials and in the effectiveness of the new military forces. (Yano Jin'ichi, *Kindai Shina shi*, Tokyo, 1940, chap. 21, *FB* 2.1.11.)

MANCHU INTERESTS AND CHINESE INTERESTS

It has been fashionable for several decades, under both the Kuomintang and the Communists, to accuse the Manchus of selling the country to save the dynasty. By using this device, conservatives have been able to advocate national revolution without social revolution, and to hold that China's modern problems can be solved only by reasserting those traditional *Chinese* values allegedly obscured by Manchu rule.[h]

Marxist scholars have found it equally convenient to distort the role of the Manchus, whose baleful influence they link with that of the imperialists[i] to explain China's "peculiar" development during the past century. By grossly exaggerating the machinations of this unholy combine, doctrinaire leftists are saved from the unorthodox conclusion that premodern Chinese society was not feudal and that more recent Chinese society has not been bourgeois. Because of the intense concern of Kuomintang and Communist historians with the role of the Manchus, few factors are more important in assaying the development of modern Chinese society. Moreover, since the Ch'ing was the only alien dynasty in Chinese history during which a restoration occurred, an understanding of the Manchu role in the T'ung-chih Restoration should clarify our understanding of what Wittfogel has called "symbiosis," the process by which Chinese and alien societies have continued to coexist, with varying degrees of mutual adjustment.

Even with the Ch'ing, the most fully Sinicized of all the alien dynasties, acculturation did not lead to simple or complete absorption. As Wittfogel points out, "political factors present until the close of the dynasty thwarted complete amalgamation."[28] That the amalgamation was never complete is obvious; it was, however, more nearly complete than is generally recognized, and the direction of the trend may in this case be the significant point. Between 1860 and 1890, the Manchu-Chinese dividing line tended to disappear. Only after the failure of the 1898 reforms were suspicions and animosities revived on both sides.[29] Manchu-Chinese conflict characterized the period before the Restoration and the last years of the dynasty. The Restoration period saw the trend reversed.

According to Wittfogel, the factors that precluded the Manchus' complete amalgamation were: (1) the persistence of the earlier military organization known as the Eight Banners, membership in which placed most Manchus out-

---

[h] Chang T'ai-yen is a good illustration of the early revolutionaries whose plan for the future of China did not go beyond elimination of the Manchus. Far from attacking the traditional society, he revered it. In a debate with K'ang Yu-wei, he insisted that the faults of nineteenth-century government were not traditional Chinese faults, but faults of the Manchus, who had always held the real power. ("Po K'ang Yu-wei," originally written in 1903 in reply to K'ang's "Nan-hai hsien-sheng tsui-chin cheng-chih shu" and reprinted by the Kuomintang in *Tang-shih shih-liao ts'ung-k'an*, No. 1, pp. 11–17.)

[i] See Chapter III.

first-born
inheritance

side normal Chinese jurisdiction, (2) the absence of primogeniture in the Manchu dynastic succession laws, (3) the Manchu dominance of the bureaucracy, especially the top posts, and (4) the general ban on intermarriage, which was not revoked until 1904.[30] However, as will be indicated further below, during the Restoration the Banner system lost most of its significance as a barrier between Manchu and Chinese, and Manchus were rapidly losing their special position in the bureaucracy. The general ban on intermarriage, although it remained on the books, lost much of its effectiveness in view of the steady revocation of all types of special Manchu protective legislation. The question of primogeniture was no longer of practical significance.

The early Ch'ing, it is true, had attempted to prevent, or at least to limit, Manchu-Chinese adaptation. After an initial period of encouraging Chinese colonization of Manchuria, policy shifted, and beginning in the early K'ang-hsi period immigration was discouraged. In an effort to preserve the Manchu homeland intact, Manchuria was by degrees closed to immigration until in the Yung-cheng period it was virtually sealed off.[31]

However, this policy of keeping Manchuria distinct from China was gradually reversed during the eighteenth century. The barrier had in any case proved weak, and the Chinese population of Manchuria had grown steadily. Moreover, the policy of reserving Manchurian land for Bannermen had been a failure, for the Bannermen were poor farmers. In these circumstances, the increasingly Sinicized Manchu rulers lost interest in preserving a Manchu cultural entity, and from the late eighteenth century onward Manchuria was by degrees assimilated to China proper. Step by step, the province of Kirin was opened, a Chinese-style local government was established at Changchun and the Chinese form of administration superseded the Manchu throughout the area. With the opening of the port of Newchwang by the Treaties of Tientsin, efforts to populate Manchuria with Chinese as a protective measure were accelerated. By the beginning of the T'ung-chih period, although certain special regulations remained on the books,[32] Manchuria was no longer cordoned off.

By the mid-nineteenth century the Manchus had long since won the support of the Chinese gentry and bureaucracy,[33] and the Taiping Rebellion drove home the identity of the two groups' interests. Friction had ceased to follow racial lines. It was a Manchu, Su-shun (and indeed the Hsien-feng Emperor himself), who saw the necessity for granting greater powers to Tseng Kuo-fan and Tso Tsung-t'ang, and it was a Chinese, Ch'i Chün-tsao, who delivered to the Hsien-feng Emperor the often-quoted warning about the potential danger to the dynasty from Tseng and his regional Hsiang Army.[34]

By 1860 China was governed by a unified Manchu-Chinese upper class whose great common aim was to preserve the Chinese cultural heritage[35] against the depredations of domestic rebellion and the threat of Western domination. Chinese social revolutionaries have correctly recognized their historic enemy, but they have incorrectly labeled that enemy alien:[36] the Manchus were inimical to the Chinese revolution not because they were Manchus in blood but because they were so consummately Chinese in culture. As the reformer K'ang Yu-wei put it, if the government of the Ch'ing had faults, they were the ancient faults of the Han, T'ang, Sung, and Ming—"It was not a special Manchu system."[37]

During the Restoration there was little substantial evidence of the later widely alleged divergencies in policy between Manchu and Chinese officials. On controversial issues Manchus and Chinese were to be found on both sides, without any significant pattern of opinion. For example, Chinese nationalists, particularly Cantonese mercantile groups, have often called the likin[j] an instrument of Manchu oppression. But the likin was devised by a Chinese, Lei I-hsien, and was favored by Lo Ping-chang and many high Chinese officials; moreover, it was vigorously opposed by many Manchus, among them Ch'üan-ch'ing. Various conflicts were involved in the likin issue: the need for increased revenues versus the unpopularity of increased taxation; the nationally controlled revenues versus the provincially controlled revenues; agricultural interests versus commercial interests in the division of the tax load; and the special interests of foreign trade versus Chinese reluctance to increase or perpetuate them. But the Chinese-Manchu issue was not involved.

Personal jealousies between officials of course existed, but not (apparently) along ethnic lines. Some factions were based on personal loyalty, others on policy views; but every faction seems to have included both Manchus and Chinese. True, a Manchu once attempted to impeach Tseng Kuo-fan on grounds of arrogance, but another Manchu, Prince Kung, refused to listen to the charges, and an edict from the Manchu throne dismissed them as entirely unfounded.[38]

By the time of the Restoration the use of Manchu, even as a secondary official language, had almost disappeared—the Manchus themselves no longer knew it. An edict of January 1862 recognized an existing situation when it exempted Manchu candidates in the examinations from translating the Chinese Classics into Manchu. By 1871 the use of Manchu was so much the exception even among border military officials that a request to write reports in Manchu was the occasion of a special edict.[39]

Most of the last restrictions[40] separating the Manchus from the Chinese were removed in 1865. The sad plight of the Bannermen themselves was made the pretext for the changes, and certainly something had to be done to adjust their formal status to their circumstances. Relaxing the restrictions had been suggested as early as the Tao-kuang period, and a number of Chinese officials had memorialized on this subject in the early years of the Restoration. Chiang Ch'i-ling

j See Chapter VIII.

memorialized in 1861, but no action was taken. Subsequently the censor Tu Jui-lien raised the problem again and asked that the Board of Revenue work out the details.[41] The governor-general of Chihli, Liu Ch'ang-yu, memorialized to similar effect, with a number of procedural suggestions designed to make certain that Banner land, when sold, would be placed on the tax rolls.[42] Finally a similar memorial from Shen Kuei-fen, then governor of Shansi and later a pivotal figure in the metropolitan Restoration bureaucracy, brought results.

Shen proposed that distressed Bannermen be allowed, for their own sake, to merge with the general population.[43] The Throne responded by instructing the lieutenant-generals of the Eight Banners and others to consult with the Board of Revenue and other boards, and to memorialize concerning their findings. The lieutenant-generals and the boards replied approving Shen's proposals. They specifically proposed that all categories of Bannermen be allowed to proceed to any province they chose, subject to the approval of the Banner commander. Legal privileges were to be waived: "In all litigation, they should be under the jurisdiction of the chou and hsien officials. If some do not attend to their own affairs and stir up trouble, they should be punished by the local officials according to the same law as the common people." They proposed also that Bannermen be permitted to register in Chinese village registers, to take the same examinations as Chinese, to enroll in the regular Chinese forces (*lü-ying*), to cultivate the land, and to engage in trade. The Emperor agreed—"Everything proposed is eminently satisfactory," said the Imperial edict—and the lieutenant-generals were ordered to carry out the new regulations.[44]

Contemporary foreigners did not miss the significance of this legislation. The editors of the *North China Herald* were aware that the Chinese had long since absorbed the Manchus.

> But we were not prepared for the sweeping legislation of the edict of which we this day publish a translation. Therein all the most cherished privileges of the Tartars are at a blow swept away.[45]

Another observer commented:

> An Imperial edict . . . abolishing the hereditary duties and peculiar courts of these troops [the Banners], permitting individuals to pursue any calling at their pleasure, and subjecting them in all matters to the ordinary tribunals of the country, thus abolishing the last distinctive mark between conquerors and conquered, excited but little interest, and is merely worth a passing remark as showing how completely the assimilation of the two races has been effected.[46]

Thus, although Wittfogel correctly points out that the ban on general intermarriage and the vestiges of the Banner system "thwarted complete amalgamation," the persistent trend *toward* amalgamation may be more significant.

It is widely held that until the very end of the dynasty the Manchus continued to dominate the bureaucracy, especially the top bureaucracy, and that as the end approached, Manchu exclusiveness increased.[47] This last is true, of course—witness the Manchu cabinet of 1911—but the trend does not appear to have been continuous. As the evidence now stands, the trend away from Manchu dominance and toward Sino-Manchu synthesis during the Restoration appears far more important historically than any lingering traces of earlier Manchu domination.

The most detailed studies of the composition of the late Ch'ing bureaucracy are still those prepared three-quarters of a century ago on the basis of data for the 1860's and 1870's. From a study of the composition of the top metropolitan and provincial hierarchies, F. S. A. Bourne concluded:

> To those who regard China as under a foreign yoke, it will seem strange that out of the 144 officials in this list, forming as they do the supreme government of the country, only 32 should be Manchus; yet such is the fact. The small share which Manchus have in the executive government will appear in a still stronger light when we note that amongst the six Ministers of the Grand Council, and the twenty-three Governors and Governors-general, there are only six Manchus. The three Kiang [Kiangsu, Kiangsi, and Anhwei] alone are more numerously represented than the Manchus—there are 47 officers of the former against 32 of the latter.[48]

These findings were confirmed by a cross-section taken in the late 1870's, which showed that all governors-general were Chinese, as were fifteen of the eighteen governors, fourteen of the eighteen provincial financial commissioners, and fifteen of the eighteen provincial judicial commissioners. Chinese dominated the lower bureaucracy as well. Ninety per cent of the officials below the rank of taotai were Chinese, 7 per cent were Manchu, just over 1 per cent were Mongol, and just under 2 per cent were Chinese Bannermen. Another set of figures dismisses the hypothesis that the Manchus may have administered the more important fu, chou, and hsien, leaving only the many unimportant districts to the Chinese.[49] These figures contrast sharply with those for the pre-Restoration period[50] and for the Ch'ing period as a whole.[k]

Admittedly these studies take no account of such relevant factors as length

---

k For the Ch'ing period as a whole, the figures are:

I. Grand Secretaries and Associate Grand Secretaries		II. The Six Boards, the Li-fan yüan, and the Censorate	
Manchus	99	Manchus	328
Mongols	18	Mongols	18
Chinese Bannermen	18	Chinese Bannermen	77
Chinese	128	Chinese	262
III. Governors-general		IV. Governors	
Manchus	209	Manchus	171
Mongols	18	Mongols	18
Chinese Bannermen	77	Chinese Bannermen	10
Chinese	288	Chinese	573

(P'an Kuang-tan, "Chin-tai Su-chou ti jen-ts'ai," *She-hui k'o-hsüeh*, I, 1 (1935), 49–98.)

of tenure in a given post, and the powers in provincial government of the Manchu generals-in-chief. Nonetheless, with every allowance for error, it still appears clear that during the T'ung-chih Restoration the Manchu and Chinese governing classes did in fact coalesce into a single Chinese-dominated governing class dedicated to the preservation of the Confucian state. Inaba has gone too far in calling the Manchus "the puppets of the Chinese" during this period.[51] They were not puppets of the Chinese; they were, for all practical purposes, Chinese.

Thus although the T'ung-chih Restoration was certainly not a nationalistic Chinese movement, neither was it a betrayal of a national movement by traitors who served an alien throne. More than the coexistence of Manchu and Chinese societies, it was very nearly a Sino-Manchu synthesis, a genuinely harmonious coalition that marked a new stage in the development of the non-national Confucian monarchy as the symbol of traditional culturalism.

The polemics of both Right and Left on the Manchu issue have failed to take account of the central point. On the Right, Chiang Kai-shek wrote that the political institutions of the Ch'ing were as great as those of the Han and T'ang and that, but for Manchu mistakes in policy, China would have advanced as Europe did.[52] In fact, the Manchu mistake was the effort to preserve in the modern period those very political institutions in which Chiang placed his faith. On the Left, Fan Wen-lan wrote with more accuracy that the Manchu and Chinese officials of the Restoration were prepared if necessary to come to terms with the West because they thought that only trade was at stake, but were opposed to the death to Chinese rebels because they knew the Confucian temples were at stake.[53] Fan realized, as Chiang did not, that the Manchu vested interest lay in the Confucian heritage. But to label their defense of this heritage "treachery" is to distort Chinese history.

For Chinese of the mid-nineteenth century the Manchu dynasty had become the protector of the Chinese national faith, and this political fact was duly noted in the chancelleries of Europe:

> Not only the gentry and educated classes, but the mass of the people regard with deep veneration the sages upon whose authority their moral and social education for so many generations has reposed. And the profession of novel doctrines, resting on the testimony of a modern and obscure individual, must tend not only to deprive the revolt of its character as a national rising against the Tartar yoke, but must actually transfer to the Tartars and their adherents the prestige of upholding national traditions and principles against the assaults of a numerically insignificant sect.[54]

As Sun Yat-sen regretfully noted, most Chinese supported the Manchus, and many gave them active support, because through the examination system the Manchus had won over "almost all the men of wisdom and learning."[55]

REGIONALISM AND CENTRALISM

The contrast between powerful regional officials and a weak central government, so obvious in China from the 1890's to the Communist conquest, has led to the view in some quarters that regionalism steadily increased from the time of the Taiping Rebellion.

There can be no question of the breakdown of central authority during the Taiping period. In Chinese theory the power of competent, semiautonomous, regional leaders was bound to grow, and in historic fact it did. In theory the central government was bound to attempt to overcome these dissident tendencies by reasserting Confucian social controls, and in historic fact it did. The first and centrifugal phase of this process has been widely discussed; the second and centripetal phase has been largely ignored.

Rebellion and restoration were complementary phases of the process of change in traditional China. The growing regionalism that had marked the early Taiping period was for a time arrested, and the centrifugal forces of an age of rebellion were transformed, by the alchemy of the Confucian ideology, into the centripetal forces of an age of restoration.

Regionalism has been ever present in China—the question is one of degree. According to a leading theorist of the Restoration, Feng Kuei-fen, centralization of power and division of power were both essential in governing the Empire. Without centralization, the vast area could not be united into a single whole, and the Empire would be divided into warring states; without division of power, the unified government could not reach down far enough to include the vast populations, and the Empire would be in rebellion.[56] The taotais, prefects, and county magistrates represented the central power; the gentry and the gentry-controlled local organizations represented the local power.[l]

After 1861 central and regional forces were for a time so channeled that they reinforced each other. Almost simultaneously, the whole ruling class, central and local alike, recoiled from the shock of domestic and foreign menace and saw in a revived, nation-wide Confucianism its only hope of survival. The examination system is best understood as an institution that sharpened this awareness of common interest, and at the same time provided it with a means of expression.[57]

Tseng Kuo-fan is often referred to as the prototype of later independent provincial leaders, and there can be no question of his enormous regional power. The critical point is this: On whose behalf did he exercise that power and to

---

[l] According to Franz Michael: "Even in the period of strongest central government, however, local autonomy could never be entirely eliminated, nor was there any such intention; for, since these local groups, especially the gentry, from which the officialdom was derived, were vital organs of social control, the problem was not their suppression but their restraint." ("Military Organization and Power Structure of China During the Taiping Rebellion," *PHR*, XVIII, 4 (1949), 470.)

what end? On the evidence—and it is voluminous—Tseng saw no conflict between his national and regional loyalties, and used his talents, powers, and prestige toward the restoration of a central Confucian state firmly grounded in local
Confucian society.^m In the chain of social pressures from bottom to top, he and
his kind were links through which the embattled gentry could make effective
their support of the central government as the mainstay of the Confucian order;
and in the chain of command from top to bottom, they were links through which
the central authority could make itself effective on the local scene. Tseng was
the greatest of the provincial leaders, but in his support of the Restoration government he spoke for all.

Conversely, high metropolitan officials shared the aims and methods of the
provincial officials. Many of them in fact held posts alternately in the capital
and in the provinces.ⁿ For example, Shen Kuei-fen, often considered the model
of a metropolitan restoration official as Tseng was the model of a provincial restoration official, actually formulated some of his chief contributions to restoration
policy when he was a provincial official, governor of Shansi. Conversely, Tseng's
power rested in part on long service at Peking before he became a regional leader.

Thus the record of the T'ung-chih period does not show a cleavage between
a metropolitan hierarchy trying to administer the whole Empire directly from
Peking on the one hand, and a series of embryonic warlords scheming to set up
satrapies for themselves on the other. On the contrary, it shows the re-establishment, for a time, of the traditional balance between central and provincial
authority. A Tseng could oppose a government that had forgotten the Confucian heritage, but never a government, however weak, which was the sole protector of that heritage.

The notion that during the Restoration period the gentry and literati opposed the Taiping rebels without being loyal to the Ch'ing, and hence refused
official posts, appears to be pure myth. The generalization is usually made without any examples of leading figures who refused government appointments;
the case of P'eng Yü-lin, sometimes cited as proof of the general statement,⁵⁸
actually demolishes it. P'eng had a long career fighting on the Imperial side.
In 1862 he accepted an appointment as junior vice-president of the Board of
War; in 1863 he was named commander of the Yangtze Navy, in 1864 junior
guardian of the heir apparent. It is true that after 1865 he preferred to remain
at home with his books, but he was nearly always a government adviser, and in
1883 he came back to active service as president of the Board of War.⁵⁹ His

---

^m See Chapters V and IX.

ⁿ Any listing of the posts held in succession by any representative group of Restoration officials
will illustrate the point. The man who was always a provincial official or always a metropolitan
official was rare indeed; cf. Bourne, "Historical Table of High Officials Composing the Central and
Provincial Governments of China," *China Review*, VII, 5 (1878–79), 324.

career, far from showing disloyalty to the Ch'ing, is striking proof that even a scholar strongly inclined toward a private life could be pulled in to support the Restoration's central machinery.

By the end of the nineteenth century the Restoration had long since failed, and the breach between central and provincial authority had widened. Provincial leaders became increasingly independent, and the central government attempted on paper to enforce extreme policies of centralization. The fragmentation of the integrated Confucian state into a series of excessively regional or excessively central factions was ultimately accomplished; it had begun with the Taiping Rebellion, but it was not a continuous process. During the decade of restoration the direction of the process was reversed, and the traditional balance between central and regional power was once again affirmed.

THE PHILOSOPHIC BASES OF RESTORATION THOUGHT[60]

It was the Confucian ideology that united the Manchus and the Chinese, the metropolitan officials and the local gentry, and that provided the chief instrument for the control of the peasantry and the framework for limited modernization.

The school of Confucian thought that dominated the nineteenth century was singularly appropriate to the political tasks of the time. The work of Han school scholars had appeared increasingly pedantic and remote as domestic catastrophe and foreign calamity mounted; revived Sung Neo-Confucianism, particularly as interpreted by the T'ung-ch'eng school, offered both solace and a means of action, especially after the Opium War.[61] Its separation of moral values from material conditions was comforting in time of trouble. And the clarity, simplicity, and emphasis on significance rather than exegesis that characterized its *ku-wen* style provided a medium for the great moral tracts of the time.[o]

From the philosophy of Chu Hsi, the Neo-Confucian revival drew the idea that whereas the "principle" on which state and society were organized had an objective existence and could not be destroyed, it assumed form only when men followed it. Accord with this objective principle was the key to successful government.[62]

From the eighteenth century on, the ideological approach of the Sung school gradually overshadowed the philological approach of the Han school. Late in the Ch'ien-lung period disciples began to flock to T'ung-ch'eng in northern Anhwei, where Yao Nai, Liu Ta-k'uei, and Fang Pao had founded a school.

---

[o] The collections on statecraft of the Sung school are in marked contrast to the monumental textual studies of the Han school. An excellent selection of examples is to be found in *Wan-Ch'ing wen-hsüan*, compiled by Cheng Chen-to, Shanghai, 1937.

From the beginning, the T'ung-ch'eng school placed less emphasis on research and more on moral teaching. Later, under Tseng Kuo-fan's influence, its attention was increasingly directed to public affairs.[63]

Tseng Kuo-fan, Lo Tse-nan, Hu Lin-i, Tso Tsung-t'ang, and many others studied under T'ung-ch'eng teachers[64] in "backward" Hunan, which had escaped the scholastic development of the Han school during its period of fashion in the traditional seats of learning.[65] The influence of the T'ung-ch'eng teaching expanded so greatly under Tseng's encouragement that it may fairly be called the doctrine of the Restoration. Although Tseng himself aimed at a broad eclecticism that would provide a synthesis of all schools, and was greatly influenced by the leading Han school scholar Ku Yen-wu, he revered a trinity of Confucius, Chou Kung, and Yao Nai and based his philosophy of government on a T'ung-ch'eng foundation.[66]

As a framework for vigorous political writing, the T'ung-ch'eng school subsequently declined. Yen Fu, K'ang Yu-wei, Liang Ch'i-ch'ao, T'an Ssu-t'ung, and other original political thinkers of the end of the century had early T'ung-ch'eng phases but later developed along other lines.[67] In the mid-nineteenth century, however, the T'ung-ch'eng school was the great rallying point of political thought, with which both morality and literature were identified. It was the seed-bed of all Restoration thinking about public affairs.[68]

THE CONCEPT OF SOCIAL STABILITY

The complementary ideas of a stable society based on the *li* (principles of social usage),[p] and of change *within* that society (*pien-t'ung*), were prominent in the Neo-Confucian ideology of the T'ung-chih period. From these two concepts were derived the values of the time: domestic and international peace; economic security through frugality rather than through expanding material welfare; social harmony and individual serenity based on Confucian social principles; cultural pride and devotion not to the Chinese nation, but to the unique way of life of the Chinese people.[69]

Observers of the Chinese scene have always been amazed at the spectacle of a vast population apparently governing itself in a peaceful, orderly, and dignified manner, and preserving intact its social institutions through crises severe enough to have obliterated other societies.

> What is the power which holds the Chinese Empire together? . . . It is expected to perish every year. . . . [But] the Empire that was full of life in the days of Melchizidec may yet outlast all the younger growths, and preserve a persistent vitality, when all the kingdoms and sceptres of Europe shall be broken and destroyed.

p I am using the translation suggested by Hellmut Wilhelm in his "Political Ideology in Nineteenth-Century China," Seattle, 1949 (mimeographed).

Now what is the bond which holds the vast incongruous mass of dominion in its place?[70]

The answer was the concept of the *li*, which lay at the root of Chinese social thought[q] and re-emerged to dominate the social thinking of the Restoration period.

The bond that held the Confucian state together was this careful hierarchical ordering of society from top to bottom, with clearly defined rights and obligations for every individual and every group. A general harmony resulted when these rights were recognized and the corollary duties performed with the state as arbiter. In the course of millennia this harmony had become the dominant motivating value of Chinese society.[71]

The strength of this bond depended on the maintenance of the Confucian ideology by the state and its general acceptance by all strata of Chinese society. Yet although the ideological issue was primary, the struggle to revive the orthodox doctrine was not a war of creeds in the Western sense: it was contended not that the people were in the first instance led astray by false doctrines, but that the weakening of the orthodox doctrine had undermined government by virtue, thus *indirectly* causing the people to rebel and to follow false doctrines. The effort to restore the orthodox doctrine was, therefore, mainly positive—an effort to restore good government and thus eliminate the causes of erroneous popular beliefs. Direct attack on false creeds was distinctly secondary, for rebel ideologies were considered symptoms, not causes. The Restoration official was a zealot with a mission and a doctrine, but not in the Western sense.

Restoration policy was based on the notion that the universe is harmonious and that human nature is good; that the chief social controls are not laws but social norms (*li*) supplemented by punishments (*hsing*). Prince Kung, in an

q The *li* as understood by traditional Chinese is very close to the "norm" as understood by contemporary social scientists: "A norm, then, is an idea in the mind of the members of a group, an idea that can be put in the form of a statement specifying what the members or other men should do, ought to do, are expected to do under given circumstances. . . . No doubt the norms accepted in a group vary somewhat from one person to another, and from one sub-group to another, and yet the *members of the group are often more nearly alike in the norms they hold than in their overt behavior.* To put the matter crudely, they are more alike in what they say they ought to do than in what they do in fact." (George C. Homans, *The Human Group*, New York, 1950, pp. 123, 126.) Traditional society was marked by an elaborate development of these norms, so much so that Kluckhohn has defined as a "Confucian state" a situation where you want to do what you have to do, and have to do what you want to do.

All observers of traditional Chinese social life have been struck by the endless gossip about the proprieties and their violation, and this is important, for according to Kluckhohn: "Where gossip is most current is where that culture is most heavily laden with values. The discussability of values is one of their most essential properties, though the discussion may be oblique or disguised—not labelled as a consideration of values." ("Values and Value-Orientations in the Theory of Action," in Talcott Parsons and Edward A. Shils (eds.), *Toward a General Theory of Action*, Cambridge, Mass., 1951, p. 404.)

essay entitled "The Principles of Social Usage as the Basis of the State" ("Li k'o i wei kuo lun"), wrote: "Those who would destroy the state must first eliminate these principles of social usage."[72] The hierarchy of society, upon which peace and the good life depended, was the result of proper attention to these principles. In Prince Kung's words, which might have been those of any member of the Sino-Manchu governing class, the foundations of the state were secure when moral authority proceeded from above and was accepted from below.[73] Conversely, confusion between superior and inferior was the basic cause of all unrest. Again according to Prince Kung: "If we seek but cannot obtain control of the Empire, what is the reason? It is because the people's aspirations are not fixed. If the people's aspirations are not fixed, what is the reason? It is because the distinction between superior and inferior is not clear."[r]

The sanction for this hierarchy, not only in ultimate philosophic terms but in daily practical terms, sprang from the moral authority of the *li*, through which men were taught and transformed. As even the *North China Herald* admitted, "the system as a system possesses the inherent power of keeping things in their places."[74] The enforcement of laws by the material power of the state was secondary. In both theory and practice government was in the main "government by virtue," and its strength depended on the moral authority of officials of all ranks and the universal acceptance of the *li*.

As a consequence of this ideological structure, the first task of the Restoration statesmen was to reassert the principles of Confucian society and to make certain of their acceptance by both the literati and the common people. The ideological heresies of the Taiping doctrine had little appeal to the educated when contrasted with the still tremendous attractive powers of the revived Confucian doctrine. Shocked by the disintegration of a cherished way of life, the literati looked to Peking for spiritual leadership; even a poor offering would have sufficed for a time, so abhorrent was the alternative. But the offering was not poor, and a revived, modified Neo-Confucian doctrine was propagated with great earnestness and vigor.

The reintegration of Chinese society at which the Restoration aimed was intended to include "the people" as well as the gentry. Under the division of labor decreed by Mencius, the people were to work with their hands in support of superior men, but they belonged to the same society. The program to consolidate their loyalty was described in two venerable slogans that pervaded the

---

[r] Prince Kung, "Chün-tzu pien shang-hsia ting min-chih lun" in *Lo-tao-t'ang wen-ch'ao*, Ch. 2, pp. 25–26.

Prince Kung was evidently a fair sociologist, for, according to Homans (*op. cit.*, pp. 366–67), social control is always lost when there is no good opinion to lose, no rank to lose because social ranks are not defined, no norms the violation of which can hurt. A society disintegrates when its norms are inoperative and it can therefore neither punish the bad nor reward the good.

political writings of the time: to make secure the people's livelihood (*an min-sheng*) and to stabilize popular sentiment (*ku min-hsin*). It was assumed that if the people's livelihood were secure and the moral leadership of "superior men" restored, popular disaffection would cease.

However, it should be noted that force (*hsing*) was never abjured. If persuasion failed, and the people ceased to play the docile role assigned them, it became not only necessary but *right* that they be punished. That was the teaching. It was no accident that Tseng Kuo-fan, the greatest philosopher and statesman of the age, was also its harshest disciplinarian.

THE CONCEPT OF SOCIAL CHANGE

The great aim of the T'ung-chih Restoration was the revival of Confucian values and institutions, but so *modified* that they might endure. There was within the accepted tradition such a wealth of diverse ideas about how to reach traditional goals that changes in method of government were possible, on the basis of precedent, within the bounds of orthodoxy.

The doctrine of change dated from the formative period of Chinese civilization[75] and was at hand to sanction reform throughout the course of Chinese history. During the T'ung-chih Restoration the doctrine, in its classic formulation from the *Book of Changes*, was cited repeatedly in memorials advocating reform: "When a series of changes has run all its course, another change ensues. When it obtains free course, it will continue long."[76]

The hopes of all supporters of the T'ung-chih Restoration, both Chinese and foreign, were centered on the traditional concept of change; for the ideas and institutions that had for two thousand years proved conducive to stability, together with a doctrine of change that had lent flexibility, gave "some ground for trusting that the regeneration of China will be accomplished, like the operation of leaven in meal, without shivering the vessel."[77] The great question was this: could change, as the Chinese had traditionally conceived it, include change of the kind that had become urgent in the 1860's?

In retrospect we can now see that Restoration statesmen had a far more dynamic conception of change than their predecessors. The writings on statecraft (*ching-shih*) of the immediate pre-Taiping period are in marked contrast to those of the Restoration period.[78] Yet the Restoration materials show a very limited notion of change when they in turn are compared with writings of the 1890's.[79] Restoration statesmen had no desire to create a new society. They wanted to restore a society that they confidently believed had been based on immutable truth and that could therefore, with adjustments, flourish in any age.

The editors of the *North China Herald* were interested in the *Book of Changes* concept and invited comment on it,[80] but they recognized that their own idea of how China should change was utterly alien to traditional Chinese thinking.[81] An experienced and frustrated missionary, Griffith John, agreed that the Chinese idea of change lacked any element of progress:

> The idea of establishing a new order of things, which shall be an improvement on the old, never enters the mind of anyone. . . . Such a change the people neither expect nor desire. All they look for is the removal of certain grievances arising from maladministration, the rectification of corrupted manners, the reformation of abuses, and the complete restoration of the primeval order. Beyond this point their hopes and aspirations never go; and a political or an insurgent chief who should attempt anything more would be an object of almost universal execration.[82]

Alcock, although aware of the limitations of the traditional Chinese idea of cyclical change, nonetheless thought it had possibilities. He quoted the *Book of Changes* to Prince Kung in an effort to find mutually acceptable terms for the gradual modernization of China, to the effect that "when a system is exhausted, it must be modified; that modified, it will work; and that working, it will endure."[83]

Robert Hart saw both the potentialities of the doctrine of change from a Chinese point of view and its limitations from a Western point of view:

> When asked if the Chinese Authorities are themselves desirous of entering on a career of improvement, and if so, in what direction and within what definite period, a categorical reply would be as much an injustice to the Western public, were it in the affirmative, as it would be to China herself, were it in the negative. To the mass of Chinese officials, the word improvement would convey no idea corresponding to that which is in the Western mind.[84]

Thomas Wade pointed out to Restoration officials that the traditional theory of change rested on assumptions that were not valid for the modern period. He granted that much of Chinese history could be interpreted cyclically, and he could understand very well why, by change, the Chinese always meant a return to the old ways. Nonetheless, he said, cyclical change of the old type was inadequate; progress *forward* was now for the first time required for the preservation of Chinese independence.[85]

 It seems plain that not even the most "advanced" statesmen of the Restoration envisaged fundamental change of the kind that later events proved essential to China's survival. In all justice they must be credited with having stretched the traditional ideology to its limits in an effort to make the Confucian system work under new conditions. Beyond those limits they could not go without losing the very values it was their whole aim to preserve. They were not stupid, or blind, or inflexible. They were simply true conservatives in a great tradition, living in an age when revolutionary institutional change proved unavoidable.

The changes for which doctrinal justification could be so readily found in the T'ung-chih period were changes in method, not changes in goal. Feng Kuei-fen anticipated by a generation Chang Chih-tung's famous maxim, "Chinese learning as the basis, Western learning for practical use." Feng did not take the naïve view that China could meet the Western challenge simply by borrowing technology. Rather, having grasped technology's contribution to the internal strength of Western society in the nineteenth century, he urged a re-examination of China's own civilization and a creation from Chinese materials of a strong modern China. This was certainly learning from the West, but it was not imitation of the West except in limited technical fields. Nineteenth-century China was clearly not the equal of nineteenth-century Europe. To overcome this inequality within the Confucian order was the aim of the Restoration.

> As to why men are unequal, it is not that Heaven endowed men [differently] and made them unequal; it is simply that men have made themselves unequal. If Heaven had endowed men [differently] and thereby created inequality, it would be shameful [for China, but] though it was shameful, there would be nothing we could do about it. Since man himself creates the inequality, it is still more shameful [for China]. But though it is shameful, there is something we can do about it. If one is ashamed, there is nothing better than self-strengthening.
>
> Now this so-called inequality [between China and the West] is a very real inequality. It is profitless to be angry about it; it is impossible to gloss it over; it is useless to talk it away.
>
> Of late, China's accumulated experience and skill have not been applied. The proper course lies in truly understanding the points of inequality. How is it that they are small, yet strong; that we are large, yet weak? We must seek the means of attaining equality; we will find that it still simply rests with man.
>
> From the point of view of present conditions:
>
> In not wasting human talent, we are inferior to the barbarian.
>
> In not neglecting the resources of the land, we are inferior to the barbarian.
>
> In having no barrier between ruler and people, we are inferior to the barbarian.
>
> In the necessary accord between name and reality, we are inferior to the barbarian.
>
> On these four points, our proper course lies in re-examination of ourselves.[86]

Chinese of the 1860's had less access to knowledge of Western civilization than Chinese of the 1890's. The alternately attractive and repulsive example of Japan was lacking, and the impact of ideas, so marked a generation later, was conspicuously absent. It is not surprising, therefore, that the response was limited in the main to the terms of the challenge: method. Western values, as they could be observed by Chinese of the sixties, were barbarous, parochial, and immature when compared with traditional Chinese values.

The aim of the Restoration was to restore to their original vigor the best of ancient institutions; there was no intention of restoring outmoded forms indiscriminately. Again in the words of Feng Kuei-fen:

> Among ancient methods of government [*fa*] some are easy to restore; others are difficult to restore. Some it is desirable to restore; others it is not desirable to restore. We can disregard those which it is not desirable to restore; but we cannot fail to restore those which are desirable, merely because it is difficult; how much less is there any excuse for not restoring those which it is both desirable and easy to restore.[87]

THE GENERAL PROGRAM OF THE RESTORATION

Convinced that the state had failed in the preceding decade to play its proper part in the universal scheme, Restoration statesmen felt urgently obliged to reexamine every institution and practice in order to recreate a working balance and harmony among them.[88] The planning of the Restoration dealt with tiny details as well as broad ethical considerations, but it was seldom trivial.

Tseng Kuo-fan was regarded by his contemporaries as the leading political thinker of the time, and he is still today considered the ablest modern exponent of Chinese conservatism. He recognized the importance of specific improvements in the fields of finance, the civil service, law, and rehabilitation projects, but he emphasized the selection and education of men of talent (*jen-ts'ai*) and the protection of the agrarian economy. Tseng repeatedly used the phrase "the people's welfare" (*min-sheng*) and forcefully restated the traditional view that agriculture was the basis of the state.[89]

Feng Kuei-fen's[90] views, although less well known than Tseng's, were widely influential in the second half of the nineteenth century and are of great intrinsic interest. In Feng's view there were three great evils responsible for China's ills: the three *li*—*li* (bureaucrat), *li* (official "red tape"), and *li* (profit); the Empire was in chaos because bureaucrats were manipulating red tape for their own profit.[91] As in antiquity the cause of rebellion was the failure of officials to understand the people. Feng wrote brilliantly on education, on technological modernization, on financial reform, on local administration, on selective borrowing from the West, on military organization—on every facet of Chinese society.

Fundamental political analysis of this type was not limited to outstanding intellectuals. The various collections of political writings of the period—memorials, essays, letters, etc.—contain literally hundreds of "master plans" for the restoration of the Confucian state and the salvation of China. A few examples should indicate something of their range and general quality.

The censor Tu Jui-lien wrote: "In a basic plan, the people's food comes first; military supplies are secondary." Fundamental social measures were needed, and he presented detailed proposals.[92] According to Liu Ju-ch'iu, a Chekiang taotai noted for his work on water control:

> In the governing of the people, agriculture comes first; in governing the people after a great rebellion, support of the people is urgent. Officials cannot support the people; the important thing is to make it possible for the people to support themselves.[93]

The former prefect Chiang Ch'i-ling presented for consideration "twelve policies"[94] ranging from the greater exaltation of Confucian studies to limitation of corruption and improved military organization. The governor of Fukien, Wang K'ai-t'ai, advocated increase in the student quotas, limitation of appointment by personal recommendation, abolition of sale of civil rank, severe re-examination of officials-designate, and greater efficiency in the army.[95]

There was general agreement on the importance of the reform of local government. In genuine Confucian political theory there could be no facile excuses attributing rebellion to outside causes and exonerating the officials. If the people rebelled, the government was at fault, particularly the local officials who were closest to the people.[96]

In summary, the majority of Chinese officials during the T'ung-chih period recognized the tremendous problems facing China and devoted their attention to fundamental reform. They did not imagine that they were improving upon the traditional and lasting principles of good government; they sought only to adjust their methods in order to realize the original aim under new conditions. The two immediate problems were the suppression of rebellion and the stabilization of foreign relations. The long-term solution of these two problems, however, involved much more than the mastery of the techniques of diplomacy and modern armament. It required in addition, as the following chapters will show, restoration of the system of government by superior civil officials; re-establishment of the elaborate network on which local control depended; rehabilitation of the economy, with attention to the interests both of the state and of the people; fundamental military reorganization; a new outlook in foreign affairs; and, in each of these spheres, education and scholarship aimed at reasserting the Confucian ideology.

CHAPTER V

THE RESTORATION OF CIVIL GOVERNMENT[a]

THE USE OF MEN

In the Confucian view the prime essentials of stable government and social harmony were the ability and integrity of officials, and this view was reflected in proverbs and common sayings[1] as well as in formal writing. To get men of the highest native ability, train their minds and mold their characters, appoint them to office on the basis of merit, and reward or punish their official conduct effectively—this was the Restoration's primary task.[2] Tso Tsung-t'ang, no armchair scholar, wrote: "Chaos in the Empire results from the fact that civil government is not properly maintained. That civil government is not properly maintained results from the fact that men of ability are not in office; that men of ability are not in office results from the fact that men's hearts are not upright; that men's hearts are not upright results from the fact that learning is not expounded."[3]

The ability of officials was considered closely related to their moral qualities. No one could with impunity suggest that a morally superior man might be incompetent in office, or that a morally inferior one might be possessed of great ability, as Ch'i-ying learned when he put forward this suggestion at the accession of the Hsien-feng Emperor: "If a man be employed in a capacity for which his talents do not fit him, though he be the 'good man' [chün-tzu], he will too probably mar his undertaking; if he be employed to do what he is able to perform, though 'the worthless' [hsiao-jen], he may still be turned to account." The edict in reply condemned Ch'i-ying's statement as evil beyond words and forcefully supported Wo-jen's presentation of the conventional view that moral worth was the supreme standard in any activity.[4]

The statesmen of the Restoration were positively obsessed with the idea of "human talent."[5] The view represented by the motto "The conduct of war rests

---

[a] The kind of government the Chinese were trying to restore was government according to the Confucian ethic by an ordered hierarchy of indoctrinated officials, selected by examination. "Civil" government (li-chih) in this sense means nonmilitary and nonecclesiastic government, but it means also a great deal more. The li-chih, like any other highly complex administrative system, could degenerate into "bureaucracy," but at its best it gave great weight to the experience, learning, and human understanding of the individual official, who was guided by broad precepts rather than by hard and fast laws and regulations. Bureaucratic red tape that impeded true civil government was a favorite target of attack during the Restoration. Feng Kuei-fen, for example, urged simplification of the regulations and of the documentary style in which they were written, so that they might be easily and fairly applied according to the dictates of common sense ("Mien hui-pi i," CPLKI, Ch. 1, pp. 6-7).

with men, not with implements" (*hsing-chün tsai jen pu tsai ch'i*) pervaded even the most technical military discussions. Similarly the effectiveness of land tax reduction in the T'ung-chih period was considered to depend upon the abilities of Hu Lin-i, Tseng Kuo-fan, and Tso Tsung-t'ang, and its subsequent failure was attributed to a lack of men. In the language of *The Doctrine of the Mean*: "When the right men are available, government flourishes; when the right men are not available, government declines."[6]

Reforms in administrative structure and procedure during the Restoration were few, and of these few only the creation of the Tsungli-yamen and the growth of the Maritime Customs Administration were important.[7] Tseng Kuo-fan's argument against redrawing and rationalizing the administrative map to make the Yangtze River a provincial boundary summed up the prevailing attitude: "In my opinion, if provincial officials are sufficiently able, then even if [provinces] straddle the Yangtze or the Huai, it will not impair the conduct of military or civil affairs. If the provincial officials are not sufficiently able, then even if we make the Yangtze a boundary, and divide the administration, it will not prevent civil and military collapse."[8]

A minor Restoration official voiced the same thought: "When extraordinary circumstances arise, we must rely on extraordinary men; and these extraordinary men will accomplish extraordinary things."[9]

THE GENERAL CHARACTER OF THE RESTORATION BUREAUCRACY

The men who suppressed rebellion and restored the Ch'ing state in the 1860's were not military men in the Western sense. They were in the main civilian officials, products of the examination system, who rose to prominence because of proven ability in *both* civil and military affairs. They were noted for their literary and scholarly accomplishments, and began the working day by practicing calligraphy.[10] Even in strictly military questions, they emphasized the human and social aspects: indoctrination, morale, and the art of leadership through the cultivation of character. Their technical military abilities were a distinctly secondary factor in their rise to power.[b]

The great majority of all Ch'ing officials rose through the examination system,[c] and the provinces that produced the greatest number of officials also

[b] See Chapter IX.

[c] The proportion compares favorably with that for the Sung period. According to Wittfogel, under the Sung system, the number of officials who reached office by way of examination was at best no more than equal to the number who were appointed on the basis of recommendation (K. A. Wittfogel, "Public Office in the Liao Dynasty," *HJAS*, X, 1 (1947), 31). In the twelfth century, according to Kracke, although most of the top officials were products of the examination system, only one-third to one-half of all officeholders had passed the examinations (E. A. Kracke, "Family Versus Merit in Chinese Civil Service Examinations Under the Empire," *HJAS*, X, 2 (1947), 103–23).

produced the greatest number of scholars.[11] In the Censorate, for example, 3,087 men held posts; of these, approximately 2,168 advanced by the "correct road"— the literary examination system—and the majority were holders of the metropolitan degree (*chin-shih*), won against heavy odds in a national competition that required half a lifetime of preparation.[12]

During the post-Taiping period, the Ch'ing bureaucracy remained a bureaucracy of scholars; even a new organization like the Hsiang Army was dominated by men trained in the examination system.[d] And the outstanding leaders of the Restoration were virtually all scholar-officials, as a review of their careers will show.

"Meritorious officials of the Restoration" (*chung-hsing kung-ch'en*) has become a stock phrase in all Chinese comment on the nineteenth century. By conservatives the phrase is used in eulogy, by Marxists in derision, by less impassioned historians as a description of fact. All agree, however, on the basic point: that a small group of "meritorious officials" in the capital and the provinces restored and prolonged the life of the traditional order.

Substantially the same names appear on all the lists: in the capital Prince Kung, Wen-hsiang, Shen Kuei-fen, and Li T'ang-chieh; in the provinces Tseng Kuo-fan, Tso Tsung-t'ang, Li Hung-chang, Hu Lin-i, and Lo Ping-chang. Most of them had had experience in both the capital and the provinces; there was no sharp dividing line.

LEADING METROPOLITAN OFFICIALS OF THE RESTORATION

At the beginning of the Restoration there was a striking change in the composition of the central government. Elder statesmen returned to high office to replace members of the discredited Tsai-yüan faction,[13] and actual control devolved upon Prince Kung[e] and Wen-hsiang. Prince Kung was severely reprimanded by the Throne in 1865, but his brief demotion does not appear to have seriously affected his power for the remainder of the Restoration. He did not become a figurehead, nor did the Empress Dowager become an autocrat, until well after the T'ung-chih period.[14]

Neither Prince Kung nor Wen-hsiang displayed any special Manchu aims or ways of thinking; their writings and their policies were what one might expect of men thoroughly steeped in the Confucian tradition. As scholars they were not in Tseng Kuo-fan's class, but as statesmen they were Tseng's metropolitan counterparts.

Wen-hsiang's writings are less reflective than those of Prince Kung; but his straightforward autobiography and his accounts of his special missions show

d See Chapter IX.
e See Chapter II.

shrewd insight, devotion to duty, and strength of moral conviction.[15] In the view of foreigners who had occasion to follow his activities, he was "the most advanced and patriotic man in the government";[16] "the most able and enlightened official, probably in the Empire";[17] "well known to be the ablest member of the Peking government";[18] "considered by the foreign legations the leading mind and ablest of the Chinese [sic] Ministers of the Tsung-le Yamun."[19]

The best-qualified observers were unanimous in their praise. In Alcock's view Wen-hsiang was "by far the most advanced among the leading ministers of the Yamen and Grand Secretariat [sic]."[20] Bruce had "never encountered a more powerful intellect."[21] According to Burlingame: "There is one great man in the government, Wen-hsiang, who is master of the situation, and who comprehends the grave condition of affairs, and earnestly and incorruptibly strives to maintain the integrity of the government."[22] According to S. Wells Williams, Wen-hsiang was "a man of most uncommonly prepossessing manner, being perhaps the most highly esteemed of all the officials who came in contact with the foreign Legations . . . a most sagacious and efficient adviser of the Government. In his death [in 1875] the Chinese Government lost an unselfish patriot and a keen observer of those things which were for the best interests of his country."[23] Robert Hart called him "one of the most intelligent and broadminded Chinese [sic] I ever knew."[24] W. A. P. Martin emphasized Wen-hsiang's "enlightened views" and his personal poverty in spite of his high position.[25]

Wen-hsiang stood equally high in Chinese esteem. Weng T'ung-ho praised his loyalty, his diligence, and his contribution to domestic and foreign policy. Chin-liang wrote that Wen-hsiang stood in history as "a main support of the Restoration" because of his courage and his profound and farsighted plans for the state.[26]

Under the protection of Prince Kung and Wen-hsiang, able Chinese officials rose to high position not only in the provincial hierarchy but in the metropolitan hierarchy as well. Prince Kung, Wen-hsiang, Shen Kuei-fen, and Li T'ang-chieh were considered to be the restorers of authority in the central government as Tseng Kuo-fan, Li Hung-chang, and Tso Tsung-t'ang were restorers of authority in regional administration.[27] To Liang Ch'i-ch'ao, the sixties were "the era of Wen-hsiang and Shen Kuei-fen."[28]

Shen Kuei-fen, who won the metropolitan degree in 1847, advanced to the Grand Council and the Grand Secretariat through a typical succession of regional *and* metropolitan posts: governor of Shantung, governor of Shansi, president of the Board of War.[29] While Chinese have generally recognized him as a leader of the Restoration, relatively little is known about him.[30] He was an effective official*ʲ*—particularly after his appointment to the Grand Council in 1867—but

ʲ On his role in the relaxation of the Banner regulations, see Chapter IV.

the record, thus far fragmentary, testifies to the fact of his prominence rather than the reasons for it.

The fourth of the great metropolitan officials of the Restoration, Li T'ang-chieh, was primarily a Neo-Confucian theorist. He won the metropolitan degree in 1822, and from then until 1860 he was variously occupied with provincial posts, private study, and organization of the militia under Tseng Kuo-fan. Although he had declined a Peking appointment in 1850, he responded to an 1862 summons.[31] Shortly after his arrival at the capital he and Wo-jen had a long discussion on "all matters," and Wo-jen went over the draft of Li's later famous memorial on "the important points in government today."[32] Li's memorial emphasized the importance of the Emperor's education, of a moral atmosphere in the capital, and of the restoration of civil government: "In my humble opinion, if we wish to pacify the rebels, we must first make the people secure. If we wish to make the people secure, we must first select upright and capable governors-general and governors."[33] Wu T'ing-tung (Hsing-ju), a provincial official and a leading exponent of Sung Confucianism, wrote that the prospects of the government were bright indeed, now that Li and Wo-jen had been given posts where they could advise on the basic principles of government and on general planning.[34]

Under the Restoration government, Li rapidly reached the official heights: vice-president of the Board of Rites, president of the Censorate, Grand Councillor. Because he left writings and corresponded with men of letters, he is better known than his colleague Shen Kuei-fen, but how his influence was exercised is by no means clear. He wrote relatively few memorials himself, although those few were widely influential. His diary for the years before he came to Peking is revealing—especially his preoccupation, in the midst of crisis, with the lessons of history[35]—but its entries after 1862 become bald notations of events, adding nothing to the *Shih-lu*. His career, as now known, chiefly indicates the important role of Neo-Confucian philisophy in Restoration politics, and the manner in which central and regional interests coalesced; everything about his career before 1862 suggests "regionalism," but he has gone down in Chinese history as a pillar of Restoration in the capital.

Some Chinese historians have written that the T'ung-chih Restoration failed because it affected mainly the high provincial officials and was not supported by the central government "except for men like Wen-hsiang who respected Tseng and Li."[36] The point is that "men like Wen-hsiang" *did* control the central government, and that the rise of able Chinese leaders in the provinces, as well as in the capital, depended on decisions made in Peking. There were diverse factions in the court, but none that could challenge the authority of Prince Kung and his colleagues.

LEADING PROVINCIAL OFFICIALS OF THE RESTORATION

The abilities of the great provincial leaders of the Restoration have received far more attention than the abilities of the central government's officials. Tseng Kuo-fan, Tso Tsung-t'ang, and Li Hung-chang are listed as the heroes—or to Communists, the villains—of the age in virtually every history of the period, and evaluation of their careers is still a perennial issue in Chinese politics.

Tseng Kuo-fan.[37] Tseng so dominated his era that an appraisal of the man becomes an appraisal of the whole Restoration, and indeed of all modern Chinese efforts at conservative reconstruction. As the issue of social revolution has come to dominate Chinese politics, estimates of Tseng himself have varied as much as estimates of the Confucian society he typified.[38] But in his own time he was the object of unparalleled, universal veneration, and given the assumptions of the Confucian state, his reputation was justified. Bland and Backhouse were not slow to find fraud and chicanery behind pious Confucian fronts, but Tseng, they wrote, "was a man of the heroic breed of philosophers which, with all its faults, the Confucian system has always produced and continues to produce to the great benefit of the Chinese people, a man whose name ranks high among China's worthies, a household word for honesty and intelligent patriotism."[39]

The customary memorials presented at the time of Tseng's death were much more than formalities; and the name by which he was canonized, "Wen-cheng kung," is one of special glory, the highest in the scale of "temple names."[40] The eulogies emphasized his personal rectitude and frugality, which gave him the force of a living, magnetic example; his courage, his wisdom, his sincerity and honesty in all dealing; and his austere devotion to duty regardless of personal interests.[41] His insistence upon returning to his native place to mourn for his mother at a critical point in his military career proved that his devotion to the Confucian ethic surpassed his political and military ambition.[g]

Tseng's whole diary breathes sternness and austerity. As a young man he had evidently enjoyed "opium, women, and improper talk"; in his early thirties he dropped opium completely, but he continued to censure himself for lapses on the other two counts.[42] No easy self-satisfaction was ever possible for Tseng. Truth and falsehood had to be as clearly distinguished as black and white. A man must understand the scheme of things, and his role in it, and devote his

---

[g] The Marxists agree with the Confucians that Tseng was revered by the "ruling classes" in China in part because of his suppression of rebellion, "but the most important reason was his ability to protect and support the Confucian doctrine." On the basis of an obviously careful study of Tseng's writings and action, Chu Ch'i-hua concluded that his life and thought remained close to the Confucian teaching; that he used its precepts to search his own soul, to teach his children, and to conduct private and public affairs. Tseng is a "traitor" to Chu, precisely because of his role in restoring Confucianism. (*Chung-kuo chin-tai she-hui shih chieh-p'ou*, Shanghai, 1933, pp. 111, 112–15, 131 ff.)

life to playing that role better. The only way lay in hard work, self-knowledge, and self-discipline; in the scheme of things success and prominence might or might not come but wisdom could be attained through one's own efforts.[43]

That Tseng himself lived by these principles has never been challenged, but he was never satisfied and constantly criticized himself for laxness. He wrote his brother that he feared he might be spending too much time in calligraphy and study at the expense of more direct duties: writing memorials and investigating officials.[44] One of his chief worries was that his children and he himself might become proud of his achievements.[45] His personal expenses were remarkably low;[46] as one foreigner noted, "He dresses in the poorest clothes and keeps no state."[47]

This tough fiber was the basis of his spectacular accomplishments in public affairs, for his family's status was not impressive and his gifts were apparently not of the first order. He made his own way by the granite determination to which he enjoined others.[48] He was unquestionably a great general. Virtually every one of his associates repeatedly commented on his extraordinary capacity as a leader of soldiers, and their view was confirmed by the outstanding Taiping general Shih Ta-k'ai.[49] His work on economic problems was remarkable.[50] He wrote on literally every subject that concerned the public welfare: army reform, agricultural rehabilitation, popular morals, foreign affairs, industrialization, education, taxation, and every variety of administrative question. His memorials were always clear, vigorous, and comparatively brief, with attention both to detail and to the basic issues involved in particular problems.[51]

Tseng has been criticized on three counts only: for excessive harshness in suppressing rebellion,[52] for yielding to foreign demands growing out of the Tientsin Massacre,[h] and for preferring his fellow Hunanese to other candidates for promotion.[53] The charge of harshness cannot be denied;[i] it was not, however, the harshness of a brute or a fanatic, but a controlled and deadly inhumanity toward weakness and evil as he saw it. The charge of yielding to foreigners is quite unjustified; he had been working toward an adjustment with the West while protecting Chinese tradition. When the Tientsin Massacre dramatically revealed the depths of latent Chinese hostility toward foreigners, he was pilloried by both sides for attempting to find some position of honorable compromise. The charge that he relied heavily on Hunanese with whom he had been long associated is correct, but not very damaging since the Hunanese in question were able officials. No evidence has been produced that either they or Tseng promoted regional interests at the expense of national interests, or that able men from other provinces found the door closed.

h See Chapter XI.
i See Chapter VI.

No critic, however intemperate, has ever suggested that Tseng was not able, hard-working, incorruptible, influential, respected, and devoted to his cause. The testimony of treaty port foreigners, who were as opposed to Tseng's policies as were the Taiping leaders, is relevant here. They recognized his extraordinary prestige throughout China, his "unprecedented amount of glory and distinction," and "his unbounded influence"; they considered him as formidable morally as Li Hung-chang was formidable physically. Although they classified him as "one of the anti-foreign, anti-progressive side," they conceded his "ability, intelligence, and political honesty," and the fact that he was "above all trickery."[54]

Foreign merchants would have derided, and rightly, the fantastic idea that Tseng was their tool; he was their most formidable enemy, but his power was based on qualities that won their admiration, grudging or otherwise. They knew very well that the source of his power was not foreign support but Chinese support, and they had some inkling of the qualities that had called forth that support. When he left the governor-generalship of Kiangsu, Kiangsi, and Anhwei in 1868, the *North China Herald* commented: "It is expected that he will be accompanied, at least as far as Yangchow, by such a following of Mandarins as never before accompanied a Vice-roy. *He has always been popular with his subordinates*, as his government was free of many of the foibles characteristic of Mandarin rule. He is strict, but men could always understand what he meant, and the consequence is that much fewer Mandarins have come to grief under him than usually happens."[55]

Halliday Macartney, who worked under Tseng's general direction, agreed with the standard Chinese and foreign view of Tseng's character. He testified to Tseng's firm refusal to relax his work schedule even after the first attack of the illness that brought his death eight days later.[56]

Tso, Li, and Other Provincial Leaders. Tso Tsung-t'ang had little distinction as a thinker, but he was no less than Tseng an outstanding practitioner of the Confucian social philosophy. He is best known for his work in establishing the Foochow Shipyard, pacifying the northwestern Moslems, and rehabilitating and trying to modernize the economy of the northwest, but his little-known accomplishments—in restoring the examination system, propagating the Confucian doctrine, and protecting the traditional agrarian economy—were of no less importance. Much of his reconstruction work compares very favorably with subsequent Chinese and Sino-foreign efforts that commanded far greater technical knowledge and material resources.

Like Tseng, Tso was respected by the foreigners who knew him; what is more, with his warm, impulsive temperament, he was liked. Similarly, he was incorruptible and indifferent to his personal fortunes. He neglected his family property and made large donations to public causes. The family was so impoverished in consequence that he urged his descendants to cultivate their patrimony as farmers and scholars.[57]

The third of the provincial triumvirate of the Restoration, Li Hung-chang, achieved his greatest fame and power after the end of the Restoration. He was less concerned with Restoration problems than Tseng and Tso, and his reputation was less based on Confucian statesmanship. In the Restoration period he was a brash young military genius whose career was furthered by Tseng. He made use of Tseng's ideas and methods, but from the beginning his specialties were foreign affairs and the army.[58] He was greatly influenced by and indebted to his adviser, the penetrating Confucian theorist Feng Kuei-fen;[59] but after Feng's death he chose different advisers and drifted away from Confucian orthodoxy.

Hu Lin-i and Lo Ping-chang often replace Tso Tsung-t'ang and Li Hung-chang in Chinese lists of the three greatest provincial leaders of the Restoration.[60] While Li, and to some extent Tso, were occupied with the problems occasioned by China's growing contact with the West, Hu and Lo were more concerned with traditional domestic problems. Hu, to whom Tseng Kuo-fan owed his career, was the most nearly comparable to Tseng and was held in his time and afterward in the same kind of veneration.[61] He was outstanding as a scholar, as a provincial governor, and as an effective Confucian general. Probably only his early death in 1861 kept his reputation from equaling Tseng's.

Lo Ping-chang shared the qualities of Tseng and Hu, but he never achieved their national prominence. His reputation rested on his extraordinary accomplishments in every field as a provincial governor, and in an integrity that after his time rapidly became obsolete in Chinese provincial administration.[j]

Able men of lesser fame occupied most of the chief provincial posts throughout the Restoration. Ma Hsin-i, as governor-general of Chekiang and Fukien and later of Kiangsu, Kiangsi, and Anhwei, was distinguished for restoring public works, for famine relief, for rehabilitating war-devastated areas, for propagating traditional learning, and for reducing the size of the armed forces. Foreigners considered him reactionary and antiforeign[k] but conceded his fairness and integrity. Kuo Sung-tao, best known for his subsequent diplomatic career, was acting governor of Kwangtung in the 1860's, and was busy pacifying the province and streamlining its administration. The work of his successor, Chiang I-li, was widely praised, and his subsequent demotion probably did not

---

[j] "He is considered by the Sze-ch'uanese to have been the last honest man who has set foot in the province." ("Notes and Queries," *China Review*, X, 1 (1881), 71.)

[k] By Chinese extremists, Ma was considered proforeign; he was assassinated in July 1870 during the widespread disturbances that followed the Tientsin Massacre.

reflect on his ability.[62] Another scholar-official, Ting Pao-chen, had a typical Restoration record: rehabilitation of Shantung following the Nien-fei ravages, flood control work along the Yellow River and Grand Canal, strengthening of local militia, improvement of coastal defenses, and reform of the salt administration. Like most of his colleagues, he had an excellent reputation for industry, integrity, and devotion to the public welfare.[63]

Although our knowledge of the Restoration bureaucracy is scarcely complete, it seems clear that there were several devoted, able, and respected Confucian officials for every such timeserver as Wu T'ang or Kuan-wen. It also seems clear that the concentration of talent in high places was greater during the Restoration than during the preceding or subsequent periods. The assemblage of talent, in theory the crucial factor in a restoration, was attained in practice during the T'ung-chih period.

THE SEARCH FOR TALENT

During the demoralization and chaos of the Hsien-feng period, the traditional system for the selection of officials—the examination system—had lost much of its effectiveness. As a result the lower ranks of the bureaucracy contained many officials who did not meet traditional standards. The able senior officials of the Restoration realized that their policies would be ineffective unless the quality of junior officials were improved, and moreover that unless the rot were checked at once, tomorrow's senior bureaucracy would be drawn from today's unimpressive lesser officials. It became, therefore, imperative to weed out the officials who had secured office in irregular ways, and to exalt the examinations once again as the correct road to high position.

Yet although there was virtually unanimous agreement among the statesmen of the Restoration that the examination system, when properly administered, afforded the best possible basis for the selection of officials,[64] it was obviously impossible to select officials entirely or automatically on the basis of objective tests alone. The system of recommendation, by which a high official sponsored the career of a promising younger man, was, therefore, an essential corollary to the examination system.

Ideally there was no conflict between the system of recommendation and the examination system; the most ardent supporters of the one strongly advocated the other. Tseng Kuo-fan, Hu Lin-i, and Tso Tsung-t'ang spent a tremendous amount of time and energy in maintaining wide contacts and in searching out new talent. To critics who attacked them on this score they made no apology; on the contrary, they defended their practice eloquently and at length.[65] Wang K'ai-yün observed flippantly that Hu sought talent but could not recognize it; that Tseng could use talent but did not seek it; and that Tso could recognize talent but not tolerate it.[66] Like most witticisms this comment is unfair to its subjects, but it illustrates the importance attached to the search for talent.

Tseng kept systematic lists of able men and encouraged them by writing to them, paying them visits, and lecturing them.[67] His formula for the restoration of civil government was to recruit widely, employ cautiously, instruct diligently, and control strictly.[68] The first step was to become widely acquainted,[l] the second to note down the strengths and weaknesses of different men and their different types of ability. Tseng's estimates were shrewd and realistic.[69] Although he believed that all talent rested ultimately on moral training,[70] he recognized that specific abilities varied, and that constant effort was needed to bring out particular latent talents and to use them appropriately. As he put it: "a *ting* of the Three Dynasties, if used to cultivate a field, is not as good as a plow."[71]

All other Restoration leaders followed similar practices,[72] agreeing with Tso Tsung-t'ang that "men all have talents and talents all have uses."[73] Immediately following the suppression of the Nien-fei Rebellion, the governor of Shantung, Ting Pao-chen, made a tour to locate talent and reported his findings.[74] Kuo Sung-tao submitted a long memorial on the able local scholars he had met— including the mathematician Li Shan-lan, who was subsequently appointed to the T'ung-wen kuan[m]—and urged that the court sponsor a great revival of scholarship by inviting local scholars to lecture in the capital, as the K'ang-hsi Emperor had done following the suppression of the Rebellion of the Three Feudatories.[75]

Feng Kuei-fen was one of the many able men who were discovered in a search for talent. Feng was brought to Nanking by Lin Tse-hsü, then governor of Kiangsu, in 1832, on the recommendation of the head of the academy where he had been studying. At an early date he showed a grasp of current affairs and economics in his essays on waterways, the salt tax, and military organization. As a result he was "recommended" in 1850 at the beginning of the Hsien-feng reign.[76] Feng's case illustrates how examination and recommendation could supplement each other in the selection of talent.

Yet the possibility of conflict between examination and recommendation was always present. Tso Tsung-t'ang wrote: "As to our country's proper course in self-strengthening, the most important thing is to discard our literary and legalistic emphasis, to employ men of real ability, to entrust these sages with the selection of high provincial officials, and to entrust the high provincial officials with the selection of local officials."[77] Such a procedure might well place the right man in the right post more quickly than the ponderous operation of the examination

---

[l] According to the diary of one of his personal aides Tseng said that whereas men of the second and third class could be "sought" and held in reserve, "men of the first class may be met; they cannot be sought out." (Ch'en Nai-ch'ien, "Tseng Wen-cheng kung yü-lu," *Ku-chin*, No. 41 (1944), pp. 27–31, based on the diary of Chao Hui-fu.)

[m] See Chapter X.

system, and would not damage the Confucian system if only men who had passed the examinations were eligible for selection. It would be particularly appealing to energetic, hard-driving administrators like Tso in an era when vigorous action was required. At the same time the possibilities of abuse were enormous if demoralization set in, or if recommendation ceased to be supplementary to examination.

As a safeguard high officials were required to back their recommendations with evidence, and were themselves held responsible for any future failings of their protégés.[78] Even so, in 1873 the censor Hu Chia-yü memorialized that the qualifications for appointment by recommendation were still too low, and that in consequence too few opportunities for advancement were open to holders of the metropolitan degree. It is worth noting that Hu complained particularly about the excessive patronage accorded the Tsungli-yamen—three times that allowed to the Grand Council itself.[79] Evidently the examination system failed to produce enough men competent to deal with the new problems, in spite of the strenuous efforts to bring Western learning into the traditional system.[n]

No one advocated abandoning the system of recommendations, but many thoughtful officials worked to keep it subordinate to the examination system.[80]

THE REVIVAL OF THE EXAMINATION SYSTEM[81]

Although the Chinese myths of high social mobility and of government by the most able and virtuous have never fully accorded with historical reality, the examination system was at its best a remarkable institution for giving reality to an ideal.[82] The T'ung-chih Restoration was marked by a resurgence of the myth and by a considerable revival of the institution.

The vastly ramifying system of examinations served the Confucian state in three ways: (1) It produced officials of intelligence who were thoroughly indoctrinated in the Confucian ethic. It doubtless checked unfettered creative thinking, but it did not, as has often been charged, load the bureaucracy with incompetent poetry writers. (2) It kept the attention of the gentry fixed on orthodoxy and provided an orthodox outlet for talent and ambition. (3) It won the support of the people by providing them with officials whose power and behavior were based on universally accepted canons rather than on wealth, birth, military power, or Imperial caprice.

The examination system had disintegrated during the Taiping Rebellion. Honorary ranks and permits to take higher examinations without first passing the lower were awarded on the basis of military accomplishment or financial contribution, and there were more and more proven cases of corruption among the examiners. As a result, at the beginning of the Restoration the bureaucracy

[n] See Chapter X.

was cluttered with two types of "upstart," merchants and military men, whose presence was undermining the whole traditional system of government. The merchants, who had in effect bought their positions, governed according to "business methods" rather than paternal benevolence; the military officials sought to control the people by force and punishment rather than by moral example.[83]

Since in the areas of strife the examinations had not been held for many years,[84] one of the first acts of officials in charge of a recovered area was to announce the resumption of examinations on schedule. On October 22, 1864, two months after the recovery of Nanking from the Taiping rebels, Tseng Kuo-fan asked that the necessary officials be sent from Peking to supervise the Kiangsu provincial examination scheduled for the winter.[85] Between 1855 and 1865 it had been impossible to hold the Kweichow provincial examination. In 1866 with peace now in sight, Chang Liang-chi requested that the Throne authorize holding not only the current 1866 examination, but the long-delayed 1855 and 1858 examinations as well.[86] After Jui-lin and Chiang I-li brought the Hakka[o] war in Kwangtung to an end and resettled the Hakkas, they, like "natives" of the province, were given the privilege of presenting one youth in twenty for examination.[87] As soon as Tso Tsung-t'ang had pacified Shensi, he announced the holding of overdue provincial examinations.[88]

As order was restored throughout the country, the examinations figured prominently in the news of the day. In 1867 Chiang I-li arranged impressive celebrations in Canton,[89] and more than twenty thousand candidates offered themselves for the provincial examination at Nanking.[90] The *Hankow Times,* amazed at the gathering of more than ten thousand men from all classes of society to participate in the Hupeh provincial examination of 1867, called the examinations "a most admirable and beneficial plan. . . . A cohesion is given to state and people beyond all conception."[91] And once again the successful provincial candidates thronged the roads to Peking to compete in the metropolitan examination for the highest degree.[92]

It was estimated at the time that every year two million candidates were taking examinations at one or another level,[p] of whom only one or two per cent were in the end successful. In the annual district examinations twenty or more candidates were selected from among the approximately two thousand[q] who competed in the average district. In the triennial examinations for the provincial degree perhaps one hundred were selected from about ten thousand applicants in the average province. Provincial degree holders competed in the triennial exami-

---

[o] See Chapter VI.

[p] According to Chung-li Chang, this estimate is too low if it is intended to include all participants at all levels (*The Chinese Gentry*, Seattle, 1955, p. 92, n. 98).

[q] According to Chang, this must be an overly high estimate based on figures for the coastal provinces; Chang's own estimate is between 1,000 and 1,500 (*ibid*., p. 92, n. 98).

nation at Peking for the metropolitan degree, and approximately one-third were successful. Between two and three hundred of those who passed the metropolitan examinations competed in the palace examination at the Hanlin Academy for the highest honors, including the title of first scholar in the Empire (*chuang-yüan*).[93]

The statutory quotas for degrees that could be awarded by the various provinces were steadily increased[94] to provide a means for rewarding military or financial contributions without weakening the examination system. The bigger a district's quota, the better its benefactors' chances to obtain a post, but through normal channels. For example, in 1865 an increased number of preliminary degrees was offered in the Shanghai and Paoshan areas on the motion of Li Hung-chang as a reward to the people for their loyalty.[95] Similarly in 1867 ten students were added to the quota of Hsingkwo hsien in Kiangsi as a reward to the people for contributing to the military treasury.[96] At the same time five students were added to the quota of Hengchow fu and three to that of Hengyang hsien, both in Hunan, as a reward for contributions toward Kiangnan naval expenses.[97] In 1872 Ting Pao-chen asked for increased quotas for both Chekiang and Kwangtung, to reward the merchants and gentry of the area for their contributions to the suppression of rebellion.[98]

This sort of premium on the military and financial strength of an area obviously had its drawbacks, among them the danger of lowering standards to fit the capacities of mediocre students. In 1868 Chang Chih-tung reported on the poor records of many students, and an edict ordered stricter maintenance of qualifying standards.[99] Nonetheless, the men most concerned at the time with the improved selection of officials generally advocated limited quota increases.

Persons familiar with the nepotism and corruption to which many modern Chinese governments have been given find it hard to believe that the examination system can have been administered with reasonable honesty. On the available evidence, however, the level of honesty compared favorably with that of western Europe at the time. The great stir caused by the discovery of irregularities in the metropolitan examinations of 1858, which resulted in the execution of the Grand Secretary Po-chün and three others, suggests that fraud was exceptional. The succession of edicts exhorting officials to observe the regulations with scrupulous care[100] indicates that constant vigilance was needed, but it should not be interpreted in reverse to mean that no vigilance was practiced.[r]

[r] On the basis of careful study, Chung-li Chang has concluded "that corruption was rife in the examination system despite the strong regulations to prevent it and the severe punishments imposed on some offenders." (*Ibid.*, p. 197.) Since Chang's illustrations can be matched by others of opposite import, as he himself points out, the conclusion any scholar may reach, in the present state of knowledge, is a matter of general judgment and insight on the basis of some implied standard of comparison.

It was the aim of the Restoration not only to exalt the examinations as the only road to prestige and power, but to increase their usefulness by modifying their content. The statesmen of the period, faced with a need for change, could always argue plausibly enough that an apparent innovation was in reality a return to neglected ancient virtues. It was widely asserted that the stereotyping of the subject matter of the examinations in the late Ming period had been a main cause of the fall of the dynasty. Hence a return to the "ancient" system, which allegedly had emphasized the substantive problems of history and society, became a main goal of the Restoration.

The supervising censor Wu Ch'uo attacked the decadent "modern" emphasis on calligraphy and prescribed style, and called for examinations based on the fundamental problems of government. The edict in reply of April 13, 1862, approved Wu's views and specified which fundamental subjects should be taken up in the three sessions of the forthcoming examinations: first, correct conduct, on the basis of the Four Books; second, fundamental moral truths, on the basis of the Five Classics; third, policy, as suggested by the lessons of ancient and modern history.[101] In this connection the young Chang Chih-tung was highly praised by the Grand Secretary Pao-yün and others for commenting on the Taiping Rebellion and other current problems in the palace examination of 1863.[102]

The 1862 edict ordered that Wu Ch'uo's principles be widely discussed (as well as applied to the examination system). Among the resulting memorials, one from a minor official, Kuei Wen-ts'an,[s] in 1864 was especially notable. According to Kuei, the excessive emphasis on form developed during the past half-century had left scholars too little time for reading the Classics and the Histories, analyzing current affairs, and striving for the true wisdom that could save the age. A shift in emphasis throughout the educational system was required to rectify the situation and to focus attention on public affairs. Of the officials of his time, Kuei remarked "they neither use what they study nor study what they use."[103] Thus this gibe, later often used against the examination system by its domestic and foreign critics, originated in constructive self-criticism within the system. The view that during the nineteenth century all substantial questions on history, government, and philosophy were dropped from the examinations[104] is quite incorrect for the Restoration period, as the following examples will show.

The questions asked at the triennial provincial examinations at Wuchang in 1867 and 1870 were a fair example of the content of the preliminary training

---

[s] Kuei, a native of Nanhai in Kwangtung, was a prolific scholar who held numerous minor posts. He had been a disciple of Juan Yüan and admired Hui Tung and other Han school scholars. On the function of scholarship in society, however, he apparently agreed with his Neo-Sung contemporaries (*Ch'ing-shih lieh-chuan*, Ch. 69, pp. 67–67b).

program for the Restoration. They dealt with the Classics, history, geography, and current administrative problems. A premium was placed on knowledge of facts, however, rather than on analysis or judgment.[105]

In the advanced examinations far more reflection and interpretation were required. In the palace examinations of 1868, Questions 1 and 2 dealt with the usage of certain characters in specific classical quotations. Question 3 listed certain books and asked whether they were suitable for the education of the Emperor. Questions 4 and 5 dealt with commentaries to *The Great Learning*. Question 6 asked why the Han and Sung schools disagreed on the importance of certain chapters of the *Classic of History*. Question 7 required a historical interpretation of the virtue of frugality among rulers. Earlier rulers had been more frugal and competent; were there distinctions other than in degree of frugality between good and bad rulers, and in the various cases was the frugality genuine or merely nominal? Question 8 asked how extravagance could be eliminated. Question 9 asked for an analysis of military training methods used in the Chou and Han dynasties. Question 10 asked why the T'ang dynasty conscription program, under which the men were soldiers for one period and farmers for two periods, in rotation, had been successful. Question 11 required an appraisal of the distribution of troops in the Sung period, when strong armies had been maintained in the capital but only weak forces were garrisoned in the provinces. Question 12 asked simply for a list of the six methods named in a certain work on the history of military training. Question 13 asked how the armies might be best improved for the least money. Questions 14, 15, and 16 dealt with the origins and development of Chinese criminal law. Question 17 asked what could be done to fulfill the Emperor's wish that no serious crimes should occur, so that there would be no need for the autumn executions.[106]

In April and May of 1867, Ting Jih-ch'ang, then financial commissioner of Kiangsu, gave a special examination designed to weed out the unfit from among the numerous purchasers of rank who were waiting at Soochow for appointment. The questions asked all concerned current administrative problems. The first session questions are not available. The two questions asked at the second session were: (1) By what plan would you propose to prevent the irregularities that exist among the under-officials of yamens? (2) What would you propose to do with the "braves" to ensure their settling down as peaceful subjects now that their services are no longer required? The two questions asked at the third session were: (1) There are now numerous candidates for official appointments, and but few appointments to give them. How would you propose to overcome the difficulty? (2) Petty officials take it upon themselves to judge cases that ought to be referred to the county magistrates. How would you propose to remedy this evil? According to foreign news reports, the examinations were written in

Ting's own presence and were strictly controlled; few of the rank purchasers were able to pass them.[107]

The examinations did not, of course, afford any final and permanent solution to the universal problem of the education of government officials. Even at their best, they were overloaded with precedent. But at their best, they produced an official far different from and vastly superior to the effete, long-nailed pedant of later caricature.

Robert Hart, in his 1865 "spectator's memorandum" to the Chinese government, pointed to weaknesses in the examination system; it had formerly been useful, he granted, but it encouraged an excessive emphasis on the reading of books and prevented provincial officials from learning the things they really needed to know.[108] The retort of Liu K'un-i, then governor of Kiangsi, was an excellent example of the Restoration view. In Liu's opinion the reading of the Histories and the Classics did not prevent the understanding of public affairs; on the contrary, the real tragedy was that modern officials often preferred poetry and essays to the study of ancient and modern government. Liu, therefore, advocated reform directed toward restoring the examination system to its ancient function and vigor.[109]

Obviously not all tendencies toward decline of the examinations could be arrested during the brief T'ung-chih Restoration. Domestic rebellion was suppressed, but the damage it had done to the examination system could not be repaired overnight. Meanwhile increasing contact with the West began to raise doubts about the relevance of the traditional learning to new problems. It was reported that in 1866 not a single candidate competed for the preliminary degree in the district that included Shanghai, and there were similar reports from other cities. A new hybrid society was emerging in the treaty ports and the coastal areas, a society in which power and position would no longer rest with the literati. The *North China Herald* commented correctly: "We have thus undermined, so far as our influence has extended, the very foundations of the Chinese political system."[110]

On the basis of evidence of this kind, it is sometimes stated that from the early nineteenth century onward the examinations, like the state they served, steadily declined. The point here is that the efforts made during the Restoration to retard this decline and to reinvigorate the traditional system were more conspicuous and more successful than has been generally supposed.

Paradoxically, the most serious impediments to the full success of these efforts came from the conservative literati. Tseng Kuo-fan at first attacked vigorously the excessive emphasis on poetry and style. But at the height of his career he seemed to lose heart, and to be reluctant to press for changes that were opposed by so many scholars.[111]

LIMITATION OF THE SALE OF RANK[t]

The "sale of rank"—that is, the award of official rank to contributors to the public funds—had existed in every dynasty since the Ch'in, but the system of contributions (*chüan-na* or *chüan-shu*) was most fully worked out during the Ch'ing. In 1673 office as well as rank had been sold to finance suppression of the Rebellion of the Three Feudatories, but generally only rank was sold. Although the country was prosperous until the end of the eighteenth century, extra funds had been needed in crises. "Contributions" increased in the Chia-ch'ing period and markedly in the Tao-kuang and Hsien-feng periods.[112]

To encourage contributions had always been regarded as an emergency measure for military expenses, river control, or relief from natural disasters;[113] moreover, the office itself was not directly offered for sale. However, rank purchasers became eligible for office and were in fact increasingly appointed to lower positions in the civil service.

Opposition of the embattled bureaucracy to the sale of rank began in the middle Tao-kuang period[114] and became vociferous by the 1860's, when leading officials considered that the Confucian state itself might be in jeopardy. Although for polemical purposes these officials may have exaggerated the extent of the damage,[u] the amount of revenue involved seemed far too small to justify the threat to the system. There was a saying in Peking that officials who had come up through the examination system were half "superior men" and half "low creatures," whereas those who had purchased rank were all "low creatures."[115]

On these grounds, it was often argued that abolition of the sale of rank was the first requirement of the Restoration. Feng Kuei-fen wrote:

> In the past ten years [the 1850's] sales of rank have been frequent, and civil government has therefore been weakened. When civil government is weakened, social ferment becomes critical; when social ferment becomes critical, the public revenues are strained; when the public revenues are strained, there is increased sale of rank. This is the way in which one rebellion leads to another. In discussion of present-day government, I consider the abolition of sale of rank to be the first principle.[116]

The dilemma of the Ch'ing was illustrated in 1862 when a censor pointed out that purchasers of rank were being appointed to substantive posts. The edict in reply ordered that henceforth no actual posts should be given to "the commercial classes." But when the Board of Revenue memorialized on the loss of income that

---

[t] On the fiscal aspects of the sale of rank, see Chapter VIII.

[u] "Only 13 officials out of 144 names in the list [which included the Grand Council, the Grand Secretariat, the Tsungli-yamen, and provincial officials above the rank of taotai] obtained their first appointment by purchase, and of these only four have reached the rank of Judicial Commissioner." (Bourne, "Historical Table . . . ," *loc. cit.*, p. 315.)

would result,[v] a second edict ordered that the "old rules" continue in force. Following this, another censor, Liu Yü-nan, memorialized that the two edicts were inconsistent; the Throne replied that the first edict concerned principle while the second was a concession to military necessity.[117]

The governor of Shantung, Yen Ching-ming, wrote several long analyses of the ramifications of the sale of rank, of its effect on civil government, and of possible methods of limiting the evil without reducing the state revenues. According to Yen, the damage had been minor as long as only a small number of ranks were sold at high prices, because a family would then invest only on behalf of an able son. But by the T'ung-chih period large numbers of ranks were sold at low prices.[118] As a result, Yen wrote, incompetent offspring of the wealthy and powerful squabbled for positions of power, while others borrowed funds to purchase office, confident of being able to repay the lender shortly. In consequence, officials could not work in peace, scholars could not study in peace, and the people rebelled. "It is not the statutory system that is harmful, but the lowering of the price."

Yen pointed out that 70 per cent of the subscriptions were for brevet rank and only 30 per cent for rank entitling the holder to office. Of the latter only one-third (or 10 per cent of the total) were for tao, fu, chou, and hsien posts. The quality of officials in these last four posts was far more important to the state than the small revenue the state might obtain from the sale of these posts. Even so, Yen did not ask that the ranks prerequisite to these offices no longer be sold, but merely that the full price be charged, and paid directly to Peking.[119]

The supervising censor Kuo Hsiang-jui reported that merchants and middlemen, the scum of the market place, were actually holding office in local government and creating great dissatisfaction among the people. An edict replied that although the sale of rank was difficult to abolish, Kuo's report of popular resentment would seem to indicate that the system was too harmful to be continued. Tso Tsung-t'ang and Shen Pao-chen had suggested that the situation be remedied by giving strict examinations to rank purchasers as soon as they reached their expected posts; the Throne endorsed this as a compromise measure that would protect civil government without reducing revenues.[120]

Some such compromise solution was generally favored. No one approved continuance of the existing system, and very few (among them the governor of Fukien, Wang K'ai-t'ai) urged outright abolition of the sale of rank.[w] Ting Jih-

---

[v] Probably more of a loss to the clerks in the Board than to the Board itself. See below, in the present chapter.

[w] Wang proposed to eliminate by examination from 70 to 80 per cent of the rank purchasers already waiting in the various yamen as officials-designate (*CHTI*, Ch. 1, pp. 36–42b). For a summary of his memorial and the edict of commendation, see *CSK*, "Hsüan-chü chih," Sec. 5, p. 14, under date 1873 (TC-12). An abstract of the memorial and the edict appears in *Translation of the Peking Gazette for 1873*, pp. 38, 41.

ch'ang, as financial commissioner of Kiangsu, weeded out a number of hopefuls in Nanking by examination as has been indicated above. The commissioner of the Office of Transmission, Yü Ling-ch'en, presented the same idea in a different form: that rank be sold only to those worthy to hold office.[121] The censor Yüan Fang-ch'eng proposed another variant: all officials-designate should be given a strict examination; those of ability and learning should then be treated as regular officials, while the others should be sent back to their native places.[122] Abolition of the system, or change in procedure so that in fact no purchaser of rank would receive a post without qualifying by examination, was also urged by the Grand Secretary Ch'i Chün-tsao; the governor of Hunan, Yün Shih-lin; the prefect of the metropolitan prefecture, Chiang Ch'i-ling; and numerous others.[123]

DISCIPLINING THE BUREAUCRACY

Although traditional political theory held that the chief guarantee of good government lay in the proper training and selection of officials in the first instance, it was recognized that officials, no matter how well selected, must be "encouraged" by a system of rewards and punishments. Officials in office were examined at regular intervals, and their activities were subject to constant scrutiny and frequent denunciation by their colleagues. The Censorate[124] was in charge of the network of surveillance, but there were internal checks throughout the administrative hierarchy.[125] Observing the almost daily investigations of the competence of individual officials and the triennial reports on the merits and demerits of all officials throughout the hierarchy, the *North China Herald* commented:

> The principles of Chinese government are enforced by such an ordered and exact gradation of rank, and each public servant is so entirely under the control of the officer above him, that it is not easy for a wrong-doer to escape detection. [In spite of abuses] the system enlists the interests of so many that it has great conservative strength. . . . It is like a network extending over the whole face of society, each individual being isolated in his own mesh, and responsibly connected with all around him.[126]

Frequent Imperial edicts urged high officials to devote more attention to investigating and reporting on the activities of their subordinates.[127] After the recapture of Nanking in 1864, Tseng Kuo-fan resumed the governor-generalship of Kiangsu, Kiangsi, and Anhwei on December 14 and immediately launched a "rigorous examination" of the activities of many officials; promotions and demotions according to his findings followed.[128]

As a rule, the governor-general or governor of a province reported his recommendations in a memorial; if these were approved by the Board of Civil Office, an edict ordered them put into effect.[129] Occasionally the Board of Civil Office found technical fault with the recommendations of a provincial governor; in that case the Emperor might either uphold the Board or confirm the governor's recommendation. If the governor's recommendation was upheld, the edict emphasized that this was a special case, not a precedent that would affect the validity of the statutes of civil office.[130]

Minor officials were most frequently demoted or dismissed on such grounds as negligence in action against lawbreakers, senility, low intelligence, deafness or other physical disabilities, frivolity, improper speech, and bad temper.[131] The charges against major officials were likely to be more serious, but there were few celebrated cases during the T'ung-chih period. In 1862 Hsüeh Huan, who was in charge of foreign relations at Shanghai, was accused by a censor of insufficient attention to military affairs, with having interests in a bookstore and a money shop, and with outraging popular sentiment.[132] The charges were investigated, and Hsüeh was demoted and transferred, but probably the administration's primary motive was to make way for Li Hung-chang.

The effectiveness of demotion and removal from office as means of controlling the bureaucracy was limited by various supplementary methods of securing reinstatement, just as the effectiveness of the examinations as a means of selecting the bureaucracy was limited by the various supplementary methods of acquiring office in the first place. In neither case was it found possible to eliminate entirely the role of money, military fame, and powerful friends, but in both cases strenuous efforts to limit the damage to civil government had some success. Provincial officials were forbidden to recommend for reappointment "permanently" discharged officials.[133] The plea of a discharged official to secure reinstatement by subscription—in fact, to convert the penalty to a fine—was subject to review by the Throne. When discharged officials were reinstated because of subscription or military merit, efforts were made to see that they were reappointed to distant provinces where their previous misdeeds were unknown and could not shake public confidence in the bureaucracy.[134]

A word should be said here about the disciplining of eunuchs, who, though they were never members of the bureaucracy, played political roles because of their palace connections. Although there was some criticism during the Restoration,[135] they did not during this decade have sufficient power to take independent action or to supplant the regular officials as agents of the Throne. When the eunuch An Te-hai was charged with assuming the symbols and functions of civil office on a trip to Shantung, Prince Kung and Ting Pao-chen promptly had him executed, in spite of the Empress Dowager Tz'u-hsi's favor.[136]

THE ATTACK ON CORRUPTION

Corruption—the misappropriation of public funds and supplies and the use of the powers of office to further private interests—must be clearly distinguished from the purchase of rank or office. The system of selling rank admitted to the official hierarchy men who were likely to be corrupt, but it was not itself a corrupt practice.

The Chinese custom of giving and receiving commissions on all public and private transactions was irregular from a Western point of view, since the terms were governed by precedent rather than written statute or contract. Yet in periods of peace, prosperity, and vigorous government, venerable custom and the "principles of social usage" afforded a fair check on abuse. In times of confusion and disillusionment, however, the Chinese system seems to have offered fewer safeguards against runaway corruption than the Western legalistic system.

Beginning with the colossal plundering of the public treasury by Ho-shen[137] in the late eighteenth century, corruption spread rapidly. The death penalty for Ho-shen did not prevent others from enriching themselves, and the Hsien-feng collapse in the face of "internal disaster and external calamity" led to a confusion and disillusionment that threatened the foundations of Confucian society. As every type of official corruption increased, the disillusion that caused it also increased in a vicious circle.

After eighty years of demoralization, no remedy seemed possible, yet in the brief T'ung-chih Restoration a number of abuses were eliminated or checked. In traditional Chinese government, corruption could not be eliminated, or even held within customary bounds, without a restoration of the traditional morale. What appeared, therefore, to be pious Restoration generalities about the elimination of corruption through moral training were in their time "realistic" discussions of the basic problem.[138]

Specific cases of corruption were attacked with vigor. Documents of the period reported constant investigation and punishment of cases of bribery. In some cases the official who was offered the bribe himself reported the case,* but usually the charges were made by censors, the members of the Hanlin Academy, provincial governors, and inspectors of storehouses. All such charges were carefully investigated, according to an elaborate procedure; if they proved groundless, the person laying the charges was punished. More often, the charges were apparently substantiated, and the accused official was punished.[139]

Although metropolitan and provincial officials of both high and low rank were accused, found guilty of corruption, and punished, lofty connections were undoubtedly used to forestall investigation or to mitigate penalties. Previous service to the state could easily be introduced as grounds for clemency. For example, in 1867 the powerful Kuan-wen, governor-general of Hupeh and Hunan, was accused of misappropriating the likin revenue, and the case was handed to the Board of Civil Office for "strict investigation and punishment." The Board rec-

---

* For example, in 1862 an edict in response to a memorial of Prince Kung ordered the punishment of the president of the Board of War, who had offered Prince Kung a bribe (*Peking Gazette*, translated in *NCH*, Feb. 22, 1862).

ommended that he be deprived of most of his titles, ranks, and salaries. However, an edict of February 15, 1867, declared that his ten years' service against the rebels far outweighed these minor crimes and softened the punishment. By May 10 he was "the Grand Secretary Kuan-wen" again, and his appointment as head of the Board of Punishments followed. Finally, on November 20, he was appointed governor-general of Chihli.[140]

Clearly the administrative system did provide some kind of a check on even the highest officials,[y] but the punishment was often mild.

A basic cause of corruption was the fact that Chinese officials were too poorly paid to devote themselves wholeheartedly to honest administration without some sort of legal supplementary income.[z] When a foreigner, Hart, pointed this out,[141] the governor-general of Kwangtung and Kwangsi, Jui-lin, and the governor of Kwangtung, Chiang I-li, retorted that whether an official was scrupulous or corrupt depended on his character; a small sum was enough for a frugal man, and no sum was enough for an extravagant one. To the Throne, however, the two officials expressed the hope that as military expenses decreased, the old higher salary scale could be restored; then honest officials would have a competence, and corrupt officials would lose their excuse for circumventing the legal penalties.[142] The importance of a realistic salary scale was widely recognized during the sixties,[143] but no real solution was found, and the problem remained to plague Chinese reformers of later generations.

THE RULE OF AVOIDANCE

According to Chinese administrative regulation, no official was supposed to serve either in his native province or for an extensive, continuous period in any province. In favor of this rule of "avoid the (native) province," it was argued that only an outsider free from the pressure of family and friends could be a just and impartial judge in local affairs. It was also obvious that an outsider was "safer," from the point of view of the central government, as being less likely to lead any local dissidence that might develop. On the other hand, it was clear that an outsider, however impartial and safe, was inevitably ignorant of local conditions[a] and hence excessively dependent on the permanent yamen clerks.[b]

[y] During the Ch'ing period as a whole the majority of all impeachments by the Censorate were directed against powerful officials above the third rank (Hsiung-fei Li, *Les Censeurs sous la dynastie mandchoue en Chine*, Paris, 1936, table on p. 128).

[z] This supplementary allowance was officially called the allowance to "nurture integrity" (*yang-lien*), and its importance is indicated by the fact that for a governor-general it amounted to between 15,000 and 25,000 taels, while his salary amounted to between 180 and 200 taels. (Williams, *The Middle Kingdom*, I, 294, citing the Red Book.)

[a] For example, Tso Tsung-t'ang found that he needed northwesterners in his northwestern campaign (Wang Chih-p'ing, *Tseng Hu Tso ping-hsüeh kang-yao*, pp. 84–85).

[b] It can be argued that the rule of avoidance had the opposite of the intended effect; that instead of keeping officials free of local embroilment, it made them wholly dependent on local clerks, so that while the officials were not "enfeoffed," the clerks were (Inaba Iwakichi, "Chung-kuo she-hui chih pen-chih chi ch'i tso-yung," *Tung-fang tsa-chih*, XIX, 17 (1922), 43).

During the Restoration many solutions to this problem were proposed. Lo Ping-chang argued that the rule of avoidance ought to be both enforced more strictly and redefined to prevent a man from holding office in the province where he had actually been brought up, regardless of whether this was officially listed as his family's original "native" province.[144] Liu K'un-i, governor of Kiangsi, also favored retention of the regulation but took a less extreme view. He conceded that military officials might with advantage be appointed to serve in their native provinces, but that with civil officials "it is difficult to be certain that they can really eliminate all partiality for friends and relatives." Liu did not favor the constant transfer of officials, however; he felt that an official of proven competence in a given area might well be kept there for long periods.[145] Jui-lin and Chiang I-li took the same position, quoting Tso Hsiung of the Later Han: "When officials are often changed, those beneath them are restless; when they are long in office, the people submit to their teaching and influence." Jui-lin and Chiang argued that to insist on frequent transfers was not to apply the rule but to abuse it.[146]

At the other extreme, Feng Kuei-fen urged that the rule itself be abolished and that an official be appointed to his native province whenever such an appointment appeared desirable. The regulation was not an ancient practice, said Feng, but a Ming[c] practice, and "I have not heard that the government of the Ming was superior to the governments of antiquity."[147]

The rule of "avoid the province" and the principle of frequent transfers were integral parts of the general theory of centralism that has dominated Chinese political thinking. Regional and local officials were never the top officials of regionally grounded hierarchies; they were rather intendants sent out to survey the local scene on behalf of the central government. Foreigners advising on China's modernization, beginning with Robert Hart,[148] have urged that this system be modified; and Chinese reformers have frequently conceded the point in principle. Yet the idea of centralism has persisted, and the governments of the late Ch'ing and of the Republic, in spite of their platforms of "local self-government," have generally done their best to see to it that provincial and local administrative power was held by "outsiders" directly responsible to the central government.

SPECIALIZATION VS. OMNICOMPETENCE

According to Chinese theory, the good official was a well-rounded "universal man." If he needed specialized assistance, he got it from a special class of men who fawned on the bureaucracy from below, who had no status in the scheme of civil government, and who were therefore unresponsive to its ideological

---

[c] According to Inaba (*loc. cit.*), the rule, in less strict form, originated with Sui Wen-ti of the seventh century A.D.

controls. The Confucian official himself was assumed to be a competent judge of policy on all matters, however complex, because government was conceived as the art of ordering human relations, not as the science of legal administration.

As the problems of government multiplied in the nineteenth century, the ever-latent weaknesses in this humanistic scheme of government were magnified. From Grand Councillor to district magistrate the official faced more complicated problems than his predecessors had ever faced, but he was still expected to provide wise solutions to them all. Foreign affairs were by no means the only new problem. The Ch'ing emphasis on precise precedents created complex legal problems; the increasing commutation of the corvée to a tax paid in silver raised difficult technical problems in finance. Neither the scholar-official nor the purchaser of rank was qualified to deal with these subjects. Yet during the Ch'ing period there were fewer alternate roads to office than had existed in the Ming period, and as the duties of every official increased, fewer subordinates within the hierarchy were available to him.

On this problem of specialization the Confucian reformer faced a fundamental dilemma. He could advocate minor adjustments, but he could not possibly advocate division of labor and specialization without destroying the essential notion of government by moral suasion through men of character.

Within the traditional system the answer was in part provided by the system of personal aides (*mu-yu*). The personal aide was a man who combined the traditional learning with legal, military, or financial competence, but who as yet had no official status. He was not supposed to appear in public, yet he often deputized for the official. Not an underling, he was expected to offer free criticism and to mitigate the perennial conflict between scholar-officials on the one hand and clerks with practical knowledge on the other.

The system of personal aides flourished particularly during the Restoration and increased the flexibility of the official system without straining it. A considerable proportion of the men came from the culturally prominent area of Shaohing; usually, however, local men were employed as personal aides, for they were familiar with local conditions and with the local dialect. For example, Tso Tsung-t'ang, a Hunanese, served as personal aide in Hunan under Chang Liang-chi and Lo Ping-chang, so effectively, it was said, that the accomplishments of Lo were the accomplishments of Tso.[149]

Yet for many purposes, no technically competent personal aide could be found, for he, like the official, had to be part of the Confucian tradition if he was to function effectively. The efforts of the Restoration statesmen to cope with the problem of specialization indicated that the officials of the time could perfectly well grasp new techniques where they chose to do so, but that the area in which they were free to make this choice and yet remain *Confucian* reformers was narrow indeed.

Other governments that have lacked specialized personnel—the Russia of Peter the Great, the Ottoman Empire, England in the late sixteenth century—have sometimes been able to employ foreigners. The Chinese government could do this only in a very limited sphere, since few foreigners could be made to fit into the Confucian system of values.

The Chinese Imperial Maritime Customs, as conceived and administered by Robert Hart, was the outstanding example of the use of foreign specialists during the Restoration,[d] and it affected only a tiny fragment of the economy of nineteenth-century China. Some foreigners were employed reluctantly in the likin and salt administrations, but none in the basic administration of the country. The attitude of foreign employees often aggravated the difficulty, but it did not cause it; no outlander, however earnest, could have played the delicate social role assigned to all officials.

THE YAMEN CLERKS

In the view of Restoration officials, the greatest danger to effective Confucian government in China was the powerful position of the yamen clerks.[150] This was a problem of long standing, but its seriousness increased with the growing complexity of government. Everywhere the Confucian civil official found himself surrounded by these clerks and dependent on their knowledge of the region he governed and the technical problems of his administration. Since few professional civil servants ever remained long enough in one post to equal their clerks' knowledge of its functional and regional problems, the clerks were often in a position to sabotage an official's policies and blackmail the people. The reformer Wang K'ang-nien later declared that the yamen clerks rather than the Emperor, the high officials, or the people, held the real power in China.[151]

The *de facto* power of the yamen clerks invalidated the premises on which the whole theory of Confucian government rested. It was taken for granted that any able man interested in scholarship and government or ambitious for prestige would attempt to make his way in the official hierarchy, where all the incentives except immediate personal gain were concentrated. Accordingly the yamen clerks were considered shrewd and unscrupulous timeservers whose careers denied every Confucian value.

In the Restoration period it is estimated that there were 1,190,000 clerks throughout the Empire. According to Feng Kuei-fen, there were at least one thousand in every board,[152] and in every board they exploited their position. In

[d] See Chapter VIII.

the Board of Revenue, for example, the clerks collected a discount from every official who came to collect his salary.[153] One of them became so rich that he was referred to as "Board Member No. 7," the statutory number being six.[154]

The clerks were denounced throughout the Ch'ing, particularly in the three great periods of reform: the late seventeenth century, the 1860's, and the 1890's.[155] The dangers were clear and constantly discussed, but few critics saw that the role of clerks was bound to increase as paper work increased, and that consequently a Confucian state could control them only by giving them status in the Confucian hierarchy, thus making them subject to its indoctrination and controls.

Feng Kuei-fen proposed a solution as radical as it was traditional. He suggested the reinterpretation and extension of true Confucian administrative principles to meet new conditions. He urged that young men with local recommendations be appointed to clerkships, there to serve a kind of apprenticeship leading to promotion into the career service.[156]

Feng's solution, if it had proved practicable, would have made the yamen clerk part of a homogeneous, extended hierarchy. To Feng Kuei-fen's suggestion that all government offices emulate the Grand Council and use "secretaries" (who had status) rather than clerks, Li T'ang-chieh replied that vested interests were strong, and that sweeping Imperial action would be required.[157] The Restoration was not an age of sweeping action. The only check on clerks remained the ambiguous one of their low social position.[e]

CONCLUSION

The Confucian theory of civil government by men of merit was severely tested during the Restoration period. It was an age of great names, standing in marked contrast to the periods that preceded and followed it. Throughout Chinese history, there had been numerous periods when "men of merit achieved extraordinary things," but the periods had always been short.[158] Although the record of the Ch'ing compared favorably enough with that of other dynasties, and although the Restoration was unquestionably one of those occasional short periods in which men of merit flourish, the results were short-lived. The system had its defects even in the best of times. As K'ang Yu-wei remarked, it led to excessive dependence on the particular qualities of particular officials: if the governor was literary, the whole province would write; if he was interested in finance, the whole province would dabble in currency reform.[159]

---

[e] "It is a significant point in the Chinese power structure that these men who were in the position of most easily abused power should have been held so low. If society had not suppressed them by despising them and depriving them of a decent social position, they might have become as fearful as wolves. But with no hope of ascending in the social scale, even if they abused their power, they would still not be too formidable." (Hsiao-t'ung Fei, *China's Gentry*, p. 80.)

A long, popular history of the Ch'ing, designed to be read aloud, reflected the universal view that the Ch'ing fell owing to an intolerable shortage of human ability.[160] The Restoration had shown traditional civil government at its best. It was an impressive performance, but as new problems multiplied, the inadequacy of its principles became painfully clear.

CHAPTER VI

THE SUPPRESSION OF REBELLION

THE GENERAL PROBLEM

The T'ung-chih reign was one of the most turbulent in Chinese history. It was marked by four major rebellions and local revolts in every province. And yet the old-fashioned Chinese chroniclers who conventionally labeled it "The T'ung-chih period of peace" were in a sense correct; for contrary to every expectation the four great rebellions were suppressed, reconstruction was launched, and some beginning was made toward removing the causes of local dissidence. In view of the magnitude of the problem, it was a stunning achievement, as the following sections will show.

Although warding off the threat of foreign conquest was the new government's most immediate task,[a] the early suppression of domestic rebellion was scarcely less urgent and fundamentally more important, for several reasons:

(1) The direct cost of the campaigns was staggering.[1] The drain on Imperial finances hindered not merely the basic program of military self-strengthening[b] but the whole civil reconstruction program of the Restoration.

(2) The indirect cost to the country at large, in terms of physical devastation, was far greater.[c] Even so stable an agrarian empire as Confucian China could not long endure such a strain.

(3) Restoration statesmen were fully aware that the disturbed state of the country invited foreign intervention. In the words of the Tsungli-yamen, "Foreign aggression has generally followed upon our failure to pacify domestic rebellion."[2]

(4) Overriding all other considerations was the obvious threat to the very existence of the Ch'ing state. The Taiping Heavenly Kingdom, with its capital at Nanking, made a direct claim to full sovereignty and central authority. The Yunnan Moslem kingdom of "P'ing-nan kuo," with its capital at Tali, claimed independence under Tu Wen-hsiu, also known as the Sultan Suleiman. Although the Nien-fei and the northwestern Moslems had no such elaborate pretensions, they were the best fighters of all, and their local chieftains controlled substantial reaches of vital territory.

The Ch'ing nightmare was that some or all of these rebels might join forces, as indeed they did to a limited extent. After 1864 the chief Nien-fei leaders were

[a] See Chapters III and X.
[b] See Chapter IX.
[c] See below, in the present chapter.

all former Taiping men; although distinct in origin, the two movements had been closely linked from 1856 on.[3] Both the Taiping and the Nien-fei had connections with the northwestern Moslems,[4] and the disturbances in Kweichow were greatly aggravated by two forays into the province by the forces of the Taiping leader Shih Ta-k'ai,[5] as well as by the existence of a full-scale Moslem revolt in neighboring Yunnan. The host of "local bandits" infesting the empire —"doctrinal bandits," "association bandits," "aboriginal bandits," "salt bandits," "gambling bandits," "horse thieves," "gunpowder dealers," and so on, down to mere "local rascals"—did not, of course, directly threaten the state; but, as the Ch'ing recognized, it was from these malcontents and rowdies that the ranks of the major rebellions were swelled.[6]

The rebellions differed greatly in geographic and social origins, in the characteristics of their leaders, and the nature of their rank and file. Their doctrines varied from the intense Christian-influenced imperial communalism of the Taiping and the fanatic New Teaching of the extreme wing of the Moslems to the simple secret-society affiliations of the Nien. The Taiping were organized as an empire, the Yunnan Moslems as a kingdom, the Nien as loosely federated mobile bands. Each rebellion had its own political and military strategy. Only the Taiping attempted great offensive campaigns in a bid for supreme power; the others confined themselves largely to attacking the failing Ch'ing power in local areas, and to defending and consolidating their base territories.

Yet there were certain similarities among the various uprisings. Each had been born of a long-smoldering local resentment, of which the Ch'ing had been aware without taking adequate remedial measures. In each case there was "a last straw"—the incessant floods in Anhwei in the 1850's, the bungling of local officials in Shensi in the early 1860's—following which the rebellion rapidly swelled to major proportions, with a more clearly defined doctrine, program, organization, and strategy. Each rebellion's first years were years of steady Ch'ing defeat, of half-hearted and self-contradictory Imperial strategies.

Finally, each rebellion reached a high point that thoroughly alarmed the government and provoked it into reassessing the situation realistically; military and political strategy was overhauled, and the new leaders of the Restoration took charge.[d] It was the central corps of great Restoration leaders (or in the case of Yunnan an immediate disciple) who suppressed all the major and most of the minor rebellions. And it was to the absence of such leadership in Kweichow that the Ch'ing failure there was attributed.

The motivations, strengths, and weaknesses of each rebellion were appraised differently, and the Ch'ing suppression strategy varied accordingly. But behind

[d] See Chapter V.

all campaigns lay the fundamental notion, as phrased by Tso Tsung-t'ang, that "a strategy of pacification that is not based on simultaneously exterminating and comforting is impossible."[7] In each case the new Restoration strategy led to a steady series of victories, culminating in a turning point—an Anking or a Chin-chi-p'u—after which the preliminary work of reconstruction could begin. None of the rebellions collapsed at the turning point, and there were further alarms and crises; but the rebel source of strength had been undermined, and the end was not far off. Having achieved domestic tranquillity, Restoration leaders were faced with the fundamental problem of preserving it. This chapter is concerned with the series of rebel-smashing campaigns—both political and military—that made the fundamental preservation effort possible.

THE SUPPRESSION OF THE TAIPING REBELLION[8]

The Taiping Rebellion, 1850–1864, was one of the major social revolutions of history. It had its origins in the southern provinces of Kwangtung and Kwangsi, where the unsettling effect of contact with the West had been most prolonged and where Hakka[e] and other minority groups were still not fully assimilated. As Ch'ing prestige and power over remote areas declined following defeat in the first Anglo-Chinese War, the great rebellion began with the famed uprising at Chin-t'ien, shortly after the accession of the ill-fated Hsien-feng Emperor.

Within three years the Taiping armies had swept up from Kwangsi and made Nanking their capital. Between 1853 and 1856 success followed success, mainly in the Yangtze valley above Nanking. Between 1857 and 1860 fighting was centered in Anhwei and Hupeh, and the Taiping fortunes continued to rise. Their defeats at the hands of Hu Lin-i and other leaders of the new regionally based armies[f] in Hupeh were more than offset by their smashing victories over the great Imperial armies of the traditional type in Anhwei. At their zenith the Taiping forces held most of central China, threatened Shanghai repeatedly, and were even able to send a spearhead toward the outskirts of Peking. In the course of fifteen years they operated in sixteen provinces and captured more than six hundred walled cities.[9]

The Taiping program called for land distribution, the development of small commerce free of the traditional monopolies, and the constitution of the Heavenly Kingdom of Great Peace as a new universal monarchy. Its doctrine was a strange blend of elements of Confucianism, Chinese secret-society teachings, primitive communism, anti-Manchu nationalism, and Christianity.[10] No other rebellion had so elaborately worked out a doctrine or so imposing a pseudo-imperial ad-

---

[e] See below, in the present chapter.
[f] See Chapter IX.

ministrative organization. And the Taiping was the only rebellion to leave a substantial documentary record of its own.[11]

The first great shock to Ch'ing complacency was the rebels' capture of Nanking in 1853. Although seven years were to pass before the necessary bold step was taken by the central government, provincial Restoration leaders began at once to develop the new armies for which the situation clearly called.[g] They also undertook an appraisal of the rebellion's causes and its weaknesses,[12] an appraisal that eventually shaped the Ch'ing counterprogram. The Taiping leaders were poor administrators, especially of rural areas; the Ch'ing offered a broad program of agrarian relief and rehabilitation.[h] Another and perhaps more crucial Taiping blunder, the alienation of the literati, has been pointed to by Chinese Communist historians as a key lesson of the Taiping Rebellion.[18]

The inadequacy of the Taiping doctrine enabled the Ch'ing to win the support not only of the literati but of other classes. Tseng Kuo-fan spoke for his generation when he said that in the Taiping areas the farmer could not freely till and pay taxes because his land belonged to God; the merchant could not trade and profit because his goods belonged to God; the scholar could not read the Classics because the rebels insisted on acceptance of the New Testament.[14] Marxist critics of Ch'ing policy concede the point in reverse language, stating that the ruling classes, though shaken, "still had the psychological implements inherited for thousands of years—human relationships, the rectification of names, and all the old ideas and practices of feudal virtue."[15]

The Taiping errors were by no means wholly psychological, however. In the period of their success the Taiping armies had failed to gain control of Hunan, the area in which their mortal enemy, the Hsiang Army, later developed. They often looted and then abandoned the cities they had captured, including strategic points like Wuhan; in consequence, their capital, Nanking, was always under pressure. And they failed, for no apparent military reason, to take Shanghai and thus gain control of all Kiangsu.

Nonetheless the Taiping forces remained formidable, and a second disaster was required to push the Ch'ing into a fundamentally new policy. This disaster came in 1860–61. The collapse of the reorganized Ch'ing forces in the lower Yangtze valley enabled the ablest of the Taiping leaders, Li Hsiu-ch'eng, to capture Hangchow, Soochow, Changchow, and all the leading cities of that vital area in swift succession. After these defeats Peking never again sent an Imperial commissioner to lead great armies of the old type against the rebels.

At the same time that allied victories in the north were leading Chinese

g See Chapter IX.
h See Chapters VII and VIII.

statesmen to a new and far more promising type of thinking on foreign affairs, Taiping victories along the lower Yangtze were producing a new approach to the problem of domestic rebellion, a new civil and military leadership, and a new army. Tseng Kuo-fan's Hsiang Army had proved its worth, and, in an unprecedented move, Tseng was placed in command over all forces in Kiangsu, Anhwei, Kiangsi, and Chekiang, with authority over both military and civil officials.

Clear Imperial ascendancy over the Taiping forces began with the recapture of Anking. The usual auspicious astronomical phenomena were noted: the sun and the moon rose in conjunction, and the five planets moved in harmony, giving rise to the saying that the general situation had changed (*chuan-chi*). The importance of the fall of Anking was indicated by the award of high honors to officials associated with the victory.[16]

Victory followed victory for the next three years. First Kiangsi was pacified, and when critical points in Chekiang and Anhwei had been recovered, Tseng Kuo-ch'üan laid siege to the rebel capital, Nanking. Li Hung-chang, Tso Tsung-t'ang, and others reconquered the lower Yangtze valley. The end of the rebellion was in sight with the fall of Soochow late in 1863 and of Changchow early in 1864. The collapse of the rebellion was as swift as its rise; only three years earlier the rebels had controlled all of Chekiang and Kiangsu and large parts of Kiangsi and Anhwei, had threatened Shanghai, and had been able to send expeditions north of the Yangtze.[17]

Throughout the spring of 1864 the *Peking Gazette* reported a steady stream of victory awards.[18] The fall of Nanking was so imminent that edicts of the spring and early summer frequently deferred various decisions "until after the recovery of Nanking." On August 1, 1864, the *Peking Gazette* announced the long-awaited triumph with fanfare. Tseng Kuo-fan received the highest honors the Throne could bestow; nearly every other high official was honored, including many who had no direct connection with the campaign. There was celebration throughout the country, and solemn ceremonies were held beginning with the repair of the temple of the founder of the Ming at Nanking.[19]

The documents pointed out with pride that since the Taiping Rebellion had been one of the most devastating in Chinese history, its suppression was one of the most glorious triumphs in Chinese history.[20] With the terrible menace of the Taiping averted, the rejoicing was in proportion to the gravity of the crisis surmounted, and confidence in the future of China was restored. "Enduring rule and lasting peace" (*ch'ang-chih chiu-an*) was the motto of the day. The records of the rebellion were compiled and studied and were seen as a "mirror'" of countless years of felicity ahead.[21] Remnants of the Taiping armies continued to operate for several years after the fall of Nanking, and Taiping fragments joined the Nien-fei and other groups, but the danger to the Ch'ing state had passed, and a new era had been ushered in.

We are here concerned with the reasons for the Taiping failure only in so far as these may shed light on the reasons for the Restoration's success. The Restoration was strongest where the Taiping were weakest: in leadership, in civil administration, and in ideology and morale. For every Li Hsiu-ch'eng on the Taiping side, there were fifty men of merit in the Restoration camp. Where the Taiping were content with merely seizing cities, the Ch'ing attended closely to the government of its territory. The Taiping blend of nationalism and religion left most Chinese cold; the revived Confucianism propagated by Tseng Kuo-fan found a ready reception. Some Taiping leaders saw the ideological danger and attempted to modify the anti-Confucian portions of their teaching,[22] but their move was too clearly opportunistic, too clumsy, and too late. The Ch'ing leaders, on the other hand, genuinely believed in what they were fighting for; once they had joined battle, their morale was far higher than their adversaries'.[23]

Foreign aid, although touted by foreigners as a chief cause of the Ch'ing triumph, was clearly a secondary factor.[i] Foreign aid perhaps hastened the decision in the final phase of fighting in the lower Yangtze valley, but it did not and could not determine it.[24]

THE SUPPRESSION OF THE NIEN-FEI REBELLION[25]

The early history of Nien brigandage in the wake of the White Lotus Rebellion is obscure.[26] Probably caused by the same factors that caused the Taiping Rebellion, it was given impetus by the Taiping disorders and local natural disasters in Shantung, Kiangsu, and northern Anhwei, the heart of Nien territory. The "great" Nien Rebellion began formally in 1853.

The meaning of the term "*nien*," to twist or knead, has long been argued. Officials at the time derived it "from the twisted greased turbans worn by the rebels as a distinctive mark."[27] Of numerous other suggested interpretations, the most plausible seems to be that "*nien*" refers to the way the original small bandit bands were subsequently "kneaded" into larger bands.[28]

After 1853 the Nien expanded rapidly from their original base in northern Anhwei into Shantung, Honan, Kiangsu, and Hupeh.[29] Although limited Imperial victories were not infrequently reported,[30] it was clear by 1862 that the Ch'ing influence was nearly nonexistent in the whole Huai basin, power in the region being divided between the Nien leader Chang Lo-hsing and the chameleon Miao P'ei-lin.[31]

In the spring of 1863 the Imperial commander Seng-ko-lin-ch'in managed to capture and execute Chang Lo-hsing, but this had little effect on the cam-

---

i See Chapter IX.

paign. Chang's nephew, the able Chang Tsung-yü, succeeded to the Nien command, and by 1864 Seng-ko-lin-ch'in had lost control of the situation. The high
point of Nien strength was reached in an 1865 campaign led by Chang Tsung-yü
and Lai Wen-kuang, which culminated in a smashing defeat of the Imperial
armies west of Tsaochow, in Shantung, and the death in battle of the redoubt-
able Seng-ko-lin-ch'in himself.[32]

The Nien organization of local chieftains was a patchwork rather than a
centralized machine and was characterized by banners and titles deriving from
general religious-society practice. The chief Nien means of expansion was to
infilter and seize control of the local corps; the objects of their limited offensives
were usually walled communities that had originally been fortified under Ch'ing
auspices as a defense against bandits.[33] In facing Ch'ing troops, the Nien-fei
originally based their strategy on a war of position; later, profiting from the
Taiping experience, they shifted to emphasis on high mobility over a wide area.[34]
Nien-fei mobility was so striking that observers diagnosed many of their successes as the work of local peasants in widely separated areas.[35] The Nien, however, were not merely roving bandits. They had wandered early to plunder, but
by 1858 their territorial core was solid and their organization, though loose, was
effective. After 1863 they were compelled to wander, but never ceased trying
to return to their base territory.[36]

The Nien leadership was excellent; Li Hung-chang attested to the courage
and ability of Lai Wen-kuang, Jen Hua-pang (Jen Chu), Chang Tsung-yü, and
others; they were said to have surpassed the Taiping in fighting ability.[37] Their
greatest source of strength, however, was their shrewd insight in meeting the
needs and hopes of the people. Before taking over a town they wooed and won the
"natural" leaders of a community; afterward they were careful not to disturb
the civilian population. They opened the prisons and humiliated hated magistrates. Once they controlled an area, they attached great importance to the maintenance of its food supply; the plunder of government convoys was not enough.
They emphasized grain production and sent detachments back from the front
to help guard and reap the crops.[38]

It was for long believed that the Nien Rebellion, in contrast to the Taiping,
was deficient in program and doctrine.[j] Chinese Marxists and Communists have
continued to cling to this notion, emphasizing the inevitable failure of a popular
uprising not guided by a doctrine.[39] Recent research suggests, however, that the
Nien had not only a political program (as indicated above) but also a definite
ideology and doctrine: "Whereas the Nien Society's White Lotus heritage had
provided a distinguishing consciousness, setting the Nien apart from ordinary

---

[j] E.g., "The rebels have no definite political cry and no coherent political creed. They are starving and they clamour for food." (*NCH*, Mar. 14, 1868.)

bandits, the participation of the gentry gave to the Nien's incipient agitation broader political consciousness and organizing power, which made a true rebellion of it."[40] The evidence unfortunately is far from conclusive, owing to the total absence of documentation from the Nien side.

Before 1865 the Ch'ing campaigns against the Nien had been total failures on both the political and military fronts. Officials reported that the villagers were supporting the Nien rather than the Ch'ing, but they appeared not to know exactly why.[41] The Ch'ing forces were defeated by popular hostility even when occasionally a victorious campaign brought them to the heart of Nien territory.

The shock that occasioned a new Ch'ing policy was the death of Seng-ko-lin-ch'in. Peking leaders, now for the first time seriously alarmed, turned to the policy that had routed the Taiping. On May 27, 1865, Tseng Kuo-fan was placed in command of all Imperial forces in Shantung, Honan, and Chihli, while Li Hung-chang temporarily replaced him as governor-general of Kiangsu, Kiangsi, and Anhwei. The crack troops of the Metropolitan Field Force (*Shen-chi-ying*) were mobilized to guard the approaches to Peking; before this, if the rebels had been able to cross the Yellow River, their path to the capital would have been almost unimpeded. Meanwhile, alarming Nien-fei victories were reported in southern Chihli, Shantung, and northern Kiangsu.[42]

At this critical juncture in the summer of 1865, Tseng Kuo-fan formulated a new basic policy for the extermination of the Nien-fei. This new policy, which was subsequently followed by Tseng's successor, Li Hung-chang, merits attention for the important part it played in later Chinese efforts to exterminate "bandits."

Tseng's plan,[43] essentially defensive, was summarized in the slogan "Make rivers the boundaries and encircle limited areas" (*hua-ho ch'üan-ti*). Tseng argued that it was suicide for the Imperial troops to attempt to "roam about" as the rebels did, since in this roaming the rebels could command ample food supplies while the Imperial troops could not. Tseng therefore established four main bases: Linhuai in Anhwei, Tsining in Shantung, Chowchiakow in Honan, and Hsüchow in Kiangsu. At first the effort was made to use these bases in the traditional manner: when one area was threatened, supplementary forces were dispatched from the other three. This strategy was useless against the mobile Nien-fei and gave way to the relentless hemming-in strategy of *hua-ho ch'üan-ti*. After three years this strategy succeeded in limiting the area of Nien-fei operations, thus rendering ineffective their greater mobility.

The Ch'ing mobilized every resource at its command. Nine supplementary garrisons were established in the four provinces. Dikes, walls, and trenches were constructed along the Grand Canal and the Yellow River. But the most important resource of all was the political insight of Restoration statesmanship.

Tseng Kuo-fan understood perfectly that the basic problem was to win back the allegiance of the people of the Nien area. As he moved north to his new command post he made the first of many careful inspections of Nien territory. Recognizing that many "good people" had followed the rebels from poverty, he tried to find out who they were, win them back, and keep them loyal by a system of merit awards and identification cards.[44] Unfortunately, the thorough intermingling of "people" and "rebels" made the basic Ch'ing policy of "simultaneously exterminating and comforting" especially difficult in the Nien areas. In consequence, Tseng's policy of "strengthening the city walls and cleaning out the countryside" was undoubtedly harsher than his parallel policies in the Taiping areas. Nonetheless, Tseng was able to cut the ties between the villagers and the Nien leaders and to re-establish the authority of Ch'ing local officials. Immediate relief was provided, and land reclamation enterprises were quickly launched. Local people were recruited into the Huai Army, the pay was good, and the troops were kept under strict control.[45] By 1867 both gentry and commoners were rallying to the Ch'ing and again were building earthworks against bandits.

The new Ch'ing strategy was not, of course, wholly successful in either the political or the military sphere for several years. In late 1865 and throughout 1866, the Nien-fei continued to win victories in mobile warfare.[46] Tseng Kuo-fan had "failed," and early in 1867, apparently at his own request, he was ordered back to the governor-generalship of Kiangsu, Kiangsi, and Anhwei. Li Hung-chang, who replaced him, continued the same general policies.[47]

The winter of 1866–67 was marked by further Nien-fei victories in both the east and the west.[k] In the Shih-tzu-p'o campaign near Sian, the western Nien-fei put all the Imperial forces of Shensi province out of action in a single day's fighting. In Hupeh the Lo-chia-chi campaign resulted in the capture of a leading Ch'ing commander, Kuo Sung-lin. The Nien-fei were able to cut him off, to blockade him, and to attack at the critical moment.[48]

Early in 1867 there was the first real danger of a pincer movement on the capital. The eastern Nien-fei, having crossed the dry bed of the Grand Canal and defeated the Imperial troops sent against them, threatened Peking from the south. If the Nien-fei of Hupeh and Shensi could force their way into Shansi, they could threaten Peking from the west. In February a series of daily edicts

---

[k] In the autumn of 1866 the Nien-fei, who at this time still consisted of many small bands, formed themselves into two main groups. Chang Tsung-yü proceeded to Shensi as leader of the western Nien-fei and established contact with the rebelling Moslems. Lai Wen-kuang and Jen Hua-pang assumed leadership of the eastern Nien-fei, operating mainly in Honan, Hupeh, Shantung, and Kiangsu. (Wu Tseng-ch'i, *Ch'ing-shih kang-yao*, Ch. 12, p. 17b; Lo Erh-kang, *Nien-chün ti yün-tung chan*, p. 18.)

indicated the capital's alarm at what was happening in Shensi, Hupeh, and Honan. Li Hung-chang was appointed governor-general of Hupeh and Hunan and ordered to stop the Nien-fei advance in Hupeh. Tseng Kuo-fan and the governor of Honan, Li Ho-nien, were both ordered to Hsüchow. Tso Tsung-t'ang was ordered to proceed at once to take command in Shensi. The gravity of the situation was reflected in the choice of such renowned commanders.[49]

In June of 1867 the war entered its decisive phase, as the main body of the eastern Nien-fei moved toward strategic Hsüchow and then into Shantung, where they could expect assistance from the long quiescent Shantung Nien-fei. An edict of June 14, 1867, commanded all armies to hold the Shantung border, but the Nien-fei broke through the Grand Canal line and into Shantung.

Shantung now became the critical area. Ting Pao-chen planned a simultaneous attack from the north and south, while Li Hung-chang, hurrying to Shantung as ordered, planned to drive the Nien-fei out onto the tip of the Shantung peninsula and slaughter them.

During July of 1867 additional government armies poured into Shantung and northern Kiangsu, and the hemming-in plan was at last really applied. Both the Yellow River and the Grand Canal were divided into sectors in an effort to prevent the Nien-fei from crossing back and forth. Li Hung-chang set up a cordon of fortifications forty li from the Shantung coast and sent to Nanking for steamers to come up the coast and shell the rebel encampments. There was a series of panics in Chefoo as refugees from the countryside reported the burning of villages. Li Hung-chang was placed in command of all forces in Shantung, and victories were reported.

In early August of 1867 government troops appeared finally to have things in hand. Li had dug and manned a one-hundred-mile ditch from Laichow to Fuping, restricting the rebels to the extremity of the Shantung peninsula. Defense preparations along the Yellow River, the Chiao-lai River, and the Grand Canal seemed in order. Li was sufficiently confident to send some of the Chihli troops back to Chihli to aid in suppressing local bandits, and he himself proceeded to the front. No escape for the Nien-fei seemed possible unless they escaped by sea, and officials were warned not to allow any boats to hover about the coast.

And then, in a surprise move on August 28, thirty thousand rebels "passed with impunity through the Imperial lines." Apparently news of earlier rebel successes had already reached the capital, for on August 27 Li Hung-chang was reprimanded and demoted; Ting Pao-chen was stripped of rank; and at least one field commander was executed.[50]

For the next three months the eastern Nien-fei appeared to be able to move at will. If Li pursued them south, they moved simultaneously north and west.

However, the basic government position steadily improved as cavalry reinforcements were brought from Manchuria, the Grand Canal line was strengthened, and the system of supply was reorganized.

The Throne refused to credit the first reports of renewed government successes, but by December 1867 there was no longer any doubt. Imperial forces scored a triumph near Weihsien; between three and four thousand rebels were killed, and the remainder fled northeast. In subsequent engagements thirty thousand rebels, including Lai Wen-kuang himself, were taken prisoner and beheaded. The best troops of the eastern Nien-fei were virtually eliminated in these actions.[51]

As the danger from the eastern Nien-fei receded in the autumn and winter of 1867, Peking's attention shifted to the western Nien-fei, who had established themselves in northern Shensi and were threatening Shansi, a vital source of food and money and the outer defense line of the approach to Peking. By raiding the Paotow area, the Nien-fei drew government forces away from the Yellow River forts to Paotow. Under Chang Tsung-yü they were then able to break through the weakened Yellow River line into Shansi and to force the main line of Imperial defense back to the Shansi-Chihli border.

All efforts were now concentrated on the defense of Chihli. The Imperial troops in pursuit of the Nien-fei from the west were so far behind them that Tso Tsung-t'ang, who had been en route to command them for many months, was ordered to proceed at once to Chihli instead and to block the advance from the east. Tso was placed in command of the Chihli troops, and the defense of Peking was entrusted to Prince Kung and the Metropolitan Field Force.

In late January of 1868, as the western Nien-fei advanced, the eastern Nien-fei, who had been "suppressed" in December and "mopped up" in early January, reappeared in force and moved from Shantung into Chihli. Li Hung-chang was held chiefly responsible for this second pincer movement on the capital, and he was deprived of his Yellow Riding Jacket, his Double-Eyed Peacock Feather, and many other honors. Tso Tsung-t'ang, Li Ho-nien, Kuan-wen, and others were also punished by edicts of February 3 and February 5.[52]

The situation was now critical. Wen-hsiang described the alarm in the capital early in 1868 as Chang Tsung-yü led his forces from Shansi along the Taihang Mountains into Chihli and reached the Marco Polo Bridge, while the Shantung Nien-fei penetrated to within a few miles of Paoting in the south. There was no panic comparable to 1853 or 1860, but stringent measures were required.[53] Plans were made for the defense of Peking, and inspection of persons moving in or out of the city was ordered. Victories were reported as well as defeats, but the bandits moved ever nearer the capital.

By early March, however, government forces appeared to be gaining ground in Chihli, and by the end of March both the western and eastern Nien-fei had moved back from the metropolitan area toward Shansi, Honan, and Shantung.

Yet bandits continued to move about freely, and heads seemed about to fall. Penalties against Li Hung-chang, Li Ho-nien, and Tso Tsung-t'ang were ordered on April 27. On May 1, Li and Tso were both warned that the favor of the court would not much longer protect them from serious punishment. And on May 9 Li was given one more month to *complete* the extermination of the Nien-fei.

In spite of these last flashes of strength, the basis of Nien power had been steadily undermined from 1865 on, and from mid-July 1868 government victories were increasingly reported. The end came when the last leader of the last handful, Chang Tsung-yü, was drowned trying to swim to safety.[54]

On August 27, 1868, the great Nien-fei Rebellion was officially declared at an end. High honors were given to all field commanders and to the Grand Councillors, every official in the empire was awarded one mark of merit, and an Imperial prince was dispatched to report the victory to the late Hsien-feng emperor.[55]

Although there was never any real chance that the Nien-fei could overthrow the Ch'ing government, they could have continued to roam north China, taking advantage of the terrain, their mobility, and their fighting skill, had it not been for the new policies of Restoration leadership. The Nien-fei lost to the Ch'ing because they lost the competition for popular support and because their mobile strategy was useless when the possibility of retreat to the west was finally blocked.[56] It was Tseng Kuo-fan who had worked out in 1865 the two policies that proved successful by 1868. Superior Ch'ing firing power after 1866, which was the only form of foreign aid involved, was a less important factor.[57]

THE SUPPRESSION OF THE NORTHWESTERN MOSLEM REBELLION[58]

There appear to have been two underlying causes of the great revolt of the northwestern Moslems in the mid-nineteenth century: (1) discrimination against Moslems by Ch'ing local officials, and (2) the influence of the fanatical New Teaching (*hsin-chiao*) in certain Moslem communities beginning in the late eighteenth century. The first cause was the more important.[59] Official Ch'ing policy had always enjoined equal treatment of Chinese and Moslems, but with the increasing Sinicization of the originally Manchu dynasty,[l] Ch'ing neutrality toward disputes between the two cultural groups became more difficult to maintain.

The Moslems of China proper were more Sinicized than those of Turkestan. Although they adhered to Islam and religious marriages, and abhorred pork, wine, and uncleanliness, they were in many respects more closely related to the

[l] See Chapter IV.

Chinese than to their Turkic coreligionists beyond the Jade Gate.[60] Yet they had had a long record of resistance to Chinese local authority, complete with popular legends of anti-Ch'ing heroes, many of them Moslem participants in Li Tzu-ch'eng's rebellion at the end of the Ming.[61] However, with the possible exception of the adherents of the New Teaching, the great rebellion of the mid-nineteenth century was less a revolt against the Confucian state than an accumulation of protests against local discrimination.

To this day the New Teaching is not fully understood. The only incontrovertible fact is that wherever it spread it was associated with intransigence and rebellion. It first developed in a dozen isolated Salar villages, west of Hochow, the "Mecca of China," on the right bank of the Yellow River, an area that played an important part in Moslem rebellions throughout the Ch'ing period.[62] Western scholars have variously claimed that the New Teaching was related to Sufism and Kaderism, modified in China because its proponents did not fully understand Islamic mysticism;[63] that on the contrary the teaching was orthodox Sunni minus the mystic contemplation associated with the central Asian Sunni groups;[64] and that it was Wahabi.[65] Japanese research on the point has been inconclusive[66] until recently, when further evidence from Ch'ing sources has been cited in support of the argument that the New Teaching leaders were Sufis.[67] Apparently neither Middle Eastern[68] nor Chinese scholars have dealt with the subject. The former prefect of Lanchow, who was reputed to be the leading authority on the rebellion, remarked later that the clash between the Old Teaching and the New Teaching had caused all the trouble, but that he could not explain the difference between the two.[69]

The New Teaching first attracted attention in 1762 when its leaders and those of the Old Teaching in the Salar areas near Sining laid charges against each other before the Chinese magistrate. The leaders of both sects were found guilty and banished from the area. In 1769 charges were renewed, and this time penalties were heavier against the New Teaching.

Smoldering unrest in the Salar area broke into open revolt in 1781, when Ma Ming-hsin, a Salar religious reformer who had traveled in central Asia, returned to preach the true faith—the New Teaching—and to lead the attack on the Old Teaching. This led to a government inspection of the area, during which an official from near-by Hochow denounced the New Teaching. The official was that night abducted and murdered, Old Teaching believers at Lanchow were assassinated, and an anti-Ch'ing rebellion was under way. Its suppression required a major Ch'ing campaign, with fierce reprisals. A second and larger revolt in 1783 was also suppressed, garrisons in the area were strengthened, mutual security bonds were required, and the New Teaching was proscribed.[70]

The New Teaching continued, however, to nourish opposition to the Ch'ing and played a leading role in the "great" Moslem Rebellion of the 1860's and 1870's. Tso Tsung-t'ang's greatest military problem, as he himself recognized, was the fanatical resistance of adherents of the New Teaching, and his greatest political problem was the reconstruction of their devastated base areas.

A certain Ma Erh was said in the Ch'ing sources to have inherited the "white cap"[m] and red gown of the Ahun [Imām][n] Mu, a leader of the New Teaching, and Mu on his deathbed was said to have ordered his sons and followers to support Ma Erh. Ma Erh himself was subsequently condemned to a lingering death, and his son, Ma Hua-lung, became the most formidable of Tso Tsung-t'ang's Moslem opponents.[71]

The immediate background of the great nineteenth-century uprising was provided by a series of trivial incidents. In 1858 in Shensi there was a quarrel about Moslem children who sold fruit at a play in a Chinese town. The Chinese magistrate refused to intervene, and, upon being petitioned for a third time by Moslem spokesmen, lost patience and ordered them beaten. Several thousand Moslems then stormed a Chinese village, with loss of life on both sides. The magistrate was recalled to Sian and troops restored order, but no Moslem believed that the government had been neutral.[72]

During 1861 and 1862, Moslem rebels were intermittently active in various parts of Shensi and Kansu,[73] and the great rebellion was launched in 1862 in southern Shensi, near Sian, in an area recently disturbed by the passage of an arm of the Taiping forces. Some six hundred Moslem troops disbanded by the governor of Honan were en route home to Kansu. At Hwachow they broke some bamboo from a garden without the permission of the Chinese owner. A crowd gathered and the militia was called out. Moslem sources claim that two Moslems were beaten to death and that near-by Moslem homes were burned that night. Officially the incident was reported as the first evidence of a widespread Moslem plot, and troops were sent in to aid the militia.[74]

Fighting spread rapidly along the Wei River, and a general Moslem uprising followed. The leader of the militia was killed, and Sian was surrounded. Pai Yen-hu and others rose quickly to prominence as Moslem leaders, and by the autumn of 1862 contact had been established with Taiping forces.[75]

[m] The references in the sources to the colors of bonnets or caps are of little help in identifying or characterizing the New Teaching. D'Ollone reported that adherents of the New Teaching sometimes wore blue bonnets, while the orthodox wore white, green, or pale blue. But the Ahun Mu's bonnet was white. In the rebellion of 1783 red bonnets were worn, but red may have been an indication of revolt rather than of doctrine (H. M. D'Ollone, *Mission d'Ollone, 1906–1909; recherches sur les Musulman chinois*, Paris, 1911, pp. 17, 247, 311–14). If bonnet colors indicated sects at all, they probably did so only locally and ephemerally. The reader who wishes this confusion compounded is referred to Marshall Broomhall, *Islam in China*, London, 1910, chap. ix.

[n] According to Martin Hartmann ("China," *Encyclopaedia of Islam*, Leyden, 1913, I, 839–54), the imāms had great power in China, where each Moslem community was independent. The caliphs were not even known of; the sharif of Mecca was known, but his authority was not recognized.

The whole of the Moslem northwest was soon in revolt, and the governor of Shensi, Ying-ch'i, called for aid. Since his first choice and the court's, To-lung-a, was occupied with the Taiping, Sheng-pao was ordered to take full charge of the new concentration of Ch'ing forces in Shensi. He was completely ineffective and early in 1863 was replaced by the able To-lung-a,[76] who launched a hard-hitting campaign in which many rebel bases were captured. Two of the commanders sent by the Taiping to aid the Moslems were killed, another surrendered, and the southern Shensi Moslem forces disintegrated. It was said that two hundred li square were stripped bare in the Ch'ing mopping up as Pai Yen-hu and others led the Moslem remnants to Kansu.[77]

This first Ch'ing success was ephemeral, however; To-lung-a was killed in 1864, and the revolt spread rapidly. Ma Hua-lung, chief exponent of the New Teaching, was in command of the area from Ningsia to Ch'in-an, including Pingliang and his native Chin-chi-p'u. Moving west, Ma Chan-ao was in command in the Hochow area, Ma Kuei-yüan at Sining, and Ma Wen-lu from Suchow west. In the following years Moslems captured Ningsia fu, Suchow, Lanchow, and many lesser cities, and the situation deteriorated by the day.[78]

By 1866 it was abundantly clear that a basic change in Ch'ing policy was urgent, but as full attention could not be given to the Nien-fei until after 1864 when the Taiping were suppressed, so full attention could not be given to the northwestern Moslems until after the Nien-fei were suppressed. Late in 1866 one of the chief figures of the Restoration, Tso Tsung-t'ang, was appointed governor-general of Shensi and Kansu for the specific purpose of suppressing the Moslem Rebellion, but his plans were not approved until September 1868,[79] and he did not reach Sian until November.

Tso and other Ch'ing leaders fully recognized that the political campaign must be based on the traditional maxim, "Do not distinguish between Chinese and Moslem; distinguish only between good and evil"—adherents of the New Teaching were of course evil. It was therefore urgent to redress cases of improper tax collection, to hear all grievances fairly, and to mete out swift punishment to unruly troops who caused disturbances among the population, for, in Tso's words, "A basic plan cannot rely on military strategy alone."[80]

The military aspect, however, had priority, and Tso faced a formidable task. His supply lines were long and passed through poor, thinly populated, hostile areas. There were few local resources to be mobilized. His opponents were not only skilled guerrilla leaders; they were religious leaders with fanatical followings, in a position to exploit age-old ethnic, cultural, and regional animosities. From 1864 to 1871 they constantly attacked the historic single line of communication to Sinkiang. The severest fighting took place along this narrow line, which passed through deserts and mountains between Mongolia and Tibet.[81]

Tso expected to be able to pacify Shensi and Kansu within five years and he succeeded.[82] Reaching Sian in November 1868, he concentrated all his forces in a three-pronged offensive drive. On the northern route, Liu Sung-shan started from northern Shensi across the Yellow River toward Suiteh in Shensi, with Ma Hua-lung's stronghold Chin-chi-p'u as his eventual goal. On the southern route, Chou K'ai-hsi moved via Tsinchow in the direction of Hochow. On the central route, Tso himself and Liu Tien proceeded from Shensi toward Kansu along the main highway.

The northern route proved to be decisive. Liu Sung-shan's first task was to clean out the "local" Moslem bandits under the leadership of Tung Fu-hsiang, later of Boxer fame, who had been disturbing the Shensi-Kansu-Suiyuan border area. When he reached Suiteh, he found that Tung's strongholds were scattered through an area lying midway between Yenan and Yülin. Liu attacked and routed the bandits in this area and pursued the fleeing remnant to their original base of Chen-ching-p'u, south of the Ordos. Tung Fu-hsiang's father and later Tung himself petitioned to surrender and were from that time loyal Ch'ing commanders. Tung's band had been independent, with little standing. After victory, as a reward for his support of the Ch'ing, he was given much of the property of the intransigent Moslem families of the area. This was the foundation of the great Tung family holdings in later decades.[83] The remaining Shensi Moslems moved west into Kansu, and by the autumn of 1869 Shensi seemed pacified. Tso then proceeded to direct his full attention to Kansu and Ningsia.

Early in 1870 Liu Sung-shan launched the first attack on a major Moslem base, Chin-chi-p'u in Ningsia—"the cradle of the New Teaching," "the fortress of the revolution," "the Medina of Chinese Islam," and Ma Hua-lung's stronghold. The Ch'ing victory and ruthless extermination of survivors was the turning point of the campaign. Ma was a tough adversary, and his followers, poorer and more ignorant than the other Moslem rebels, considered their leader an incarnation of the spirit, equal or superior to Mohammed, and informed on every subject by divine revelation.[84]

It was a savage campaign. Liu's first attack failed with heavy losses, among them Liu himself. Ma Hua-lung's position improved, and he was able to send forces into Shensi to raid Tso's lines of communication. When Pai Yen-hu came to Ma's support, the Peking authorities, seriously alarmed, countered by ordering Li Hung-chang to the front. Tso, however, managed to retrieve his own position. He appointed Liu Chin-t'ang, the nephew of Liu Sung-shan, to the Chin-chi-p'u front command. Liu, ruthless and bent on revenge, promptly cut the Yellow River dikes and closed a tight ring around the town. Early in 1871 Chin-chi-p'u fell; whether Ma Hua-lung surrendered it to save what was left of the starving population is not clear. In any case, there was no question of amnesty.

Ma's whole family was executed by "lingering death," his house was razed, and henceforth no Moslem was allowed to live in Chin-chi-p'u. Ma's remote relatives were transported to virtually certain death in Heilungkiang, after the government had first ascertained that there was no trace of the feared and hated New Teaching in that province.[85]

The recapture of Chin-chi-p'u was the first great victory of the northwestern campaign. Tso reported vividly and triumphantly the complete destruction of the town and the execution of the bandit leaders. High honors and praise were heaped on Tso, and awards were made to all who had shown merit in the campaign.[86]

After the capture of Chin-chi-p'u, the Imperial troops clearly held the ascendancy in the northwest, and Peking was impatient for final victory. Tso reported advance scouting operations in the direction of T'ung-kuei-p'u in Kansu, and he was now trying to win the remaining less fearsome opposition to his side. Edict after edict warned him not to waste time with invitations to surrender, not to think only of ruling by soothing, but to seize the opportunity now offered for total military victory.[87]

In view of the terrain, Tso can scarcely be accused of dawdling. An edict of April 22, 1871, reported the capture of T'ung-kuei-p'u. Here Ch'ing policy was much milder. Although a number of rebel leaders were given refuge in near-by fortified Moslem settlements, there was no general sack and massacre, but rather a proclamation urging the "good Moslems" to turn in the "unchangeable" rebels they were sheltering.[88]

New victories followed,[89] and Hochow was the next major target. There had been talk of a negotiated surrender at Hochow for several years;[90] Ma Chan-ao, the Moslem commander there, had successfully held out against the Ch'ing commander Chou K'ai-hsi, but he was no longer confident of final Moslem victory. On the Imperial side, Tso Tsung-t'ang wanted to avoid another siege like Chin-chi-p'u; he offered an amnesty and Ma surrendered. There were some punishments, but Hochow was spared Chin-chi-p'u's executions, banishments, and wholesale transfers of population. A number of leading Hochow Moslems were given government titles and offices; Ma Chan-ao's family later became the most powerful in Kansu Moslem society.[91] At Sining, Ma Kuei-yüan had lost ground even before Liu Chin-t'ang's forces arrived in December 1872. Some of the Sining Moslems were executed, some surrendered.[92] Ma Kuei-yüan and his remaining supporters fled to Payenyungko, whose capture was subsequently announced on April 7, 1873.[93]

The final phase of the campaign for the pacification of the northwestern provinces of China proper began with the drive to recover Suchow, which had been held by Ma Wen-lu since 1865. Ch'eng-lu's forces had supposedly been advancing on Suchow for many years, and virtually every edict on the Moslem Rebellion included a rider ordering Ch'eng-lu to take the city. Ch'eng-lu was finally recalled and sentenced to death, and in the summer of 1872 Tso launched a new campaign for the capture of Suchow. In the autumn of 1873 he took personal command at the walls, and the city fell in November. The burning, executions, and general slaughter exceeded even those at Chin-chi-p'u.[94] A few Suchow Moslems, including Pai Yen-hu, escaped to Sinkiang and thence to Russian territory, where their descendants still live.[95]

In this most dramatic of Restoration campaigns, offers of Russian aid were declined. Apart from certain private loans negotiated by Tso Tsung-t'ang,[o] no Western aid was necessary.

The recapture of Suchow completed the pacification not only of the northwest but of all China proper. The Taiping, Nien-fei, southwestern Moslem, and various local rebellions[p] had all been suppressed earlier, and the Middle Kingdom was at peace.

THE PACIFICATION OF YUNNAN[96]

From the Ch'ing point of view, the revolt of the southwestern Moslems in the so-called Panthay Rebellion seemed far away. Tseng Kuo-fan declared that, although Yunnan was the most remote province in the empire and Kweichow the poorest, the Emperor would defend every subject and every foot of soil; but the plan he recommended showed little knowledge either of Yunnan and Kweichow or of the Moslems.[97]

Rebellion had been seething in Yunnan well before the rise of Tu Wen-hsiu in the 1850's. Officials were spread thin, and the villages seemed as remote from the hsien government as the hsien from the provincial government or the provincial government from Peking. Bandits always flourished, especially near the borders, and stood in no fear of officialdom. The land tax and army requirements were unusually high, and the levies bore even more heavily on the Moslem population of the province than on the Chinese. Justice could not be properly administered owing to the great distances involved, the corruption of the clerks, and the notorious incompetence of the provincial bureaucracy. The Moslems complained particularly that local officials were biased in adjudicating Moslem-Chinese disputes.[98]

Most of the disturbances in Yunnan originated in local riots at various mines. By the mid-nineteenth century, as the population of the province multiplied, the veins worked by Chinese were exhausted and they turned to the more remote

---

[o] See Chapter VIII.

[p] For the last two, see following sections. Tso Tsung-t'ang's campaign in Sinkiang, not completed until 1877, is outside the period of the present study.

but richer veins to which they had driven the Moslems in earlier years. There were riots at a silver mine in 1845, and the great uprising began in the winter of 1855–56 at a gold mine. Accounts of the precise circumstances vary, but, in any case, matters got out of hand before the magistrate took action, and in February 1856 Moslem villages were burned with considerable loss of life. When the local Chinese appealed to Kunming (Yunnanfu) for aid, the Moslems retaliated, and most of their leaders escaped arrest. This led many Chinese to believe that a general Moslem uprising was imminent, and to forestall this subordinate officials ordered a preventive massacre of Moslems for May 19, 1856. The governor-general, apparently powerless to block his subordinate's order, committed suicide, and his successor had no better luck. The Chinese population, supported by the officials, ran amok, and the Moslem and other non-Chinese elements rose in general rebellion.[99]

Moslem power developed rapidly. Ma Ju-lung's forces attacked the capital, Kunming, in 1857 and cut off its food supply. In the following year Tu Wen-hsiu captured Tali in the west and made it his capital, which it remained for fifteen years.

Ch'ing officials in Yunnan in the late 1850's were totally inept; instead of suppressing rebellion, they enlarged it. In the general demoralization following the Moslem uprising of 1856, even the magistrates of districts loyal to the government abandoned their responsibilities and fled to the capital. The Kunming officials were at best weak, irresponsible, and suspicious of each other; the record shows an astonishing list of assassinations, suicides, and abrupt removals from office. Among the governors-general and governors of the period, one was murdered, one was a' suicide, one lost his mind, one refused to enter the province to take up his duties, and several had to be recalled for gross incompetence. Huang Ts'ung, ordered by Peking to organize new regional military forces along the pattern established by Tseng Kuo-fan, failed completely and committed suicide.[100]

At this time the "Grand Priest" Ma Te-hsin (also known as Ma To-sin, Ma Te-hsing, or Ma Fu-ch'u)[101] was in command of the whole rebellion, with two subordinates who at the outset accepted his authority: Ma Ju-lung (also known as Ma Hsien)[102] in eastern and southern Yunnan, and Tu Wen-hsiu in the west.[103] There were certain similarities between the Yunnan leaders and the northwestern Moslem leaders: Tu Wen-hsiu fought to the end like Ma Hua-lung at Chin-chi-p'u; Ma Ju-lung, like Tung Fu-hsiang, was won over and became active on the Ch'ing side. Ma Te-hsin, an outstanding religious leader who managed to maintain a kind of neutrality, had no counterpart in the northwest. The son of a merchant in the Tali area, Ma had had first a Chinese and then an Islamic education. He had made the pilgrimage to Mecca, traveled in

Egypt, and spent two years in Constantinople before returning to Yunnan in 1846. Ma Ju-lung, a Moslem of good family, had studied Arabic with Ma Te-hsin (they may have been relatives) and had passed the examinations for the degree of military licentiate. When the great rebellion broke out, he was working as a mine supervisor, and his brother was killed in the first massacre. By all accounts he was an extremely able soldier. Tu Wen-hsiu, inspired by the Taiping Rebellion, had greater dreams; he made Tali the capital of his kingdom, P'ing-nan kuo, used elaborate state seals, and erected a Forbidden City where Ming dynasty dress was worn.[104]

In spite of their early association as leaders of the Moslem population, there may have been important differences in doctrine between Ma Te-hsin and Ma Ju-lung on the one hand and Tu Wen-hsiu on the other. The learned and devout Ma Te-hsin felt that the beliefs of Islam must be kept pure and not submerged in the general Chinese outlook on life, but saw nothing in these beliefs that conflicted with the Confucian teaching. The Chinese provincial commander-in-chief, who was also the director of education in Yunnan, with the rank of recorder of the Hanlin Academy, wrote in 1859 (HF-8) that Ma Te-hsin was a superior man; that the way of life he advocated in his *Ssu-tien yao-hui* was precisely the way of the five Confucian relationships and the orthodox virtues. The governor of Yunnan wrote similarly. Ma's Moslem disciples wrote that he not only taught Moslems what their faith really meant, but also demonstrated to Confucians the true character of Islam, pointing out where its teachings resembled those of the *Book of Changes,* Confucius, Mencius, the great Neo-Confucians, and the famed Chinese poets, and how much they differed from the teachings of Mo Ti and Yang Chu and other unsettling doctrines.[105] Ma Ju-lung was a close follower of Ma Te-hsin and a perfect example of what Restoration leaders thought of as a "good Moslem," to be won over by benevolence, conciliation, and fair treatment.

Tu Wen-hsiu was different. Before 1860 he accepted Ma Te-hsin's authority, and until his death still accorded him the respect due to his religious rank. Yet he would not follow him. D'Ollone suspected that Tu may have been converted to the New Teaching; from the strange answers he received from the Moslems he interviewed at Tali he was convinced that the New Teaching had flourished there but that the living memory of holocaust prevented anyone from admitting it.[106]

In 1860, the year of crisis in Yunnan as in China at large, the Ch'ing cause appeared hopeless. Moslem forces could move at will through two-thirds of the province, and the capital was under siege. But at the eleventh hour Governor Chang Liang-chi succeeded in negotiating an agreement with Ma Ju-lung; when Ma occupied Kunming in 1861, he occupied it as a Ch'ing general, and the entry of the Moslem troops was orderly.[107]

Although the pacification of all Yunnan required another twelve years, Ma Ju-lung's shift in allegiance turned the tide. Since he does not appear to have been bought off, his motives have been the subject of much speculation. Perhaps he realized even at the height of his power that in the end the Moslms could not defeat the Ch'ing and that protracted fighting would wreck the province. Insight of this sort apart, to a former military licentiate, the offer of rank and authority within the Ch'ing system must have been tempting; and the system itself, committed to distinguishing between good and evil rather than between Chinese and Moslems, had its attractions. Finally Ma Ju-lung may have split with Tu Wen-hsiu over the New Teaching.

Whatever his motives were, Ma Ju-lung became and remained an effective leader of the Ch'ing forces. Ma Te-hsin, although he refused to accept a Ch'ing title, generally associated himself with Ma Ju-lung.[108]

Despite Ma Ju-lung's surrender, the Ch'ing campaign at first made little headway. There were new uprisings in 1862, and the governor-general, P'an To, was assassinated in 1863.[109] Officials capable of winning over other Moslems were lacking, and there was violent enmity between the famed anti-Moslem Ch'ing commander Ts'en Yü-ying and Ma Ju-lung and his men.[110] Ma Ju-lung remained loyal, but the situation deteriorated steadily. An outstanding Restoration official, Lao Ch'ung-kuang, was finally appointed to succeed P'an To, and Ma Te-hsin agreed to go to Tu Wen-hsiu to urge his surrender on the ground that he would fare better as an Imperial official than as the sultan of an independent but war-torn area. Tu received Ma, but was not persuaded.[111] He advanced on Kunming, and Lao Ch'ung-kuang died of illness with the capital again under siege.

Peking now fully recognized the seriousness of the situation, and the appointment of a governor-general was taken up by the Grand Council, the Grand Secretariat, the Six Boards, and the Nine Ministries. Unable to spare the governor-general of Szechwan, Lo Ping-chang, the authorities appointed Liu Yüeh-chao, a young native of Siangsiang trained by Tseng Kuo-fan.[112]

The situation continued critical throughout the summer and autumn of 1868. The battle seesawed, but Tu Wen-hsiu's besieging troops were weakened by disease and shortage of food, and Ma Ju-lung, as a Moslem himself, was able to exploit differences among them and to break their morale. The siege was finally lifted in the autumn of 1869, and Tu's Moslems were thenceforth in retreat until their final defeat in 1873.[113]

The next four years were marked by a merciless campaign on the part of Ts'en Yü-ying, backed by Ma Ju-lung's diplomacy, with Liu Yüeh-chao attempting to curb Ts'en where necessary and to give substance to Ma's promises to the Moslems.[114] One by one the Ch'ing forces captured Tu's fifty-three walled cities that stretched across Yunnan from Szechwan to the Kweichow border; finally they reached Tali. When the city was captured in January 1873, Tu committed suicide, and after three days of murder, pillage, and arson, the entire population of fifty thousand was dead or missing.[115] A single band of rebels is said to have escaped to the mountains of the Sino-Burmese border, where its descendants live today.[116]

The Ch'ing success in Yunnan, like the earlier Ch'ing successes, was primarily a political triumph. To be sure, as rebellion was suppressed elsewhere, more troops were available for Yunnan, and Ma Ju-lung and Ts'en Yü-ying were both splendid fighters in their different ways. More basic, however, was the fact that men like Lao Ch'ung-kuang and Liu Yüeh-chao could win and hold the allegiance of leading Moslems by offers of peace, justice, and reconstruction. In this respect Tu Wen-hsiu's shortcomings greatly aided the Restoration effort. Although Tu had begun by emphasizing the union of Moslems and Chinese against the Ch'ing, he never quite trusted any Chinese and was afraid to give authority to his own most devoted Chinese general. As time went on, he became more sect-minded and attempted to enforce Islamic customs in food, clothing, and worship. This cost him most of his Chinese following and much of his Moslem following. As dissension in his areas mounted, the gentry, including most of the Moslem gentry, rallied to the Ch'ing, seeing in the Ch'ing program for rectifying local abuses and assuring all subjects equal status a viable alternative to rebellion.[117]

No adequate information is available on the role of foreign aid in the Yunnan campaign. It has been alleged that the French sold munitions to Ts'en Yü-ying and helped him manufacture arms and train troops at Kunming,[q] and that the arms so produced were superior to the European-manufactured arms that Tu Wen-hsiu bought from the British in Burma. But there is also evidence that in the main Tu's overtures were rejected by the British, who decided that in Yunnan as elsewhere British interests coincided with Ch'ing interests.[118] All that can be safely said is that although France and England supported the Ch'ing side, either exclusively or in the main, the outcome was decided not by this aid but by a complex of internal forces, in which the Yunnan Moslem response to the Restoration offer of peace with justice was the crucial factor. If outside material aid saved Yunnan, it was the aid of Szechwan province.

[q] A certain Jean Dupuis, who was later instrumental in the French capture of Hanoi in 1873, appeared in Kunming in 1868, became a close friend of the governor-general and others, and in 1870 was commissioned to suppress the rebels on the Annamese border. The main significance of this episode appears to have been Dupuis' use of his status as delegate of the "Emperor of China" (who was suzerain of Annam) to extend French power at China's expense. (V. Hoskiaer, *Les Routes commerciales du Yunnan*, Paris, 1883, reprinted from *Geographisk Tidsskrift* of the Royal Danish Geographical Society, pp. 6–7.)

THE PACIFICATION OF LOCAL REVOLT

In addition to the four major rebellions, the Restoration government had to contend with local revolt in virtually every province. Even "reliable" Szechwan was not wholly exempt. Except in Kweichow, however, where a long series of unco-ordinated or loosely co-ordinated outbreaks amounted in sum to a major rebellion, these local disturbances were dangerous primarily because (1) they rendered more difficult the general civilian reconstruction program; and (2) these "local rowdies" were regularly recruited by the major rebellions.

Kweichow[119] had been in ferment from the late Tao-kuang period. To the general grievances lying behind all unrest at the time were added the specific grievances of the non-Chinese Miao tribes and the influence of the near-by Taiping and Yunnan Moslem forces. Sporadic outbreaks occurred between 1854 and 1858, and between 1858 and 1867 revolt was widespread. Altogether there were fifty-four uprisings, during the course of which six-sevenths of the towns of Kweichow were captured and recaptured, some of them many times. Some of the revolts were Miao, some Chinese, and some Moslem.[120]

In the early 1850's, when the young Hu Lin-i[r] was a prefect in Kweichow, he listed three causes of the disorders: improper civil administration, inadequate military force, and discrimination against the Miao. Some thought Hu might have saved Kweichow, but he was later made governor of Hupeh, leaving Kweichow during the crucial years to a governor inadequately trained in the "principles of proper government," who allowed the abuses to continue.[121]

As long as the great rebellions raged, Peking ignored local revolt in Kweichow; not until 1867 could some attention be given to the province. Governor Tseng Pi-kuang reported that the Kweichow rebels were so poorly organized that if he were given funds to organize local forces and able commanders to lead them, the province could be easily pacified.[122] Funds and commanders were sent; on the surface, the Chinese uprisings were brought to an end in 1868, and the Miao and Moslem ones in 1872–73.[123]

The perennial antics of the salt bandits and the government troops pursuing them across the north China plain supply comic relief in the grim story of the major rebellions. Sometimes there were reported to be a "few hundred"; hundreds and then tens were reported killed by vastly superior government forces, and again there would be "a thousand." Victories were reported, but the bandits always reappeared.[124] As immediate causes of this absurd situation, officials referred to rivalry among commanders, inadequately trained troops, and lack of cavalry to take the offensive against the mobile bandits.[125] A more fundamental cause, according to an edict of January 1, 1868, was that the bandits

---

[r] See Chapter V.

apparently had little trouble recruiting constant replacements from among the common people; if this was true, there was no possibility of suppressing them by force alone.[126]

Restoration officials were extremely concerned about the problem of the salt bandits, partly because they were depriving the government of a much-needed source of revenue,[s] partly because it was feared that they might join the Nien-fei.[t] In the view of Ch'ung-hou, one of the officials most directly involved, proper countermeasures depended upon enlisting the aid of the local gentry.[127]

Disturbances reported from Manchuria throughout the Restoration were clearly trivial in character. Edicts frequently referred to horse thieves, wood thieves, and unorthodox religious sects.[128] The number of mounted bandits gradually increased until in 1866 there were said to be some thirty thousand, organized in twenty bands; but Wen-hsiang's campaign to suppress them was quickly successful.[129] The situation was so well under control that the military governor at Mukden, Tu-hsing-a, could be ordered to proceed to Chihli with his best cavalry at the height of the alleged disturbances.[130]

Similar local disorders were reported from central China in the wake of the Taiping Rebellion. Occasionally villages were burned, and some secret societies were involved, but most of the incidents described smacked more of rowdyism than of insurrection.[131]

Local bandits in remote Kwangsi appeared even less important to Peking. Efforts were made to suppress them, and the army Feng Tzu-ts'ai built up for this purpose was later of importance in the Franco-Chinese War. Generally speaking, however, Restoration officials paid less attention to the Annamese frontier than to China's northern frontiers. Fleeing Chinese bandits, including the Taiping remnants later led by Liu Yung-fu, found easy refuge in Annam.[132]

Disturbances in Kwangtung, arising largely from conflicts between Hakkas[u] and "natives" of the province, were viewed more seriously because of the major role played by Hakkas in leading the Taiping Rebellion.[133] The chief local fighting took place between 1856 and 1867, and since Ch'ing officials recognized that the "natives" were often at fault, conciliation played an important part in pacifi-

---

[s] See Chapter VIII.

[t] The Nien-fei leader Chang Lo-hsing was believed to have come from a wealthy family of salt smugglers (*Chiao-p'ing Nien-fei fang-lüeh*, Ch. 3, p. 4b).

[u] The Hakkas (*k'o-chia*, guests) had been settled in a portion of Shansi-Honan-Anhwei before the Eastern Chin. Subsequently they had migrated five times, ultimately settling deep in Kwangtung and Kwangsi and on Hainan and Taiwan. A number of special characteristics continued to distinguish them from the Chinese among whom they were settled: the maintenance of large joint families representing all occupations, with large family landholdings undivided; great adventurousness, courage, even bravado; limited class distinctions; a major social and economic role for women; and a tendency to take extreme and unadaptable positions on all issues. (Lo Hsiang-lin, *K'o-chia yen-chiu tao-lun*, Hingning, Kwangtung, 1933, pp. 63–64 and Ch. 7, *passim*.)

cation. Governor Chiang I-li declared an amnesty in 1866, provided for reconstruction, and displayed considerable vision and generosity.[134] The subsequent activities of the Hakkas in the Kuomintang notwithstanding, the Restoration program appears in this case to have been successful for a time, and the officials concerned were duly rewarded.[135]

FIRST STEPS TOWARD RECONSTRUCTION

Restoration leaders were primarily concerned not with whether this or that rebellion could seize power (after the Taiping Rebellion passed its peak in 1861, it was clear that none could), but with how the areas where Ch'ing military control had been reasserted could be truly pacified. In the words of Tso Tsung-t'ang, the aim was to plan for several centuries of peace and happiness, not merely to seize the momentary benefits of victory.[136]

The first problem was what to do with the rebels who survived. In traditional theory rank-and-file rebels were not criminals; they were the common people who in times of maladministration and consequent suffering could be "seduced" by wicked leaders.[137] The liquidation of rebellion, therefore, required ruthless extermination of the ringleaders, but amnesty for the rank and file.[v]

The difficulty lay in ascertaining who were the good people (including some of the leaders) who were capable of reform, and who were the irreconcilables who would surrender for the purpose of infiltration only. The penalty was severe against a commander who indulged in needless executions of the weary and repentant. Yet any commander who misjudged the enemy's intentions and accepted the surrender alive of unreconstructed rebels was in even greater danger of Peking's wrath, since under the system he was held responsible for the future behavior of those he pardoned.[138]

For the Taiping leaders, there could be no question of clemency; they were considered to have offended against the laws of nature and man.[w] But in general, amnesty for the mass of the rebel following and for civilian collaborators with the enemy was readily granted. The literati who had served the rebels were usually pardoned on the ground that they had had no alternative to collaboration during

---

[v] On this point Bruce reported: "I gather from His Excellency Wen-siang's remarks, that the Governor [Li Hung-chang] entertains very different feelings toward the bulk of the insurgents and toward the men of Kwan-tung and Kwang-si, the originators of the insurrection. The latter are looked upon as dangerous characters, whose submission is merely nominal, and who will be ready, on any favourable opportunity, to recommence their malpractices. . . . The former, who consist chiefly of natives of the Central Provinces, are looked upon as forced into the rebellion, and readily obtain pardon and relief on submission, as in the instances quoted in his despatch. I apprehend that public opinion in China approves of this distinction." (Bruce to Russell, Feb. 12, 1864, *China. No. 7. (1864)*, p. 3.)

[w] On the execution of the Taiping leaders who surrendered at Soochow, see Chapter IX. Tseng Kuo-fan asked how one could possibly be tolerant toward men who had caused such disaster and who should have been executed years earlier (*Tseng Wen-cheng kung hsüeh-an*, Shanghai, 1925, pp. 379–80).

a prolonged rebel occupation. An effort was made to distinguish between voluntary and involuntary collaboration;[139] among the "involuntary collaborators" forgiven were the cavalry forces that had been cut off and compelled to join the Nien-fei at the time of Seng-ko-lin-ch'in's death.[140]

Moreover, in the early years pardon was offered quite freely to local leaders of rebel bands. Some of the leaders who surrendered to the first anti-Nien commander, Sheng-pao, remained loyal, but a number changed sides many times, notably the perennial turncoat Miao P'ei-lin. As Ch'ing policy stiffened, Miao was executed, and Sheng-pao was punished for his poor judgment.[141] Pursuit of the Nien leaders was uncompromising in the later phases of the campaign, but a general, if cautious, amnesty was offered to the Nien rank and file in August 1868.[142]

Somewhat different factors were involved in the Moslem rebellions. Chinese officials convicted of collaboration with the rebels were executed,[143] but the Ch'ing could afford no such attitude toward the Moslem leaders themselves. In the central provinces, if the Ch'ing could rally the gentry, it could undermine the power of the rebel leaders. In the Moslem areas, the very local leaders on whom the reassertion of Ch'ing power must depend were likely themselves to be rebel leaders. A bold policy to win over the Moslem leaders and gentry was therefore essential. Furthermore, since most of them were fighting local abuses rather than the Ch'ing state and society, conflicting interests could usually be reconciled. Tung Fu-hsiang and Ma Chan-ao in the northwest and Ma Ju-lung and Ma Te-hsin in the southwest were instrumental in the Ch'ing reconquest of those areas; numerous lesser leaders followed them in surrender, and, after proving their loyalty, were given property and rank.

The policy of pardon was not without risk, and Peking constantly ordered more careful investigation of the true intentions of the Moslems who asked to surrender.[144] Yet except at such die-hard strongholds as Chin-chi-p'u and Tali, the policy of pardon proved an effective and essential corollary to military action against Moslem rebels.

In local disturbances, surrender was readily accepted. Only in Kweichow were there serious problems in ascertaining the "sincerity" of the repentant bandits, especially the Miao.[145]

Execution of ringleaders and pardon for the mass by no means liquidated a great rebellion, however. Before an area could be truly stabilized, vast displaced populations had to be resettled and the framework of orderly political, economic, and social life restored. These tasks, difficult of achievement in any circumstances, were enormously complicated by the staggering degree of destruction that had occurred.

On the scene confronting the Restoration government in the areas recovered from the Taiping, there is vivid testimony from foreign eyewitnesses. The rebellion

> had even altered the face of the country; destroyed its communications; deflected its rivers; broken down its sea defences. During its continuance smiling fields were turned into desolate wildernesses; 'fenced cities into ruinous heaps.' The plains of Kiang-nan, Kiang-si and Cheh-kiang, were strewn with human skeletons; their rivers polluted with floating carcasses; wild beasts descending from their fastnesses in the mountains roamed at large over the land, and made their dens in the ruins of deserted towns; the cry of the pheasant usurped the place of the hum of busy populations; no hands were left to till the soil, and noxious weeds covered the ground once tilled with patient industry.[146]

> The scenes of misery and ruin which have been disclosed as they have been driven back from Shanghai, surpass any accounts before published of the horrors of war; and the wretched inhabitants of the districts which Gordon has lately recovered have been driven to cannibalism to satisfy the cravings of hunger.[147]

Nanking was wrecked:

> the Tartar city appeared more like a dense jungle than a city. Houses and walls had been razed. The ground afforded an excellent cover for game and would probably attract sportsmen in that view; but no one looking at it at the present moment would have thought it was a city.[148]

In some areas, two-thirds of the population was lost, and the devastation dwarfed the damage done during the Japanese invasion and the civil war following World War II.[149]

The destruction was not limited to the Yangtze valley. Parts of the north China plain and much of Kweichow, Yunnan, and the northwest lay in ruins when the Nien-fei, Miao, and Moslem rebellions were finally suppressed, their prostrate populations stunned into passivity for two generations. It has been estimated that nine-tenths of Shensi's Moslem population and two-thirds of Kansu's disappeared; the remainder was uprooted and resettled. The death toll may have exceeded three million. Forty years later travelers shuddered at the sight of great empty walled cities.[150] In Yunnan, an estimated three hundred thousand Moslems were killed outright.[151] The total population of the province appears to have declined by between four and five million, or more than half.[152] There was a nearly total destruction of property in all but three hsien of the province.[153] Nearly five million people died in Kweichow, and property damage there was astronomical. Casualties among civilian officials were particularly heavy.[154] The Miao lost their lands and either became tenants or retreated into the mountains; sixty years later they still turned pale at the mention of the past.[155] Even in the local Hakka uprisings the death toll has been estimated at five hundred thousand to six hundred thousand lives.[156]

In the face of destruction of this magnitude, it was essential that troops be disbanded as rapidly as feasible, that survivors be resettled on abandoned land, that land titles be clarified, that morale be restored, and that emergency relief be provided. That anything could be salvaged was a near miracle, yet a great deal was accomplished, and quickly.

The chief agrarian program of the Restoration was carried out in the areas recovered from the Taiping.[x] In the Nien areas, Tseng Kuo-fan worked from the outset for the rapid restoration of normal economic life;[157] as early as the autumn of 1868 taxes had been remitted and reconstruction had begun. Ch'ung-hou's relief work in eastern Chihli was particularly notable.[158] A foreign observer reported:

> About two weeks back, Chung-how returned from an inspection of the districts lately occupied by the rebels. He reinstated the different officers in their posts and arranged disputed matters regarding the possession of certain properties, restoring everywhere the imperial authority, and releasing the owners of the land from paying taxes.[159]

Ting Pao-chen carried out a similar program in Shantung.[160]

In the northwest Tso Tsung-t'ang's first problem was to resettle the truly destitute. After the sack of Chin-chi-p'u early in 1871 Tso moved at once to succor the displaced persons, the women left without family, the old and the sick. Typically, he had the Sacred Edict reprinted and read aloud throughout both Chinese and Moslem communities of the area. He reserved a portion of the silver his forces seized for the purchase of food, seed, land, and draft animals for surrendering Moslems, and he memorialized on the need for further provisions of this type.[161]

These measures were not directed solely toward civilian rehabilitation; they were in part military measures designed to secure Tso's rear. The methods used were often harsh and occasionally ruthless; lenient measures, it was felt, would only encourage unregenerate rebels to surrender, infilter the resettled areas, and organize new uprisings.[162]

Tso's policy even at its mildest had no place for Moslem cultural autonomy; he was dedicated to the idea of Sinicization. He dissipated the authority of the Moslem chiefs and let their powers accrue to the local officials, and he hammered at the Confucian ethic. But although the rule was stern, it was not the rule of the sword. From a Confucian point of view, Moslem religious leaders misled the common people. Once the fighting ceased, the remedy lay—as it lay elsewhere in China—in the selection of good local officials, the proper administration of justice, attention to the people's welfare, and, above all, guidance in the principles of social usage.[163]

[x] See Chapter VIII.

Efforts at the rehabilitation of Yunnan began in 1872, before the capture of Tali. Despite the usual difficulty over property titles resulting from the loss of records, the recovery was remarkable. Deserted towns were repopulated and commerce, mining, and agriculture were quickly resumed.[164] Yunnan prospered enough in subsequent decades to attract immigrants from other parts of China. It was no model province, but the authority of Peking was again recognized and the basis for separatism destroyed.

In Kweichow the issue was less happy. There was no great fault in the Ch'ing diagnosis of the causes of the rebellion or in the plans for reconstruction. The underlying cause was felt to be the fact that "the Kweichow Miao peoples do not understand the Confucian ethic."[165] "If we wish to put an end to the Miao evil, we must first transform the Miao into Chinese."[166] Hence the rehabilitation programs all emphasized closer contact between officials and Miao, an increase in the number of political subdivisions, more schools, public granaries, relief, tax reform, strengthening of the pao-chia system of collective responsibility, and reduction in the number of troops, especially those from outside the province.[167] But in practice Miao lands were confiscated to provide for the resettlement of Chinese, even though not the Miao themselves but their un-Sinicized state was held responsible for their defection. Even in the Chinese settlements confusion and unease persisted.[168] The Restoration prescriptions for the liquidation of rebellion assumed that programs would be administered by officials of outstanding ability and insight who could appeal to deep-rooted Confucian social patterns or, in the minority areas, create them. In Kweichow, unfortunately, there was no counterpart of Tso Tsung-t'ang.

The problem of reconstruction in other areas of local revolt was relatively simple. A movement was launched to break down the separate Hakka settlements and to provide more adequately for the Hakkas in the general Restoration program in Kwangtung.[169] In Manchuria destruction had been minor—a field trampled, some carts requisitioned. Reconstruction was simply a matter of providing tax exemption proportionate to the damage.[170]

In every area, from the utterly devastated to the mildly disturbed, the immediate measures taken were intended to restore confidence and to get people back to work. They were the prelude to plans for long-term reconstruction in all spheres of public and private life, as the following chapters will show.

CHAPTER VII

THE RE-ESTABLISHMENT OF LOCAL CONTROL[1]

SOURCES OF THE TRADITIONAL EQUILIBRIUM

The Restoration's success or failure depended on how far the traditional society could be reintegrated on the local level without detriment to the government's new plans for limited modernization in the fields of war and diplomacy. Owing to the peculiar character of local control in traditional China, the attempted compromise faced fundamental difficulties that in the end proved insurmountable.

Organized institutions of local control certainly existed, but their effectiveness depended to an unusual extent on persuasion. The civilian bureaucracy was not sufficiently staffed to maintain order without the acquiescence of the population,[a] and troops were stationed only at a relatively small number of widely separated strategic points. Moreover, the very idea of direct control ran counter to orthodox political theory.[b] A magistrate traditionally maintained control by taking advantage of local social forces, specifically by using the local gentry as a bridge between himself and the vast mass of the population within his jurisdiction. This reliance on the gentry was universally held to be not only inevitable but right and proper. A magistrate so circumstanced was in no position either to play off gentry and people against each other or to champion the cause of the people against the gentry.

The system of local control through the gentry reached its full maturity during the first two centuries of Ch'ing rule. In the mid-nineteenth century virtually every observer was struck by the stability of the local communities, which apparently governed themselves without in any way undermining the central authority. Alcock, the British minister to China during the Restoration, noted

---

[a] According to S. Wells Williams, in all the eighteen provinces, with a population numbered in the hundreds of millions, there were fewer than two thousand officials above the rank of assistant district magistrate (*The Middle Kingdom*, I, 438). According to Chung-li Chang: "The total number of civil and military officials at the capital and in the provinces has been given as approximately 27,000. Of this number, approximately 20,000 were civil officials, and 7,000 were military officers. Among the civil officials, approximately 2,000 were key regional and local officials, and 1,500 were key educational officials." (*The Chinese Gentry*, p. 116.) Administrative responsibility thus rested with approximately two thousand regional and local officials.

[b] "The authoritarianism of the central government was in cases and at times truly autocratic, yet that regime was in theory based on moral authority rather than force; the teachings of the Confucians made the point again and again; the fact that an ideal other than absolutism existed influenced the facts, just as the ideal of social equality between all men influences the facts in the United States." (Robert Redfield, Introduction to Hsiao-t'ung Fei, *China's Gentry*, pp. 11–12.)

that the "Confucian Empire," alone among the empires of history, was not based on military power, religion, or superstition.[2] Another British official reported after an extensive inland journey that although the Empire might be weak, "the wonderful organization and arrangement visible everywhere was especially remarkable."[3] This "wonderful organization and arrangement" was based on the universal acceptance of the Confucian ideology. Everyone (including the Emperor) and every group (including the central government) strove to play its proper Confucian role. In the words of Hu Lin-i: "The issue of order or chaos in the Empire does not go beyond the two words 'gain' [*li*] and 'morality' [*i*]. When men's hearts long for gain, there is chaos; when men's hearts long for morality, there is order."[4] Military action, although sometimes necessary, was a superficial remedy; the fundamental remedy was the local application of the principles of civil government.

This venerable, harmonizing, moderating yet authoritarian, society-centered ideology was nearly perfectly suited to the maintenance of ultimate central control in a vast and physically decentralized empire. When the system was working, the gentry accepted their role with its attendant privileges and responsibilities. They "did not try to control political power in their own interest but endeavored rather to put forward a set of ethical principles which should restrict the force of political power." The peasant too was indoctrinated and recognized his place in the total scheme.[5]

The state secured the acquiescence of the local population not only by intensive indoctrination, but by guaranteeing the legal and economic privileges of the gentry on the one hand and supporting social welfare measures designed to relieve the peasantry on the other. To both classes the state claimed to offer a peaceful and orderly society with a place for all, prosperous and just according to accepted standards. Control through persuasion was supplemented by control through a network of collective responsibility and through a highly developed legal system. In all types of control the quality of the local official was of prime importance. He must not only be a competent administrator in all fields; he must in his own person embody the Confucian teaching that was the ultimate sanction of authority.

In the mid-nineteenth century domestic rebellion and foreign encroachment had undermined the quality of the Confucian civil service, threatened the established interests of the gentry, and given rise to widespread popular doubts, first about the state's good faith, later about the validity of the traditional ideal itself. Yet the inertia of the traditional system was so great that something had been preserved even during the worst years. Statesmen of the Restoration considered it their task to rebuild the old society on its remaining foundations.

THE EFFORT TO RESTORE THE GENTRY'S FUNCTION[b]

Traditionally, the gentry[c] had been useful to the government because of their influence with the people and to the people because of their influence with the government. If their loyalty was essential to the state, so was the state essential to the preservation of their economic, social, and legal privileges.

Since the literati formed the core of the gentry, gentry families encouraged their more talented members to study for the examinations. The whole class was thus subject to constant Confucian indoctrination.[d] It was a small minority,[e] but it was distributed fairly evenly throughout the country and capable of exerting influence in virtually every village.

The gentry formed an open class. To the peasant, the gentry's way of life was the right way; his highest aspiration was to contribute toward his family's advancement to gentry status. The successful merchant tried to acquire gentry status by converting his money into land or his time into learning.[f] Able men who had asserted themselves in other classes were steadily drawn into the gentry and thus neutralized.[g] The way was relatively open: witness the now notorious case of Wu Hsün, a peasant boy of the late nineteenth century, who made a

---

[c] There has been considerable controversy over the definition of the term "gentry" (*shen-shih*). I use it here in the sense in which it is generally used in nineteenth-century Chinese sources and in twentieth-century Chinese monographs, to denote the whole social class which, from the ownership of land, derived the leisure to become educated and thus eligible for public office. Since it was an open class with multiple determinants of membership, a simple working definition seems adequate for present purposes. The shortcomings of Chung-li Chang's strict definition of the gentry as degree-holders are summarized in M. Freedman's review of *The Chinese Gentry* in *Pacific Affairs*, XXIX, 1 (1956), 78–80.

[d] On how the examination system was used to keep members of the gentry studying orthodox teachings throughout their lives, see Chang, *The Chinese Gentry*, pp. 165–82; Chung-cheng Chow Li, *L'Examen provincial en Chine* (*hiang che*) *sous la dynastie des Ts'ing*, Paris, 1935.

[e] No estimates are available of the size of the whole gentry, and estimates of the proportion of degree-holders to the total population of China in the second half of the nineteenth century are at best rough. According to Bourne ("Historical Table . . . ," *loc. cit.*), there were alive at any one time:

Winners of first place in the Palace Examination (*chuang-yüan*)   14
Holders of the metropolitan degree (*chin-shih*)   4,900
Holders of the provincial degree (*chü-jen*) 21,698

According to Chung-li Chang (*The Chinese Gentry*, pp. 102, 122, 125):

Holders of the metropolitan degree   2,600
Holders of the provincial degree who did not go on to the higher degree 10,000
Holders of the preliminary degree (*sheng-yüan*) 910,597

Since the total population of China was nearly four hundred million, there can be no doubt that degree-holders were a small minority.

[f] See Chapter VIII.

[g] According to Hsiao-t'ung Fei, "The gentry class is in fact a safety valve in social changes. Conservatism becomes the rule of Chinese society, and China as a culture is singular in the history of human kind in its stability and perpetuation." (*China's Gentry*, p. 12.)

fortune in commerce, entered the gentry, and ended up founding schools for classical study and aiding the Ch'ing in local security problems.[h]

The record of the gentry's activity in public affairs is quite remarkable. They were constantly engaged in raising funds for roads, bridges, dikes, etc.; in organizing local defense; in moral instruction and guidance; in the arbitration of disputes; and in charitable enterprises.[7] Although these activities were related to production, none was in itself immediately productive. Moreover, they had a political character; their effective discharge required not special technical knowledge but rather a savoir-faire in the handling of men.[8] The gentry's leadership in these activities and their connections with the government gave them considerable influence over the peasantry. The peasant "had to support the gentry, but the scholar-official of the class he supported was useful to him in negotiating with the representatives of the imperial power to prevent the infliction of extreme hardship."[9]

In these circumstances the local official could not discharge his duties without the support of the gentry.[10] The *Handbook for Local Officials* pointed out that the people did not understand or accept official orders unless these were explained to them by the local gentry, in whom they had confidence.[11] As an experienced nineteenth-century observer put it:

> the literary class in China hold the functions of both nobles and priests, a perpetual association, *gens aeterna in qua nemo nascitur,* holding in its hands public opinion and the legal power to maintain it. The geographical isolation of the people, the nature of the language, and the absence of a landed aristocracy combine to add efficiency to this system; and when the peculiarities of Chinese character, and the nature of the class-books which do so much to mould that character, are considered, it is impossible to devise a better plan for insuring the perpetuity of the government, or the contentment of the people under that government.[12]

The years of rebellion that preceded the Restoration shook the whole hierarchy of status and substantially modified the gentry's feeling of responsibility toward the state. Luckily for the Ch'ing, the Taiping rebels had failed to offer the gentry any viable alternative to the Confucian system; hence the way was open for the central government to recover its hegemony.

Tseng Kuo-fan urged that the gentry be encouraged by awards and recognition to reassume their traditional role.[13] Edicts spoke in the highest terms of the gentry; eulogies of those who had remained loyal during the rebellions were published, and memorials to the dead were erected.[14]

As a second means of consolidating gentry status and loyalty, the state scrupulously respected all the gentry's traditional legal and economic privileges.[15]

---

[h] The story of Wu Hsün received an accolade in Communist China until Party spokesmen made clear its reprehensible character. The literature on the subject is now voluminous.

The *status quo ante* in land titles was restored, and land tax relief was directed primarily toward the relief of landlords.[i] The right of the gentry to appeal to Peking against provincial and local officials was confirmed. For example, an elderly holder of a minor degree in Shansi felt that he had been taxed unduly. When his appeal to the county magistrate failed (the clerks, he alleged, had distorted the evidence), he appealed to the prefect, then twice to the governor, and eventually all the way to the Throne.[16] Similarly, a gentleman whose property had been seized by the Nien-fei was unable to reclaim it after their suppression. When the gentleman got no satisfaction from the local officials, a censor carried his case to the Throne, and an Imperial committee of investigation was appointed.[17]

Gentry requests were not always granted, but they never went unheeded. When a Kiangsu holder of a provincial degree sent an intermediary to the Censorate to petition for raising the water-mark on a local lock, the request was denied, but only after the Censorate had memorialized on the degree-holder's behalf, and the Throne had referred the matter to three of the highest officials in the country for consideration.[18]

Actually, the general restoration of the Confucian social order and the vigorous revival of Confucian teachings were more important to the gentry than any specific measures. More interested in order and status than in political power, the gentry had throughout history thrown their weight to Confucian monarchs against unruly peasants and to Confucian peasants against unruly monarchs. That they would continue to do so was not only an article of faith but a perfectly reasonable assumption; for the Confucian system, although produced in ancient, feudal China, had in the course of two millennia become a "complete system of the interests, the aspirations, and the ideas of the literati-officials."[19] The system conferred status upon them, sanctioned it, and perpetuated it; they could ask no more than that the system itself be propagated. Accordingly, encouragement to scholarship and learning was one of the chief political policies of the Restoration.

THE REVIVAL OF SCHOLARSHIP AND LEARNING

The revival of scholarship and learning was intended to reinforce Ch'ing local control in several ways. First, as has been noted above, the gentry were loyal not to the state as such but to a state that protected the institutions and values on which their own position depended. The Ch'ing, as a non-Chinese dynasty, was under a particular compulsion to demonstrate its adherence to those institutions and values. Second, the gentry's influence over the peasantry depended in part upon peasant indoctrination in the Confucian teaching. If

[i] See Chapter VIII.

the peasants were to respond to ideological controls, they must continue to believe in the worth of their heritage. Third, the non-Chinese minorities and the population of the frontier areas had to be controlled more closely in an age of domestic unrest and foreign war; Ch'ing statesmen were convinced that Confucian indoctrination was an excellent means for bringing them into line.[20] Fourth, Restoration statesmen were acutely aware of the need for more "men of talent" in government, men whose Confucian training would guarantee both their ability and their moral influence.

Before the Taiping Rebellion, semiofficial schools, academies, libraries, and local literati clubs had been scattered throughout the country. Although founded and maintained by local literati, these institutions were under official patronage.[21] During the years of rebellion the state had been obliged to use its energies in other ways; the great libraries had been looted, scholars were out training troops, and public funds could scarcely be spared for educational purposes. Measures to correct this situation were more than pious formalities; they were of urgent practical importance.

The record of the Restoration in the rebuilding of these schools and academies was impressive. Feng Kuei-fen, who had great influence on high officials of the period, constantly urged not only the rebuilding of destroyed academies but the building of new ones, especially free ones.[22] Early in the Restoration provincial officials were ordered to rebuild academies and to return their endowment lands as rapidly as the various areas were recovered. In 1864 Ting Jih-ch'ang, then taotai of Su-Sung-T'ai (the circuit comprising Soochow, Sungkiang, and Taitsang), founded the Lung-men Academy in Shanghai. In 1865 Tseng Kuo-fan and Li Hung-chang were ordered to restore the academies of Nanking and Changchow, nearly all of which had been destroyed. In 1867 Wu T'ang, as governor-general of Fukien and Chekiang, presented a plan for the restoration of the academies of those provinces. The Hupeh director of education, Chang Chih-tung, established the Ching-hsin Academy, and subsequently Wang K'ai-t'ai established the Chih-yung Academy.[23]

The special problem of indoctrinating the incompletely Sinicized minorities received considerable attention. As Tso Tsung-t'ang by degrees recovered control of Shensi and Kansu in the late 1860's, he memorialized on the importance of developing educational institutions in hitherto neglected Kansu, in order to provide a basis for lasting peace in the province. He founded or restored a long list of academies. Tso also provided special scholarships for Mongols and Moslems in an effort to bring these minorities into the Chinese ideological orbit.[24] The director of education for Shensi and Kansu gave a detailed account of regional problems, pointing out that for the development of public morals, men of talent were needed; to produce men of talent, schools were needed.[25]

There were similar efforts in the Miao areas of Kweichow and the Hakka areas of Kwangtung.ʲ Although the Manchus were in most respects scarcely comparable to the other non-Chinese minorities, special steps were taken to improve the education of the children of Bannermen. In Chihli, Ch'ung-hou memorialized on the need for state-supported schools since the old privately supported schools had degenerated.[26] The censor Tu Jui-lien agreed, pointing out that although the Bannermen faced many difficulties, learning was more important than food and clothing.[27]

The authorities concerned themselves not merely with the pro-forma establishment of schools but with the effectiveness of the schools' administration,[28] and above all with what they taught. All the great scholar-officials of the time, notably Tseng Kuo-fan, Wo-jen, Li T'ang-chieh, and Kuo Sung-tao, delivered long and reflective pronunciations on this vital matter. Li T'ang-chieh spoke for them all when he argued that going through the motions of study was not enough, that the education of the literati was the foundation of the reform of customs, and that the literati must therefore study the right books in the right way.[29] Chang Chih-tung founded the Ching-hsin Academy to encourage what he considered *genuine* study, a subject on which he had a great many ideas.

The revival of scholarship also required the rebuilding of libraries. More than half of the five-hundred–odd great private libraries of the Ch'ing period had been located in Kiangsu and Chekiang, where the Taiping iconoclasts had been strongest. With the Restoration, officials and gentry joined forces to recover and rehouse the scattered volumes. The brothers Ting Ping and Ting Shen reassembled a considerable proportion of the books that had belonged to the Wen-lan ko, destroyed in the capture of Hangchow; these later became the nucleus of the Kiangsu Provincial Library. Another Chekiang scholar-official, Sun I-jang, was able in the 1860's to buy copies of lost Chinese books in Japan, where Western interests were now predominant (a sidelight on the difference between the Meiji Restoration and the T'ung-chih Restoration).[30]

The Classics and Histories were reprinted, and new books on government were published. In 1864 Tseng Kuo-fan established a printing office at his Anking headquarters, where officers of disbanded armies were employed as collators under the direction of distinguished scholars.[31] Other printing offices were set up at Nanking, Soochow, Yangchow, Hangchow, and Wuchang.

As governor of Kiangsu, Ting Jih-ch'ang subsidized the printing of works to be used in local administration.[32] Topical digests of the lessons of history were presented to the Throne and received commendation.[33] In the northwest, mainly at Lanchow, Tso Tsung-t'ang subsidized the publication of important books as part of his regional reconstruction program. He emphasized the Clas-

ʲ See Chapter VI.

sics, arguing that they (1) provided the standards of personal conduct, (2) taught the lessons of community life, and (3) made regular and uniform the thought of the common people.[34]

As rebellion was pacified, the censors urged that the reprinting of the Classics be speeded. In areas where fighting had been intense, there was some delay owing to the destruction of the printing blocks themselves; but while the preparation of new editions took time, it gave high officials an opportunity to provide suitable employment for needy local scholars.[35] The government availed itself of every opportunity to give encouragement and aid to this group.[k]

The program to revive scholarship and learning was expected to affect the common people as well as the gentry. It was assumed, for example, that a turbulent populace would be calmed by the reissue of books on proper behavior.[l] The literati were encouraged in their studies in part because they provided moral instruction for the peasantry.[36] At that time the literati still lived throughout the countryside; talent had not yet been drained off into the cities.[37] In every area local scholars spent their lives studying and lecturing,[38] and there were "winter-three-months" schools for the poor.[39] There is no doubt that the Confucian teaching penetrated to the lowest ranks of society; that "the teachings of the ancient sages reached the peasants through these scholars and redefined again and again the sense of moral purpose which peasant and gentry had in common."[m]

As propagation of the Confucian teaching was considered the basic means of local control, so the spread of frivolous or heterodox teachings was considered the cause of unrest. The counterpart of Ting Jih-ch'ang's subsidies for the publication of useful works was his campaign against novels. In his proclamation banning *The Dream of the Red Chamber*, the *Shui-hu chuan*, and some hundred other works, he stated: "Morals (customs) are the mere outward expression of the mind within; so that we may fairly attribute the rebellions of late years to the impure literature now prevalent, which in secret is fomenting every dissension."[40] It is clear from the frequent exhortations against novels, theatricals, gambling, mixed gatherings, and so forth that any frivolity was regarded as inconsistent with the austere Confucian code.[41] Political satires were also dangerous. In 1867 the appearance of a collection of satirical poems caused great consternation, and high officials engaged in a futile attempt to locate the author.[42]

---

[k] On the sponsorship of Western learning, see Chapter X.

[l] For example, in the Tientsin area, the people were quarrelsome and *therefore* books on the principles of social usage were reprinted and lectures were given (*Ching-men tsa-chi*, Ch. 1, pp. 41–42).

[m] Robert Redfield, Introduction to Fei, *China's Gentry*, p. 11. This point was striking to contemporary foreign observers. Alcock, for example, referred to the "thoroughly popular works of Confucius and Mencius" and observed: "there is current among all classes of Chinese . . . a fund of knowledge on all the practical duties and relations of life." ("The Chinese Empire in Its Foreign Relations," *Bombay Quarterly Review*, No. 6 (1856), p. 228.)

Popular religious beliefs and practices were similarly suspect. Although certain types of "loyal" local gods and spirits[n] could be fitted into the Confucian system, the state took pains to prevent the development of popular movements outside the system. The later famous Elder Brother Society (Ko-lao hui) was ordered suppressed in all provinces.[43] When the censor Wang Shu-jui proposed that of the temples destroyed during the rebellions, only those devoted to the gods of the land be rebuilt,[44] the *North China Herald* commented: "It is worthy of note that the reasons urged for this step are entirely of a political character, viz., the prevention of large gatherings of the people."[45] Even a sect claiming a Confucian affiliation—the Huang-yai chiao in Shantung—was exterminated in 1866 on grounds of suspected heterodoxy.[46]

THE APPEAL TO THE PEOPLE: SOCIAL WELFARE POLICIES

The state's chief persuasive means of controlling the common people was its program of social welfare and relief.[47] Few governments have ever made such a fetish of loving the people as did the autocratic government of the Chinese Empire. Traditionally, the stability of the state depended on the welfare of the people. The people were the basis of the state; "they should be loved by the sovereign as a man loves his life."[48] Prince Kung wrote that Heaven gave birth to the people and set up "superior men" to shepherd them. At the top of the hierarchy the Emperor governed the people on behalf of Heaven; the Emperor served the Universe, not the Universe the Emperor.[49]

Tseng Kuo-fan wrote that the bankruptcy of the state might be borne, but that loss of the people's affections was an irreparable calamity. History showed that an auspicious era such as that of Sui Wen-ti (A.D. 589–605) might end in chaos and rebellion, whereas one beginning poorly like that of Han Chao-ti (86–76 B.C.) might lead to glory—depending on how the people were treated. Tseng emphasized the lesson of the first sixteen years of the K'ang-hsi reign (1662–77), when in spite of the strain on the treasury and the Rebellion of the Three Feudatories, the Emperor so loved the people that they were bound to him by ties of sentiment that could not be loosened.[50] This notion that statesmanship must inevitably be concerned with the people's reaction, that government was essentially government of the people, permeated all political writing of the time.[51]

As the supervising censor Chu Ch'ao put it, "To love the people (*ai-min*) requires deeds as well as words."[52] Traditionally "love of the people" had been

---

[n] When Imperial representatives worshiped at a local shrine, the *North China Herald* commented: "The political gain secured by the government by this sort of worship is also very visible. The people along the road praise the Emperor for his parental interest in their welfare. They expect an increase in local prosperity from the service offered by so high a personage as the Son of Heaven to their local divinity, and become more contented with their rulers." (Sept. 28, 1867.)

demonstrated primarily by the enactment of measures intended to preserve domestic peace and order and to protect agriculture, and only secondarily by direct
state intervention in matters of social welfare and public relief. In normal times
families and communities had been able to care for their own unfortunates in a
remarkably effective manner.[53]

Yet even in stable times the state had been considered responsible for providing special relief in emergencies, and since the normal standard of living was
marginal, emergencies had not been rare. In the 1860's, when natural calamities
added to war, rebellion, and their aftermath seemed to make necessary more and
bigger special measures of relief, a few statesmen seem to have become dimly
aware that certain not fully understood dislocations in the old society might
require more systematic public welfare policies on a permanent basis.

Although natural calamities of substantial proportions were a regular oc-
currence and regularly required extraordinary relief,[54] all the existing welfare
agencies were severely tested by the drought and subsequent flood in north China
in 1867 and 1868,[55] in areas already hard pressed by the campaign against the
Nien-fei. In the early summer of 1867 drought caused a general crop failure, the
consequences of which were aggravated by the drying up of many water transportation routes and the loss of millet stalks for fuel.[56] Master plans for relief
poured into Peking,[57] and as the price of food soared, the normal winter free
distribution of rice gruel was continued through the summer.[58]

The governor-general of Chihli and the prefect of the metropolitan prefecture were ordered to take direct charge of operations, to compile statistics, to find
work, to facilitate migration to other areas, and to establish more orphanages.
Rice brought in from the south was in some cases distributed free on recommendation of the Board of Revenue; in others it was added to the limited supply
available for sale through normal commercial channels.[59] Special measures were
taken to check misappropriation of relief funds and supplies.[60] Private contributions were solicited, evidently with enough success to give rise to a racket in
which "local rascals" impersonated the collectors of contributions.[61] New soup
kitchens and other free food distribution centers were established, committees
to survey needs were sent out, reserve grain from undamaged areas was sent into
the famine areas, and all over north China public and private relief agencies
mushroomed.[62] As the crisis continued into the winter of 1867–68, the distribution
of cooked rice was supplemented by allotments of rice grain and money to certain
areas, on the basis of their population.[63]

Relief operations on this scale were complex. The immediate problem was
to save lives, but good will and largesse had to be supplemented by careful planning. Free kitchens could not be established at random, for fear the poor would
mob them, exhaust their supplies, and start rioting. If relief grain were bought

anywhere in north China, the price would simply rise further, since the shortage was genuine and not the result of hoarding. Therefore, rice had to be bought in the south. This required measures to ensure more efficient transportation and price control to prevent the flow of rice to the area of highest market price.

Above all, there was the problem of making certain that the relief actually reached the people for whom it was intended.[64] Data on this point are scarce, but one may safely infer that a substantial effort was made on behalf of the general public welfare, and that this idea of relief was everywhere accepted and approved. An on-the-spot observer saw the roads thronged with carts of grain sent in for free distribution by the central government and wrote in glowing terms of the exertions of both officials and gentry.[65]

Beyond immediate relief, officials proposed a series of public construction projects based on the principle "use work to replace charity" (*i kung tai chen*). This, it was pointed out, would both help the people and take care of rebuilding the various water works, town walls, and public buildings destroyed during the fighting.[66]

There were numerous other public and private social welfare activities during the Restoration period. Tseng Kuo-fan was a vigorous proponent of granaries supported by local wealthy families.[67] A British consul noted that, in proportion to their means, the Chinese were quite as generous as the British.[68] The Shanghai taotai established a house of refuge for destitute people without family support.[69] There was general acceptance of the idea of the public responsibility for providing adequate orphanages and nurseries and for preventing the drowning of baby girls.[70] Competent officials were quick to act in a crisis; in 1867, for example, when there was an explosion in the Hankow arsenal in which some eight hundred people were reported killed, the governor-general was observed on the spot, taking personal charge of relief operations.[71]

Public health was not ignored. When an outbreak of plague was reported, investigation and diagnosis were ordered.[72] The state attempted to prevent excessive delays in burial,[73] even though matters of birth, marriage, and death were normally left entirely to the family. Local officials arranged for free vaccination in Nanking, Soochow, and Shanghai, and the Shanghai taotai even provided fruit and fish with which the very poor might reward their children for submitting to the needle.[74]

I emphasize these details here because there has been a widespread tendency to suppose that in traditional China each family was interested exclusively in the welfare of its own members,[o] and that the state considered such questions

---

[o] It seems likely that the unity of the extended family and the exclusiveness of the village in Chinese society have been exaggerated in conventional writing on the subject. (See Fukutake Tadashi, *Chūgoku nōson shakai no kōzō*, enlarged edition, Tokyo, 1951. FB 8.1.8.)

as disaster relief, poor relief, public health, and child welfare as beyond its proper concern. This was not so. Both private citizens and the government were attentive to the general welfare. In normal times local agencies handled things adequately, but the state was always ready (and expected) to take action in a crisis. After the failure of the Restoration, public welfare was neglected not because the idea was lacking but because the old institutions for its expression, being part and parcel of the old order, were inadaptable to the new.

THE WEB OF COLLECTIVE RESPONSIBILITY

The Confucian system of control through persuasion was reinforced by a series of group organizations designed (1) to ensure conformity and (2) to provide a direct channel through which the state could tap the food and manpower resources of the village. The most important of these instruments were the pao-chia system of collective responsibility and its corollary, the li-chia system of tax collection. In each administrative area public registers were kept, recording the population census. Ten families constituted a *p'ai*, one hundred families a *chia*, and one thousand families a *pao*, and all members were responsible for each other's actions. Although the families constituting a unit nominated its head, their choice was confirmed by the magistrate, and the pao-chia officers functioned only at the pleasure of the magistrate.[75]

The question of the origin of the pao-chia system and of its relation to the clan and family systems has remained highly controversial. It was not originally supported by the Confucians, who argued for administrative control through the family.[76] However, from the Sung period onward, as the great families declined and the texture of the Chinese gentry altered, the organization of neighboring households became an increasingly important supplement to the social cohesion created by family units.

Wang An-shih (1021–86) encouraged the development of the pao-chia as a means of centralization and of providing public security without a large standing army. Intense peasant resistance led to its failure, and Wang was replaced by Ssu-ma Kuang's conservative clique. The system flourished again during the Ming period and was in theory always supported by the Ch'ing government.[77] By the nineteenth century, however, it had declined into an ineffective instrument of local control, and its revival became one of the chief aims of the Restoration.

Whatever the relation between the family system and the pao-chia system may have been in earlier periods of Chinese history, during the Restoration the two systems were seen not as alternative but as corollary instruments of local control. The men who were most prominent in the effort to revive the pao-chia were the great Confucian literati. Li T'ang-chieh wrote that the pao-chia system was essential to assuring harmony between officials and the people.[78] Tseng

Kuo-fan, perhaps the system's most prolific protagonist, praised it as a gradual remedy, one that would calm the people as order and firm guidance soothed a child recovering from a long illness.[79]

Feng Kuei-fen urged the reinstitution of both the clan system and the pao-chia system; they were useful, he said, because they could reach where the government could not. According to Feng, the pao-chia system was the warp and the ancient clan system (*tsung-fa*) the woof of Chinese society. In ancient times during the Hsia, Shang, and Chou dynasties, Chinese society had been cohesive but had later disintegrated. In Feng's view, the clan law could be used to restore union in the clan; the pao-chia regulations could be used to restore union in the state; and the two forms of union thus achieved would restore Chinese society to its former heights.[80]

Feng's views on this were typical.[81] Wherever bandits appeared, the state ordered the enforcement of the pao-chia regulations as a means of detaching the bandits from the common people and thus depriving them of food and shelter.[82] The censor Wang Shu-jui wrote that the Taiping and Nien-fei rebellions could never have broken out if the pao-chia regulations had been enforced.[83] The censor Chu Ch'eng-lan made the same point about the various lesser rebellions of the Chia-ch'ing period, adding that the system might be used to restrain the activities of bandits' relatives.[84]

The militia system was a closely related local institution, operating through the same channels. It was designed to protect an area against wrongdoers from outside, as the pao-chia was designed to weed out wrongdoers within the area. However, officials of the Restoration period were dubious about the militia system,[85] which was costly and aroused local antagonism. The general view of the time seems to have been epitomized in a phrase that Tseng Kuo-fan repeated at every opportunity: "Put the emphasis on the group organization afforded by the pao-chia system, not on the military drill required in the militia system" (*chung tsai t'uan, pu tsai lien*).

Appraisals of the pao-chia system of the nineteenth century have been clouded by twentieth-century polemics.[p] Although it was certainly not a form of local self-government,[86] the pao-chia officers were local people, neighbors and kinsmen, in a position to intervene with the authorities. Moreover, the system appears to have contributed to the public order and security upon which agrarian prosperity depended.[87]

Some such system as the pao-chia was obviously essential in the administration of a centralized agrarian state. It provided an effective and cheap sup-

---

[p] Chinese scholars of our time frequently describe the whole nineteenth-century pao-chia system as nothing more than an ineffective attempt at terrorizing the population, and as having no social utility. Quite apart from the current political implications of varying interpretations of the pao-chia system, it is possible that they are incautiously attributing to the system at earlier dates those features which were prominent in it at the turn of the century.

plement[q] to local control through the gentry, and at its best it was a relatively mild system of surveillance. In the period of disintegration that followed the Restoration, however, its harshest features assumed prominence; it came to irritate the population without controlling it, and ultimately fell apart altogether under the strain of basic reform attempts.

THE ROLE OF LAW

Confucian ideological and institutional controls are quite clearly incompatible with any notion of the supremacy of the law in the abstract, or of absolute human and property rights that transcend particular circumstances. It is quite erroneous, however, to suppose that traditional Chinese law was limited to criminal law, as the term is popularly understood in the West, or that it had little to do with maintaining social control.

From the point of view of Roman law, Chinese jurisprudence confused law and morality.[88] The principles of social usage, natural law (*li*), and positive law (*fa*) were considered aspects of the same universal harmony. Preservation of this harmony depended in the first instance on moral teaching, moderation, and compromise; but the state stood ready to enforce, if necessary, observance of the whole codified canon of proper behavior.[89]

The judicial system was designed not to maintain absolute or abstract rights of the state or its citizens, but to avert or resolve actual conflicts. By "justice," a Chinese magistrate understood specific justice in view of all the specific factors of a given case, rather than justice according to logical categories:

> for although the judges profess to be guided by certain principles of justice, decisions are greatly affected by local custom, and even more so by the particular circumstances of the case under consideration, such decision standing entirely by itself and not, as in Europe, professing to stem from a portion of one harmonious system.[90]

"Chinese law does not assume that one can be right or wrong in the abstract."[91]

From this effort to make law specifically equivalent to justice by very fine definitions and distinctions came a code and a system of judicial procedure that were admirable instruments of control within the stable traditional society. At the same time, it was largely this preoccupation with law as specific justice that blocked the development of a law susceptible of wider application, the kind of law that would have held its ground as the traditional society disintegrated.[92]

This vast accumulation of detailed prescriptions for all conceivable situations did not rely on oral tradition or on an accumulating body of judicial opinion.

[q] A well-informed Communist writer referred to the units with a kind of admiration as Tseng's "cadres" (*kan-pu*). (Chu Ch'i-hua, *Chung-kuo nung-ts'un ching-chi ti t'ou-shih*, Shanghai, 1936, pp. 469–70).

The whole of the law, including equity, was in the code. The adjustments allowable on grounds of politics or morality were also in the code. There was no judge; no counterpart, that is, to the Western civil judge, who creates law not by applying precise statutes but by interpreting recognized general doctrines. There was only the magistrate, an administrative official. He had to weigh a variety of factors, but these were the specific circumstances of the individual case, not the abstract legal relations involved. A "superior man" was required for the post, but not an independent judiciary.[93]

The Chinese code included both civil and criminal law. In form the code was a criminal code; it covered only those acts considered to be crimes against the state, and made no legal provision for disputes presumed to concern private parties only. Hence the erroneous notion that China had no civil law. Actually, there was no type of dispute in which the Chinese state was not interested, so that Chinese "criminal" law in fact covered the whole range of behavior covered by "civil" law in the West, including such matters as the institution of an heir, the management of orphanages, mortgages and sale of mortgaged property, conveyancing of land, even the establishment of a memorial gate to a chaste widow.[94] Civil suits were simply treated as involving criminal offenses; for example, a suit to reclaim a horse or a field would charge the defendant with theft, or mischief to property.[95] The state was never disinterested.

A French authority has defined civil law as "a rule of conduct upon a subject of common interest prescribed to all citizens . . . by which it commands, under certain penalties or subject to certain rewards, what each citizen ought to do or not to do or to permit for the common good of society."[96] If we accept this definition, the Chinese code must certainly be characterized as a highly developed civil code. If civil law is taken to mean continental law, as the common law lawyers use the term, then Chinese law is clearly civil rather than common.[97] It can also be characterized as public law, as contrasted with private law.[98] As an instrument of local control, Chinese law covered the whole range of human relations. It placed no excessive emphasis on felonies and misdemeanors; it was a binding, written code, enforceable and enforced; and its punishments were not retributive against the individuals, but imposed to protect society.

It never occurred to Restoration statesmen to make basic changes in the code. The Ch'ing recodification of the traditional code under the Shun-chih Emperor lasted until the post-Boxer constitutional reforms. The new editions issued during the T'ung-chih period showed no evidences of innovation.[99]

Like all conservatives, officials of the T'ung-chih period distrusted legislative activity and directed their attention to administrative improvement. They occupied themselves with specific problems in the administration of justice,[100] with abuses of the system rather than defects in it. The most frequent causes of complaint were delay in the handing down of decisions, interference by the yamen clerks in the judicial process, the abuse of local police power, and the harshness of penalties.

The slowness of justice was widely considered one of the main causes of popular unrest and was constantly condemned by competent administrators.[101] An edict of 1866 pointed to the hardships caused by delay.[102] The prefect of the metropolitan prefecture considered legal delays a major threat to local tranquillity.[103]

A second major problem was the position of the yamen clerks.[r] In the view of competent foreign observers, a Chinese official usually heard a case fairly; the difficulty was to get the case before him: "However willing the judge may be to decide rightly, subordinates have not the same scruples, and those subordinates are the channels through whom, only, approach to the judicial chair is possible."[104] A generation later, in a memorial on legal reform, Chang Chih-tung and Liu K'un-i, who had advanced from promising young officials of the Restoration period to elder statesmen of the Reform period, still wrote: "It is very necessary to do away with these clerks, only then can such things be stopped."[105] Some relief was afforded by the censors, who provided a channel of judicial appeal to the central government in instances in which the clerks were blocking appeal through normal channels.[106]

A third problem was law enforcement. The Chinese system had been reasonably efficient in normal times;[s] but in the turbulent mid-nineteenth century there were signs of considerable laxity[107] and of abuse of police power at the lower levels. According to the censors, the police robbed the people, accepted bribes to change the reports of crimes, and so forth.[108] There is no evidence, however, of any general breakdown of law and order. Reports of improper police administration on one occasion were balanced by reports of especially competent administration on another. Ting Jih-ch'ang had an outstanding reputation in this respect as taotai at Shanghai.[109]

The fourth problem was the much-discussed harshness of penalties.[110] Following the rebellions even the most convinced advocates of government by example, persuasion, and group pressure urged strict and severe punishment. Yet the Chinese system was not without safeguards for the accused. The code was severe, but provided for clemency on grounds of equity, politics, and morals.[111] The censors appear to have continued to exercise their traditional

---

[r] See Chapter V.

[s] "A system which can lay its hand on a criminal or suspected person in any yamun or in any cottage, if he be a Mandarin with a coral button or a coolie staggering under his burden, must of necessity excite fear. But it is not the slavish fear of men living in the land of an inquisition. It is a fear based on the firm conviction that laws are on the whole good and righteous." (*NCH*, Aug. 14, 1868.)

function of limiting abuses by publicizing them, and the human rights of prisoners in jail were recognized.[112]

In short, with all its obvious imperfections the Chinese legal system was an admirable instrument of local control during the Restoration. Experienced foreign observers agreed that "There is far greater security for life and property in the majority of towns and villages than in our metropolis."[113] The difficulty that eventually caused the system's collapse proved to be simply this: "the Chinese conception, whatever may be its intrinsic value, is poorly adapted to the economic and social organization of the modern world."[114]

KEYSTONE OF THE SYSTEM OF LOCAL CONTROL: THE LOCAL OFFICIAL

In a feudal empire, the suppression of rebellion rests with the feudal lords; in an empire divided into administrative districts, the suppression of rebellion rests with the local officials.

—Tso Tsung-t'ang[115]

He who is an official is a bitter man; to do the work of an official is a bitter business. He who considers official status a pleasure can never be a good official.

—Wo-jen[116]

For more than two thousand years China had been not a feudal empire but a unified empire divided into administrative districts. In each district full powers of government were held by a man appointed by and directly responsible to the central government. He maintained relations with the gentry, encouraged scholarship and learning, took charge of relief operations, controlled pao-chia activities, and interpreted and enforced the law. In the Chinese view, when the local official was an able man, these various institutions of local control were effective; when the local official was incompetent, they were useless—the gentry were alienated, learning was a mockery, relief was maladministered, the pao-chia system rubbed people the wrong way, and the law could not be enforced. Ting Jih-ch'ang's memorials on the importance of appointing the right man to local office were representative:

> If we obtain the men, there is control; if we lose the men, there is chaos. This has been true from ancient times; it is even more urgent today.

> The Empire is an accumulation of chou and hsien. If we get the right man in one hsien, one hsien will be under control; if we get the right man in every hsien, the Empire will be under control.[117]

In the same vein, the governor of Shantung, Yen Ching-ming, memorialized: "From antiquity, without careful selection of local officials, it has never been possible to govern the Empire."[118]

Emphasis on the quality of local officials was not, of course, a Restoration innovation. The compiler of the *Handbook for Local Officials* of the Tao-kuang period was transmitting a venerable political doctrine when he wrote: "All the affairs of the Empire have their origin in the chou and hsien. If the chou and hsien are properly managed, there is nothing in the Empire which is not properly managed."[119] However, there was a new urgency in the Restoration concern. The *Handbook for Local Officials* was reissued with some fanfare, and in a new preface Li Hung-chang pointed out that after years of turmoil the responsibilities of the district magistrates were even greater than usual.[120] To an official on his way to take up a local post, Wo-jen wrote of the devastation of the Yangtze valley and of the enormous responsibility consequently devolving upon local officials. To restore stability, he wrote, the local official must encourage study, search vigorously for new talent, and observe an austere impartiality in fixing rewards and punishments. Laxness in this last respect, usually the result of local pressures, had been one of the chief defects of local government in recent times.[121]

Nearly every memorialist urged that local officials be appointed solely on the basis of the examination system. Although important at every level of government, restoration of the examination system[t] was nowhere so important as in local administration. Local administrators were more numerous than their superiors, and they dealt more directly with more people. It was an administrative platitude that neither the gentry nor the common people could be controlled unless the local official himself was steeped in the Confucian tradition.[u] As Tseng Kuo-fan put it, when the local official is not a "superior man," both the gentry and the people are upset, and disorder results.[122]

A foreign missionary testified to the loss of control that followed whenever the traditional system for selecting the "wisest and best" for local posts was abandoned:

> Literary merit, notwithstanding the increasing number of cases of bribery, is still the real ground of promotion. Any great departure from this rule invariably brings down the wrath of the people upon the head of the offending magistrate; and most serious disaffection will certainly follow any general departure from old-established principle and practice. Many, indeed, trace the disturbances, which for the last ten years have been threatening the overthrow of the Manchow dynasty, to the fact that wealth, rather than merit, is in so many cases becoming the step to official promotion.[123]

t See Chapter V.

u It is generally true that the moral authority of the leader of any group is essential to his power; that although his rank carries the presumption that his orders will be obeyed, these must conform to the norms of the group. If they do not conform, they will not be obeyed and the status of the leader will in consequence decline. (George Homans, *The Human Group*, New York, 1950, p. 187.)

Fully conceding the lamentable necessity of conferring office upon some otherwise unqualified men in recognition of their military and financial contributions, Restoration officials advised that these "outsiders" should never be appointed district magistrates without the strictest supplementary examination.[124] The memorialists presented ample evidence that incompetent local government led to widespread disorders. Li T'ang-chieh remarked that only the indoctrinated local official could promote that harmony between government and people which would deprive seditious elements of issues for agitation.[125] In the summer of 1867 the governor-general of Kwangtung and Kwangsi, Jui-lin, was enjoined to use especial care in the appointment of local officials because banditry had been only recently suppressed in that area.[126] Even a strictly military figure like Seng-ko-lin-ch'in reported on disturbances caused by incompetent local government and the resulting damage to his military operations.[127] The Board of Civil Office periodically prepared a list of all the counties of the Empire, annotated to indicate those where particularly able magistrates were needed. The importance attached to considerations of this kind was shown in edicts correcting and amending the Board's list.[128]

Again and again memorialists pointed out the direct connection between the policies of local officials and the stability of the Empire. Feng Kuei-fen wrote: "there is nothing evil in human nature . . . the people are not born to rebel; but if the people are not nourished and are not taught, rebellion results." As cold and hunger caused rebellion, so local governments could prevent it by providing for adequate food, clothing, shelter, and moral training.[129] Wo-jen wrote that never in history had hungry people been tranquil, and that only an able official could see to it that his people were provided with food.[130]

According to the censor Wang Tao-yung, local incompetence caused all the woes of the state by rendering ineffective the pacification efforts of high civil and military officials.

> In government nothing is more important than to tranquilize the people. To tranquilize the people, it is first necessary to investigate the officials. The investigation of officials must begin with the chou and hsien magistrates. Wisdom or the lack of it in chou and hsien magistrates is the basis of order or chaos in the Empire.

Wang described in some detail the errors in policy committed by "city slickers" (*shih-ching chih t'u*) and military men when they were entrusted with local government. As a result of such appointments, "civil government daily disintegrates . . . In my opinion current events today are like a long-standing illness; in order to cure the symptoms, we must first tranquilize the people in order to fortify the basis of society." According to Wang, the people could be tranquilized only if local officials were appointed solely according to the examination system, not because it guaranteed the wisdom of the successful candidate (he admitted that it did not) but because it served to clarify and stabilize the structure of society in accordance with traditional precepts.[131]

By this theory there clearly could be no precise formula for successful administration, and the *Handbook for Local Officials* did not attempt to offer one. Officials were rather advised that their posts were established for the benefit of the people; that unless the people were actually benefited they could not be controlled; and that local officials' decisions involved the whole course of administration from beginning to end and covered both major and minor questions. Administration would be successful, and control would be maintained, when the official gave his constant and earnest attention to all the affairs of his district, acting flexibly in the light of accumulated Chinese experience, which was summarized for him at some length.[132]

Since the local official's administrative responsibilities were extensive,[133] his *Handbook* gave detailed consideration to some of the more predictable practical matters: office procedure, budget, and personnel; the problems of agriculture and sericulture, including water control, forestry, fertilization, land tenure, and the land tax; social welfare and relief; the care, education, and moral indoctrination of the young, including orphans; crime and its punishment; local defense; and so forth.

What the local officials were doing and ought to be doing in all these various fields was the subject of constant discussion and debate at the upper levels of government. Local government was under constant review, especially by the censors, and sweeping advice was offered. The censor Yu Pai-ch'uan, for example, pointed out quite correctly that the re-establishment of local control required accelerated relief measures, strengthening of the pao-chia system, and more careful attention by senior provincial officials to the conduct of local officials within their jurisdiction.[134] The censor Ma Yüan-jui urged local officials to find means: (1) to eliminate corruption, illegal taxes, and unemployment, for "to provide a means of livelihood for the common people is to eliminate the source from which bandits come"; (2) to improve the judicial procedure, for "if we wish the Empire to have no rebellious people, we must see to it that the Empire has no resentful people"; (3) to demand less from the people in the way of supplies and manpower, since people without adequate means of livelihood become the prey of agitators, and "in this case the fault does not rest exclusively with the people"; (4) to improve the means of communication, so that edicts concerning the people's affairs could be immediately proclaimed in every village and discussed in every household.[135]

A local official with a country gentry background and long Confucian training would obviously be more likely to succeed in these tasks than one who was appointed in recognition of his military or financial services to the state.*ᵛ* Where the Confucian official was to acquire technical operating competence in so many fields was another matter; how to become intimately familiar with local conditions in an area where his tenure was made intentionally short was still another.*ʷ* The whole system of civil government was intended to place all local authority in the hands of a single man who would be free of local pressures and above narrow technical preoccupations, a microcosmic philosopher-king whose humanistic vision would encompass horizontally the whole of the Empire and vertically the whole of society.

As noted earlier, this system of government gave enormous unofficial power to the "permanent technical staff," i.e., the yamen clerks, and especially the runners, who were familiar with local conditions and operating details. The yamen clerks were considered particularly harmful in local government, where they could most readily abuse their position—for example, by extorting special payment from those who came to pay taxes, since the magistrates rarely understood the intricate local tax registers. Cases of this kind could be, and were, reported to the Throne,[136] but abuses remained frequent.*ˣ* In consequence, as the technical problems of local government became more complicated, more numerous, and more important, increasing power was relegated to or usurped by men who not only had no Confucian training, but were completely enmeshed in local pressures and prejudices.*ʸ*

Statesmen of the Restoration generally assumed that the power of the clerks would once again be held within bounds as soon as local government and local society were stabilized along traditional lines. The revolutionary idea that specific authority might be delegated to a *responsible* subordinate with specific competence seldom occurred to them. When it did occur, it was rejected by most as alien to the traditional social life they sought to restore.

ᵛ For example, as the censor Yüan Fang-ch'eng pointed out, the basic problem of the time was the revival of agriculture and sericulture, subjects about which people who purchased rank would know nothing (*CHTI*, Ch. 2, pp. 14–15; *THTKTI*, Ch. 20, pp. 4–5). Yüan, a native of Kiangtsing hsien, Szechwan, won the metropolitan degree in 1853 (HF-3).

ʷ See Chapter V.

ˣ The Censor Yu Pai-ch'uan, after describing the general corruption of yamen clerks, wrote: "This is an outline of conditions in the government offices in the capital; but the harm caused by yamen clerks in the provinces is even more unspeakable." (*CHTI*, Ch. 8, pp. 14–15b.) The Nien-fei were able to bribe clerks and runners to give misinformation to magistrates who were trying to restore order, and even to become yamen runners themselves (Ssu-yü Teng, "The Nien-fei," chap. 2).

ʸ Hart warned the Chinese government of precisely this. Of the refusal to appoint men to their native provinces or to leave them long enough in one place to acquire local knowledge, he wrote: "The corruption that this rule seeks to prevent arises from this rule; with the result that the most obedient people in the whole world have finally become insubordinate and rebellious." (Hart's 1865 memorandum to the Chinese government, *IWSM-TC*, Ch. 40, p. 15.)

THE WESTERN IMPACT ON LOCAL CONTROL

China's developing contacts with the Western world were bound to threaten the whole system of local control. For one thing, it was neither legal nor logical to apply Chinese law to foreigners and their expanding activities. Consequently, in carrying out certain treaty provisions, local officials were obliged to act against the basic principles of traditional local administration. Moreover, employment with foreigners, particularly in the foreign concessions, offered an escape from the net of collective responsibility. As time went on, new ideas threatened the hegemony of the Confucian teaching. Young men of talent increasingly wondered whether an official post at the end of a long and arduous training was the highest goal to which man might aspire. Above all, the whole position of the gentry and literati was threatened.

The administration of justice collapsed in the trading towns and especially in the treaty ports. Not content with being themselves outside Chinese jurisdiction, the foreigners also attempted to secure extraterritorial legal privileges for their business employees and their converts.[137] Moreover, the swollen population of these cities was drawn from all over the Empire; uprooted people felt less constrained by old pressures. The magistrate was deprived of his channels of control: families were separated, neighbors did not know neighbors, and the men of greatest influence were not the gentry, but men of uncertain background, the newly prominent compradors.[138]

Most of the international problems of the time were essentially problems in Chinese local administration, since the Sino-Western treaties were mainly concerned with stipulating what local conditions foreign missionaries and businessmen wanted. Responsible local officials were torn between their duty to the Throne, which insisted on observance of the treaty provisions, and their duty to the people under the Confucian system. Many an official was faced with the necessity of destroying his own effectiveness as a magistrate by issuing orders that alienated the gentry and ran counter to popular custom.

The most serious problem the Restoration government faced in local control was the increased xenophobia of the local gentry. Every cautious step the central government took to improve its diplomatic position threatened to alienate this group, whose loyalty was essential. The local official who impressed foreigners as having a sound knowledge of Victorian commercial requirements was scarcely the man to protect the economic interests of the gentry; his very appointment would threaten their social position. And a man known to foreigners for his broadminded tolerance of Christian evangelism or Western political ideas could not lead the Confucian revival.

Missionaries were given to provoking debates designed to demonstrate publicly the "ignorance" of the literati. The consequence was an implacable and mounting hostility not only toward missionaries, not only toward all foreigners, but toward the Chinese "modernizers," whom the local literati succeeded in labeling as traitors. There was pressure to prevent young men from taking the T'ung-wen kuan examinations.[z] When Kuo Sung-tao went home to Hunan before beginning his diplomatic mission in Europe, he was attacked and his boat was burned following a gathering in the local Confucian temple. Tseng Chi-tse met a similar reception.[139] During the examination sessions, where the literati were assembled, there was always a noticeable increase in antiforeign incidents.[140] Unofficial proclamations calling for the general expulsion of foreigners bore unmistakable signs of literati authorship.[141]

The Restoration government could not possibly attempt to break down the Confucian prejudices of the literati, for the survival of the traditional state depended on the resurgence of these ideas. At the same time, the survival of any state at all appeared to depend on coming to terms with the foreigners. In these circumstances the government attempted to secure faithful observance of the treaties wherever this could be done without outraging gentry sentiment. For a time—until the Tientsin Massacre—the government appeared to be making some progress in its effort to persuade the literati to accept limited institutional change and to follow Peking where foreign affairs were concerned.[a] But it was quite definitely a matter of persuasion. Restoration leaders were aware that they governed effectively only with the consent of the governed; that the power of the literati to resist innovation was firmly based in the power of the literati over the people in a Confucian society.

The central government, high provincial officials, and the great literati could on the whole envision a process of gradual conservative modernization and accommodation, with changes in the outward form but not in the essential core of Chinese life. But the rank and file of the gentry were mired in a slough of trivia. With their eyes on the local scene and its immediate problems, they could not see through the millennial accumulation of detail to the enduring bases of the Confucian system. They insisted on the total preservation of the existing order, and in so doing precipitated its total loss.

[z] See Chapter X.
[a] See Chapter XI.

CHAPTER VIII

THE REHABILITATION OF THE CHINESE ECONOMY

THE TRADITIONAL POLITICAL ECONOMY

Economics was a major concern of all Chinese governments and had a place in the education of statesmen. What they studied, however, was closer to the "political economy" of the mercantilist age than to the "economics" we study today.[a] Economic questions were held to be inextricably intertwined with all the great questions of politics and morals. Statesmen believed that they could control economic developments and subordinate them to political purposes; in short, that economics could be made to follow politics rather than vice versa. Restoration economic policy, following the pattern of Restoration policy in other spheres of government action, was based on the assumption that the traditional economy could be made to flourish again by the intelligent adaptation of the traditional Chinese principles of political economy. The security of the agricultural producer was the essential aim of political economy in a country in which nearly the whole population derived its income directly from the land, and in which the land tax had traditionally provided the great majority of the state's funds. The principle "exalt agriculture" (*chung nung*), and its corollary "disparage commerce" (*ping shang*), had been emphatically reiterated in the Classics and Histories, and agriculture continued to be regarded as not merely the only feasible basis for the Chinese economy, but the only desirable basis.[1]

There was no notion, however, either of expanding agricultural production and increasing the agrarian-based revenues, or of a "prosperous" agrarian economy in the modern Western sense. The Restoration's goal was an austere

---

[a] This chapter is a survey of the economic policies of the Restoration government; it is not intended as a study of the structure and functioning of the late Ch'ing economy. The reader who feels that the material presented on the causes and consequences of these policies is insufficiently precise would do well to remember that the field has been scarcely explored, and that scholars today must still use the same records of which S. Wells Williams wrote long ago, "All these calculations are approximations, which, although easily made up, cannot be verified to our satisfaction" (*The Middle Kingdom*, I, 290–92), and of which Thomas Taylor Meadows wrote:

"My experience of the Chinese Empire teaches me that it is impossible to obtain from Chinese sources materials for Tables of the kind alluded to that are not worse than valueless; worse, namely, because they would misinform inquirers, while no Tables only leave inquirers uninformed.... Statistics could be furnished in large quantities, and in all the usual varieties, and the materials could be exhibited in Tables of different headings, one showing this, the second that, and the third the relation of this to that, and so forth; all this could be done if one were perfectly indifferent to furnishing what was false." *China. No. 4. (1864)*, p. 1.

and stable agrarian society in which a strongly inculcated ideal of frugality curbed the cost of government, the luxuries of the gentry, and the material aspirations of the peasantry.[2]

Where frugality was coupled with shrewd management, it was felt that no economic crisis could arise. So experienced and able a political economist as Wang Ch'ing-yün wrote in 1850:

> In these days all classes, high and low, are downcast, and alarmed at our poverty. Your Majesty's servant does not find ground for alarm. Without looking for additional means of producing wealth, let but that which the state possesses be properly administered, and what suffering will there be from poverty?[3]

The Ch'ing financial machinery, which in the main followed the Ming system, was cumbersome by modern standards, but it was highly developed and had proved effective in earlier times. When the government could maintain peace and provide conditions conducive to sound agricultural practice, it could raise the money it needed without putting intolerable pressure on the people.[b] The Board of Revenue and related offices, however, were poorly equipped to deal with the declining revenues and rising expenditures of a period of crisis.

Before the Hsien-feng period (1851–61), the four main sources of Ch'ing revenue had been the land tax, the grain tribute, the taxes on domestic commerce, and the salt monopoly. Such miscellaneous Ming taxes as the Ch'ing retained yielded too little to be of economic importance. The land tax alone had provided two-thirds of the total revenues. Its rate was fixed in perpetuity: in a series of edicts between 1712 and 1745 the Ch'ing had solemnly promised that it would never be raised.[4] The grain tribute quotas were also fixed, and the quotas for the customs and the salt monopoly could not easily be raised. In these circumstances the Ch'ing had relied in minor emergencies on the reserve accumulated in prosperous years, and on the sale of rank and occasionally of minor office.[5] Although the new expenditures required by the mounting domestic and foreign problems of the nineteenth century posed a real challenge to the old order, there was no recognition of the need for new and expanded sources of permanent revenue until well into the Kuang-hsü period.[6]

The very idea of developing commerce into an important source of revenue was unthinkable. The literati had always regarded as parasites all those, except of course themselves, who did not produce food directly; and fearing the development of a rich rival class, they had consistently and effectively fought against all development of commerce and industry.[7] State monopolies, price

---

[b] There had been deficits in the early decades of the Ch'ing period, but from the end of the seventeenth century to the middle of the nineteenth, regular reserves had been accumulated in prosperous years (Lo Yü-tung, *Chung-kuo li-chin shih*, Shanghai, 1936, I, 2–3).

regulation through the ever-normal granaries,[c] recurrent attacks on usury, punitive tax policies, and ideological molding had done their work well. Compared with the Chinese merchant class, the pre-Meiji Japanese merchant class was strong, and the late medieval European merchant class a colossus.

State measures aside, China's high degree of local self-sufficiency provided little incentive to the development of commerce. Although some agricultural specialization had long been recognized in the use of such terms as "silk districts" and "cotton districts,"[d] every village was expected to produce nearly every article it needed, and every family to work in many crafts. Gentry families as well as peasant families wove; Tseng Kuo-fan in his family letters inquired closely into the cloth output of the ladies of his household. Only in the silk-growing districts was there a relatively small group of professional specialists, people who did nothing but weave. The other "specialists"—potters, masons, carpenters, metal workers—were mostly farmers who in the slack seasons produced primarily for their own and their neighbors' use. Money existed, but it was not a money economy; fairs had developed widely from the late Ming on, but it was not a market economy. The stability of this "natural" economy was augmented by the general esteem for frugality, by the nonacquisitive ideal, by the real economic interdependence of peasantry and gentry, and by the relative security the system afforded to both classes.

The role of foreign commerce had traditionally been even more limited than that of domestic commerce. It was felt that no imports could make up for the drain of bullion and of such useful articles as tea and silk. Mining had existed from the earliest times, but its importance was still discounted in the nineteenth century, partly because of its disruptive social effects, partly from a moral feeling that since no one had planted mineral wealth, no one was entitled to harvest it.[8]

It can be argued that the proven technological bent of its people would have brought China to the threshold of the industrial age, except for the crushing weight of the state and of an ideology opposed to social innovation,[9] for "premodern" technology had been developed to a remarkable degree. Nineteenth-century observers noted, as had the Jesuits before them, that the Chinese "work mines, amalgamate metals, and work them in all sorts of ways—work them, in some instances, as the foremost nation of Europe *cannot*."[10] They could, for example, rejoin severed silver perfectly, carve agate, repair holes in cast iron, and handle stupendous sizes and weights with no more equipment than the wedge, the lever, and the wheel. The processes used in printing and in the manu-

[c] Grain, bought up in years of surplus and low price, was stored in these granaries, to be sold at fixed prices in years of scarcity and high price. For details see Lien-tching Lu, *Les Greniers publics de prévoyance sous la dynastie des Ts'ing*, Paris, 1932.

[d] I am indebted to Professor Motonosuke Amano for calling my attention to the use of such terms in Hsü Kuang-ch'i's *Nung-cheng ch'üan-shu* and similar sources.

facture of silk, tea, porcelain, and paper demonstrated their facility in practical invention. Hsiao-t'ung Fei has put the point succinctly:

> Knowledge of the natural world was knowledge for production and it belonged to farmers, craftsmen, and others who depended on it for earning their living. Ethical knowledge, on the other hand, was an instrument in the possession of those who used their minds to rule the people.[11]

Ch'ing policy not only did not depart from the time-honored principles of political economy, it carried them to new heights. As Western traders became more importunate, desperate efforts were made to forestall the development of a foreign trade of real importance. And internally, during the Ch'ing period as a whole,[e] the state encouraged the development of the small owner and established relatively strict controls over large landholders and their employment policies. Numerous latter-day special privileges were abolished as "un-Confucian," and there was a marked tendency for tenants to become full and free owners, in accordance with the traditional principles of political economy.[12]

ECONOMIC COLLAPSE DURING THE HSIEN-FENG PERIOD, 1851–61[f]

The economic stability—prosperity according to traditional standards—that had characterized the first century and a half of Ch'ing rule did not come to an abrupt end with the accession of the Hsien-feng Emperor. A slow deterioration in almost all fields had set in at the end of the eighteenth century.[13] Cyclical change in the economy appeared to follow the general pattern of the dynastic cycle;[g] the prosperity of the K'ang-hsi and Ch'ien-lung periods was followed by the private hardship and public deficits of the Chia-ch'ing and Tao-kuang periods. As rebellion increased, less land could be cultivated and there was less grain for the people. The state could not collect the full land tax, yet ever greater revenues were needed to provide for increased military expenditures. As waterworks were neglected and farmers recruited, the acreage of cultivated land declined further and in some areas famines began to occur.

The Ch'ing government, increasingly dependent upon corrupt and incompetent officials, faced additional economic problems created by the growth of foreign trade. Household industry, on which the peasant depended for essential supplementary income, was disturbed by imports of Western cotton cloth. Since these imports and others were paid for in silver, the price of silver rose and the value of copper cash expressed in silver declined from 1800 onward. Since taxes

---

[e] Although at the outset a number of large Ming estates were confiscated for the benefit of Manchus (Chu Po-k'ang and Chu Tzu-shou, *Chung-kuo ching-chi shih-kang*, Shanghai, 1946, Ch. 12), Manchu privilege was a minor aspect of Ch'ing land policy.

[f] On the general crisis of the Hsien-feng period, see Chapter II.

[g] See Chapter IV.

and other contributions were computed in silver, the hoarding of silver followed and forced its price still higher.[14]

The Taiping Rebellion dealt a shattering blow to the declining Ch'ing economy. The area of land under cultivation declined sharply, and according to some contemporary estimates the population declined by half:[15] "Vast tracts in the interior of China which were at one time covered by wealthy cities and cultivated fields are now wildernesses."[16] In all Anhwei, for example, only one fu, two chou, and three hsien were not devastated.[17] When eventually the once fertile and populous provinces of Kiangsu and Chekiang were recovered by the Imperial forces, Western observers were appalled at the vast stretches of abandoned land and at the plight of both landlord and peasant: "Their fields lie waste, and they have neither the means to till nor to plant them. . . . Many districts are almost as open to immigration as newly discovered countries."[18]

As military expenses soared, the land tax and the grain tribute—mainstays of the revenue—could not be collected in many of the richest areas of central China. For example, according to Thomas Wade:

> This province, Kiangsu, should contribute by law nearly 1,500,000 piculs, say 90,000 tons a year. The demand made on it in this year [1859] was but for 400,000 piculs and the Provincial Treasurer declared himself unable to promise more than 250,000 piculs. Even this quantity he has failed to make up. The land taxes are almost everywhere in arrears, and subscriptions, to be repaid in rank, as the local proclamations show, have yielded far less than the authorities had conceived themselves as entitled to expect.[19]

It was estimated that during the 1850's the Peking grain requirement was never more than one-third filled, and that by 1857 it was only one-tenth filled.[20]

In these circumstances, the hard-pressed Imperial government could seldom meet its normal obligations.[21] Public works were generally neglected.[22] As the situation deteriorated, often even the troops could not be paid.[23]

The remedies attempted were panic-born, halfhearted, and mutually inconsistent. A few tax increases were attempted,[24] but the government honored its commitment never to raise the land tax and continued the traditional policy of offering tax relief to distressed areas.[h] A new tax on commerce, the likin, was introduced, and the sale of rank was accelerated, but receipts were disappointing.

The value of copper in relation to silver continued to fall, and as supplies of copper from Yunnan were cut off by the Moslem Rebellion,[i] the value of rice in relation to copper also fell. In order to make his usual income in money, the peasant had to market an increasing amount of rice. Since the peasant sold his

---

[h] Karl Marx compared the Ch'ing tax remissions for 1853 to those offered Austria in 1848 ("Revolution in China and Europe," *New York Daily Tribune*, June 14, 1853, reprinted in *Marx on China*, London, 1951, p. 3).

[i] See Chapter VI.

rice for copper while silver remained the standard in which taxes were computed, the actual taxes he paid increased sharply.[25] In addition, beginning in 1853 the government was compelled to resort to a policy of deliberate inflation. Paper notes that inspired no confidence were introduced, and copper cash were reminted into coins of larger denomination. Iron cash were coined, counterfeiting became widespread, and by degrees all money except silver became virtually valueless outside Peking. By 1861 the value of Imperial notes had decreased to 3 per cent of face value, that of provincial notes to 4 per cent. The general lack of public confidence was reflected in the stagnation of Chinese business and in the exorbitant rate of interest that prevailed.[26]

THE GENERAL ECONOMIC PROGRAM OF THE RESTORATION

The Restoration period was as crucial in modern Chinese economic history as it was in China's political history. With the traditional economy apparently collapsing, and with new leaders in power who knew something of the triumphs of the Industrial Revolution in the West,[27] the time might have seemed ripe for a change (that it seemed so to Europeans in China we have seen earlier). Yet although the new government was an "enlightened government," concerned about the welfare of the people,[28] there was no attempt to lay the foundations of a modern economy, no economic program comparable to that of the Meiji Restoration in Japan.[29]

This does not mean that economic questions were slighted by Restoration leaders. On the contrary, Tseng Kuo-fan, Li Hung-chang, Tso Tsung-t'ang, Hu Lin-i, and some of their colleagues earned a place in the history of Chinese economic thought,[30] and not for quaint fantasies but for grappling with the realities of production and distribution. They were interested, however, in restoring the "strength and wealth" of the traditional economy, not in enhancing the strength and wealth of the country at the cost of its traditional institutions.[31]

Every act of the state in the realm of economics was judged by its contribution to the twin goals of traditional political economy: the finances of the state and the people's livelihood (*kuo-chi min-sheng*). This was not a new idea, but it was given a new emphasis in the Restoration period. Ch'ung-hou argued the case for developing irrigation in eastern Chihli in these terms, as did Su T'ing-k'uei the case for cultivating the old bed of the Yellow River. Increased expenditures toward the control of the Yellow River were justified in the same *kuo-chi min-sheng* terms: a flood destroyed the livelihood of the people over a vast area, and it led to banditry, then to rebellion, and eventually to pacification campaigns that were more costly to the state than engineering works. In newly recovered areas, the importance of giving due weight to both state finances and the people's livelihood was particularly emphasized.[32]

The improved method of collection by which Hu Lin-i reduced the land tax in Hupeh became a model, and rightly so; it seemingly promoted both the state's welfare and the people's. Shen Pao-chen was praised on the same grounds when he improved the method of collecting the Kiangsi land tax.[33] In the subsequent reduction of the Kiangsu land tax, which led to knottier problems, discussion centered on means of reconciling the two aims. Adam Smith would have approved these Confucian principles of public finance as eminently sound in the circumstances.

There are two reasons for emphasizing what Restoration officials meant when they said that the finances of the state and the people's welfare were mutually dependent and of equal importance in all calculations of economic policy. First, insistence on any such doctrine is rare in premodern autocracies. And second, the modern ring of the words[j] is deceptive. The Restoration conception of the welfare of the state and of the welfare of the people has very little in common with Western capitalist and socialist conceptions.

Restoration leaders, like their predecessors, saw agriculture as the only possible basis of the people's livelihood and the state's finances. They never questioned the priority of rural reconstruction. In one of his letters of instruction to local officials, Tseng Kuo-fan wrote:

> During the years of fighting, the livelihood of the gentry, merchants, and artisans has not been entirely destroyed; but as to the farmers, there is no man who is not in distress, no locality that is not in distress. If the farmers suffer too long, the fields will be barren and uncultivated. If the army has no food, it will certainly give trouble to the people. If the people have no food, they will certainly follow the bandits. If the bandits have no food, they will become roving bandits and create disorder on a large scale, and there will be no end to it. Therefore the first duty of hsien and chou magistrates today is to "exalt agriculture."[34]

To "exalt agriculture," however, meant to provide the people with the opportunity to survive by diligent farming; there was no notion that greater productivity, greater leisure, and a higher standard of living were in any way desirable. After pointing out that no government had survived without providing for the people, Prince Kung went on to praise frugality and condemn greed: "Teach the people frugality so that their incomes will suffice."[35]

It is important to note that the nonacquisitive ideal was *a fortiori* applicable to the gentry. Tseng Kuo-fan's diary and family letters are filled with such statements as "to build houses and buy land is an odious practice for officials"; the effort to accumulate property for one's sons and grandsons he also condemned.

---

j The ring is as modern to Chinese as to Western ears. "Min-sheng" became Sun Yat-sen's term for the third of the Three People's Principles, and was later widely used in both Nationalist and earlier Communist economic programs.

He sent stern instructions to his son concerning the proper behavior for the son's bride: the new daughter-in-law must proceed early to the kitchen and spend her leisure in weaving; she must on no account be allowed to believe that because she was born to wealth and high position she could avoid hard work.[36]

This was of course far from egalitarianism. The Confucian version of the nonacquisitive ideal enjoined upon a man the frugality appropriate to his class and circumstances; it counseled not against privilege or status, but against the socially disruptive effort to increase wealth. Among the great families and the small—whether of scholar, farmer, artisan, or merchant status—there was none that would not flourish if it were frugal, none that would not decline if it were extravagant.[37]

The government, like the gentry and people, was expected to curb extravagance and to avoid grasping for new sources of wealth. The pomp and glory of Imperial Peking notwithstanding, the state itself recognized the precept that luxury and waste were abhorrent, and that the search for new sources of wealth was morally reprehensible and would surely destroy the Confucian political economy. No government was ever farther from the notion that increasing production, increasing revenues, and increasing consumption are healthy signs.

Most Restoration memorials on economic problems began with a statement on the need for greater economy. As Wo-jen put it, the revenues of the state are fixed; if more were spent for an extravagant Imperial wedding, less would be available for the serious purposes of government.[38] Palace expenditures were the subject of constant criticism, and whatever steps were in fact taken, it is of some importance that the court was kept constantly on the defensive and invariably issued orders to eliminate unnecessary luxury.[39]

The genuine importance attached to frugality in government was illustrated in the Te-t'ai incident, which all the chroniclers and textbook writers have listed as one of the half-dozen great events of the Restoration, ranking with the suppression of the Taiping Rebellion and the founding of the Tsungli-yamen. In 1868 the censor Te-t'ai presented to the Throne a plan worked out by Kuei-hsiang, an official of the Imperial Household Treasury, whereby the palace gardens could be restored to their original state without using Treasury funds. The proposal was proceeding along routine channels through the Grand Secretariat, when suddenly a memorial from the Grand Council indignantly condemned it. According to the Grand Council, the plan proved to involve the ingenious increase of taxes in the area just outside Peking by taxing the acreage, the village, *and* the household. The final edict, which stripped Te-t'ai of office and banished Kuei-hsiang to Heilungkiang, declared the plan to be an extreme case of the loss of proper feeling, not "love of the people" but oppression. The Ming dynasty had increased taxes, the edict continued, but the Ch'ing had learned the lesson and would abide by the principle of perpetual nonincrease of taxes decreed by the earlier Ch'ing emperors.

Imperial extravagance may have continued, but it never passed unprotested. In 1872 (TC-11) the governor-general of Kiangsu, Kiangsi, and Anhwei, Li Tsung-hsi, urged the cessation of repairs to the Yüan-ming yüan, which had been destroyed by the allies in 1860, so that the grave problems remaining before China might be solved and restoration (*chung-hsing*) finally achieved.[40]

The principle of "disparaging commerce" was a natural corollary of the Restoration principles of exalting agriculture, anathematizing the profit motive, and extolling frugality. The rationale behind the principle was frankly stated by Hsü Tzu, a prominent historian and local official noted for his resistance to the Taiping Rebellion: "When the profits of commerce are small, those who plow and weave will be numerous." Hsü had observed that commerce was easier and more profitable than farming; where it flourished, the people left their looms and plows and flocked to the towns to trade. To Hsü and his generation this was demonstrable proof that the time-honored injunctions against commerce were essential to the protection of the agrarian Confucian society.[41]

Foreign trade was viewed as even more dangerous. There was not even the temptation of new and superior consumers' goods, for European exports did not rival in beauty and durability the products long available in China. That they were cheaper did not appear to statesmen of the time as an advantage if the lower prices meant the bankruptcy of China's cottage industry.

Most abhorrent of all were the machines for improved manufacture and communication. Restoration leaders cannot be accused of a primitive shying away from fearsome monsters. The new devices doubtless did appear demonlike to some countrymen, but official resistance to them was based on two reasoned convictions: (1) that an increase in their use would tighten the foreign hold on China, and (2) that the new means of easy private enrichment for Chinese merchants with foreign connections would destroy the stable, frugal, traditional ordering of society.

The Europeans who were pressing for economic modernization recognized as well as the Chinese who were resisting it what was at stake: nothing less than the whole of the traditional civilization. The *North China Herald* agreed with the mandarins on where the issue lay: "Experience has proved to them how insidious is the advance of Western civilization, how fatal to the stability of their national institutions."[42] And a promoter wrote:

> Shall we any longer mask the real face? . . . It is towards the extermination of so-called Chinese philosophy, and the extinction of the powers of the "literati," we must bend all our efforts, before the natural riches of one of the finest quarters of the globe can be brought to light and made use of for the mutual benefit of mankind.[43]

A half century later, when a series of efforts at conservative reform had failed, and modern machines and modern ideas had destroyed the Confucian society without providing a new structure of community and national life, the Restoration contention that preservation of the traditional civilization required unwavering opposition to economic modernization received inverted support from Li Ta-chao, co-founder of the Chinese Communist Party. Li taunted the leaders of a Confucian revival in 1920:

> If you can smash all the economic relations of the modern world and restore the ancient life of closed frontiers and self-sufficiency; if you can sweep out all Europe's material culture and its dynamic civilization, and restore the motionless life of antiquity, then of course the new ideas cannot develop.[44]

In 1920 the effort to shield China from the industrial age and its consequences was stupid. In 1860 it may have been futile, but it was not stupid.

The Restoration economic program was a series of efforts to revive the agricultural economy to a point where it could continue to serve as the mainstay of the people's livelihood and the state's finances. As the sections that follow will show, devastated lands were restored to cultivation and new lands were brought into cultivation, in part by water control. Some efforts were also made to increase the productivity per acre. At the same time the land tax was reformed, in the hope that a more equitable system might bear less heavily on the people and still yield adequate revenue.

Through the likin, the salt gabelle, and loans and contributions, the non-agricultural sections of the traditional economy were taxed as much as the traffic would bear, partly to increase revenues, partly to discourage commerce. China's new and growing foreign trade was lightly taxed only because the tariff was fixed by treaty. The maritime customs revenue proved quite useful to the Restoration government, but it did not occur to the government to encourage foreign trade in the hope of increasing revenues.

In the realm of monetary and fiscal policy, the currency was stabilized after a fashion, and the government tried to tighten its control over the collection and expenditure of revenues. But although government costs continued to rise, the rise was never recognized as marking the beginning of an era of perennially costly government. The new expenses were attributed to temporary emergencies; if frugality were observed, normal conditions would return, and a fixed and relatively light tax on a fairly stable level of agricultural production would once again suffice.

AGRARIAN POLICIES

Increase in the Area Under Cultivation. During the 1860's Chinese officials were primarily concerned with increasing the total area under cultivation, obviously a sound policy at a time when vast areas of arable land had been deserted and large population shifts were taking place. They were interested only slightly in increasing the per acre productivity, since traditional methods of cultivation were intensive; and not at all in increasing per capita production, since work on the land had to be found for millions of refugees, surrendered rebels, and demobilized soldiers.

The problem facing the Restoration government as rebellion receded was staggering. S. Wells Williams wrote:

> The face of China in 1865 was perhaps as wretched as that of Central Europe after the Peace of Westphalia; indeed a more general desolation could hardly be imagined. Nevertheless the rapidity with which its inhabitants not only resumed their occupations as best they could, but rebuilt dwellings and reorganized trade, startled even their habitual disparagers into praise and testified to the marvellous recuperative powers of this much despised civilization.[45]

Resettlement followed immediately upon military recovery all through the Yangtze valley and other devastated areas.[46] European eyewitness accounts confirm the official Chinese reports: "Within the year the settlement of the districts lately disturbed by the rebellion has proceeded. Accounts from Soochow and Hangchow as also from the provinces of Cheh-kiang, Anhwei, and Kiang-si speak of returning prosperity . . ."[47] The population of Kiukiang, for example, estimated at no more than eight thousand at the beginning of 1862, stood at forty thousand the following September. In the spring of 1864 agriculture was resumed in the Soochow area while the peasants were still living in sheds of matting. Obstructions in the river were removed, bridges were repaired, and produce from the surrounding area was reported pouring into the city even before martial law was relaxed.[48] By the end of 1866 Governor Ma Hsin-i could report that immigrants had poured into Chekiang and that agriculture and sericulture were in a satisfactory condition in all but the most seriously damaged areas of the province.[49]

Although this flow of population into the recovered areas was in part spontaneous, Ch'ing officials are entitled to considerable credit for the series of "homestead acts" by which they encouraged resettlement. Throughout the Kiangnan region, deserted lands were confiscated and resold at moderate prices. Preference was given to those with sufficient funds to purchase outright and to begin cultivation at once, but other refugees were offered land, seed, and equipment through loans whose terms made possible full repayment and clear title within three years. After interviewing families who had immigrated to Kiangnan from Hupeh, surprised Europeans admitted that this program "shows such a knowledge of political economy as we are not accustomed to connect with the ordinary transactions of the Chinese Government." Apparently in some instances land was given free to those able to undertake its cultivation.[50] In others the settlers were allowed to retain as much as 70 per cent of their crops.[51] Agricultural resettlement offices (*chao-keng chü*) were established to encourage group organization, to distribute seed grain and tools, and to supply the destitute with a monthly food grain ration until the first crop was harvested.[52] A general order was issued to all provincial officials to actively recruit displaced persons to cultivate land, and throughout the country placards appeared inviting the landless to migrate to areas where agricultural labor was needed.[53]

Although the initiative was nominally taken by such leading officials as Li Hung-chang in Kiangsu, Kiangsi, and Anhwei, and Tso Tsung-t'ang in Chekiang and Fukien, the co-operation of prominent local leaders figured largely in the success of the program.[k]

The reclamation of abandoned lands inevitably affected the system of land tenure. As the country recovered, many landowners and peasants who had fled to distant parts of China gradually returned to their native places. In Anhwei, for example, which had been a "wilderness studded with ruins," recovery was well under way in the hands of immigrants when many of the original owners reappeared; riots followed and the legal difficulties were virtually insoluble. The litigation was rendered more complex by the fact that often the landlord retained basic ownership only, leaving the peasant the right of perpetual cultivation and the privilege of selling this right as he chose.[54]

In all the resettled areas there was confusion, the clarity of land titles was obscured, and there was some black marketing in rebel land. In these circumstances it was difficult to carry out the announced policy of restoring the *status quo ante* wherever possible, with meticulous respect for land titles.[55] Although a society of freeholding farmers remained the Ch'ing goal,[56] some landlords seem to have taken over the holdings of relatives, friends, and neighbors who had disappeared. More than this, there was a tendency for "entrepreneurs" (*yeh-hu*) with funds to buy abandoned lands and to become unrestricted owners of land cultivated by tenants without perpetual rights.[57]

Ch'ing officials, whose immediate aim was to get the land back into production, failed to see that the tenants who poured into the devastated areas from land-hungry areas were glad enough for a chance to become farm laborers or tenants again, and that by unintentionally giving landlords a chance to increase their holdings the various homestead acts were creating a land system diametrically opposed to the Restoration goal.

---

[k] E.g., Li Chen-ling, who took first rank among the metropolitan degree-holders in 1840 (TK-20). His work in his native place, Chinkiang, was regarded as outstanding, and his appointment to the Hanlin Academy was deferred, at Li Hung-chang's request, until resettlement at Chinkiang could be completed (*Peking Gazette*, July 3, 1865, translated in *NCH*, Sept. 16, 1865).

The Restoration policy of opening new lands to cultivation along the frontier from Manchuria to Sinkiang was a corollary to the policy of reclaiming abandoned lands in the interior. In Manchuria this was a reversal of earlier policies designed to protect the Manchu homeland from agriculturalization and Sinicization, and to guard the nomadic tribal interests of the Mongols, whose support against the Chinese had been considered essential by earlier Ch'ing rulers. By the time of the Restoration, however, Manchu separate interests had largely disappeared.[1] Occasionally the old prohibitions were enforced, but the major effort was to use the underpopulated borders to resettle refugees, to increase food production, and to increase receipts from the land tax. Where "prohibited" land was found to be illegally cultivated, the Restoration government tended to legalize the cultivation and to tax it.[58]

In Sinkiang seeds, animals, and implements were provided in the hope of encouraging refugees to return, and to resume and extend their farming.[59] The colonization of Inner Mongolia, under the authority of the Mongol princes with the sanction of Peking, proceeded rapidly. In 1863 Jui-lin was authorized to invite farmers to begin cultivating more than 8,000 ch'ing (121,040 acres) of reserved Banner land near Weichang in Jehol. The land was sold on credit, and the program quickly expanded beyond the original limits planned. The government tried to prevent unauthorized, *ad hoc* extensions, but it made no effort to reverse the marked trend of the times toward the settlement of frontier areas.[60]

Although there were more reservations about the colonization of Manchuria than about the colonization of Mongolia or Sinkiang, the pattern was the same. Illegal cultivation was investigated and reported, but specific exceptions were increasingly allowed. The reasons for extending cultivation were the same as elsewhere: to increase the food supply, to increase taxes, and to settle refugees, wandering gold miners, and others who might otherwise cause trouble. As the trees were chopped down and wildlife disappeared, the Peking government was less concerned with keeping up the hunting preserves of early Manchu emperors than with collecting current and back taxes.[61]

The few existing studies of increases in the area of cultivated land during the Ch'ing period do not give separate figures for the 1860's. In 1869 the Board of Revenue merely reported that although the increases were gratifying, there was still room for improvement.[62] All that can be safely said is that the loss in acreage under cultivation caused by the rebellions was quickly made up, and that the long-term Ch'ing increase in acreage continued.[63]

Productivity Per Acre. The Restoration program to increase the area under cultivation was accompanied by a lesser program to increase the per acre production of food and textile fibers. In spite of China's traditional intensive agri-

[1] See Chapter IV.

cultural technology and the generally abundant supply of farm labor, improved methods of farming aroused quick interest when they seemed suited to the existing rural economy. Feng Kuei-fen urged the use of foreign agricultural machinery in the southeast, where after the rebellions "men are few and the land is a wilderness";[64] and at least one Chinese ordered a steam plow after seeing a picture of one.[65] Tso Tsung-t'ang devoted considerable attention to improved methods of cotton growing and sericulture in Chekiang and Fukien, and to cotton growing, animal husbandry, wool production, and reforestation in Shensi and Kansu.[66]

Under the direction of the provincial treasurer of Fukien, scientific sericulture was systematically promoted. Astonished foreign observers reported:

> Silkwinding machines and other appliances connected with the rearing of the insects, etc., have been got ready and are now placed at the disposal of the public. Persons of all classes within and without the city desirous of growing cotton, planting mulberries or rearing silk worms can obtain from the committee the seeds, insects, etc., as they may require together with the necessary appliances for rearing.[67]

There was certainly no chance of revolutionizing Chinese agriculture by introducing improved methods of cultivation; cultivation was already far too intense for that. But it is worth noting that there was apparently little resistance to such technological improvements as were feasible.

Water Control. Water control could make possible the cultivation of arid or submerged lands[68] and could multiply the yield of marginal lands. A long period of decreasing attention to waterworks had preceded the years of rebellion; during those years the dikes of virtually every river and lake in China had broken.[69] Hence the repair of old waterworks and the construction of new and improved systems became a cardinal point in Restoration planning.

"A mou reclaimed is a mou gained" was Ch'ung-hou's reaction to the waste lands of eastern Chihli, where the great waterworks of earlier periods had gradually fallen into disrepair in the course of the preceding century.[70] Pien Pao-ti reported that between Tientsin and Ningho water control would make arable 15,000 acres of grain land where there was now no sign of human habitation.[71] Plans were approved for constructing waterworks to reclaim a further 60,000 acres in two other circuits of Chihli, and for experimental irrigated rice culture elsewhere in Chihli.[72] Similar programs were undertaken in Shantung, Shensi, Szechwan, and other provinces.[73]

Waterworks of the Restoration period were of a wide variety of types. There were reservoirs, often built at considerable cost with stone brought from a distance.[74] In the coastal provinces sea walls had to be repaired to prevent the inundation of farm lands with salt water.[75] One of the sea walls was intended to protect not agriculture but the stocks of materials at the Foochow Shipyard.[76] Inevitably a disproportionate amount of effort was expanded on minor construction designed to prevent floods near the Imperial palaces and tombs.[77]

Attention was concentrated, however, on possible ways of preventing the perennial ravages of the Huai and Yellow rivers. In 1866 (TC-5) considerable interest was aroused by the publication of a book advocating the return of the Huai River to its old bed. In the following year the author, one Ting Hsien, persuaded the officials with jurisdiction over the Huai valley[m] to set up a general office in charge of Huai engineering.[78]

The great water control problem of the Restoration, as of all periods of Chinese history, was the control of the Yellow River.[79] In the early nineteenth century the Yellow River was following its southern course, reaching the sea on the south side of the Shantung peninsula as it had for centuries.[80] A serious rise in its bed was noticed but ignored, and between 1851 and 1855 the river made a series of disastrous shifts to a northern course. Large areas of fertile farm land were lost, lines of military communication were broken, and the vital Grand Canal became dangerous and even unnavigable at many points.[81]

At the outset of the Restoration provincial officials launched a series of efforts both to lower the bed and to rebuild the dikes.[82] In 1864 T'an T'ing-hsiang and the censor Hu Chia-yü memorialized on the importance of extending this work regardless of the high cost.[83] In 1866, after further floods, the governor of Shantung, Yen Ching-ming, inaugurated an ambitious public works program, using the labor of refugees from the flooded areas.[84] This program was later carried forward by Ting Pao-chen.

The proposals and reports issued during these years show a growing awareness of the magnitude of the total problem of controlling the river, and of the need for a co-ordinated large-scale program.[85] Early in 1867 the governor-general of Chihli put forward a multiprovince plan,[86] and later in the year Tseng Kuo-fan presented a master plan for returning the river to its southern bed. Contemporary foreign observers considered his blueprint bold and technically sound and found it "a refreshing contrast to the apathy which appears so generally to characterize the Chinese Government and its subordinates."[87]

Tseng, with his experience in the highest central and provincial posts and with his influence over all factions, was groping for a new formula for co-ordination, one that would reconcile ultimate central control with regional initiative and responsibility. The centralist early Ch'ing had increased the authority of

---

[m] The governor-general of the Kiangsu, Kiangsi, and Anhwei, Tseng Kuo-fan; the director-general of the grain transports, Chang Chih-wan; and the governor of Kiangsu, Kuo Po-yin.

the director-general of the Yellow River in an effort to create workable machinery for administering multiprovince, multipurpose waterworks;[88] but this post had steadily declined in importance in the decades prior to the Restoration, when many of its functions were taken over by the provincial governments of Chihli, Shantung, and Honan. With the Restoration there was a clamor to abolish the post of director-general, since "at the present time all are people's dikes; there are no government works."[89]

Tseng's effort at a compromise solution failed. Nothing was done in time to check the great flood of 1867–68,[n] and after a brief flash nothing further was heard of Tseng's master plan for the Yellow River. Apparently it was never repudiated; it was simply not carried into effect, possibly because of mounting expenses in the campaign against the Nien-fei. The general office for the control of the Huai, unable to compete with the armies for funds, also suspended activity, and water control continued to be dealt with in piecemeal fashion.[90]

Reform of the Land Tax. In Restoration economic policy, adjustment of the land tax and grain tribute systems was second only to the resumption and extension of cultivation in its importance to both the state's finances and the people's welfare. This section refers primarily to the land tax, but many of the same problems were raised, often in the same documents, in connection with the grain tribute. The grain tribute quotas, like those of the land tax, were in many areas excessive, and their reduction was urged. In both the grain tribute and the land tax, levies beyond the quota were commonplace, and the great families abused their influence. In both cases the method of collection was inefficient and costly, and investigation and control were difficult.[91] In the grain tribute there were in addition special problems that arose from the capital's dependence on grain shipments from the provinces.[92]

In Chinese histories the reduction of the Kiangsu land tax is invariably listed as one of the half dozen great events of the Restoration era. This was, however, by no means the sole instance of land tax reduction: the reduction for the whole country has been estimated at 30 per cent.[o] It was an axiom of the Restoration

---

[n] See Chapter VII.

[o] In these estimates for the whole country, the distinction between reduction in rates and quotas and decline in receipts from other causes is not always clear. Since the comparisons are between the period before the outbreak of great rebellions and the period following their suppressions, inability to collect taxes in rebel territory does not figure as a source of error. In some instances decline in quotas may have resulted from decline in production as well as from the intent to relieve the population. It is clear, however, that there was a substantial intentional reduction, and that this intentional reduction was a special characteristic of the T'ung-chih reign: note the concentration of documents of T'ung-chih date in the land tax sections of all the classified collections of Ch'ing documents. (Lo Yü-tung, "Kuang-hsü ch'ao pu-chiu ts'ai-cheng chih fang-ts'e," *Chung-kuo she-hui ching-chi shih chi-k'an*, I, 2 (1933), pp. 189 ff.; and Wu T'ing-hsieh, *Ch'ing ts'ai-cheng k'ao-lüeh*, 1914, p. 18b.)

that political control could not be effectively reasserted until the burden of the land tax was lightened and more equitably distributed.[p]

In 1723 the land and poll taxes had been fused into a single tax, the *ti-ting yin*.[93] Shortly thereafter, as noted above, this tax was fixed by Imperial edict, never to increase. However, "special" taxes on land began almost immediately, and early in the Hsien-feng period there was inaugurated the notorious surtax on land (*t'ien-fu fu-chia shui*), which did not fall within the purview of the Ch'ing's self-restraining edicts.[q]

With the spread of the Taiping and other rebellions, the government's total land tax receipts declined sharply owing to loss of territory and rupture of communications. The provincial treasurer of Kweichow, for example, reported a steady decline from 1854 on, until finally "the treasury was as empty as if scoured."[94] In these circumstances, the areas still under Ch'ing control found themselves subject to desperate and unprincipled *ad hoc* levies.[95]

The new Restoration government was alert to the dangers of this situation and responsive to local pressures. Taxes were widely remitted or reduced on an emergency basis. Day by day and year by year edicts ordered paternal tax concessions to areas that had suffered from flood, drought, and war.[96] Although the request for a tax reduction usually originated with the stricken area, Peking also took the initiative by inviting such requests[97] or by refusing to authorize a levy contemplated by officials in a distressed area.[98]

More important, the regular land tax rates were by degrees reduced in certain areas.[99] Hu Lin-i set the pattern in his reduction of the Hupeh land tax.[100] In the spring of 1864 Governor Yen Ching-ming secured the abolition of the Shantung land surtax.[101] Ma Hsin-i secured concessions for Kinhwa fu in Chekiang;[102] Tso Tsung-t'ang for Shaohing, Ningpo, and the Hang-Chia-Hu circuit[103] (comprising Hangchow, Kashing, and Huchow); Jui-lin and Chiang I-li for Canton;[104] and so forth.

The Restoration's agrarian policy, and indeed the general issue of the feasibility of conservative agrarian reform in modern China, were epitomized in the reduction of the Kiangsu land tax. Step by step rates were reduced in virtually all counties of the province.[105] The history-making case was the reduction of the

---

[p] E.g., memorial of the censor Ting Shou-ch'ang: "In my opinion, if we wish to chill the courage of today's bandits, we must first win back the hearts of today's people; if we wish to win back the hearts of today's people, we must first reduce the heaviest tax rates." (*Chiang-su sheng chien-fu ch'üan an*, 1866, Ch. 2, p. 4b.) See also the memorial of the censor Wang Tao-yung, *CHTI*, Ch. 3, pp. 7–8b.

[q] Between 1724 and 1812 the reported acreage under cultivation increased by about 15 per cent, while the reported receipts from the land tax increased about 24 per cent (my estimates, based on tables in Wang Ch'ing-yün, *Hsi-ch'ao chi-cheng*, Ch. 3, pp. 20–22). Unfortunately no figures are given for the period after 1850. See also Executive Yuan, Rural Reconstruction Commission, *T'ien-fu fu-chia-shui tiao-ch'a*, Shanghai, 1935, pp. 19–24.

land tax in the Su-Sung-T'ai circuit; so important did the government consider this move that it dispatched the edict of authorization at a speed of 500 li per day—an express rate ordinarily reserved for orders to armies in campaign—and published the documents on the case amid extraordinary fanfare.[106]

In the Yangtze valley, particularly in the Su-Sung-T'ai area, special taxes on land had increased steadily and disproportionately for centuries,[107] but before 1820 there had been no outspoken opposition to them. Flourishing silk production had enhanced the general prosperity of the area; moreover, the near-by Manchu garrisons were at that date still an effective police force.[108] However, as the rural economy declined in the course of the Tao-kuang period and the feebleness of the Manchu garrisons became patent, there were popular riots and collection of the full quota became increasingly difficult. Since this was the region that had suffered most from the Taiping Rebellion, the Restoration government favored it with especially swift remedial measures.

The formal proposal for the reduction of the Su-Sung-T'ai circuit land tax was made by the director of the Court of Imperial Entertainments, P'an Tsu-yin, and a supervising censor of the Fukien circuit, Ting Shou-ch'ang.[109] In typical Restoration phraseology they urged that the proposed new land tax regulations would be in accordance with the changing times, and would benefit both state and people.[110] Li Hung-chang and Tseng Kuo-fan memorialized in support, citing the abnormally heavy tax rates in the area and its present devastation. The area's high proportion of untaxed government land, which had mounted steadily, added to the difficulties of the private landowners who carried the tax load.[111] An edict of July 7, 1863, authorized the reductions in principle and established an office to work out the details.[112]

Much of the credit for the political and economic insight evident in the handling of the Kiangsu land tax reduction belongs to Feng Kuei-fen. It was he who insisted on a really substantial reduction in the basic rates, approximately two-thirds, and who distinguished most carefully between optimistic general orders to reform and specifically effective procedures.[118]

The central government was constantly and correctly suspicious that authorized tax reductions might not be carried into effect. It was less important, Peking declared, to reduce the legal rate than to reduce the amount actually paid by the people. At the time some lands paid no taxes[r] while other lands paid taxes far

---

[r] Unreliable li-chia officials were responsible for compiling the tax registers. Although much of the unregistered and hence untaxed land was in the frontier provinces, there was a great deal in China proper. According to a Board of Revenue memorial of 1872 (TC-11), reviewing the period since 1854 (HF-4), some 20,000 acres of "black land" had been discovered within the metropolitan prefecture itself and subsequently registered (*WHTK*, p. 7528). For further materials, see *ibid.*, pp. 7519, 7521. For the procedure in a specific case, see edict of Aug. 2, 1868, *SL-TC*, Ch. 235, pp. 29b–30.

above the legal rates, the excess being pocketed by the collectors.[114] On one occasion, Ting Jih-ch'ang, having discovered that the yamen clerks were misrepresenting the legal rates, countered by publicizing the rates more widely.[115]

Abuses in collecting the land tax were hard to discover and correct, since the collectors were not Imperial agents but officers of the li-chia system, in which the influence of the leading landowners was paramount.[116] However, the li-chia officers were not entirely independent; they operated under the authority of local and provincial officials, who were ordered to prevent the wealthier families from escaping their just share of the tax quota. At this period it was not revolutionaries but the Imperial government itself that railed at the "tax monopolies of the big families."[117]

In view of the failure of conservative land reform in modern China, it would be easy to underestimate the signal importance of the Restoration accomplishment. In the six provinces of the Yangtze valley the land tax was lowered by some ten million taels per annum,[118] to the vast benefit both of human well-being and of the land recovery program.[119] At the same time, the state's tax receipts from the area were safeguarded by an accelerated campaign against corruption.[120] Both the state's revenues and the people's welfare appeared to have been served.

And yet the Restoration reforms obviously failed to provide a viable land system for modern China, since after twenty or thirty years of growing prosperity and stability, the old evils reappeared more acutely than ever. The weaknesses in the program that contributed to its failure appear to have been as follows, in reverse order of importance:

(1) The legislation was imperfectly drafted. The obnoxious miscellaneous taxes were not rationalized, and the continuing high price of silver, in which the taxes were in the end paid to the government, nullified a portion of the benefit.[121]

(2) The systematic national land survey and graduated tax scale urged by Fêng Kuei-fen—and independently by Robert Hart—were ignored.[122]

(3) The land program of the Restoration, like all other programs of the time, depended for its effectiveness on capable officials. In their obsession with government by "men of ability," Restoration leaders did not think in terms of impersonal systems that would work reasonably well regardless of who staffed them. In the early years, when officials of immense personal authority could get their orders carried out with enthusiasm along the whole line down to the county magistrates,[123] the system worked well. Unfortunately, as in other eras of Chinese history, the concentration of talent was short-lived; the bureaucracies of the generations following were run-of-the-mill, and their more inconvenient orders were easily sidetracked in the bypaths of Chinese administrative procedure.

(4) The fatal weakness of the Restoration land program was its failure

to deal with the growing problem of tenantry and the larger landowners' abuse of their position. Virtually every official was concerned with means of taxing *owners* according to a just and uniform scale of rates,[124] but only Feng Kuei-fen saw the urgency of reducing land *rents* as well. In the 1863 documentation on the Su-Sung-T'ai circuit land tax reduction there was no mention of tenants. In 1868 limited rent reductions for three counties in Kiangsu were ordered on Feng's insistence, but apparently these were the only such reductions.[125]

RESTORATION ATTITUDES TOWARD TRADITIONAL COMMERCE

Despite its limitations, the Restoration land program was a general program; it encompassed production and distribution, the peasant's income and the state's revenues, the long term as well as the short term. For the nonagricultural sections of the economy—deemed parasitic excrescences, economically trivial, socially and politically harmful—there was no general program at all.[s] The people engaged in these pursuits remained people, and as such were entitled to a little of the all-embracing compassion of the Throne; but the pursuits themselves were entitled to no encouragement or protection. If the state could tap some of this wealth, well and good, for that much of the tax burden would be transferred from agriculture. If the tapping destroyed the source of the wealth, so much the better. All circumstances affecting the prosperity of agriculture were the proper subject of earnest consideration; what circumstances might affect the development of trade and manufacture was never even formulated as a question. In the Restoration view, the likin, the sale of rank, loans, and up to a point the salt administration were little more than convenient instruments for the *ad hoc* seizure of private wealth.

The Likin and Other Commercial Taxes. Commercial taxes had been heavy at the beginning of the Ch'ing period, but they were gradually lightened from the K'ang-hsi reign onward, along with taxes on agriculture, in an effort by the Ch'ing to consolidate the loyalty of its alien subjects. However, as government expenses mounted in the mid-nineteenth century, increased taxes on commerce offered the obvious remedy.[126]

By far the most important of the taxes on commerce was the notorious likin, devised in 1853 by Lei I-hsien, the commander of a local anti-Taiping force near Yangchow. In 1854 the central government authorized the collection of the likin throughout Kiangsu, and by 1857 it was in force in most of China. Likin receipts provided perhaps one-third of the support of the troops that suppressed the Taiping Rebellion.[127]

The likin was a tax—nominally *ad valorem*—on the sale of goods; since it was most often collected on goods being transported or otherwise offered for

---

[s] With the partial exception of the salt system. See below, in the present chapter.

sale but not yet sold, multiple taxation of the same goods was commonplace. Unlike the traditional taxes, the likin was spent as it was collected by local and provincial officials, with little effort at systematic reporting.[128]

Criticism of the likin began almost immediately, chiefly on the ground that the lack of supervision encouraged corruption. In 1861 the Board of Revenue made its first and last effort to set up a centrally controlled likin system for the whole country. The procedures it promulgated were not followed, and only one or two provinces reported collections.[129] The reforms attempted thereafter were less ambitious.

Demand for the abolition of the likin increased after the recapture of Nanking seemed to herald an era of decreasing military expenditures. The chief spokesman against the likin was Ch'üan-ch'ing, senior vice-president of the Censorate. He argued that all the special war taxes had given rise to abuses, could not be brought under central control, and were no longer necessary; that with the return of peace the traditional taxes should provide adequate revenue. He also expressed concern over the mounting popular opposition to the likin in areas such as Canton, where commercial interests were prominent.[130]

The defenders of the likin did not deny these abuses; they had never regarded the likin as anything more than a temporary tax, to be abolished as soon as the revenue it provided could be spared. They argued simply that the revenue had continued to prove essential, and that what was necessary was an effort to check the worst abuses.

There was general agreement on the importance of preventing the mushrooming of small branch likin stations, which were the most difficult to supervise. Lo Ping-ch'ang and Mao Ch'ang-hsi argued that abuses would be limited if only the provinces and not the counties were authorized to collect the likin.[131] In response to this view, an edict of August 31, 1864, ordered the abolition of all branch likin stations, and stricter control of the major stations until such time as the military situation permitted their abolition.[132]

When this order proved only partially effective, edicts continued to announce that the collection of the likin by local officials was illegal.[133] Yet a large number of branch likin stations were in fact closed during the late T'ung-chih period, and the administration of the remainder was apparently somewhat improved.[134] According to Beal, the Restoration saw "the nearest approach to the abolition of *likin* attained during the Ch'ing period."[135] This was a typical Restoration achievement: no drastic changes were made, yet considerably more was accomplished than in the decades that followed. The worst abuses were checked, and a return to the days before the likin was necessary seemed imminent.

The likin has been frequently condemned as providing regional warlords with financial independence; as throttling the development of Chinese capitalism and indeed of the whole national economy; as the major source of the subsequent paralyzing corruption of the bureaucracy; and as designed to plague foreigners. It has less often been noted that the likin was supported by some of China's most distinguished statesmen, on grounds that were far from unreasonable in terms of Restoration aims. Its proponents—among them Tseng Kuo-fan, Lo Ping-chang, Mao Hung-pin, Kuo Sung-tao, and Liu K'un-i—argued that agriculture was carrying too heavy a burden, that the comparatively easy profits of commerce were not contributing their share to mounting military expenses; and that although the merchants might chafe, the people welcomed the likin.[136] The only alternative to the likin, these men argued, was an increase in the land tax, and this was unthinkable. History proved them right, for when after seventy-five years of agitation the likin was finally abolished in 1931, commerce was "freed," but the land surtax, borne largely by the peasantry, soared.[137]

The likin was by no means the only tax in force on commerce.[138] According to the supervising censor Wang Hsien-ch'eng, the special shop tax and the special household tax were more burdensome to the people of Kiangsu than the likin.[139] The variety of commercial taxes and the tendency to regard all goods in sight as fair game[t] resulted in multiple taxation, because the same goods were made subject not only to a number of different taxes but to the repeated levying of the same tax.[u]

The Chinese complained about the commercial taxes because there were no enforceable regulations for their collection, not because of their adverse effect on the general development of Chinese commerce. Only foreigners, with their very different views, thought in the latter terms, and their statements were ambiguous. On the one hand, they declared the taxes deadly not only to the development of their own enterprises[v] but also to Chinese businesses.[140] On the other, they testified abundantly to a revival of Chinese commercial life despite the tax system;[141] according to one foreign report, explaining a decline in land values and trade in extraterritorial Shanghai, "the thousands of natives who thronged the streets of the foreign settlements at Shanghai shook off the enforced yoke of cleanliness and municipal ordinances, and hastened back to dirt, liberty and Soochow."[142] These reports are not consistent with the notion that crippling commercial taxation destroyed the possibility of profitable Chinese business. If

---

[t] "The Chinese Government, while they come upon the moneyed interest in the way of forced loans and contributions, think, like the Americans, an increased tariff a good way of meeting extraordinary expenditure; and the people are of the opinion that indirect taxation, by imposts on articles of consumption not absolutely necessary to their existence, presses more lightly upon them than any other." (*NCH*, July 31, 1868.)

[u] It was said that P'eng Yü-lin verified the situation by traveling incognito in a small empty boat; taxes were nonetheless demanded (Ch'ai O, *Fan-t'ien-lu ts'ung-lu*, Ch. 5, pp. 24–25). For reports of similar occurrences at the Ch'ung-wen gate of Peking, see *SL-TC*, Ch. 217, pp. 11b–12.

[v] See Chapter XI.

few Chinese reports suggest any such revival, it must be remembered that commerce was simply not the subject of reports.

The Restoration government had no policy of encouraging the revival of commerce; nor did it hesitate to adopt any otherwise desirable measure solely on the ground that it would injure commercial interests. Yet clearly it did not embark on a general program designed to throttle commerce. In the first place, any such drastic action would have led to trouble, particularly with foreigners and their Chinese protégés, and the Restoration government wanted no added trouble. Second, the Restoration leaders' training did not teach them how to cope with commercial matters, except in the most elementary way. Third, and most important, Restoration leaders did not spend much time thinking about commerce, not even about its evils. After a few disparaging remarks and punitive orders, their attention returned to agriculture. Commerce was not worthy even of systematic eradication.

The Salt Monopoly.[w] Unlike the likin, the salt monopoly was considered a permanent feature of the Ch'ing economy; the documents on its operation and on Restoration efforts to reform it are voluminous. Yet the salt program of the time, unlike the land program, seemed to lack guiding principles. Reports and proposals concerning land, for all their intricate detail, were organized around a few main ideas and aims; the writers had their subject in hand. Salt documents, by contrast, were scarcely more than a vast welter of unorganized detail on administrative abuses, high prices, loss of revenue, excess profits, and bankruptcy.[143] There were seldom clear lines of argument that appealed to accepted axioms of political economy,[x] for the salt monopoly, though often rationalized, had never been an honored Confucian institution. On the contrary, throughout the ages the appeal to Confucian principles had been made chiefly by its opponents.

Prior to the nineteenth century the transportation and sale of salt had been the monopoly of a small group of designated salt merchants in each area, who worked closely with the officials, were heavily taxed, and were extremely influential. For example, eight great licensed salt merchants dominated the trade and banking of the whole Huai-nan area. For the Ch'ing period as a whole, salt pro-

---

[w] Outside of agriculture and minor retail trade, the traditional Chinese economy was dominated by monopolies. It was generally taken for granted that the right to engage in any substantial enterprise should be licensed by the state, that a considerable proportion of the earnings should go to the state, and that in return the right of exploitation should be exclusive. Only the salt monopoly was involved in the general economic policy of the Restoration, but the granting of other monopolies was a popular form of raising revenue, and some of them, notably the Formosa camphor monopoly, caused international complications.

[x] Would-be reformers of the Szechwan salt system, for example, appealed merely to an edict of 1651 that had ordered strictly just collection of the salt taxes and provided a popular right of appeal through the Censorate (*Ssu-ch'uan yen-fa chih*, chüan shou, pp. 1–1b). This is in sharp contrast to the broad principles of political economy around which discussions of the land tax were organized.

vided one-fourth of all revenues, and the Huai-nan area provided 40 per cent of this.[144] The system, rotten from the middle Ming, had virtually collapsed by 1830.

In 1832 the great salt reformer T'ao Chu[y] introduced the salt ticket (*p'iao-yen*) system, under which anyone could buy a ticket (*p'iao*) to transport and sell salt (*yen*).[145] The purpose of the ticket system was to break the monopoly of the hereditary salt merchants and to increase sales, thus making possible a reduction in tax rate and price without loss of revenue.[146]

According to the new system, the producer of salt paid a special rent or tax on the land he used, and deposited the salt he produced on it at a government depot where it was purchased by a salt merchant. The merchant kept on hand a number of tickets of widely varying costs, which permitted him to buy from one hundred to five hundred catties of salt per ticket. He sold the salt thus purchased on a designated scale of rates in designated areas.[147]

Although the ticket system spread rapidly, it failed to become a uniform system for the country. Portions of various older systems remained in force in some areas; in others there was a tendency for the new purchasers of tickets to become lesser monopolists in their turn; in still others the government itself sold the salt directly.[148] Any remaining vestige of coherence in the Ch'ing salt system was destroyed by the Taiping Rebellion. In some areas production was wrecked and equipment destroyed or scattered; in others flourishing production was equally disastrous, for there was no means of transporting the salt to the areas in which its sale was licensed.[149] On the eve of the Restoration the salt merchants were bankrupt, the revenue was inadequate, and the supply to consumers was short.[150]

Restoration memorials on the reform of the salt system presented a bewildering mass of detailed proposals applicable to specific cases only; for as Tso Tsung-t'ang put it, "the evils are not of one day or of a single origin." There were remnants of all the varying systems that had prevailed in varying areas at varying periods. Not even the abuses were uniform.[151]

In principle the enforcement of the ticket system was the Restoration goal.[152] The most generally accepted view was well stated by Chih-kang after he had traveled down the Grand Canal with Burlingame en route to the Occident.[z] Under the ticket system, said Chih-kang, salt is easy to buy, the people are benefited, and the revenues reach the government; under the older licensed monopoly (*yin-yen*) system, the officials of the salt monopoly grow rich, but salt is expensive, smuggling is encouraged, and there is little benefit to the state.[153]

---

[y] T'ao Chu is regarded as one of the three great salt reformers of all Chinese history, the other two having lived in the Ch'un-ch'iu and T'ang periods respectively (Tseng Yang-feng, "Chung-kuo yen-cheng chih tung-hsiang," *Tung-fang tsa-chih*, XXXIV, 7 (1937), 77–78).

[z] See Chapter XI.

In practice, however, the adjustments of the principle to particular circumstances were so extensive as to obscure the principle being adjusted. Tseng Kuo-fan, for example, granted that Tso Tsung-t'ang's application of the ticket system in Fukien and Chekiang had broken up the older monopolies, but argued that the system's spirit had been lost since in disturbed times only the big merchants were in a position to obtain tickets and engage in the trade.[154]

Tseng himself, perennially eclectic, attempted a compromise, the so-called license-ticket (*yin-p'iao* or *p'iao-fan*) system, in which the tickets were valid for a longer period and for a number of transactions and in which the areas of sale were strictly fixed. Tseng seems to have favored licensing a larger number of salt merchants than the older monopoly system had licensed, so as to diffuse the profits somewhat; but a smaller number than the original ticket system licensed, so that smuggling could be more tightly controlled. His system was designed to protect salt merchants by guaranteeing a relatively high selling price, by providing official assistance in transportation, and by reducing the amount of capital required to engage in the trade, but at the same time, to prevent them from becoming too rich or powerful.[155]

Unfortunately Tseng's longer-term tickets quickly came to be regarded as permanent licenses, valid for the lifetime of the holder and even inheritable. When receipts from the sale of tickets declined in consequence, Li Hung-chang tried another adjustment: he attempted to increase the number of occasions on which the purchase of tickets could be required and yet at the same time to supervise the system more closely.[156] Apparently only Feng Kuei-fen advocated fundamental reform of the whole salt system with a view to increased sales at lower prices with a minimum of government controls.[157]

The practical operation of the salt monopoly during the T'ung-chih period is an even more confused subject than the conglomerate proposals to reform it. Large-scale and organized salt smuggling is attested to by the campaigns against the "salt bandits."[a] Smuggling on a small scale was presumably universal, since the law allowed any "poor" person under fifteen or over sixty years of age to deal in forty catties of contraband salt per day without penalty.[158]

Year in and year out the government had difficulties with the salt merchants. In some instances local officials demanded excessive payments from the merchants; in others the merchants refused to sell at the fixed prices. Sometimes the merchants refused to engage in the trade, and the officials had to handle transportation and sale directly.[159]

The government also had trouble with the salt producers. In one of the salt-producing districts of Chihli, for example, production fell sharply; the local

a See Chapter VI.

producers were said to fear that the Restoration effort to reimpose centrally controlled taxes and controls was the first step toward government confiscation of their salt fields.[160] There were a number of tax riots in the salt-producing areas of the lower Yangtze valley. In one of them an official was murdered ("executed") by a crowd carrying banners reading "The officials force the people to rebel."[161]

To all these domestic difficulties with the salt monopoly there were added difficulties with foreigners who longed to import cheap foreign salt. Alcock argued that without a monopoly salt would be cheaper; that the import duties on a larger volume of cheap foreign salt would yield more revenue than the existing taxes on a smaller volume of expensive domestic salt; and that the Chinese engaged in the salt trade could turn to some more secure and profitable occupation. He pointed out that all these benefits had followed when the restrictions on importing foreign salt into British India had been removed.

Prince Kung's reply to Alcock's proposal affords a nice illustration of some basic economic ideas of the Restoration. He insisted that revenues would decline because a treaty tariff on imported salt would be lower than the tax rate on domestic salt under the monopoly; he failed to grasp Alcock's point about increased volume. On the question of alternative and more profitable employment for Chinese salt producers and merchants, he wrote:

> Simple as the people of China are, these would certainly not submit to be, as the British Minister's despatch suggests, turned into cultivators of jute, abandoning a certain means of livelihood for wages in prospective, nor is there any quantity of vacant ground for them to till.[162]

The Tsungli-yamen's success in maintaining the salt monopoly in the face of foreign pressure[b] was a triumph of Restoration foreign policy, not of Restoration economic policy. Although the revenues from salt were somewhat increased, the full quotas were never reached. The grievances of producers, merchants, and consumers continued. Many improvements were attempted, sometimes with the revenue foremost in mind, sometimes with primary attention to the plight of the producers or merchants or consumers of a particular area.[163] But since there was no clear policy to which the specific measures had reference, controls were applied at cross purposes.[c]

Sale of Official Rank. The sale of rank and privilege was not new; since the unification of the Empire there had been arrangements for making payments

---

[b] See Chapters X and XI.

[c] Reluctance to overhaul the salt administration continued. On the eve of the Revolution of 1911 the cry was still "The salt administration should have been reformed long ago." (*Kuo-feng pao*, I, 5 (1910), 15.)

to secure advancement and to avoid penalties in the bureaucracy. The Ch'ing "contribution" (*chüan-na* or *chüan-shu*) system[d] for tapping commercial wealth[e] was, however, the most elaborate in Chinese history.[164] During the K'ang-hsi period *office* was sold, but for a short time only, in order to raise funds to suppress the Rebellion of the Three Feudatories. During the Ch'ien-lung period the elaborate Ch'ing system for the regular and systematic sale of *rank* was fully worked out.

As rebellion spread in the early nineteenth century, the sale of rank supplied revenue which, though relatively small in amount, was essential. As more ranks were offered for sale, the saturation point was quickly reached and the ranks began to decline in value. Larger and larger numbers were sold, yet the total receipts continued to decline.[165] The loss of revenue from this source was one of the factors leading to the introduction of the likin.

In theory the sale of rank did not undermine the examination system, for it did not put the purchaser in office; it merely enabled him to bypass some of the preliminary qualifications for competing in the examinations. In fact, however, there was no doubt that the sale of rank was tending to discredit the bureaucracy in the public eye and to reduce its effectiveness.[f] Restoration statesmen argued vociferously that revenue from this dubious source was of relatively little importance,[g] and that the effort to sell more and more ranks must cease. Rather than abolition of the system, however, they urged the sale of fewer ranks at a higher price.[166] In their eyes there was nothing objectionable about coaxing money from rich merchants with traditional ambitions by offering them honors without power, but clearly this could be neither an important source of funds nor a major means of mobilizing commercial wealth.

POLICIES TOWARD ECONOMIC DEVELOPMENT

Restoration leaders were as little interested in modernizing the Chinese economy as they were in encouraging the commercial elements in the traditional economy. Their aim was the restoration of the old order, and they were intelligent enough to see that most of the new Western techniques for speeding pro-

---

[d] Properly speaking, *chüan-shu* was one of the types of *chüan-na*, but the terms are generally used interchangeably (Lo Yü-tung, *Chung-kuo li-chin shih*, I, 3).

[e] Ambitious sons of the gentry normally had the education to proceed through the examinations in the normal way, scorned purchased rank, and seldom had large sums in cash to spare. The opposite often held for the sons of merchants. There were exceptions, however. I am indebted to Chaoying Fang for the information that Li Tz'u-ming sold his family land to purchase his early ranks.

[f] On the political aspects of the sale of rank, see Chapters V and VII.

[g] They were probably correct, but the facts of the case have not been adequately investigated. (Edwin G. Beal, "The Origin of *Likin*," ms. cited with author's permission, pp. 44–47.) T'ang Hsiang-lung, "Tao-kuang ch'ao chüan-chien chih t'ung-chi," *She-hui k'o-hsüeh tsa-chih*, II, 4 (1931), 432–44, gives numerous statistical tables, but the relation of the *chüan-na* revenue, which is given for various periods and areas, to the total revenue of those areas and periods, is not clear.

duction and distribution and increasing consumption were certain to disturb its stability.

Improved Communications. In the absence of modern communications, China's size and rugged terrain have posed serious problems to economic reformers. Officials of the sixties, however, were interested in improved communications only in so far as they might affect maritime defense and the food supply of the capital.[167] For these ends the reopening of the Grand Canal and the use of steamers in coastal waters seemed essential. Railways and telegraph lines, on the other hand, which were known to have opened up India to accelerated Western military and economic penetration,[168] seemed dangerous even to the practically minded.

The foreign argument that rapid communications were essential to the functioning of the free market fell on deaf ears. To Westerners of the time it was unthinkable that the price of rice land, for example, should be ten times as high near Ningpo as it was in the Tsinghwa district of the same province.[169] With railways, there would be no difficulty about the labor supply or market outlets for devastated Tsinghwa. Chinese officials, on the contrary, although they devoted great attention to resettlement, had no desire to make it possible for the Chekiang population to wander about uprooted in response to market shifts. Merchants who operated in accordance with the laws of supply and demand were "low fellows who aim at profit."[170]

The foreign argument that modernized communications were an inevitable part of general economic development, that one change must lead to another in an interrelated modern economy, was understood in a sense opposite to the sense in which it was put forth. Restoration leaders took it as a warning that one concession would lead to another until the whole fabric of the traditional economy was destroyed.

All Chinese officials agreed on the prime importance of reopening the Grand Canal and the lesser canals of the southeast. These were the traditional and safe routes for transporting rice, copper, and other tribute to the capital; they also provided a traditional and safe livelihood for hundreds of thousands of Chinese. Yet although canal works proceeded steadily throughout the Restoration, and although the effort to control the Yellow River was directed as much toward protecting the Canal from its ravages as toward preventing floods,[171] it proved impossible to restore the canal system to a point where it could perform its vital pre-1853 functions. Hence the emphasis in discussion shifted to the development of coastal transport to supply Peking and north China.

Opponents of the use of the sea route argued that it was vulnerable to foreign attack, that China was short of seagoing vessels, that long-established interests along the canal were threatened by the competition, and that riots among unemployed canal boatmen were increasing. Proponents of the sea route pointed out that canal transportation was slow, dangerous, and costly, and in the absence of effective control of the Yellow River, subject to total disruption. Moreover, since foreigners used the sea route, it seemed unreasonable to deny it to Chinese.[172] The issue was brought to a head by drought and flood in the north in 1867–68. It was essential that large quantities of grain be brought into the stricken areas by the quickest and cheapest transportation available. Provincial officials were ordered to ship the tribute rice by sea,[173] and even private grain merchants were authorized to use the tax-free sea route.[174]

Arguments in favor of the increased use of steamers in coastal waters easily won out.[175] Foreign merchant steamers had long sailed these waters, and Chinese naval steamers were coming into use.[h] Although Chinese merchants were for a time nominally forbidden to use steam transport, the paper prohibition was soon relaxed.[176] If steamers were used at all, they had to be used universally, for the junks could not compete in coastal waters.[i] Up and down the coast large junks were being sold for one-tenth or even one-twentieth of their cost.[177] The Chinese government's effort to check this trend by offering subsidies to junkmen in the form of higher rates for the transport of grain[178] was short-lived, for by the time it took effect the advantages of steam navigation in coastal waters had become generally recognized. By 1867 even the literati were traveling north by steamer for the examinations at Peking.[179]

Foreign proposals to use steamers on inland waterways met with far greater resistance.[j] Foreign steam navigation on rivers, canals, and lakes posed a military threat as well as a threat to the domestic economy, and to Chinese it seemed to offer no compensating advantages.[180]

Merchant shipping owned and managed by Chinese was slow to develop. The government was opposed, and little Chinese capital appears to have been available for investment; what capital there was for this purpose belonged chiefly to wealthy Chinese merchants of the port cities, who preferred to invest it in foreign shipping.[181] The accidents and misfortunes that marked the history of the Shanghai Steam Navigation Company, founded in 1862, were the accidents and misfortunes of British and American commercial expansion.[182] They had little to do with the rehabilitation of the Chinese economy.

The dismal history from 1872 on of the first Chinese enterprise in this field,

---

[h] See Chapter IX.

[i] According to Consul Gibson's report on the trade of Tientsin: "The more enlightened Chinese merchants no longer patronize them. . . . Thus the competition of foreign vessels, coupled with the operations of the insurance offices, is rapidly driving the junk off the face of the ocean." (*China. No. 4. (1864),* p. 25.) See also, Consul Caine's report on the steady decline of the junk trade at Swatow, June 20, 1863 (*ibid.,* p. 55).

[j] See Chapter XI.

the China Merchant Steam Navigation Company, suggests that Restoration leaders were not missing any good bets in their reluctance to encourage such developments.[183]

The proposed introduction of railways raised more serious problems than steam navigation, even on inland waters. The most commercially minded Chinese were gravely alarmed at the prospect of unemployment, disturbance of the graves, expropriation of precious farm land for rights of way, virulent opposition from the literati and peasantry, and the increase of foreign influence. Although foreigners often conceded that these arguments had some foundation,[k] they considered the hazards minor, certain as they were that in the end railroads always led to progress and prosperity. According to J. Ross Browne, who succeeded Burlingame as American minister: "A single mile of railroad would do more within ten years for the elevation and advancement of China than all that the teachings of political theorists and nationalists would be able to accomplish in a century."[184] The *North China Herald* summed up the conflicting attitudes as follows: "To us, railways mean free intercourse, enlightenment, commerce and wealth; to the mandarins, they suggest rowdyism, the overthrow of time-honored custom and tradition, disturbance and ruin."[185]

Chinese officials of the time knew what railways could do, and were not uninterested in new contraptions. A British attaché who visited the residence of an official of the Board of War reported that his host, "Yang lao-yeh," was an avid amateur photographer; that he collected guns, telescopes, and thermometers; and that he served curaçao. He also, it seems, favored railways, but the grounds he gave for his interest are instructive: "Indeed he spoke to me about constructing a tramway and telegraph over his property in Shantung for the convenience of communicating with his tenants and agents."[186]

For railways as more than toys, Restoration officials had no use. Their nightmare was the dimly perceived shape of a new China, its social fabric shattered by a network of steel rails owned and controlled by foreigners. A few like Shen Pao-chen, Kuo Sung-tao,[187] and Li Hung-chang believed that the best defense for China was to build and control its own railways; but most of their colleagues considered railways an explosive force too dangerous to handle at all.[l] There was no responsible official who thought of the introduction of

---

k "It is easy to understand the apprehension with which a regency views a change so gigantic as the introduction of steam would effect, in a country already discontented and disturbed; and the anxiety of its members that, not in their time, should the deluge arise." (*NCH*, Mar. 23, 1867, commenting on a letter from Alcock in the same issue, reviewing conversations with Prince Kung.)

"Nor is there any prospect that the thousands who must be thrown out of work will find employment through a larger demand springing up for produce, when its transport becomes easier; for every available inch of the soil of China is already tilled to the exclusion even of pasturage." (*Ibid.*, Sept. 3, 1864.)

l See Chapter XI.

railways as part of a general program of economic modernization and development. Subsequent history lent weight to the Restoration argument; the first serious Chinese railway project, launched in 1882, ran into difficulties far greater than had been encountered by early projects in Japan or India.[188]

The proposed introduction of a telegraph system raised virtually the same issues as the introduction of railways, but in a less acute form. Chinese officials liked to look at model telegraph sets, but if a foreigner put up real poles, they were pulled down.[189] In 1869 the Tsungli-yamen refused Alcock's request for authorization of a coastal telegraph line. When Wade repeated the request the following year, arguing that the proposed line would merely connect seaports and therefore could have no effect on China, an answering edict specified that all the lines must be in water and the terminals on ships.[190]

Chinese officials understood the importance of efficient communication for administrative purposes and were at pains to maintain the speed of the traditional courier service.[191] They could see no need for communication more rapid than this. As they pointed out, foreign complaints at the slowness of Chinese communications arose from the fact that foreigners considered trade of basic importance.[192] Foreigners wanted to receive commercial news from their agents immediately; to give orders to buy and sell in the interior on the basis of the latest shifts in the world market. They wanted to move more and more goods faster and faster.

The Restoration government wanted no part of this. Once the traditional land and water communications were restored and supplemented by coastal steamers, all the activities that seemed important to Chinese officials would be quite adequately served.

Foreign Trade and Its Revenues. It was not until long after the Restoration that Chinese officials considered foreign trade an important aspect of the national economy.[193] Before the Opium War the Ch'ing had considered foreign trade useless. Ricci had observed in the sixteenth century that "everything which the people need for their well-being and sustenance, whether it be food or clothing or even delicacies and superfluities, is abundantly produced within the borders of the kingdom and not imported from foreign climes."[194] And Alcock had confirmed in 1856 that China

> is perhaps the only empire in the world, at the present day, that may be said to be by nature independent of all extraneous supplies or interchange of products with other countries, and perfectly *self-sufficing* in the fullest sense of the term. . . . Commercially speaking, then, we cannot entertain the hope of holding out a lure to China sufficiently enticing to induce her to close her eyes to any dangers or prejudices inseparably connected with her foreign relations.[195]

As the famous letter of the Ch'ien-lung Emperor to the King of England remarked, the outside world could offer China mere baubles, interesting only for their novelty and of no use to society. Such foreign trade as existed was looked on as a gracious concession.[196]

Following the Opium War, to the scorn of foreign products was added a growing fear of the domestic dislocations and foreign wars to which the trade appeared to lead. As early as the K'ang-hsi period Chinese officials had known of Western conquests in other parts of the globe. Events of the first half of the nineteenth century seemed to them to indicate that China was next.

This attitude toward foreign trade persisted, with modifications that will be indicated below, throughout the Restoration. Britain's commerce was certainly less feared than France's support of Catholic missions or Russia's territorial ambitions, and Chinese anxieties were in some measure relieved by the Co-operative Policy. But all this was negative. No Chinese of importance shared the widely held foreign view that increased foreign trade offered China's best hope of economic prosperity. In the words of Liu K'un-i, "Foreign trade is harmful to our best manufactures."[197] When foreign trade, like every other economic activity, was judged by its effect on the people's well-being and the state's revenues, Chinese officials found it wanting.

Confused appraisals of "the Chinese" attitude toward foreign trade have often resulted from a failure to distinguish clearly between Chinese officials, literati, and landed gentry on the one hand, and a small group of Chinese merchants—"compradors"—in the port cities on the other. These merchants waived their standing in society[198] and emerged as shrewd and able businessmen, quick to learn and readily able to compete with foreigners for the profits of foreign trade. As the *North China Herald* drily remarked:

> If the protection of native interests be the motive which impels the Chinese Government to still shut against foreigners every possible door of ingress into the interior, reflection founded on recent experience should convince them that their subjects are perfectly capable of guarding themselves. The cry from all the outposts, that trade is passing completely into the hands of Chinese, should remove all fear of injury to Chinese merchants from foreign competition.[199]

Chinese merchants worked their way steadily and rapidly not only into the coastal trade but into the direct import trade. They began to charter their own steamers and to protect themselves with marine insurance. They soon knew as much of foreign markets as the foreigners did, and incomparably more of Chinese markets. In the interior they took advantage of their lower transportation and operating costs and guild organization to bankrupt their foreign competitors. By the mid-1860's all reports agreed that in every port Chinese now handled most of the foreign trade. The foreign merchants remained dependent on their compradors, but the compradors no longer needed the foreigners.[200]

The trend appeared to be to "reduce the position of the foreign merchant almost to that of an agent working into the hands of native dealers."[201]

> Clearly, a new order of things must be inaugurated, now that we have to encounter so much keen competition from the Chinese traders, who have already monopolized the Tientsin trade, and are gradually driving us out of the Yangtze trade. Even much of the opium import from Hongkong is on Chinese account; and foreigners have for some time given up to natives, the business carried on between the ports of Newchwang or Chefoo, and Amoy or Swatow.[202]

The number of British residents in China was expected to decline as the Chinese took over trade, and the Foreign Office had to justify the very maintenance of its consular establishments on long-term considerations of general British foreign policy.[203]

As Chinese merchants claimed an increasing share of the profit from China's foreign trade, the foreign trade itself increased considerably.[m] How much this benefited the Chinese economy is debatable, for the following reasons: (1) Although the Chinese market for foreign goods disappointed foreigners by its limited size,[204] imports were still sufficient to threaten the cottage manufactures that provided the peasants' margin of subsistence.[205] (2) The ratio of exports to imports declined, and after 1864 China's balance of trade became perennially unfavorable.[206] (3) Although the export trade presumably stimulated production, "the people at large . . . complain that the result has been an increase in the value of those articles."[207] (4) Although the revenue from the maritime customs was useful, much of it went to pay for the military preparations, wars, and indemnities to which the Chinese believed that foreign trade had given rise.[n] Wen-hsiang was probably telling the truth when he said to Hart, whom he greatly admired: "We would gladly pay you all the increased revenue you

[m] Year	Net imports	Net exports	Total
1864	51,293,578	54,006,509	105,300,087
1865	61,844,158	60,054,634	121,898,792
1866	74,563,674	56,161,807	130,725,481
1867	69,329,741	57,895,713	127,228,454
1868	71,121,213	69,114,733	140,235,946
1869	74,923,201	67,143,988	142,067,189
1870	69,290,722	61,682,121	130,972,843

From Chong Su See, *The Foreign Trade of China*, New York, 1919, Appendix II, and *China. No. 11. (1869)*. Figures are in Hackwan taels, the value of which in 1864 was 6/8 sterling; in 1867, 6/3 sterling.

[n] *In* 1860 Heng-ch'i claimed that the annual revenue from foreign trade of some four million taels was paltry in comparison with the indemnities that China had had to pay for the foreign wars that had opened China to commerce: 21 million in 1842, 6 million in 1858, 10 million in 1860 (Parkes to Elgin, Oct. 20, 1860, *Correspondence Respecting Affairs in China. 1859–1860*, p. 236).

have brought us, if you foreigners would go back to your own country and leave us in peace as we were before you came."[o]

Certainly no Chinese would have agreed with the statement made in Parliament by a spokesman of the China trade that: "In truth the Central Government is a gorgeous mockery, to be likened to Nebuchadnezzar's golden image with feet of clay, and it would collapse tomorrow but for the contributions to its Peking Treasury of more than 3,000,000 sterling annual customs duties."[208]

The Chinese Imperial Maritime Customs Administration[209] had its origins in the efforts of consular officials to collect customs duties from their nationals on behalf of China during the disordered occupation of Shanghai by the Triad Rebels in 1854. In 1858 the Treaties of Tientsin provided for the establishment of a uniform Imperial customs service, staffed in part by foreigners and under the direction of a foreign inspector-general responsible to the Chinese central government. By 1864 there were some four hundred foreign employees concerned not only with collecting the duties but with the compiling of statistics, the lighting of the coast, harbor improvements, patrols against pirates, and a variety of administrative reforms. The inspector-general, Robert Hart, emerged as the major figure of the nineteenth century in Sino-foreign relations.

The Maritime Customs may safely be cleared of the Communist charge that it was the tool of foreign interests.[210] Foreign merchants of the sixties maintained an unceasing fire of criticism both against Hart, "who has succumbed to the fatal attraction of Chinese intercourse, and is as completely Chinese in his sympathies as the Chinese themselves,"[211] and against the entire Customs staff in all ports, for their enforcement of Chinese regulations.[212]

Chinese officials, for their part, were quick to recognize the administrative efficiency of the Customs.[p] Hart received repeated Imperial honors for his assistance to the Chinese in controversies with merchants and consuls, and for administering the Customs service in a manner thoroughly satisfactory to the Chinese government. In 1866 a long list of Customs officials received honors, on the motion of Li Hung-chang, because of a substantial increase in the revenues.[213]

As customs revenue increased[q] and no further foreign wars followed, Chi-

---

[o] His "exact words," "a few years after the inauguration of the Customs," according to Juliet Bredon, *Sir Robert Hart*, New York, 1919, p. 221. Freeman-Mitford got the same impression from others: "the mandarins, at any rate, would rather return to the old state of things, have nothing to do with us and our treaties, and sacrifice the revenue that accrues to them from their customs." (Aug. 7, 1865, *The Attaché at Peking*, p. 118.)

[p] For example, the governor of Hunan, Mao Hung-pin, was pleasantly surprised to discover that the foreign regulations against smuggling were "even" stricter than the Chinese, and proposed that they be extended to cover all Chinese trade (memorial of Mar. 5, 1862, *IWSM-TC*, Ch. 4, pp. 29b-31).

[q] Tls. 7,845,365 in 1864; tls. 9,425,656 in 1868 (*China. No. 11. (1869)*, p. 2). The figures given in See, *The Foreign Trade of China*, Appendix V, vary slightly.

nese officials gradually came to see how useful this new revenue could be. In 1862, for example, Hart pointed out that it could be used to pay for foreign military equipment, enabling the government to avoid foreign loans and gifts; he helped the Tsungli-yamen prepare the plan to this end that was submitted to the Throne.[214] The Shanghai customs revenues were important enough to be cited as a major reason for keeping the city out of Taiping hands.[215] After 1866, when the indemnities imposed by the Conventions of Peking had been paid off from the Customs Forty Per Cent Account (*ssu-ch'eng yang-shui*), the account was still continued, and a substantial uncommitted sum was thereafter available in Peking.[216]

In Chinese eyes the most important use to which the revenues of foreign trade could be put was emergency military financing. Staple revenues were otherwise assigned, and the idea of loans, on which the government would pay interest, was abhorrent. Even the modernizers—Shen Pao-chen, for example—never dreamed of using borrowed funds to increase production so that repayment might be made from profits.[217] The few small, short-term loans that were arranged in the early years of the Restoration were last resorts in military crises. The borrower was the official concerned, not the Chinese government; the lender was a private foreign concern, not the Chinese public or a foreign government.[218]

Even these modest arrangements aroused considerable anxiety.[219] Grave alarm was felt in 1867 when Tso Tsung-t'ang negotiated the first of a series of larger loans of longer term[220] to finance his campaign in the northwest,[r] which was a deficit area even in normal times. The loans were approved, but every effort was made to keep the sum at a minimum, history having shown that the acceptance of loans was usually the forerunner of foreign intervention and control. The availability of the Customs Forty Per Cent Account was of great importance here.[221]

The government needed the customs revenue so urgently that methods of avoiding delay in the transmission and clearance of Customs checks were the subject of an Imperial edict.[222] Yet nowhere does one find a memorial urging measures to increase these obviously useful revenues by stimulating an increased volume of foreign trade. From the beginning to the end of the Restoration, so far as the documentary record shows, the Chinese government was interested in the customs collection as an administrative problem, not in foreign trade as an economic problem. Hart and his associates "milked" foreign trade more effectively than Chinese officials had ever dreamed was possible, and they turned in their full receipts. For this they were honored, and their technical suggestions were listened to with respect.[223] Their more general suggestion that the

[r] See Chapter VI.

over-all economic structure of the Empire be revised with a view to expanding commerce went unheeded.[s]

Mining and Industry. The notion that mining might play an important role in the Chinese economy was less alien than the notion that foreign trade might do so. Mining had existed from the earliest times, and its advantages and disadvantages to society had been argued throughout history. In the late Ming the conclusion had been reached that mining was socially harmful, and a subsequent edict of the late seventeenth century (K'ang-hsi 22) stated flatly: "Mining does not benefit the locality; if anyone hereafter seeks permission to mine, it is not to be granted."[224]

There were exceptions, however. Salt mining was of course essential, and the Ch'ing promoted the mining of needed copper in Yunnan and of gold in Mongolia and Sinkiang. As early as the Tao-kuang period there were economic theories that emphasized the importance of mining in general to the national economy.[225]

Yet fear of the disruptive social consequences of mining lingered,[226] not to be widely repudiated until the Kuang-hsü period.[227] During the summer and autumn of 1868 there was a gold rush in the Chefoo area, and mining by small groups of foreigners and Chinese, said by the Tsungli-yamen to be Cantonese,[228] was reported elsewhere in Shantung. Chinese officials were ordered to stop the Chinese, and foreign consuls were asked to check foreign participation in these illegal enterprises.[229] Eventually troops were ordered into the areas concerned, to stop the mining by force if necessary.[230]

On the whole, however, there was less resistance to mining during the Restoration than to any other form of economic development. Local officials were reported to have encouraged the development of private coal mines near Tientsin. Chinese were reported to have taken the initiative in opening coal mines west of Peking, with the help of foreign technical advisers. Letters from Chinese readers to the *North China Herald*'s vernacular edition, *Pen-ti hsin-wen-chih*, reflected a heated controversy over the relative merits and demerits of mining.[231] Tseng Kuo-fan, Li Hung-chang, and a number of other high officials soon became willing to experiment with modern mining, provided the foreigners employed were technicians under Chinese control.[t] As Feng Kuei-fen put it, if the right men were used to develop mining, the people need not be disturbed; in foreign countries mining was a normal procedure and did not cause unrest;

---

[s] See Chapter XI.

[t] See Chapter XI. Alcock noted the Chinese unwillingness to accept most of the innovations urged by foreigners, "if I except coal mines, some of which they are willing to work themselves with foreign machinery and superintendence" (*China. No. 12. (1869)*, p. 9); he believed that the Chinese were correct in opposing foreign investment in mining, unless there were guarantees against intervention (*China. No. 5. (1871)*, pp. 112–13, 123–24).

and according to foreign books, the foreigners would open mines in China if the Chinese did not.[232]

The difficulty lay in China's inability to find an effective method of organizing mining enterprises. The ores could not be profitably mined except on a large scale and with the use of modern technology. Perhaps the foreign technicians could be controlled, but could foreign capital, readily available, also be controlled? Very little Chinese capital—public or private—appears to have been available for investment in mining,[233] and effective managers and technicians were lacking. When at the end of the Restoration the revival of Yunnan copper mining was attempted, the system employed, commercial management with official supervision (*kuan-tu shang-pan*), was a total failure.[u] Neither private interests nor the state, nor the two in combination, appeared able to mobilize the capital and the entrepreneurial talent required for effective modern mining.

If Restoration statesmen showed some interest in mining, as well as a necessary toleration of commerce, that was the limit of their concern. Industry they ignored altogether. The T'ung-chih reign is conventionally considered the first period in the development of modern Chinese industry, but there was at that time not the glimmer of an idea that industrialization would ever go beyond the building of ships and the manufacture of arms. Even Feng Kuei-fen, when he urged the manufacture of foreign implements, meant only implements of war.[234] The initial performance of military industry was impressive but of brief duration; none of the men who sponsored the arsenals and shipyards of the Restoration ever conceived of using the machine and the factory system to increase general production.[v]

THE MACHINERY OF PUBLIC FINANCE

The Problem of Central Fiscal Control. The elaborate fiscal machinery of the Ch'ing had never been fully under central control. The collection of taxes had been farmed out, and although the central government knew

[u] Yunnan copper production, under the old system of state mines, had declined steadily from the mid-eighteenth century in consequence of maladministration. Not a catty was mined for nearly twenty years because of the Moslem Rebellion. When the area was finally pacified, the way was open for a new system, but the one that was tried ran into every imaginable difficulty. There was a shortage of capital, of managers, and of mine labor; the margin of profit allowed to mines working on government contract was very low; funds were short, even for repairs; and there was constant interference by corrupt officials. See Yen Chung-p'ing, *Ch'ing-tai Yün-nan t'ung-cheng k'ao*, Shanghai, 1948, pp. 26–48; "Notes and Queries," *China Review*, XII, 2 (1883), 135; Ch'en Ts'an, *Huan-Tien ts'un-kao*, Ch. 1, p. 18.

[v] See Chapter IX. If Tso Tsung-t'ang is an exception, which I am inclined to doubt, the "industrial" portion of his career belongs to the post-Restoration period. On Tso's sponsorship in the northwest of a woolen mill, a sugar refinery, iron mines, etc., see Gideon Chen, *Tso Tsung-t'ang*, pp. 57–78; and Chen, "Tso Tsung-t'ang, the Farmer of Hsiang-shang," *loc. cit.*, pp. 219–25.

whether or not the prescribed quotas reached Peking, it had no sure way to tell what sums beyond the quota were collected and pocketed. The allocation of funds was under the direct control of the central government, but the accounting methods of the time allowed leeway, to say the least, in actual expenditures.[w] Anyone familiar with the sources will agree with the editor of the Empire's last great encyclopedia of government that China's public finance was as confused as tangled silk.[235]

The Board of Revenue, like all the central boards, was subdivided into a complex series of bureaus each with both a geographical and a functional responsibility.[236] This cumbrous system had worked well enough in stable times; but in an era in which limited resources had to be made to support agricultural rehabilitation and military and diplomatic modernization programs, tighter central controls were essential.

At the outset the Restoration government lacked even the traditional central controls. The tax system was so complex[x] and the supervision of disbursements so unsystematic that the weakening of the central authority during the Taiping Rebellion had led to chaos. Restoration efforts to restore the essentials of central control met with some success, enough to check temporarily the trend toward regionalism in public finance. Typically, however, the Restoration program was concerned with reinstituting the older Ch'ing system, not with creating a financial agency capable of promoting China's economic development.

The first step was to improve the collection of taxes. No one suggested that agents of the Imperial government collect taxes directly, that the eminently successful practice of the Maritime Customs be followed in other sections of the economy. The Restoration program was limited to publicizing the legal quotas on the traditional taxes, asking for fuller reports from the provinces,[237] and improving the quality of local officials.[y] In the case of the likin, for which there were no quotas and no traditional system of reports, the Board of Revenue could only try to reduce the number of likin stations and hope eventually to institute supervision of those that were left. Although many of the reports and sums sent to Peking continued to be incomplete and late,[238] the government's cam-

---

[w] A careful South Manchuria Railway study on Ch'ing finance indicates the pitfalls that await the economic historian, and warns that although the structure of Ch'ing institutions of public finance may be studied in full, no reliable estimates of the actual amounts expended can be compiled (Matsui Yoshio, *Shinchō keihi no kenkyū*, SMR, 1935, Preface. FB 7.13.2).

[x] To the intricate major taxes discussed above were added a host of even more complicated minor taxes; multiple taxes on tea, wine, mining, medicine, bamboo, and so forth (*WHTK*, pp. 7955, 7964, 7983); James T. K. Wu, "The Impact of the Taiping Rebellion upon the Manchu Fiscal System," *PHR*, XIX, 3 (1950), 265–75; C. J. Stanley, "Chinese Finance from 1852 to 1908," *Papers on China*, III (1949), 1–23.

[y] See Chapter VII.

paign was not a total failure. Partly in consequence of improved methods of tax collection, the government's total receipts were greater than they had been in the Tao-kuang period before the great rebellions began.[239]

Officials of integrity were appointed wherever possible, and efforts were made to improve accounting procedures. Estimates of cost on routine matters were challenged, investigated, and discussed.[240] Misappropriations of funds nonetheless occurred, and funds were not always actually spent as the government intended they should be, but the Restoration campaign was on the whole fairly effective. There were no great scandals like those of the Ch'ien-lung period or the second and third regencies of the Empress Dowager.

Again Restoration officials were content with patching up the old machinery; they never thought to overhaul the system. Only Feng Kuei-fen saw further, and proposed that there be a public accounting of all public funds; that every office be required to post statements of receipts and expenditures, and that the people be encouraged to report any discrepancies they noted; that weights and measures be standardized; and that government-supported agencies, including the Imperial Clan Court, operate on fixed budgets.[241] Since these were measures that would have increased the wealth and power of the central government without disturbing the traditional moral, social, and economic order, the failure to devote serious attention to them must be reckoned as a major shortcoming of the Restoration.

Money and Banking. Restoration measures in the field of money and banking were likewise a patchwork. The stability of the traditional monetary system had depended on the stability of the silver-copper ratio and on adequate supplies of both metals.[z] In the half century before 1850, the drainage of silver and the decline in copper production had destroyed this ratio; by 1850 the price of silver was even more inflated than that of copper. During the Hsien-feng period, as noted earlier, deliberate debasement of the copper currency and the issue of nonconvertible paper and iron money reduced the Ch'ing currency system to chaos. Reconstruction was scarcely feasible until some degree of monetary stability was restored.

The main problem was to stabilize the copper currency. Tseng Kuo-fan proposed that the central government promulgate an annual fixed silver-copper ratio for the whole country, and that the value of copper in terms of silver be

---

[z] Although silver and copper were both unlimited legal tender in Ch'ing China, the fiscal system was not truly bi-metallic because of the dominance of silver in the major sectors of the economy. Most of the silver was imported, and most of the copper from the eighteenth century onward was mined in Yunnan (Chang Te-ch'ang, "Chin-tai Chung-kuo ti huo-pi," *Jen-wen k'o-hsüeh hsüeh-pao*, I, 1 (1942), 72–73). On the currency system of the Ch'ing in general, see Wang Ch'ing-yün, *Hsi-ch'ao chi-cheng*, Ch. 5, pp. 1–25.

supported by increasing the demand for it in the major sections of the economy: troops might be paid partly in copper, copper might be accepted for a portion of taxes, and so forth. Feng Kuei-fen also proposed that the use of copper be greatly extended.[242]

Unfortunately, the enforcement of a fixed silver-copper ratio proved virtually impossible in the decentralized Chinese economy. No matter what rate was fixed, some interests would be adversely affected and some local economies would be disturbed. For example, whereas the traditional ratio (and the one used in official calculations) was 1/1000, throughout most of Honan the market rate was said by Governor Chang Chih-wan to be 1/2500 or 1/2600. Had the market rate been announced as official, the real value of Honan taxes would have more than doubled. Moreover, although this was not mentioned in memorials, the lucrative business of buying silver at official rates and selling it on the open market would be undermined. On the other hand, unless the ratio was fixed and enforced, an ordinary person would still have to buy his silver at black market prices but pay taxes calculated on the assumption that he had bought silver at the official price. In the Honan case the censor Lü Hsü-ch'eng proposed fixing the ratio at 1/3000, arguing that the people would benefit from the uniformity and that the government rather than the tax collectors would receive the surplus represented by the old difference between the official ratio and the market ratio. This proposal was dismissed as "harmful and impractical," and the governor's proposal to maintain the old official rate on paper was accepted, for disturbance of the economy could not be risked.[243]

In the view of Restoration officials, the effort to stabilize the value of copper in terms of silver was hindered not only by the continuing rise in the value of silver but perhaps even more by the continuing shortage of copper, which made it impossible to mint a sufficient supply of coins with equal face and intrinsic values. An edict of 1867 (TC-6) declared that the copper supply had become an even more urgent question than the supply of tributary rice, and frantic but largely unrealistic efforts were made to bring more copper to Peking. The government insisted that large quantities of copper were being hoarded and, taking no note of the total cessation of copper mining in Yunnan, kept repeating the annual production quotas of the various mines. Complex administrative arrangements were made to buy Yunnan copper in Szechwan and Hunan.[244]

The Restoration government next authorized provincial officials to resume imports from Japan, which had supplied much of China's copper before the development of the Yunnan mines in the late seventeenth century, but little if any proved available from this source.[245] The country was searched for minor mines in accessible locations, but with little result. Finally the governors of the coastal and Yangtze valley provinces were ordered to buy up copper coins and to ship them to Peking, in lieu of the customary tax silver, for reminting.[a]

Such measures, although they could clearly provide no lasting solution, were all the Restoration government could manage. Even when suppression of the Yunnan Moslem Rebellion finally made it possible to put the copper mines back into operation in 1874, production in the first year was only one-twelfth what it had been in a good eighteenth-century year, and subsequent efforts to develop the mines were ineffective.[246]

The fact that in these circumstances the currency situation did nonetheless improve seems evidence of the limited role of money in the traditional economy, rather than of the success of any specific plan. The circulation of forged silver and spurious cash seems to have been reduced somewhat. The value of copper coins in terms of silver gradually rose.[247] Prices had been rising gradually for several decades and speculation increased local fluctuations,[248] but there is nothing to suggest that inflation continued at any very rapid rate. The sterling value of the tael was maintained at approximately 6/5. The drop to 3/3 in 1895 began after the Restoration and was gradual.[249]

The banking system of the Restoration was as ill-adapted to a modern economy as the monetary policy of the period. The Shansi banks were the fiscal agents of the government from the early years of the Restoration; and although they were far from primitive and excited some foreign admiration, their remittance system was not up to covering the cost of Tso Tsung-t'ang's campaign, for which large amounts of bullion had to be transported to the northwest. There was no general organization or clearinghouse; the different banks merely assisted each other, and depended on a reciprocal demand for credit. Moreover, the whole system was loosely controlled; its functioning depended on men, not method. If the men proved unreliable, the system suffered.[250]

The officials in charge of the system were appointed for short terms. They never thought of developing credit over a long period, or of using credit to expand production. They merely tapped the banks for the government's needs, and their own. Since the banks, like other traditional Chinese institutions, were able to operate only by maintaining a network of friendly connections with officials, they offered them easy credit with no security.[251] Modern banking practices were introduced by the Hongkong and Shanghai Banking Corpora-

---

[a] Officials were cautioned to keep this information from the public. The measure, which was also intended to remove spurious cash from circulation, was limited to provinces where sea transport could be used to ship the bulky coins. (Edict of Nov. 30, 1867, replying to a memorial of the Board of Revenue, *SL-TC*, Ch. 215, pp. 17–18b.) Ma Hsin-i sent 100,000 strings of cash from Chekiang; he was ordered to investigate whether this had upset the Chekiang economy, and if not, to send more (edict of May 1, 1868, *SL-TC*, Ch. 228, pp. 31–32). Li Han-chang sent 200,000 strings from Hupeh and Hunan, and undertook to try to secure copper ore from the Shih-i mines in Hupeh (edict of Apr. 12, 1868, *SL-TC*, Ch. 227, pp. 13b–14).

tion, but its activities were limited to the port cities and had little significance for the Chinese economy as a whole.[252]

There was no sign of the emergence of native banks capable of supplying the credit needed for economic modernization in a country where capital was scarce and scattered. In the government there was not only no interest in the subject but no recognition of the problem.

Military Finance.[b] The basic limitations of the Restoration fiscal system were most immediately evident in the field of military finance. The traditional revenues controlled by the central government covered only the expenses of the Banners and the regular Chinese forces. There were no standard procedures for financing the new armies of regional origin that constituted the Restoration's major fighting forces. These armies had ceased to be mere local forces and were often fighting far from their home provinces; no matter, they had to be supported largely from the likin and other provincially controlled revenues. To make things worse, a single province could seldom support its own forces, even when it was allowed to hold back for this purpose taxes due the central government. Yet since there was no effective central control of the new revenues, Peking could do little more than juggle the supposed resources of the different provinces.

The money for a single military operation had to be dredged up from a wide variety of sources. If Manchuria required a large lump sum, it might come from funds in the possession of the Board of Revenue, the provincial salt revenues, the overdue Shantung land tax, overdue Honan taxes, and the Shanhaikwan customs.[253] If the forces in Kansu were in urgent need, they might be supplied half by Shansi, Shantung, and Honan, half by Hunan and Kiangsi, with Szechwan sending rice.[254] Shansi, Shantung, Honan, and Chihli might be jointly ordered to send funds to the garrisons in Mongolia and Sinkiang.[255] This procedure was used not only for frontier military finance, but in the heart of the country as well; on one occasion Kiangsi, Chekiang, Hunan, and Hupeh were jointly ordered to supply the requirements of troops in northern Kiangsu.[256]

Only rarely was the Board of Revenue able to advance funds to the army in need immediately, and later itself attempt to collect from the provinces.[257] Generally there was no more immediate source of funds than the provinces, no quick emergency procedure even when unpaid, cold, hungry troops refused to attack in Kweichow, when the Sinkiang garrisons were reported out of food, when starving troops threatened mutiny in Kansu or even on the outskirts of Peking.[258]

When the Board of Revenue tried to inform the Throne which provinces

---

[b] On military finance in the context of the problems of central military administration, see Chapter IX.

could afford to contribute, or to keep account of the sums owed by the provinces to each other,[259] it found its information inadequate; sometimes a province was merely ordered to send what it could afford.[c] It is obvious that many orders were issued more in hope than in expectation, and most had to be repeated.[260] Since funds were usually sent directly from the contributing agency to the receiving agency, and since bullion shipments were subject to physical hazards, the Board of Revenue had no certain means of ascertaining exactly what was sent and what arrived.[261] Rivalries were common, and it was taken for granted that loans might not be repaid. Moreover a hard-pressed command was tempted not to forward funds received en route to another command but to keep them.[262]

It was obviously impossible to control the expenditure of funds collected and apportioned in this haphazard manner. The Board of Revenue might hear of some particularly scandalous waste and report it, but no close supervision was feasible. In the circumstances it is remarkable that the campaigns against the various rebellions were fought to successful conclusions. Somehow substantial funds were collected, transmitted, and in good measure spent for the purpose for which they were intended.

The immediate danger passed as internal peace was restored, and the armies were progressively disbanded or reduced in size. Yet the Restoration experience with military finance demonstrated how little provision there was for emergencies. The government's achievements in financial reform seem meager alongside its failure to see the importance of expanded sources of revenue and of a fiscal system that could be systematically administered by the central government.

THE PROBLEM OF ECONOMIC STAGNATION

As the study of modern China is an underdeveloped area of historical scholarship, so the study of economic growth is an underdeveloped area in economics. This being so, comments on the absence of economic growth in nineteenth-century China are doubly hazardous. We have not even rough estimates of the gross national product, much less any means of determining how it was used. We not only know little of shifts in the employment of the labor force, we actually lack reliable general population figures,[263] and there has been no work done on the historical population of China with reference to any feature other than its size. We know neither the total receipts from the various taxes and from various areas, nor the total expenditures of the various government agencies. We lack not only statistical material but descriptive material as well. We do not know precisely how a number of agencies of government functioned, or precisely what many of the terms used in the documents mean.

---

[c] For example, an edict of March 16, 1867, ordered all provinces to send funds to Tso Tsung-t'ang; it was specified that the least disturbed provinces should send the most, and vice versa, but the governor in each case was to fix the amount (*SL-TC*, Ch. 196, pp. 26b–28).

On the other hand, economists have cautioned that studies of the economics of growth must not be limited to the Western European framework; that the study of remote times and places, in spite of the relative paucity of data, is necessary; and finally that any study of growth requires an analysis of sociological and ideological factors that are not fully subject to measurement even in the contemporary West.[264]

In retrospect it is clear that the T'ung-chih Restoration did not lay the foundation for a modern economy as did, for example, the contemporary Meiji Restoration in Japan. Perhaps we can get at our subject best by ascertaining which of the circumstances associated with economic growth in Japan and elsewhere were lacking in China.

(1) Natural resources would appear to have little bearing on the case, for China is far better supplied than Japan and many other modernized economies with arable land and essential minerals.

(2) The question of the portion of the national income available for investment is more complex, but certainly premodern China was not so poverty-stricken that her whole product was necessary simply to keep her population alive. In spite of the forces that militated against the accumulation of wealth, substantial amounts were accumulated in the salt monopoly, the traditional banks, the pawnshops, domestic trade, foreign trade, and the "savings" of officials. During the 1860's there was a net profit of 20 or 25 per cent in many types of business.[265] In foreign trade, although the balance of China as a whole was generally unfavorable, there was a substantial favorable balance in certain areas. For example, Maritime Customs reports showed that in a period of less than five years some forty million pounds sterling were presumably paid in in specie in the tea-producing areas near Foochow. As contemporary Westerners commented: "The amount is sufficient to cause an immense stimulus to enterprise and trade if it were only available."[266]

(3) The crux of the matter appears to lie in the manner in which wealth was spent. Abramovitz has pointed out that "there is no specific instinct for capital accumulation," that "the energy and ability which in some societies are directed toward religion, politics, art, or war are in the developed capitalist milieu channeled into business."[267] In the Confucian milieu, energy was channeled into politics and the associated literary studies, and liquid funds were used to buy land, endow libraries, and found poetry societies; there was no competing goal of any importance.[d] The salt merchants wanted to become literati, not entrepreneurs on a larger scale, and they were remarkably successful in shifting roles.[268] Investment in commerce appears to have been limited to the hiring of a few

---

[d] As late as World War II there was no place in the social order of interior China for the business type. For a case study, see Kuo-heng Shih, "Social Implications of Tin Mining in Yunnan," *Pacific Affairs*, XX, 1 (1947), 53–61.

shop assistants; investment in manufacture was virtually nonexistent. The officials had begun as landlords; when they retired, they became landlords again. The merchants attempted to become landlords as rapidly as possible.[269] The competition to invest in land forced the price of land upward, but it did not lead to any important changes in agricultural production. There was little interest in specialized cash crops. Moreover, despite the increasing concentration of ownership, the cultivation of land was increasingly fragmentized. There was little chance to use more capital and less labor to achieve an increased output;[270] on the contrary, just to maintain output came to require more labor, owing to increasing fragmentation and loss of productivity caused by the long-term decline of water control.

Thus nineteenth-century Chinese agriculture was capitalist only in the sense that land could be freely bought, sold, rented, or cultivated with hired labor. Moreover, although land rents were dangerously high from a social point of view, they were too low from an economic point of view. They did not lead to the accumulation of large sums that might be available for subsequent industrial development.[271]

(4) The same factors that limited the accumulation of wealth and channeled what was accumulated into land also limited the development of a supply of entrepreneurial talent. The true industrial or commercial entrepreneur was a rare and despised creature. The typical merchant of nineteenth-century China was scarcely more likely than the landlord-official to become an entrepreneur.[e] This was as true of the rising comprador as it was of the salt merchant and hong merchant whom he had replaced in importance. Unlike his predecessors, the comprador had personal relations with officials rather than formal relations with the government; he was a man without family or government backing; he managed his own affairs and amassed great wealth; but unless he went overseas, he did not go on to engage in industry.[272] The early compradors were almost completely divorced from production; the later ones were concerned with it not as entrepreneurs but as moneylenders. Through loans for consumption, not production, the comprador monopolized the sale of goods produced by traditional cottage manufacture. His profits went not into the expansion of production but into more consumption loans and eventually into land. The artisan himself had no opportunity to accumulate capital for the expansion of production.[273]

According to Abramovitz, all studies of underdeveloped economies demonstrate precisely this point: that although there is potential opportunity for gain

---

[e] Owing to the low esteem in which the merchant and his business problems were held, records were not even kept; Chinese investigators have had great difficulty in locating data. (Wang Shu-han, "Liang-Huai yen-wu yü ch'ien-chuang," *Ching-chi hsüeh chi-k'an*, II, 3 (1931), 118–207. On the importance of this field, see Marion Levy and Kuo-heng Shih, *The Rise of the Modern Chinese Business Class; Two Introductory Essays*, New York, Institute of Pacific Relations, 1949.

and savable income, the leading elements are interested in political or other non-productive activities, and that the normal desire of businessmen is to move into this class.[274] By contrast, members of the less mobile Japanese merchant class devoted their talents, over a period of centuries, to improving their position as businessmen.

(5) It was doubtful whether the Confucian state had the power to initiate and guide a program of economic development. The authority of the whole bureaucracy and of the Throne itself was limited to the traditional social context. There were no transcendent sanctions, no hierarchy of loyalties that would prevail regardless of altered policies. Japan had a network of feudal loyalties that guaranteed obedience to any orders that certain authorities might give, including orders to modernize the economy. In Japan, loyalty to the state was loyalty to a particular ruling house, to a particular group of islands, to a particular race of men. It could be made demonstrably clear that henceforth this state could best be served by factories. In China, by contrast, loyalty to the state was loyalty to the Confucian way of life; any suggestion that the Confucian way of life could be served by factories, being patently preposterous, would have carried no weight at all.[275]

(6) Nineteenth-century China lacked the type of labor force generally associated with economic growth. Its labor force was indeed the largest in the world, and generally characterized as honest, sober, industrious, frugal, and intelligent, with the most highly developed manual dexterity yet known. However, the Confucian insistence on self-sufficiency and low consumption held the division of labor within narrow fields. The efforts of a number of local officials in the Ming and Ch'ing periods to promote local textile manufacture failed because of this universal insistence on family and village self-sufficiency.[276]

Moreover, although the life of a peasant was hard, it was relatively secure. He was not driven off the land in search of a living; on the contrary, his labor was needed except in the slack seasons. As a peasant, he had considerably higher status than he would have if he left the land. He had been thoroughly taught to prize this status, and such independence as he had, above the prospect of increasing his wealth beyond his customary modest requirements. When several generations later the peasant did finally take a factory job, he was inclined to work only long enough to acquire a small sum; after that he returned to his village, preferring autonomy and social standing to further economic advance.[277]

(7) Emphasis on self-sufficiency and low consumption impeded not only the development of a labor force suited to industry, but also the development of markets for industrial products. Moreover, communications were poor and in the economy as a whole money and credit were not readily available to supplement barter.

Certain foreign machine-made goods found a limited market, but markets capable of absorbing a little of the product of the Industrial Revolution in England were quite incapable of stimulating an industrial revolution in China.

(8) In technology, it was not the level of knowledge but the limitations on its use that impeded economic growth in nineteenth-century China. As has been shown above, Chinese traditional technology remained of a high order, in spite of a decline in some fields, and knowledge of Western technology was readily available. The Restoration was one of the great periods for Chinese translation of foreign scientific works, but the new knowledge was not applied to economic development, and a half century of stagnation in the Chinese adoption of Western technology followed.[f]

Foreign technical specialists were readily available, and there were precedents in the K'ang-hsi period for their employment as skilled individual craftsmen;[278] Alcock urged Restoration officials to follow the pattern of Peter the Great in this respect.[279] All in all, however, there was no way in which nineteenth-century European engineers could be used to advance an industrial economy in a society that had no room for industry.

(9) Several other conditions associated with economic growth elsewhere were lacking in nineteenth-century China. China had a highly developed legal system with a written code,[g] but there was little provision for abstract property relations or for nonpersonal contracts. Private mercantile property was highly vulnerable and lacked the minimum legal protection afforded by the late medieval western city.

The amount of money in circulation seems to have been limited and to have grown very slowly from the seventeenth to the nineteenth century. Mid-nineteenth-century experiments with paper money were a total failure, as indicated above. The limited and rigid currency system of a "self-sufficient" agrarian economy not only was not reformed and expanded as foreign trade developed; it actually deteriorated somewhat.[280] The existing credit facilities could do little to remedy this situation. There was in nineteenth-century China no sign of the development of the kind of financial institution that sped the industrialization of Japan, Germany, and Russia.[281] Neither the Shansi banks nor any of the other existing financial institutions could be used for such purposes.

Yet all this falls short of really explaining economic stagnation in nineteenth-century China, for there is not one of these various obstacles to economic growth that has not been overcome by determined governments of other underdeveloped countries at one time or another. Whatever one may say about preferences for investment in land, inculcation of ideals of self-sufficiency and frugality, or the

---

f See Chapter IX.
g See Chapter VII.

weakness of credit institutions, China did have the basic resources of land, minerals, labor, and wealth. She also had orderly government and long experience in commercial organization.

Was there, perhaps, some other crucial circumstance? Was the government of the time uninterested in the economic welfare of the country? Obviously not. Were the traditional revenues so ample that new sources of revenue seemed unnecessary? On the contrary, although the Ch'ing government did not become "insolvent" until after 1894,[282] the importance of taxes on commerce to supplement the land tax should have been abundantly clear during the Restoration. Between the 1840's and the 1870's the receipts from the land tax declined an estimated 30 per cent, yet the total revenue increased from an estimated thirty or forty million taels in the pre-Taiping period to some sixty million in 1874, of which an estimated twenty-nine million was supplied by the new taxes, notably the likin and the maritime customs duties.[283]

On all the evidence, the Restoration government could not interest itself in economic development because economic development had no place in the moral, social, and political order it sought to restore. Officials clung to the belief that the new expenditures were extraordinary expenditures, that the need for new sources of revenue was temporary. The swollen armies would be disbanded, the West would recede, and with a few modifications China would return to the days when the salt monopoly had yielded nearly twice what taxes on commerce yielded and both were dwarfed by the land tax.

Gerschenkron has pointed out that the more "backward" an economy, the more powerful the ideology of progress "required to grease the intellectual and emotional wheels of industrialization."

> To break through the barriers of stagnation in a backward country, to ignite the imaginations of men, and to place their energies in the service of economic development, a stronger medicine is needed than the promise of better allocation of resources or even of the lower price of bread. Under such conditions even the businessman, even the classical daring and innovating entrepreneur, needs a more powerful stimulus than the prospect of high profits. What is needed to move the mountains of routine and prejudice is faith—faith, in the words of Saint-Simon, that the golden age lies not behind but ahead of mankind.[284]

Restoration China, far from having a passionate faith that the golden age lay ahead of mankind, saw in the Confucian social order of the past the zenith of human achievement, and in the Western economic order of the present and future only a hideous new savagery designed to render a return to the true golden age forever impossible.

CHAPTER IX

THE SELF-STRENGTHENING MOVEMENT

Fundamental military changes, unlike fundamental economic changes, seemed to Restoration leaders not only desirable but absolutely necessary. Although of necessity rebellions in progress had to be suppressed and imminent foreign aggression checked by whatever means were at hand, virtually all the political and military leaders of the period recognized that the long-term security of the state required an almost complete reorganization of the military. The effort to go beyond *ad hoc* remedies to sound long-term policies resulted in the much-discussed "self-strengthening movement."[1]

Military reforms of the Restoration period were of two general types: (1) those aimed at giving armed forces of new types a suitable place in the Chinese domestic order, so as to heighten troop morale, ensure popular support for the army, and reinforce the loyalty to the Ch'ing state of the rapidly developing regional military forces; and (2) those aimed at making China the military equal, in arms and training, of the contemporary West.

The military reorganization was successful up to the point at which it conflicted with the essential requirements of the traditional society. Domestic rebellion was brought under control, separatism was for the time checked, and modern armaments were effectively introduced. The reorganization program produced indoctrinated scholar-generals who were technically competent to devise and carry out a new strategy, heightened the army's morale and increased its popular support, introduced improved methods of military finance and supply, reduced the size of the standing army sharply, improved its quality, and modernized its equipment.[2] And yet the program failed; it proved impossible to fit a modern army into the Confucian order. True military modernization proved to require greater changes than the Ch'ing was willing to make: basic changes in the class structure, the system of values, the tax system, and the principles of organization of the Empire's administrative hierarchy. Statesmen of the time understood the importance of improved ships and guns, and showed that China could make them. But the goal of the self-strengthening movement was broader: to defend the traditional society against barbarian onslaught and internal subversion. The first triumphs notwithstanding, it soon became clear that to reach this goal, to create sufficient military power to defend China, was to imperil the cherished order the statesmen sought to preserve.

THE CH'ING MILITARY SYSTEM BEFORE THE RESTORATION[3]

The once mighty Manchu striking force—the Banners—had gradually declined into a horde of parasites no longer capable of performing elementary military functions. According to a contemporary observer: "The men were as heterogeneous as their clothes. Old and young, strong and decrepit, half blind or whole deaf, none seemed too miserable objects for service."[4]

A similar fate had overtaken the regular Chinese forces (*lü-ying* or "green battalions") under the direct command of the Board of War of the central government. Their decline began late in the eighteenth century, as increasing corruption led to loss of fighting morale. Neither the Chia-ch'ing nor the Tao-kuang Emperor had been temperamentally suited to major institutional reform. When the Taiping Rebellion broke out in 1850, the regular forces had had no experience of a sustained campaign since the White Lotus Rebellion forty years earlier.[a]

During the Taiping Rebellion the regulars proved virtually useless. Their low rations had not been increased as the cost of living rose. The Board of War in Peking had lost the ability to enforce its orders, and command had become increasingly decentralized. Troops were assigned to a variety of petty duties in post stations and elsewhere, and it had become nearly impossible to assemble them for training or active service. The system of transfer, according to which they were moved about in small groups rather than in combat teams, undermined whatever working efficiency and *esprit de corps* might have developed. Training was formal, without real content. Padded enlistment rolls were usual, and the entire organization was permeated with a flabby bureaucratic spirit. In consequence, the central government found itself dependent upon untrained, mutinous troops who refused to fight, strained the treasury, went over to the rebels, and regularly outraged the civilian population by acts of pillage.[5] As Hart remarked in his 1865 memorandum to the Chinese government,[b] the Imperial troops advanced only when the rebels had already retreated, and reported a great victory when they had killed a few peasants. If the rebels did not retreat, the troops did.[6]

THE NATIONALIZATION OF THE NEW REGIONAL ARMIES

As the old-style Imperial forces collapsed in the course of the 1850's, local and later provincial leaders were organizing the gentry and more prosperous peasantry into effective fighting units of a new type. The Restoration was by no means an exclusively metropolitan movement; it had its regional and local manifestations in various spheres, including the military. The central govern-

---

[a] Land fighting in the Opium War was very limited.
[b] See Chapter XI.

ment's problem was not to suppress these local groups, but to keep them in line in spite of their *de facto* independence of the Board of War.ᶜ Within a surprisingly short period of time a new national military program was under way, based on the lessons learned in bringing the various rebellions under control.

The recruitment of regionally based armies in time of crisis was not new in Chinese history. At the end of the Ming period and again during the Ch'ienlung and Chia-ch'ing periods, especially-recruited "private armies" had supplemented the central government's military forces. However, the Hsiang and other new armies of the Restoration period differed from the earlier literati-led farmer armies in two important respects:

(1) The new armies were larger, stronger, more cohesive, and more independent. The commander-in-chief personally selected the officers, 83 per cent of whom were Hunanese in the Hsiang Army, for example, and each officer recruited his soldiers from his own native district, sometimes from his own clan. With the battalion of 500 or less as the unit, close attachments were formed. The army and the groups within it were handled somewhat like a Confucian family, with much emphasis on moral instruction and guidance. Moreover, the new armies were supported by local revenues, independently of the central government. Pay and rations were generous—triple the normal standard of the time. The battalion commander was personally responsible for withholding a large portion of each man's pay and sending it to his family at home. The personal ties thus developed further encouraged a fighting spirit, because no one wanted to be ashamed to return home.

(2) In earlier crises the traditional military forces had maintained their vigor so that the temporary regional forces could be disbanded once rebellion was suppressed. After the Taiping period the efforts to revitalize the regular forces failed and the Banners were in effect abandoned, so that there was little military counterweight to the regionally based armies.⁷

The ominous trend that the new armies suggested was not overlooked by contemporary observers. Foreigners, noting that Li Hung-chang and Tseng Kuo-fan could easily have established themselves as independent warlords, supposed that they might actually do so. According to the *North China Herald*, "the provincial army called into being by the rebellion in Kiangsu, will yet, we imagine, play the most important part in the future of China."⁸

These predictions overlooked the powerful centripetal forces of the restored

ᶜ "There was enough material to organize a large-scale rebellion, but there were enough conservative local groups to build up resistance against it. The question was, who would succeed in getting more support from these groups—rebellious leaders, or government leaders, who, taking advantage of, and using the strength of the reformist gentry group, would bring it, at a price, to the government side." (Franz Michael, "Military Organization and Power Structure of China during the Taiping Rebellion," *PHR*, XVIII, 4 (1949), 475–76.)

Confucian state, which tended to hold the obvious centrifugal forces in check. The leaders of the Hsiang and other new armies were literati, men who had a profound interest in the preservation and strengthening of the existing state.[d] As Lo Erh-kang has put it:

> It is evident that the position of the Hsiang Army developed originally from self-defense; but because of the interdependence in destiny of the literati and the Emperor, [its leaders] were compelled at the same time to rally to the defense of the Ch'ing government.[9]

Chinese political figures of a later generation have used varying adjectives to characterize this rallying of the regional literati and gentry to the Ch'ing Restoration state, but they have all recognized the phenomenon. To the Nationalists after 1927, it appeared as a glorious model and the key to the manipulation of social forces in twentieth-century China.[e] To a Youth Party leader it symbolized the supremacy of national ideological interests over private or regional material interests.[10] In the view of a Marxist specialist on Ch'ing social history, Tseng used the Confucian doctrine to attract and hold the local bullies (Tseng's "upright gentry"), and these in turn hoodwinked the peasantry into supporting the Ch'ing.[11] In the uncolored language of the leading Chinese authority on the subject, "the Emperor made use of them [the regional gentry and scholar-generals] to support the dynasty, and they depended on the Emperor to maintain their own privileges."[12]

THE NEW MILITARY LEADERSHIP

Restoration leaders were convinced that success in military affairs, even more than in other fields, depended primarily on getting the right men. And as in other spheres, professional capacity without moral superiority was regarded as not only useless but dangerous.[f] In his diary, Tseng Kuo-fan repeatedly emphasized the moral character and training of the Confucian system as virtually the sole basis for the selection of officers. If a military leader did not display justice, humility, and vision, the troops would not obey him. He must be scrupulously honest: "not a copper for private luxury; not an employee for personal reasons." He must rise early and follow a strict schedule; otherwise the business of the army would be neglected. Understanding the leader's fear-

---

[d] There was, of course, some variation among the armies. The leaders of the Huai Army, for example, were less indoctrinated than those of the Hsiang, and they were sometimes more loyal to an immediate superior than to a principle.

[e] See Chapter XII.

[f] Professional military capacity was not ignored, however. Discussion of the talents of various commanders figures largely in the correspondence of the period, as well as in official reports. Analysis of ability was generally shrewd and by no means limited to generalities about "the superior man." E.g., Tseng's audience with the Empress Dowager in January 1869, in *Tseng Wen-cheng kung ta-shih chi*, compiled by Wang Ting-an, Shanghai, 1876, Ch. 4, pp. 6b-8b.

lessness, the troops would follow him courageously, like younger brothers guided by an older brother's example. It was axiomatic that under good commanders, there were no poor soldiers. And most important, a military unit trained and disciplined according to these principles would attract popular support.[13]

Tseng was not merely moralizing when he talked about the primacy of moral training in military affairs; he was discussing the realities of the Restoration period. The Hsiang Army, for which we have statistics, was dominated by indoctrinated literati. And since the Huai and other armies that went on to defeat the Nien-fei and the northwestern Moslems were largely built around units of the old Hsiang Army,[14] it may reasonably form the basis for generalizations about the Restoration's military leadership.

The majority of the officers of the Hsiang Army had grown up as fellow students in the Neo-Confucian revival of the mid-nineteenth century.[15] Fifty-seven per cent had begun their careers as literary candidates. What is more significant, the officers in the highest-ranking 10 per cent were all products of the literary examination system; only in the lowest-ranking category did the number of military candidates exceed the number of literary candidates.[16] Had this not been so, the integration of military reorganization with civil reconstruction would have been impossible. As it was, the military commanders' training and indoctrination made it certain that the social aspects of military questions would receive full attention, and that the new armies would not turn against any government that remained an effective protector of the Confucian order.

The senior military officers of the Restoration were loyal officials who understood the broad problems of national reconstruction; they were also competent military men. In spite of the low esteem in which the Chinese traditionally held military achievement, men of outstanding ability and prestige were generally available to take charge of major operations in time of crisis. This was particularly true during the Restoration. There were many others besides the great names of Hu Lin-i, Tso Tsung-t'ang, Li Hung-chang, and Tseng Kuo-fan.[17] Wen-hsiang was notably successful in training and commanding the Metropolitan Field Force, as was Ch'ung-hou in reorganizing the Tientsin troops. Liu Ch'ang-yu, who was frequently reprimanded for his defeats, nonetheless impressed foreign observers as an outstanding military administrator.[18] To-lung-a, Tu-hsing-a, Liu Sung-shan, and Seng-ko-lin-ch'in—men of widely differing types—had in common their proven military competence.

THE SHORTAGE OF COMPETENT MIDDLE-GRADE OFFICERS

Although the Restoration produced outstanding commanders of armies, the officer corps as a whole proved inadequate to the challenge of military modernization. This has been the perennial weakness of Chinese armies of the past century, recognized by Chinese and foreigners alike. The *North China Herald*, which had a correspondent at Li Hung-chang's headquarters, wrote that the better-equipped Imperial troops were nearly always outmaneuvered by the rebels except when Li himself was present; that the campaign would not have dragged on so long if Li had had better officers.[19] On the eve of the war with France, observers still saw weakness in officers as the chief problem of the Chinese army.[20]

After 1860, as China attempted to modernize her military establishment, the weakness of the officer corps became far more serious a hazard than it had been under the traditional order, because of the greatly increased importance of officers in modern warfare:

> Under the native system of drill, which consisted principally in a vigorous flourishing of flags at a distance, and in every man acting as fancy dictated if close quarters were by chance come to, the ignorance of the officers was less important. Their men, from long habit, never expected to see a commander in the neighborhood of danger, and the latter did not disappoint them. But under the foreign system of drill, the presence of an officer is necessary, and the attempt to teach the men foreign tactics, while the superior officers make no effort to learn the simplest word of command, simply results in bewilderment.[21]

Leading statesmen of the Restoration saw the problem and set about trying to solve it. In 1862 the Tsungli-yamen secured Imperial approval for a plan under which officers of both Chinese and Manchu forces would be thoroughly trained by foreign officers in foreign tactics. Chinese officers could then train and command Chinese troops. It was recognized that "to train soldiers we must first train officers," and the plans were carefully worked out. Frequent edicts ordered that military talent be sought out, and numerous proposals on this score were put forward.[22] Feng Kuei-fan, for example, advocated restoring the military examinations to their "original" importance, and encouraging, through these, the promotion of able men from the ranks.[23]

Plans of this type, sound though they may seem, were hopelessly visionary. In point of fact, Chinese society was divided into peasants who fought and an upper class whose values precluded rigorous military drill and front-line leadership. The plans failed not because policymakers were blind to the need for modern officers, but because there was no existing class that could produce such officers. Sergeants and corporals frequently learned to handle their men properly, but seldom got promoted; men whose social status qualified them to be officers under the Chinese system were technically as incompetent as ever after three years of modern training.[24] The status that was a prerequisite to command produced qualities that were irreconcilable with effective command under new conditions.

The inability to produce an adequate officer corps did more than hamper the program of training; it also wrecked other parts of the Restoration plan for self-strengthening. Corruption of middle-grade officers[25] rendered ineffective the plans for improved supplies and better pay. The troops still had to forage, and popular resentment continued. The new arsenals and shipyards, after an initial spurt of growth, stagnated and then declined. The high command was compelled to undermine discipline by tolerating irregular conduct on the part of able junior officers, because they were so urgently needed. Ch'en Kuo-jui, for example, disobeyed direct orders but was explicitly tolerated.[26] The central government was aware that a large proportion of the field reports it received were pure fabrication;[27] inept men glorified themselves, and capable men covered up for their subordinates for fear that worse ones would be sent to replace them. Victory or defeat could usually be verified, but it was impossible to get the full facts.[28]

There was no way to close the crucial gap by employing foreign officers. Foreigners were accepted as technical specialists, but they could not possibly perform the political, social, and ideological roles that were a prerequisite to effective military leadership, a lesson the West has been slow to learn.

TROOP MORALE AND POPULAR SUPPORT

The problem of keeping the troops loyal to the state, and the people behind the troops, not only was basic to the whole program of military reform, but involved the total political and social program of the Restoration. Clearly, ill-treated troops fighting for no cause tended to be mutinous, and little popular support could be expected for armies that looted territory and then abandoned it to rebels. Verses posted anonymously in Hangchow in 1860 expressed the popular attitude:

> When the bandits arrive, where are the troops?
> When the troops come, the bandits have vanished.
> Alas, when will the troops and bandits meet?[29]

All the leaders of the period were alert to the need for competing effectively with the rebel forces for popular support; for in their view the best military plan was useless in the face of popular opposition.[f] Tseng was alarmed at reports that government troops were more disruptive in the countryside than the rebels: "I fear that if we once lose the people's support, we will not be able to get it back." In Tseng's view, rebels were hated just because in their contempt for the people they raped, robbed, burned, and killed; the government troops were respected for rescuing and calming the people (*pai-hsing*); when the troops caused injury to the people, they were no different from bandits and rebels. Hu Lin-i wrote that the common people were the foundation of the army; yet soldiers angrily abused villagers who had treated them with courtesy and respect:

---

[f] The specific problems in connection with each campaign against a rebellion are discussed in Chapter VI.

"Soldiers exist for the purpose of protecting the people. If they do not love the people, why need we have soldiers?"[30]

An edict of 1867 called attention to a report that the people of north China feared the Imperial troops more than they feared the rebels.[31] Foreign observers pointed out that the peasants had been supplying correct information to the rebel forces but dangerously misleading information to the Imperial forces.[32] Newly recruited armies en route to the front frequently clashed with civilians.[33] For example, during the campaign against the northwestern Moslems, boat owners refused to transport troops.[34] Week after week and year after year Imperial edicts recorded looting and pillaging by troops. Officers enforced discipline only feebly and frequently participated in the looting themselves, selling the goods in Tientsin and elsewhere.[35]

Immediate measures, such as burning the boats of recalcitrant owners, did not solve the problem; more basic matters were involved. Unless the ideology of the whole society could be reinvigorated, troops and people would not find a common interest in defending it. Unless the troops were adequately paid and supplied, looting could not be controlled; the Imperial financial structure was involved as well as the quality of army officers.

The Hsiang Army and the other new armies of its type were developed along lines designed primarily to assure troop morale and popular support. Tseng Kuo-fan insisted that the people must be convinced that they fared better with the troops than with the rebels, and that this was in the first instance a question of morale and ideology. Three-quarters of a century later Chinese armies were still being taught Tseng's song on "loving the people": "Oppressed people welcome the Imperial troops," and so on. Tseng's effective "Summons to Punish the Yüeh Rebels" emphasized the utter incompatibility of the Taiping doctrine and the customary Chinese way of life.[36]

Tseng's basic aim was to "protect the community and to support Confucianism."[37] For this purpose, the indoctrinated Hsiang Army was an admirable instrument, since the indoctrination induced not only an attitude of loyalty to the central government but also a code of behavior certain to win widespread popular support in mid-nineteenth-century China. The leading Chinese authority on the Hsiang Army has called it "an army of farmers led by literati." This combination, eminently appropriate to the time and place, made a magnificent fighting force under the banner of revived Confucianism.[38]

The efforts of other military leaders to raise morale and ensure popular support followed the pattern established by Tseng for the Hsiang Army. Tso Tsung-t'ang's handling of the Ch'u Army during the northwestern campaign was a good example. Tso administered his army efficiently, enforced strict discipline, and lived himself under the same conditions as his troops. He compelled his troops to pay market prices for food and assigned them to tree planting and other enterprises of benefit to agriculture. He inaugurated a reconstruction program as soon as an area was recaptured.[39]

It is not easy to say exactly what this mass of documentation exhorting to "love of the people" proves,[h] but it seems clear that it cannot be dismissed entirely as meaningless verbiage. Take the case of the recall and imprisonment of Ch'eng-lu, a ranking commander in the campaign against the northwestern Moslems. Tso Tsung-t'ang reported that Ch'eng-lu's troops had abused the people, treating upright villagers as traitors; on the basis of this report the censor Wu K'o-tu pressed the case in Peking.[40] Tso was understandably eager to replace a commander who had long been stalemated, and perhaps glad to remove a potential rival from the scene. The point is that the charge of mistreating the common people seemed to Tso not only a proper basis for indicting a general, but a better basis than demonstrable incompetence. It should also be remembered that Wu K'o-tu later showed the importance he attached to considerations of traditional morality by committing suicide in protest against the filial impiety of the Kuang-hsü succession.

For study of these problems of loyalty, dissidence, and social cohesion, what men say is as important as what they do. A doctrine in which belief is widely and consistently professed is usually a surer key to the ethos of an age than a list of lapses from that doctrine.[41] It is true that in the end the Ch'ing failed to create lasting popular support for its armies; it is no less true that Restoration leaders recognized the dimensions of the problem and made strenuous and intelligent efforts to solve it. These efforts did not save the old order forever, but they did undercut popular support for the rebellions and make possible a period of domestic order and stability.

THE ABORTIVE EFFORT TO REINVIGORATE THE REGULAR ARMY

Although the military history of the Restoration is largely the history of new armies of the Hsiang type, programs affecting the old armies deserve brief mention. By the time of the Restoration, the Banners were recognized as inept and outdated; it was proposed that they be gradually absorbed into civilian life rather than rehabilitated as fighting units.[i] Some effort, however, was made to rebuild the Chinese regulars as modernized national armies. As mentioned

---

[h] Marxist writers have made devastating use of the diatribes of Restoration leaders against government alienation of the people. They do not have to quote critics of the Ch'ing; they can and do quote the Restoration leaders themselves to prove abuse of the population by the army (e.g., Chu Ch'i-hua, *Chung-kuo chin-tai she-hui shih chieh-p'ou*, Shanghai, 1933, p. 129; Ch'ien Hung, "Nien chün . . . ," *T'ai-p'ing t'ien-kuo ko-ming yün-tung lun-wen chi*, Peking, 1950, pp. 132–35). It is worth noting that for this purpose they generally use the same passages as do the eulogists of the Restoration, who are less impressed with the admitted abuses than with the evident effort to eliminate them.

[i] See Chapter IV.

earlier, the new regional armies were directly under the control of their generals, and hence only indirectly, even tenuously subject to central control.[j] In these circumstances it was natural that the central government should attempt to counterbalance them with revitalized Imperial forces under the immediate command of the central Board of War.

After the recapture of the rebel capital of Nanking in 1864, officials in the capital and in the provinces memorialized urging the progressive disbandment of the regional armies' "braves" and their re-enrollment in a reformed Imperial army. Tseng Kuo-fan himself immediately took the initiative in disbanding his Hsiang Army. If this step was in part a political maneuver to which he was pressed, the available evidence indicates that it was also a statesmanlike act in support of the Ch'ing state and in accord with his own political principles.[42]

Yet although Tseng and his colleagues gave formal support to the effort to restore the regular army, they doubted that the effort would come to anything. Enormous difficulties stood in the way. Morale was poor. Finances remained inadequate, and corruption and padding of rosters continued. The methods of indoctrination and training used so effectively with the "braves" had little effect on the regulars except in Chihli.[43] Thirty years later another generation of reformers still pointed to the Imperial army as an excrescence, whose support exhausted the people without providing them with any reliable defense in return.[44]

THE MILITIA

It was inevitable that the Restoration should also bring with it an effort to revive the militia system, since this was sanctioned by tradition[k] and appeared

[j] K'ang Yu-wei subsequently used a number of instances from the Restoration period to establish his point that the governors-general, who were often at the same time Grand Secretaries, outranked the administrative boards to such an extent that the president of the Board of War often knew only the number of regular troops of which he was theoretically to dispose, but nothing of their actual numbers and disposition (*K'ang Nan-hai wen-ch'ao*, Shanghai, 1916, ts'e 4, pp. 32–43).

[k] According to Lei Hai-tsung, the loss of the ancient identity of soldiers and people, institutionalized in the militia, is the key to China's historic decline since the Eastern Han. In his view, between the Ch'un-ch'iu and the Han periods the army and people, originally inseparable, became first distinct and then opposed. Chinese history became passive, governed by pressures of natural disaster, population growth, and attacks from outside. Hence there could be no long-term development in Chinese history, but only the fluctuating cycles of order and disorder and the makeshift use of foreign troops. Only in the first great century of Sui-T'ang was there true conscription and hence a true national revival. Wang An-shih was one of the few who understood that China's only hope lay in the remilitarization of the people and especially of the literati. (Lei Hai-tsung, "Chung-kuo ti ping," in *She-hui k'o-hsüeh tsa-chih*, I, 1 (1935), 1–47. See also Lei's "Wu-ping ti wen-hua," *ibid.*, I, 4 (1936), 1005–30. Both articles are reprinted in his book *Chung-kuo wen-hua yü Chung-kuo ti ping*, Changsha, 1940.)

Without quibbling over terminology, it should be noted that Ch'ing chroniclers sometimes found the precedent for the nineteenth-century militia not in antiquity but in the suppression of the An Lu-shan Rebellion of the eighth century A.D. (editor's preface to the chapter on militia, *WHTK*, p. 9617).

to many to fill a current need. In the ideal Chinese state of antiquity, at least as seen through Restoration eyes, soldiers and peasants had been identical; farmers had equipped themselves and defended their homes. Sizable standing armies had not been needed.[45] On the practical side, a good militia system would both save money and increase local control. Moreover, it would solve many of the government's knottier transportation and communication problems by assuring the constant presence of armed forces in remote places, for example in Kansu, to which it was always difficult to transport troops and supplies.[46]

For these reasons, Hart, along with various Chinese Restoration planners, urged the extension of the militia system.[47] Widespread efforts were made,[48] but most of them were dismal failures; contrary to hopes, local funds and popular support were not forthcoming. Tseng's success with the Hunan militia was the exception rather than the rule, and Tseng himself came to consider the system impracticable and unwise, too heavy a burden on the people and readily susceptible to abuse by the gentry.[49] In addition, conflict between regular army and militia was frequent and serious.[50]

The Hsiang and other new armies of the Restoration have sometimes been erroneously identified with the local militia. On the basis of a careful study, Lo Erh-kang has refuted emphatically the notion that Tseng used the militia to suppress the Taiping Rebellion—the notion that the Hsiang Army *was* the Hunan militia.[51] As the Hsiang Army developed, the Hsiang-hsiang militia died.

Restoration military leaders did succeed in raising morale and securing popular support, but they did so by creating indoctrinated regional armies and making them in effect subordinate to the central government. The extension of the militia system was a different and secondary program, and a failure. Neither the Restoration government nor its heirs succeeded in making every village secure from "bandits," at low cost, by working a local militia into the pao-chia system.*[l]*

CENTRAL MILITARY ADMINISTRATION*[m]*

After the Taiping Rebellion the Board of War was never again able to exert direct control over the major military activities of China.[52] As the regionally based armies came to dominate the scene, provinces became increasingly reluctant to supply men and treasure to other provinces. And even where the will to co-operate was present, the way was often lacking.

After finding it impossible to rehabilitate the old Imperial forces, the central government concentrated on gaining the substance of national military administration without the form. This design, envisoned as depending on "men

---

[l] See Chapter VII.

[m] On the problems of military finance as an aspect of general fiscal policy, see Chapter VIII.

of ability" and a patchwork of adjustments, was far from absurd; everything indicated that the scholar-generals in the provinces would automatically take account of the national military situation as a whole, and some of them did. A generation later, K'ang Yu-wei insisted that only Hu Lin-i really rose above his region and acted in the national interest,[n] but K'ang was campaigning for tight administrative centralization. A less impassioned review of the outstanding military careers of the Restoration suggests that although individual efforts to act in the general interest could not make up for the absence of centralized control, they were sufficient to make possible a number of large-scale, well coordinated military campaigns.

However, the government's effort to create a rational system of military administration encountered what proved in the end to be insuperable difficulties.[53] The biggest difficulty was China's economy, which Restoration leaders did their best to keep stable, stagnant, and incapable of expansion. The cost of armies had been high in proportion to the total income of China's agrarian economy even before the introduction of expensive new arms during the Restoration. The support of one cavalryman for one year had required the revenue of seven hundred mou of land,[54] the total holdings of perhaps thirty-five farm families. Modern armies would require still more money, too much money for a stable agrarian economy to provide.

In consequence, the usual step in an emergency had been to order provinces with alleged surpluses to supply funds to armies fighting in deficit provinces. After years of civil war, however, there was little prosperity anywhere, and much of what supplies could be scraped together was lost in transit owing to the clumsy system of transport. Not only silver bullion but grain was moved excessively long distances.[55] The supplies that arrived were generally short, and there was confusion concerning their allocation.[56] The system according to which Ma Hsin-i was ordered to send 50,000 taels to Tso Tsung-t'ang or half a dozen provinces were ordered to supply Li Hung-chang with a million taels[57] was satisfactory to no one.

The responsible officials clearly understood the fundamental importance of finance and supply,[58] and recognized the shortcomings of the system as it operated. Theoreticians like Feng Kuei-fen pointed to the necessity of full information on military expenditures as a prerequisite to a rational budget;[59] accordingly the central government in 1862 (TC-1) ordered all armies to report quarterly to the Board of War.[60] In 1864 the Grand Secretariat and the Board of Revenue

---

[n] In Kang's view, "In general, the governors-general and governors considered protecting their own territories to be their task; beyond their borders they had no responsibilities; for this they took no thought. For the general situation of the Empire, they made no provision." (*K'ang Nan-hai kuan-chih i*, n.p., n.d., pp. 6–9.)

jointly requested an accounting from all provinces.[61] Edicts of 1867 and 1868 repeated the orders for full reports and for field investigations.[62] This plan, however admirable in theory, was unrealistic, and the orders went unheeded. In the course of eight years only two provinces—Hupeh and Szechwan—sent in regular reports.[63]

Tseng Kuo-fan, who believed that the Nien-fei could never have invaded Chihli if finances had been sound, devised a plan more appropriate to existing conditions. Typically, he proposed "an adjustment in accordance with the times" in order "to change weakness into strength." Under the present confused system, he wrote, nearly every province was responsible for some contribution to the military expenditures of nearly every other province. He urged that certain "base areas" be designated and assigned the sole and total responsibility for supplying specified military areas. He suggested the upper Yangtze valley as the base for the Kiangnan area, Szechwan as the base for Yunnan, Hunan as the base for Kweichow, and so forth.[64]

In attacking confusion of responsibility, Tseng was attacking an important weakness in all Chinese administration, and in other respects also his plan was a good one for its time. The Restoration came to an end before it could be given a fair trial. For the long run, however, it seems in retrospect that the radical concepts of an expanding economy with expanding revenues, of a national military budget and a centralized administration, were as necessary to China as they were repugnant to China's leaders.

REDUCTION IN THE SIZE OF THE ARMY

The problem of finance was closely related to the question of the size of the Chinese army.[65] Since funds were limited, a modernized army would have to be a small one: on this point there was virtually universal agreement during the Restoration. Tso Tsung-t'ang pointed out that if useless and fictitious troops could be eliminated those that remained could be trained more adequately.[66] Tso ignored, as did others, the local constabulary duties that supposedly occupied so many Imperial troops. Hart, in his famous 1865 memorandum° to the Chinese government, suggested that a trained army of 90,000 men—5,000 for each province—would be stronger and more economical than the ragged million enrolled at that time.[67] Despite some reservations on details, the high officials asked to comment on the memorandum were in general agreement with Hart.[68]

Feng Kuei-fen suggested that between three hundred thousand and four hundred thousand troops would be sufficient; he pointed out that England and France had achieved world power with relatively small standing armies.[69] Wen-

° See Chapter XI.

hsiang also urged the training of smaller, more effective forces. On the basis of his experience as commander of the campaign to pacify south Manchuria in 1866, he concluded that a properly trained force of two thousand men could defeat a rebel force of thirty thousand men. He attributed past defeats to the failure of responsible officers to deal effectively with problems of organization, training, and morale.[70]

The censor Wang K'ai-t'ai pointed out that the government had spent billions on the regular army to no avail; so large a number of men simply could not be made into good soldiers with the funds available. Since they earned too little to support their families, troops in the so-called training camps were more occupied with earning a living than with military training. Wang worked out detailed proposals for reducing the number of troops, increasing pay, and reorganizing the training camps.[71]

Reduction in the total size of the armed forces having been accepted as policy, there remained two main problems in its execution: (1) it was dangerous to reduce the number of troops rapidly in areas where there was still fighting; (2) disbanded troops roaming the countryside would constitute a threat to public order. However, rebellion was gradually being brought under control, and in 1864 (TC-3) Li Hung-chang was able to discharge half of his sixty thousand Kiangsu provincial troops.[72] Portions of the Kwangtung armies were disbanded early in 1868.[73] At the same time the governor-general of Fukien and Chekiang, Ying-kuei, was permitted to discharge thirteen thousand of the thirty-five thousand troops in the Chekiang Army, and to increase the pay of the rest.[74] In May 1868, Kuan-wen blocked a proposal to disband six inefficient Chihli armies and to use the sum saved for supplies to the better armies.[75] This, however, was only a postponement; a second edict confirmed the principle that the size of all armies should be decreased as rapidly as practicable.[76]

Preventing disbanded troops from stirring up local disturbances was a harder problem. In some cases disbandment did not appear to be worth the risk. For example, discharged soldiers from Pao Ch'ao's army caused such tension in the Yangtze valley in 1865 that when the problem came up again in 1867, it was decided to disperse his soldiers among other armies rather than risk creating a body of *rōnin*.[77] Wherever considerable numbers of troops had been disbanded, a vigilant watch had to be maintained.[78]

Significant steps were taken, however, to facilitate the return of ex-soldiers to peaceful civilian life. Ch'ung-hou's program to achieve this end was noteworthy.[79] Similar measures were taken in Shantung following the Huai Army's victorious campaign against the Nien-fei.[80] Ting Pao-chen ordered that the disbanded troops whose native places were in Shantung be given back their old jobs as farmers, artisans, or merchants, and that arrangements be made through the pao-chia system to see that there were no wanderers to start trouble. He asked the central government for travel funds for soldiers whose native places were in other provinces.[81] The outstanding and most widely acclaimed example was Tseng Kuo-fan's demobilization of the large forces that had pacified the lower Yangtze valley. Tseng devised and put into effect a plan whereby the more turbulent soldiers were incorporated into the new Yangtze Navy and the remainder received not only terminal pay, but free, carefully arranged transportation back to their native places and assistance in rehabilitation.[82]

MODERNIZATION OF ARMAMENT

Generally speaking, officials of the sixties opposed only such technological change as seemed likely to lead to social change. Virtually all of them readily conceded the advantage of using Western-type ships and guns. The memorials advocating the manufacture of modern arms emphasized that this was simply a craft, which Chinese could learn.[83] A Gunpowder Office (attached to the Board of Works)[84] and other similar offices had long existed for the production of military equipment. The adoption of more effective Western methods was merely a technical improvement.

An interest in Western arms had begun to develop among a few private citizens and provincial officials in the 1840's, but their efforts to introduce improved arms received little support from higher authorities. In the opinion of the Tao-kuang court and bureaucracy, producing Western weapons would cost too much and would endanger established interests. During the Hsien-feng period, the Chinese government became even more conservative and intransigent. However, the interest in Western arms was never entirely lost and began to revive sharply in the early 1860's as the lessons of campaigns against both rebels and foreigners were driven home.[85]

The important new element in the armaments program of the sixties was the sustained interest of the highest metropolitan and provincial officials. Prince Kung and Wen-hsiang were enthusiastic supporters of the various projects that mushroomed in widely different parts of the Empire.[86] Tso Tsung-t'ang, who understood the importance of social, political, and economic reconstruction, wrote: "But from the standpoint of urgency, the casting of guns ranks first; and dredging rivers, drilling wells, and manufacturing woolen cloth come next."[87] Even Tseng Kuo-fan, who held the view that the conduct of war depended on men rather than on arms, devoted some of his best efforts to the modernization of arms.

In the self-strengthening movement, the chief emphasis was placed on developing shipyards and arsenals where China could manufacture her own arms. The Chinese government was persistently suspicious of foreign governments' offers to give or sell China arms.

The Beginnings of a Modern Navy. From the time when Western steamers were used to transport the Hsiang Army from Anking past the Taiping river defenses to Shanghai, the importance of modern ships was recognized by both central and provincial authorities.[88] Many of the ships used at the outset were leased or purchased abroad, but the affair of the Lay-Osborn Flotilla, to be described below, confirmed the Chinese in the determination to manufacture their own ships.

The optimism of Tseng Kuo-fan, who believed in 1861 that steamers could be successfully introduced within a year or two,[89] proved unjustified, but even so the sixties were the most promising decade in modern Chinese naval history.[90] The Chinese navy of the time was a modest one, of course, consisting largely of armed junks and sampans until after 1868, but it proved useful against rebels and pirates from the beginning of the era. It was used by Tu-hsing-a to block Li Hsiu-ch'eng's advance toward Woosung, and by Tu-hsing-a and Tseng to check the Taiping raids from Nanking across to points on the north bank of the Yangtze.[91]

The more formal Yangtze Navy was organized during the summer of 1865 with six senior officers, 798 junior officers, and twelve thousand enlisted men. Its annual budget of more than sixty million taels was to be supplied by the likin offices of the Yangtze valley. Its administrative regulations were drawn up by P'eng Yü-lin and Tseng Kuo-fan. The majority of the officers were selected by Tseng, but other high provincial officials were able to register recommendations with the Grand Council.[92] Tseng's chief difficulties in developing the Yangtze Navy were the lack of competent naval officers and the preoccupation of provincial authorities with land armies.[93]

The Kiangnan Arsenal. The Kiangnan Arsenal,[94] formally established in 1865, was the most impressive of China's efforts to manufacture modern arms. In the T'ung-chih period it was peerless in east Asia and one of the great arsenals of the world, and by 1870 China seemed to be rapidly coming abreast of the West. This prospect was never realized; seventy years later, having never surpassed the 1870 level of the Kiangnan Arsenal, China had fallen disastrously behind the West and Japan.[95]

The history of the Kiangnan Arsenal began with Tseng Kuo-fan's unsuccessful attempt to set up an arsenal at Anking in 1863. A few months later Li Hung-chang easily convinced the Tsungli-yamen that a first-class arsenal was needed in the lower Yangtze valley.[96] Li himself went to Shanghi to find foreigners to teach the manufacture and use of arms, "to make the foreigners' special skills China's special skills."[97]

The best proofs of the effectiveness of the Kiangnan Arsenal are the detailed reports of foreigners who inspected its accomplishments on the spot and who at the outset certainly were not prejudiced in the Chinese favor. In 1866 Li Hung-chang was described as having "enormous magazines," "vast numbers" of rifles and guns, "arsenals which for extent may vie with those of the most powerful nations of Europe." In 1867, only two years after the founding of the Arsenal, the *North China Herald* stated: "It is now in such an efficient condition, that all the tools and machinery needed is manufactured in the shop." In 1868 the first modern-style gunboat built by Chinese was successfully launched, and the construction of others was planned.[98]

The Kiangnan Arsenal represented a high degree of innovation in broad policy as well as in technology. The work of its translation bureau and language school is well known. In the opinion of a distinguished Chinese scientist of today, the works translated there exceeded in quality those translated in all China during the subsequent half century.[99] At each of the machine shops young Manchus were observed studying applied mechanics. The Chinese directors were described as able and well-trained. The three hundred Chinese employees were paid from four to eight times the prevailing wage for farm and coolie labor, they received their pay direct, and they worked an eight-hour day.[100]

The Foochow Shipyard. The achievements of the Foochow Shipyard were another example of the speed with which Restoration China was able to solve the purely technical problems of a modern army and navy. Founded by Tso Tsung-t'ang when he was governor-general of Fukien and Chekiang, the Shipyard was related to Tso's program of regional reconstruction as well as as to his general plan for coastal defense.[101] In the beginning two courses of study were offered: engineering and the French language, and navigation and the English language. In 1873 (TC-12) the director proposed to expand the curriculum to include chemistry, metallurgy, and international law.[102] Tso was willing to employ foreigners until Chinese could be trained, but he was emphatic about the importance of training Chinese to replace them as rapidly as possible.

When Tso left to command the expedition to pacify the northwest,[p] he was succeeded as director of the Shipyard by Shen Pao-chen. Shen was selected not only because of his proven ability but also because as a member of the Fukien gentry he would find it easy to secure local co-operation. Chou K'ai-hsi and Tso's French protégé, Prosper Giquel, were named Shen's assistants.[103] During Shen's term of office, 1867–74, both progress and prospects were great. Fifteen vessels were built, and a large number of competent young men were trained.[104]

---

p See Chapter VI.

Among the early students was the enormously influential translator Yen Fu. Giquel appeared to have good reason for predicting of these students:

> in a few years they will certainly supply China with engineers and superintendents of departments, capable of carrying out the construction of all styles of ships and engines which she could desire, and with naval officers as experienced as those of any other nation.[105]

An observer from the British Museum deplored the emphasis on applied science at the expense of basic scientific studies, but reported that

> about 300 young Chinamen are here engaged in studying navigation and mechanics under the superintendence of between sixty and seventy teachers, artisans, etc., most of whom are French. A half-pay English naval officer presides over the school of navigation, and has so far succeeded with his pupils as to be able to provide good and efficient native crews and engineers for the steamers employed on Government duty along the coast. Already several transports carrying guns, and gunboats, have been successfully launched from the dockyard, and others are rapidly approaching completion. The former vessels have been employed in carrying the imperial grain to the north, and although they are manned and officered by natives, it is noteworthy that no accident has yet befallen any of them.[106]

After 1874 the Foochow Shipyard, like most of the other creations of the Restoration, gradually declined. There was some active opposition to it, and Chang Chih-tung later charged the conservative literati with sabotaging it by a whispering campaign,[107] but the chief difficulty appears to have been loss of vigorous leadership and general apathy.[108] Founding the Shipyard had required courage and imagination on Tso's part. In operating it, Shen had needed all his perseverance and prestige. After Shen's time, the directors were subordinates in the provincial hierarchy, lacking in status. Their requests for funds went unheeded, and they obtained little co-operation from other provinces. Costs mounted as Western naval design became more elaborate, and the post-Restoration central government lacked the determination and the ability to afford sustained support.[109].

The Kiangnan Arsenal and the Foochow Shipyard were conspicuous examples of a general trend. Tso Tsung-t'ang was famous for his work in the manufacture of arms in the far northwest. The Tientsin arsenals, under the management of the taotai, employed two thousand workmen, including some foreigners and many artisans from southeast China. According to a contemporary Chinese description, "the noise can be heard for miles around."[110] Other arsenals were developed at Hangchow and elsewhere.[111]

Foreign Drill. An essential part of the modernization program was training Chinese troops to use the new weapons. In the port cities and occasionally in the interior, training programs proved that a Chinese peasant could be made into a first-class modern soldier within a very short time. Ch'ung-hou's training program in Tientsin produced creditable results.[112] The mobile and well-equipped Metropolitan Field Force was designed for the protection of Peking, south Manchuria, and the Imperial tombs, but it could be rushed to trouble spots anywhere in Chihli.[113] And as deep in the interior as Yunnan and Kweichow, Chinese troops were drilled by a foreigner, William Mesny, beginning in 1861.[114]

One portion of the Restoration program to improve the technology of war was based on Manchu and Mongol rather than on Western models. Experience had proved the urgency of greater mobility, and in consequence the cavalry was greatly expanded. Manchurian cavalry units were built up and were used in various parts of China proper. At the same time many commanders in China proper began to develop their own cavalry.[115]

With great and gifted generals, alert troops, a promising arms industry, and a very creditable training program, China's new armies lacked only one essential: an officer corps capable of the routine fulfillment of the duties of modern warfare. Dependent upon one generation of great leaders, they disintegrated when those leaders were gone.

THE CHINESE ATTITUDE TOWARD FOREIGN MILITARY AID

Although suspicious of all foreign military aid, T'ung-chih officials distinguished between aid controlled by the Chinese government and aid controlled by foreign governments, i.e., intervention. They were willing to employ individual foreigners and to accept foreign-manufactured arms as temporary measures until China had built her own arsenals and trained her own officers and troops, but only on the condition that this temporary aid should remain under strict Chinese control.

The Employment of Foreign Officers. The Chinese attitude toward the employment of foreigners was clear and consistent. The foreign officer or technical specialist must accept a Chinese appointment and be solely responsible to the Chinese government. Moreover, he could not expect a special status but must take an appropriate place in the regular hierarchy.[116]

The career of Frederick Townsend Ward, the American organizer of the Ever-Victorious Army, is a good example. Ward held a Chinese rank, was considered by the Chinese government to have become a Chinese subject, and was subordinate to the usual provincial military authorities. He achieved noteworthy victories and was duly rewarded, Chinese style. Nonetheless the Chinese government remained apprehensive about him, and repeatedly cautioned provincial officials to see that he did not gain too much authority or prestige.[117]

At the time of Ward's death in 1862, another American officer, Henry Andrea Burgevine, was high in Chinese favor because of his victories and his reported wish to become a Chinese subject.[118] When Burgevine, who succeeded to Ward's command, later openly flouted Chinese authority and deserted to the rebels, Li Hung-chang ordered his arrest—for treason. From the foreign point of view, Li's action threatened the principles of extraterritoriality, even though there was little foreign support for Burgevine himself. From the Chinese point of view, the issue was sovereignty and the right to control the alien instruments of military progress.[119]

An Englishman, Charles George "Chinese" Gordon, later the famous General Gordon who died at Khartoum in 1885, seems to have come closest to meeting the Chinese government's standards for foreign officers in Chinese employ, perhaps because Gordon was less of a free-lance adventurer than the others and more convinced a supporter of the Ch'ing cause. After being appointed by Li Hung-chang to the command of the Ever-Victorious Army early in 1863, Gordon led the army in a series of victories culminating in decisive assistance to Li Hung-chang in the recapture of Soochow in December 1863. He received due credit in Li's report, was commended by the Throne, and was awarded 10,000 taels.[120] Bruce reported, apparently correctly: "There is no affectation in the cordial expressions of good will with which the Prince and his associates in the Foreign Board invariably mention his [Gordon's] name."[121]

The Chinese problem in making use of an officer like Gordon arose not only from the question of sovereignty but from differences between the Chinese and English codes of behavior. Gordon helped secure the surrender of Soochow by promising to spare the lives of its Taiping leaders. But when they had surrendered, Li promptly proceeded to execute them because, as doctrinaire leaders of insurrection, they could not safely be re-educated to the proper way of life. Although Gordon's motives may have been mixed, he considered that his word of honor had been sacrificed to unprincipled Chinese opportunism. To the Chinese, every principle required the extermination of the Taiping leaders, and Gordon was simply being stubborn in an unintelligible, irrational, foreign way.

In these circumstances, the Chinese set about controlling Gordon by "ensnaring" him; he was given free rein in relatively minor matters but kept under strict control where serious issues were involved.[122] Complications were avoided by the Tsungli-yamen's skillful approach to the British minister.[123] Arrangements were made for Hart to explain to Gordon the difference between the Chinese and English notions of a soldier's honor. Successfully "ensnared," Gordon went back to work. After the recapture of Changchow, further honors were heaped upon him, including a Yellow Riding Jacket and the rank of provincial commander-in-chief.[124]

A number of other Western officers accepted Chinese commissions and contributed to Chinese military progress: d'Aiguebelle, Giquel, Le Brethon, Roderick Dew, Protet, and others.[125] Their achievements were duly recognized, provided they remained suitably modest and tractable.[126] As their numbers increased, the Chinese government devised a special decoration, the "Double Dragon Precious Star," with which to reward them, presumably in order to avoid excessive increases in their Chinese rank.[127]

The use of foreign technical experts in the arsenals and dockyards raised the same problems as the use of foreign field officers. In Chinese eyes no skill the foreigners could offer was worth the slightest concession of sovereignty. They were employees of the Chinese government, to be used in the program of military modernization until competent Chinese could be trained. Giquel, a protégé of Tso Tsung-t'ang and Shen Pao-chen, and Halliday Macartney, a protégé of Li Hung-chang, were outstanding examples of foreign technicians who adapted themselves to Chinese requirements. In his memorials Tso spoke of Giquel with astonishingly informal affection, and Shen later saw to it that his work was recognized.[128] Macartney thoroughly deserved and enjoyed Li's confidence.[129]

Neither Macartney nor Giquel was a mere technician. Their influence on the high Chinese officials whom they served was pronounced. Li went so far as to deputize Macartney to co-operate with the prefect of Nanking on any international issues that might arise during Li's absence from the province.[130] These men and others like them were able to extend their influence because they did not claim it as a right.

British officials and British home opinion generally sympathized with the Chinese view of the proper position of foreigners in the employ of the Chinese government. Alcock wrote: "The Chinese will have nothing to do with foreigners as the protégés of their respective governments; and they are right." He argued that foreigners could help modernize China only if their governments refrained from all interference.[131] British home public opinion agreed. In discussing British subjects overseas, the *Economist* wrote: "Our Government entirely declines to interfere for their protection against the laws of the country in which they may settle, or the decrees and proceedings of the Government with which they may have taken service."[132]

Foreign residents in China generally took a different view. According to the *North China Herald*, foreign employees of the Chinese government must be independent of Chinese officials if they were to be effective; otherwise their skills would be smothered by the weight of the Chinese bureaucracy: "Equally with the Imperialists as with the rebels, the full value of a European was seldom evoked, because the Chinese are too fond of directing him how to impart the instruction he is paid to communicate."[133]

The Purchase of Foreign Arms. Foreign arms were urgently needed until such time as the Chinese-manufactured supply became adequate. Throughout Europe men made fortunes selling war-torn China (and the war-torn United States) surplus Crimean War arms, most of them made obsolete by changes in standard European equipment.[134] The Chinese problem was to get the arms without risking political involvement. A program for training Chinese troops in the use of arms imported from Russia in 1861–62, originally planned for Kiakhta on the Mongolian-Siberian frontier, was transferred to Peking when the Imperial agent at Urga reported that Russian influence thereabouts might be excessive.[135]

The affair of the Lay-Osborn Flotilla[136] best illustrates the Chinese position. Early in 1862, following the loss of Ningpo and Hangchow to the Taiping forces, a series of urgent edicts ordered the Tsungli-yamen and Yangtze valley officials to follow up the previous summer's preliminary discussions with Hart on the possibility of purchasing foreign warships for naval attack on the rebels.[137] The various foreign envoys resident in Peking were informed of the plan in the hope of forestalling their objections.[138] Subsequently, H. N. Lay, the former inspector-general of the Chinese Imperial Maritime Customs, then on sick leave in England, was instructed to use Chinese funds to purchase a number of naval vessels to be manned by a British crew under the command of Captain Sherard Osborn.[139]

The arrival of the Flotilla in China in 1863 raised dramatically the basic question of how foreigners could best be used in the Chinese military program. In the Chinese view, Osborn was an associate to a Chinese officer and employed to increase China's naval strength without subjecting China to foreign direction.[140] Lay and Osborn, on the contrary, considered themselves the makers rather than merely the implementers of policy, and had no notion of simply offering their technical services to help the Chinese government attain its own objectives. As a result, Lay was dismissed and the Flotilla rejected.[141]

Contemporaries placed varying interpretations on the episode of the Flotilla. The British minister had no doubt that Lay, impatient of the inevitable slow course of persuasion, aimed at obtaining

> the sole command of the most certain sources of the Imperial revenue and of the most efficient branch of its executive . . . The Chinese Government, however, comprehended at once the scope and bearing of this scheme and look upon it as an insidious attempt to take the administration out of their hands.[142]

The United States agreed with this interpretation.[143]

Lay and Osborn, who despised the Chinese, led a vicious attack on Bruce for supporting the increasingly independent Chinese attitude.[144] Gumpach completely overlooked the Chinese government as a factor and adopted the near-lunatic view that America had engineered the opposition to Osborn and that Bruce was currying favor with Washington.[145] W. A. P. Martin reached the unpenetrating conclusion that since the Flotilla had offered a prospect for the study of science, its dismissal was a "backward step."[146] The *North China Herald* reluctantly conceded that the Chinese government was within its rights, but regretted that the Chinese action looked "like a blow aimed at the present system of foreign interference,"[147] which of course it was.

In retrospect, and on the evidence, it seems clear that Chinese metropolitan and provincial officials "rejected the fleet, not because it was a hated foreign implement, but because the hated foreigner wanted to retain control of it."[148]

Foreign Intervention on Behalf of the Chinese Government. The Co-opera-tive Policy[q] led foreign governments to offer military aid, but the Chinese government was prepared to accept this aid temporarily and reluctantly, and in "remote corners" only. No documents support the view that the Ch'ing was willing to sell the country to save the dynasty. Edict after edict stated that although foreign troops might render temporary assistance in Shanghai, because Shanghai "lies secluded in a corner of the sea," the chief reliance must be placed on Chinese troops.[149] In the Chinese view England and France were being "permitted" to aid in campaigns against bandits in the lower Yangtze valley, but the danger of their presence on Chinese soil must never be forgotten.[150]

As on so many other subjects, it was Tseng Kuo-fan who wrote the ablest analyses of the risks involved in accepting foreign military aid. In December 1860 he memorialized: "From time immemorial barbarian assistance to China, when followed by barbarian success, has always involved unexpected demands."[151] He vigorously opposed the use of foreign units in the campaigns to retake Soochow, Changchow, and Nanking, believing that the long-term political hazards of such an arrangement would easily outweigh its military advantages.[152] Tseng's view was supported at court, and he was ordered to speed up the campaign in order to deprive the British of a pretext for sending in Indian troops.[153]

Tseng's views were widely shared.[154] Some men, like Yüan Chia-san, went further and opposed the use of foreign forces even in the defense of Shanghai. Yüan argued that if the Ch'ing forces could win victories in the interior, they could also win at Shanghai; that the foreigners knew that the government was winning and offered aid merely to gain concessions.[155]

A few Chinese were less reluctant to use foreign aid. Certain "gentry" of

q See Chapter III.

Kiangsu and Chekiang petitioned for foreign protection, and Hsüeh Huan negotiated with the British on their behalf. Hsüeh got permission to use foreign troops in the protection of Shanghai, but even Hsüeh was not prepared to concede to foreign forces the right of autonomous action in China.[156]

The recapture of Nanking marked the end not only of the Taiping menace, but also, apparently, of the threat of Western intervention. The Tsungli-yamen reminded Wade that he and Bruce had always urged China to rely mainly upon herself; now at last no further foreign aid would be necessary. Wade was asked to communicate this happy development to Bruce in England so that the British public might respect China.[157]

The Chinese were as opposed to offers of Russian assistance as they were to offers of assistance from the maritime powers. In 1866 when the Ili garrison was begging for help against the Moslem rebels, a member of the Tsungli-yamen, Tung Hsün, wrote in his autobiography that it "was absolutely not permissible" to allow Russia to help defend Ili.[158] Throughout the affair, the Tsungli-yamen seemed less concerned with the danger of Moslem insurrection than with the danger of Russian aid against the insurrection.[159]

During the Nien-fei Rebellion individual foreigners sometimes suggested the use of foreign troops to restore order, but no serious proposals were made. It was generally recognized that Chinese of all types were firmly opposed to the presence of foreign troops on Chinese soil. Wen-hsiang, noting that foreign troops cost twice as much as Chinese troops, said: "If we do not provide for their expenses, how can they be for our use? If we have the necessary funds, how can it be that we have no men of our own?"[160] Tseng Kuo-fan granted that the T'ang dynasty had made good use of Uighur troops, but pointed out that these troops had been used only in conjunction with Chinese troops. Tseng summarized the Restoration attitude toward foreign intervention with a neat metaphor: it was permissible for a man to have his essays "polished" by someone else, but not to send a substitute to take his place in the examination hall.[161]

It is worth noting that Restoration statesmen considered that foreign good offices in arranging a truce were a form of foreign intervention, and these too they refused. The British, whose interests required the liquidation of the Taiping Rebellion as quickly as possible, offered to send British naval vessels up the Yangtze to proclaim an amnesty and to give British sponsorship to the truce. Wade invited Wen-hsiang and others to the British Legation to discuss the matter. The Tsungli-yamen rejected the offer; they considered a truce desirable but insisted that it should be proclaimed by the Chinese government acting entirely independently.[162]

There is no evidence to support the view widely held among doctrinaire Marxist scholars that the Restoration supinely invited foreign aggression. It seems unnecessary to comment on Fan Wen-lan's statement that Prince Kung's attitude was a "base psychology of treating the foreigners as gods," that Li Hung-chang was the puppet of England, Tso Tsung-t'ang the puppet of France, and Tseng Kuo-fan at once the puppet of England, France, and America.[163]

CONCLUSION

For the brief period of the Restoration, China made remarkable progress along both the main lines of military reform: the regional foci of military power were transformed into flying buttresses of the Ch'ing state, and improved arms were produced. A half century later the Hsiang Army appeared in retrospect as a "historical miracle,"[164] and China's accomplishments in the 1860's in the sphere of military modernization appeared no less striking. Prosper Giquel wrote in 1872 that China was rapidly becoming a formidable adversary; that the whole official class was determined to restore China's international position; that the output of factories and shipyards was impressive and that Chinese-built warships would soon equal the highest European standards; that Chinese military power was vastly different from what it had been in 1860.[165] According to a London *Times* review of Restoration achievements, such great changes had occurred in the Chinese army since 1860 that the well-known earlier accounts by Wade, the Abbé Huc, and others had become irrelevant.[166]

China threw more war materiel than France into the Franco-Chinese War of 1883–85; more than Japan into the Sino-Japanese War of 1894–95. Defeats proved that something essential was still lacking, something other than firing power. For after brilliant initial achievements, armies of the Hsiang type, which were supposed to mobilize regional forces in support of the central power, degenerated into warlordism.

The weakness of later Chinese armies was thus no simple malady that could be remedied by supplying them with modern equipment. Modern arms China had long since been able to make; what she could not do was use them effectively. A modernized army with a competent officer corps would have disrupted the very social order the new arms were designed to protect. With the arms unused, or improperly used, the very capacity to manufacture them declined. Thus China's subsequent defeats seem to have been caused by the inadaptability of her social system, of which the later shortage of arms was a symptom and not a cause. Military reform programs failed because they were based on faulty ideas of what needed reforming.

China's disintegration in the early twentieth century into a series of regions governed by quasi-independent warlords has customarily been attributed to the rise of powerful provincial armies during the Restoration. Certainly the shift of military power to the new armies was potentially dangerous to the central government, as has been shown above, and it cannot be denied that they contained the seeds of warlordism. During the Restoration, however, it was by no means a foregone conclusion that they would eventually become warlord armies rather than the regionally based national armies their founders envisioned.

It is misleading to argue that because armies of this type later drifted away from a crumbling central authority, this was the aspect of greatest significance at the time they were first formed, in the 1860's. This fallacy overlooks the aims that guided the actions of provincial leaders of the Restoration. They were interested not in securing satrapies for themselves, but in assuring the survival of the Confucian order; only later, when the Confucian order was clearly doomed, did the disastrous *sauve qui peut* attitude become common. During the Restoration, when there appeared to be great hope for the old order, no one worked more fervently to realize that hope than the prototype of powerful provincial leaders, Tseng Kuo-fan.

CHAPTER X

THE MODERNIZATION OF CHINA'S SYSTEM OF FOREIGN RELATIONS

The most immediate danger confronting the Chinese government during the crisis years of 1859–61 was foreign aggression. To ward off this danger, the statesmen responsible for the management of barbarian affairs faced the problem of grafting onto the traditional idea of the state and the traditional machinery of administration a series of radically new concepts and institutions. There is no more dramatic indication of the vitality that the traditional state still possessed at this late date than the speed with which the Restoration government mastered the Western system of diplomacy and used it to serve Chinese ends.

THE TRADITIONAL CHINESE VIEW OF FOREIGN POLICY

Chinese skill in the peaceful ordering of international relations was no new development. The tributary system,[1] which included all the world known to China, had proved through centuries to be an enduring and effective system of international organization, a hierarchy in which the place of each people was determined by the degree to which it was permeated and transformed by the Confucian doctrine. The magnetic center of this Confucian world order was China, from which civilizing influences radiated to all nations. In the ideology that held the system together, little account was taken of the manner in which Chinese civilization had throughout its history been influenced by contact with non-Chinese peoples. The dogma as formulated in the Chinese Classics was: "I have heard of men using the doctrines of our great land to change barbarians, but I have never yet heard of any being changed by barbarians."[2]

The term barbarian (*i*) meant simply "not yet Sinicized"; the barbarians had an accepted place in the world scheme, below that of the partially Sinicized peoples. The Chinese Emperor recognized the status of the sovereigns of tributary states and of their peoples, and bestowed upon them the immense moral and material benefits of Chinese civilization. The tributary states in return sent tribute missions that gave substance to the universal pretensions of the Chinese Emperor.

The Confucian orthodoxy assumed that there was nothing inherently evil in human nature, including the barbarian nature. If the barbarian could be reformed by education, then tolerance and kindness were the basis of a sound foreign policy. Prince Kung enjoined his fellow countrymen to hate the evil that a barbarian might do but not the barbarian himself; to be "kind to men from afar" in accordance with the Classics, to the end that the myriad nations might be tranquilized, that China might flourish, and that government by virtue might prevail throughout the world.[3]

Although leaders of the Restoration were quick to learn that the tributary system, which had been seriously disrupted during the years of rebellion, could never be rebuilt into an effective means of controlling the Western powers, the system still had considerable value in the conduct of China's relations with other Asian countries.[4] Therefore, while a new system was constructed for dealing with the West, the old system was revived for dealing with Asia; where both the West and Asia were involved, as in the French invasion of Korea in 1866, China used the old and new systems in combination.

One of the marks of the Restoration was the resumption of tributary missions along routes that had long been closed by fighting and were now reopened.[5] Foreign observers were amazed at these demonstrations of Chinese skill in ruling by prestige the far-flung peoples "who continue to worship the shadow after the substance has departed."[6] The *North China Herald* of November 19, 1864, commented: "It is singular that notwithstanding its material weakness, the Chinese Government contrives to maintain unimpaired the suzerainty over neighboring states which it acquired in former days, under more energetic emperors."[a]

Not only the Restoration conservatives but the Taiping revolutionaries as well continued to apply the concepts of the tributary system to some types of international relations. When a British warship visited Ningpo after its recapture by the Ch'ing, officers found an apparently authentic copy of a Taiping edict on world affairs. According to this document, the Taiping leaders envisioned a universal state under the Taiping Emperor. Hereditary foreign consuls would be recognized by China, would be awarded seals, and would be supervised by a Chinese foreign director:

> The affairs of foreign states will be directed by the Director under our orders. The various affairs of the foreign states will be settled by the consuls. The consuls will all obey the order of the foreign Linguist Director, who will direct them.[7]

Thus at the beginning of the Restoration, Chinese conservatives and revolutionaries held a common concept of a Sino-centric universal state. In the light of this basic concept, the efforts of the Western powers to advance their interests were bound to be regarded as insubordination, or, if force was used, rebellion.

---

[a] A quarter of a century later experienced travelers were still impressed with the control exerted by small numbers of Chinese civil officials far out in central Asia and at the Chinese skill in "ruling by effect" (Capt. Frank E. [later Sir Francis] Younghusband, *The Heart of a Continent*, London, 1896, p. 306 and *passim*).

The traditional Chinese foreign policy had regularly been parallel to domestic policy: soothe the obedient, chastise the rebellious.[8]

In 1859 Bruce had recognized these "maxims of China in regard to intercourse with foreign nations" as "the key":

> The subjects of foreign nations residing in China are represented as belonging to barbarous tribes, and living by trade (of all occupations the one in least repute among the Chinese), as devoid of civilization, and ignorant of the rules of reason, and by all means to be confined to the outskirts of the country.
>
> According to the maxims of the Government they are entitled to no rights beyond those accorded by the favour of the emperor; and though circumstances and the weakness of the Government have led it to acquiesce in the concession of considerable privileges to foreigners in distant sea-ports, it is remarkable in proving how tenaciously it holds to its traditions that it always classifies as acts of rebellion the measures of coercion adopted by foreign governments to obtain redress for wrongs done to their subjects.[9]

This traditional system of international relations had for twenty years ceased to work to the satisfaction of either Chinese or Westerners. From the foreign point of view, constant recourse to the use of force locally was a costly and ineffective means of protecting foreign interests.[b] From the Chinese point of view, no policy could be implemented because the foreigners were insensible to reasoning based on Chinese political thinking. Applied to the European barbarians, the principles of the tributary system proved unworkable. In this dilemma the Chinese did not, as has often been charged, sit apathetically repeating Confucian platitudes to a contemptuous West. Instead, they learned the Western system of international relations and adapted it to Chinese needs.

During the crisis of 1860 the Chinese decided to abandon the futile effort to control a physically stronger enemy by the routine assertion of Confucian moral authority, and to appeal instead to the enemy's own moral standards. They were sufficiently acute observers to see that the foreigners granted the validity of moral arguments based on international law, Western public law, written agreements, and common-sense justice. The Chinese attempt to use these European counterparts of the Confucian ethic to control foreign activity in China was the essence of Restoration foreign policy. From the negotiations following the flight of the Hsien-feng Emperor,[c] Prince Kung had concluded that the barbarians kept their pledged word, and that for the time being at least peaceful coexistence was possible.[10]

THE TSUNGLI-YAMEN[11]

The establishment early in 1861 of a modern foreign office, the Tsungli-yamen, was the most striking institutional innovation of the Restoration period. The structure of the Chinese bureaucracy had been fixed for centuries by statute

---

[b] See Chapter III.   [c] See Chapter II.

and precedent, and a tremendous inertia made change difficult. Yet the system was not so moribund as to rule out executive reorganization in an emergency. At the outset, the yamen was no more than a weak and informal association of individually prominent statesmen, but its function was quickly expanded and its status consolidated. The Tsungli-yamen of 1865 was a very different institution from the Tsungli-yamen of 1861. Its intimate association with the Grand Council is no argument against its importance in its own right, but rather reflects a typical Restoration effort to modernize the functioning of the Confucian state without perceptible effect on its basic structure. The device worked well for the duration of the Restoration. Later, when the traditional state disintegrated and powerful provincial officials like Li Hung-chang assumed all the powers of government, the Tsungli-yamen, like the central government of which it was an organ, lost its effectiveness.

Before 1861 there had existed no office concerned solely with the conduct of China's foreign relations. The Board of Rites had responsibilities far beyond the handling of relations with the tributary states. The Li-fan yüan (Mongolian Superintendency) and various other agencies considered their handling of relations with Russia as a minor duty. The shock of the defeat of 1860 and the burning of the Yüan-ming yüan forced a reconsideration of policy.

An edict ordered Prince Kung to take charge of the peace negotiations and appointed Kuei-liang and Wen-hsiang as his chief assistants. Prince Kung himself co-opted Ch'ung-hou and Ch'ung-lun. Heng-ch'i and Lan Wei-wen made the approaches to the allied representatives, and a number of other officials also worked under the direction of the Imperial appointees.[12] Memorials on foreign affairs poured in from the provinces, and copies were sent to the new office for consideration. Its responsibilities increased rapidly after the Treaties of Tientsin were finally ratified and foreign envoys took up residence in the capital.

Early in 1861 Prince Kung, Wen-hsiang, and Kuei-liang memorialized on the need for a new foreign policy to meet a new type of barbarian problem.[13] On January 20, 1861, Prince Kung secured approval for the establishment of a formal and permanent office for the handling of foreign affairs; he communicated his new status to the foreign envoys and received their congratulations.[14] For the first time a single organ of government had charge of all relations with Western powers. The superintendents of trade for the three northern ports and the five southern ports respectively were placed under the jurisdiction of the Tsungli-yamen.[15] Although, like the metropolitan boards and high provincial officials, the superintendents could consult each other on problems involving foreigners and memorialize directly, copies of their correspondence were forwarded to the Tsungli-yamen, as were copies of relevant central government documents.[16]

At the beginning Prince Kung was assisted only by Wen-hsiang and Kuei-liang, but the addition of other members was envisioned from the outset.[17] There was no fixed number; first there were three, later six, and by 1869 ten members.[18] Their titles varied at first but were gradually standardized. The earlier appointees were princes, ministers, and heads of boards who held concurrent appointments to the Tsungli-yamen. As time went on, new members tended to be specialists in foreign affairs holding a single appointment.[19]

For the first three years the internal organization of the yamen fluctuated, but its structure was formalized by the reorganization of 1864. The system enacted at that time lasted until 1901.[20] Some overlapping jurisdictions and historic anachronisms persisted, but the system was a relatively modern and functional one, resembling the Republic's foreign ministries more closely than anything in the pre-1860 Ch'ing system.[d] The yamen suffered less than the other organs of government from the antiquated Ch'ing system of public finance because many of its expenditures were chargeable to other agencies. For example, since the chief members of the yamen held concurrent appointments, their salaries and expenses were paid not by the yamen but by the various traditional offices to which they were concurrently assigned. Many other expenses were paid directly from Maritime Customs revenues.[21]

The Chinese government made a great effort to increase and confirm the prestige and authority of the Tsungli-yamen. The important role it was expected to play was made clear in the first year of its existence, when the Prussian representative asked it to request permission for foreigners to enter the walled cities of Canton and Chaochow, near Swatow. The edict in reply expressed concern lest foreigners think that the Tsungli-yamen was lacking in authority to take action, and instructed the yamen to correct this impression by taking appropriate measures on its own authority.[22] Hsüeh Huan in Shanghai complained that he was now ignored by foreign officials, who would deal only with Peking in spite of the fact that he was the superintendent for ten ports in six provinces.[23]

Once established, the Tsungli-yamen came to have a vested interest in the further development of international relations. To a certain extent its interests became opposed both to those of more conservative, antiforeign local officials and local gentry, and to those of the more conservative organs of the central government. The foreign envoys had almost become its protégés. There thus developed a community of interest between the Tsungli-yamen and the diplomatic corps against aggressive foreign merchants and missionaries on the one hand and Chinese obscurantists on the other. The Sinicization of foreign diplomats[e] was paralleled by the Westernization of the Tsungli-yamen.

d The Chinese Communist historian Fan Wen-lan dismisses the Tsungli-yamen as an organ of no importance, as the Li-fan yüan under another name, having a "nobility-bureaucratic-comprador character" (*Chung-kuo chin-tai shih*, Hongkong, 1949, I, 203–4).

e See Chapter III.

In consequence, the local use of force by subordinate British officials embarrassed Alcock *because* it embarrassed Prince Kung in his relations with the rest of Chinese officialdom. During the Formosan incident of 1868, when a British consul had resorted to "gunboat diplomacy," the action was reported directly to the Throne by the governor-general of Chekiang and Fukien. Alcock, who certainly got his information from the Tsungli-yamen, reported to the Foreign Office:

> the course followed by the Vice-roy of Fukhien in addressing his memorial direct to the throne, has no doubt placed, as it was intended, the Prince and his Foreign Board, of which he is president, in a very unpleasant position, as being answerable for the foreign relations maintained, and in some degree therefore held responsible for the humiliation thus inflicted by 2 subaltern officers of a foreign power. . . . [In cases of this kind, the Tsungli-yamen] were themselves on their trial before the Court and the other Boards. . . . It was necessary that the Prince should at once be able to show that, if any wrong had really been committed by the subordinate officers of a foreign power, in violation of treaty or international law and usage among civilized states, Her Majesty's Representative here would be prepared, after due investigation, to give satisfaction, and, as far as possible, to afford redress for any injury inflicted.[24]

The community of interest between foreign officials and the Tsungli-yamen against the extremists on either side was urged by Prince Kung in a shrewd memorandum to Alcock in 1868:

> The purpose of the Chinese trader is to concede as little as possible to the foreigner, and to seek his interests alone; while the foreign trader aims at his own advantage, without regard to the condition of the native merchant. Each, in short, is careful of his own interest, without thought of the other's welfare. . . . Such being the disposition of the trading class, it rests with officials to act in accordance with the principles of justice, considering both sides of a question, and inclining to neither, by which means a speedy arrangement may be concluded.[25]

It has been responsibly charged that the organization of the yamen was faulty; that it did not permit specialization; that its members spent too much time drinking tea with foreign envoys and too little in the serious study of international affairs, of which they remained absurdly ignorant; that essentially they were conservatives reflecting the traditional outlook of the Grand Council and the boards on which they served.[26] These statements are true in a sense, but they do not make up a balanced appraisal of the Tsungli-yamen. The organization was faulty, but it marked a considerable advance over previous machinery for handling foreign affairs; more specialization was permitted than had been permitted before, and at that time the specialist was not regarded as the ideal statesman in either Europe or China. The members of the yamen were doubtless leisurely, but their success depended on developing intimate, cordial relations with the foreign envoys, most of whom were also accustomed to leisurely social intercourse.*ƒ* They were certainly conservatives, but their conservatism was not the same as the conservatism of the officials in the capital who pilloried the yamen, or of the angry literati in the provinces who mobbed Kuo Sung-tao, the first minister to England.

RESTORATION SPECIALISTS IN INTERNATIONAL AFFAIRS[27]

During the 1860's men of established position like Prince Kung and Wen-hsiang rapidly developed a competence in foreign affairs, and new appointments to the Tsungli-yamen were increasingly based on experience and ability. In the course of ten years changes in the personnel of the yamen were even more striking than changes in its structure and function. Its members quickly came to represent all the varied kinds of knowledge, prestige, and power useful in making and carrying out foreign policy: the Imperial family, the major branches of the central government, the middle bureaucracy, traditional scholarship, knowledge of the Western world, military experience, and experience in the secretariat of the yamen.

There is little foundation for the contention that the ranking members of the Tsungli-yamen were in effect honorary appointees who devoted little attention to foreign affairs. Prince Kung's responsibilities in other spheres of government were extensive, but his own writings and those of foreigners who knew him show that he was a "man of mental vigor and bold resolve," following coherent principles of foreign policy and capable of negotiating skillfully. His personal and official rank greatly strengthened the position of the new yamen within the Chinese bureaucracy and added to its prestige in foreign eyes. Wen-hsiang, "probably the ablest man who ever held a seat in the Tsung-li Yamên," was nominally second to Prince Kung within the yamen and in fact often its acting head, and his work in the Tsungli-yamen was his major responsibility. When his health failed in 1870, he attempted to resign from all his offices except the Tsungli-yamen. He was gradually relieved of his command of a Manchu Banner and of the Metropolitan Field Force, of his presidency of the Board of Works, and of several lesser offices; but until his death he remained in the Tsungli-yamen.[28]

In its first year the Tsungli-yamen was admittedly a Manchu organization, following the pattern of Manchu metropolitan dominance of the pre-Restoration

---

ƒ Foreign reports on diplomatic life in the sixties are filled with accounts of endless visits between the foreign envoys and the members of the Tsungli-yamen; of long, serious conversations as well as of the cordial exchange of social amenities (e.g., *NCH*, Mar. 9, June 8, 1861; Jan. 30, 1864; Oct. 19, 1867). To the Throne, the Tsungli-yamen members explained that they returned calls as a method of "haltering" the barbarian (e.g., Apr. 23, 1863, *IWSM-TC*, Ch. 15, pp. 2b-3), but on the evidence the method was enjoyable as well as effective. In the provinces, officials having contact with foreigners took their cue from Peking; the Shanghai taotai regularly awarded a cup to be shot for at the volunteer rifle meetings, and a Ningpo taotai turned over the lower floor of his house for meetings of the North China Branch of the Royal Asiatic Society (*NCH*, June 17, 1865; Sept. 29, 1866).

period rather than the Restoration pattern of Manchu-Chinese coalescence.[g] The salt controller Ch'ung-lun, the skilled negotiator Heng-ch'i,[h] and the scholarly Grand Secretary Pao-yün were excellent representatives of Manchu civilian officialdom, but of little else.

The picture changed quickly as Chinese of varying backgrounds were added. The first Chinese appointee, Tung Hsün, became a member simultaneously with the last of the high-ranking Manchu appointees, Pao-yün. At the time of his appointment Tung Hsün was a junior vice-president of the Board of Revenue. As associate general editor of the *Shih-lu* for the Hsien-feng period, he was widely read in the documents on all phases of recent Chinese history.[29] A friend and neighbor, W. A. P. Martin, admired his vigor and flexibility of mind and personality.[30] On his sixtieth birthday in 1866, Tung Hsün received unusually high official honors as a reward (according to an informed younger contemporary, Weng T'ung-ho) for his outstanding achievements in the field of China's foreign relations.[31]

The appointment of the distinguished geographer Hsü Chi-yü to the Tsungli-yamen in 1865 was striking evidence of the rapid change that had taken place in the Chinese handling of foreign affairs. The appointment was startling because Hsü and his well-known work on foreign countries, the *Ying-huan chih-lüeh*, symbolized that nascent Chinese interest in the Western world which had proved so signally inconsequential twenty years earlier. Although the geography Hsü published in the forties was "an immense stride in advance" in knowledge of the West, he had been first demoted and then in 1851 removed from office in disgrace.[32] His official recognition in 1865 and the reissue of his book with a preface by Tung Hsün[33] were signs of a new age.

The significance of Hsü's appointment was not fully understood by Westerners, but its importance was not overlooked.[i] S. Wells Williams commented

---

[g] See Chapter IV.

[h] On Heng-ch'i's remarkable talents, see Chapter II and Harry Parkes's full accounts of his conversations with Heng-ch'i, *NCH*, Mar. 23, Mar. 30, and Apr. 13, 1861. Announcement of Heng-ch'i's promotion, *NCH*, Jan. 24, 1861; obituary, *NCH*, Mar. 9, 1867.

[i] E.g., "The *Peking Gazette* has just announced an appointment in the Chinese Foreign Office (The Tsung-Li Yamen), which is said to be the most important event, as far as foreign relations are concerned, that has taken place since the signature of Lord Elgin's treaty. A mandarin of the name of Hsü has been named one of the high Ministers of the Office. This man some years ago was in high office in the Province of Fohkien, and while there, he, with the help of certain American missionaries, wrote a work on the geography of the world, in which he examined foreign institutions and men with an interest which no Chinaman had ever before shown. His two favourite heroes were Napoleon and Washington. The book was written in a popular form and had a large sale. After he had been in office three years, he came to Peking to pay his respects to the Emperor, and during his visit was degraded on the plea that he had not conducted his government well, but really on account of the new views put forward in his book, and of his admiration and intelligence of foreign affairs. Now, for the very qualities which before brought him into disgrace, he is raised to the dignity of a red button of the third rank, and appointed to a vacancy in the Board of Foreign Ministers . . . Hsü's acceptance of office is looked upon as the beginning of a new era in our intercourse with the Chinese." (Freeman-Mitford, *The Attaché at Peking*, pp. 181–82.)

at length in his dispatches. Seward, then Secretary of State, replied: "The importance which you ascribe to the appointment of Seu Ki-yu to a post in the Foreign Office seems to be well founded."[34]

One cannot attach great importance to Tung Hsün's rendering Longfellow into Chinese verse,[35] or to Hsü Chi-yü's writing a eulogy of Washington, for which he received a portrait of his subject as a gift from the American government.[36] Yet details of this kind indicate a considerable change in the character of Chinese official contact with the West.

During the later years of the Restoration, three Chinese officials who had had typical successful careers were appointed to the Tsungli-yamen. T'an T'ing-hsiang had been governor-general of Chihli and junior vice-president of the Board of Revenue.[37] Mao Ch'ang-hsi had been president of the Board of Civil Office, vice-president of the Censorate, and commander of the campaign against the Honan rebels.[38] Shen Kuei-fen, who had also held a succession of provincial and metropolitan offices, was one of the pivotal figures of the Restoration.[j] These appointments served both to neutralize much of the opposition to the yamen and to educate the established hierarchy in some of the new problems of foreign policy.

As the Tsungli-yamen expanded, the importance of its secretariat increased. In 1864 all the agencies of government had been invited to recommend candidates; from the resulting list thirty Chinese and thirty Manchus had been selected as yamen secretaries.[39] These secretaryships quickly became apprenticeships for policy posts. In 1869 a secretary, Ch'eng-lin, became a minister of the yamen;[40] and in 1872 he was joined by a second secretary, Hsia Chia-hao.[41] Subsequently Ch'eng-fu, Li Chao-t'ang, Chou Chia-mei, and other secretaries rose to positions of responsibility because of their training in the yamen.[42]

Experience in foreign relations became equally important in the careers of a number of Chinese officials outside the Tsungli-yamen. Ting Jih-ch'ang's extraordinary career resulted from his supposed skill in foreign affairs as well as from Li Hung-chang's patronage.[43] Li Feng-pao was promoted from the Foochow Shipyard to be minister to several European countries.[44]

S. Wells Williams found China's new foreign affairs specialists "men of acute minds" who were making an intelligent effort to preserve the Confucian state by limited modernization. In his view, when they failed, they failed because they "were placed between the two great pressures of a warped and bigoted multitude of literati wedded to the old regime and the ministers of the outside powers . . . representing armies and navies which had been found invincible."[45]

Kuo Sung-tao, himself a product of the Confucian system, went further

_____
j See Chapter V.

than his colleagues in his effort to bridge the gap between Chinese tradition and the West. He argued that foreign contacts had been of benefit to China, and that the foreigners' intentions were good.[46] In a classic review of the principles of Restoration foreign policy, written about 1875, he emphasized the many common interests between China and the West, the many instances of honorable compromise in recent years.[47]

In examining the qualities of these men as foreign affairs specialists, it is important to remember that for each of them—even for Hsü Chi-yü,[k] even for Kuo Sung-tao[l]—China's domestic affairs remained the primary concern. Foreign affairs did not outweigh domestic in Chinese political thinking until much later.[m] Communist historians have been very wrong to dismiss these men as a "foreign affairs clique," "a new production of the Tientsin Treaties," through whose agency the foreign invaders transformed old-style militarists into new-style militarists.[48]

CHINA'S ACCEPTANCE OF THE TREATY SYSTEM

Before 1860 no Ch'ing statesman had regarded treaties as desirable. Even if specific terms had been favorable (and they were not), they would still have been limitations on the vaguely defined Imperial prerogatives of the tributary system. When tributary illusions were shattered by Western attack, a few officials, notably Ch'i-ying,[49] had developed the beginnings of a new strategy by which China might use the treaties to control the foreigners, provided China herself observed them scrupulously. However, efforts of this type had always been short-lived and without lasting results.

The ratification of the Treaties of Tientsin in 1860 marked more than a return to the Ch'i-ying policy. In the following decade the Ch'ing government accepted and mastered the principles and practices of Western diplomacy and succeeded in using them as the main bulwark of Chinese sovereignty.

Nearly every document concerned with foreign affairs in the 1860's included a careful statement of the bearing of the treaties on the case under discussion. Where there was a treaty stipulation on the matter, the decision was automatic according to law; where a case was not clearly covered by treaty, however, the

[k] Even after he was appointed to the Tsungli-yamen, he memorialized more about the details of bandit movements in Shansi than about international relations. Seward was quite wrong to consider Hsü's appointment as a proof of "the advance in China of the sentiments of Western civilization," but he was right to consider that it marked a considerable change in Chinese policy. See Hsü Chi-yü, "Sung-k'an hsien-sheng tsou-su," in *Sung-k'an hsien-sheng ch'üan-chi*, preface 1915; Seward to Williams, Mar. 6, 1866, *U.S. Arch. China. Instructions*, I, 392.

[l] Kuo's memorials covered domestic affairs fully; his statements on foreign affairs are important but infrequent. See his *Yang-chih shu-wu ch'üan-chi*, 1892, "Tsou-su." His remarkable ideas on foreign policy are to be found in his later *San hsing shih shu-tu*, Shanghai, 1908.

[m] Note the sharply increasing proportion of material on foreign affairs in the Kuang-hsü period, *THTKTI*, Ch. 18.

issue was debatable according to politics. The principle was clearly stated on many occasions: treaties had the force of positive law. If foreign demands were based on treaties, they were to be granted regardless of where China's immediate interests might lie, because her long-term interests depended on the sanctity of treaties.[50]

There is no recorded instance in which the officials responsible for foreign affairs advocated the violation of a treaty during the T'ung-chih Restoration.[51] On the contrary, the Chinese documents, which were never intended for publication, record innumerable instances of the Tsungli-yamen's insistence on strict observance of the law. The yamen refused to protest against a survey of the north China coast by a British ship in 1866; British navigation rights were guaranteed by treaty.[52] When Wen-hsiang was in charge of the purely domestic task of suppressing bandits in southern Manchuria, he devoted particular attention to maintaining order in the Yingkow area, remarking later: "It is a place where foreigners trade; it had to be protected."[53] On the delicate question of the new Sino-Russian frontier following the cession of the Maritime Province, Heilungkiang officials were ordered to change their system of border inspections so as to avoid the chance of trespassing on what had become Russian territory.[54] On the minor but irritating problem of renting commercial premises in the ports, local officials were instructed not to interfere because the right to rent was guaranteed by treaty.[55]

This new policy of accepting and upholding treaties did more than deprive the Western powers of legitimate grievances that might be used as occasions for punitive action. It enabled the Chinese government to reverse the function of the treaties and to use them to limit the activities of foreigners to treaty specifications. Before 1860 the treaties had represented the minimum privileges that foreigners could expect—a line from which they could press forward in the further opening of China. During the 1860's the minimum became the maximum—a line behind which the Chinese government could find security. Japan at this early date posed a problem for Chinese diplomacy precisely because Japan was not a treaty power, and thus not subject to the usual sort of representations in regard to Japanese activities in Korea.[56]

The use of treaties to "halter" the barbarian was not entirely new in the history of Chinese diplomacy. In 1845 Ch'i-ying was instructed to try to prevent British ships from proceeding to Korea by arguing, and correctly, that no treaty had provided for the opening of Korea.[57] Even in 1859–60 a minority faction had urged acceptance of the Treaties of Tientsin.[58] But it was only after 1860 that it became standard Chinese policy to uphold the treaties and to insist that foreigners do likewise.

This new Chinese diplomatic strategy was most effective against the Western powers with whom China's relations were entirely modern in character. By appeal to the treaties, smuggling and illegal maritime trade could be checked and the coolie trade to some extent controlled.[59] Foreign efforts to legalize the import of salt were frustrated, and the establishment of a French salt dealer in Shanghai was closed down.[60]

The success of this policy was indicated by widespread indignation among foreigners in the ports. Treaties, they wrote, had once been minimum rights to be extended by negotiation. They had become precise legal documents, and the Western powers had accepted the Chinese view that any privilege or right not specifically conceded by China could be firmly withheld by China.[61]

THE INADEQUACY OF TREATIES IN RELATIONS WITH RUSSIA[62]

The new Chinese foreign policy was only partly successful where Russia was concerned.[n] The regulation of Russian overland trade was largely under the jurisdiction of the Russian minister in Peking, with whom the Tsungli-yamen could negotiate as skillfully and effectively as it negotiated with the representatives of France, England, or the United States. The formal delimitation of the long Sino-Russian frontier from Korea to Sinkiang also could be made subject to the new system of treaty relations. The third and most serious issue in Sino-Russian relations in the 1860's, however, was the competition for the allegiance of the non-Chinese minorities and the attendant Russian pressure and intrigue along the border. Here the Tsungli-yamen was nearly helpless, for authority and responsibility rested not with the Russian minister in Peking but with the Siberian governors.[63]

The Russian overland trade, which excited such envy among merchants in the treaty ports,[o] posed no great problem to China.[p] In 1862 the Tsungli-yamen and Balliuzek signed a provisional agreement, reached by mutual compromise. In the next three years no serious difficulties were encountered, although certain minor changes in the text proved necessary. In these negotiations the Tsungli-yamen, chiefly represented by Heng-ch'i, was at its best; by fourteen months of adept and imaginative maneuvering it succeeded in blocking the Russian effort to use the pretext of textual revision to throw the whole of Mongolia open to trade on a large scale.[64] Problems continued to arise, but adjustments proved relatively easy to make, and in 1869 a final agreement was reached and signed by the Tsungli-yamen and Vlangali.[65]

[n] See Chapter III. The present section is a study of the application in one field of the new Chinese skills and attitudes in foreign affairs, based on Chinese archival materials. It is not a proper account of Chinese-Russian relations in full, since I have been unable to locate the corresponding Russian archival material.

[o] See Chapter XI.

[p] According to Freeman-Mitford (*The Attaché at Peking*, pp. 263–64), the trade was carried on at a loss, the real interest being territorial.

Border delimitation was a more difficult question. Between 1862 and 1864 territorial disputes were common, and both sides frequently complained of violations all along the frontier. Chinese officials were constantly being ordered to the Sinkiang frontier to check on strayed Russian herds, or to the Heilung-kiang frontier where Russians were alleged to have crossed over to cut grass.[66] The Tsungli-yamen tried to be meticulous: while protesting the slightest Russian infringement,[67] it also was severe with Chinese who were attracted, often by mining possibilities, to the forbidden border zones.[68] When the fault appeared to lie with Russian border authorities, the Tsungli-yamen tried to follow the policy it used so successfully with England; it asked the Russian minister to request that his government reprimand the border officials concerned. The yamen found the minister co-operative, but he claimed to have no authority over border affairs.[69] Chinese border officials were regularly ordered to follow the yamen's instructions,[70] but the Russian foreign ministry never took the hint. On one occasion the yamen gave the Russian minister a letter of protest in Manchu, addressed to the "Russian Grand Secretary." When Wen-hsiang later called at the Russian Legation for a reply, he was told that there had been no answer from the governor-general of Western Siberia.[71] Only rarely could the yamen report that Russia had accepted responsibility for a disturbance and had agreed to send troops to maintain order on its side of the border.[72]

Even so, the Chinese considered that Sino-Russian treaties were useful enough to be worth preserving. An edict of September 7, 1863, ordered Chinese border officials to yield to Russian demands, and on no account to take any retaliatory action that could be construed as violation of the treaty; if China resisted Russia, she would be defeated, *and* the treaty would be destroyed; it was better to yield voluntarily and at least still have the treaty.[73]

Negotiations for fixing the border continued. An agreement reached in 1864 was embodied in the Protocol of Chuquchak,[74] which provided a workable basis for settling disputes. Disputes continued, but solutions were negotiated before they reached serious proportions,[75] and a "final" delimitation of the northwest frontier was reported on September 10, 1869.[76]

Unfortunately for China, neither the trade agreement nor the border agreement provided clear points of reference for fixing the shifting allegiance of the non-Chinese minorities of the northwest, where Russian success in winning allies among the minorities had all but destroyed the traditional basis of Chinese power. It is important to note just how thinly held that territory was.[77] In 1863 the acting Tartar General at Uliasutai, Lin-hsing, reported that on the critical frontier between Kobdo and Uliasutai there were only twenty-four garrisons, manned by a total of *six* regular officers, thirty Mongol princes, and 890 troops. At the most, there could be no more than fifty men at any one guard post. In

Uliasutai itself there were only 240 regular (*lü-ying*) troops and a Manchu garrison of thirty-three. None of these could be spared for guard post duty. Linhsing therefore emphasized the critical importance of the orientation of the Mongols of the surrounding area, of which he gave a detailed description. He concluded that if Uriankhai (Tannu-Tuva) could be kept loyal to China, Russian designs could be blocked.[78]

Lin-hsing described a situation that prevailed throughout the Sino-Russian border region. Everywhere the theoretical quota of Chinese troops was small, and the actual numbers smaller still. Garrisons were mutinous.[79] Funds and supplies were years in arrears.[80] As far as the Chinese knew, Russian influence over the Kazakhs had begun in 1824 when the Russians "kidnaped" a Kazakh khan, whom they still held in 1863; the extension of Russian influence had been noted in the increasing use of the Russian language among the Kazakhs.[81] Chinese documents of the early sixties contained frequent reports on increased Russian activity in Mongolia and Chinese Turkestan.[82]

The Tartar General at Uliasutai, Ming-i, reported that the Russian policy was threefold: (1) to "entice" the Mongols, (2) to "overawe" Chinese officials, (3) to attack. In Ming-i's view, the immediate Russian aim was to secure the allegiance of the Mongols and to open a direct route to Kashgar.[83]

The outbreak of the Moslem Rebellion in the northwest heightened the danger of Russian influence on the non-Chinese minorities, and Russian propaganda exacerbated local Chinese-Moslem friction.[84] As the rebellion spread, Kazakhs who had aided the Moslems found refuge in Russian territory.[85] Faced with loss of their lands, even the Solun, with their long record of faithful service to the Ch'ing, fled to Russian territory.[86]

To check this Russian infiltration, the Chinese tried every method except the one that might have offered some chance of success. Representations were of course made to the Russian minister,[87] but in these the Tsungli-yamen had no confidence. When a border official beset with difficulties wrote that the chief hope of solution must rest with the Tsungli-yamen, the yamen replied that the border officials themselves must do the solving, since the Russian minister had no authority over Russian border officials.[88]

Specific incidents were usually dealt with according to the circumstances. When Kazakhs fled to Russian territory, efforts were made to have them driven back to Chinese territory, where they could be punished by Mongol princes loyal to China.[89] The case of the Solun, who had been pressed by loss of livelihood, was different. Lands for resettlement were offered them, together with funds to restock their herds, and an official mission was dispatched to negotiate their return.[90]

Above all, Chinese policy was aimed at neutralizing the Russian influence on the nomads. The traditional method of wooing tribal leaders with offers of rank continued. Great importance was attached to getting the support of the Mongol princes confirmed.[91] When Russia claimed the territory of a Kazakh khanate, the lowest orders of nobility were quickly given hereditary rank.[92] All Chinese border officials were instructed to do their utmost to negotiate workable alliances with local leaders.[93] A special proclamation, warning against Russia, was issued to the vital Uriankhai area,[94] and Tarbagatai officials issued a similar proclamation to the Mongols of that area.[95]

Nonetheless, according to the reports of Chinese officials, Russian propaganda remained more effective than Chinese counterpropaganda.[96] Edicts praised the theory of checking Russia by forming Chinese-Mongol alliances; to secure Mongol co-operation would be "to take away the firewood from under the pot." But, the Throne continued, the Russians seemed able to move about everywhere and to impress the Mongols with their strength. Russians had recently succeeded in abducting thirteen men from a Mongol garrison, showing clearly that Chinese-Mongol defense alliances were based not on fact but on empty words.[97]

Faced with this grave trend, China considered it inadvisable to attempt military retaliation even where local victory was certain.[q] The Russian general military strength along the border was greater than the Chinese; Russian political policies had proved more effective, and Ch'ing statesmen were intelligent enough to see that, in any event, the allegiance of the Mongols must be voluntary if it was to be useful. What the Ch'ing leaders could not see was that their traditional enticement—the chance to move gradually from the outer darkness to the twilight zone of Chinese culture, with increased status in proportion to their degree of Sinicization—could no longer compete with the Russian offer of more power and higher standing for Mongols as Mongols.

Chinese policymakers deplored but recognized the fact that China had no "lever" after the Russian success with the Kazakhs and Buriats, and that the Chinese bargaining position had been further weakened by the threat of Russian aid as Moslem insurgents captured the cities of Sinkiang. The only promising policy was, therefore, (1) to cultivate good relations with the nomads where possible, yet guard against their probable treachery; (2) to improve border control and inspection; and (3) above all, to exalt the treaties and to continue to negotiate without making concessions that Russia might later exploit.[98]

q For example, the fighting Lama Kun-ko-cha-lo-ts'an was very useful against unruly Kazakhs, but his habit of raiding Russian territory gave rise to diplomatic complications that in the Chinese view more than offset his local usefulness. High officials of the area were ordered to pay the compensation asked by Russia, to see that the border was clearly marked, and to keep Kun-ko-cha-lo-ts'an under control. (*SL-TC*, Ch. 209, pp. 21–22; Ch. 218, pp. 9b-11; Ch. 225, pp. 8–9b; Ch. 230, pp. 17–18; Ch. 231, pp. 6–7.)

THE INTRODUCTION OF INTERNATIONAL LAW

To make effective use of treaties, Chinese officials were obliged to become acquainted with international law, so as to base their arguments on premises acceptable to Westerners. Although no formal declaration of adherence was issued, the Chinese adjustment to this new theoretical scheme of international relations was rapid. W. A. P. Martin, who made the first published translation into Chinese of a work on international law, wrote in its preface:

> To its [international law's] fundamental principles, the Chinese mind is prepared to yield a ready assent. In their state ritual as well as their canonical books, they acknowledge a supreme arbiter of human destiny, to whom kings and princes are responsible for their exercise of delegated power; . . . The relations of nations, considered as moral persons, and their reciprocal obligations as deduced from this maxim, they are thoroughly able to comprehend.[99]

Similarly, the Tsungli-yamen reported that although international law was not identical with Chinese law, it contained many principles that China could readily adopt.[100]

In the early sixties Hart had translated certain portions of international law and had expounded its principles to the Tsungli-yamen. The members, especially Wen-hsiang, had been greatly interested and had appointed a commission of four scholars to work with Martin on a complete translation of Wheaton.[101] The finished work, with a preface by Tung Hsün, was presented to the Throne on January 27, 1865.[102]

Martin's translation was a sign of a change in outlook that had proceeded rapidly from the beginning of the Restoration. From the outset the members of the Tsungli-yamen had shown a talent for closely reasoned argument. Their analysis of the Russian treaty in 1862 had indicated a grasp of the legal implications of each clause.[103] Li Hung-chang's masterly justification of the arrest of Burgevine, prepared for foreign consumption in 1863,[r] was based solely on international law, with particular attention to the American government's view of foreigners serving in the Confederate forces.[104] The Chinese government strengthened its legal position against its own insurgents by denying the use of its ports to insurgent Confederate cruisers, and Secretary of State Seward expressed his gratification at the "just appreciation of international comity thus manifested."[105]

In these circumstances, Western supporters of the Restoration could easily persuade the Tsungli-yamen that the study of Wheaton would be as useful to Chinese as the study of the Ch'ing code (*Ta-Ch'ing lü-li*) had been to foreigners.

---

[r] See Chapter IX.

First, however, the cautious yamen tested the idea. The members studied a little and worked out a series of arguments with which they confronted the Prussian envoy when he next made demands. To the satisfaction of the yamen, "he hung his head and had nothing to say." Thereupon the yamen issued an official edition of the *Wan-kuo kung-fa* ("International Law") and distributed three hundred copies to officials concerned with foreign affairs.[106]

Chinese skill in this new field continued to grow. The negotiation of the Mesopotamian treaty in the summer of 1865 was of importance mainly for the opportunity it afforded for displaying the new Chinese diplomacy.[s]

The French expedition against Korea in 1866 was a more interesting case, because it involved both international law and the tributary system. The Board of Rites, guided by the Tsungli-yamen, handled communications with Korea according to traditional forms. But in dealing with France, and eventually the other Western powers, the yamen concentrated on the type of reasoning the foreigners found convincing, and wasted little time on the forms.[t] Chinese policy statements showed an excellent understanding of such subjects as the technical meaning of blockade and the duties and rights of neutrals.[107]

Foreign residents, annoyed at the Chinese "talent for casuistry which enables them to combat foreign wishes so successfully," began to rue the day the Chinese had discovered "those flowery meads of diplomacy where they so highly excel." In the end the foreigners conceded: "We must make up our minds to see the Chinese in future contesting acts to which they are opposed on grounds which we ourselves recognize."[108]

THE ADVANCEMENT OF WESTERN LEARNING

At the beginning of the T'ung-chih period, Chinese officials had known little of the Western world or even of some parts of China that were important in foreign relations. It was said that they were ignorant of the very names of foreign countries and confused Macao (*Ao-men*) with Australia (*Ao-chou*). In the 1862 negotiations with Russia, the members of the Tsungli-yamen found that they did not know where Lake Baikal was. By their own report, they knew too little of finance to offer an opinion on the regulations for the Maritime Customs, and very little of the geography of the Yangtze valley or of the conditions

---

[s] "They have shown in these negotiations that they have read their translation of Wheaton's *International Law* with profit, and they have departed from old precedents in a way which was enough to make the old conservatives' tails stand on end." (Freeman-Mitford, *op. cit.*, pp. 175–76.)

[t] E.g., "In the French proclamation there are as usual phrases which slander China without justification. But the said country does not understand the rhythm of a Chinese sentence. It is not worth while to wrangle with them about it." (Tsungli-yamen memorial, Dec. 20, 1866, *IWSM-TC*, Ch. 46, p. 13b.)

prevailing in the ports.[109] This initial lack of information was, however, a short-coming that could be overcome within the Confucian tradition. Study of the problems of government had been the core of traditional education; all that was needed was to expand the concept of government to include international relations.

The effort to understand the West was not, of course, entirely new. Works such as the *Hai-lu*, the *Hai-kuo t'u-chih*, and the *Ying-huan chih-lüeh* had been in circulation for many years.[110] There had long been a Russian-language school in Peking,[111] and numerous Chinese in the treaty ports had had business contacts with foreigners. However, the information available from these sources was limited. Moreover, unless a knowledge of foreign affairs could be introduced into the heart of the official system, there was the great danger that such knowledge might become a monopoly of the compradors, for whom the traditional official had the greatest contempt. Feng Kuei-fen was particularly apprehensive on this score.[112]

The introduction of Western studies in Japan provided another reason for introducing them in China. In 1863 the Censorate presented to the Throne the proposal of a district magistrate-designate that all officials whose work concerned foreign affairs be required to pass an examination on the geography, topography, customs, government, and produce of foreign countries. The petitioner reported his alarm at hearing that the Japanese had sent a mission to study shipbuilding and armament in Russia and America for ten years. To counter this increase in Japanese strength, he suggested that China set up suitable training centers in Hongkong, Amoy, Foochow, and Shanghai on the model of the provincial academies. The Tsungli-yamen approved the plan for training future officials, but was unwilling to require the new knowledge of officials already in office.[113]

During the Restoration the effort was made to develop new knowledge in China without sending Chinese abroad to acquire it. It was not until 1871 that Yung Wing succeeded in persuading Tseng Kuo-fan and Li Hung-chang to send the first group of students abroad under his direction, and the project was later discontinued.[114] Foreign works were translated at an increasing rate.[115] Tseng Kuo-fan attached a translation bureau to the Kiangnan Arsenal,[u] and a number of other government offices were fitted out with similar branches. The Tsungli-yamen pointed out that new maps and new statistics were especially needed in the handling of foreign affairs.[116]

In the course of twenty-five years, China's attitude toward foreign books had changed. When Russia had presented books to China in 1845, they had

[u] See Chapter IX.

merely been stored in the archives.[v] When the United States sent a gift of books in 1869, the Tsungli-yamen was interested; it also recalled the Russian books and requisitioned them for study.[117] Foreigners in China noted these and other "symptoms of a tendency to inquire into the reasons of things which were before deemed unworthy of notice."[118]

By the end of the T'ung-chih period, the Tsungli-yamen, which had originally limited its interest in the West to immediate considerations of technology and international law, had begun to urge a broader understanding of Western society. In commenting on the stationing of Chinese envoys abroad in 1875, it emphasized

> not simply the transaction of business in which Chinese and foreigners may be jointly concerned. . . . Men's minds, in fact, must have free access to each other before angry collisions between them can be prevented. If there are to be no collisions between them, they must thoroughly acquaint themselves each with the other.[119]

The reading of foreign newspapers and public documents to keep abreast of current world affairs was a striking innovation. For the study of foreign books for basic learning there were Chinese precedents; but in China there had never existed any source of information comparable to the nineteenth-century Western press. Yet as early as 1862 the former chief supervisor of instruction memorialized on the importance of reading foreign newspapers in order to discover the foreigners' intentions.[120] Hsüeh Huan regularly relayed to Peking press accounts of foreign activities in central China, although he claimed to doubt the reliability of the clippings.[121]

Chinese officials put their new knowledge to effective use in solving problems of widely varying types.[w] During the French invasion of Korea in 1866, the Tsungli-yamen studied Western criticisms of the French action and used them with notable success.[122] Chinese officials on all levels were quick to locate foreign news reports and other documents that might weaken the foreign posi-

---

[v] The Chinese government had apparently not requested these Russian books; the Russians sent them in appreciation for some 800 Chinese stitched volumes on Buddhism that had been sent earlier on Russian request. Of the 357 works, all in Russian, half dealt with Russian history, geography, and military science, one-fifth with philosophy, one-fifth with medicine and forestry, and the rest with religion, poetry, etc. There was some discussion in the Grand Council about accepting the books and about priorities for translating them, but apparently nothing was done. See the account by Ho Ch'iu-t'ao (author of the *Shuo-fang pei-sheng*) in "O-lo-ssu chin-ch'eng shu-chi chi," with list attached, in *CSWP*, Ch. 74, pp. 10–25; and Wen Kung-chih, *Chung-O wen-t'i chih ch'üan-pu yen-chiu*, Shanghai, 1929, p. 83.

[w] Proposals on the manner in which the new knowledge might be used came first from Shanghai, but Peking quickly approved. Merchants were approached to put pressure on ministers, and vice versa. Traditional European power rivalries were studied with a view to using the barbarian against the barbarian: Russia might be used to investigate smuggling on the Yangtze; Spain and England might be useful to China where Portuguese Macao was concerned. E.g., *IWSM-TC*, Ch. 3, pp. 49–50; Ch. 11, pp. 10b–12; Ch. 15, p. 36.

tion in China. For example, in 1859 W. A. P. Martin wrote a letter casting doubt on the good faith of the allies. Years later Tung Hsün was found to have a Chinese translation, presumably made from the Blue Book text.[123] A missionary in central China wrote:

> Our Viceroy is a very intelligent man, and anti-foreign to the backbone. He knows just as well as I do all that has been said in the House of Lords, and all that has appeared in the *Times* on missionaries and the missionary enterprise. He sees that we are despised and distrusted and knows that we are at his mercy.[124]

Alcock commented on the increasing tendency of the yamen to observe world affairs. He thought the yamen had probably found in the British press one of its favorite arguments against the extension of missionary activity: that alien Buddhist proselyters would probably meet with considerable popular hostility in England.[125]

This new Chinese habit of newspaper reading forced British officials for the first time to take account of the effect of the foreign press on Chinese policy. The negotiations for the revision of the British Treaty of Tientsin* were jeopardized by the extravagant views expressed in the press by merchant groups. According to Alcock: "The Foreign Board, here, gets translations made of such documents as these, when made public, and habitually have laid before them the comments of the local press and their more salient articles." On this occasion the Tsungli-yamen, outraged at what it read, inclined toward intransigence. To limit the damage, Alcock ordered all British consuls to publish repudiations of the merchants' view.[126]

Restoration officials learned to use the press not only as a source of information about foreigners but as an instrument to give foreigners the desired impression of China. Hence, they became sensitive to foreign press accounts of themselves. It was generally believed at the time that Li Hung-chang had been very much aware of foreign criticism of his execution of the Taiping leaders who had surrendered at Soochow, and that he released an impounded foreign ship, the *Tsatlee*, in order to improve his press relations.[127] Chinese officials frequently took exception to news stories printed about China; on one occasion the Tsungli-yamen ordered the local taotai to warn the *North China Herald* against making libelous remarks about Chinese officials.[128]

THE T'UNG-WEN KUAN AND THE MODERNIZATION OF CHINESE EDUCATION

Adapting China's highly developed traditional system of education to new needs was a basic problem of the Restoration. In modernizing education, as in modernizing foreign policy, the important thing was learning new skills. It

---

* See Chapter XI.

was a cardinal principle of the Confucian state that officials should be selected on a competitive basis from among the young men who had shown the greatest proficiency in the study of government. Foreign relations would be dangerous to this traditional political system only if they could not be absorbed into it. If they were to be absorbed, they would have to be handled by competent officials with a regular status in the hierarchy without reliance on the merchants of the ports.

The compilers of the dynastic history, the *Ch'ing-shih kao*, dated the beginnings of China's new school system from the beginning of the T'ung-chih Restoration.[129] In 1862 the T'ung-wen kuan[130] was established in Peking for the purpose of training selected young Bannerman in foreign languages. In 1863 Li Hung-chang established the Kuang fang-yen kuan in Shanghai on precisely the same model, and in 1864 Jui-lin established a similar school in Canton. In 1866 Tso Tsung-t'ang founded the Ch'uan-cheng hsüeh-t'ang at Foochow for the study of English, French, navigation, and engineering. Each of these institutions grew rapidly from modest beginnings and rapidly expanded its functions.

It is worth noting that Chinese rather than foreign initiative was predominant in this first phase of educational reform, and that the emphasis was placed on creating schools in China rather than on sending students abroad. As early as 1860 S. Wells Williams had suggested that the $200,000 remaining from the Chinese indemnity might be used

> as a fund for establishing a school of a high rank in China where the natives of that Empire can be taught the languages and science of Western countries, under the tuition of competent men, with the object of making them serviceable to their own countrymen and government.[131]

Nothing came of this proposal—contrast the importance of the Boxer indemnity in the development of Chinese education forty years later. In 1865 American Presbyterians founded at Tengchow the institution that later became Cheeloo University, and in 1871 American Episcopalians established the future Hua-chung University at Wuchang,[132] but these and similar institutions became important only under the altered circumstances of a later era. During the Restoration Protestant missionaries concerned themselves more with translating religious texts than with introducing Western knowledge in general. Catholic missionaries, who had earlier devoted their main attention to scholarly work in China, withdrew from the educational field during the Restoration.[133]

The outstanding example of the Chinese effort to modernize Chinese education in the 1860's was the T'ung-wen kuan. By its establishment, Restoration officials hoped to incorporate the new learning into the old system, thereby ultimately strengthening that system against Western expansion and its Chinese shock troops, the Cantonese compradors. Feng Kuei-fen argued that the new subjects should become recognized and esteemed fields of learning and should be included in the examination system.[134] Since the compradors were also a new element in the traditional class structure, Feng's opposition to their advance represented a fusion of the class and cultural interests of the bureaucracy.[y]

The Tsungli-yamen had originally hoped to use Chinese teachers in the T'ung-wen kuan, but soon discovered that even in Shanghai and Canton no qualified teachers of foreign languages were available.[135] The decision in 1862 to use foreigners to teach China's future officials seemed hazardous; anxiety over ideological penetration was overcome only when Wade reassured the yamen that foreigners could be found who would not teach Christianity.[136]

The Tsungli-yamen was determined that the new school should provide effective training and should avoid the weaknesses of the old Russian-language school, which during its long career had yielded no results whatever.[137] The original plan called for between ten and twenty-four students of about fifteen years of age, but their number expanded rapidly. Their progress was tested by regular examinations, and they were expected, after the first year's diligent study, to gain additional practice by translating incoming dispatches.[138]

The schools established at Shanghai and Canton followed the Peking pattern. Li Hung-chang, like the Tsungli-yamen earlier, pointed out that foreigners had been studying Chinese for more than twenty years and that a number of them could read the Chinese Classics, Histories, and official documents. In contrast, very few members of the Chinese bureaucracy or gentry could read foreign languages; most of them were forced to rely on interpreters who might not be trustworthy. Morever, it was necessary for Chinese officials to study the subjects that foreigners considered important, with a view to understanding the foreigners' intentions. Hence a good foreign language school was urgently required. With their great native ability, Chinese could easily learn new subjects.[139]

As long as only languages were taught, there was routine progress.[140] But the implications of the T'ung-wen kuan were far from routine, and as this became clear to the extreme conservative faction, there was a vociferous (if temporarily unsuccessful) protest. The Tsungli-yamen's successful defense of its stand on education exemplifies the degree to which the conduct of foreign affairs had been modernized within the old order.

On January 28, 1867, the Tsungli-yamen proposed that an additional school be established to teach engineering, astronomy, and mathematics to students training for government service. The yamen argued that science was the basis

---

[y] The career of Feng's eldest son, Feng Fang-ch'i, illustrates the policy for which the father worked. Fang-ch'i passed the metropolitan examinations in 1868, was immediately registered as a secretary of the Tsungli-yamen, and became a Maritime Customs official (*Feng Ching-t'ing hsing-chuang*, p. 17; *Eminent Chinese*, p. 243).

of Western technology, and that *fundamental* knowledge was essential to China's program of self-strengthening. Foreign instructors were to be selected, and the whole scheme had Hart's approval.[141] The *North China Herald* took the announcement as a sign that Chinese exclusiveness was at last really giving way and conceded the possibility that the Chinese, if trained in Western science, might develop "real intelligence" in addition to their admittedly excellent memories.[142] On February 25, 1867, Hsü Chi-yü was appointed director of the expanded school.[143]

When the new plan became known, the extreme conservative opposition under the leadership of Wo-jen mobilized immediately.[z] A Shantung censor, Chang Sheng-tsao, speaking for Wo-jen, stated the literati's case:[144] the examination system was based on literature, not on technical subjects; astronomy and mathematics were the proper concern of the Observatory and the Board of Works and should not be introduced into the education of officials; officials should be trained in the classic principles of government and their application; science was a technical skill, the concern of subordinates if of anybody, and should not be elevated to a recognized position within the sphere of true learning.

The Throne backed the so-called liberal faction, and in an edict of March 5, 1867, laid down the principle that astronomy and mathematics now were a proper part of the education of a Chinese scholar, that science was more than "cleverness," that students could learn to use Western methods without abandoning the way of the sages.[145] This was the very essence of the T'ung-chih Restoration: radical innovation within the old order.

The opposition did not yield easily, and in March 1867, the Grand Secretary Wo-jen himself began the major attack. As early as 1850 Wo-jen had written a famous memorial contrasting fundamental ethical teaching with this same "cleverness." In the intervening years he had been president of several boards, a tutor to the Emperor, president of the Censorate, and chancellor of the Hanlin Academy. He was an authority on the prevailing Confucian orthodoxy and the recognized leader of the opposition to Prince Kung and Wen-hsiang; for some time the Tsungli-yamen had been trying to neutralize his opposition by getting him appointed to its own ranks.[146] Rumors spread rapidly. Couplets were hung in the city bemoaning the loss of state policy and the abandonment

---

[z] T. F. Tsiang has interpreted the episode as a conflict between the Manchu Prince Kung, who controlled the T'ung-wen kuan, and Wo-jen as the representative of the literati who had no part in the T'ung-wen kuan (Chiang T'ing-fu, *Chung-kuo chin-tai shih*, Changsha, 1938, pp. 66–67). That was not the precise issue. Literati of the type of Tseng Kuo-fan and Feng Kuei-fen, who saw that the old order could not continue to exist unmodified, supported the T'ung-wen kuan; the mass of the literati, however, could not follow the Restoration leadership without loss of status, and it was these whom Wo-jen represented.

of respect for the philosophers when alien breeds became teachers. In Imperial audience Wo-jen remained bitter and intractable.[147]

Thus the apparently minor issue of teaching science brought to a head the whole latent conflict between Restoration leaders and the majority of the literati. It illustrated the magnitude of the change that had almost imperceptibly taken place in the thinking of the leaders in the course of a few years. The issue was clearly defined, and the highest officials in the Empire were involved.

In a memorial of March 20, Wo-jen attacked the teaching of mathematics and astronomy on principle: good government came not from men of specialized training but from men of character.[148] The Tsungli-yamen countered by sending Wo-jen copies of the views of Tseng Kuo-fan and others in support of the T'ung-wen kuan.[149] Wo-jen then shifted his ground and suggested that if Western subjects must be taught, they might at least be taught by Chinese instructors. The Tsungli-yamen replied that few Chinese had the necessary competence. When an edict ordered Wo-jen himself to nominate qualified Chinese, he replied that he had no acquaintances in the scientific field.

At the end of April the Tsungli-yamen summarized its case and repeated its refutation of Wo-jen's basic principle. The yamen's position was approved by the Throne, which instructed the T'ung-wen kuan to proceed with the enrollment of students who could pass the qualifying examination for the scientific courses.[150] Once more Wo-jen himself was ordered to serve in the Tsungli-yamen, and again he refused on the ground that he would make mistakes. His refusal was not at first accepted, but somehow he avoided appearing at his new post.[151] Eventually a face-saving formula was worked out; owing to his "illness," Wo-jen was relieved of all his duties except those of Grand Secretary. This automatically excused him from the Tsungli-yamen.[152]

The drought of 1867 offered Wo-jen's party a chance to renew the battle. In traditional Chinese political theory a natural calamity was interpreted as the result of some error in policy, and it was the Emperor's duty to correct the error so as to restore the harmony of the universe.[a] The extreme conservatives seized the occasion to claim that the Tsungli-yamen's action had disturbed the natural

---

[a] Drought and flood were always given a prominent place in the Imperial records, but in most cases the political remedy ordered was rather general, e.g., that officials should cultivate frugality and speak the truth (*CSK*, "Pen-chi," Ch. 21, p. 5b). This notion that "nature and morality are mutually dependent" still persisted in 1931; the Nationalist government was accused of causing the widespread calamities of that year by its disregard of Confucian principles of government, though in name it honored the sage. (See Chapter XII.)

In many primitive and peasant societies, "The assumption is that unless all the rules of society are observed, nature will not yield her fruits." (George Homans, *The Human Group*, New York, 1950, pp. 327–28.) Yet though the idea itself is not peculiar to China, it was nowhere else developed into a governing principle of a long-lived empire.

harmony and caused the drought. On these grounds a chou magistrate-designate, one Yang T'ing-hsi, proposed the closing of the T'ung-wen kuan in order to bring rain. Yang claimed that the Tsungli-yamen had usurped power and had influenced the Emperor to ignore his proper advisers, the censors. He then proceeded to the main point, the inadaptability of Western civilization to China's needs.[153]

Yang's argument was ridiculed in the edict in reply, but the Throne expressed concern over the powerful clique (*tang*) that might be behind him. Wo-jen was warned by name to remember the obligations of an official. The edict went on to reaffirm in positive language the government's determination to support the Tsungli-yamen's policy, citing the careers of Tseng Kuo-fan and Li Hung-chang to prove that Confucian learning could be combined with Western learning. The edict concluded that there was no need for the Hanlin Academy to restrict itself to literary subjects.[154]

Once the principle was made clear, the blow was softened. The Tsungli-yamen offered to resign, but the resignation was refused. Yang for his part was not reprimanded, on the ground that the Emperor did not wish to discourage officials from offering advice. Instead Yang was invited to draw up a memorandum on self-strengthening. When Chung P'ei-hsien, a reader of the Grand Secretariat, suggested that Wo-jen and his party had been reprimanded for pointing out errors in government, an edict in reply denied this and stated that Wo-jen, although misinformed, had been genuinely and properly concerned with the public welfare.[155]

In spite of these efforts to preserve the dignity of the opposition, official policy was made perfectly clear in an extraordinary series of vigorous Tsungli-yamen memorials and equally vigorous edicts. Translations of many of the documents were printed by the Maritime Customs and reproduced in the press and in Western documentary compilations. The importance of the episode was widely recognized. Burlingame reported developments to Washington, where the State Department admired both the strategy and tactics employed by the Tsungli-yamen.[b] There is no foundation for the charge that Burlingame forwarded to Washington only the edicts that were critical of Wo-jen, without the alleged final decree that reversed the government's position.[156] There was no such final reversal.

At the height of the Restoration, in 1867–78, there appeared to be good

---

[b] On the effort to appoint Wo-jen to the yamen, William Hunter, a ranking State Department official, commented: "This was certainly an ingenious expedient for getting rid of political opposition and securing the services of an opponent." On the general issue Seward wrote: "The proceedings described in these papers are exceedingly interesting and manifest a strong tendency on the part of the Imperial Government towards assimilation to the institutions and customs of Western nations." (*U.S. Arch. China. Instructions*, I, 460, 454; dated July 24 and July 6, 1867, respectively.)

reason for the nearly universal optimism concerning the future of the T'ung-wen kuan. W. A. P. Martin wrote: "It was no small triumph for the college to survive an attack led on by the champion of the literati aided by such portents as they were able to evoke from the discord of the elements."[157] According to the *London and China Express*:

> The whole civilized world has a stake in its [the T'ung-wen kuan's] success. . . . Why not educate Chinese in China, combine native with foreign learning, and endeavour to turn out men versed in modern science, but also fitted by literary attainments to fill magisterial offices, to become provincial governors, and perhaps eventually Presidents of Boards?[158]

The *North China Herald* found throughout the documents on the case a "spirit which it is a positive refreshment to perceive."[159]

After the defeat of the Wo-jen faction, the affairs of the T'ung-wen kuan appeared to be proceeding smoothly[160] as far as the Chinese were concerned, and not to have been greatly affected by the confusion among the foreign staff caused by a suit for fraud against Hart in connection with the school.[c] The distinguished mathematician Li Shan-lan joined the teaching staff in 1868. A colleague wrote of Li: "His faith, if he had any, was a compound of West and East. Professing to be a Confucian, he was an eclectic, grafting ideas alike from India and the Occident on the doctrines of the Chinese sage."[161] Examinations in mathematics and science became a matter of routine, and both the number of students and the status of the school increased.[162]

And yet the T'ung-wen kuan was in the end a failure, a failure for which contemporary foreign explanations were wide of the mark. Some found fault with the school's avoidance of religious instruction,[163] but this circumstance favored its success as a Chinese institution. Others argued that the foreign instructors spent too much time studying Chinese subjects: "The Peking College for the instruction of the Chinese in English literature has become the Peking College for the instruction of the English in Chinese literature."[164] Here again, the instructors' interest in China, if it had had any effect at all on the school, would have contributed to its stability and served to allay Chinese hostility.

Chang Chih-tung, who had just begun his distinguished official career at the time of the T'ung-wen kuan episode, wrote thirty years later that the school had

---

[c] Gumpach sued Hart for damages, claiming that, in accepting employment in the T'ung-wen kuan he had been defrauded by Hart's description of the Tsungli-yamen as a ministry of state. (For Gumpach's account of the trial, see his "The New University of China," in *The Burlingame Mission*, pp. 772–73.) The morale of the foreign staff fell when the British Supreme Court at Shanghai, though dismissing most of the charges against Hart, did fine him. The Privy Council later reversed this judgment in accordance with the English legal principle of the immunity of the sovereign, arguing that the Court had no jurisdiction over any act committed by Hart as the agent of the Chinese sovereign. (Stanley F. Wright, *Hart and the Chinese Customs*, chap. xii, "The Tung Wen kuan and the von Gumpach Case.")

been sabotaged by a whispering campaign conducted by narrow-minded and conservative literati. It withered in a hostile climate of opinion, as Restoration leaders were succeeded by lesser men, and there were no further innovations in Chinese education until after 1895.[165]

Until recently, Chinese historians have generally referred to the founding of the T'ung-wen kuan as an important step in the modernization of China but have not seriously considered the causes of its failure. Chinese Communist historians, who have lately inquired into the matter, have concluded that the school was an anti-Chinese imperialistic tool serving the interests of Manchus and foreigners. According to Fan Wen-lan, the aim of the Tsungli-yamen clique was to build up a body of translators and compradors and to keep the control of foreign affairs in Manchu hands. In Fan's (and Wo-jen's) view, the school encouraged worship of foreigners and contempt for Chinese; it failed because Li Hung-chang and other strong dissidents broke away from this Manchu-Western imperialist axis.[166]

The optimists of the sixties who thought they were witnessing a profound and fundamental change in Chinese culture were not so wrong as this. The T'ung-wen kuan failed, like so many innovations of its time, because as it grew it came to challenge the basis of the Confucian state. Jui-lin, Grand Secretary and governor-general of Kwangtung and Kwangsi, pointed to the fundamental obstacle: the students of the new schools were neglecting their Western studies and were attending mainly to traditional studies, which remained the qualification for provincial office.[167] Jui-lin urged that some means of changing this situation be found, but no means could possibly be found short of revolutionary change in the character of the Chinese state and its officials. High officials could try their hand at innovation, but they lacked the power to coerce the literati and gentry. Even if they had had this power, they could not, as Confucian statesmen, have chosen to use it.[d]

CONCLUSION

The Restoration success in modernizing foreign relations was noteworthy. In writing a formal preface to the collection of Chinese documents on foreign relations for this period, the Grand Secretary Pao-yün wrote: "The thirteen-year reign was bright and glorious. This book [the *I-wu shih-mo*] offers a golden mirror of it."[168] The *I-wu shih-mo* certainly does in fact record not the

---

[d] From what anthropologists have discovered of the general circumstances in which new skills and attitudes are learned without social disruption, one can say that the T'ung-wen kuan could not have succeeded. According to Robert Redfield, ventures of this sort fail where there has been a recent effort by one group to dominate the other, where there is serious economic competition along ethnic lines, where there is color prejudice, etc. This and related material is summarized in A. Irving Hallowell, "Socio-psychological Aspects of Acculturation," in Ralph Linton (ed.), *The Science of Man in the World Crisis*, New York, 1945, pp. 171–200.

customary easy reassertion of China's traditional pretensions in foreign affairs, but something far more important: the labored working out, with many setbacks, of a modern foreign policy. By necessity and by choice, the main lines of the policy were civil, but the long-term importance of military strength was not forgotten.

At the end of the 1860's China's international position was stronger than it had been at any time since 1840, stronger also than it was to be again for nearly a century. Direct foreign military intervention had virtually ceased; the forward movement of Western commercial enterprise had come to a halt; there was some talk of the rendition of extraterritoriality; and the beginnings of nationalism were not supplanting but reinforcing traditional ethnocentric culturalism.

Restoration foreign policy had succeeded in protecting Chinese interests without damage to legitimate foreign interests. The groups that had looked forward to the early and complete incorporation of China into the world of nineteenth-century commerce were bitter, as were those who had thought of conquest and annexation. Yet if imperialist dreams were shattered, the actual position of the typical foreign resident was greatly improved.[e] Fifteen ports, and in addition Peking, were open to him for residence. Nearly everywhere he found safe conditions of travel and courteous treatment. The physical plant for the conduct of trade was improving each year with the construction of docks, the increased use of steamers, the firm establishment of an efficient Maritime Customs service, and various procedural innovations. The officials with whom he had to deal were becoming better informed; if he had a legitimate grievance and stated it reasonably, he would probably receive a fair hearing. The French, never easily satisfied with the performance of Asian governments, conceded that the signs of the times were encouraging.[169] Harry Parkes characterized the new look in Sino-foreign relations very fairly as "a sort of husband and wife arrangement, with slight incompatibilities of temper on both sides."[170]

During the Restoration both Chinese and foreign officials were convinced that China's domestic problems were paramount and that if these could be solved, foreign relations would present no serious difficulties. By this, Alcock and his colleagues meant that foreign interests depended on peace, order, effective central control, and domestic economic prosperity. Prince Kung, Tseng Kuo-fan, Tso Tsung-t'ang, and others meant that whereas domestic weakness and disorder invited foreign intervention, domestic strength commanded foreign circumspection.

---

[e] "In effect, a comparison of the position of foreigners in China twenty years ago, with that which they now hold, will probably surprise many who complain most loudly of Chinese obstinacy and stupidity." (*NCH*, Jan. 16, 1868.)

Two events of the summer of 1870 marked the end of Restoration foreign policy: the British rejection of the Alcock Convention, and the Tientsin Massacre. Although these disasters may appear at first glance to be failures of the new Chinese diplomacy, each was in fact the result of developments outside the sphere of Chinese foreign policy. The reluctant decision of the British government to withhold ratification of the Alcock Convention was the result of direct pressure by British merchants on the British home government. The Tientsin Massacre was an explosion of local xenophobia, ignited by literati and local officials whose status was threatened by the Western intrusion. Such accidents apart, the Tsungli-yamen had devised ways of dealing satisfactorily with the conventional subject matter of international relations. It was helpless where the immediate requirements of foreign policy ran counter to the fundamental requirements of the Confucian order, as the following chapter will show.

CHAPTER XI

NEAR VICTORY AND DISASTER

THE FIRST EFFORT AT AN EQUAL TREATY

As the preceding chapter has indicated, the Restoration government had from 1861 onward accepted China's existing treaties with the West, and by adopting Western diplomatic methods had even succeeded in turning some of the treaty terms to its own advantage. But the government's ambitions went further: although the Treaty of Tientsin[a] was no longer the nightmare it had seemed in 1858,[1] the next step was to get its most objectionable clauses revised and to establish a new and "equal" treaty basis for Sino-foreign relations. Any adjustment was bound to be difficult, for the requirements of expanding Western commerce affected the whole of Chinese society and in many instances ran directly counter to the Restoration domestic program.

Foreign residents in China understood little of this. They were buoyantly committed to a policy of throwing the whole of China immediately open to unrestricted contact with Western commerce and religion. They held that the Treaties of Tientsin offered them too few rights, and that even some of these were in practice withheld by the wily machinations of the Tsungli-yamen and the pro-Chinese prejudices of British and American diplomats.[b]

British officials, by contrast, were haunted by the hazards of the road ahead. Alcock, with his strong sense of history, his broad experience, and his wide reading in current affairs, was intensely aware that what he was witnessing was no ordinary diplomatic spectacle, but "such a revolution as has never been seen since the world began." From the Mediterranean to the Pacific, he saw the molds being cast for the modern Asian states of the future. He did not suppose that Great Britain could either retard or force their growth, or even shape it to her own designs.

> The world's experience since history began has shown, that although colonies may be transplanted from a parent stock, civilization itself cannot be transferred wholesale from one people to another, either by the sword or by Treaties. It is something that must grow in the soil where it is to take root, and from small beginnings. It must adapt itself to the climate and soil and all its surroundings; and in turn, as years give it strength, it modifies them also; and so, by mutual and reciprocal action, they form, sooner or later, one consistent and harmonious whole.

[a] Since British interests dominated foreign interests in China, the phrase "Treaty of Tientsin" refers to the British treaty, unless otherwise specified.
[b] See Chapter III.

If China were willing to make the hitherto untried experiment of a sudden and total reversal of all these conditions, and at one and the same time lay down railroads and telegraphs; work all her mineral resources by foreign agencies and machinery; adopt free trade in its fullest development; burn all the books of Confucius; adopt new creeds; and embrace the foreigner as a brother; or any other utopian and wild scheme of universal assimilation—does any one suppose peace and prosperity would be the immediate result, or that by such impatient processes a stable State could be built up on the crumbling ruins of the old—the oldest polity and nation now standing erect in modern times? Can any one believe this who has ever read a page of the history of the race and its civilization?[2]

In saying that the West could not and should not coerce, Alcock was by no means saying that Western statesmen had no responsibilities, that they might as well wait until the dust settled. On the contrary, he believed that there were critical moments in history when its course for decades to come might depend on the insight and generosity with which a few critical diplomatic decisions were made. As he studied the Chinese scene he came to believe that the years 1868–70, when a reform government seemed to be gaining strength, were such a moment for setting the tone of modern China's relations with the West. Yet although the vision was grand, he did not expect to achieve it by dramatic strokes, for "negotiators must in general deal with facts as they are and the actual condition of things, and not as they may be at some future period."[3]

The great fact of the 1860's was that the government of China and the makers of opinion were intensely suspicious of Western imperialism. For this, Alcock's prescription was to negotiate patiently, to concede graciously, and to make truly extraordinary efforts to understand and represent the Chinese case. He thought he saw signs of Chinese willingness to co-operate in negotiations based on mutual concessions,[4] and he was bitter at the merchants' refusal to respond to that willingness.

When negotiations for the revision of the British Treaty of Tientsin were about to begin, he told the merchants: "All treaty stipulations imposing loss or wrong upon one side for the advantage of the other were likely to be evaded by the party injured, and always proved a fertile source of trouble and misunderstanding."[5] In retrospect, when the effort to negotiate China's first "equal" treaty in 1869 had failed, he wrote:

> That we were dealing with the Peking Government on equal terms was greatly overlooked by the mercantile communities in China. It was supposed that the revision would offer chances for further privileges; and it never seemed to occur to them that the Chinese might take a very different view, and claim a right to profit by the first opportunity that had occurred since the occupation of Peking by the allied forces, to cancel or limit the privileges previously extorted from them under pressure and as the price of peace.[6]

The unratified Alcock Convention of 1869 was a genuine attempt at treaty revision based on bilateral concessions, as will be shown further below. When Alcock told Wen-hsiang that he had been much criticized for allegedly not demanding enough for the West, Wen-hsiang replied: "Yes, no doubt; I see what your newspapers say sometimes. I, too, am accused of being a renegade and only wearing Chinese clothes."[7]

In Alcock's summing up, neither side had got its larger demands, but the Chinese government had proved more flexible than British merchants. Although he granted that the merchants were to some extent justified in suspecting the ultimate purposes of the Chinese government, he insisted that without good faith treaties would be pointless, and the world would relapse into barbarism.[8]

THE THREE INTERESTED PARTIES

The Treaty of Tientsin satisfied no one. Conflicts of interest and outlook between the Chinese government, the British government, and British merchants and missionaries were reflected in every sphere of Sino-foreign relations.[9] The priorities the three parties assigned to the various issues, however, were quite different. British merchants were concerned first with lower taxes on foreign trade and with enforcement of the transit tax clause of the Treaty of Tientsin; and second with the general opening of the interior to foreign residence, steam navigation, mining, and railways. They were not particularly concerned with the questions of audience, the sending abroad of Chinese envoys, and Chinese domestic reform. Missionary organizations were primarily concerned with the unrestricted right to inland residence, travel, and evangelical work. The British government and British officials supported the merchants' complaints against unreasonable and discriminatory taxation of British trade in violation of written agreements, but they were strict constructionists; they refused to challenge China's right of taxation except where a specific commitment had been made. Unlike the merchants and missionaries, they had serious doubts about the wisdom of opening the interior of China. The audience question no longer seemed urgent to them, but they attached great importance to getting Chinese diplomatic missions sent abroad. The great issue in their view was domestic reform in China; upon this, they felt, the solution of all the specific problems of Sino-foreign relations must ultimately depend.

Audience and the sending of envoys were generally the first items on any Chinese agenda of foreign affairs because they touched the dignity of the Throne and the State, but the tone in which they were discussed indicates that they were in fact secondary concerns. Most important to the Chinese was the missionary question, which scarcely interested the merchants and was of interest to the

British government primarily because of the sharp Chinese reaction. To the Chinese, the second question was the introduction of railways and steam navigation in the interior, and foreign capital investment. Foreign residence and travel in the interior were of somewhat less importance and the transit tax a matter of almost no concern.

The flaming question of the twentieth century, extraterritoriality, loomed relatively small in the eyes of all three parties.

THE ISSUES AS THE FOREIGNERS SAW THEM

Transit Duties. Foreigners as a whole were concerned chiefly with the liability of the goods of foreign trade to Chinese domestic taxation.[c] To the merchants this was "perhaps the most important question of all in connection with the treaties."[10] Article 10 of the Treaty of Nanking, 1842, had provided vaguely for the optional commutation of all inland levies on imports to a single payment, the amount of which was never fixed. Article 28 of the Treaty of Tientsin, 1858—the "Elgin transit clause"—had attempted to remedy this vagueness by specifying that Chinese domestic tax rates be announced in advance, and that all Chinese domestic transit taxes on the goods of foreign trade might be commuted, at the trader's option, to a single tax of $2\frac{1}{2}$ per cent ad valorem.

From the beginning Article 28 proved unworkable;[11] for one thing, there was sharp disagreement over its meaning. The subject was hotly debated in Parliament as well as in the Chinese ports.[d] At what point did native products destined for export become "goods of foreign trade" and hence become privileged? At what point did foreign products, once imported, cease to be "goods of foreign trade" and hence become unprivileged? What privileges did payment of the treaty transit tax ensure? Exemption from all local Chinese taxes, or merely from local *transit* taxes? What provision was there to prevent extralegal collection by Chinese local officials? What provision was there to prevent fraud by foreign merchants? The *North China Herald* had some reason for observing: "The compilers [of the Tientsin Treaty] evidently knew nothing of the Chinese fiscal system, or they must have perceived the impracticability of two rates of taxation on the same produce working side by side."[12]

The consul in Shanghai took the view that unsound as the Chinese tax

---

[c] See Chapter VIII.

[d] Government supporters argued that Elgin had from the beginning recognized the distinction between local taxes and transit taxes and had intended to protect foreign trade only from the latter; if this was so, none of the evidence presented on the local taxation of the goods of foreign trade represented a violation of the transit tax clause of the Treaty of Tientsin. The China trade bloc denied this interpretation. The Foreign Office spokesman then conceded that the original purpose of the transit tax clause had been to exempt imports from all internal levies, but supported China's reinterpretation as justified by British merchants' fraudulent sale of transit passes to Chinese domestic merchants. (*Hansard*, Vol. 197, pp. 1786–90, 1795–97, 1800.)

structure might be, "it must be changed in some other way than as the incidental result of a commercial treaty."

> . . . one cannot see how such an intricate and extensive system of inland dues, extending from the Great Wall to the extremities of Hainan, can be thoroughly and effectually controlled to suit all the requirements of foreign commerce, without the assumption of a supervisory power over the whole internal administration of the country.[13]

Angry merchants did not agree. They insisted that the transit passes issued under Article 28 exempted their goods from all inland charges, from the likin as well as from domestic transit taxes.[e] From all the ports they cried that Chinese local officials were defrauding them of their treaty rights, and in some ports the merchants had the support of their consuls.[14]

By contrast, British diplomats supported the Chinese contention that the treaty transit tax did not provide exemption from such local taxes as the likin,[15] and they were even more outraged than the Chinese at the open scandal of a black market in transit passes operated by British merchants.[16] No nineteenth-century Englishman could approve of the likin; it violated all the accepted principles of fiscal policy. But although British officials lost no opportunity to advise the Chinese to reform their tax system,[17] they did not believe that such a reform could be forced by treaty. As Alcock told the merchants of Kiukiang, no matter how unwise and unjust the Chinese system of domestic taxation might be, the British had very little legal right to interfere with it; and as for regulating so intricate a domestic question, the British had no power whatsoever. He urged the merchants to cease quibbling over rights that were at best purely nominal, and to assist him in working out an arrangement that would be practicable in the existing circumstances.[18]

"*Opening the Interior.*" From the foreign point of view, the second great problem in the operation of the Treaty of Tientsin was raised by Article 12, which specified that foreigners might rent houses, churches, hospitals, and so forth throughout China at the prevailing rates. British officials stated that this clause did *not* give foreigners any general right of unrestricted residence in the interior; that if that had been intended, there would have been no need to enumerate the open treaty ports.[19]

British merchants generally took the opposite view. They insisted that Article 12 had "opened the interior" and that they were being denied their treaty

---

[e] Not only did the Shanghai Chamber of Commerce argue that Chinese conveying the goods of foreign trade should be allowed the protection of transit passes; it even defended the sale of transit passes to Chinese engaged in purely domestic trade, on the ground that the whole tax policy of the Chinese government was illegal and immoral (*China. No. 4. (1870)*, pp. 14–15, 18–20; *Minutes of the Annual Meeting of the British Chamber of Commerce*, Shanghai, July 27, 1861; *Minutes of the Annual General Meeting of the Shanghai General Chamber of Commerce*, Aug. 23, 1865).

rights.[20] They were no longer pressing for the opening of additional treaty ports, for overexpansion had already caused them serious business losses.[f] Instead they now hoped to reduce overhead by reducing the number of branch establishments in the various treaty ports and at the same time to expand the volume of business by unrestricted access to the interior. They were convinced that if they could travel and take up residence at will, they could somehow regain their former prosperity; that if they could personally supervise all transactions, the goods of foreign trade would be taxed less.

The merchants had no clear answer to the argument that such business as foreign firms had carried on in the interior had not proved particularly profitable; that they were ill-equipped to compete with Chinese firms outside the ports; that the increase in the total volume of imports into China had benefited producers in England and consumers in China rather than merchants in either.[21] When in 1868 Alcock invited the merchants to specify their needs, they sent expeditions into the interior and wrote voluminous replies. But instead of recommending specific steps, they confined themselves to general enthusiasm for the vision of a China through which their trade would flow at will and for the opening of a land route through to India.

The degree to which the Treaty of Tientsin had opened the Yangtze River to foreign commerce was the subject of particular controversy. Article 10 had provided for the opening of three Yangtze ports—later named as Chinkiang, Kiukiang, and Hankow—and Prince Kung had memorialized at the time that this was the most dangerous clause in the treaty.[23] After several British reconnoitering expeditions a map was made, and in March 1861 the British, with Chinese concurrence, published "Provisional Regulations" for navigation on the Yangtze by foreigners. British merchants interpreted these steps as meaning that the Yangtze was fully open as far as Hankow and anticipated that now "the opening of China will commence in real earnest."[24] British officials denied it and gave their support to the first Chinese ruling on the subject,[g] in spite of the merchants' outrage.[25]

The British government and British officials upheld the Chinese view that the Treaty of Tientsin had *not* provided for the opening of all China to foreigners; they questioned the wisdom of trying to exercise even such rights as were

---

[f] "Experience has shown the opening of new ports to be far less advantageous than was ever thought. The tendency of foreign trade is to centralize in Shanghai." (*NCH,* Oct. 12, 1867.)

[g] The "Revised Regulations on the Trade of the Yangtze Kiang" were issued on September 10, 1862, as the result of negotiations between Prince Kung, Hart, Bruce, and Burlingame. Foreign trade was declared specifically limited to the three open Yangtze ports. Moreover, whereas river boats were authorized to proceed as far as Hankow, ocean-going vessels were ordered to stop at Chinkiang. See Chung-chi Wang, *La Navigation du Yang-tseu,* Paris, 1932, pp. 82–89; Sargent, *Anglo-Chinese Commerce and Diplomacy* . . . , pp. 146–47. See also *Correspondence Respecting the Opening of the Yang-Tze–Kiang River to Foreign Trade,* 1861, *passim.* See also Chapter III.

guaranteed by the Treaty, and they considered the merchants' enthusiasm for extending these rights totally impracticable.[h]

Extraterritoriality. In the 1860's extraterritoriality was an issue only where residence in the interior was concerned. Since the Chinese government did not want foreigners in the interior on any condition, it used the argument that foreigners were not subject to Chinese law; but the legal aspects of the situation were more important to Alcock than they were to the Tsungli-yamen. To Alcock it was outrageous that foreigners should expect to be exempt from Chinese law in the interior: "Such unequal and incompatible conditions might possibly be imposed by force upon a conquered nation, but can never be the result of negotiations; nor could they, in my opinion, be carried into effect, without great danger to the existing Government and Empire."[26]

As Sino-Western contact in the ports expanded, the problem was to set up legal machinery that would offer foreigners the protection and redress to which they were accustomed, and would at the same time confirm ultimate Chinese authority. As British officials recognized, it was inevitable that there should be many grievances on both sides where there was "no common ground of action in laws, customs, or creed on which the judgments of a mixed tribunal can be founded."[27]

No one urged that foreigners in the ports be made subject to Chinese law as it existed; in both principle and procedure Chinese law lacked the firm safeguards for the accused and the convicted that nineteenth-century Europeans held to be the universal rights of man; moreover, it had no commercial code suited to the type of commercial litigation in which foreigners were regularly involved.[i]

The first solution had been consular jurisdiction over nationals of the treaty powers, whose extraterritorial rights were fully outlined in Articles 15–19 of the

---

[h] The "Return of the Import Trade at the Port of Tientsin" for 1862 pointed out that the requirements for successful trade in the interior included a knowledge of the spoken language, acquaintance with Chinese usage, and complete honesty. Cantonese compradors were useless. When the typical foreign merchant attempted to operate in the interior:

"The consequence is obvious; a misunderstanding arises between the foreign traders and the natives, the intervention of the local authorities is requested, the local authorities when not corrupt are generally stupid, and endless troubles and complications are thus generated, which it requires months to settle. Trade, of course, under such circumstances, is not to be thought of. Both foreigners and Chinese within this district are at present far too ignorant of each other to render the operation of this right of access into the interior of much importance to the merchant." (*China. No. 4. (1864),* pp. 35–36.)

Alcock agreed with this general view. See Alcock to Stanley, May 5, 1868, *China. No. 5. (1871),* pp. 135–39; and Alcock to Stanley, May 21, 1868, *China. No. 3. (1869),* p. 1.

[i] In Jardine Matheson's experience, "The Chinese possess a code of moral but none of civil law; all disputes concerning property or commercial obligations are decided by them according to crude, puerile notions of equity, and their officials are rarely free from at least the suspicion of bribery." (Memorial of Jardine's, Nov. 28, 1867. *China. No. 4. (1870),* p. 32.)

British Treaty of Tientsin. British authorities were to have jurisdiction when both parties were British or when the accused was British. A Chinese crime against a British subject was to be punished by the Chinese authorities according to Chinese law. Disputed cases were to be referred to the consul for decision. Consuls were subsequently given limited standing in Maritime Customs prosecutions,[j] since British merchants had complained that they had no effective channels of appeal against arbitrary fines or confiscations ordered by an agency of the Chinese government.[28] Consular jurisdiction soon proved inadequate, and there began almost immediately the long slow process of creating new and independent judicial institutions suited to local conditions. By an Order in Council of 1865, the Supreme Court of Shanghai was established with "extraordinary original jurisdiction . . . to hear and determine any case, civil or criminal, between British subjects or where the defendant was a British subject."[29] Although the court had the support of the merchant community,[30] it was not their tool. Chief Justice Sir Edmund Hornby ruled that extraterritoriality was not exemption from obedience to Chinese law; it meant only that British violators of Chinese law were to be prosecuted in a British court by the British Crown *on behalf of the Chinese Crown.*[k]

The Chinese authorities appeared to accept the judgments of the court as fair. Although they had long been aware of British criticism of the extreme penalties of the Chinese criminal law,[31] they had earlier demanded, to no avail of course, that these penalties be imposed on foreigners convicted of crimes against Chinese. Now they demanded no more than what the foreign public generally regarded as reasonable and proper punishment.[32]

New legal institutions developed steadily. Soon there was general agreement that British consuls should be deprived of their remaining legal functions, their place being taken by a high-ranking mixed court;[33] for Chinese plaintiffs had found it difficult to plead their cases before a British consul or the British Supreme Court, and British plaintiffs had found it difficult to plead their cases before Chinese magistrates.[l] The first experiment was a mixed court to handle

---

[j] The system promulgated jointly by Wade and Prince Kung on October 27, 1865, provided that disputed customs cases were henceforth to be settled by the joint action of the consul, the superintendent of the port, and the foreign commissioner of customs. The Customs might then appeal to the Tsungli-yamen, and the consul to the British minister at Peking. Subsequently, by the "Rules Agreed upon Between Sir Rutherford Alcock and the Prince of Kung for Joint Investigation in Cases of Confiscation and Fine by Custom-House Authorities," Peking, May 31, 1868, the system was altered to give the Customs more authority in cases of confiscation, the consul more authority in cases of fine. Hertslet, *Treaties,* Vol. I, No. 9.

[k] See Chapter III.

[l] As early as 1860, Bruce had seen the advantages of a mixed court, but at that time Chinese officials were unwilling to function publicly on an equal basis with foreigners (Bruce to Russell, April 7, 1860, *Correspondence Respecting Affairs in China. 1859–1860,* No. 22).

cases in which the plaintiff was foreign and the defendant Chinese.[m] It was also proposed that a mixed court be given jurisdiction when the plaintiff was Chinese and the defendant foreign.[34] As to procedure, British officials advised against any attempt to introduce the elaborate and expensive European system because it was opposed to the Chinese system of arbitration founded on custom.[35] The chief problem in placing British defendants under the jurisdiction of a mixed court was the absence of a commercial and civil code suited to the new conditions. The British believed that from the experience of the mixed court a new code could be gradually developed, one that would meet Western standards without violating the Chinese penal code or Chinese custom.[36] Although the *North China Herald* urged the Chinese to adopt the Code Napoléon as a solution,[37] British officials were, in legal as in other matters, slow to recommend the wholesale substitution of European ways for Chinese ways; they looked for a Chinese foundation. For example, Alcock investigated the question of the responsibility of guarantors in Chinese law, on behalf of the Shanghai Chamber of Commerce, and he informed the Chamber:

> The Chinese have no written code of commercial law. In the absence of a statute law, there is, as with ourselves, a common law founded on immemorial usage, and having the force of law by general reception and accordance, though never reduced to writing or embodied in any edict or statute.[n]

Until a code could be prepared, jurisdiction over British defendants (but not plaintiffs) in mixed cases would have to continue to rest with the British Supreme Court. But the trend of thinking was clearly indicated when the British consul urged the British judge always to request the assistance of the taotai until such time as it became feasible to yield jurisdiction.[38]

Related problems were raised by the administration of the foreign settlements and concessions. Everyone agreed that orderly municipal government was needed; the question was, from whom should the authority of the governing body be derived. No one at this date, Chinese or foreign, proposed that the Chinese try to set up the actual machinery for administering the affairs of a body of foreigners with extraterritorial rights. But at the other extreme, there was

---

[m] A Chinese subprefect was to reside permanently within the International Settlement to "decide all civil and commercial suits between Chinese residents within the settlement, and also between Chinese and foreign residents in cases where Chinese are defendants, by Chinese law." (Rules for the Mixed Court at Shanghai, instituted April 20, 1869, Hertslet, *Treaties*, Vol. II, No. 129. Review of its activities, *China. No. 5. (1871)*, pp. 163–70.)

[n] Alcock's letter and enclosed notes on the subject from Prince Kung and Wen-hsiang, *NCH*, June 19, 1868. Alcock was correct in concluding that Chinese bondsmen had to honor their bonds and that this and similar facts would make possible the development of a working commercial code that would be satisfactory to both foreigners and Chinese. He was quite mistaken, however, in equating the Chinese idea of custom with the British idea of the common law. Although neither was codified, they were based on opposite conceptions. (See Chapter VII.)

no responsible support for the idea that the settlements should be independent "free cities."[39]

The 1854 Shanghai Land Regulations had become clearly inadequate and had to be revised, for if each consul merely governed his own nationals, there would be little room for experiment and development, and there would be numerous practical difficulties.[40] Yet the consular body as a whole could not function as a supranational administrative body, since each consul was the direct agent of his own government.[o]

The main concern of British officials was that ultimate Chinese authority over Shanghai should be emphatically reasserted. From the beginning of the Restoration, Bruce had been on guard against the development of any idea that Shanghai was quasi-independent territory.[41] When the land regulations were revised in 1866 and confirmed in 1869, Alcock took the same view.[p] He held that the Emperor of China had delegated authority to the Shanghai Municipal Council, which consequently derived its powers from China.[42]

The Status of Foreign Envoys. The historic questions of the residence of foreign envoys in Peking and the manner of their reception in Imperial audience did not prove to be major problems in the 1860's. The right of residence had been confirmed,[q] and although its confirmation did not work the miracles that had once been expected,[r] it contributed to the founding of the Tsungli-yamen and to friendly contact between Chinese and foreign officials.[s]

Originally the British had considered that the question of the residence of

[o] When Li Hung-chang offered to give the consular body as a whole jurisdiction over unrepresented foreigners, the foreign envoys at Peking insisted that no consul could arrest the nationals of another state (*NCH,* Jan. 30, Feb. 20, 1864).

[p] Seward described Alcock's purpose as "adjusting them in a manner which may result in doing away with the semblance of territorial authority now exercised by England, France and the United States in Shanghai." (Seward to Williams, April 7, 1866, *U.S. Arch. China. Instructions,* I, 396–97.) Contemporary French criticism of the revised land regulations is not persuasive. Maintaining their own concession under strict consular control, they argued that the Municipal Council, as an oligarchy not bound by treaty obligations, was a greater threat to Chinese sovereignty than a concession governed by a single consul (Drouyn to Bellonet, June 18, 1866, *DD,* 1867, No. 8).

[q] Articles 2–7 of the British treaty had provided that either country might appoint an envoy to the other, and that the envoy would be accorded the treatment customary in Western capitals. Although Elgin had agreed in October 1858 that the British minister would not for the present insist on living in Peking, this concession was withdrawn when ratification of the treaty had to be forced. Article 2 of the Convention of Peking, 1860, confirmed the right of residence, and early in 1861 Bruce arrived to begin the first routine diplomatic assignment to the Chinese capital. (Russell to Bruce, Jan. 6, 1861, *Correspondence Respecting Affairs in China. 1859–1860,* No. 116.)

[r] "It used to be a cardinal article of faith among Europeans in China during the fifties that if once we could throw Peking open to foreign diplomacy all would be well. That was to be the sovereign cure for all the ills of which we had to complain. We should be in touch with the Emperor and his court, and we could not fail to convert the most recalcitrant of mandarins to the adoption of our Western civilization." (Freeman-Mitford, *The Attaché at Peking,* Preface, p. xliv.)

[s] See Chapters III and X.

envoys in Peking was inseparably connected with that of their reception in Imperial audience without the kowtow. To Elgin in 1860:

> The Emperor's affectation of superiority is not, in itself, of much consequence to other Sovereigns; but it has an unfavourable bearing as regards the validity of the Treaty rights which they obtain from him on behalf of their subjects, because it imparts to them in some sort the character of concessions made of pure grace by a Suzerain to vassals, and enjoyed, therefore, under some not very definable conditions of fealty.[43]

After 1860 audience seemed much less important to the British. When Bruce arrived in 1861, he was instructed not to insist on exercising his right in this respect.[44] The *North China Herald* noted this with approval: "England can well afford to waive this ceremony. She *cannot* afford to fight for it."[45] As the British ceased to demand audience, the Chinese became increasingly willing to grant it. Although the first audience was not held until 1873, the negotiators on both sides had come to regard the question as a largely formal one, on which mutually satisfactory compromise was relatively easy.

Christian Missions.[46] Christian missionary activity was fundamentally the most serious problem in Sino-foreign relations, and the failure to solve it during the Restoration was dramatically represented by the Tientsin Massacre of 1870. Yet oddly enough the issue took a minor place in the negotiations for the revision of the Treaty of Tientsin, because British officials and the Tsungli-yamen were in a substantial agreement that belied the explosive forces beneath on both sides. The British wanted no more than the vague freedom of Christian teaching and practice that was guaranteed by Article 8 of the Treaty of Tientsin, and the Tsungli-yamen had no intention of trying to withdraw so small a concession.

British officials considered missionaries as more presumptuous than merchants, as representing no substantial British national interest, and as dangerous to the stability of China. Alcock wrote in 1869:

> They [the Chinese] may dislike the merchant, but the missionary they fear; and where the former might trade or travel peacefully, the latter is not allowed to preach or settle himself. The one they regard as a trafficker, more or less intrusive, whose presence in the interior, with his extraterritoriality, they could well dispense with; but the other as creating an *imperium in imperio* fatal to the authority of the Emperor. And are they so far wrong in their conclusion?[47]

Neither Alcock nor other British officials were prepared to support an expanding missionary program.

The Tsungli-yamen for its part was prepared to accept a certain amount of missionary work as inevitable, but it could not control anti-Christian outbreaks. The late 1860's were marked not only by a "paper war against missionaries,"[48] but by a steady procession of incidents in which churches were looted and foreign missionaries and Chinese converts were beaten and killed. Although Catholic missions deep in the interior were the chief victims,[49] British Protestant establishments were also attacked.[50]

As the atrocity stories mounted, the Foreign Office reiterated its policy of "forbearance and conciliation."[51] The British government did not, of course, believe Chinese tales of cruel and inhuman practices on the part of Christian missionaries, but it recognized that if missionaries were indiscreet, anti-Western elements could easily impress such tales upon the Chinese populace. It was argued in Parliament that if missionaries irresponsibly forced their way into the interior in these circumstances, they had no one but themselves to blame for the resulting tragedies.[52]

These views permeated British officialdom, from Clarendon through Wade and Alcock down to a consul on Formosa who told the missionary victims of a riot there "that the opinions of the people cannot be altered by any mandates of the authorities, and that they must either live down these reports, as has been done in other places, or quit the island for a place where their labours would be more thankfully received."[53] Alcock did not suppose that the missionaries would withdraw from China en masse. He thought friction could be gradually reduced if they acted circumspectly, with due respect for Chinese sentiment, and if they did not claim residence in the interior as a right but asked for it as a privilege.[54] Wade went further; he considered inland residence inadvisable in any circumstances and advised the missionaries to abandon evangelism and to try to convert the upper classes by teaching nonreligious subjects.[55]

British missionaries expressed their opposition to the government view in full voice. Under the most-favored-nation clause they wanted the same rights of owning lands and buildings in the interior that they believed the French Treaty of Tientsin gave to Catholics.[56] They also had an important answer to Alcock's contention that missionary work was subversive of the established Chinese order:

> you dwell much on the political and revolutionary tendencies of Christianity, and argue that, as the missionary, from the very nature of the doctrines he teaches, must of necessity teach revolution, he ought to be restrained from going into the interior, and you leave the impression on the reader of your despatch that it would be decidedly for the peace of China if Christianity and its emissaries were excluded from the country. . . . Christianity may be revolutionary of customs and opinions, but it is not seditious. . . . *But the very presence* of Anglo-Saxons in the East is revolutionary, and therefore we are warranted in arguing that if Christianity is to be banished because of its tendency to produce changes, the British and American Governments ought to recall every Anglo-Saxon in China. . . . If the despotic Governments of the East are to be left unimpaired, if nothing must be done which is at all likely to interfere with the ideas on which they are founded, then we have

no right to bring to China the laws or the commerce of Christendom, and force the Chinese to accept them. Both are revolutionary in such countries as China and Japan. Both break up the established order of things. . . . The settlement in Peking of a British Minister at the point of a bayonet, and the demand that he shall be treated as Ambassadors in the West are treated, are far more subversive of all the Chinese ideas of government than the teachings of missionaries. . . . China, it is admitted on all hands, needs a revolution.[57]

Alcock, of course, knew that this was true, that contact with the West was starting China along a new and unknown road. But he believed that the change would be less hazardous to both China and the West without the irritation and fear to which missionary teaching gave rise.[58]

FOREIGN ADVICE ON THE "REGENERATION OF CHINA": THE WADE-HART PROPOSALS

To British diplomats of the 1860's the "regeneration of China" was the overriding issue in diplomacy. The Co-operative Policy, as we have seen, was designed to create external conditions favorable to reform. Alcock, Wade, and Hart went further and attempted to suggest certain domestic measures to the Chinese government. On November 6, 1865, Hart presented to the Tsungli-yamen a "spectator's memorandum" (*p'ang-kuan lun*); and on March 5, 1866, Alcock presented a similar memorandum by Wade, together with a supporting statement of his own.[59]

Hart apologized for commenting as an outsider but remarked that the whole face of the Lu-shan mountain could be seen only by a man standing at a great distance. He then plunged into the gist of his argument: China, which had been great when the nations of Europe amounted to nothing, was now weaker than any of them. Why? Because in the modern period she had failed to solve her domestic problems. Since Sino-Western contact was an unalterable fact of the future, China could keep her dignity and her very independence only by repairing her domestic shortcomings.

Most of the shortcomings to which Hart referred were already being discussed among Restoration officials themselves, as earlier chapters have indicated. Among Hart's points in this category were the following: Provincial officials were transferred too rapidly and were not appointed to their native provinces, where they knew the dialect, the people, and the conditions. The yamen clerks had far too much power. The army was weak because its rosters were padded with the names of the old, the weak, and the very young; because morale was low and training anachronistic. The classical education of officials, originally admirable, had in the course of time become empty of useful content. The land tax, the salt gabelle, the salary scale, and the general fiscal structure of the Empire were in urgent need of reform. And China could strengthen her international position by granting Imperial audiences and sending Chinese envoys abroad.

Hart also made a number of suggestions that Chinese statesmen of the time were not making. He was sharply critical of the censors, whom he called the wrong eyes and ears for the Throne, men who contributed to the corruption of officials and did not hear the people's anger. He attacked the whole theory of government by men of ability, arguing that too many and too varied duties were expected of a single man. And he urged Sino-foreign co-operation in the expansion of trade, the building of railways, and so forth, as the best means of promoting the people's prosperity.

After reviewing recent examples of Sino-foreign friction, Hart concluded that as China's difficulties in foreign affairs today arose from her previous failure to solve domestic problems, so the failure today to solve foreign problems would cause domestic problems in the future. China's enormous population, he wrote, is civilized, industrious, and peacefully inclined, and the West stands ready to help: "If policies are altered, China can become the leader of all nations; if policies are not altered she will become the servant of all nations. Thus will the future's domestic affairs depend upon your handling of today's foreign affairs."

The Tsungli-yamen, although finding Hart's memorandum worthy of careful study, did not present it to the Throne at that time because it was not official, i.e., it did not come from the representative of a foreign power.[60] Alcock's note and the Wade memorandum, however, required official attention.

Wade reviewed recent Chinese history in more detail than Hart had done, pointing to the spread of rebellion, the growth of secret societies, and other signs of weakness. He had studied the memorials and edicts published in the *Peking Gazette* since 1845, and found that they attributed popular unrest and the weakness of the government primarily to the incompetence of officials and secondarily to natural calamities. But having identified these causes, Wade charged, Chinese officials had made no attempt to combat them. Rather they had taken the view that the cycle of flourishing and decay was normal in all history, complacently noting that in the past at the height of disorder a hero had always appeared with the strength to pacify rebellion and restore the ancient way of life.

Wade granted that the Chinese cyclical view was a correct interpretation of China's past; the nineteenth century was another matter. Could not China's officials see that domestic affairs and foreign affairs were now inextricably intertwined, that if the dynastic cycle were allowed *now* to take its course, there would be no mere period of decay, for the West would intervene to protect its interests? "If one country intervenes, the rest will intervene. In that event need one ask whether China will be sovereign and independent, or partitioned among other countries?"

After that dire threat, Wade offered hope: decay was not inevitable. The literati and gentry were loyal, after all, and the bandits were simple folk. If

China would take foreign advice in certain fields, there need be no catastrophe.

Wade denied the charge, lodged as early as this, that foreign governments were interested less in reforming than in controlling China. He insisted that England had no territorial ambitions, pointing out that in 1860, when the British and French could have taken anything they wanted, they had aided the Chinese government against its internal enemies and had withdrawn their troops as soon as a treaty was signed. This had promoted trade, of course, but it was surely no way to acquire territorial control.

Wade's specific suggestions were similar to Hart's. China needed adequate revenues, internal peace, and sufficient military strength to prevent foreign aggression. These could be attained through reform, economic modernization, modern military training, foreign loans, and the establishment of medical and other schools. Chinese legations abroad could protect China's international interests by arguing over the heads of the foreign envoys in Peking to their home governments.

The conclusion of Wade's memorandum was an eloquent plea to China to heed the example of the conquest of Burma, of Indo-China, of Russian Asia; to cease thinking that the old days could ever return, to move forward with the Western world, to use its help until China was strong, then to stand alone. "To sum up, if you move forward, you can flourish again and be strong; standing still will surely lead to collapse beyond recall."

A word must be said here about the proposals for economic development that these memoranda contained. Hart, Wade, and Alcock were looking for a *modus vivendi*. In this effort, they emphasized to the Tsungli-yamen the long-term importance of modernization. To their own merchants and the home government, they emphasized the dangers inherent in hasty and carelessly planned modernization. It was a matter of tactics, and the inconsistency was on the surface only.

The Tsungli-yamen's reaction to these memoranda is worth careful attention. In a memorial of April 1, 1866, the yamen condemned as threats what Wade and Hart had phrased as predictions. At the same time it was careful to point out that the memoranda contained worth-while suggestions that ought to be discussed by all the high officials of government. The phraseology was devious, but the import was clear enough: Although we personally find these ideas as distasteful as do our colleagues in other branches of government, we must formulate some positive policy that takes account of them in one way or another.[61] The Grand Council took the view that since the government could not be certain of the motives of Wade and Hart, China should follow some of their suggestions to please them but avoid accepting their whole plan.[62]

When these various documents had been presented to the Throne, an edict summarized the issues and ordered ten leading officials[t] to deliberate and to memorialize without delay, "distinguishing what can be done immediately, what can be done by degrees, and what is definitely harmful and unacceptable."[63] The Tsungli-yamen did not want the discussion of basic issues confused by recriminations over certain minor grievances mentioned by Wade and Hart, such as the Chinese delay in granting permission for foreigners to enter the walled city of Chaochow, to erect churches, to open warehouses, and to establish customhouses. Therefore in a supplementary memorial of the same date, April 1, the yamen asked for and received an edict to provincial officials to clear up without delay any minor matters mentioned in the memoranda to which there was no fundamental objection.[64]

The memorials in reply commenting on the Wade-Hart proposals varied in general tone and in specific recommendations.[65] Everyone favored self-strengthening; everyone disliked missionary activity, which Wade and Hart had not mentioned except with reference to limited treaty obligations; everyone mistrusted railways, seeing in them a means of foreign penetration and control. On the other proposals, however, there was a range of opinion. Kuan-wen and Ma Hsin-i, suspicious of any foreign suggestion, interpreted the proposals as proof that foreigners feared China. Kuan-wen argued that Wade and Hart merely wanted lucrative advisory posts for themselves and other nonmerchant foreigners; he thought that China should be generous in this respect while preparing for a showdown. Ma wrote that the main strength of the Chinese government was the Chinese people, upon whom it could count to resist foreigners to the death.

Ch'ung-hou's views were at the other extreme. He pointed to the success of the Maritime Customs, the troop training program, and the arsenals as proof that many foreign methods could be turned to good use. Tso Tsung-t'ang shared neither the enthusiasm of Ch'ung-hou nor the hostility of Kuan-wen and Ma Hsin-i. He was obsessed with the importance of steamers but feared railways as much as his colleagues. Other foreign devices he considered attractive but useless toys: "it is not important whether we have them or not." He reported that when one of his French technical advisers at the Foochow Shipyard, Baron de Méritens, had brought a telegraph set to show him, he had been amused, had bought it, and had had it stored in the Foochow prefectural treasury! For Tso it was the foreigners' possession of steamers and steamers only that made China vulnerable; if China too had these, the West could be held at bay.[u] Jui-lin,

---

[t] Tseng Kuo-fan, Kuan-wen, Tso Tsung-t'ang, Jui-lin, Li Hung-chang, Liu K'un-i, Ma Hsin-i, Cheng Tun-chin, Kuo Sung-tao, and Ch'ung-hou.

[u] The general import of Tso's memorial is somewhat twisted by his irritation at the fact that the Wade-Hart proposals had come from Englishmen rather than from Frenchmen, whom he much preferred, provided they were anticlerical.

Chiang I-li, and Liu K'un-i took a similar view of modern technology; railways were anathema, but such things as steamers and Western arms could be quite useful. Devices such as telegraphs and looms were unimportant either way, for they had "no relation to the basic principles of government."

There was considerable feeling among the memorialists that to send envoys abroad might be useful to China, and that some compromise procedure might be found for granting Imperial audiences to foreign envoys in Peking.[v] Ma Hsin-i, however, objected violently, apparently because he misunderstood the use of the term "plenipotentiary" with reference to envoys. He argued that the foreign envoys would become the rulers of China, whereas China's envoys would have merely an empty name.

The memorialists were at pains to point out that many of the proposals for domestic reform were already under consideration, and that some were already being carried out. What was needed was not change (*pien-keng*) but adjustment (*pien-t'ung*) and putting in order (*cheng-tun*). As Jui-lin and Chiang I-li put it, in government (*cheng-chih*) a distinction must be drawn between *cheng*, "politics," in which the fundamental wishes of the people must be followed (that is, the Confucian society must be preserved); and *chih*, "administration," in which questions of mere method may be decided in accordance with time and place.[w]

On the basis of this distinction, there was general support for continuing to adjust the land tax, for reducing the power of clerks, for decreasing the size of the army and improving its quality, for increasing official salaries, and for standardizing the coinage. Opinion was divided on the advisability of appointing officials to their native provinces.

Hart's basic criticism of the principle of government by men of ability trained in the Classics was acceptable to no one. It was one thing to say, as the Chinese themselves did, that the particular content of the training had become overly literary; it was another to propose administration by specialists rather than by nonspecialist "superior men." Jui-lin and Chiang I-li said that Hart on this had the point of view of a man who sat in a well to look at the sky. Since the T'ang and Sung periods it had been proved that the examination system produced officials of outstanding competence; in recent years alone there had been Hu Lin-i, Tseng Kuo-fan, Tso Tsung-t'ang, Lo Ping-chang, Li Hung-chang, and Shen Pao-chen. In ancient times it had not been the custom to re-

[v] The memorialists also suggested more careful study of the West; specifically, it was suggested that China bribe foreign informants, circulate information about the West through all branches of government, and try to take advantage of rivalries among the Western powers.

[w] This is the same distinction that Sun Yat-sen later drew between the broad powers of *cheng*, which belonged to the whole people, and the day-to-day administrative powers of *chih*, which belonged to the government.

proach high officials for their ignorance of financial or military details. For less important subjects there were lower officials, just as there were servants who prepared the altars for worship.

Men like Wade and Hart stood somewhere between the Chinese and the Western worlds. They admired much of the Chinese heritage, but they were no eccentrics in flight from their own age. They understood the meaning of the nineteenth century and the relentless force of the Industrial Revolution. They were attempting, and not always with optimism, to control and direct the forces engendered by a collision between two civilizations.[x]

British diplomats were not remiss in pressing for specific steps, as the negotiations for the revision of the Treaty of Tientsin showed. Their maneuvers, however, must be examined in the light of the broad political ideas behind the negotiations, ideas that were discussed in much of the British diplomatic correspondence, but were most fully stated in the Wade-Hart memoranda.

BRITISH PREPARATIONS FOR TREATY REVISION

The Treaties of Tientsin had provided for optional revision after ten years. As the time approached, Alcock set himself two tasks: to persuade the Tsungli-yamen to accept certain limited reforms in the fields affecting foreign affairs, and to persuade British merchants to adjust their demands to what was feasible from the Chinese point of view.[66] His first effort in the first direction was his support of the Wade-Hart proposals. To achieve his second purpose, he began by making a tour of the treaty ports in the late spring of 1867 to inform himself in detail of the merchants' views.[67] At each port views were freely expressed, and these views were elaborated in numerous meetings and petitions for the next three years.[68]

In general import these various documents were similar. Only Newchwang was satisfied with the way things were going.[y] In all the other ports, "there could not be a more fertile theme for mutual condolence among foreigners than the shortcomings of the Chinese government."[69] The merchants held these "shortcomings" to be violations of the spirit, if not the letter, of the Treaty of Tientsin; they wanted a new and aggressive British minister who would force the Chinese to observe the Treaty's provisions as the merchants interpreted them. In the words of the Shanghai General Chamber of Commerce,

[x] In 1902 the Empress Dowager reportedly told Hart she regretted that more of the advice he gave in the 1860's in his memorandum had not been accepted, for subsequent events had proved him correct. Juliet Bredon, *Sir Robert Hart*, New York, 1909, p. 111.

[y] The *North China Herald* commented wryly that Newchwang must be "a small mercantile paradise," for the merchants there had reported that "The province is peaceable; sword-racks have disappeared; the river is well-buoyed; the approach well-lighted; the pilots are models of sobriety and skill; illegal taxation is unknown; and the taotai is an incarnation of even-handed justice and integrity." (Jan. 24, 1868.)

The design of the Treaty was, by throwing open the producing and consuming districts to foreign capital and energy, and by fostering a closer communication between the Chinese people and Europeans, to introduce an element of progress into our trading relations, previously shackled by innumerable artificial and unjust obstructions.

The chief need was not for new privileges but for "confirmation and extension of those already granted." According to the Chamber, Alcock had punished foreigners for the slightest infraction of the treaty,[z] but had said not a word against wholesale Chinese violation of its major provisions, "the maintenance of the dignity and prestige of the Chinese government seeming to weigh more with the foreign authorities than the spirit of the Treaty or the claims of justice." Any treaty would fail, whatever its terms, "if the privileges granted by it be not scrupulously and vigilantly protected against the constant opposition of a government as subtle in design as unscrupulous in action."[70] Jardine, Matheson and Co. took the same view: the Treaty of Tientsin was fundamentally sound, but its privileges should have been gradually extended. Instead many of the privileges already conceded were now being withheld by China; "forbearance is now costing England more than it brings in."[71]

Specifically the merchants demanded the right of unrestricted residence in the interior *with continuing extraterritoriality*;[a] reorganization of the Chinese system of local taxation with the convenience of foreign trade as the chief end in view; Chinese adoption of a written code of civil law based on European principles; the right of steam navigation on all inland waterways, with the Yellow River as well as the Yangtze fully opened to trade; the right to engage in the construction of railways, telegraph lines, and mines; the right to import salt; standardization of the Chinese currency; formal recognition by the Chinese government of the independent jurisdiction of foreign municipal councils in the international settlements; and increased powers for consuls including consular review of the decisions of the Maritime Customs.

As the merchants vented their feelings, each new memorial was angrier and more demanding than the last, until finally even the *North China Herald* poked fun at the exaggerated nature of some of the complaints, pointing out that in fact the position of foreigners had greatly improved in recent years. Foreigners were never satisfied, never thankful; their motto was "accept every concession with a growl."

> The moment . . . an important step is gained, we take advantage of it quietly, and fasten upon the remaining grievances under which we labour, so as to preserve in undiminished strength and purity those valuable feelings of exasperation

---

[z] See Chapter III.

[a] There was some variation of view on this point. Hongkong merchants were the most extreme; some groups were willing to settle for limited rights in the interior.

against the Chinese and their misdeeds, which compel us to urge on our schemes for benefitting them, and ourselves, in the opening up of the Middle Kingdom.[72]

The merchants also had certain technical grievances in regard to bonded warehouses, drawbacks, tonnage dues, harbor improvements, and coastal lighting, complaints that were readily subject to remedy by negotiation. But the major demands of the merchants were of such a revolutionary character that they could not possibly be attained by mere pressure and insistence. As Alcock told the merchants, they were

> measures which either presuppose complete command of the country, or the willing cooperation of its government. The first means the disintegration of a great Empire; the second a mutual agreement between the high contracting parties. Which of these do the memorialists contemplate?[73]

The merchants never answered this question. While they did not recommend an expedition to conquer China, they were quite unprepared to accept the notion that revised treaty terms would require the consent of the Chinese government; that short of conquest, the only path open to British officials was skilled bargaining and persuasion. The treaty ports had in fact not yet "recognized" the Chinese government, and when they saw the lines along which Alcock proposed to proceed, they wrote:

> The revision is to be a mutual adjustment of terms, in which the wishes of the Chinese Government are to have exactly the same weight on the one side as the interests of progress, civilization and commerce on the other. If that is the spirit in which the Treaties are to be revised, there is little hope of any satisfactory results . . . If we had limited our aspirations concerning the China trade to that which the Chinese Government should have "spontaneously granted or willingly conceded," the whole commerce might still be carried on by two or three merchants living at Macao on sufferance, and tolerated at Canton under degrading conditions for a month or two in the tea season.[74]

The British government took a very different view. It agreed with Alcock that negotiation based on mutual concession offered the only possibility for the peaceful adjustment of Sino-foreign relations, and it was determined to have no more China wars. As the negotiations were about to begin, Foreign Secretary Stanley instructed Alcock:

> I am glad to see that you are prepared to take into account the interests, the feelings, and to a certain extent the prejudices, of the Chinese Government and people. The true policy to be advocated is that which, by mutual forbearance, shall combine the suffrages of both parties in some common system, which, though it may not be the best in the abstract, yet may have in its favour that it does not, without some palpable corresponding advantage to Chinese interests, clash with their existing habits and fixed opinions, but enlists the good will of the majority in its favour.[75]

CHINESE PREPARATIONS FOR TREATY REVISION

From its founding in 1861 the Tsungli-yamen had attempted to keep informed about foreign opinion concerning China. Its members were familiar with foreign complaints on such subjects as transit passes, and they knew what British merchants were saying in the press. They had studied the Wade-Hart proposals, and they were aware that the British Treaty of Tientsin was subject to revision in 1868.

Early in 1867 the Tsungli-yamen raised the problem of treaty revision in a letter to Li Hung-chang. Li replied that in his opinion the foreigners would certainly bring pressure to bear and that it would be difficult for China to attain her own objectives. The Tsungli-yamen saw China's weakness as an added reason for preparing the Chinese case carefully. Tseng Kuo-fan was also consulted but did not reply. The yamen staff was then ordered to prepare a classified analysis of the terms of the Treaty of Tientsin, noting the additions, deletions, and modifications that would be to China's advantage.[76]

When Alcock left for his tour of the ports in early May of 1867, the yamen became acutely aware of its own inadequate knowledge of recent developments in the ports; Tseng Kuo-fan and Ch'ung-hou were therefore ordered to select officials intimately familiar with the conditions of foreign trade in the southern and northern ports respectively, and to send them to Peking the following autumn.

In its first formal memorial on treaty revision, on June 16, 1867, the Tsungli-yamen pointed out that once a treaty clause had been agreed to, every character in it constituted an ironclad precedent; that it would therefore be extremely difficult to persuade the foreigners, whose ambition and cunning were boundless, as was well known, to agree to give up any of the privileges they had acquired in previous treaties. It would also be difficult to keep them from wrangling about introducing railways and telegraphs, about abolishing the salt monopoly, and about allowing steam navigation on inland waterways. Great skill and determination would be required to hold their advance within bounds.[77]

In these difficult circumstances, the Tsungli-yamen proposed to strengthen its position by consulting high provincial officials on the principles of foreign policy. In this way the yamen hoped both to protect itself from the criticism of more conservative Chinese officials and to impress foreigners by speaking for the whole bureaucracy. Moreover, it expected that a general consultation would produce a more informed and uniform policy. Pointing to the disastrous results in the past of apathy and quarreling over foreign policy, it called for a united front on treaty revision.[78]

The Tsungli-yamen prepared a circular letter on the main problems of treaty revision, and an edict of October 12, 1867, ordered the Grand Council to send copies speedily to eighteen high officials for their comment.[79] Since negotiations would probably begin early in 1868, replies were to reach Peking before December 10.[80] The edict cautioned officials to give serious attention to a policy suited to the circumstances, since pen and tongue were China's only weapons.[81]

The yamen's circular letter pointed out that the barbarian question was one of long standing; that China had made one mistake after another until it was now obvious to all that the situation was critical. The barbarians, once weak and remote, had become strong through superior weapons and were now near neighbors as a result of improved communications. In 1860, the yamen continued, China's position had been so desperate that it had been necessary to accept the Treaties of Tientsin as a last resort. Many points in them had been unsatisfactory, but the only possible policy had been to observe the treaties in good faith while seeking a means of controlling the foreigners. The times were difficult, but China's present problems could not be solved by empty talk of the Way and its Power (*tao-te*) or by idle tears. It was easy enough, the yamen thought, to point out things that should never be allowed to happen; the problem of the moment was to suggest realistic means to keep them from happening.[82]

The Tsungli-yamen attached to its circular letter an outline of the chief issues likely to be discussed in the forthcoming negotiations: (1) receiving foreign envoys in Imperial audience; (2) sending Chinese envoys to foreign countries; (3) introducing railways and telegraphs; (4) establishing foreign warehouses in the interior, arranging for inland travel and residence, and allowing steam navigation on inland waterways; (5) importing foreign salt and developing coal mines; (6) extending Christian missionary activity.[83] The replies from provincial officials followed this outline.[84]

Although this entire correspondence was supposed to be secret, there was a leak. Tseng Kuo-fan's memorial was accurately summarized and reviewed in the *North China Herald* on June 13, 1868, and its contents were reported to the American Department of State in July.[85] A translation of the full text was published in the *North China Herald* on September 11. The Tsungli-yamen was alarmed, and an edict ordered increased caution in the handling of secret documents.[86]

The negotiations were not imperiled by the leak, for Tseng's memorial was widely admired, even by those who disagreed with his position. There were no other leaks. When foreigners discussed the "Tsungli-yamen's treaty revision circular," they were talking about another circular letter sent to the superintendents of customs at the various ports. This circular dealt not with the great issues of foreign policy, but with the details of the tariff and the customs administration. Tseng Kuo-fan was asked to assemble the superintendents' replies on these minor points and to review them.[87]

THE ISSUES AS THE CHINESE SAW THEM

Audience. Although the audience question had ceased to be important to foreigners, to the Chinese it was, for ceremonial reasons, the first problem to be discussed. In 1858 they had been intransigent.[88] By 1868 this seemed a point on which concession was possible. The Tsungli-yamen's argument in favor of granting audiences illustrates the flexibility of Chinese conservatives in the diplomatic field. The yamen argued that the precedents of ancient Chinese history were not instructive here because of changes in ceremony during the Sung period. It then quoted Han Yü to the effect that Chinese ceremonies were performed only by those barbarians who had been civilized (Sinicized); none of the barbarians of the present had risen to the Chinese level, and there was therefore no point in attempting to control them by Chinese rites, such as the kowtow.

The majority of replies to the Tsungli-yamen circular agreed that it would be politic for China to concede audience without kowtow. Tso Tsung-t'ang wrote emphatically that the audience the Western powers asked was no more than reasonable, since China had already recognized them as equals.

In court circles there were still objections, but not among officials in a position to make policy. The first audience did not take place until 1873, chiefly because of the special problems raised by the regency of the two Dowager Empresses. When the T'ung-chih Emperor approached his majority, the views of the Tsungli-yamen and high provincial officials easily outweighed the conventional opposition.[89] Wen-hsiang handled the arrangements with England, France, Japan, and Russia, and the first audience in the modern manner was finally held on June 29, 1873.[90]

Chinese Envoys. The Tsungli-yamen argued in favor of sending Chinese envoys abroad on two grounds: (1) it was necessary to study the behavior of the enemy, and (2) by appealing directly to foreign governments, China might persuade them of the justice of her case. The yamen had been eminently successful in appealing to consuls to reprimand unruly merchants, and to ministers to reprimand unruly consuls, all in terms of international law. Its members were shrewd enough to realize that the home governments were removed from the irritations of on-the-spot negotiations, and that Chinese envoys abroad could appeal to foreign offices to reprimand ministers.[b]

The majority of provincial replies agreed with the Tsungli-yamen that the

---

[b] While the Burlingame Mission was abroad, Prince Kung delicately intimated to Alcock that he would trust Alcock's sense of justice in the handling of a certain Chinese complaint, *rather than instruct the Chinese envoy to make representations to the British home government* or to the representatives of other powers. Alcock commented: "They are making progress in their diplomatic education, it is very obvious"; he added that the sending abroad of Chinese envoys "affords the best security, perhaps, the Chinese can have for the abstinence from wrongful acts of any one foreign representative or government." (*China. No. 3. (1869)*, p. 33; see also p. 36.)

sending abroad of envoys might be conceded in principle.[91] Tseng Kuo-fan was chiefly concerned to have it clearly understood that the envoys would be sent at China's discretion; others were concerned at the shortage of Chinese capable of filling ambassadorial posts. Tso Tsung-t'ang had no reservations. He agreed with both the Tsungli-yamen's arguments and added that able envoys could be selected from among the merchants and gentry of Kiangsu, Chekiang, and Fukien who had become versed in foreign affairs; he warned against the employment of Cantonese, whom for all their knowledge of the West he regarded as frivolous, deceitful busybodies.

Railways and Telegraphs.[c] The Tsungli-yamen's circular letter based its opposition to the introduction of railways and telegraphs on three grounds: (1) China would lose control of strategic military areas; (2) graves would be disturbed and the principles of geomancy (*feng-shui*) violated; (3) the people's welfare would be endangered. Since foreigners had not been impressed by the second argument, the yamen proposed to emphasize the third. Even if the government could bring itself to tolerate these innovations, the people would destroy them: "the anger of the people is impossible to withstand."[d]

The replies from provincial officials agreed unanimously that on no account should foreigners be accorded the right to build railways and telegraphs in China, because the government could not defy popular opinion.

Opening the Interior. The yamen's letter pointed out that the whole purpose of the treaty port system was to set aside special areas in which China could safely allow the foreigners the exemptions they sought from Chinese law and Chinese taxes. As long as foreigners claimed such privileges, they could not be allowed free access to the interior. The yamen had already offered to "open the interior" if foreigners would accept Chinese jurisdiction and pay all local taxes.[e] This the foreigners had refused to do.

As to steam navigation of inland waterways, the yamen argued not only that countless Chinese would lose their livelihood in the competition, but that there would be many tragic accidents on the narrow, crowded rivers and canals. In spite of the legal prohibitions, many foreigners were already engaged in illicit trade in the interior. If China showed any tendency to concede, they would quickly overrun the country.

The provincial replies agreed with the yamen unanimously.

---

[c] On the general Restoration opposition to economic development, see Chapter VIII.

[d] As evidence, the Tsungli-yamen could point to the destruction by the populace of telegraph lines erected illegally by Englishmen at Woosung and on Pagoda Island near Foochow.

[e] In these circumstances China could easily nullify the "opening" without violating the treaty, by levying confiscatory taxes and fines and by refusing to issue travel passports on convenient, specific pretexts.

Importing Salt and Mining Coal. The yamen pointed out that although salt was contraband under Article 3 of the 1858 trade regulations, foreign smuggling was common. There could be no relaxation of the prohibition, for the revenue of the salt monopoly[f] was essential. The provincial replies agreed; although two officials suggested that foreigners be granted formal permission to engage in the trade, they outlined conditions that could have led only to bankruptcy.

As to mining,[g] the Tsungli-yamen pointed out that it would endanger the people's welfare and violate the principles of geomancy. Yet the yamen's language left the way open to compromise. The majority of the provincial replies opposed mining, but rather gently: the ringing denunciations used against railways and steam navigation in the interior were lacking. A minority, including Tseng Kuo-fan and Shen Pao-chen, advocated exploitation of mines by the Chinese government with foreign machinery and technicians. Li Hung-chang agreed and went a little further: foreign mining concessions might be tolerated if the foreigners would observe Chinese regulations and pay Chinese taxes.

Christian Missions. Discussion of the mission question was moderate. Its moderation, in view of the secret character of the correspondence, tends to disprove the charge that responsible officials of the central or provincial governments either provoked or condoned the antimissionary outbreaks that culminated in the Tientsin Massacre.

Early in the Restoration the Tsungli-yamen had memorialized to the effect that even Christian converts were children of the Emperor; that missionaries, though interfering, were often well-meaning; and that therefore litigation affecting Christians should be handled promptly and justly. It was so ordered, and in the following years there were repeated memorials and edicts in the same tenor.[92] The yamen did not welcome missionaries, of course, but it had for several years justified its strategy of tolerance on two grounds: (1) China could afford to yield to foreigners on minor points in order to win their support on major ones, and (2) prohibitions would merely stimulate missionary activity. "To forbid them to go to Yunnan is to invite them to do so."[93]

Even the French granted that the yamen was doing its best: it had given proof of its intention to observe the treaties; the most recent death of a French missionary had been the result not of ill will in Peking but of factional rivalries in the provinces.[94]

Christianity in the 1860's was attacked not (as it had once been) by officials, but by the populace and non-office-holding lower literati; it was menaced not by proscription but by mob riot.[95] During the Restoration period high officials con-

---

[f] See Chapter VIII.
[g] See Chapter VIII.

cerned themselves chiefly with preventing missionary interference in Chinese local government.[h]

It was otherwise on the popular level, where the roots of anti-Christian feeling were deep and complex.[i] It appears to have been widely believed that missionaries kidnaped children for their orphanages, that girls were held in the convents by force, and that noxious drugs were administered in the hospitals. Among the gentry it was said that whereas merchants merely stole China's wealth, missionaries tried to steal the people's hearts.[96] On the limited evidence thus far available, it seems probable that the lower literati took the lead in sowing suspicion and in provoking mass violence.[j]

The Tsungli-yamen's circular letter appeared to take a calm and resigned view of the situation. It pointed out that there was now no possibility of prohibiting Christianity, for China had granted the right of Christian teaching in a treaty, and several published Imperial edicts had expressly confirmed this right. Moreover the doctrine was harmless. On these two points, the provincial replies agreed.

The difficulty, the yamen continued, was that among missionaries there were troublemakers as well as good men, and the troublemakers shielded their converts from Chinese jurisdiction and interfered constantly in local administration. To prevent this the yamen had two suggestions. (1) Officials might be appointed to supervise Christian activities in the same way that Buddhist and Taoist activities were supervised. Provincial officials were not enthusiastic about this, fearing that it might institutionalize Christianity. (2) The local gentry and people, while appearing to accept Christianity, might quietly renew their efforts to strengthen the Confucian orthodoxy. This would be a "prohibition that did not appear to be a prohibition."

[h] See Chapter VII. Vivid illustrations of the degree to which Catholic mission affairs had become intertwined with local administration are to be found in a memorial of the acting governor of Kweichow, Chang Liang-chi, reporting his nearly hopeless effort to untangle local cases about which the French minister had protested to the Tsungli-yamen (April 16, 1866, *IWSM-TC*, Ch. 41, pp. 22–26). Particularly difficult problems were raised by missionary interference in the governing of the non-Chinese minorities (*ibid.*, Ch. 34, p. 24).

[i] The Chinese Communist resuscitation of nineteenth-century myths about missionaries may be worth noting. Four of the present Communist charges were current in the 1860's: (1) that missionaries violated the treaty limitations on inland residence and "sneaked into the interior" illicitly; (2) that missionaries, notably French missionaries during the T'ung-chih period, claimed administrative rights; thus interfering in China's domestic affairs; (3) that missionaries engaged in espionage; (4) that missionaries murdered innocent common people. A fifth Communist charge is, however, somewhat contradictory: that missionaries such as W. A. P. Martin and S. Wells Williams aided the Ch'ing government in oppressing the Chinese people. The Communist case was succinctly stated by Hsieh Hsing-yao in *Jen-min jih-pao* (Peking), April 13, 1951; NCNA English version, entitled "How did imperialism use religion for aggression on China?" in *Current Background* (American Consulate General, Hongkong), No. 68, April 18, 1951.

[j] For example, one of the main issues in the Yangchow incident of 1868 was whether or not the gentry had taken advantage of their immunity from punishment by local officials to agitate against foreigners. See *China. No. 10. (1869)*, pp. 2, 11, 17, and *passim*. The Chinese documentation on the Yangchow incident is to be found in *Ch'ing-chi chiao-an shih-liao*, I, 5–15. See also Chapter III.

Although provincial officials naturally agreed that the Confucian orthodoxy should be strengthened, they did not appear particularly alarmed by Christian activities, nor was there any suggestion of a holy war. Nearly everyone concurred with Tseng Kuo-fan's view, that Christianity as a doctrine was not important enough to worry about. The behavior of Christian converts was a problem in local control, and local *ad hoc* remedies could be worked out.[k]

THE BURLINGAME MISSION[97]

At the time when the Tsungli-yamen and high provincial officials were discussing the advantages of sending envoys abroad, the first tentative experiment had been made. In 1866 Pin-ch'un and others had been appointed to accompany Hart on a visit to Europe for the express purpose of learning about Europe first-hand. Tung Hsün, in his preface to Pin-ch'un's account of the journey, described it as China's first diplomatic mission.[98] Although Pin-ch'un was neither distinguished nor high-ranking, foreigners at the time were correct in considering the precedent an important one, and the correspondence between Alcock and the Foreign Office on the matter was extensive.

In October 1867 the Tsungli-yamen asked provincial officials for advice on sending envoys abroad; on November 21, without waiting for replies, it secured the appointment of Anson Burlingame, then United States minister to China, as "Imperial envoy charged with the conduct of China's international relations."[l] According to the yamen's memorial recommending the appointment, the initial suggestion had come from Burlingame himself, but the memorial also referred to frequent conversations with Hart.[99]

The yamen reviewed its earlier statements on the advantages to be gained for China by appointing envoys to foreign capitals. Unfortunately no suitable Chinese was available, and in any event the appointment of a Chinese would raise special difficulties. Yet, the yamen continued, it had investigated Western diplomatic practice and found that envoys were not necessarily nationals of the countries they represented; moreover, Hart's management of the Maritime Customs had proved that nationality was less important than sincerity and mutual good faith. Everything the yamen knew of Burlingame was favorable: he had been cordial and helpful since he first came to China in 1861, and on an earlier trip home he had pleaded the Chinese case.

As the yamen saw it, the essential point was to have a clear understanding

---

[k] In the course of the discussions of the Wade-Hart proposals, Liu K'un-i had suggested that missionaries be required to turn in to the magistrate the names of converts, on the pretext that persons using false names were being investigated; this would frighten the converts away (memorial of May 29, 1866, *IWSM-TC*, Ch. 41, pp. 43–50). Similar ingenious schemes, which would have discouraged converts without giving the treaty powers any substantial cause for complaint, must have occurred to many Chinese officials.

[l] Or, in Morse's version, "Ambassador Extraordinary, accredited to all the courts of the world" (Morse, *Relations*, II, 188).

with Burlingame: he was to be appointed for one year; he was to oppose all proposals harmful to China and to be slow to assent to those which seemed favorable; he was not to make agreements without first securing the yamen's consent. According to the yamen, Burlingame had agreed to these terms on November 18.

In a second memorial of the same date, November 21,[100] the yamen stated that although America was the most peaceful and cordial of the three great powers that dominated the Occident,[m] England and France must also be represented if China was to win their support. The yamen knew an appropriate Englishman, John McLeavy Brown, Chinese Secretary of the British Legation, and had obtained his consent. On the choice of a Frenchman, the yamen had heard from Hart that Emile de Champs, a French commissioner in the Maritime Customs who had accompanied Hart to Europe the preceding year, was sound and reliable. The yamen also proposed to attach one or two of its own secretaries to the mission.[n] On November 26 the yamen recommended Chih-kang, a Manchu who held the Single-Eyed Peacock Feather and had been designated for a Customs appointment, and Sun Chia-ku. Politically they were of no importance, but they were described as well-informed, well-connected, diligent, and of suitable temperament.[101]

The announcement of the Burlingame Mission was major news in foreign circles.[102] At the outset it was widely approved, but approval quickly gave way to disgust as news came in of the "pro-Chinese" principles to which Burlingame had secured the assent of the British and American governments.[o] Even Alcock,

---

[m] Only a few weeks earlier the Tsungli-yamen had referred to Russia, rather than the United States, as the third leading power of the Occident (*IWSM-TC*, Ch. 50, p. 25).

[n] In the first memorial the position of the foreign assistants was referred to as *sui-wang*, subordinate; that of the Chinese assistants as *t'ung-wang*, co-ordinate. After consulting with Burlingame the yamen subsequently proposed that all Chinese officials who were members of the mission be given the rank of imperial envoy. Brown and de Champs were made first and second secretaries of the mission respectively. According to the yamen, they had to have some rank; if it were too low, they would not accept it; if it were too high, it would be inappropriate; therefore a new rank was invented. (*Ibid.*, Ch. 52, pp. 5–6.)

[o] According to the *North China Herald*, the Burlingame Treaty was "solemn, pompous and trifling"; a mission with excellent prospects was now "on the high road to ruin from the injudicious advocacy of the head Mandarin, Mr. Burlingame himself." (Sept. 19, 1868; see also *ibid.*, Sept. 11, 1868.)

The chief criticism of the China merchants was that Burlingame was perpetuating dangerous illusions about China's willingness to reform (Hongkong Chamber of Commerce to Clarendon, Jan. 21, 1870, *China. No. 6. (1870)*, No. 3). See also Michie, *The Englishman in China*, II, 212 ff.

The extreme anti-Burlingame view was this: "the Burlingame Mission, although originally planned by the confidential adviser of the Tsung-li Yamen, Mr. Hart, for the purpose only of throwing dust into the eyes of Europe, of gaining time for the Chinese Government to prepare an armed resistance to the just demands, urged upon its stagnating policy by the spirit of Western progress and civilization, and of securing certain commercial and fiscal advantages to China at the expense of England, assumed from the first moment of its prospective realization the graver character of a diplomatic fraud and a conspiracy against the dignity of the Western sovereigns and the independence of their states." (Gumpach, *The Burlingame Mission*, p. 175.)

who had had high hopes of the mission when it was appointed, called the Washington Treaty of 1868—the "Burlingame Treaty"—reactionary, and for a time thought it useless to proceed with treaty revision negotiations if the Chinese were going to be encouraged by such exaggerated statements.[103] Burlingame took the opposite view, that the Washington Treaty had encouraged the Tsungli-yamen to be more liberal than it would otherwise have been in the negotiations for the revision of the British treaty.[p]

The Tsungli-yamen reacted favorably to the activities of the Burlingame Mission and approved the Washington Treaty, but neither made as much stir[104] in China as the Wade-Hart proposals and the Alcock Convention. When the news of Burlingame's death in Russia reached Peking, he was generously rewarded,[105] but in retrospect his mission appears to have been important chiefly for firmly establishing the precedent in China of sending envoys abroad. It was the Alcock Convention and not the Washington Treaty that attempted to make cautious improvements in the existing conditions.

THE NEGOTIATIONS FOR TREATY REVISION

The formal negotiations that led to the Alcock Convention began just as the replies to the Tsungli-yamen circular on foreign policy were beginning to come in, and as the Burlingame Mission was preparing to set out. On January 2, 1868, John McLeavy Brown, recently appointed first secretary to the Burlingame Mission and hence now a Chinese official, called at the Tsungli-yamen bringing the first draft of the British proposals. In a long introductory despatch Alcock urged the Chinese to build on the K'ang-hsi example and to emulate Russian self-strengthening through Westernization. He praised the appointment of the Burlingame Mission as a first step and elaborated at length upon the Russian experience. Although Alcock certainly did not put forward the merchants' case for the opening of China as his case, he emphasized the impatience of the Western temperament and warned that if the merchants' legitimate grievances were not attended to promptly, grave difficulties would follow.

All this was prefatory. As working proposals, Alcock put forward six rather modest suggestions that he thought would benefit British trade and satisfy well-founded merchant complaints without raising serious problems for China. The great issues of the Wade-Hart memoranda and the Tsungli-yamen circular were

---

[p] "[The conciliatory Chinese attitude] is sufficient answer to those who but recently declared that China would avail itself of the action of the Western powers in its favor, to restrict rather than enlarge the privileges of foreigners. This favorable result was not fully arrived at until the Chinese government had fully comprehended the treaty made with the United States, and the full effect of the action of the British Government—against the aggressive spirit of its own subjects—not until after Lord Clarendon had severely censured many of the British officials in China for unjustifiable action at Yang-chow, Swatow, and Formosa." (Burlingame to Bismarck, Jan. 4, 1870, *U.S. Arch. China. Notes,* Vol. I.)

not raised. Alcock's proposals concerned: (1) enforcement of the transit pass system on foreign imports; (2) certain specific reductions in the tariff; (3) allocation of part of the transit tax duties collected by the Maritime Customs to the provincial authorities, as compensation for their loss of revenue from domestic transit taxes; (4) the use of small steamers by foreigners conveying their own goods on inland waterways; (5) the opening of several additional Yangtze ports for loading and unloading; (6) the establishing of bonded customs warehouses in the treaty ports.

The Tsungli-yamen, observing that nothing was said about railways and telegraphs, found all this so trivial that it did not memorialize on treaty revision for more than a year; and when it did, it apologized for troubling the Throne with trade regulations.[106] The yamen participated in the preliminary negotiations on its own authority. A five-man mixed commission was set up in late January consisting of two junior British representatives, Hugh Fraser and Thomas Adkins; two junior Chinese representatives, Hsia and Tsai;[q] and Robert Hart, who clearly was in the pivotal position.

As the negotiations opened, Alcock's position was as follows. The big questions—introduction of railways and telegraphs, residence in the interior, importation of salt, development of mines by foreigners, etc.—went beyond treaty rights. They were not essential to British trade, they raised serious problems for the Chinese domestic economy, and they would require readjustment of the whole extraterritorial system.[107] Moreover, the time was not ripe for raising such questions, for reports of the staggering debt with which the Egyptian Khedive, Isma'il, had been deftly saddled had evidently reached Peking.[108] The Tsungli-yamen, seeing Egypt starting down the road to foreign tutelage by way of bankruptcy, could not possibly be persuaded that foreign loans for economic development could safely be repaid from earnings. On January 1, 1868, Alcock reported to the Foreign Office:

> It would be a mistake to suppose that the experience of the Pasha of Egypt and the questions to which the privilege of making the Suez Canal has given rise have been lost upon the Chinese Government. They are as much alive as the Pasha himself can be to the danger and inconvenience attaching to such enterprises with foreign capital, and Government protection as a contingency.[109]

Alcock believed that his cautious proposals would reassure the Chinese and at the same time adequately protect British trade. He concluded:

> Finally, although we do not usually make any parade of Utopian theories for the regeneration of the world as a principle of government and national policy, or seek the advance of civilization and Christianity by schemes of reconstruction

---

[q] Their names appear only in the British documents; in the Chinese documents they are nameless. In later meetings various Suns, Kaos, and Chungs are mentioned as present, but again only in the British documents.

for other countries, there is something to be said from this point of view. It is not at all events to be entirely overlooked that a policy dictated by the more tangible interests of commerce and in harmony with the law of nations . . . [is also the policy most likely to bring about the regeneration of China].[110]

The meetings of the mixed commission proceeded smoothly. On March 2 Alcock sent in a note suggesting that if the Tsungli-yamen approved, the commission might work out a code of commercial law suitable for application in all mixed cases.[111] At the first formal meeting of the commission on March 3, the Chinese agreed to the bonded warehouses and to the enforcement of the transit tax clause of the Treaty of Tientsin. They could not agree to the immediate abolition of the likin, owing to the decline in receipts from the land tax and the impossibility of floating a government loan. They agreed, however, to work out means for redressing any damage that foreign merchants suffered from the likin, and to abolish the likin when domestic peace was fully restored.[112]

Alcock then added a number of radically different items to the agenda, partly for bargaining purposes[r] and partly in the hope of making the terms of the revision acceptable to the other treaty powers.[s] He argued that missionaries were a more disturbing factor than merchants; that since missionaries had been given the right of inland residence by the French Treaty of Tientsin, merchants should be accorded similar rights.[113] He proposed that imported goods, no matter who owned them, be exempted from all domestic Chinese taxation.[t] He urged the commission to discuss railways and telegraphs, mining concessions, the importation of foreign salt, the abolition of the camphor monopoly, the payment of customs duties in silver locally current rather than in Haekwan taels, and so forth.

In the meetings of the commission between April and September, both parties bargained skillfully. The Chinese agreed to consider permitting nonsteam navigation by foreigners on specified inland waterways, but were adamant against a general concession on the point. They agreed readily to adjustment of the tariff, to the construction of landing stages on the Yangtze, to payment of duties in local silver, to the abolition of the camphor monopoly, to the joint working out of a commercial code, and to the development of mines with foreign

[r] The Tsungli-yamen reported that Alcock's courteous requests had been alternated with threats, but that later the threats had ceased (memorial of Feb. 2, 1869, *IWSM-TC*, Ch. 63, pp. 1–7b).

[s] Alcock reviewed this point in a dispatch to Stanley of December 6, 1868. He himself had wanted to limit the issues to his original agenda and had introduced these added questions at the instance of other diplomats. His dispatches of September 8 and November 9 must therefore be read "rather as conveying the general sense in which my colleagues desired the matter to be pressed than by my own individual convictions." He reiterated his belief that inland residence, steam navigation of inland waters, foreign ownership of mines, etc., would at this point be harmful to British interests as well as to Chinese interests. He also repeated his fears concerning the dangers he felt were inherent in French policy on missions, referring to a confidential dispatch of December 4 (*China. No. 5.* (*1871*), No. 76; see also Nos. 74, 75).

[t] He proposed at the same time that the British agree to limit the exercise of this right (*ibid.,* pp. 192–93).

machinery and technical supervision, provided the mines remained Chinese property. On the allocation of a portion of the customs revenue to the provinces, the Chinese first refused, then agreed to consider the matter, and in the end flatly refused. They also flatly refused to yield on importing salt, introducing railways and telegraphs, and opening the whole interior.

The crucial practical question was whether or not some workable system could be devised for protecting the goods of foreign trade from internal transit taxes in excess of the 2½ per cent provided for by the Treaty of Tientsin.[u] Various formulas were discussed, and finally an agreement that satisfied both parties was reached. Foreign goods were to pay the import and transit duties simultaneously at the port of entry without option, after which they might circulate freely; native produce destined for export was to pay double transit duties at the first barrier, the surplus being refundable upon proof of export within three months. From the Chinese point of view, these rather simple adjustments would prevent most of the fraud and confusion that the transit pass system, with its original options, had allowed; from the British point of view, the goods of foreign trade would be taxed no higher than the Treaty of Tientsin intended they should be.[114]

By the autumn of 1868 the outstanding issues were those on which Alcock had never intended to insist, and agreement in principle appeared to have been reached. Alcock testified to the "evidences of good will so constantly given" throughout discussions that had proceeded "without acrimony or a sign of irritation on either side."[115] If a convention could have been quickly signed and ratified, its effect on the future course of Sino-foreign relations might have been very great. Routine affairs could have been handled with substantially less friction, and major questions could have been deferred in the hope that their solution might become less difficult. More important than what the agreement said was how it was reached. Neither side had yielded on its own vital interests or tried to force such a concession from the other. In a relatively relaxed discussion, the negotiators had discovered where mutually acceptable working agreements were possible, and had phrased the potential agreements clearly. This was the first international agreement—and the last for many decades—that any Chinese government ever regarded as beneficial and well worth signing.

---

[u] Following the June 27 meeting of the mixed commission, Alcock noted: "The difficulties of the Tsungli-yamen, and the necessities of the country, have been fully recognized by the British Minister, and there is every desire on his part to avoid embarrassing discussions, or pressing for impracticable measures, either beyond or within the limits of existing treaties. But this one question of an assumed right of the Chinese government to tax foreign trade *ad libitum* at the ports is one of principle, and of such vital moment to the interests of commerce that a British Minister can have no discretionary power in protesting against it as a violation of the Treaty in the face of which it is certain no counter-proposition of the Chinese government to increase the tariff rates on tea and silk has a chance of being entertained." (*Ibid.*, p. 212.)

Difficulties began almost at once, however. Alcock had to persuade the British government to override a mounting wave of opposition from the China trade interests at home,[116] and in China hostile comment from the merchants was interfering with the conduct of the negotiations. If these were to continue, Alcock had to publicly dissociate the government from the merchants' views, and with Stanley's approval he did so in stinging terms.[117] On the other side, the Tsungli-yamen had to persuade conservative Chinese leaders that this new departure offered real hope.

At this juncture, during the autumn of 1868, a series of violent antiforeign outbreaks in various parts of China[v] almost persuaded Alcock that the merchants were right after all, and that in international relations the Chinese understood nothing but force. He felt that Burlingame's extravagant statements abroad had been interpreted by the Chinese as meaning that they could now do exactly as they pleased, and be damned to the foreign devils. In a moment of despair, he stepped out of character and sanctioned "gunboat diplomacy" in the Yangchow incident.[118]

This shift in outlook was of brief duration; Alcock had returned to his role of negotiator even before Clarendon reminded him that any local use of force was contrary to basic British policy toward China. He secured Chinese assent to foreign steam navigation on Poyang Lake, and hoped for some Chinese concession on limited residence in the interior and on the ownership of mining enterprises, although he did not consider these points essential. At the end of 1868 he was ready to drop the questions of railways, telegraphs, and the importation of salt, and to turn the draft agreements over to the Foreign Office for decision.[119] In doing so, he stated that although he himself had at times recommended the introduction of railways and telegraphs, general inland steam navigation, and inland residence, these innovations were less important than solution of the transit tax question, and were in any case entirely impracticable for the present.[120]

When the terms of the draft convention became fully known, the merchants' opposition increased. They particularly decried Alcock's failure to get them rights of inland residence equivalent to those of the French and the Russians.[121] Alcock replied sharply that the Russian and French rights were by no means so clear as British merchants were prone to assume. Some Russians did in fact live in the interior,

> but it is permissive and not claimed as a right; and I believe they are simply left alone because they give no trouble, speak and live and dress like Chinese, and have no Canton boys or compradors to get into quarrels with the people, and then beard the authorities as being under foreign protection and not amenable to their

[v] See Chapter III.

jurisdiction. . . . The objections [to inland residence] appear to be insuperable in connection with extraterritorial rights. The Tsungli-yamen state that . . . if the foreign merchant claims the one, he must forego the other in common justice to their own people.[122]

Yet in the face of concerted opposition Alcock himself sometimes doubted the advisability of England's acceptance of his draft as a formally revised treaty, binding for ten years. To Clarendon he wrote that England could not now withdraw from China and that past wrongs could not now be undone; yet the use of force would be folly. The viable alternatives appeared to be to accept the present terms or to postpone revision and let matters drift.[123]

The Foreign Office and the Board of Trade expressed emphatic approval of the results Alcock had obtained, and authorized their incorporation into a convention. If the Chinese could be persuaded to accept the terms as temporary articles, which they had so far refused to do, so much the better. There would be less outcry from the China trade. If the Chinese continued to refuse, then Alcock was instructed to sign the convention as a formal revision of the Treaty of Tientsin, binding upon both parties for ten years.[124]

While the Foreign Office was considering the draft of the Alcock Convention early in 1869, the Tsungli-yamen was attempting to secure Imperial approval. The yamen did not consider that formal negotiations were under way until Alcock began to use an official seal on his memoranda in November 1868, and it did not memorialize until after Alcock had submitted the draft to the Foreign Office. On February 2, 1869, the yamen presented the relevant despatches and memoranda to the Throne, together with a careful memorial reviewing the negotiations step by step.[125]

The yamen began by stating that during these negotiations the foreigners had been insatiable as always. It was at great pains to point out how firm it had been in resisting all proposals to introduce railways or open the interior. But the yamen reported its attitude as having been flexible: sometimes its negotiators had been stubborn, sometimes they had yielded readily, sometimes they had simply ignored questions raised. By these tactics the yamen had secured Alcock's consent to certain changes that would undoubtedly benefit China; but on some points, where there was no real harm to China, the yamen had voluntarily conceded. On the whole, its members thought they had secured a diplomatic victory, and they wondered whether the British would in the end sign a treaty that clearly did not satisfy British merchants' demands. The yamen did not want to trouble the princes and ministers with the details of trade regulations, but it sought approval for its new policy of negotiation.[126]

During February the Imperial princes, the Grand Council, and the Grand

Secretariat were given copies of the documents on treaty revision, and their advice poured in.[127] The tenor of these memorials was somewhat different from that of the Tsungli-yamen memorials. The princes and ministers approved the yamen's policy, but they felt something should have been said about military preparations. Diplomacy made it possible to control the foreigner through the principles of social usage (*li*); self-strengthening would make it possible to control him by arms. Neither could be forgotten, for although there were negotiations now, war loomed in the future.[w]

The Tsungli-yamen replied that it agreed, and it reviewed the history of its various recommendations on troop training, arsenals, and naval shipyards. It had not, it said, discussed military preparations in its earlier memorial because their importance was self-evident; war and diplomacy were parallel, not contradictory, policies. Yet for all this elaborate disclaimer, one gets the impression that the Tsungli-yamen was trying to say that the time had arrived for a new approach to international affairs. Military strength must certainly be built up and held in reserve, for the French were fierce, the Russians treacherous, and the Germans perverse and deceitful. Yet the British were less arrogant, and here was proof that they could be moved by tongue and pen; and the Americans were proving relatively gentle. Was it not barely possible, the yamen's memorial suggested, that diplomacy might now be considered something more than verbiage designed to ensnare the barbarian until China was strong enough to annihilate him?[128]

In the spring of 1869 the Tsungli-yamen, considering that its position had been approved, became so impatient to sign the convention that it accused Alcock of delaying tactics.[129] Alcock, however, felt that he must in some way make the convention more acceptable to British merchants. He again proposed that the convention be considered articles without time limit; the Chinese refused. He made a sudden last-minute effort to break the Chinese salt monopoly.[130] The Chinese called this a "tactic of exhaustion," accused Alcock of breaking his pledged word, and countered by demanding the right to a Chinese consul at Hongkong and certain limitations on missionary activities.[131] In September and early October the negotiations threatened to collapse entirely until Hart and Wen-hsiang discussed all the issues personally, without intermediaries. All the evidence agrees on Hart's crucial role.[132]

Following these conversations, the additional demands were withdrawn on both sides. The Chinese agreed to accept the convention as articles without a

[w] Prince Shun and Wo-jen also specifically urged stricter control of missionaries, especially of their orphanages, and police inspections of foreigners in China. The yamen declared both these measures inadvisable (secret memorial of Feb. 24, 1869, *IWSM-TC*, Ch. 64, pp. 17–21).

time clause in return for the British agreement to say nothing further for the moment about Imperial audiences or regulation of the coolie trade.[x] The convention was signed in Peking on October 23, 1869, and on November 20 Hart was awarded the rank of financial commissioner (*pu-cheng-shih*) for his services to China in the revision of the English treaty.[133]

The significance of the Tsungli-yamen's support of the Alcock Convention has been variously interpreted. Wang Te-chao[134] believes that Prince Kung had learned that the barbarians kept their word and that hence peaceful coexistence was for a time possible. But according to Wang, there was no real change in aim; the program was to get rid of the Taiping, the Nien-fei, Russia, and England in that order. Chinese Communist scholars take an almost opposite view. Hu Sheng[135] notes the marked change in the view of Ch'ing officials between 1860, when the signature of the Convention of Peking had been regarded as a disgrace, and 1870, when Tseng Kuo-fan could memorialize on ten years of peaceful relations and mutual good faith, and Kuo Sung-tao could write of international law and enlightened Western colonial systems as new and peaceful forms of international relations. Hu takes this to mean that Kuo was quicker than the mass of the literati, who called him a traitor, to see that traditional China could survive only if it submitted to the "imperialist world order of international law."[y]

A third interpretation seems the likeliest, namely, that a real change in outlook did occur; that this was not treasonable and shameless submission to the West, but an intelligent effort to find a secure and dignified place for the traditional Chinese state in the modern world community.

TERMS OF THE ALCOCK CONVENTION

The Alcock Convention marked a major turning point in the history of Sino-foreign relations, not only in the way it was negotiated but in its form and substance. The language used—"Great Britain on the one part agrees . . . ; China on the other part agrees . . ."—is in marked contrast to that employed in

[x] Article 5 of the Convention of Peking had guaranteed to Chinese subjects the right of emigration, and the British desire to control the abuses of the coolie trade, which were an international scandal, would not at first glance appear to conflict with the Tsungli-yamen's interests. However, promulgation of regulations meant institutionalizing the coolie trade. The yamen preferred to let the abuses continue rather than to risk discussing such an inflammatory issue. Thus it was a concession by the British to assent to China's nonratification of the 1866 "Convention to Regulate the Engagement of Chinese Emigrants by British and French Subjects," drawn up by Prince Kung, Alcock, and Bellonet, even though the convention itself improved the position of the wretched emigrants (text in Herslet, *Treaties,* I, No. 10).

On the bargaining on these last-minute points, and the Chinese agreement to a convention without a time clause, see Alcock to Clarendon, September 30, 1869, *China. No. 5. (1871),* No. 150.

[y] This last remark was not included in the original 1948 edition of Hu's book; it was added in 1952.

the Treaty of Tientsin (1858) or the Chefoo Convention (1876). The difference in tone is particularly striking in the Chinese versions.[136]

Article 1 attached an important qualification to the most-favored-nation principle, under which every power had previously been able to claim all the privileges that any other power had wrested from China. Henceforth British subjects could participate in the advantages accorded nationals of another power only if they accepted the conditions under which those advantages had originally been accorded.[z]

Article 2 declared that China and England might each appoint consuls in the territories of the other. England had long enjoyed this right; China now acquired the right to establish a consulate at Hongkong. This was not empty talk about equality of diplomatic rights; it was a real issue, for the residents of Hongkong were strongly opposed to a Chinese consulate there, whereas Chinese officials believed that such a consulate could be of great help in the control of smuggling.[137]

Article 3 provided at last a solution to the problem of greatest concern to British commerce as a whole: Chinese domestic taxation of British textiles. It provided that textiles should be subject to the import and $2\frac{1}{2}$ per cent transit duties simultaneously at the port of entry, without option and regardless of destination. After this they were to circulate freely in the nine provinces containing treaty ports, paying no additional tax of any type; in the other nine provinces, they were to pay all domestic taxes. Alcock believed that the payment of a small domestic tax on all imports, whether they were going to the interior or not, was the simplest solution and well worth the risk, for the likin alone had been as high as 90 per cent in some ports.

> All other concessions are, comparatively speaking, unimportant, if this one advantage can be secured, immunity from local and irresponsible taxation, and I think the arrangements now contemplated offer a fair hope of all foreign textile fabrics, which form the great bulk of the import trade, being so emancipated.[138]

Hart agreed: "a most important concession."

Article 4 provided an equally simple and fair-minded solution of the problem of taxing Chinese produce destined for export. Henceforth, such produce was to be subject to all domestic taxes, but vouchers were to be given. If the produce were exported, the Maritime Customs at the port of exit would refund any sum collected in excess of $2\frac{1}{2}$ per cent. Both Hart and Alcock considered this an advantage to both parties: the sale of transit passes would be stopped, the futile effort to apply differing tax rates to the same produce in the interior would

---

[z] It has been said that Article 1 of the Alcock Convention completely eliminated the elements of unilateral privilege in the most-favored-nation principle (See, *The Foreign Trade of China*, pp. 185 ff.). This may be an overstatement, but it was a long step in that direction.

cease, and the merchant engaged in legitimate export trade could claim his refund from an agency that always had funds in hand, had foreigners on its staff, and was organized along Western administrative lines. Moreover the Tsungli-yamen at the last moment agreed to apportion to the provincial authorities seven-tenths of the transit taxes henceforth collected at the ports.[a]

Alcock believed that by Articles 3 and 4:

> The transit-pass system, liable to such grievous abuse by foreign merchants, has, at the same time, been almost entirely superseded—entirely so for the bulk of the imports in the nine provinces, and in native produce for export, in all—under conditions which, by dispensing with all distinction between native and foreign trade, leave to the provincial authorities the rights they are accustomed to exercise of inland taxation, and an interest in the increase of foreign trade, while it secures the foreign merchant from all surcharge over the Tariff rate for transit of 2½ per-cent more effectively than any system of protection by transit passes could do in such a country as China.[139]

To the criticism that the Chinese would not abide by such terms, and would find means of evading their new responsibilities, Alcock replied that the Tsungli-yamen had thoroughly, and voluntarily, approved the new arrangements; that provincial officials now had a reason for an interest in foreign trade; that the merchants would have a far better chance of reclaiming against overcharges on exports than they had ever had before, even if a few local officials did refuse vouchers; that on imports 2½ per cent was a very small sum to risk, in view of the sweeping and unequivocal character of the Chinese concession.[140]

By Article 5, Chinese produce shipped from Hongkong to a treaty port would be subject to all inland duties, but Chinese produce shipped from a treaty port to Hongkong could claim export privileges. Alcock believed that the export privileges would benefit Hongkong sufficiently to compensate for the decline of smuggling that would follow the appointment of a Chinese consul to the island.

Article 6 provided for the opening of Wenchow and Wuhu, in return for the closing of Kiungchow on Hainan, which Alcock regarded as useless in any event. The Tsungli-yamen, however, stood firm against the opening of Ichang, "the gateway to the upper Yangtze" and the port in which British merchants were most interested. Articles 7 and 8 specified certain technical improvements in the collection of tonnage dues and the turning in of manifests for ships of British register. In both instances there were mutual concessions. Articles 9, 10, and 11 provided similar mutual concessions in customs fines and confiscation, licensing of pilots, and refunding of drawbacks on re-exported foreign goods.

---

[a] British merchants had argued that the treaty transit tax replaced provincial and local taxes; that hence if receipts from it were forwarded to Peking, local officials would surely try to recoup their losses by extralegal exactions (e.g., Chairman of the Shanghai General Chamber of Commerce to Medhurst, Feb. 1, 1869, *China. No. 12. (1869)*, pp. 5–6).

By Articles 12 and 13, the Tsungli-yamen won two important points: increases in the export duty on silk and in the import duty on opium. As Alcock said, "we have had to give something in return." He did not believe that the increase would affect the volume or the profits of the trade, and he thought the Chinese had a good case: "Considering that they desired to double the duty on tea, silk, and opium, and had a direct interest in doing so, I think they showed great moderation in being finally contented with so little."[141]

The Tsungli-yamen was firm in its refusal to allow a general right to steam navigation on inland waterways, but in return for the tariff concessions it agreed to allow an experiment with steam on Poyang Lake. Furthermore, foreigners were granted the surprising right to navigate all the inland waterways of the country in foreign-owned boats of the traditional Chinese type. According to Alcock, this was "perhaps the largest concession ever gained from any independent country." China also conceded a conditional and qualified right of temporary residence in the interior. Alcock wrote to the dean of the diplomatic corps:

> I consider that these two privileges, limited as they are, and far removed from steam navigation and right of permanent residence which the merchants demanded, make no inconsiderable advance in opening up the country. If British and other merchants will only act on what they allow quietly and judiciously, as do the Russian merchants in some of the tea districts, giving no trouble to the authorities, and exciting no alarm or hostile feeling among the people, they will have little cause to complain that the privileges fall far short of their wants.[142]

To the Foreign Office he reported:

> The conditional and qualified right of temporary residence, and inland navigation in foreign-owned vessels, if judiciously and quietly worked, will, I am satisfied, give foreign merchants all they can reasonably desire, and quite as much as they are in a position to turn to any good account at present. It is too much to expect, however, that they will think so.[143]

To Alcock, one of the convention's most important provisions was the Chinese assent to the adoption of a written code of commercial law. He saw this not only as a contribution to orderly business transactions, but as the first of three steps toward the abolition of extraterritoriality itself. On the record, it is clear that Alcock saw in extraterritoriality the dangers that others recognized half a century later. Certain limited legal reforms by China would make possible an agreement placing foreigners and their interests under Chinese jurisdiction.[144] In reporting the signing of the convention to the Foreign Office he wrote:

> The adoption of a written code of commercial law . . . is more important for what it may lead to, than for any immediate results. From a commercial to a civil and criminal code, founded on European principles, and an international

court for its administration in all mixed cases, there are but two steps; and these once gained, extraterritoriality may be dispensed with.[145]

THE REJECTION OF THE ALCOCK CONVENTION

Although the Tsungli-yamen had been anxious lest Alcock fail to sign the convention, once he had signed they considered his action final and assumed that ratification would follow automatically. Clearly the yamen's knowledge of Western diplomatic procedure was still incomplete, but its assumption was a reasonable one in the circumstances. For thirty years foreign governments had required the Chinese government to accept agreements signed by its qualified representatives; surely in this instance the British minister was a qualified representative, and nine months earlier he had submitted the drafts to the British government for approval.

It seems clear that the Tsungli-yamen considered the Alcock Convention a diplomatic victory for China. The memorial reporting its signature stated that the yamen had conceded several points at the last moment because Alcock was returning to England and the next British minister might be more difficult to handle.[146] The yamen then began to press for early ratification, a striking change from previous negotiations, in most of which foreign governments, after many delays, had had to force ratification. For the first time the Chinese government was eager to ratify a treaty.

On the Chinese side, the signature of the convention had been considered final and binding; the seals used were those of the Emperor, Prince Kung, and the presidents of four boards and of the Li-fan yüan.[147] In a memorial of January 26, 1870, the Tsungli-yamen repeated its view that the signature had been final, since both sides had used the seals of office and since procedures for putting the terms of the convention into effect had been covered in a subsequent exchange of despatches.[148] The convention had been promulgated in the provinces with scrupulous attention to every detail.[149] The yamen was aware of the British merchants' opposition to the convention, but reported to the Throne that the views of foreign merchants were not the same as the views of foreign governments.[150]

Meanwhile British mercantile opposition to the convention was mounting to a new pitch.[151] Along with the expected roars of rage from merchants in China and chambers of commerce in England, one firm, Sassoon and Company, protested to the Foreign Office "on behalf of Indian interests."[152]

Alcock's rejoinder was that men with a true interest in Imperial commerce would not agree with the China merchants:

no country or Western government has ever before made such liberal concessions to foreign trade. In how many countries, it may be asked, are all goods for personal and house consumption of foreigners, all ship and dock stores, admitted duty free? In how many Western countries are foreign ships allowed to share in the coasting trade without differential duties, or in the right of navigating all inland waters? Apart from the rights of extraterritoriality, which may be held to be something exceptional and only to be exacted in dealing with Eastern powers, it may yet be asked in how many European states is there perfect toleration in religion, and freedom to teach any creed or faith, however subversive of existing religions, institutions, and forms of worship. Or lastly to go back to material and commercial interests, in what country is there a Custom-house tariff so moderate in regard to foreign trade as that of China?[153]

He insisted that the Chinese had been far more generous than the merchants realized:

Indeed, the total prohibition of opium, the restriction of missionaries from inland residence, and the abolition of all extraterritoriality being the three cardinal points and chief objects of desire with the Chinese Government and all the official hierarchy, it must be matter of congratulation that they have not insisted upon any one of these . . . Besides the small increase in duty on these two articles [tea and silk], nothing has been conceded on our part but the plainest of all international rights, if there is to be any principle of reciprocity recognized in our relations with China, viz., the right to appoint consuls in the British dominions. . . . I think the advantages we have gained so far preponderate over the little that has been yielded, as to leave no doubt on the subject.[154]

Merchants in England did not agree, any more than did those in China. Merchants and others meeting in London concluded that the Treaty of Tientsin had best be left unrevised. They insisted that by the Alcock Convention Britain was conceding more than China; that the treaty port system was unsatisfactory and that the whole interior must be opened; that bonded warehouses would be of little use if they were owned by the Chinese government; that the provisions for inland travel and residence and exemption from transit taxes were a reduction in the privileges already granted by the 1858 treaty; and so forth. In brief, "The Convention forms the first distinct evidence of a retrograde policy in China."[155] Similar meetings were held and similar resolutions passed in Glasgow, Leith, Manchester, Macclesfield, Halifax, Liverpool, Belfast, Edinburgh, Dundee[156]— wherever an interest in the myth of an ever-expanding China trade could be drummed up.

The other treaty powers were less violent on the subject of the Alcock Convention than the British merchants, but except for the United States they opposed its ratification. Alcock, feeling that if the concessions to which he had agreed affected British subjects only, they would rankle the more, vainly attempted to persuade his colleagues in the diplomatic corps at Peking of the desirability of a general European agreement.[157] The French replied that there was no assurance that the provincial authorities would honor the commitments undertaken by the Tsungli-yamen.[b] They were courteous but they believed that formal treaty revision should be postponed; for their part, they reserved the right to renegotiate in the following year, 1870, particularly with reference to the rights of Catholic missionaries.[158] Prussia likewise reserved the right to independent revision of its treaty relations in 1872.[159] The Russian envoy, although conceding that the Tsungli-yamen's concessions had been more extensive than he had dared hope, found them insufficient to meet Russian merchants' requirements. He objected to the increased duty on tea and to the failure to make provision for depots in the interior. As for transit taxes, he suggested that foreigners might agree to pay all of them provided they were announced a year in advance.[160] Belgium, Spain, and the Netherlands undertook to follow Great Britain pro forma.[161] American support was more enthusiastic,[162] but cooled with the appointment of J. Ross Browne to succeed Burlingame.[c]

It was not pressure from other powers, however, that blocked the Alcock Convention. In the end, and against its own better judgment, the British government yielded to pressure from British merchants and refused ratification. Spokesmen for the China trade, who had challenged Alcock's policy from the beginning of the negotiations, renewed their protests early in 1870.[163] Clarendon rebutted their arguments with considerable force; he had the support of the Board of Trade, and he was not without sympathizers in Parliament.[164] Alcock was called home to England for consultation, and the government delayed action as long as possible. Yet there was no gainsaying the merchant opposition in the end. Shortly before his death in June 1870, Clarendon, without altering his own views of the merits of the convention, advised the government that ratification in the face of such opposition would be impolitic.[165] Alcock admitted defeat and urged the government to attribute nonratification to certain supposed difficulties with France rather than to merchant opposition; acknowledging the merchants' power to force a reversal of policy not only would lead to "a great deal of ill-feeling and distrust at Peking,"[166] but would seriously weaken England's future position in China.

The death of Clarendon and the Tientsin Massacre in June 1870 sealed the British government's decision to reject ratification.[167] In response to a question in Commons on July 7, the Undersecretary for Foreign Affairs stated that the Alcock Convention would not be ratified.[168] Granville, who succeeded Clarendon, announced that Alcock had negotiated the convention under instructions

---

[b] Tso Tsung-t'ang's French protégé, Prosper Giquel, was an exception. He applauded Alcock's stand and advised against a separate French attempt at treaty revision (*La Politique française en Chine depuis les traités de 1858 et de 1860*, Paris, 1872, pp. 14–25).

[c] See Chapter III.

from Clarendon, who had thought the revision "a great advance on the existing state of things."[169] To Alcock he wrote:

> Her Majesty's Government much regret that the view taken by the Mercantile Associations in this country, and in China, of the probable benefits of that Convention . . . has not coincided with the view which Her Majesty's Government had hoped would be taken of it.[170]

In Shanghai there was rejoicing:

> It is only a few brief months since Sir Rutherford Alcock explained here, in person, the provisions which he had embodied in a supplementary treaty; and ever since that time there has been a continuous flow of memorials, resolutions, and letters from the numerous mercantile bodies interested, condemning the proposed arrangement and urging on Her Majesty's Government the importance of refusing to ratify it. . . . In the present case, the influence that has been exerted has been sufficient to induce the British Government to withhold ratification in deference to the opinions of the opposing merchants, and in direct opposition, not only to the views of Sir Rutherford Alcock, *but to those which they themselves entertained.*[171]

There can be no real proof of the ultimate effect of the rejection of the Alcock Convention. It can be argued that the merchants' victory was limited, that it was reversed by 1871, and that the foundations of the Clarendon policy were not affected,[172] for powerful voices in Parliament continued to assert that the Chinese government's weakness was the result of foreign pressure, that Chinese antiforeignism was quite understable in view of foreign behavior, and that foreign intervention would lead to anarchy.[173] It can also be argued, and is by the Communists, that the rejection stripped British policy of its grandiloquent pretensions to fairness, for there was no difficulty about ratifying the Chefoo Convention, which offered China nothing.[174] Only one thing is certain: if there was ever a time when the ominous growth of Sino-Western distrust might have been nipped, 1869 was that time. Alcock knew it and he convinced his government. But when the chips were down, a government that had been more aware of the mainstreams of history than most temporized with strident chambers of commerce. Its sense of responsibility blunted, it let slip a chance that it knew might not come again.

As to the immediate effect of the rejection, it would be going too far to say that it caused the antiforeignism that took shape in the Tientsin Massacre.[175] Antiforeign riots had swelled before the Alcock Convention became an issue. Yet Wade reported again and again, "it is beyond dispute that the difficulties of the Legation are infinitely multiplied by the rejection of the Convention of 1869"; he described Wen-hsiang as "thirsting for revenge because of the discredit and inconvenience our rejection of the Convention has occasioned."[176] Of all this there is of course no mention in Wen-hsiang's diary, or in the writings of the other Chinese officials closely concerned. If the hypothesis is correct that the Tsungli-yamen was tentatively introducing a radically new view of China's foreign relations, then the rejection made fools of the yamen's members in Chinese eyes and no comment on it could be expected. Not until six months later, on January 21, 1871, did the yamen break its silence. English merchants had considered the convention too favorable to China, it said, and this was proof of the importance of the merchant class in British society; more important, it was an omen of greater pressure from all foreign powers in future negotiations.[177]

The Margary affair[d] and the Chefoo Convention of 1876 were sequels not of the Alcock Convention but of its rejection. Following Margary's death, the British attitude toward China stiffened. In a postscript to Margary's journal Alcock wrote:

> There is a Nemesis attaching to failure in the East which no Asiatic power can afford to disregard. However questionable may have been our right, in an international point of view, to insist on the concession of a free passage and trade with Yunnan and Burmah originally, we could have very little choice left afterwards. . . .
>
> Renewed and successful effort is the only alternative if we would avoid a total loss of the moral power, by which, far more than by superior force, we govern in the East and enjoy both security and commercial privilege.[178]

In the Chefoo Convention of 1876,[179] signed by Wade and Li Hung-chang, the British government still refused to go along with the major demands of British merchants, on the ground that

> They, in general, involve enterprises which, in my opinion, cannot be healthfully undertaken independently of the free action of the government. Such enterprises cannot, it is true, be given effect to, without foreign aid, if not foreign capital; but it is not desirable to force them upon the country.[180]

The Convention therefore was limited to: (1) settlement of the Margary case, (2) the code of diplomatic behavior, (3) the administration of justice in the treaty ports, and (4) revision of the commercial regulations.

Both sides knew that China could never use the Chefoo Convention to right past wrongs; nor could she any longer refuse new concessions—the opening of the upper Yangtze, for example. Any moderation in terms was by grace of the British. Only Hart's position had not changed; when the Tsungli-yamen asked

---

d Margary was murdered in Yunnan while exploring a possible land route to Burma. His journal generally praised Chinese officials for their courtesy and helpfulness, in spite of occasional corruption and inefficiency, but of "the people" he wrote: "It is the nature of Chinamen to give in to anything which asserts its superiority. A kick and a few words in his own tongue telling him he is an ignorant boor will make a common Chinaman worship you. . . . Singly or in small groups they are the pink of civility, but a mob is rather dangerous." (*The Journey of Augustus Raymond Margary, from Shanghai to Bhamo and Back to Maniwyne*, London, 1876, p. 131.)

his advice, he prepared a careful exposition of Chinese and foreign needs and grievances, together with a series of practical suggestions for their adjustment by mutual concession.[181] But this time British officials ignored his recommendations.

The Chefoo Convention marked the fixing of the unilateral pattern in Sino-foreign relations. It was not a new pattern; it was essentially the pattern of the Treaties of Tientsin, and of the preceding treaties that had opened China to Western intercourse on Western terms. The Alcock Convention had represented an effort to alter that pattern in a number of important particulars.

In 1868–69 modern China was able for the first time to negotiate a treaty as a sovereign state under no immediate coercion.[e] In 1860 Prince Kung had written:

> the insecurity of peace, as negotiated during many years past, has been entirely owing to the fact that peace has always been negotiated in the presence of an armed force, and that it has been impossible to have explanation of the different conditions of the Treaty article by article, the consequence of which has been doubt and suspicion on both sides.[182]

The Alcock Convention was the first, and is still one of the few, Chinese-foreign agreements negotiated with mutual consent. Alcock considered that establishing the principle of peaceful negotiation was far more important than the specific terms of the convention:

> Hitherto we have only attempted to make Treaties with China after an appeal to arms, under which they have succumbed. Now, for the first time, there is an opening for negotiation on a totally different basis, one of mutual interests and friendly relations, and this change of circumstances must materially affect, if not wholly govern, the progress of affairs as well as the things attainable.[183]

> I am persuaded that on no other basis can permanent relations of amity and commerce be maintained. There must be reciprocity of benefits as well as a spirit of fairness and desire for mutual accord. We may not get all that could be desired by strictly adhering to such a policy, nor obtain the most reasonable concessions as promptly or fully as we desire. But such as are obtained will be more willingly upheld by the central Government, and therefore less likely to be evaded by the provincial authorities, or rendered nugatory by indirect means.[184]

THE TIENTSIN MASSACRE[185]

The missionary question was the most serious problem in conservative reform, for the domestic program would fail unless the gentry and literati were encouraged to lead a Confucian resurgence in every locality, and the new foreign policy would fail if this Confucian resurgence led to excessive xenophobia.

---

[e] I refer here to the period after the "opening" of China. The Treaty of Nerchinsk and other earlier treaties are irrelevant in this connection.

Foreigners at the time often believed that the central government secretly encouraged the antiforeign outbreaks,[186] but the documentary evidence is to the contrary.

The increase in the privileges of Catholic missionaries after 1860 led to increased friction and ill will.*f* Catholic accounts of the activities of the Tientsin Mission in the 1860's reveal quite clearly why feeling was so high: young girl converts entered convents and refused to see their families, missionaries were able to prevent investigation by the local authorities, and so forth.[187] Suspicion of missionary activities was not limited to local officials. When the Alcock Convention was submitted to the Chinese government early in 1869, Prince Shun and Wo-jen had urged that a clause limiting missionary activities be included, and in particular that the missions be forbidden to operate orphanages. The Tsungli-yamen discussed this suggestion in a secret memorial. It agreed that the mission issue was the most difficult of all, but advised that any restrictive measure would be interpreted by foreigners as interference with freedom of religion, and might cause a Sino-foreign incident.[188] What was required was some means of regularizing the position of Christianity, and the possibilities were being explored.[189]

Into this calm atmosphere at Peking in the early summer of 1870 came first a warning from Ch'ung-hou, superintendent of trade for the three northern ports, that trouble was brewing in the port of Tientsin, and then on June 23 the report of a catastrophe that has remained a living memory for Chinese and old China hands alike.[190]

The makings of an explosion lay ready at hand in Tientsin, where there was a legacy of bitter feeling against the French troops that had been quartered there from 1860 to 1863. Other French actions fed the bitterness: the French Consulate was a former Imperial villa, and in June 1869 the French cathedral of Notre Dame des Victoires was dedicated on the site of a razed Chinese temple. Tensions mounted from the beginning of June 1870, when a number of Chinese arrested by the district magistrate confessed to having kidnaped children for the orphanage of the Sisters of St. Vincent de Paul. Zealous to save more children than the local Chinese wanted saved, the Sisters had been ignorant and imprudent enough to offer a small sum of money for each child brought them. It seems quite probable that these rewards encouraged kidnaping; certainly the local Chinese believed it. Rumors had been spreading rapidly since May, and the Sisters reported growing hostility from groups that had until recently been friendly. To the normal high death rate in the orphanage—the result of the Sisters' eagerness to take in dying children for baptism and Christian

---

f According to Giquel, the 1860 privileges were costly in good will, and the older missionaries would have preferred to return to the pre-1860 status (*La Politique française en Chine* . . . , pp. 26–47).

burial—were added the effects of an epidemic that broke out in June. When Chinese broke into the cemetery at night and disinterred the bodies, wild tales spread.

With local Chinese demanding an inspection of mission premises, the taotai called on the French consul, Henri Fontanier, on June 19. Apparently Fontanier persuaded the taotai that the charges against the Church were false, but the district magistrate was harder to handle. In an angry meeting the consul insisted that the magistrate was the fomenter of the trouble; the magistrate insisted that the consul was concealing the evidence. On the following day the ranking Imperial official of the area, Ch'ung-hou, intervened personally. In a friendly call, he persuaded the consul that the simplest way to disprove the charges against the Church was to allow an inspection. Evidently Fontanier was thinking of a quiet tour by high dignitaries at some future date; the district magistrate thought otherwise.

On the following morning, Ch'ung-hou and Fontanier were reporting to their respective superiors that a nasty situation had been resolved in the nick of time, when news reached the consulate that the taotai, the prefect, and the magistrate were outside the cathedral demanding entrance. In an act of fantastic folly, Fontanier, accompanied by his chancellor, rushed to Ch'ung-hou's office, struck the table with his sword, fired twice at Ch'ung-hou without hitting him, and as office attendants tried to grasp him, broke up cups and chairs and, as Ch'ung-hou put it, "used indecorous language." Infuriated by the effort to seize him, Fontanier refused to listen to the warning that a large crowd had gathered outside. It was no mob of ragamuffins, but an organized band of local officials, gentry, and respectable householders. He rushed into the crowd, the chancellor clearing a path with his sword. As the district magistrate started toward Fontanier (to attack him, in the French version; to rescue him, in the Chinese version) Fontanier fired at the magistrate and killed one of his attendants.

Hideous as the vengeance was, it might easily have been worse. The two French officials were ripped open on the spot. The crowd then set fire to the consulate, the cathedral, the orphanage, and the rest of the premises, and killed and horribly mutilated ten French Sisters, two French priests, seven foreign residents, and a number of Chinese converts.

At a time when responsible Western diplomats were summoning every reserve of wisdom to allay Chinese suspicion, one French consul closed his eyes to everything except France's role as protector of the Church. At a time when high Chinese officials were eating wormwood to avoid international incidents, one stubborn district magistrate closed his eyes to everything except the swell of local Chinese feeling against missionaries. In an afternoon a decade's work was undone.

China might well rejoice that there were no telegraph lines nearer than Kiakhta (on the Siberian frontier) and Ceylon. The news did not reach Europe until July 25, ten days after the outbreak of the Franco-German War. If it had arrived more promptly, another China war might have followed. As it was, warships from Far Eastern stations moved rapidly to Tientsin, and strong voices in Paris and Rome called for drastic punishment. Chinese troops were ordered to battle stations and retired commanders were called back into active service.[191]

The Tsungli-yamen gave the case its undivided attention for the next three months. In his capacity as governor-general of Chihli, Tseng Kuo-fan was sent to Tientsin to conduct the investigation, which, under foreign pressure, resulted in the execution of some sixteen Chinese[192] and the dispatch of Ch'ung-hou to France as head of a mission of apology.[193] Knuckling under to foreigners, said the Chinese; shielding the real perpetrator—the government of China—said the French.

Although war was avoided, both sides remained uneasy. In the following year the Tsungli-yamen attempted to get the treaty powers to agree to a clear definition of missionary rights and responsibilities. On February 9, 1871, the Tsungli-yamen sent Wade the same communication it had sent Alcock in 1869, stating that converts were often disreputable local characters, that missionaries had poor relations with the local gentry and officials, that where hostility was intense the government could not prevent violence. To remedy this, the yamen proposed a series of regulations; and various other means of controlling missionary work by according Christianity some regular place in the established order were widely discussed at the time.[194]

These views were eventually incorporated in a circular letter from the Tsungli-yamen to the envoys of all treaty powers.[195] The British government was inclined to agree with the Tsungli-yamen, but France and the United States were opposed.[196] According to Catholic sources, the basic fault in the Tsungli-yamen's reasoning was that it proposed that the Church stand in the same relation to the Chinese state as it stood in relation to European states, that is, that the state should have the right to inspect orphanages, control passports, and so on while the Church refrained from interference in civil administration. To the missionary this was absurd, since the Chinese state was not civilized.[197]

Wade, as chargé d'affaires, was pilloried by China hands for "his well-known sympathy with the fatal policy which has encouraged the recent outbreak,"[198] but to the Tsungli-yamen it seemed that his former friendly attitude had changed.[199] This was scarcely surprising, for as S. Wells Williams put it: "In short, the whole history of the riot—its causes, growth, culmination, results and repression—combine as many of the serious obstacles in the way of harmonizing Chinese and European civilizations as anything which ever occurred."[200] In the end, no solution could be found, and as foreign interests in the interior grew, xenophobia remained close to the surface.[g]

THE END OF THE RESTORATION

Treaty revision provided a cross section of the chief issues of the Restoration: whether or not the British government would continue to develop the Co-operative Policy in the face of opposition from British merchants and European powers; whether or not, through limited domestic reform, the Restoration government could stabilize the economy, make administration effective, revive the Confucian ideology, and build up an adequate military force; in sum, whether men who believed that there was much of enduring value in the Chinese tradition could adjust that tradition to the requirements of a new age.

By 1870 much had been accomplished in every field, and yet the signs of failure were soon thereafter apparent. The country became weaker rather than stronger; sycophants filled the posts lately held by the great Restoration statesmen; and the successful foreign policy of the sixties gave way to an era of ever more humiliating treaties, loss of territory, and—in all but name—loss of sovereignty itself. Historic periods rarely begin or end on particular days, but as the recapture of Anking and the founding of the Tsungli-yamen had symbolized the beginning of the Restoration, so the rejection of the Alcock Convention and the Tientsin Massacre symbolized its end.

[g] The Chinese Communists have made much of the Tientsin Massacre. They argue not only that Fontanier's death at the hands of the "broad masses," led by "patriotic youths," was fully justified, but also that charges of hypnotism and murder in the mission were proved by the investigation, and that the people's patriotism grew as these things became known. E.g., Chu Ch'i-hua, *Chung-kuo chin-tai she-hui shih chieh-p'ou*, Shanghai, 1933, pp. 132–40; Hu Sheng, *Ti-kuo chu-i yü Chung-kuo cheng-chih*, Peking, 1952; *Jen-min jih-pao*, Peking, April 13, 1951.

CHAPTER XII

THE HERITAGE OF THE RESTORATION

The failure of the T'ung-chih Restoration demonstrated with a rare clarity that even in the most favorable circumstances there is no way in which an effective modern state can be grafted onto a Confucian society. Yet in the decades that followed, the political ideas that had been tested and, for all their grandeur, found wanting, were never given a decent burial. Battered and decayed as they are, they have been revived by political leaders who in the face of the evidence insist that the Restoration was a success and that in its heritage lies the key to political control in twentieth-century China.

The accession to power of the Kuomintang in 1927–28 marked the end of the era in which revolutionary strains had been dominant in the party's program and the beginning of one of the most interesting and instructive of the many efforts in history to make a revolution the heir of ancient tradition.[a] The Kuomintang effort is noteworthy for four reasons: (1) the rapidity with which its course was reversed; (2) the magnitude of the gulf between the Confucian system the Kuomintang sought to restore and the national and social revolution that the party had lately led to victory; (3) the full and uninhibited adherence of Chiang Kai-shek and other leaders not only to the values of the traditional society, but to the specific institutions in which these had been embodied; and (4) a well-documented, persistent, and self-conscious effort on the part of these leaders to win the competition with the Communists by applying in the mid-twentieth century precisely the means the Imperial Chinese government had applied against the Taiping Rebellion in the mid-nineteenth.

 As the new rulers of China, Kuomintang leaders searched China's past for ways of dealing with economic decline, social dissolution, political incapacity, and armed uprisings; and they seized upon the T'ung-chih Restoration as a model. Whereas the Kuomintang in its revolutionary days had regarded itself as the heir of the great Taiping Rebellion, the Kuomintang in power identified itself with the Imperial government and its seeming successes.

Chiang Kai-shek and his colleagues attributed the achievements of the T'ung-chih Restoration to the stern moral character and insight into the working of the Confucian social process that had characterized the heroes of the age, notably Prince Kung, Tseng Kuo-fan, Tso Tsung-t'ang, and Hu Lin-i. They saw that

---

[a] I am indebted to the editors of the *Far Eastern Quarterly* for permission to use here a portion of my article, "From Revolution to Restoration: The Transformation of Kuomintang Ideology," *FEQ.* XIV, 4 (1955).

the Restoration had involved not politics alone but the whole of Chinese life; not only the suppression of rebellion, the selection and control of officials and the training of armies, but also the norms of behavior in ordinary social life, personal relations outside as well as within the family, the role of women, the relation between the generations, the choice of jobs, the demand for goods, the forms of recreation. To Kuomintang leaders, Confucian ideas in their Restoration form appeared relevant to twentieth-century problems of domestic tranquillity and international security. They did not see that the Restoration, for all its brilliance, had in the end failed precisely because the requirements for maintaining the Confucian social order and the requirements for ensuring China's survival in the modern world had proved quite fundamentally opposed.

The issue of Confucianism as a social principle and of the T'ung-chih Restoration as a guide to its revival were squarely joined in the Kuomintang-Communist struggle for the control of China's destiny. According to the co-founder of the Chinese Communist Party, Ch'en Tu-hsiu:

> The question of Confucianism relates not only to the Constitution; it is the basic question of our people's actual life and ethical thought. The essence of Confucianism is that the "principles of social usage" (*li*) are the basis of our country's ethics and politics. Their preservation or destruction is a question our country must soon resolve, and it should be resolved before questions of the form of the state or of the constitution.[1]

The Communists studied the lessons of the Restoration almost as carefully as did the Nationalists, and dubbed it "a counterrevolution achieved with foreign support." In the Communist view, the Kuomintang exaltation of the Restoration and the virtual canonization of Tseng Kuo-fan were fraudulent and futile efforts to anesthetize youth, the fabrication of a legend out of whole cloth by fascist theoreticians.[2]

As they made their bid for power, the Communists called the conflict in the interpretation of Tseng's character and career one of the battlefronts in the struggle between the "democracy-demanding Chinese people and the property-owning classes." They insisted that Sun Yat-sen, like all true revolutionaries of the early Kuomintang, had repudiated Tseng and had considered himself the younger brother of the Taiping leader Hung Hsiu-ch'üan.[3]

In contrast to the Communists' doctrinal consistency—i.e., their implacable opposition to Confucianism in general and to the T'ung-chih Restoration in particular—dominant Kuomintang views shifted and varied in the years of the party's rise to power. The issues of a Confucian society vs. a modern society, of restoration vs. revolution, had not been sharply posed until the years of heightened intellectual and social ferment after 1916. Among early Kuomintang leaders, including Sun Yat-sen and Chang T'ai-yen, the issue of nationalism had been primary; the establishment of the republican capital at Nanking had been a vindication of the Ming dynasty rather than of the Taiping Rebellion. Indeed Chang's views seem to have differed from those of his monarchist political opponents largely on the question of the nationality of the chief of state. And although Sun himself was sharply critical of those who saw nothing but the nationality issue, he considered the revolution of 1911 not as a break in the main course of Chinese history but as a continuation of five thousand years of glory.

As late as 1915, when Yüan Shih-k'ai assumed autocratic powers, the Kuomintang's own argument against the pretender to the Confucian monarchy and the "stabilizing" figure of the age rested on essentially Confucian grounds. The leader of the uncompromising armed opposition to Yüan, "Martyr of the Revolution Ts'ai Sung-p'o" (Ts'ai O) himself selected maxims from the works of Tseng Kuo-fan and Hu Lin-i, and issued them to his revolutionary forces as basic indoctrination material. In his preface Ts'ai wrote that where values and morale were concerned, discussion of the present was less useful than transmission of the teachings of antiquity; that although antiquity was sometimes too remote to be directly relevant, Tseng and Hu had lived only a half-century ago, so that what they had to say was of urgent importance today.[4]

After 1915, however, Chinese history moved rapidly. In the years following the May Fourth Movement of 1919, a Communist-Nationalist coalition centered at Canton gained strength. In 1924 the first congress of the reorganized Kuomintang issued a radical declaration that provided the basis of a common program with the Communists.[5] Mikhail Borodin was at the height of his influence and the young Chiang Kai-shek, recently returned from the Soviet Union, was military commander at the revolutionary Whampoa Academy, with Chou En-lai as director of the political department. It was in these extraordinary circumstances that Chiang selected for the Academy's textbook his own enlarged version of Ts'ai O's selections from the maxims of Tseng Kuo-fan and Hu Lin-i,[6] and it was to this step that Chiang's later success was subsequently attributed.[7]

In his preface Chiang wrote that the reason for the success of the Restoration and the failure of the Taiping Rebellion was not difference in ability, for in ability the Taiping heroes Hung Hsiu-ch'üan, Shih Ta-k'ai, and Li Hsiu-ch'eng were the equals of the Restoration heroes Tseng Kuo-fan, Hu Lin-i, and Tso Tsung-t'ang. In Chiang's view, Tseng had been the leader of the age because he acclaimed virtue and embodied proper personal conduct. It was because of this that Chiang took Tseng for his master.

Chiang observed that he himself had been studying the works of Tseng and Hu for some time, and had earlier decided to "postpone" writing the history of the Taiping Rebellion he had once intended as a guide to his comrades, and to compile instead a selection of the works of Tseng and Hu. For convenience he was using Ts'ai O's compilation as a basis, but he had made certain additions, particularly with reference to mental discipline, and had included selections from the works of Tso Tsung-t'ang as well. And Chiang concluded:

> Alack! The words of Tseng, Hu, and Tso are the voice of true experience in governing men, the things I wish to say but cannot put into words . . . I wish to present a copy to each of my comrades in the Academy so that in future there will be a foundation for the command of the army and the government of the country.[8]

In 1924 Chiang Kai-shek's view of the army of the revolution as the stabilizer of Chinese society along Restoration lines contrasted sharply with most of the published statements of the Kuomintang's position. There were a few like Tai Chi-t'ao who were already urging the use of the party organization "to restore the spirit of our ancestors and thus cause the country to flourish."[9] But Chiang's own position was still ambivalent. In 1924 at Whampoa he lectured on Tseng and stability but he also lectured on revolution.[10] There was nothing about the Confucian order in his manifesto to the nation of August 1926.[11] In 1933-34 he lectured only on stability and the Confucian code of behavior.[12] In 1924, although Chiang extolled Tseng, his references to the Taiping Rebellion were polite.[13] In 1932 he spat upon it.[14] And in 1933-34 at Lushan, Chiang took his stand not only against the Communists and the Taiping Rebellion but against all the rebellions in Chinese history, going back to the Red Eyebrows and the Yellow Turbans.[15] His cause was one with the cause of Hu Lin-i, he proclaimed, because: "If we do not exterminate the red bandits, we cannot preserve the old morals and ancient wisdom handed down from our ancestors."[16]

The full turn in the Kuomintang position took place between 1924 and 1928, and Chiang was always ahead of the party. The proclamations of the first two congresses of the Kuomintang were revolutionary documents. In the first (1924), the enemies of the party were specified as the constitutional clique, the federal autonomy clique, the compromisers, and the groups dominated by businessmen. The manifesto of the second congress (1926) was similar but more sharply anti-imperialist in the Marxist sense. The enemies of the party were the warlords, the bureaucrats, the compradors, and the local bosses. With the third congress in 1929, the picture changed and the enemies of the party became the "agents of red imperialism."[17] Radicals now either reformed their outlook or left the party, and many of those purged in earlier years returned to the fold.[18]

Even at the high tide of the northern expedition there were already those who called Chiang Kai-shek today's Tseng, who compared General T'ang Sheng-chih to Hu Lin-i.[19] When the Communist Propaganda Corps called on Chiang, its leader was struck by the fact that the phrases, the procedure, the whole atmosphere already suggested the traditional rulers of China.[20] The Communist view of the alternatives before the Kuomintang late in 1926 was illustrated in a poster hung at the Peasants' Association in a small town near Nanchang. On one side was a Confucian temple, on the other the "world park," featuring Marx, Lenin, and a vacant third position. In the center a man in Chinese Nationalist uniform was carrying the portrait of Sun Yat-sen toward the Confucian temple. The legend read: "Sun ought to be in the world park but Tai [Chi-t'ao] wants him in the Confucian temple."[21]

Public and avowed veneration for Confucius was resumed in 1928. As late as 1927 a mob had dragged a straw effigy of Confucius through the streets of Changsha and beat and burned it,[22] and the National Government itself had on February 15 ordered the abolition of official Confucian rites and turned the funds over to public education on the grounds that

> The principles of Confucius were despotic. For more than twenty centuries they have served to oppress the people and to enslave thought. . . . As to the cult of Confucius, it is superstitious and out of place in the modern world . . . China is now a Republic. These vestiges of absolutism should be effaced from the memory of citizens.[23]

The vestiges were not effaced for long. On November 6, 1928, Chiang Kai-shek was urging his officers to spend their leisure in the study of the Four Books.[24] In 1931 Confucius' birthday became a national holiday. Nationalist troops were ordered to give special protection to all local Confucian temples.[25] Recognition increased by degrees, culminating in the recanonization of Confucius in 1934 when Yeh Ch'u-ts'ang was sent as the official delegate of the National Government to take part in the ceremonies at the Confucian temple at Küfow,[26] now revived as a national shrine.

The Kuomintang never ceased talking about revolution. It merely redefined the term in a precisely opposite sense. As Ch'en Li-fu said in 1935, the "new" to which the revolution must lead was new in the sense that the Chou dynasty was new, new in the sense of slow adjustment and renewal of ancient and unchanging principles.[27] The official party history declared that Taiping thought was contrary to the spirit of Chinese culture, of which the Kuomintang was the true revolutionary carrier.[28] The party elder Chang Chi told the party's Central Training Corps in 1943 that the rejection of the sage kings and loyal ministers of the past that had characterized the early period of the revolution had been an error of youth, one that the party had long since corrected.[29] In these circumstances, T'ao Hsi-sheng wrote, as well he might, that the historic origins of the Kuomintang were subtle and confused, for the party was "the heir of both the Taiping Rebellion and Tseng Kuo-fan."[30] By 1953 the confusion had disappeared and reversal in the meaning of revolution was complete. According to T'ao: "Revolutionaries are scholars who take the statecraft (*ching-shih*) studies of the late Ming and early Ch'ing as their basis, but who have also imbibed Western thought."[31]

The change in the orientation of the Kuomintang was marked by a growing cult of Tseng Kuo-fan. In 1922 it had been difficult to believe that Tseng had been dead only fifty years, so much had Chinese life apparently changed.[32] By 1932 he seemed very much alive again; his works were reissued in large volume and discussions of his life and its meaning filled the new books and magazines. Again and again Tseng was described as the leading official of the restoration of the Ch'ing house and the pillar of the Restoration; the greatest man in modern Chinese history because he preserved not only the Ch'ing house but China; the greatest statesman of the Restoration, even greater as a thinker; a man of grand vision who renovated the old society.

After 1928, selections from Tseng and Hu became virtually part of the Kuomintang's party canon. New compilations and new editions of Ts'ai O's original compilation poured from the presses. Orders to study the maxims became a routine part of lectures by party leaders to army officers.[33] Ts'ai himself was increasingly identified with the Restoration, and he became a "model for youth" because he combined Tseng's "capacity" (*tu*), Tso's ability, and Chiang Chung-yüan's courage.[34]

This apotheosis of Tseng, and of Chiang Kai-shek as a greater Tseng, was not unprotested, but the critics had little effect. Repeatedly in times of crisis Chiang called on the nation to rise taking Tseng as its model. Tseng was every-thing: the symbol of spiritual mobilization in the war against Japan,[35] the consummate military commander, the embodiment of party discipline,[36] the arbiter of the academic world,[37] the proof incarnate that every man might through diligence and moral firmness rise to the heights.[38]

The choice of the Restoration as a model was logical enough once the Kuomintang leaders had ceased to consider the party a spearhead of revolution and had come to regard it as an instrument for restoring order. With their new outlook, they declared that the new period of revolutionary construction required qualities opposite to those needed in the preceding period of revolutionary destruction. The revolution could now go forward only if the party purged itself of the evil tendencies left over from its earlier history and concentrated on re-establishing the fixed and secure relationships of the Confucian order.[39] And the main and obvious feature of the Restoration was that these Confucian relationships had been re-established in the face of a revolutionary threat, and that order had thereby been restored.

The new Confucians of the Kuomintang were men of action, not philosophers. Chiang Kai-shek might quote the whole of the "great harmony" passage of the *Record of Rites* to the People's Political Conference,[b] and other leaders might refer in passing to any appropriate classical dictum, but Kuomintang leaders did not attempt to expound the Confucianism of the party in theoretical terms. They pulled from Confucianism, on an *ad hoc* basis, whatever seemed likely to promote internal order. Reasonably enough, their chief emphasis, like that of the Restoration leaders, was on the principles of social usage (*li*) and the associated virtues of "righteousness" (*i*), "integrity" (*lien*), and "sense of shame" (*ch'ih*).

There is little point in attempting a systematic analysis of exactly what the Kuomintang meant by *li, i, lien,* and *ch'ih*. They were discussed incessantly in party literature, but never very precisely or reflectively. Chiang Kai-shek instructed party workers that *li* meant precise and meticulous behavior in accordance with the unchanging principles of nature, society, and the state.[40] He told army officers that *li* and the associated virtues of *i, lien,* and *ch'ih* were the only sources of order, discipline, vision, and courage in the army, the best defense against the loss of loyalty which, as Tseng Kuo-fan had pointed out, was the great cause of all rebellions.[41] He told the general public not what these virtues were in positive terms, but what their absence entailed: in the absence of *li*, there was inattention to order, discipline, and rules; in the absence of *i*, there was lack of good faith and neglect of duty; in the absence of *lien*, there was confusion between right and wrong, between public and private; in the absence of *ch'ih*, there was imperceptiveness and irresolution.[42]

Although the philosophic meaning of this version of the doctrine of the rites is confused and scarcely worth discussion, its political and social meaning is clear enough, and worth careful attention. The thing that is really being discussed all the time is the means of ensuring social stability and popular discipline. In the view of the Kuomintang ideologists, Confucianism was the most effective and cheapest means ever devised by man for this purpose. They saw that the Confucian order had held together because certain canons of behavior had been hammered in by precept and example so effectively that deviation from them was nearly impossible. In the Kuomintang view the content of these canons mattered less than reviving the habit of behaving in accordance with fixed and unquestioned rules. The canons once accepted,, the opposition to Kuomintang

---

[b] The text of Chiang's address quoting this passage, which he called China's supreme political theory and the goal of national reconstruction, appears in *Tung-fang tsa-chih*, XXXVI, 6 (1939), 56. The meaning of the passage, made famous by K'ang Yu-wei and beloved by Sun Yat-sen, has become the subject of considerable controversy. To many who have read it casually, it has seemed to represent a liberal and democratic utopia. It has been praised by the Kuomintang—portions of it were set up in neon lights in Nanking in 1946 to celebrate the convening of the National Assembly—and attacked by the Chinese Left. Leading Japanese scholarly opinion considers the doctrine highly authoritarian. There can be little doubt that Chiang himself so regards it. For the text see James Legge (trans.), *The Li Ki*, Oxford, 1885, pp. 364–66. For an analysis see Itano Chōhachi, "Kō Yū-i no daidō shisō," in *Kindai Chūgoku kenkyū*, Tokyo, 1948, pp. 167–204 (*FB* 2.6.3).

control would presumably end. That the disciplinary effectiveness of Confucianism was dependent on its whole content and its whole context seems never to have occurred to them.

What has sometimes been called Chiang Kai-shek's idealism stemmed from this belief that indoctrination and habit are more effective than physical force in social control. In the mid-1930's, as economic crises and Japanese threats mounted, he stated that if the classic virtues had been more assiduously cultivated in recent years, China would not then be facing either domestic or foreign difficulties.[43] As his armies fell back before the advancing Japanese in 1939, he blamed neglect of the doctrine of the rites and urged that the nation save itself by putting a renewed emphasis on loyalty and filial piety.[44] And when, in 1950, his armies had retreated to Formosa, he attributed the Communist victory primarily to the Kuomintang's loss of morale. He replaced the morally discredited Central Executive Committee with a new Central Reform Committee with the charge: "We must inherit our five thousand year old culture and make it a guide in human progress."[c]

Chiang's insistence that the decisive element in human affairs, and in the flourishing and decay of civilizations, is the moral purpose of men, is good Confucian doctrine and more particularly good Restoration doctrine. But in Chiang's conception of this moral purpose and of the legacy from which it springs there is an important new element. For Chiang the Confucian way of life has lost its traditional rational and universal qualities and it has become imbued with a romantic nationalism. It has supreme value because it is Chinese, the source of *our* great past, the promise of *our* great future. There are not one but two anomalies in the statement that the task of the revolution is "to revive our Chinese culture, to restore our people's ancient virtues, to proclaim our Chinese national soul."[d]

Out of all these five thousand years of which Chiang talked, it was the T'ung-chih Restoration that held his attention. As he took command of the anti-Communist forces in the critical battles in Hupeh in 1932, his thoughts turned to Hu Lin-i, whom he eventually came to consider as even greater than Tseng Kuo-fan.[e] The Communists, he reflected, were nothing like so formidable a foe as the Taiping had been. He meditated about the way in which Hu

---

[c] Chiang's exact words on the causes of the Nationalist defeat were: "The disastrous military reverses on the mainland were not due to the overwhelming strength of the Communists but due to the organizational collapse, loose discipline, and low spirits of [Kuomintang] Party members." (Speech of July 22, 1950, authorized English translation in *Selected Speeches and Messages of President Chiang Kai-shek, 1949–1952*, Taipei, Office of the Government Spokesman, 1952, pp. 45–54.)

[d] *Lu-shan hsün-lien chi* (1933–34), n.p., n.d., II, 84. Chiang's nationalistic Confucianism marked the culmination of a process that had alarmed Liang Ch'i-ch'ao as early as 1902 (Liang, "Lun pao chiao chih shuo," Chinese text and French translation in Léon Wieger, *Chine moderne*, Sienhsien, 1921–31, I, 161–71).

[e] According to Chiang, Hu was the author of the plan that Tseng and all the other Restoration leaders used, but he died too young to achieve the fame he deserved (*Lu-shan hsün-lien chi*, II, 241–45).

had pacified the area, turned defeat into victory, and overcome his environment. If Hu's principles could be mastered, they could become "the ultimate guiding principles for our suppression of the Communists today."[45]

Although in theory the new Kuomintang policy was modeled on Restoration policy in all fields, in practice the Kuomintang emphasized Restoration lessons with respect to local control, military leadership and strategy, and revival of the Confucian ideology. Restoration principles in other fields—notably economics— were almost entirely ignored. It is true that Chiang quoted with approval Hu Lin-i's version of the classic principle: "If civil government is weakened, then the people's livelihood has nothing on which to depend. Even though you kill a thousand bandits a day, you will not remedy the general situation."[46] But Chiang also instructed party workers that it was an error to quote the Classics to the effect that adequate food and clothing were prerequisite to virtue. On the contrary, Chiang stated, the people must first be virtuous; only then would they have the moral strength to obtain food and clothing.[f]

For the Kuomintang, agriculture was the basis of the state in theory, but the Kuomintang documentation lacks the Restoration emphasis on water control, public works, reduction of the land tax, and control of currency and speculation in the interest of the agrarian economy. Evidently Kuomintang leaders did not agree with Restoration leaders that the Confucian virtues flourish only in an agrarian society, that industry and commerce are profoundly disruptive of the traditional way of life. The new Confucian revival was supposed to march hand in hand with a three-year plan for commercial and industrial development. As the "Confucian" governor of Kwangtung put it in a stormy interview with Hu Shih: "In building production, we may use foreign machines, foreign sciences, even foreign engineers. But for building men we must have roots; and these roots must be sought within China's ancient culture."[47]

By contrast with its relative neglect of Restoration precedents in economic policy, the Kuomintang gave close attention to certain aspects of Restoration local control. In 1930 in Kiangsi, where the Red armies had their bases, it seemed to the Kuomintang that control could best be reasserted by applying Tseng Kuo-fan's three basic principles: strict law enforcement, revival of the pao-chia system, and organization of the gentry. This was "the best model in history for learning how to exterminate Communists."[48]

Chiang and other leaders reiterated these principles and repeatedly tried to put them into effect.[49] Logically enough, they tried to build up the position of the gentry. Old privileges were restored and new ones added in the hope that

---

f *Min-chung yün-tung fang-an fa-kuei hui-pien*, n.p., ca. 1936, II, Appendix, p. 6. Chiang here attributes this "error" to Kuan-tzu, but it is Mencius who is most often quoted on the necessity of meeting the people's economic needs before the virtues are taught. (James Legge (trans.), *Mencius*, Oxford, 1885, pp. 148–49). It was presumably impolitic to attack Mencius by name.

the gentry might once again play its traditional role of maintaining local order and indoctrinating the peasantry. In 1939 Chiang Kai-shek wired all regional and local government and party officials to remind the gentry throughout the country that, in the words of the *Analects*, when the wind moves, the grass bends; that the gentry could educate beyond where government orders could reach; that the country could be saved only if the gentry recovered their "true national spirit" and remembered that "for several thousand years our country has considered loyalty and filial piety as the basis of the state."[50]

Revival of the pao-chia system of collective responsibility and the related militia system was as important in the Kuomintang program of local control as reinstatement of the gentry. Ch'ing statements on the pao-chia were carefully studied and reissued for the guidance of army officers and local officials, with particular attention to the plan of "strengthening the walls and clearing out the countryside" which was first developed for the suppression of the White Lotus Rebellion. The compilations reissued by the Kuomintang emphasized that in the defense of villages, the pao-chia and the militia must function together, the one preventing traitors from operating within the area, the other warding off outside attack. In this, "the poor serve with their strength, the rich contribute money, and separate families are banded together in large groups." This last arrangement, the party noted, is the very essence of the system.[51] The Kuomintang evidently accepted the Ch'ing arguments without reservation. Its leaders ordered the full reinstitution of the pao-chia system, against which they as revolutionaries had once railed, with particular attention to its use in Communist-infested areas.[52]

The Kuomintang gave less emphasis than the Restoration leaders to good local government in connection with local control. In Kuomintang sources, there is relatively little attention to the slowness of justice, the interference of the clerks, and other abuses that Restoration leaders considered major causes of local dissatisfaction and revolt. Although the Kuomintang in theory considered the quality of officials to be a matter of major importance,[53] the Restoration emphasis on the quality of local officials was lacking. Moreover since the actual machinery through which these men of ability were supposed to be selected, trained, and controlled had long since collapsed, Kuomintang discussions of the subject often lacked practical point.

The second field in which the Kuomintang modeled itself closely on the Restoration was military leadership and strategy. From the time Chiang first used Ts'ai O's book as a text at the Whampoa Academy in 1924, Nationalist army officers were urged to study the careers of Restoration leaders. As Ts'ai O put it, and others have repeated, the Restoration experience shows that the essential qualities of a good commander are: (1) a sense of public duty, and consequently a respect for the troops; (2) fearlessness in the face of death; and (3) indifference to fame. Ts'ai noted that whereas Westerners valued genius in military men, Tseng and Hu had emphasized the good heart, and had thereby transformed an era of catastrophic rebellion into an era of immortal glory.[54]

If the officers of the Nationalist army have fallen short of this goal, it has not been for want of instruction.

Restoration precedents also dominated Kuomintang thinking about strategy.[55] Although the campaigns against the Taiping furnished the chief lessons, those against the Nien-fei were not neglected. In analyzing the various campaigns, the Kuomintang consistently drew the lessons from the Ch'ing side. The party was interested not in learning how the Nien-fei might have avoided being trapped, but in mastering the relentless *hua-ho ch'üan-ti* hemming-in strategy by which the Ch'ing trapped the rebels. In 1930 Chiang Kai-shek ordered that all the proclamations and reports—even the troop songs—of the Ch'ing campaign against the Nien-fei be compiled, for the specific purpose of using similar methods against the Communists.[56] In 1948, researchers in the Ministry of National Defense were still hopefully studying this problem. Disconcertingly enough, the conclusion was drawn that the secret of Ch'ing success lay less in superior firepower than in the attention Tseng Kuo-fan and others devoted to assuring popular support of the government by appointing good local officials and disciplining troops.[57]

The Kuomintang effort to use Restoration models in local control and in military affairs obviously required an intensified campaign to revive the Confucian ideology, and one was accordingly launched. It took many forms: the works of Tseng Kuo-fan were reprinted and assigned for study in the schools; Confucian ceremonies were publicized; a flood of books and articles on the traditional virtues were published; manifestoes by selected professors on the preservation of the Chinese heritage were issued;[58] and there was even a government-ordered "Read the Classics" movement, promulgated from the "cradle of the Nationalist revolution, Canton."[59] Liberal comment might be scathing,[60] but Hu Shih was expelled from Kwangtung for lecturing against this movement and threatened with the loss of his civil rights.[61] To counter the left-wing pamphlets and the learned Marxist treatises that offered new solutions for the country's ills, special popular editions of traditional works were released in the most disturbed areas, and books in conflict with the doctrine of the rites were banned.[62]

With the movement to revive the Classics went its corollary—a movement to discourage education in the modern humanities and social sciences. With Chinese studies as the basis, it was argued, only science and technology need be borrowed from the West. Both Hu Shih and T. F. Tsiang warned that this was a reversion to a Restoration formula that history had proved unworkable,[63] but Kuomintang leaders thought otherwise. In their view, history had *not* discredited the T'ung-chih Restoration. According to Chiang Kai-shek, a little science might be useful, but Chinese education, like Chinese civilization, had a special basic character, and this could be best preserved through studies of Tseng Kuo-fan and Hu Lin-i.[64]

The Restorationism of the Kuomintang cannot be dismissed as a joke. For all its foolishness, it was the ideology of the only political movement that ever had a chance of successfully competing with the Communists, and the character of the competition was gravely affected by the persistence of the doctrine of the rites. Although the Kuomintang was far from monolithic, on this point there was little protest either from the splinter parties associated with it, or from the partially independent regional military leaders.[g]

Within the Kuomintang itself there were fissures but not on this point. Li Tsung-jen, leader of the Free China opposition to Chiang Kai-shek, declared from New York in 1950:

> After Chiang Kai-shek, it was thought any change was for the better. But after one year of trial, the people found that whereas Chiang Kai-shek was only interested in money and in depriving the people of their material well being, the Communists aim at depriving them of their soul.

But Li, like Chiang, went on to reassert the hard core of the Confucian social doctrine:

> For over 4000 years the Chinese people were knitted together by a moral code, apart from a common written language, the same blood strain and a cultural heritage. The code of morals expounded by Confucius and the rest of our sages is the only reason Chinese exist as a people and as a country. This code of morals distinguishes Chinese from other people by defining the correct relationship between parents and children, husband and wife, brother and sister, teacher and student, friend and friend.[65]

This might easily be Prince Kung writing on the principles of social usage as the basis of the state.[h]

[g] The leader of Shansi, Marshal Yen Hsi-shan, had his own personal Restoration model, Hsü Chi-yü, who in addition to his well-known career as a geographer and statesman (see Chapter X) had also been prominent in organizing Shansi's resistance to the Taiping and Nien-fei rebellions (see Yen's November 1915 preface to his publication of Hsü's complete works, *Sung-k'an hsien-sheng ch'üan-chi*). Subsequently Yen established what was called the Confucian administration of "the model province" of Shansi (see texts sympathetically assembled and translated in Wieger, *Chine moderne*, IV, 335–58). Ideas reminiscent of the Restoration have characterized the policy statements of most of the other regional military leaders. Even Feng Yü-hsiang considered that Tseng Kuo-fan's methods of troop training, his personal austerity, his love of study, and his diligent attention to duty were worth admiration and emulation. Feng moved toward the Communists, but in his own army he used Tseng's army songs about loving the people. (Feng, *Wo ti tu-shu sheng-huo*, n.p., 1947, I, 145, 153–54.)

[h] See Chapter IV.

The whole of the neo-Restoration of the Kuomintang was a dismal failure, a far sadder spectacle than the T'ung-chih Restoration it tried to copy. Local control was not reasserted. Army morale was not restored. There was never really any effort to revive the Confucian economy. And above all there was no resurgence of Confucian values and mores.

To call this distorted echo the last stand of Chinese conservatism would be to insult a magnificent tradition. True Chinese conservatism made its last stand in the 1860's, when, with England holding the ring, the West stood back to applaud a new government to which a galaxy of extraordinarily able officials had rallied; when the first modern Chinese foreign office made diplomacy an effective instrument of the state; when great rebellions were put down and agrarian rehabilitation was undertaken in earnest; when inflation was checked, revenues were increased, and taxes were lowered; when newly formed military forces showed high morale and a remarkable ability to make and use the most advanced Western arms; when the bases of the Confucian faith were resoundingly reaffirmed from the Imperial palace in Peking to remote villages on the fringe of the Chinese cultural world.

The T'ung-chih Restoration failed because the requirements of a modern state proved to run directly counter to the requirements of the Confucian order. In some individual issues this conflict was clear, in some muddy, but the basic choice became increasingly clear: with the Confucian heritage, or with the demonic new world of expanding national power. Restoration statesmen, and the last few genuine Chinese conservatives who followed in their steps, chose to remain with the Chinese heritage. It was precisely this heritage—and not a nation in the Western sense—that it was their chief aim to protect. The *Chung-kuo* of which they wrote with such feeling was more a way of life than a country. They have been accused of flabby indifference to their people's decline, but the accusation is unjust. They sought to avoid the fate of India, Burma, Annam, and Egypt, and later, when Japan's success became evident, to master Japan's secret, but they found the price too high. To the makers of the T'ung-chih Restoration adjustment that yielded, as it must have yielded to be effective, on the essentials of the Confucian society, was no alternative to extinction, but extinction itself.

ABBREVIATIONS

Ch.	The basic unit of a Chinese book, usually *chüan*, occasionally *chang* in twentieth-century works.
CHTI	*T'ung-chih chung-hsing ching-wai tsou-i yüeh-pien.*
Cordier, *Relations*	Henri Cordier, *Histoire des relations de la Chine avec les puissances occidentales, 1860–1902*, Paris, 1901–2, 3 vols.
CPLKI	Feng Kuei-fen, *Chiao-pin-lu k'ang-i.*
CSK	*Ch'ing-shih kao.*
CSPSR	*Chinese Social and Political Science Review.*
CSWP	*Huang-ch'ao ching-shih wen hsü-pien.*
CTLT	*Huang-ch'ao cheng-tien lei-tsuan.*
DD	France. Ministère des Affaires Etrangères, *Documents diplomatiques.*
Eminent Chinese	*Eminent Chinese of the Ch'ing Period*, edited by Arthur W. Hummel, Washington, D.C., 1943, 2 vols.
FB	John K. Fairbank and Masataka Banno, *Japanese Studies of Modern China; a Bibliographical Guide to Historical and Social Science Research on the 19th and 20th Centuries*, Rutland, Vermont, and Tokyo, 1955.
FEQ	*Far Eastern Quarterly.*
Hansard	*Hansard's Parliamentary Debates*, third series.
HF	Hsien-feng period, 1851–61.
HJAS	*Harvard Journal of Asiatic Studies.*
IWSM	*Ch'ou-pan i-wu shih-mo.*
JNCBRAS	*Journal of the North China Branch of the Royal Asiatic Society.*
KH	Kuang-hsü period, 1875–1908.
Morse, *Relations*	Hosea Ballou Morse, *The International Relations of the Chinese Empire*, London, 1910–18, 3 vols.
NCH	*North China Herald and Supreme Court and Consular Gazette.*
Papers on China	Harvard University, China Regional Studies Program, *Papers on China*, mimeographed annually for private distribution.
PHR	*Pacific Historical Review.*
SL	*Ta-Ch'ing li-ch'ao shih-lu.*

TC	T'ung-chih period, 1862–74.
THL	*Tung-hua hsü-lu.*
THTKTI	*Huang-ch'ao Tao Hsien T'ung Kuang tsou-i.*
TK	Tao-kuang period, 1831–50.
U.S. Arch. China. Instructions, etc.	United States. Department of State. Archives. China. *Instructions,* etc.
WHTK	*Huang-ch'ao hsü wen-hsien t'ung-k'ao.*

I have attempted to use *op. cit.* and *loc. cit.* only where the work in question has very recently been cited in full. Where the full citation is not near at hand in the Notes, the reader should consult the Bibliography.

NOTES

CHAPTER I

1. *Oxford Universal English Dictionary*, II, 375.
2. The case is summarized in Russell Kirk, *The Conservative Mind, from Burke to Santayana,* Chicago, 1953, pp. 7–8 and *passim.*
3. So characterized by Kirk, *ibid.,* p. 75.
4. One of the best short analyses of the modern Confucian position is Shen Yü-ch'ing, "Lun ju-chia ti fa-lü kuan," *Tung-fang tsa-chih,* XXXVIII, 5 (1941), 27–32. This is a well-annotated, critical comparison of Confucian principles with the general principles of modern Western thought.
5. Hsiao-t'ung Fei, *China's Gentry,* Chicago, 1953, p. 74.
6. Joseph Levenson, " 'History and Value,' the Tensions of Intellectual Choice in Modern China," in Arthur F. Wright, ed., *Studies in Chinese Thought,* Chicago, 1953, pp. 146–94; and Levenson, *Liang Ch'i-ch'ao and the Mind of Modern China,* Cambridge, Mass., 1953.
7. See Mary C. Wright, "From Revolution to Restoration, the Transformation of Kuomintang Ideology," *FEQ,* XIV, 4 (1955), 515–32.
8. Several facets of this question are explored in Lionel Trilling, *The Liberal Imagination,* New York, 1953.
9. Ralph Linton, "Present World Conditions in Cultural Perspective," in Linton, ed., *The Science of Man in the World Crisis,* New York, 1945, p. 203.
10. Some of the current sociological and anthropological findings on this point are summarized in Linton, *loc. cit.,* pp. 201–21, and in A. Irving Hallowell, "Socio-psychological Aspects of Acculturation," *ibid.,* pp. 180–94.
11. Alcock to Stanley, Dec. 23, 1867, *China. No. 5. (1871),* p. 83.
12. *Ibid.,* p. 83.

CHAPTER II

1. The autobiography of the Manchu statesman Wen-hsiang, who later became a pivotal figure in the T'ung-chih Restoration, includes a description of the spread of the rebellion, the panic in the capital, and the flight of metropolitan officials. Wen-hsiang, "Wen Wen-chung kung tzu-ting nien-p'u," shang, pp. 19–20, in *Wen Wen-chung kung shih-lüeh,* 1882; see also Wang Te-chao, "T'ung-chih hsin-cheng k'ao," in *Wen-shih tsa-chih,* I, 4 (1941), 21–22.
2. Ch'en Ch'i-t'ien, *Hu Tseng Tso p'ing-luan yao-chih,* Shanghai, 1932, pp. 3–4.
3. *NCH,* Jan. 28, 1860.
4. *Correspondence with Mr. Bruce, Her Majesty's Envoy Extraordinary and Minister Plenipotentiary in China,* pp. 41–44, and *Further Correspondence with Mr. Bruce . . . ,* p. 2.
5. On the various Anglo-French expeditions in connection with the negotiation and ratification of the Treaties of Tientsin, 1857–60, see W. C. Costin, *Great Britain and China, 1833–1860,* Oxford, 1937, chaps. vi, viii; Henri Cordier, *L'Expédition de*

Chine de 1857–58 . . . , Paris, 1906; Laurence Oliphant, *Narrative of the Earl of Elgin's Mission to China and Japan in the Years 1857, '58, '59*, London, 1860; Stanley Lane-Poole, *Sir Harry Parkes in China*, London, 1901, chaps. xii, xiii; Morse, *Relations*, Vol. I, chaps. xxiv, xxv, xxvi; and Charles Cousin de Montauban, *L'Expédition de Chine de 1860; souvenirs du Général Cousin de Montauban, Comte de Palikao*, Paris, n.d.

6. Wen-hsiang, ". . . nien-p'u," shang, pp. 28b–31b, *loc. cit.*

7. *Ibid.*, pp. 32–33. The translation of the second paragraph is slightly abridged.

8. *Ibid.*, p. 33b.

9. Tung Hsün, *Huan-tu-wo-shu lao-jen tzu-ting nien-p'u*, 1892, Ch. 1, p. 30. Other memorials of August and September, 1860, were found by the allies when they captured the Yüan-ming yüan. Translations are included in *Correspondence Respecting Affairs in China. 1859–1860*, presented to Parliament 1861, pp. 259–68. Documents on the allied occupation of 1860 and the resulting Chinese discussions of policy are included in *Shih-liao hsün-k'an*, No. 17, pp. 589–600, and No. 18, pp. 630–38b.

10. Ward to Cass, June 29, 1860, *U.S. Arch. China. Despatches*, No. 19.

11. For interesting accounts of the impact of the expedition and of the subsequent settlement, see *Chang kung hsiang-li chün-wu chi-lüeh*, compiled by Ting Yün-shu and Ch'en Shih-hsün, 1910, Ch. 6, *passim*. There are vivid glimpses of Peking during the occupation of 1860—the swarms of foreigners shopping outside Ch'ien-men, etc.—and indications of the literati's reaction in the diary of the censor Liu Yü-nan, edited by Meng Sen ("Ch'ing Hsien-feng shih-nien yang-ping ju-ching chih jih-chi," in *Shih-hsüeh chi-k'an*, No. 2 (1936), pp. 179–93). Dr. Rennie noted some of the aftereffects in his diary for 1861; see D. F. Rennie, *Peking and the Pekingese* . . . , London, 1865, Vol. I, chap. 1.

12. Chiang T'ing-fu provides a good summary in "Chung-kuo yü chin-tai shih-chieh ti ta pien-chü," *Ch'ing-hua hsüeh-pao*, IX, 4 (1934), 783–827.

13. *Correspondence Respecting Affairs in China. 1859–1860*, pp. 175, 179, 181–82. Costin, *op. cit.*, p. 330. Gros to Thouvenel, date line Pali-Kao, Sept. 22, 1860. *DD*, 1860, p. 251.

14. *Correspondence Respecting Affairs in China. 1859–1860*, p. 237. For a Chinese view of Parkes's captivity, see extracts from Weng T'ung-ho's diary in Chin-liang, *Chin-shih jen-wu chih*, n.p. [1935?], pp. 48–49.

15. For the text of the British Convention of Peking, signed by Prince Kung and Lord Elgin, see Godfrey E. P. Hertslet, ed., *Treaties, etc. Between Great Britain and China and Between China and Foreign Powers* . . . , 3d ed., London, 1908, Vol. I, No. 8.

16. Gros to Thouvenel, Oct. 26, 1860, *DD*, 1860, pp. 255–56; Cordier, *Relations*, I, 1–3, 11; Charles de Mutrécy, *Journal de la campagne de Chine, 1859–1860–1861*, Paris, 1862, II, 40, 44–46.

17. Russell to Elgin, Nov. 27, 1860, *Correspondence Respecting Affairs in China. 1859–1860*, p. 177. See also footnote *d*.

18. Elgin to Russell, Nov. 13, 1860, *Correspondence Respecting Affairs in China. 1859–1860*, pp. 254–55, and enclosures attached, p. 257; Mutrécy, *op. cit.*, II, 121–22.

19. Quoted in Cordier, *Relations*, I, 49. See also Mutrécy, *op. cit.*, II, 122–23.

20. The best short account, carefully documented, is Chang Ts'ai-t'ien, *Ch'ing lieh-ch'ao hou-fei chuan-kao*, n.p., n.d., Ch. 2, pp. 71–74. See also J. O. P. Bland and

E. Backhouse, *China Under the Empress Dowager*, London, 1910, chaps. ii, iii; Cordier, *Relations*, I, 119–30; D. C. Boulger, *A Short History of China*, London, 1893, pp. 307–11.

21. The edict was published in the *Peking Gazette* of Aug. 23, 1861; a full translation appeared in *NCH*, Sept. 21, 1861. The authenticity of the document has never been confirmed. A second edict was promulgated Sept. 11, 1861 (*CSK*, "Pen-chi," Ch. 21, p. 1b).

22. *CSK*, "Pen-chi," Ch. 21, p. 1.

23. *Ibid.*, Ch. 21, p. 1b. *WHTK*, pp. 9233–36. Li T'ai-fen, *Chung-kuo chin pai-nien shih*, Shanghai, 1914, I, 93–95. Tung Yüan-shun's memorial was translated in *NCH*, Nov. 16, 1861.

24. *SL-TC*, Ch. 5, pp. 26–29b; summary in *CSK*, "Pen-chi," Ch. 21, pp. 2–2b.

25. Edict of Nov. 8, *SL-TC*, Ch. 6, pp. 15–15b; edict of Nov. 9, *ibid.*, pp. 22 ff.; summarized in *CSK*, "Pen-chi," Ch. 21, p. 2b. Extensive translations in *NCH*, Nov. 23, 1861.

26. Jan. 18, 1862. *CSK*, "Pen-chi," Ch. 21, p. 4.

27. *WHTK*, pp. 9873–74. *IWSM-TC*, Ch. 2, pp. 9b–10. Hsüeh Fu-ch'eng, "Chi Hsien-feng chi-nien Tsai-yüan Tuan-hua Su-shun chih fu-chu," in *Chung-kuo chin pai-nien shih tzu-liao*, edited by Tso Shun-sheng, Shanghai, 1926.

28. Guy Boulais, *Manuel du code chinois*, Shanghai, 1924, pp. 28–31.

29. *SL-TC*, Ch. 6, pp. 23b, 24b–26b.

30. *CSK*, "Pen-chi," Ch. 21, pp. 2–2b.

31. The Tsungli-yamen could present to the Throne the records of courteous and satisfactory correspondence with the recently menacing imperial powers, e.g., *IWSM-TC*, Ch. 2, pp. 47–48.

32. Juliet Bredon, *Sir Robert Hart; The Romance of a Great Career*, London, 1910, pp. 61–63.

33. *NCH*, Sept. 21, 1861.

34. *Ibid.*, May 10, 1862.

CHAPTER III

1. Text of Burlingame's letter and editorial comment, *NCH*, July 9, 1864.

2. Review of the achievements of the Co-operative Policy, *ibid.*, May 12, 1866.

3. Review of the history of the policy, *ibid.*, Dec. 24, 1867.

4. Elgin to Malmesbury, May 9, 1858, *Correspondence Respecting Affairs in China*, presented to the House of Commons following the request of Feb. 16, 1860.

5. Costin, *Great Britain and China*, pp. 332–40.

6. The need for a new policy based on careful appraisal of the actual state of affairs in China was outlined by Rutherford Alcock in "The Chinese Empire and Its Destinies," *Bombay Quarterly Review*, Oct. 1855, p. 246.

7. [Rutherford Alcock] "The Chinese Empire in Its Foreign Relations," *Bombay Quarterly Review*, Apr. 1856, p. 237.

8. Alcock to Stanley, Nov. 15, 1867, *China. No. 5. (1871)*, p. 57.

9. C. A. Bodelsen, *Studies in Mid-Victorian Imperialism*, New York, 1925, p. 45.

10. For a general account of the anti-imperialist movement in England in this period, see *ibid.*, pp. 14–45. See also Alexander Michie, *The Englishman in China During the Victorian Era* . . . , London, 1900, II, 165. The evidence is against Kier-

nan's conclusion that Britain would have set about conquering China except for a series of accidents (E. V. C. Kiernan, *British Diplomacy in China, 1880 to 1885*, Cambridge [England], 1939, pp. 313–14). There was a positive and definite British policy of avoiding action that might lead to an attempt to conquer China.

11. Grey, Lords, reviewing the history of British policy, Mar. 9, 1869, *Hansard*, Vol. 194, pp. 944–46.

12. Carnarvon, Lords, Feb. 26, 1857, *ibid.*, Vol. 144, pp. 1311–21.

13. *Marx on China, 1853–1860, Articles from the New York Daily Tribune*, London, 1951, p. 20.

14. *The Times* (London), Feb. 20, 1861, reprinted in *NCH*, April 20, 1861.

15. Michie, *op. cit.*, II, 197–209.

16. For an account, from a missionary point of view, of this clash in England between the missionary societies and the Foreign Office, see R. Wardlaw Thompson, *Griffith John. The Story of Fifty Years in China*, London, 1906, chap. x. Thompson had been Secretary of the London Missionary Society.

17. Clarendon, Lords, Mar. 9, 1869, *Hansard*, Vol. 194, pp. 937–44.

18. Somerset, Lords, Mar. 9, 1869, *ibid.*, pp. 933–37.

19. Grey, Lords, Mar. 9, 1869, *ibid.*, pp. 944–46.

20. Otway, Commons, July 13, 1869, *ibid.*, Vol. 197, pp. 1798–1801.

21. "Retrospect of the Tenth Year of Hienfung," *NCH*, Feb. 16, 1861.

22. *NCH*, Nov. 28, 1868.

23. Bruce to Russell, Apr. 7, 1860, in *Correspondence Respecting Affairs in China. 1859–1860*, No. 22; *ibid.*, Nos. 23, 25; Bruce to Alston, Dec. 31, 1860, quoted in Costin, *Great Britain and China*, pp. 341–42; A. J. Sargent, *Anglo-Chinese Commerce and Diplomacy . . .* , Oxford, 1907, pp. 143–44.

24. Russell to Elgin, Apr. 17, 1860, *Correspondence Respecting Affairs in China. 1859–1860*, pp. 29–30.

25. Gros to the French minister of foreign affairs, July 11, 1860, as related by Gros to Elgin, July 17, 1860, *ibid.*, p. 89.

26. These views are extensively and forcefully stated in the works of Johannes von Gumpach, *The Treaty Rights of the Foreign Merchant and the Transit System in China*, Shanghai, 1875, and *The Burlingame Mission*, Shanghai, 1872.

27. Clarendon to Alcock, Jan. 13, 1869, *China. No. 1. (1869)*, p. 5.

28. *NCH*, Jan. 7, 1865.

29. *Ibid.*, Feb. 14, 1863.

30. Text of Hammond's note in *ibid.*, Apr. 25, 1863. For further material on the revised Yangtze regulations, see Chapter XI.

31. *Ibid.*, Dec. 27, 1862, and Mar. 28, 1863. For further discussion of British efforts to compel Westerners to abide by treaties, see Grace Fox, *British Admirals and Chinese Pirates, 1832–1869*, London, 1940, chap. vii.

32. E.g., *NCH*, Jan. 10, 1863; July 2, 1864.

33. *Ibid.*, Dec. 2, 1865.

34. *Ibid.*, Jan. 6, 1866.

35. *Ibid.*, Jan. 31, 1868. Examples can be multiplied.

36. *Ibid.*, Sept. 25, 1868.

37. Stanley to Alcock, Aug. 16, 1867, *China. No. 5. (1871)*, p. 8.

38. Winchester to Alcock, Nov. 7, 1867, *ibid.*, p. 31.

39. The immediate British background is summarized in Fox, *op. cit.*, chap. iii, Sec. 1, "General Principles of British Naval Policy in China."

40. For an uncharacteristic statement urging forceful action, see Alcock to Stanley, Nov. 10, 1868, *China. No. 5. (1871)*, No. 74. Note that this was written at the height of the antiforeign demonstrations. See also Michie, *op. cit.*, II, 221–22.

41. Report in *NCH*, Jan. 31, 1868.

42. *China. No. 2. (1869)*, *passim*. Also reported in *NCH*, Aug. 28, Sept. 11, Sept. 19, Sept. 25, Oct. 3, Oct. 13, Nov. 24, and Dec. 8, 1868.

43. *NCH*, Sept. 11, Oct. 3, Oct. 13, and Nov. 24, 1868.

44. *Ibid.*, Nov. 24, 1868.

45. Clarendon to Alcock, Jan. 14, 1869, *China. No. 2. (1869)*, No. 18.

46. For a detailed review of the incident, see *NCH*, Dec. 28, 1868; Gibson to Alcock, Dec. 14, 1868, *China. No. 3. (1869)*, pp. 7–12. The background of the antiforeign feeling was the foreign effort to break the camphor monopoly. See Holt to Alcock, Oct. 14, 1868, *China. No. 6. (1869)*, p. 2.

47. *China. No. 3. (1869)*, pp. 24–26.

48. *Ibid.*, pp. 21–22.

49. Clarendon to Alcock, Apr. 23, 1869, *China. No. 9. (1869)*, p. 5.

50. Keppel to Robertson, Feb. 2, 1869, *China. No. 7. (1869)*, p. 7; minutes of the interview, Jan. 25, 1869, *ibid.*, pp. 5–6.

51. Hammond to the Secretary of the Admiralty, Mar. 24, 1869, *ibid.*, pp. 11–12. Admiralty reply quoted, *ibid.*, p. 21.

52. Alcock to Stanley, Feb. 5, 1869, *China. No. 3. (1869)*, pp. 36–37.

53. *Hansard*, Vol. 195, pp. 131 ff.

54. *Ibid.*, Vol. 195, pp. 577–79.

55. *Ibid.*, Vol. 199, pp. 1870–72.

56. Clarendon to Alcock, Apr. 19, 1869, *China. No. 8. (1869)*, p. 5.

57. *Hansard*, Vol. 205, pp. 562–63.

58. *Ibid.*, Vol. 144, pp. 1515, 1742 (Feb.-Mar., 1857).

59. Report of hearings, *Regina* v. *Reynolds and Holt*, *NCH*, Oct. 21, 1865.

60. E.g., Prosper Giquel, *La Politique française en Chine depuis les traités de 1858 et de 1860*, Paris, 1872, pp. 1–14.

61. E.g., Francis Garnier, "Le Rôle de la France en Chine et en Indo-Chine," *Revue Scientifique de la France et de l'Etranger*, 2d Series, 5th year, No. 15 (Oct. 9, 1875), pp. 337–46. The article is dated Shanghai, Aug. 9, 1873.

62. Costin, *Great Britain and China*, p. 335. Cordier, *Relations*, I, 43–48.

63. "Affaires politiques; exposé des affaires politiques et commerciales," *DD*, 1867, No. 8, p. 16.

64. "Exposition des affaires politiques," Nov., *DD*, 1869, No. 12, pp. 14–15.

65. Drouyn to Bellonet, June 18, 1866, *DD*, 1867, No. 8; *ibid.*, No. 10, p. 19; Burlingame to Fish, Paris, Sept. 18, 1865, *U.S. Arch. China. Notes*, Vol. I.

66. The chief studies of Russian-Chinese relations at this period are A. Buksgevden, *Russkii Kitai; ocherki diplomaticheskikh snoshenii Rossii s Kitaem*, I. *Pekinskii Dogovor 1860 g.*, Port Arthur, 1902; Chi Tsai Hoo, *Les Bases conventionelles des relations modernes entre la Chine et la Russie*, Paris, 1918; Agnes F. C. Chen, "Chinese Frontier Diplomacy: The Eclipse of Manchuria," *Yenching Journal of Social Studies*, V, 1 (1950), 69–141.

67. On the background, see A. K. Korsak, *Istoriko-statisticheskoe obozrenie torgovykh snoshenii Rossii s Kitaem*, Kazan, 1857; Gustav Cahen, *Some Early Russo-Chinese Relations*, Shanghai, 1914. Earlier works have been superseded by Mark Mancall, "Major-General Ignatiev's Mission to Peking, 1859–1860," *Papers on China*, X (1956), 55–96.

68. According to Agnes F. C. Chen, *loc. cit.*, p. 116, the Russians gained their ends by manhandling the Chinese envoy and by concealing differences between the Russian and Chinese texts. In her opinion, the contrary view of T. F. Tsiang (Chiang T'ing-fu) that the Ch'ing yielded supinely reflects primarily his desire to discredit the Ch'ing. Compare Chiang T'ing-fu, *Chung-kuo chin-tai shih*, Changsha, 1938, pp. 56–61, and Chiang, "P'ing *Ch'ing-shih kao* pang-chiao chih," Part 1, in *Pei-p'ing Pei-hai t'u-shu-kuan yüeh-k'an*, II, 6 (1929), 483–84.

69. Agnes F. C. Chen, *loc. cit.*, pp. 120–25; Cordier, *Relations*, I, 94–95.

70. Mutrécy, *Journal de la campagne de Chine*, II, 123–25.

71. See A. Popov, "Tsarskaia diplomatiia v epokhu Taipinskogo vosstaniia," *Krasnyi Arkhiv*, No. 21 (1927), pp. 182–99, based on pre-1860 Russian archival material.

72. E.g., Seward to Burlingame, Sept. 9, 1863, *U.S. Arch. China. Instructions*, I, 289–90; Burlingame to Seward, Dec. 12, 1863, *Foreign Relations of the United States, 1863*, Part 2, p. 837; Seward to Burlingame, Sept. 14, 1864, *U.S. Arch. China. Instructions*, I, 312–13; Fish to Burlingame, Sept. 17, 1869, *U.S. Arch. China. Notes to*, pp. 8–9. Tyler Dennett, *Americans in Eastern Asia*, New York, 1922, chap. xxii.

73. Seward to Williams, Nov. 20, 1866, *U.S. Arch. China. Instructions*, I, 418–24.

74. Seward to Burlingame, March 6, 1862, *Foreign Relations of the United States, 1862*, p. 83; Seward to Burlingame, Sept. 9, 1863, *U.S. Arch. China. Instructions*, I, 289–90.

75. June 6, 1868, *U.S. Arch. China. Notes to*, pp. 2–7.

76. See Seward to Burlingame, Aug. 18, 1864, *U.S. Arch. China. Instructions*, I, 309, and Sept. 2, 1863, *ibid.*, 285–86.

77. On the reaction in Peking to Browne's arrival, see Alcock to Stanley, Nov. 23, 1868, *China. No. 5. (1871)*, No. 75. For a defense of Browne, see Paul H. Clyde, "The China Policy of J. Ross Browne, American Minister at Peking, 1868–1869," *PHR*, I, 3 (1932), 312–23. Browne stated his own position to Alcock Dec. 17, 1868 (*China. No. 5. (1871)*, pp. 258–60).

78. S. Wells Williams, *The Middle Kingdom*, New York, 1907, II, 699.

79. *NCH*, May 2, 1863; Oct. 27, 1866; Aug. 21, 1867.

80. *Ibid.*, Mar. 5, 1864.

81. "The Chinese Empire and Its Destinies," *loc. cit.*, p. 223.

82. Nov. 8, 1867, *China. No. 5. (1871)*, p. 63.

83. Gumpach, *The Burlingame Mission*, pp. 236–37.

84. *Correspondence Respecting Affairs in China, 1859–1860*, pp. 78–80. *The Chinese and Japanese Repository*, Sept. 12, 1864, II, 75–76.

85. E.g., *NCH*, May 9, Nov. 24, 1868. Gumpach, *The Burlingame Mission*, chap. xi.

86. *NCH*, July 5, 1867.

87. *Ibid.*, Mar. 23, 1867.

88. *Ibid.*, July 5, 1867.

89. *Ibid.*, June 2, 1866.

90. *Ibid.*, Sept. 25, 1868.

91. Alcock to Stanley, Dec. 23, 1867, *China. No. 5. (1871)*, p. 2.

92. *NCH*, Oct. 24, 1863.

93. See exchange of letters between Keswick and Winchester, *NCH*, Feb. 24, 1866.

94. Letter of Jan. 24, 1868, *NCH*, Jan. 31, 1868.

95. A. B. Freeman-Mitford, *The Attaché at Peking*, London, 1900, p. xlix.

96. *NCH*, Aug. 19, 1865.

97. Gumpach, *The Burlingame Mission*, p. 3.

98. Wade's 1854 memorandum cited in Stanley F. Wright, *Hart and the Chinese Customs*, p. 111.

99. Michie, *op. cit.*, II, 134. On Wade's views, see also Baron de Méritens, *Notes upon Mr. Wade's Memorandum Regarding the Revision of the Treaty of Tientsin*, Hongkong, 1871, Preface and p. 11; "Mr. Wade on China," *China Review*, I (1872–73), No. 1, pp. 38–44, and No. 2, pp. 118–24.

100. Described in *NCH*, Nov. 10, 1868.

101. See Chiang Tun-fu's essay on the Hart memorandum in *CSWP*, Ch. 104, pp. 1–46. Chiang was a close associate of the mathematician Li Shan-lan and of the reforming journalist Wang T'ao.

102. E.g., memorial of Ma Hsin-i, then governor of Chekiang, Nov. 27, 1866, *IWSM-TC*, Ch. 45, pp. 44b–45b.

103. Fan Wen-lan, *Chung-kuo chin-tai shih*, Hongkong, 1949, I, 207–8. As evidence Fan offers a criticism of Tsungli-yamen dilatoriness by Wade.

104. Hu Sheng, *Ti-kuo chu-i yü Chung-kuo cheng-chih*, Shanghai, 1948, and Peking, 1952, pp. 38, 41–47, 49, 51–55, 67.

105. Alcock to Medhurst, Mar. 23, 1869, in *China. No. 12. (1869)*, p. 9.

CHAPTER IV

1. Sun Chia-kan in Wo-jen, *Wo Wen-tuan kung i-shu*, n.p., 1875–76, Ch. 1, pp. 29 ff.; shou, chüan-hsia, p. 21b.

2. *CSWP*, Ch. 15, pp. 1–2.

3. *THTKTI*, Ch. 4, p. 8.

4. Hsüeh Fu-ch'eng, "Chung-hsing hsü-lüeh," essay dated 1868, shang, p. 3b, in *Yung-an wen-pien*, Ch. 2, in *Yung-an ch'üan-chi* (printed 1884–98). Since the quotation is *not* from the *Book of Changes*, the *Tso-chuan*, or the *Classic of History*, and no satisfactory source is suggested in the *P'ei-wen yün-fu*, I have simply translated *ch'uan* as "tradition."

5. Etienne Balázs, "La Crise sociale et la philosophie politique à la fin des Han," *T'oung-pao*, XXXIX (1949), 123–24. The use of a cyclical calendar probably encouraged this cyclical tendency in the history of ideas.

6. See James Legge (trans.), *The She King or the Book of Poetry*, in two parts, Oxford, 1893–95, Prolegomena, pp. 31–33, and text, pp. 77 and 541–45.

7. The term restoration was also occasionally applied to certain other periods. On the use of *chung-hsing* for the first year (A.D. 317) of the Eastern Chin dynasty and the astronomical phenomena that were taken as signs of restoration, such as the appearance of a supernatural seal in the shape of a chi-lin and multiple rings around the sun, see *Chin-shu chiao-chu*, Peking, 1928, Ch. 6, pp. 3b, 9b–10b. As an era name,

chung-hsing was also used by the Western Yen for the years A.D. 386–394 and by the Southern Ch'i, the Northern Wei, the Southern T'ang (A.D. 958), and the Nan-chao (897[8]–901[2]). See *Tōyō rekishi daijiten*, VI, 76, and *Lien-mien tzu-tien*, I, 68–68b. Hsiung K'o, *Chung-hsing hsiao-chi*, deals with the reign of Sung Kao-tsung (1127–1161).

8. Otto Franke, *Geschichte des Chinesichen Reiches*, Berlin, 1930–48, I, 149–50; Ung-Bing Li, *Outlines of Chinese History*, Shanghai, 1914, pp. 26–28; Friedrich Hirth, *Ancient History of China*, New York, 1908, pp. 157–71; Edouard Chavannes (trans.), *Les Mémoires historiques de Se-ma Ts'ien*, Paris, 1897–1905, I, 276–78, 285. The reign of Hsüan-wang was described as a restoration in the dynastic history, eulogy to the "Hsüan-ti chi"; cf. Homer Dubs (trans.), *History of the Former Han Dynasty*, Baltimore, 1938–44, II, 265. The term was also used in the biography of Liu Hsiang, the essay on rites and music, etc. See references in *Lien-mien tzu-tien*, I, 68–68b.

9. Franke, *op. cit.*, p. 150. The Eastern Chou is not referred to as a restoration.

10. The most thorough study of the period is focused on the rebellion rather than on the restoration. See Hans Bielenstein, *The Restoration of the Han Dynasty*, reprinted from the Museum of Far Eastern Antiquities, Stockholm, *Bulletin* No. 26, 1954. Bielenstein concludes (p. 165): "Wang Mang's rule never quite replaced the Han dynasty in the minds of the people, and thus his reign represents an interregnum rather than a new dynasty. . . . If Wang Mang's dynasty had lasted, the memory and glory of Han would slowly have faded away. As it was, the Yellow River brought Wang Mang to his fall early enough to save the Han dynasty."

11. René Grousset, *Histoire de la Chine*, Paris, 1942, pp. 81–84, 112; Ung-Bing Li, *op. cit.*, pp. 83–84; Franke, *op. cit.*, I, 388–95; Balázs, "Crise sociale . . . ," *loc. cit.*, pp. 89–91.

12. Balázs, "Crise sociale . . . ," *loc. cit.*, pp. 95–105.

13. See references in *Lien-mien tzu-tien*, I, 68–68b, to the Annals of Kuang-wu and various biographies.

14. Arthur Waley, *The Life and Times of Po Chü-i, 772–846 A.D.*, London, 1949, p. 40.

15. *Ibid.*, p. 4.

16. The preceding account is based on Henri Maspero, "Les Régimes fonciers en Chine," *Receuils de la Société Jean Bodin*, II (1937), "Le Servage," pp. 291–92; Franke, *op. cit.*, II, 457–63; Ung-Bing Li, *op. cit.*, pp. 147–48; Grousset, *op. cit.*, pp. 207–9. The most illuminating treatment of the background is to be found in Edwin G. Pulleyblank, *The Background of the Rebellion of An Lu-Shan*, London, 1955.

17. Wang Shih-to's eulogy of Hu Lin-i, prepared on behalf of Kuan-wen, in *Wang Mei-ts'un hsien-sheng chi*, 1881, Ch. 6, p. 4. Other Restoration eulogies are included in Ch. 12 and the final unnumbered chüan of the "Wai-chi."

18. Tseng's memorial, n.d., as governor-general of Kiangsu, Kiangsi, and Anhwei, *CHTI*, Ch. 7, p. 11.

19. Memorial of Ma, Mar. 15, 1869, *IWSM-TC*, Ch. 64, p. 26.

20. Memorial of Li, 1872 (TC-11), *THTKTI*, Ch. 2, pp. 13b–14.

21. Eulogy of Tseng Kuo-fan, *CHTI*, Ch. 6, pp. 4b–5.

22. See Bibliography.

23. *CHTI*, compiler's preface.

24. *WHTK*, p. 10068.

25. Preface to the poetry section of Kuo's *Yang-chih shu-wu ch'üan-chi*.

26. For a classic statement by Wo-jen, 1852 (HF-2), on the manner in which the virtue of the sovereign enables the whole system of government to operate, see *THTKTI*, Ch. 3, pp. 10–10b. See also memorial of the censor Wu Hung-kan, Mar. 8, 1873, *Translation of the Peking Gazette for 1873*, Shanghai, 1874, p. 25.

27. Chang Ts'ai-t'ien, *Ch'ing lieh-ch'ao hou-fei chuan-kao*, n.p., n.d., Ch. 2, pp. 70–77; Chaoying Fang in *Eminent Chinese*, pp. 295–300.

28. Karl A. Wittfogel and Chia-sheng Feng, *History of Chinese Society. Liao*, Philadelphia, 1949, pp. 10–15.

29. Li Chien-nung, *Tsui-chin san-shih nien Chung-kuo cheng-chih shih*, Shanghai, 1934, pp. 48–49.

30. Wittfogel, *Liao*, pp. 10–15.

31. Wu Hsi-yung, "Chin-tai tung-pei i-min shih-lüeh," *Tung-pei chi-k'an*, No. 2 (1941), pp. 24b-29; Inaba Iwakichi, *Shinchō zenshi*, Tokyo, 1914, II, 487–97 (*FB* 2.1.4); Sudō Yoshiyuki, *Shindai Manshū tochi seisaku no kenkyū* . . . , Tokyo, 1944 (*FB* 3.2.2).

32. Hsiao I-shan, "Ch'ing-tai tung-pei chih t'un-k'en yü i-min," *Tung-pei chi-k'an*, No. 4 (1942), 37 leaves; Franklin L. Ho, "Population Movement to the Northeastern Provinces in China," *CSPSR*, XV (1931–32), 346–50; Otake Fumio, *Kinsei Shina keizaishi kenkyū*, Tokyo, 1942, pp. 238 ff. (*FB* 7.1.3); Yano Jin'ichi, *Manshū kindai shi*, Tokyo, 1941, chap. 1 (*FB* 4.7.2); Inaba Iwakichi, *Manshū hattatsu shi*, Tokyo, 1942; H. E. M. James, *The Long White Mountain or a Journey in Manchuria*, London, 1888, pp. 148, 150 ff.

33. On the efforts of the K'ang-hsi Emperor to mitigate Sino-Manchu friction as early as the seventeenth century, see Hellmut Wilhelm, "The Attitude of the Early Ch'ing Scholars Toward the Manchus," paper read before the Far Eastern Association, New Haven, Conn., April 1949 (mimeographed). On the question as a whole, see Abe Takeo, "Shinchō to Ka-i shisō," *Jimbun Kagaku*, I, 3 (1946), 137–59 (*FB* 6.3.2).

34. Liu Fa-tseng, *Ch'ing-shih tsuan-yao*, Shanghai, 1914, pp. 117–18; Yano, *Kindai Shina shi*, chap. 21; Chin-liang, *Ch'ing-ti wai-chi*, n.p., n.d., p. 138. I am indebted to Chaoying Fang for amplification of this material.

35. On the triumph of the pro-Confucian over the anti-Manchu spirit, see Li Chien-nung, *Chung-kuo chin pai-nien cheng-chih shih*, Shanghai, 1948, I, 86–87. On the reflection of Manchu-Chinese assimilation in the popular fiction of the nineteenth century, see Wen-djang Chu, "The Policy of the Manchu Government in the Suppression of the Moslem Rebellion . . . ," Ph.D. dissertation, University of Washington, 1955, p. 9. Ms. cited with author's permission.

36. On the general tendency of nomadic invaders to ally themselves with, and thus strengthen, the conservative elements in Chinese society, see Tamura Jitsuzō, "Ajia shakai no kōshinsei to yūboku minzoku to no rekishiteki kankei," in *Yūboku minzoku no shakai to bunka*, Kyoto, 1952, pp. 1–8 (*FB* 1.5.17).

37. K'ang, "Nan-hai hsien-sheng tsui-chin cheng-chih shu," as quoted in *Tang-shih shih-liao ts'ung-k'an*, No. 1, pp. 11–17.

38. Edict of Mar. 3, 1867, *SL-TC*, Ch. 195, pp. 28b–29b. One of Tseng's most trusted subordinates was a Manchu, T'a-ch'i-pu.

39. Edict translated in *NCH*, Mar. 1, 1862; edict of Mar. 31, 1871, *SL-TC*, Ch. 305, p. 4b. Further illustrations of the complete victory of the Chinese over the Manchu language are to be found in Miyazaki Ichisada, "Shinchō ni okeru kokugo mondai no ichimen," *Tōhōshi Ronsō*, I (1947), 1–56 (FB 3.1.2).

40. For background on the special status of Bannermen, and limitations on their occupations, see Wang Ch'ing-yün, *Hsi-ch'ao chi-cheng*, Ch. 4, pp. 46–56.

41. Memorial of Tu Jui-lien, n.d., *CHTI*, Ch. 3, pp. 17–19b.

42. Liu's memorial, July 9, 1864, *Liu Wu-shen kung i-shu*, 1902, Ch. 6, pp. 10–12. Background is included in this and in Tu's memorial.

43. Text of Shen's memorial, n.d. [before July 23, 1865], *CHTI*, Ch. 3, pp. 1–4b.

44. Edict of July 23, 1865, *SL-TC*, Ch. 144, pp. 2b–4. English translation, in which date given is July 26, 1865, in *NCH*, Aug. 26, 1865, and *JNCBRAS*, II (1865), 139–40. For extensive further documentation on the relaxation of the Banner regulations, see *CSWP*, Ch. 34, pp. 6–10b and *passim*, and *THTKTI*, Ch. 31, pp. 10b–11b and *passim*.

Curiously enough Wang Hsien-ch'ien overlooked the importance of this edict, perhaps because the situation had long been taken for granted. The *Tung-hua hsü-lu* merely notes tersely the "enlargement of the regulations under which Bannermen may proceed to all provinces to earn their living." July 23, 1865, *THL-TC*, Ch. 48, p. 1. *THL* usually includes the full text of important documents.

45. *NCH*, Aug. 26, 1865. This article was considered of sufficient interest to be reprinted in the *Chinese and Japanese Repository*, III, 541–42.

46. Thomas W. Kingsmill, "Retrospect of Events in China and Japan During the Year 1865," *JNCBRAS*, II (1865), 139.

47. On Manchu dominance of the bureaucracy in the late Ch'ing, Wittfogel cites Hu Shih, P. C. Hsieh, Brunnert and Hagelstrom, and De Harlez. None of these offers persuasive data on this point. Wittfogel's own published figures are limited to the year 1893 (*History of Chinese Society. Liao*, Philadelphia, 1949, Introduction).

The Chinese Communist historian Fan Wen-lan, in commenting on the Restoration period, also makes the flat statement that Manchus dominated the central government and usually held 60 to 70 per cent of the provincial governor-generalships and governorships as well (*Han-chien k'uai-tzu shou Tseng Kuo-fan ti i-sheng*, 1944, p. 1).

48. F. S. A. Bourne, "Historical Table of the High Officials Composing the Central and Provincial Governments of China," *China Review*, VII, 5 (1878–79), 314–29. The table on p. 315 includes the Grand Council, the Grand Secretariat, the Tsungli-yamen, and all provincial officials above the rank of taotai with the exception of the Literary Chancellors. On the Chinese dominance of both the metropolitan and the provincial bureaucracy during the Restoration, see Ling T'i-an, *Hsien-T'ung Kuei-chou chün-shih shih*, Shanghai, 1932, Part 1, pp. 18–18b.

49. "The Share Taken by Chinese and Bannermen Respectively in the Government of China," *China Review*, VI, 2 (1877–78), 136–37. The tables are based on the Red Book, presumably for 1877.

50. See John K. Fairbank, "The Manchu-Chinese Dyarchy in the 1840's and '50's," *FEQ*, XII, 3 (1953), 265–78.

51. Inaba, *Shinchō zenshi*, II, 523 (FB 2.1.4). See also Inaba, *Manshū hattatsu shi*, pp. 439–41.

52. Chiang Kai-shek, *China's Destiny and Chinese Economic Theory*, edited by Philip Jaffe, New York, 1947, pp. 47–48.

53. Fan Wen-lan, *Chung-kuo chin-tai shih*, Hongkong, 1949, I, 202. On this Fan quotes Kuei-liang, Prince Kung, and Tseng Kuo-fan.

54. Bruce to Russell, Aug. 1, 1860, *Correspondence Respecting Affairs in China. 1859–1860*, p. 91.

55. Sun Yat-sen, "Third Lecture on Nationalism," *San Min Chu I; The Three Principles of the People*, translated by F. W. Price, Shanghai, 1929, pp. 55–59.

56. Feng, "Fu hsiang-chih i," *CPLKI*, Ch. 1, pp. 10–12b.

57. The point is elaborated in Meadows, *The Chinese and Their Rebellions*, p. 48.

58. Vincent Y. C. Shih, "The Ideology of the T'ai-p'ing T'ien-kuo," *Sinologica*, III, 1 (1951), 14.

59. For an outline of P'eng's career, see Ssu-yü Teng in *Eminent Chinese*, pp. 617–20. For treatment of P'eng as a Restoration leader combining military and literary abilities, see Ch'ai O, *Fan-t'ien-lu ts'ung-lu*, Ch. 5, pp. 20b–31b. Hsü Pin, "Tseng Hu t'an-wei," Part 15, in *Kuo-wen chou-pao*, VI, No. 45 (1929).

60. For general accounts, see Ch'ien Mu, *Chung-kuo chin san-pai nien hsüeh-shu shih*, Shanghai, 1937; Ch. 12 deals with Tseng and Lo Tse-nan. Ch'ien Chi-po, *Hsien-tai Chung-kuo wen-hsüeh shih*, Shanghai, 1933; a long section on Wang K'ai-yün includes extensive treatment of philosophy in the T'ung-chih period. Hellmut Wilhelm, "The Background of Tseng Kuo-fan's Ideology," *Asiatische Studien*, III, 3/4 (1949), 90–100, is a brilliant introduction to Restoration thought.

61. Hsün Ho, "Hsin hsüeh p'ien," in *Chung-ho*, I, 1 (1940), 7; pp. 1–9 provide a general review of the scholarship of the period.

62. Feng Yu-lan, "Chu Hsi che-hsüeh," *Ch'ing-hua hsüeh-pao*, VII, 2 (1932), 18–21 and *passim*.

63. Wu Wen-ch'i, "Chin pai-nien lai ti Chung-kuo wen-i ssu-ch'ao," in symposium of same title, *Hsüeh-lin* monograph series, No. 1, 1940, pp. 1–10.

64. Liang Ch'i-ch'ao, in *Ch'ing-hua hsüeh-pao*, I, 1 (1924), 32–34.

65. Lo Erh-kang, *Hsiang-chün hsin-chih*, pp. 63, 75–80.

66. Wu Wen-ch'i, *loc. cit.*, pp. 6–8; Hsü Pin, "Tseng Hu t'an-wei," Part 16, *Kuo-wen chou-pao*, VI, No. 50 (1929); Ai Na, "Hsiang-hsiang hsüeh chi," *Chung-ho*, V, 7–8 (1944), 1–14.

67. On the decline of the T'ung-ch'eng school, see in addition to the above works, Hu Shih, "Wu-shih nien lai Chung-kuo chih wen-hsueh," Shen-pao kuan Fiftieth Anniversary Publication, Vol. II, *Wu-shih nien lai chih Chung-kuo*, Shanghai, 1922, pp. 3–5; Hiromu Momose in *Eminent Chinese*, pp. 870–72; Henri Van Boven, *Histoire de la littérature chinoise moderne*, Peiping, 1946, pp. 7–8.

68. The most interesting single collection of materials of this type is Wu T'ing-tung (Hsing-ju) (1793–1873), *Cho hsiu chi*, 1871 (TC-10). During the Restoration, Wu, a leading philosopher, was first financial commissioner of Shantung, then judicial commissioner of Chihli. The work includes correspondence with Wo-jen, Tseng, and others, and essays on the thought of the Sung and later periods. The prefaces and postfaces deal with ideas more than with texts. His letters to his grandsons and his discussions with the family tutor are particularly revealing.

69. Representative statements are legion. Two classic memorials of Wo-jen, of 1862 (TC-1) and 1872 (TC-11), are fair examples (*THTKTI*, Ch. 2, pp. 4, 11, 13b).

70. *NCH*, Aug. 14, 1868.

71. See Arthur F. Wright, "Struggle vs. Harmony: Symbols of Competing Values in Modern China," *World Politics*, VI, 1 (1953), 31–44; Derk Bodde, "Harmony and Conflict in Chinese Philosophy," in Arthur F. Wright (ed.), *Studies in Chinese Thought*, Chicago, 1953, pp. 19–80.

72. Kung ch'in-wang, I-hsin [Prince Kung], *Lo-tao-t'ang wen-ch'ao*, n.p., 1867–68, Ch. 1, p. 5.

73. *Ibid.* For Tseng Kuo-fan's views on the *li*, see Hellmut Wilhelm, "The Background of Tseng Kuo-fan's Ideology," *Asiatische Studien*, III, 3/4 (1949), 96–97.

74. *NCH*, Aug. 14, 1868.

75. The *Book of Changes* and its commentaries have been considered major examples of dialectical philosophy. For an introduction, see Richard Wilhelm, *I Ging, Das Buch der Wandlungen*, Jena, 1924; Hellmut Wilhelm, *Die Wandlung, Acht Vorträge zum I-Ging*, Peiping, 1944; A. A. Petrov, *Van Bi: Iz istorii kitaiskoi filosofii*, Moscow, 1936, reviewed at length by Arthur F. Wright, in *HJAS*, X, 1 (1947), 75–88.

76. James Legge (trans.), *The Yi King*, Oxford, 1882, p. 383. For representative examples of the frequent use of this quotation in many contexts, see memorial of the governor of Fukien, Wang K'ai-t'ai, on abolition of sale of rank, *CHTI*, Ch. 1, pp. 36–42b; memorial of the censor Ch'en Hung-i, *ibid.*, Ch. 2, pp. 31–32b; letter of Li Hung-chang to the Tsungli-yamen, 1864, in *Chin-tai Chung-kuo wai-chiao shih tzu-liao chi-yao*, compiled by Chiang T'ing-fu, Shanghai, 1931 *et seq.*, I, 365; Hsü Chi-yü on reform of salt administration, *Sung-k'an hsien-sheng wen-chi*, p. 10.

77. Williams, *The Middle Kingdom*, II, 742. This is the concluding sentence of the book.

78. If one compares the general tone of the documents and essays in the *Kuo-ch'ao wen-lu* and the *Huang-ch'ao ching-shih wen-pien*, both of the Tao-kuang period, with that of *CSWP*, for example, the T'ung-chih materials seem by contrast bold, inquiring, even radical.

79. Compare the materials from the 1860's with those from the 1890's in *THTKTI*, *WHTK*, or any of the several classified compendia of documents and essays covering both the T'ung-chih and Kuang-hsü periods.

80. *NCH*, Apr. 28, 1860. Editorial comment on a letter signed W. H. O. The writer stated that in the view of his Chinese friends the fall of dynasties in China was the result of "their non-appreciation of the maxim of yih . . . that (when a system is) exhausted it should be modified; modified it will act; so acting it will endure."

81. *Ibid.*, Mar. 4, 1867.

82. Letter of late 1869, in R. Wardlaw Thompson, *Griffith John*, London, 1906, pp. 253–54.

83. *China. No. 5. (1871)*, p. 96.

84. Robert Hart, "Mr. Hart's Note on Chinese Matters," Peking, June 30, 1869, reprinted as Appendix II to Gumpach, *The Burlingame Mission*, pp. 876–77.

85. Chinese text of Wade's memorandum, received by Tsungli-yamen Mar. 5, 1866, presented to the Throne April 1, 1866, *IWSM-TC*, Ch. 40, pp. 23–36.

86. Feng Kuei-fen, "Ts'ai hsi-hsüeh i," *CPLKI*, Ch. 2, pp. 70b–71. In this essay Feng proceeds to analyze with great insight the way in which certain kinds of Western learning might be grafted on to a Chinese base, provided the Chinese base were itself

re-examined and restored. Huang Ts'ui-po's comment that Feng is in this passage advocating the adoption of Western culture, as Itō later urged in Japan, is wide of the mark indeed (Huang Ts'ui-po, "Ch'i-shih nien ch'ien chih wei-hsin jen-wu Feng Ching-t'ing," *Chung-shan wen-hua chiao-yü kuan chi-k'an*, IV, 3 (1937), 979).

This general problem is ably analyzed in Hellmut Wilhelm, "The Problem of Within and Without, a Confucian Attempt in Syncretism," in "Chinese Reactions to Imported Ideas, a Symposium," *Journal of the History of Ideas*, XII, 1 (1951), 48–60.

87. Feng, preface to *CPLKI*, pp. 2b–3.

88. E.g., edict, n.d., in *Peking Gazette*, translated in *NCH*, Dec. 21, 1860; *THTKTI*, Ch. 1, pp. 12b–23; edicts of Sept. 2 and Sept. 3, 1868, *SL-TC*, Ch. 238, pp. 10–11b and pp. 16b–17b.

89. A useful account of Tseng's views on these subjects is found in Ho I-k'un, *Tseng Kuo-fan p'ing-chuan*, [Shanghai] 1937, which is topically arranged. See also Chiang Hsing-te, *Tseng Kuo-fan chih sheng-p'ing chi ch'i shih-yeh*, Shanghai, 1939; Hsiao I-shan, *Tseng Kuo-fan*, Nanking, 1946, p. 177; Ch'en Ch'i-t'ien, *Hu Tseng Tso p'ing-luan yao-chih*, Shanghai, 1932, pp. 4–6.

90. On Feng, see Huang Ts'ui-po, *loc. cit.*, pp. 969–91; Momose Hiromu, "Fū Kei-fun to sono chojutsu ni tsuite," *Tōa Ronsō*, No. 2 (1940), pp. 95–122 (*FB* 2.5.1); Inaba Iwakichi, *Shina seijishi kōryō*, Tokyo, 1918, pp. 284–302 (*FB* 2.1.3). For Tseng Kuo-fan's high opinion of Feng, see Tseng's letter to Feng, reproduced as a preface to the 1898 edition of *CPLKI*. Chinese Communist scholars have been interested in Feng as a product of the "reformism of the upper intelligentsia," but have been inclined to dismiss him as a "landlord-bureaucratic intellectual," e.g., Shih Hsün and others, *Chung-kuo chin-tai ssu-hsiang chiang-shou t'i-kang*, Peking, 1955, p. 52.

91. Feng Kuei-fen, "Sheng tse-li i," *CPLKI*, Ch. 1, pp. 14b–16b.

92. *CHTI*, Ch. 3, pp. 17b–19b.

93. 1869 (TC-8), extract in *WHTK*, p. 7618. Liu is identified in Chang Nien-tsu, *Chung-kuo li-tai shui-li shu-yao*, Tientsin, ca. 1931, pp. 150–51.

94. Memorial of Apr. 17, 1862, *CSK*, "Pen-chi," Ch. 21, pp. 5b–6.

95. *CHTI*, Ch. 1, pp. 36–42b.

96. E.g., memorials of the following: the censor Yu Pai-ch'uan, *CHTI*, Ch. 8, pp. 14–15b; the censor Ma Yüan-jui, *ibid.*, Ch. 1, pp. 17–19; the censor Wang Tao-yung, *ibid.*, Ch. 3, pp. 7–8b; Seng-ko-lin-ch'in, *ibid.*, Ch. 8, pp. 10–11; proposals of Li Shu-ch'ang and Li T'ang-chieh, *Eminent Chinese*, p. 483.

CHAPTER V

1. Li Kao, "Chung-ch'ang T'ung ti cheng-chih ssu-hsiang," *She-hui k'o-hsüeh chi-k'an*, IV, 3/4 (1924), 1.

2. On the general theory, see Prince Kung's essay "On the primacy in government of human ability" (Wei cheng i jen-ts'ai wei hsien lun"), *Lo-tao-t'ang wen-ch'ao*, Ch. 2, pp. 17b–19. See also Wo-jen's essay on the essentials of civil government, *Wo Wen-tuan kung i-shu*, chüan-mo. See also *CSK*, "Hsüan-chü chih," Sec. 4, pp. 9–9b, on the selection of men of talent as the basis of government.

3. Quoted in Ch'in Han-ts'ai, *Tso Wen-hsiang kung tsai hsi-pei*, Shanghai, 1946, p. 160.

4. Thomas F. Wade (trans.), *Decree of the Emperor of China Asking for Coun-*

sel, and the Replies of the Administration, 1850–51 . . . , London, 1878, pp. 24–28, 33, 35.

5. One cannot open the memorials of any official without quickly seeing an example. For statements by numerous leaders, see *CSWP*, Chs. 16 and 18, and *THTKTI*, Chs. 21–23. The memorials of Manchus are in the same vein as the memorials of Chinese. The point was elaborated in Hsüeh Fu-ch'eng, "Chung-hsing hsü-lüeh," 1868, in *Yung-an ch'üan-chi*, Ch. 2.

6. E.g., quotations in Wang Hsin-chung, "Fu-chou ch'uan-ch'ang chih yen-ko," *Ch'ing-hua hsüeh-pao*, VIII, 1 (1932), 5; Hsia Nai, "T'ai-p'ing t'ien-kuo ch'ien-hou Ch'ang-chiang ko-sheng chih t'ien-fu wen-t'i," *ibid.*, X, 2 (1935), 473.

7. With these two exceptions, the documents on administrative structure and procedure of the T'ung-chih period concern trivia. See *WHTK*, pp. 8733–8913, 8940, 11212–13.

8. Memorial of Tseng opposing the proposal of the censor Ch'en T'ing-ching, *CHTI*, Ch. 7, pp. 11–11b. Examples of this argument can be multiplied; e.g., memorial of Jui-lin and Chiang I-li, July 30, 1866: "The fault rests with the men, not with the law." (*IWSM-TC*, Ch. 42, p. 62.)

9. Chin Chao-t'ang, preface dated 1862 to *Chang kung hsiang-li chün-wu chi-lüeh*, 1910, Ch. 1, p. 1.

10. Ch'ai O (*Fan-t'ien lu ts'ung-lu*, Ch. 5, pp. 30–31b) has assembled illustrations of this point. Hai-yü lao-yü (pseud.), "Shuo Tseng Ti-sheng lun tzu," *Kuo-wen chou-pao*, VI, No. 36 (1929), is made up of excerpts from Tseng Kuo-fan's remarks on calligraphy in his diary. In a postface, the compiler quotes a man who had observed the general practice of calligraphy by Restoration leaders.

11. P'an Kuang-tan, "Chin-tai Su-chou ti jen-ts'ai," *She-hui k'o-hsüeh*, I, 1, (1935), 70 and *passim*.

12. Derived from figures given in T'ang Chi-ho, "Ch'ing-tai k'o-tao kuan chih jen yung," *She-hui k'o-hsüeh ts'ung-k'an*, I, 2 (1934), 153–62.

13. See *CSK*, "Chün-chi ta-ch'en nien-piao," hsia, pp. 11 ff. On the Tsai-yüan conspiracy, see Chapter II.

14. Translations of the "Edict Degrading the Prince of Kung," of Apr. 2, 1865, in *The Chinese and Japanese Repository*, III (July 1, 1865), 351, and in *NCH*, Apr. 22, 1865. Further edict, *NCH*, Apr. 29, 1865. For a translation of the edict of reinstatement of May 8, 1865, see *NCH*, June 3, 1865. For a translation of the edict of Nov. 1, 1865, expunging the April edicts from the record, see *NCH*, Dec. 9, 1865. For chronological outlines of Prince Kung's degradation and reinstatement, see Wu Tseng-ch'i, *Ch'ing-shih kang-yao*, Ch. 12, pp. 11–11b, and Yin Luan-chang, *Ch'ing-chien kang-mu*, Shanghai, 1936, p. 687.

15. See his collected works published in 1882 under the title *Wen Wen-chung kung shih-lüeh*, 4 chüan.

16. Freeman-Mitford, *The Attaché at Peking*, p. 85.

17. Letter of the Professor of English (not otherwise identified) at the T'ung-wen kuan to *NCH*, Jan. 25, 1870, quoted in Gumpach, *The Burlingame Mission*, p. 656.

18. *NCH*, Feb. 29, 1868.

19. Tientsin correspondent in *NCH*, Dec. 14, 1867.

20. Alcock to Stanley, Jan. 1, 1868, *China. No. 5. (1871)*, p. 114. Presumably the Grand Council was meant.

21. Quoted in W. A. P. Martin, *A Cycle of Cathay*, pp. 360–63.

22. Burlingame to Seward, Oct. 25, 1862, *Foreign Relations of the United States, 1863*, Part 2, p. 831.

23. Williams, *The Middle Kingdom*, II, 715.

24. Juliet Bredon, *Sir Robert Hart*, New York, 1909, p. 221. On the close relations between Hart and Wen-hsiang, see Stanley F. Wright, *Hart and the Chinese Customs*, pp. 198–99.

25. Martin, *A Cycle of Cathay*, pp. 360–63.

26. See excerpts from Weng T'ung-ho's writings in Chin-liang, *Chin-shih jen-wu chih*, n.p., n.d., p. 50; Chin-liang, *Ssu-ch'ao i-wen*, n.p., n.d., p. 17b.

27. E.g., Liu Fa-tseng, *op. cit.*, p. 117; Lo Yüan-kun, *Chung-kuo chin pai-nien shih,* [Shanghai] 1933, I, 169; Ch'en Huai, *Chung-kuo chin pai-nien shih-yao*, Canton, 1938, Ch. 10.

28. Liang Ch'i-ch'ao, *Li Hung-chang*, n.p., n.d., p. 5.

29. Bourne, "Historical Table . . . ," *loc. cit.*, p. 324; *Eminent Chinese*, p. 100.

30. There are no studies of his career, and apparently he left no collected works. His memorials are scattered through such collections as *THTKTI, CSWP*, and *WHTK*. The frequent but brief *SL* references provide a very limited picture of the man. I have discovered only one of his writings other than scattered memorials—a narrative of his journey to Kwangtung in 1861–62 as an examination official: Shen Kuei-fen, "Shen Wen-ting Yüeh yao jih-chi," *Chung-ho*, I, 4 (1940), 95–103; I, 5 (1940), 79–84; I, 6 (1940), 92–98.

31. H. S. Tseng in *Eminent Chinese*, pp. 485–86.

32. Li's diary, *Li Wen-ch'ing kung jih-chi*, Ch. 16, under dates May 26 and June 11, 1862.

33. Text in Li's works, *Li Wen-ch'ing kung i-shu*, Ch. 1, pp. 1–8; also in *THTKTI*, Ch. 1, pp. 12b–13b.

34. Wu T'ing-tung, *Cho hsiu chi*, Ch. 9, p. 19b.

35. *Li Wen-ch'ing kung jih-chi*, Ch. 15, under dates Aug. 12–23, 1861.

36. Chin Chao-tzu, *Chin-shih Chung-kuo shih*, Shanghai, 1947, pp. 122–23. Gideon Chen also frequently contrasts the reactionary court with the progressive viceroys, but gives no evidence (e.g., *Tso Tsung-t'ang*, p. 84).

37. There is no shortage of material for the study of Tseng. His voluminous published writings are available in many editions, and he also figures largely in the writings of his contemporaries. Yet two earlier works in English (by W. J. Hail and Gideon Chen) deal with limited aspects of his career, and the numerous Chinese and Japanese studies to date are less than full and balanced biographies.

38. Mary C. Wright, "From Revolution to Restoration: The Transformation of Kuomintang Ideology," *FEQ*, XIV, 4 (1955), 515–32. See also Chapter XII.

39. Bland and Backhouse, *China Under the Empress Dowager*, pp. 64–65.

40. On the meanings of the various "temple names" and their relative distinction, see Hsü Pin, "Tseng Hu t'an-wei," Part 3, *Kuo-wen chou-pao*, VI, 29 (1929), 3. For an amusing account of the specific virtues the various "temple names" of Restoration statesmen were intended to indicate, see also *Chung-ho*, I, 4 (1940), 103.

41. See, for example, the eulogistic memorial of the governor of Kiangsu, Ho Ching, in *CHTI*, Ch. 6, pp. 1–8, and other similar memorials in the same collection.

42. Ojima Sukema, "Sō Koku-han," in Yoshikawa Kōjirō (ed.), *Chūka rokujū meika genkō roku*, Tokyo, 1948, pp. 267–81, based on Tseng's diary.

43. I have used the "classified" edition of Tseng's diary, where excerpts are arranged by subject rather than date: *(Hsin-shih piao-tien) Tseng Kuo-fan jih-chi lei-ch'ao*, Shanghai, 1923, pp. 39, 40, 135–216, and *passim*.

44. Letter to Tseng Kuo-ch'üan in *Tseng Wen-cheng kung hsüeh-an*, p. 372.

45. *Tseng Kuo-fan jih-chi lei-ch'ao*, pp. 146–47.

46. Chu Ch'i-hua calls Tseng a murderer and worse, but, when using Tseng's figures on the cost of living in Peking, warns the reader that these may be unrealistically low "because Tseng himself was very frugal and spent little." (*Chung-kuo chin-tai she-hui shih chieh-p'ou*, Shanghai, 1933, p. 16.)

47. A. Egmont Hake, *Events in the Taeping Rebellion*, London, 1891, p. 463.

48. Ch'en Ch'ing-ch'u, preface to *Tseng Ti-sheng chih tzu-wo chiao-yü*, Chungking, 1942; Wilhelm, "The Background of Tseng Kuo-fan's Ideology," *Asiatische Studien*, II, 3/4 (1949), 94.

49. Chiang Hsing-te, *Tseng Kuo-fan chih sheng-p'ing chi ch'i shih-yeh*, pp. 166–68.

50. T'ang Ch'ing-tseng, "Tseng Kuo-fan chih ching-chi ssu-hsiang," *Ching-chi hsüeh chi-k'an*, V, 4 (1935), 52–60.

51. See references to Tseng's memorials on various topics throughout the present book.

52. This charge is made in all Communist works.

53. E.g., Cordier, *Relations*, I, 446–47.

54. *NCH*, Jan. 7, Aug. 5, Dec. 9, 1865; Aug. 28, 1868. See also Sept. 19, 1868. *Daily Press*, reprinted in *NCH*, Sept. 11, 1868.

55. *NCH*, Oct. 31, 1868; italics mine. For a general appraisal of Tseng on the occasion of his transfer to Chihli, see *ibid.*, Oct. 27, 1868.

56. Cordier, *Relations*, I, 446–47. For an anthropologist's analysis of Tseng's personality, see Francis L. K. Hsu, *Under the Ancestor's Shadow*, New York, 1948, pp. 282–84.

57. "Historical Notes," *I-ching*, No. 15, p. 15. See also Hsü Pin, "Tseng Hu t'an-wei," Parts 11–14, *Kuo-wen chou-pao*, VI, Nos. 40–43 (1929); Ch'ai O, *Fan-t'ien lu ts'ung-lu*, Ch. 5, pp. 8–20; Ch'in Han-ts'ai, *Tso Wen-hsiang kung tsai hsi-pei*, concluding eulogy and *passim*.

58. In Li's collected works (*Li Wen-chung kung ch'üan-chi*, edited by Wu Ju-lun, 1908), "Tsou-kao," Chs. 1–16 deal with the T'ung-chih period. They concern precise and concrete problems, such as the recovery of the bean trade for Chinese merchants, rather than the nature of the threat to Confucian society.

59. See Li's memorial of Apr. 22, 1870, acknowledging Feng's help, *ibid.*, "Tsou-kao," Ch. 16, p. 24.

60. See, for example, the edict of Dec. 17, 1861, enjoining all provincial degreeholders throughout the country to take Tseng Kuo-fan, Hu Lin-i, and Lo Ping-chang as their models (*CSK*, "Pen-chi," Ch. 21, p. 3b).

61. Ch'ai O regarded Hu as *the* great man of the era (*Fan-t'ien-lu ts'ung-lu*, Ch. 5, pp. 1–7b), and K'ang Yu-wei honored him particularly (*K'ang Nan-hai kuan-chih i*, n.p., n.d., Ch. 6, pp. 5–6). See also Hsü Pin, "Tseng Hu t'an-wei," *loc. cit.*, especially Part 2.

62. For accounts of Chiang's work, see *NCH*, Oct. 19, 1867, and Mar. 4, 1868. On the investigation, see *SL-TC*, Ch. 207, pp. 20b–22; Ch. 216, pp. 5–7; Ch. 217, pp. 11–11b; Ch. 219, pp. 18b–19.

63. Outlines of the careers of all these men may be found in *Eminent Chinese*.

64. Tseng Kuo-fan argued this point at greater length than any other official. For summaries of his views, see Ho I-k'un, *Tseng Kuo-fan p'ing-chuan*, pp. 317–69, and Chiang Hsing-te, *Tseng Kuo-fan chih sheng-p'ing chi ch'i shih-yeh*, pp. 149–52.

65. On this point, see Ch'en Ch'i-t'ien, *Hu Tseng Tso p'ing-luan yao-chih*, Ch. 3; Wang Chih-p'ing, *Tseng Hu Tso ping-hsüeh kang-yao*, pp. 65–75 and *passim*.

66. Quoted in Ch'in Han-ts'ai, *Tso Wen-hsiang kung tsai hsi-pei*, pp. 160–61.

67. For illustrative notations in Tseng's diary about the people he interviewed, see *Tseng Kuo-fan jih-chi lei-ch'ao*, pp. 126–36; Chiang Hsing-te, *op. cit.*, pp. 145–49. Tseng's lectures to his staff after meals are recorded in the diary of one of his personal aides, Chao Hui-fu. See Ch'en Nai-ch'ien (ed.), "Tseng Wen-cheng kung yü-lu," *Ku-chin*, No. 41 (1944), pp. 27–31.

68. Letter to Tseng Kuo-ch'üan, in *Tseng Wen-cheng kung hsüeh-an*, pp. 368–71.

69. For examples, see *ibid.*, pp. 293–309, and Tso Kung, "Tseng Kuo-fan p'ing-i tang-shih jen-wu," in *Ku-chin*, No. 41 (1944), pp. 29–32.

70. *Tseng Wen-cheng kung hsüeh-an*, "Hsüeh-shu lei," *passim*.

71. Quoted in Wang Chih-p'ing, *op. cit.*, p. 80.

72. See memorials by Tseng, Hu Lin-i, Liu Ch'ang-yu, and others reporting on able men in their own provinces (*THTKTI*, Ch. 1, pp. 29–32b and *passim*).

73. Quoted in Wang Chih-p'ing, *op. cit.*, p. 81.

74. Memorial of Oct. 3, 1868, in *Ting Wen-ch'eng kung tsou-kao*, Ch. 6, pp. 17–18, and *THTKTI*, Ch. 21, pp. 5b–6.

75. Kuo, *Yang-chih shu-wu ch'üan-chi*, "Tsou-su," Ch. 10, pp. 1–3. Kuo's memorial is undated, but he would not have called Li a local scholar after his appointment to Peking.

76. *Feng Ching-t'ing hsing-chuang*, n.p., n.d., pp. 2–3.

77. Memorial of July 14, 1866, *IWSM-TC*, Ch. 42, pp. 45–48; for Tso's views on the need for "irregular methods" in the northwestern crisis, see also Wang Chih-p'ing, *op. cit.*, pp. 85–88.

78. For examples of recommendations and of the action taken, see *SL-TC*, Ch. 202, pp. 18b–19; Ch. 204, pp. 24b–25b; Ch. 206, pp. 18b–19; Ch. 207, pp. 28b–29; Ch. 208, pp. 4–5; Ch. 214, pp. 18–19; and *WHTK*, p. 8506, edicts of 1862 (TC-1) and 1863 (TC-2).

79. *Translation of the Peking Gazette for 1873*, p. 68.

80. E.g., memorial of Wang K'ai-t'ai, *CHTI*, Ch. 1, pp. 36–42b.

81. Miyazaki Ichisada, *Kakyo*, Osaka, 1946 (*FB* 6.7.1) is an admirable survey of the system.

82. For a classic description see Wang Ch'ing-yün, *Hsi-ch'ao chi-cheng*, Ch. 1, pp. 32b-52b. See also W. A. P. Martin, "Competitive Examinations in China" (written in 1868, reprinted in Martin, *The Chinese; Their Education, Philosophy and Letters*, New York, 1893); Williams, *The Middle Kingdom*, I, 565–66; Chung-li Chang, *The Chinese Gentry*, Seattle, 1955, Part 3.

83. Memorial of the censor Wang Tao-yung, *CHTI*, Ch. 3, pp. 7–8b.

84. Shen Kuei-fen, who as senior vice-president of the Board of Rites went to

Canton in 1861 as an examination official, commented in his diary of the journey that very few examinations had been held recently in the places through which he passed ("Shen Wen-ting Yüeh yao jih-chi," *loc. cit.*, Part 1).

85. *WHTK*, p. 8453; and Chiang Hsing-te, *Tseng Kuo-fan chih sheng-p'ing chi ch'i shih-yeh*, p. 158.

86. *WHTK*, pp. 8453–54. Edict of authorization, Apr. 2, 1867, *SL-TC*, Ch. 197, pp. 20b–21.

87. *WHTK*, p. 8571, dated 1866 (TC-5); see also Chang, *The Chinese Gentry*, pp. 79–80.

88. *WHTK*, p. 8454, dated 1869 (TC-8). See also Tso's memorial of 1873 (TC-12) on his efforts to extend the examination system in the northwest (*THTKTI*, Ch. 42, pp. 2–3).

89. Described in *NCH*, Oct. 19, 1867.

90. *Ibid.*, Sept. 28, 1867.

91. See article from *Hankow Times*, reprinted in *NCH*, Nov. 4, 1867. In 1870 between eight thousand and nine thousand candidates, of whom sixty-one were successful, were reported to have participated in the Hupeh examinations ("A Translation of Examination Papers Given at Wu-ch'ang," *China Review*, II, 5 (1874), 309–14). For further similar examples, see Chang, *The Chinese Gentry*, pp. 167–70.

92. Tientsin correspondent, *NCH*, May 30, 1868.

93. Martin, "Competitive Examinations in China," *loc. cit.*, pp. 40–53; for more detailed figures, see Chang, *The Chinese Gentry*, Part 2.

94. For increases authorized between 1867 and 1870, see *WHTK*, p. 8453.

95. *Peking Gazette*, Aug. 5, 1865, translated in *NCH*, Sept. 16, 1865.

96. *SL-TC*, Ch. 194, p. 14b.

97. *Ibid.*, Ch. 194, pp. 23b–24.

98. *THTKTI*, Ch. 42, pp. 6b–7 and *passim* for similar materials. For further examples, see Chang, *The Chinese Gentry*, pp. 83–92.

99. Sept. 13, 1868, *SL-TC*, Ch. 239, pp. 20b–21b; see also Chang, *The Chinese Gentry*, p. 92.

100. E.g., *WHTK*, pp. 8453–54.

101. *Ibid.*, p. 8453; *SL-TC*, Ch. 22, pp. 25–26b.

102. *Eminent Chinese*, p. 27.

103. *THTKTI*, Ch. 42, pp. 3b–4.

104. Chang, *The Chinese Gentry*, pp. 174–82; Inaba Iwakichi, "Chung-kuo she-hui chih pen-chih chi ch'i tso-yung," *Tung-fang tsa-chih*, XIX, 17 (1922), 45–46.

105. On the 1867 examinations, see *Hankow Times*, reprinted in *NCH*, Nov. 4, 1867. On the 1870 examinations, see "A Translation of the Examination Papers Given at Wu-ch'ang," *China Review*, II, 5 (1874), 309–14.

106. Edict of May 13, 1868, *SL-TC*, Ch. 230, pp. 1–4.

107. *NCH*, May 23, 1867. Tseng Kuo-fan also emphasized the need for reducing the number of officials-designate who were saturating the official hierarchy. See Ch'en Kung-lu, *Chung-kuo chin-tai shih*, Shanghai, 1935, I, 236–37.

108. *IWSM-TC*, Ch. 40, p. 15.

109. *Ibid.*, Ch. 41, pp. 43–50.

110. *NCH*, Apr. 14, 1866; Chang, *The Chinese Gentry*, p. 92, offers similar evidence.

111. Chang Chih-tung, *Ch'üan hsüeh p'ien,* "Pien Fa," translated in Ssu-yü Teng and John K. Fairbank (eds.), *China's Response to the West.* Cambridge, Mass., 1954, p. 170.

112. On the history of the sale of rank, see Feng Kuei-fen, "Pien chüan-li i," *CPLKI,* Ch. 1, pp. 17b–19b; Lo Yü-tung, *Chung-kuo li-chin shih,* Shanghai, 1936, I, 3–9; Hsü Ta-ling, *Ch'ing-tai chüan-na chih-tu,* Peking, 1950, Preface, Chs. 1 and 5.

113. *CSK,* "Hsüan-chü chih," Sec. 7, p. 1.

114. Chao Feng-t'ien, *Wan-Ch'ing wu-shih nien ching-chi ssu-hsiang shih,* Peiping, 1939, pp. 182–83.

115. Feng, "Pien chüan-li i," *loc. cit.*

116. *Ibid.*

117. *WHTK,* p. 8531.

118. Yen's statement on the increased number of sales at greatly reduced prices was confirmed by figures given in *NCH,* May 23, 1867.

119. *CHTI,* Ch. 2, pp. 21–24. For this and another memorial by Yen on the same subject, see *WHTK,* pp. 8531–33.

120. *WHTK,* p. 8531.

121. *CHTI,* Ch. 1, pp. 25–26b. Yü was from Fengtien, *chin-shih* of 1844 (TK-24).

122. *WHTK,* p. 8533, dated 1868 (TC-7).

123. *Ibid.,* pp. 8531–33.

124. On the organization of the Censorate, see T'ang Chi-ho, "Ch'ing-tai k'o-tao tsu-chih yen-ko," *Hsin she-hui k'o-hsüeh chi-k'an,* I, 1 (1934), 67–74; on its function, see T'ang Chi-ho, "Ch'ing-tai k'o-tao chih kung-wu kuan-hsi," *She-hui k'o-hsüeh lun-ts'ung,* I, 2 (1934), 207–13. See also Charles O. Hucker, "The Traditional Chinese Censorate and the New Peking Regime," *American Political Science Review,* XLV, 4 (1951), 1041–57; Hsiung-fei Li, *Les Censeurs sous la dynastie mandchoue (1616–1911) en Chine,* Paris, 1936.

125. On the statutory system of rewards and punishments of the Board of Civil Office, see Boulais, *Code chinois,* pp. 28–31, 40–46; Williams, *The Middle Kingdom,* I, 449.

126. *NCH,* Aug. 14, 1868.

127. E.g., *WHTK,* 1866 (TC-5), p. 8514.

128. *NCH,* Dec. 31, 1864.

129. For examples, see *SL-TC,* Ch. 194, pp. 21b–22, 33; Ch. 195, pp. 30–30b; Ch. 196, pp. 28–28b, 41b–42; Ch. 213, pp. 27–28; Ch. 214, pp. 21b–22b; Ch. 219, pp. 26–26b; Ch. 220, pp. 25–25b, 29b–30; Ch. 223, p. 7b; Ch. 225, pp. 5b–6b; Ch. 227, pp. 26–27; Ch. 233, p. 19; Ch. 240, pp. 24b–25.

130. E.g., *ibid.,* Ch. 233, pp. 18b–19.

131. *Ibid.,* Ch. 210, pp. 22–23; Ch. 213, pp. 11–11b; Ch. 214, pp. 11b–12; Ch. 216, pp. 23b–24; Ch. 220, pp. 21b–22; Ch. 234, pp. 9b–10b. S. Wells Williams lists six "official" faults: lack of diligence, inefficiency, superficiality, lack of talent, superannuation, and disease (*The Middle Kingdom,* I, 449).

132. *SL-TC,* Ch. 22, pp. 9–10; Wu Tseng-ch'i, *Chiang-shih kang-yao,* Ch. 12, p. 9b.

133. *WHTK,* p. 8531. Permanent discharge for a serious offense was here distinguished from ordinary discharge, the duration of which was not specified in the original judgment.

134. On this last point, see the memorial of the governor-general of Szechwan, Ch'ung-shih, *CHTI*, Ch. 2, pp. 29–30, and *SL-TC*, Ch. 195, pp. 29b–30.

135. E.g., Memorial of the censor Wen-ming, *CHTI*, Ch. 8, pp. 12–13b.

136. Ting Pao-chen, *Ting Wen-ch'eng kung tsou-kao*, Ch. 7, memorials 1, 2, and 4, autumn 1869.

137. See Knight Biggerstaff in *Eminent Chinese*, pp. 288–90.

138. E.g., joint memorial of three senior statesmen, Ch'i Chün-tsao, Wo-jen, and Li Hung-tsao, *CHTI*, Ch. 1, pp. 1–2. From the Restoration point of view, it was appropriate that such a memorial be the first document in a collection of Restoration materials.

139. For examples, see *SL-TC*, Ch. 195, pp. 31–31b; Ch. 201, pp. 27–27b; Ch. 203, pp. 19–19b; Ch. 206, pp. 4b–5, 5–5b, 25–26, 28b–29; Ch. 208, pp. 1b–2; Ch. 210, pp. 9b–11, 25b–26b; Ch. 211, pp. 8, 10b–11; Ch. 212, pp. 5–5b, 11–12; Ch. 213, pp. 11b–12, 13b–14; Ch. 214, pp. 4–5, 16–16b, 17b–18; Ch. 217, pp. 5–5b, 15b–16, 18–18b; Ch. 224, pp. 1b–2, 2–2b; Ch. 225, pp. 20–20b, 20b–22, 34–34b; Ch. 227, pp. 32b–33; Ch. 229, p. 16; Ch. 231, pp. 9b–10, 18–19; Ch. 232, pp. 16b–17, 31b–32; Ch. 234, pp. 20–21; Ch. 237, pp. 11–12; Ch. 239, pp. 10–10b.

140. For the case, see *ibid*, Ch. 194, pp. 20–21b; Ch. 200, p. 17; Ch. 202, pp. 4–5b; Ch. 215, p. 16b.

141. Hart, "spectator's memorandum," 1865, *IWSM-TC*, Ch. 40, pp. 19–19b.

142. Memorial of July 30, 1866, *IWSM-TC*, Ch. 42, pp. 58b–65b, item 8.

143. E.g., Feng Kuei-fen, "Hou yang-lien i," *CPLKI*, Ch. 1, pp. 7–9, and memorial of Wang K'ai-t'ai, *CHTI*, Ch. 1, pp. 36–42b.

144. *CHTI*, Ch. 2, pp. 27–30.

145. Memorial of May 29, 1866, *IWSM-TC*, Ch. 41, pp. 43–50.

146. Memorial of July 30, 1866, *ibid*., Ch. 42, p. 60.

147. Feng, "Mien hui-pi i," *CPLKI*, Ch. 1, pp. 6–7.

148. Hart, "spectator's memorandum," *IWSM-TC*, Ch. 40, p. 14.

149. See Charles J. Stanley, "The Mu-yu in the Ch'ing Dynasty" (ms. cited with author's permission). Ch'üan Tseng-yu, "Ch'ing-tai mu-liao chih-tu lun," *Ssu-hsiang yü shih-tai*, No. 31 (1944), pp. 29–35, and No. 32 (1944), pp. 35–43.

150. On the types of clerks, and the regulations concerning them and their functions, see Lienche Tu Fang, "A Preliminary Study of the Clerks, Yamen Runners and Personal Aides in the Ch'ing Officialdom" (ms. cited with author's permission). See also Naitō, *Shina ron*, pp. 46–48 (*FB* 1.4.1); Williams, *The Middle Kingdom*, I, 442, 478–79.

151. *Huang-ch'ao ching-shih wen hsin-pien* (to be distinguished from the *hsü-pien* (*CSWP*) hitherto cited), Shanghai, 1901, Ch. 18, shang, p. 12.

152. Feng, "I li-hsü i," *CPLKI*, Ch. 1, pp. 12b–14b.

153. *SL-TC*, Ch. 195, pp. 11b–12b.

154. Board of Punishments' report on a censor's charges in *Translation of the Peking Gazette for 1873*, p. 101.

155. Ku Yen-wu, Feng Kuei-fen, and Wang K'ang-nien may be taken as typifying the three eras. For representative statements by each, see *Chung-ho*, II, 10 (1940), 95. More extensive examples are to be found in the sections on clerks in *CSWP*, *CTLT*, and *WHTK*.

156. Feng, "I li-hsü i," *loc .cit.*

157. Li T'ang-chieh, *Li Wen-ch'ing kung i-shu*, Ch. 2, pp. 29–30.

158. For a review of the theory of the upright official and its political effectiveness in Chinese history, see Chang Shun-ming, "Hsün-li yü hsün-li chih cheng-chi," in *Cheng-chih ching-chi hsüeh-pao*, III, 2 (1935), 225–48.

159. K'ang Yu-wei, *K'ang Nan-hai wen-ch'ao*, Shanghai, 1916, ts'e 4, pp. 28–43b.

160. Ku Yüeh-tung, *Ch'ing-shih t'ung-su yen-i*, Shanghai, 1921, ts'e 8, pp. 56–56b.

CHAPTER VI

1. On the direct cost of the campaign against the Nien, see the figures in *Chiao-p'ing Nien-fei fang-lüeh*, compiled by an Imperial commission under the direction of Prince Kung, completed in 1872, Ch. 320, p. 42b. See also Chapters VIII and IX.

2. Memorial of Aug. 20, 1864, *IWSM-TC*, Ch. 27, p. 26b. On the relative importance in Chinese eyes of foreign aggression and domestic rebellion, see also *NCH*, Mar. 3, 1860.

3. Kuo T'ing-i, *T'ai-p'ing t'ien-kuo shih-shih jih-chih*, Shanghai, 1947, I, "Fan-li," 2; Lo Erh-kang, *Nien-chün ti yün-tung chan*, Changsha, 1939, pp. 14–18; Ssu-yü Teng, "The Nien-fei and Their Guerrilla Warfare," unpublished ms. cited with author's permission, chap. 3; Ch'ien Hung, "Nien-chün," in *T'ai-p'ing t'ien-kuo ko-ming yün-tung lun-wen chi*, Peking, 1950, pp. 122–25, based mainly on Li Hsiu-ch'eng's diary.

4. E.g., *SL-TC*, Ch. 194, pp. 15–17; Ch. 195, pp. 32–33; Ch. 196, pp. 3–4; *THL-TC*, Ch. 62, pp. 43b–44; Lo Erh-kang, *Nien-chün ti yün-tung chan*, p. 18.

5. Ling T'i-an, *Hsien-T'ung Kuei-chou chün-shih shih*, Shanghai, 1932, Part 5, Secs. 3 and 4.

6. E.g., Ch'ung-hou reported that arrested salt-bandit leaders had confessed that they had intended to join the Moslem rebels (edict of Mar. 17, 1868, *SL-TC*, Ch. 225, pp. 24–24b).

7. Quoted in Wang Chih-p'ing, *Tseng Hu Tso ping-hsüeh kang-yao*, p. 9.

8. Documents on the Taiping dominate the *SL* and other general collections of Ch'ing documents, as well as the memorials of contemporary statesmen. The chief specialized collections are *Chiao-p'ing Yüeh-fei fang-lüeh*, compiled by an Imperial commission under the direction of Prince Kung, completed in 1872, 420 +2 chüan; and *P'ing-ting Yüeh-fei chi-lüeh*, compiled by Tu Wen-lan, 1865 preface by Kuan-wen, printed in 1871 (TC-10), 22 chüan.

The most useful works for the general student are the earlier works of Lo Erh-kang: *T'ai-p'ing t'ien-kuo shih-kang*, Shanghai, 1937; and *T'ai-p'ing t'ien-kuo shih ts'ung-k'ao*, Shanghai, 1947 reprint of 1943 edition. The chief events are briefly but adequately summarized in Li Chien-nung, *Chung-kuo chin pai-nien cheng-chih shih*, Shanghai, 1947, I, 87–98. Good maps illustrating the campaigns, as well as extensive annals, are to be found in Kuo T'ing-i, *T'ai-p'ing t'ien-kuo shih-shih jih-chih*, Shanghai, 1947, 2 vols.

For the enormous standard bibliography on the Taiping Rebellion, see Ssu-yü Teng, *New Light on the History of the Taiping Rebellion*, Cambridge, Mass., 1950, and Vincent Yu-chung Shih, "Interpretations of the Taiping Tien-kuo by Noncommunist Chinese Writers," *FEQ*, X, 3 (1951), 248–57. On the massive collection, No. 2 in its documentary series, published by the Chinese Historical Commission (*T'ai-p'ing t'ien-kuo*, Shanghai, 1952, 8 vols.) and six other Chinese Communist publications on the subject, see review articles by Teng and by Mary C. Wright in *FEQ*, XII, No. 3

(1953). In the unending stream of more recent Communist publications, those by Lo Erh-kang are noteworthy. His *T'ai-p'ing t'ien-kuo shih-shih k'ao* (Peking, 1955) is a critical review of the evidence on a number of famous moot points in Taiping history. His *T'ai-p'ing t'ien-kuo shih-chi tsai-ting miao-chi* (Peking, 1955) and his *T'ai-p'ing t'ien-kuo shih-liao pien-wei chi* (Peking, 1955) deal with the authenticity of controversial texts. The latter is substantially different in content from his 1950 *T'ai-p'ing t'ien-kuo shih pien-wei chi.*

9. Yin Luan-chang, *Ch'ing-chien kang-mu*, Shanghai, 1936, p. 685.

10. See Eugene P. Boardman, *Christian Influence upon the Ideology of the Taiping Rebellion, 1851–1864*, Madison, Wis., 1952, chaps. ii and iii.

11. For a Chinese Communist listing of all the known sources from the Taiping side, including manuscripts abroad and materials preserved only in foreign translations, see Jung Meng-yüan in *T'ai-p'ing t'ien-kuo ko-ming yün-tung lun-wen chi*, compiled by the North China University Historical Research Institute, Peking, 1950, pp. 148–65. For facsimile reproductions of a number of documents, see Kuo Jo-yü (ed.), *T'ai-p'ing t'ien-kuo ko-ming wen-wu t'u-lu*, cheng, hsü, pu pien, Shanghai, 1952–55.

12. The Ch'ing appraisal of the Taiping Rebellion, as a basis for policy decisions, was set forth in *Tsei-ch'ing hui-tsuan*, compiled by a commission under the direction of Chang Te-chien, compiler's preface 1855, 4 chüan. For Wen-hsiang's analysis, see his ". . . nien-p'u," *Wen Wen-chung kung shih-lüeh*, Ch. 2, pp. 19–20. See also *P'ing-ting Yüeh-fei chi-lüeh*, Ch. 18, p. 23 and appendixes.

13. E.g., Yang Sung and Teng Li-ch'un, *Chung-kuo chin-tai shih ts'an-k'ao ts'ai-liao*, Yenan, 1940, I, 517–18; Chao Ch'un, *T'ai-p'ing t'ien-kuo*, n.p. [Honan], 1951.

14. Hu Che-fu, *Tseng Kuo-fan*, Chungking, 1944, pp. 21–22; Ch'en Ch'i-t'ien, *Hu Tseng Tso p'ing-luan yao-chih*, pp. 8–10.

15. Chu Ch'i-hua, *Chung-kuo chin-tai she-hui shih chieh-p'ou*, Shanghai, 1933, p. 105.

16. *WHTK*, p. 10849; Liu Fa-tseng, *Ch'ing-shih tsuan-yao*, Shanghai, 1914, p. 118.

17. Li Hung-chang's detailed reports on this phase of the campaign are included in *Li Wen-chung kung ch'üan-chi*, "Tsou-kao," Chs. 1–6, arranged chronologically; *IWSM-TC*, Ch. 22, pp. 3b–4; *Peking Gazette*, n.d., translated in *NCH*, Feb. 6, 1864.

18. *Peking Gazette* of Apr. 9 and Apr. 16, translated in *NCH*, May 28, 1864; *Peking Gazette* of Apr. 30, translated in *NCH*, June 4, 1864; *Peking Gazette* of May 12, translated in *NCH*, June 25, 1864; *Peking Gazette* of May 21, translated in *NCH*, June 18, 1864.

19. On the recovery of Nanking, see edicts of Aug. 1, Aug. 2, *et. seq.*, as translated in *NCH*, Aug. 27, Sept. 3, 1864; Mar. 1, Mar. 4, Mar. 11, and Mar. 18, 1865. The course of the whole rebellion was reviewed in these edicts. Much of the *NCH* material is summarized in Cordier, *Relations*, I, 226–34. See also Yin Luan-chang, *Ch'ing-chien kang-mu*, Shanghai, 1936, p. 684.

20. Memorial of Kuan-wen and Tseng Kuo-fan, July 26, 1864, translated in *NCH*, Feb. 18, 1865.

21. Preface to *P'ing-ting Yüeh-fei chi-lüeh.*

22. Boardman, *op. cit.,* pp. 35, 123–26, and chap. iii, *passim.*

23. Li Chien-nung, *Chung-kuo chih pai-nien cheng-chih shih*, Shanghai, 1947, I, 98–103.

24. George E. Taylor, "The Taiping Rebellion; Its Economic Background and Social Theory," *CSPSR*, XV, 4 (1933), 612–13.

25. The Nien-fei Rebellion, until recently the least-known, is now perhaps the best-known of the nineteenth-century rebellions, owing to the appearance of Siang-tseh Chiang's excellent study, *The Nien Rebellion*, Seattle, 1954. There is also an earlier unpublished study by Ssu-yü Teng, "The Nien-fei and Their Guerrilla Warfare," ms. cited with author's permission.

On the basic Ch'ing sources, the bibliography in Chiang's study is reasonably complete, except for the curious omission of the *SL*, which contains a great deal of material not to be found in the local histories, the histories of particular armies, or the collected writings of the chief leaders. Among accounts by contemporary foreigners, a long article from the *Hankow Times* (reprinted in *NCH*, May 6, 1867) is of particular interest.

Neither Chiang nor the Chinese Historical Commission has been able to discover records from the Nien side; the latter's documentary collection (*Nien-chün*, Shanghai, 1953, 6 vols.) consists of selected Ch'ing sources.

The most useful of the Chinese monographs is Lo Erh-kang's very short *Nien-chün ti yün-tung chan*, Changsha, 1939. The most interesting of the Japanese accounts is the highly uneven study to be found in Sano Manabu, *Shinchō shakai shi*, Tokyo, 1947, Part III, Vol. II (*FB* 2.1.4). There has been little or no Nationalist publication on the Nien; the recent Communist publication has been enormous, but on the whole popular in character.

26. Some information is to be found in Chiang, *The Nien Rebellion*, pp. 1–5; Teng, "The Nien-fei," pp. 6–7; Lo Erh-kang, *Nien-chün ti yün-tung chan*, pp. 14–18; and Sano, *op. cit.*, Part III, Vol. II, pp. 33–41.

27. Memorial of the governor of Shantung cited in "Notes and Queries," *China Review*, XII, 3 (1883), 207.

28. The evidence is reviewed in Chiang, *The Nien Rebellion*, pp. 7–8.

29. Teng, "The Nien-fei," chap. 2.

30. E.g., *CSK*, "Pen-chi," pp. 2, 5, 5b.

31. Chiang, *The Nien Rebellion*, pp. 75-102.

32. Lo Erh-kang, *Nien-chün ti yün-tung chan*, pp. 37–41; Wu Tseng-ch'i, *Ch'ing-shih kang-yao*, Ch. 12, pp. 11b–12.

33. On the Nien organization, see Teng, "The Nien-fei," chap. 3; Chiang, *The Nien Rebellion*, Part 1.

34. Lo Erh-kang, *Nien-chün ti yün-tung chan*, pp. 1–13, 23–26.

35. *NCH*, Feb. 23, 1867.

36. Chiang, *The Nien Rebellion*, p. 44.

37. Lo Erh-kang, *Nien-chün ti yün-tung chan*, p. 18; Teng, "The Nien-fei," chap. 3; *Huai-chün p'ing-Nien chi*, compiled by Chao Lieh-wen, n.p., n.d., Ch. 10, p. 13b.

38. Chiang, *The Nien Rebellion*, pp. 40–42 and Tables 1 and 2.

39. E.g., Chu Ch'i-hua, *Chung-kuo chin-tai she-hui shih chieh-p'ou*, p. 108; Chu, *Chung-kuo nung-ts'un ching-chi ti t'ou shih*, pp. 471–73; Chang Wen-ch'ing, *Nien-tang ch'i-i*, Shanghai, 1952; Ch'ien Hung, "Nien chün . . . ," *loc. cit.*, pp. 121, 125.

40. Chiang, *The Nien Rebellion*, p. 52.

41. *Ibid.*, pp. 86, 100.

42. Wu Tseng-ch'i, *Ch'ing-shih kang-yao*, Ch. 12, pp. 11b–12; Wen-hsiang, ". . . nien-p'u," *loc. cit.*, Ch. 3, p. 44b; *Peking Gazette* of Apr. 18–28, translated in *NCH*, May 27 and June 17, 1865.

43. The account of the new strategy in these two paragraphs is based on the following studies: Lo Erh-kang, *Nien-chün ti yün-tung chan*, pp. 50–58; Wu Tseng-ch'i, *op. cit.*, Ch. 12, pp. 12b–13; Sano, *op. cit.*, Part III, Vol. II, pp. 89–91. The new strategy was eulogized in the preface to Chao Lieh-wen's *Huai-chün p'ing-Nien chi*. According to Chiang, *The Nien Rebellion*, p. 100, "We can call this a new phase, not because the Nien were suppressed three years after the entry of Tseng but because his entry made their suppression possible."

44. Chiang, *The Nien Rebellion*, pp. 100–103. For text of Tseng's proclamation on this subject, see *Tseng Kuo-fan chiao-Nien shih-lu*, compiled by Lu Ti-p'ing, compiler's preface 1930, pp. 7–9.

45. Chiang, *The Nien Rebellion*, pp. 100–131. See also report of Chefoo correspondent in *NCH*, Jan. 16, 1868.

46. Lo Erh-kang, *Nien-chün ti yün-tung chan*, pp. 18–20; Chiang; *The Nien Rebellion*, pp. 103–6; *NCH*, July 15, 1865, and Feb. 3, 1866; article from *Hankow Times*, reprinted in *NCH*, Jan. 5, 1867.

47. Teng, "The Nien-fei," chap. 5, attributes Tseng's request to resign to the pressure of public opinion. See also Chiang, *The Nien Rebellion*, pp. 114–15; Wu Tseng-ch'i, *op. cit.*, Ch. 12, p. 13.

48. Lo Erh-kang, *Nien-chün ti yün-tung chan*, pp. 20–22, 45–49.

49. Wen-hsiang, ". . . nien-p'u," *loc. cit.*, Ch. 3, pp. 47b–48; *SL-TC*, Ch. 194, p. 4b and *passim*; Ch. 195, pp. 1–15. For campaign maps, see Kuo T'ing-i, *T'ai-p'ing t'ien-kuo shih-shih jih-chih*, Appendix IV.

50. This account is an abridged summary of daily documents that fill most of the *SL* from Ch. 198 to Ch. 208. See also special articles in *NCH*, July 5, July 19, July 22, July 27, Aug. 16, Aug. 21, Sept. 14, Oct. 25, 1867; Chiang, *The Nien Rebellion*, pp. 123–26.

51. This summary is based on the daily records that fill most of the *SL*, Ch. 209 to Ch. 220. See also *NCH*, Dec. 24, 1867, Jan. 5, Feb. 15, 1868; Teng, "The Nien-fei," chap. 3.

52. *SL-TC*, Ch. 202, pp. 14b–15; Ch. 203, pp. 19b–20b; Ch. 204, pp. 7b–9, 19–19b, 28–29b; Ch. 205, pp. 3–4b, 14b–15, 24–25; Ch. 206, pp. 15–15b, 16–16b, 26b–28; Ch. 207, pp. 13–14, 18b–19b; Ch. 214, pp. 8b–10; Ch. 216, pp. 32–33b; Ch. 217, pp. 6b–7b; Ch. 218, pp. 11b–12b, 16–17b; Ch. 220, pp. 5–6, 7–9, 12–13, 16b–20b; Ch. 221, pp. 2–3b, 13–13b, 24–28; Ch. 222, pp. 2b–4b.

53. Wen-hsiang, ". . . nien-p'u," *loc. cit.*, Ch. 3, pp. 58–61.

54. This summary of the final phase of the campaign against the Nien-fei is based on the daily documents that fill most of the *SL*, Ch. 224 to Ch. 238. See also the special reports in *NCH*, Mar. 14, Apr. 24, May 9, June 27, 1868; *Shan-tung chün-hsing chi-lüeh*, Ch. 9, pp. 1–9.

55. *SL-TC*, Ch. 237, pp. 30–34; Ch. 238, pp. 1b–2; *NCH*, Sept. 5, Sept. 11, 1868.

56. Lo Erh-kang, *Nien-chün ti yün-tung chan*, p. 50.

57. On Li Hung-chang's use of improved Western arms, see Chiang, *The Nien Rebellion*, pp. 116–22.

58. Studies on the Northwestern Moslem Rebellion, in either Chinese or foreign

languages, are far rarer than those on the Taiping or, if we include recent publications, the Nien-fei. The scarcity of information is indicated in Claude L. Pickens, *An Annotated Bibliography of Literature on Islam in China*, Hankow, 1950.

The standard short documentary history of the suppression of the rebellion is *P'ing-ting kuan-lung chi-lüeh*, compiled by Yang Ch'ang-chün, 1887. This work deals mainly with the period 1864–73. The long official history *P'ing-ting Shen Kan Hsin-chiang Hui-fei fang-lüeh*, 320 chüan, compiled by an Imperial commission under the direction of Prince Kung, covers 1855–1889. *SL* materials are of course abundant, and these have been the basic source for the present section. The chief earlier Chinese studies of Islam in China, all general in character, are Chin Chi-t'ang, *Chung-kuo Hui-chiao shih yen-chiu*, Peiping, n.d., [1935?]; Fu T'ung-hsien, *Chung-kuo Hui-chiao shih*, Changsha, 1940; Pai Shou-i, *Chung-kuo I-ssu-lan shih kang-yao ts'an-k'ao tzu-liao*, Shanghai, 1948.

The study of Chinese Moslem history has received considerable encouragement under the Chinese Communists. Volumes III and IV of the Chinese Historical Commission's *Hui-min ch'i-i* (Shanghai, 1952, 4 vols.) are devoted to northwestern uprisings throughout the Ch'ing period, with emphasis on the nineteenth century. According to the editor-in-chief, Pai Shou-i, who has long been a leading authority on Chinese Moslem history, no such publication would have been possible under the Nationalists. *Hui-min ch'i-i* offers virtually no documents from the Moslem side; the Ch'ing documents appear to be faithfully reproduced, including the use of the dog radical beside the character for Moslem. Other recent Communist publications include Pai Shou-i, *Hui-hui min-tsu ti hsin-sheng*, Shanghai, 1951; Ma Hsiao-shih, *Hsi-pei Hui-tsu ko-ming chien-shih*, Shanghai, 1951; and a number of vivid elementary accounts such as Tuan I, *Tsi-pei Hui-tsu ti fan-Ch'ing tou-cheng*, Shanghai, 1954. The Western literature is thin, as the references below will indicate, the most substantial source being H. M. D'Ollone and others, *Mission d'Ollone, 1906–1909; recherches sur les Musulmans chinois*, Paris, 1911. The only monographic study is Wen-djang Chu, "The Policy of the Manchu Government in the Suppression of the Moslem Rebellion in Shensi, Kansu, and Sinkiang from 1862 to 1878," Ph.D. dissertation, University of Washington, 1955, ms. cited with author's permission.

59. Pai Shou-i, *Hui-hui min-tsu ti hsin-sheng*, pp. 43, 62.

60. Fu T'ung-hsien, *op. cit.*, pp. 112–14.

61. Pai Shou-i, *Hui-hui min-tsu ti hsin-sheng*, pp. 43–45.

62. D'Ollone, *op. cit.*, pp. 245–46, 275, 307–11.

63. D'Ollone based this view on burial customs and on what he interpreted as a typically Sufist emphasis on the opposition between "interiorism" and "exteriorism" (*djaouri*, corrupted in China to *chaiherinye*); *ibid.*, pp. 273–77, 307–11.

64. In taking this view, Martin Hartmann challenged D'Ollone's observations and equated *chaiherinye* with *djahriye*, to pray aloud. It should be noted that Hartmann's article ("China," *Encyclopaedia of Islam*, Leyden, 1913, I, 839–54) is inaccurate on several well-established points, but he may be correct here.

65. J. J. M. De Groot, *Sectarianism and Religious Persecution in China*, Amsterdam, 1903, II, 311–29, based on Chinese texts that are included

66. Dazai Matsusaburō, *Shina Kaikyōto no kenkyū*, Dairen, 1924, avoided the question of the doctrinal affiliations of the New Teaching. Iwamura Shinobu reviewed the various Western theories and after his own extended field investigations

as far west as Paotow, concluded that the distinctions between the conservative Old Teaching, the reformist New Teaching, and the separatist New New Teaching (*Hsin hsin chiao*) were still so unclear as to require further systematic field research before their doctrinal affiliations could be established (*Chūgoku Kaikyō shakai no kōzō*, Tokyo, 1950–51, chap. 5. *FB* 6.4.7).

67. Saguchi Tōru ("Chūgoku Isuramu no shimpi shugi," *Tōhōgaku*, IX (1954), 75–92) describes the New Teaching as ritualistic mysticism characterized by prayers with head-shaking, chanting, miracles, and the worship of saints.

68. There are no references or hints in the works of A. J. Arberry and H. Lammens.

69. D'Ollone, *op. cit.*, pp. 267–68.

70. Pai Shou-i, *Hui-hui min-tsu ti hsin-sheng*, pp. 45–52; D'Ollone, *op. cit.*, p. 274; Saguchi, *loc. cit.*; Dazai, *op. cit.*, pp. 74–80.

71. Wu Tseng-ch'i, *Ch'ing-shih kang-yao*, Ch. 12, pp. 23b–24.

72. Pai Shou-i, *Hui-hui min-tsu ti hsin-sheng*, pp. 65–66.

73. E.g., *CSK*, "Pen-chi," Ch. 21, pp. 2, 4b, 6, 6b.

74. Chin Chi-t'ang, *Chung-kuo Hui-chiao shih yen-chiu*, pp. 191–94; Pai Shou-i, *op. cit.*, pp. 66–67; *CSK*, "Pen-chi," Ch. 21, p. 7b.

75. Pai Shou-i, *op. cit.*, pp. 66–67; Ma Hsiao-shih, *Hsi-pei Hui-tsu ko-ming chien-shih*, Shanghai, 1951, pp. 1–15. Ma emphasizes the Taiping aid, citing Lai Wen-kuang's autobiography and other sources. Further details on the various incidents are narrated in Wen-djang Chu, *op. cit.*, chap. 2.

76. Pai Shou-i, *op. cit.*, pp. 69–70. For a fuller account of Ch'ing strategy in the first two years, see Chu, *op. cit.*, chaps. 3 and 4.

77. Pai Shou-i, *op. cit.*, pp. 69–70; Ma Hsiao-shih, *op. cit.*, pp. 15–32. For further details on To-lung-a's campaigns, see Chu, *op. cit.*, chap 5.

78. Pai Shou-i, *op. cit.*, pp. 67–68; Wu Tseng-ch'i, *Ch'ing-shih kang-yao*, Ch. 12, pp. 5b, 9b, 10b–11, 12; *NCH*, Feb. 15, 1868. Materials on the Moslem rebels, February 1867 to September 1868, are heavily concentrated in *SL-TC*, Chs. 195–240. It is not feasible to reproduce the detailed references here. See also Wen-djang Chu, *op. cit.*, chaps. 6 and 7.

79. *SL-TC*, Ch. 239, pp. 7–8b.

80. E.g., *SL-TC*, Ch. 194, pp. 15b–17; Ch. 209, pp. 15–16b; Ch. 241, pp. 10–12b; Ch. 229, pp. 22–22b; Ch. 308, pp. 11–12b; Wang Chih-p'ing, *Tseng Hu Tso ping-hsüeh kang-yao*, pp. 6 ff.

81. D'Ollone, *op. cit.*, pp. 252–56.

82. For the complex details of Tso's campaigns in China proper, see Wen-djang Chu, *op. cit.*, chaps. 8 and 9, and chap. 10, Secs. 1–3.

83. Wu Tseng-ch'i, *op. cit.*, Ch. 12, pp. 19b–21; D'Ollone, *op. cit.*, pp. 271–72.

84. D'Ollone, *op. cit.*, pp. 273–74. The point was frequently made in Tso Tsung-t'ang's memorials.

85. Pai Shou-i, *Hui-hui min-tsu ti hsin-sheng*, pp. 70–71; Ma Hsiao-shih, *op. cit.*, pp. 38–44; Wu Tseng-ch'i, *op. cit.*, Ch. 12, pp. 21–23b; *SL-TC*, Ch. 307, pp. 14b–15b; D'Ollone, *op. cit.*, p. 273; W. L. Bayles, *Tso Tsung-t'ang*, Shanghai, 1937, chap. ix.

86. Edict of Mar. 22, 1871, *SL-TC*, Ch. 304, pp. 2–3b, 5b. See also battle scene labeled "Hui-fei," No. 13, depicting the victory (in possession of author).

87. E.g., *SL-TC*, Ch. 304, pp. 5b–7b, 9–10, 14–15b; Ch. 308, pp. 11–12b.

88. *Ibid.*, Ch. 306, pp. 5b–6b; Ch. 307, pp. 2b ff.; Ch. 308, pp. 11–12b. Battle scene labeled "Hui-fei," No. 14, depicting the capture of T'ung-kuei p'u (in possession of author).

89. The *SL* materials are concentrated in Chs. 302–10.

90. E.g., edict of June 24, 1868, *SL-TC*, Ch. 233, pp. 10–11b; Mar. 22, 1871, Ch. 304, pp. 5b–7.

91. D'Ollone, *op. cit.*, p. 236; Pai Shou-i, *op. cit.*, pp. 71–72, 90–92.

92. Wu Tseng-ch'i, *Ch'ing-shih kang-yao*, Ch. 12, pp. 23b; Pai Shou-i, *op. cit.*, p. 72.

93. See battle scene labeled "Hui-fei," No. 15 (in possession of author).

94. See battle scene labeled "Hui-fei," No. 16 (in possession of author); Wu Tseng-ch'i, *op. cit.*, Ch. 12, pp. 26–26b; Pai Shou-i, *op. cit.*, pp. 72–73.

95. D'Ollone, *op. cit.*, p. 268, based on the deposition of a literatus who had specialized on the Moslem Rebellion; confirmed by Ch'ai O, *Fan-t'ien-lu ts'ung-lu*, Ch. 5, p. 14, and Pai Shou-i, *op. cit.*, p. 73.

96. The revolt of the southwestern Moslems is the least studied of the nineteenth-century rebellions. The official documentary account is *P'ing-ting Yün-nan Hui-fei fang-lüeh*, 50 chüan, compiled by an Imperial commission under the direction of Prince Kung, completed in 1896. It is far shorter than the parallel accounts of other rebellions. The *SL* materials are abundant, but reflect the lesser Ch'ing understanding of what was happening in the southwest. Materials on the campaign to the turning point in 1868, which is the chief concern of the present section, are to be found throughout Chs. 196–228.

Fewer major officials served in Yunnan, hence less material is available from individual collections of memorials. Volumes I and II of the Chinese Historical Commission's *Hui-min ch'i-i* (Shanghai, 1952) deal with the Yunnan rebellion. Although a few fragmentary materials from Tu Wen-hsiu's kingdom are included, the main contents are excerpts from *P'ing-ting Yün-nan Hui-fei fang-lüeh*, from Ch'ing memorials, and from nonofficial accounts from the Ch'ing side.

Such local archives as were preserved in the Yunnan Provincial Library have apparently not been published. There is one excellent Chinese monographic study, Ho Hui-ch'ing, "Yün-nan Tu Wen-hsiu chien-kuo shih-pa nien shih-mo," published in five parts in *I-ching*, Nos. 12–16, 1936.

The chief Western sources are H. M. D'Ollone, *Mission d'Ollone, 1906–1909*, and the firsthand account of a Chinese Imperial Maritime Customs official who was in Yunnan from 1870 to 1873: Emile Rocher, *La Province choinoise du Yün-nan*, Paris, 1879–80, 2 vols. Marshall Broomhall, *Islam in China*, London, 1910, chap. viii, is based on Rocher. Georges Cordier, *Les Musulmans du Yunnan*, Hanoi, 1927, says little about the rebellion.

97. Memorial of 1865 (TC-4), *CSWP*, Ch. 83, pp. 6–7.

98. Ho Hui-ch'ing, *loc. cit.*, Part 1, pp. 9–12; Wang P'ei-ch'in, "Tu Wen-hsiu ko-ming chün ti t'uan-chieh wen-t'i," in *T'ai-p'ing t'ien-kuo ko-ming yün-tung lun-wen chi*, pp. 136–37, citing local histories; Dazai, *Shina Kaikyōto no kenkyū*, pp. 92–97.

99. Wang P'ei-ch'in, *loc. cit.*, pp. 137–38; Rocher, *op. cit.*, II, 29–57; Pai Shou-i, *Hui-hui min-tsu ti hsin-sheng*, pp. 53–56.

100. Rocher, *op. cit.*, II, 45, 55–56; Ho Hui-ch'ing, *loc. cit.*, Part 1, p. 10, and Part 5, p. 31.

101. According to a memorial of Ts'en Yü-ying, quoted in Ho Hui-ch'ing, *loc. cit.*, Part 1, p. 12. See also varying forms in prefaces to his translation, *Ho-yin Ma Fu-ch'u hsien-sheng i-shu Ta-hua tsung-kuei Ssu-tien yao hui*, reprinted in 1927.

102. He was referred to as Ma Ju-lung after his surrender to the Ch'-ing (Dazai, *op. cit.*, p. 94).

103. Rocher, *op. cit.*, II, 55; Pai Shou-i, *op. cit.*, pp. 53–56.

104. Rocher, *op. cit.*, II, 46–54; Pai Shou-i, *op. cit.*, pp. 56–58; Broomhall, *op. cit.*, p. 131; Wang P'ei-ch'in, *loc. cit.*, pp. 138–44; Ho Hui-ch'ing, *loc. cit.*, Part 1, pp. 12–16, Part 2, pp. 34–36.

105. Various prefaces, including Ma Te-hsin's own preface of 1865 at the age of 72 to *Ho-yin Ma Fu-ch'u hsien-sheng i-shu Ta-hua tsung-kuei Ssu-tien yao hui* and other shorter works. I have been unable to identify the original works of which these are allegedly translations. They may rather be Ma's own interpretations of the meaning of Islam, for which he would not, of course, claim original authorship.

106. D'Ollone, *op. cit.*, p. 206.

107. Rocher, *La Province chinoise du Yün-nan*, II, 71–72; Pai Shou-i, *Hui-hui min-tsu ti hsin-sheng*, pp. 56 ff.; Dazai, *Shina Kaikyōto no kenkyū*, p. 94.

108. D'Ollone, *op. cit.*, p. 206; Rocher, *op. cit.*, II, 72–77; Pai Shou-i, *op. cit.*, p. 53.

109. Rocher, *op. cit.*, II, 78; Ho Hui-ch'ing, "Yün-nan Tu wen-hsiu chien-kuo shih-pa nien shih-mo," *loc. cit.*, Part 1, p. 10.

110. E.g., *SL-TC*, Ch. 211, pp. 14–15; Ch. 240, pp. 30b–32.

111. Rocher, *op. cit.*, II, 82–83; Pai Shou-i, *op. cit.*, pp. 57–58.

112. *SL-TC*, Ch. 209, pp. 25–27; Rocher, *op. cit.*, II, 123.

113. *SL-TC*, Ch. 224, pp. 49–50; Ch. 227, pp. 12–13b, 30–31; Ch. 228, pp. 5b–7b; Ch. 231, pp. 2b–3b; Ch. 233, pp. 1b–2b; Ch. 234, pp. 18b–19b; Ch. 236, pp. 1–3b; Ch. 237, pp. 19–20; Ch. 239, pp. 12–14; Ch. 241, pp. 16b–18. Rocher, *op. cit.*, II, 110–17; Pai Shou-i, *op. cit.*, pp. 57–58.

114. Rocher, *op. cit.*, II, chaps. v–vi; Pai Shou-i, *op. cit.*, pp. 57–62; Ho Hui-ch'ing, *loc. cit.*, Part 3, pp. 36–39; Wang P'ei-ch'in, "Tu wen-hsiu ko-ming chün ti t'uan chieh wen-t'i," *loc. cit.*, p. 143; Chaoying Fang, in *Eminent Chinese*, pp. 742–46. Fang, in *Eminent Chinese*, pp. 742–46.

115. Rocher, *op. cit.*, II, 178–86.

116. Pai Shou-i, *op. cit.*, p. 62.

117. Wang P'ei-ch'in, *loc. cit.*, pp. 138–41, 145–46; Ho Hui-ch'ing, *loc. cit.*, Part 2, *passim*, Part 5, pp. 29–31; Pai Shou-i, *op. cit.*, pp. 57–58; D'Ollone, *op. cit.*, pp. 1–2.

118. Dazai, *op. cit.*, pp. 92–97; Pai Shou-i, *op. cit.*, pp. 62–63; Rocher, *op. cit.*, II, 111–13.

119. The official documentary history is *P'ing-ting Kuei-chou Miao-fei chi-lüeh*, compiled by an Imperial commission under the direction of Prince Kung, completed in 1896, 40 chüan. The present section is drawn largely from a comprehensive study, with extensive documentary inclusions, Ling T'i-an, *Hsien T'ung Kuei-chou chün-shih shih*, Shanghai, 1932, 5 parts in 8 vols. There is virtually nothing in Western languages; F. M. Savina's scholarly *Histoire des Miao* (Hongkong, 1930) makes no reference to the nineteenth-century rebellions.

120. Ling T'i-an, *op. cit.*, Part 1, p. 9, detailed chronology on pp. 10–18. On the Chinese rebellions, see Part 2, shang, chung, hsia; on the Miao rebellions, Part 3, shang, hsia; on the Moslem rebellions, Part 4.

121. *Ibid.*, Part 1, pp. 4–8.

122. *SL-TC*, Ch. 217, pp. 22b–23b.

123. Ling T'i-an, *op. cit.*, Part 5, p. 1; Wu Tseng-ch'i, *op. cit.*, Ch. 12, pp. 24b–26.

124. See documents scattered throughout *SL-TC*, Chs. 205–26.

125. *Ibid.*, Ch. 214, pp. 23–24; Ch. 215, pp. 25b–27, 29–29b; Ch. 216, pp. 8b–11; Ch. 217, pp. 5b–6b.

126. *Ibid.*, Ch. 218, pp. 14b–16.

127. *Ibid.*, Ch. 226, pp. 18b–20; Ch. 227, pp. 6b–7b.

128. See documents scattered throughout *SL-TC*, Chs. 195–241.

129. Wen-hsiang, ". . . nien-p'u," *loc. cit.*, Ch. 3, pp. 47b–52; *Peking Gazette* of Dec. 21, Dec. 22, 1864, translated in *NCH*, Mar. 4, 1865.

130. *SL-TC*, Ch. 229, pp. 16b–17.

131. *NCH*, Mar. 23, Apr. 8, 1867; *SL-TC*, Ch. 197, pp. 8–9b; Ch. 198, pp. 23b–24b; Ch. 203, pp. 10b–11; Ch. 206, p. 6b; Ch. 220, pp. 14b–15; Ch. 226, pp. 2b–4.

132. In addition to scattered *SL* references, *SL-TC*, Chs. 204–30, see memorial of Feng Tzu-ts'ai, 1868 (TC-7), *WHTK*, p. 9533.

133. All the first-rank Taiping kings except Hung Ta-ch'üan were Hakkas. Lo Hsiang-lin, *K'o-chia yen-chiu tao-lun*, Hingning, Kwangtung, 1933, p. 2 and Ch. 8, *passim.*

134. *Ibid.*, pp. 3–4; *China Mail*, reprinted in *NCH*, Jan. 29, 1867; biography of Jui-lin, *Ch'ing-shih lieh-chuan*, Ch. 46, pp. 36–39.

135. *SL-TC*, Ch. 196, pp. 36–36b; Ch. 197, pp. 23–24b; Ch. 199, pp. 11b–12b; Ch. 202, pp. 10–11; Ch. 232, pp. 2b–3.

136. Quoted in Wang Chih-p'ing, *Tseng Hu Tso ping-hsüeh kang-yao,* p. 9.

137. For a typical statement of this view, see memorial of the Honan director of education, 1863 (TC-2), in *THTKTI*, Ch. 23, pp. 18–18b.

138. E.g., *SL-TC*, Ch. 196, pp. 6–6b; Ch. 211, pp. 15b–16b; Ch. 216, pp. 34b–35b; Ch. 221, pp. 5–6, 17b–18; Ch. 229, p. 7; Ch. 237, pp. 8b–9, 18b–19; Ch. 240, p. 19b.

139. E.g., edict of 1862 (TC-1) in regard to Anhwei, *WHTK*, p. 8570.

140. *SL-TC*, Ch. 218, pp. 27–28.

141. Chiang, *The Nien Rebellion*, pp. 92–96; Teng, "The Nien-fei," chap. 3; *Peking Gazette*, translated in *NCH*, Oct. 24, 1863.

142. *SL-TC*, Ch. 236, pp. 20–21.

143. E.g., the case of a district magistrate and others in Kansu, *SL-TC*, Ch. 304, pp. 4b–5.

144. On Tung Fu-hsiang, *SL-TC*, Ch. 232, pp. 6b–7b; on Ma Chan-ao and the Hochow Moslems, *ibid.*, Ch. 304, pp. 5b–7. The factors in other cases are outlined in Ch. 196, pp. 35–36; Ch. 229, pp. 11b–13, 22–22b; on the Sining Moslems, Ch. 306, pp. 4b–5b.

145. E.g., *ibid.*, Ch. 223, pp. 11b–12b; Ch. 225, pp. 25–27; Ch. 229, pp. 3b–4b.

146. Thomas W. Kingsmill, "Retrospect of Events in China and Japan During the Year 1865," *JNCBRAS*, II (1865), 143.

147. *NCH*, Apr. 30, 1864.

148. Alabaster's report to the NCBRAS, *NCH*, Aug. 6, 1864.

149. Morton H. Fried, *Fabric of Chinese Society. A Study of the Social Life of a Chinese County Seat*, New York, 1953. Fried's data is for Chuhsien, Anhwei, and is based on local records and the accounts of local scholars.

150. Pai Shou-i, *Hui-hui min-tsu ti hsin-sheng*, pp. 73–74; Ma Hsiao-shih, *Hsi-*

pei Hui-tsu ko-ming chien-shih, p. 3; H. M. D'Ollone, *Mission d'Ollone, 1906–1909*, pp. 250, 256, 280–81, and *passim*.

151. Georges Cordier, *Les Musulmans du Yunnan*, p. 22.

152. Ho Hui-ch'ing, "Yün-nan Tu Wen-hsiu chien-kuo shih-pa nien shih-mo," *loc. cit.*, Part 5, pp. 31–33, citing *Yün-nan hsü t'ung-chih kao*; Pai Shou-i, *op. cit.*, pp. 62–63.

153. Ho Hui-ch'ing, *loc. cit.*, Part 5, pp. 31–33; Rocher, *op. cit.*, II, 29–30; D'Ollone, *op. cit.*, p. 6.

154. Ling T'i-an, *Hsien T'ung Kuei-chou chün-shih shih*, Part 5, pp. 37–37b. Full data are given in tabular form.

155. Hsüeh Shao-ming, *Ch'ien Tien Ch'uan lü-hsing chi*, Shanghai, 1938, pp. 25–26.

156. Lo Hsiang-lin, *K'o-chia yen-chiu tao-lun*, pp. 3–4.

157. Chiang, *The Nien Rebellion*, pp. 106–7.

158. E.g., *SL-TC*, Ch. 238, pp. 8–8b. See also Chapter VII.

159. *NCH*, Nov. 24, 1868.

160. Ting, *Ting Wen-ch'eng kung tsou-kao*, Ch. 6.

161. Text of Tso's memorial, *CSWP*, Ch. 18, pp. 5b–6b, and four edicts of Mar. 22, 1871, *SL-TC*, Ch. 304, pp. 2–7b; *THTKTI*, Ch. 25, pp. 9b–10b. For further details, see Wen-djang Chu, "The Policy of the Manchu Government in the Suppression of the Moslem Rebellion . . . ," chap. 10, Sec. 4.

162. Pai Shou-i, *op. cit.*, p. 70; D'Ollone, *op. cit.*, p. 256; Ma Hsiao-shih, *Hsi-pei Hui-tsu ko-ming chien-shih*, pp. 74–82; *SL-TC*, Ch. 196, pp. 35–36; Ch. 229, pp. 11b–13, 22–22b; Ch. 232, pp. 6b–7b; Ch. 233, pp. 10-11b.

163. *SL-TC*, Ch. 304, pp. 2–7b.

164. Rocher, *op. cit.*, II, 176–78.

165. Ling T'i-an, *Hsien-T'ung Kuei-chou chün-shih shih*, Part 5, p. 1, quoting Tseng Chi-feng.

166. *Ibid.*, Part 5, p. 6b, quoting Ch'en Pao-chen.

167. *Ibid.*, Part 5, *passim*.

168. *Ibid.*, Part 5, p. 37b. Ling based this conclusion on an examination of records of litigation in Kweichow for the sixty years following the suppression of open rebellion. These showed persistent confusion in both family and community matters.

169. Lo Hsiang-lin, *Ko-chia yen-chin tao-lun*, pp. 3–4.

170. Wen-hsiang, ". . . nien-p'u," *loc. cit.*, Ch. 3, pp. 52b–54.

CHAPTER VII

1. On the general problem of Ch'ing local control, see Matsumoto Yoshimi in Wada Sei (ed.), *Shina chihō jichi hattatsushi*, 1939, pp. 128–82 (*FB* 3.4.1); Kano Naoki, *Dokusho san'yo*, Tokyo, 1949 reprint, pp. 133–76 (*FB* 3.4.7); Kung-ch'uan Hsiao, "Rural Control in Nineteenth Century China," *FEQ*, XII, 2 (1953), 173-82; Wang Ch'ing-yün, *Hsi-ch'ao chi-cheng*, Ch. 2, pp. 17–22.

2. [Rutherford Alcock] "The Chinese Empire and Its Destinies," *Bombay Quarterly Review* (Apr. 1856), p. 249.

3. Oxenham's report, Mar. 1, 1869, in *Reports of Journeys in China and Japan Performed by Mr. Alabaster, Mr. Oxenham, Mr. Markham, and Dr. Wells of Her Majesty's Consular Service in Those Countries*, 1869, p. 21.

4. Quoted in Ling T'i-an, *Hsien T'ung Kuei-chou chün-shih shih*, Part 1, p. 6b.

5. Hsiao-t'ung Fei, *China's Gentry*, pp. 36, 77.

6. The best-documented study of the modern Chinese gentry is Chung-li Chang, *The Chinese Gentry*. Among the most important studies that take a different view are: Hsiao-t'ung Fei, *China's Gentry*; Fei's now classic essay, "Peasantry and Gentry," *American Journal of Sociology*, LII, reprinted by the Institute of Pacific Relations, New York, n.d.; Wu Han and Fei Hsiao-t'ung, *Huang-ch'üan yü shen-ch'üan*, Shanghai, 1948; Negishi Tadashi, *Chūgoku shakai ni okeru shidōsō*, Tokyo, 1947 (*F.B.* 8.3.2); Etienne Balázs, "Les Aspects significatifs de la société chinoise," *Asiatische Studien*, No. 6, pp. 77–87.

7. For a detailed analysis, see Chang, *The Chinese Gentry*, pp. 51–70 and Tables 33–35.

8. Balázs, "Les Aspects significatifs de la société chinoise," *loc. cit.*, pp. 83–86. Balázs also points out that a society of this type in which the elite control the technician invites corruption, nepotism, and a totalitarianism that kills invention.

9. Robert Redfield, Introduction to Fei, *China's Gentry*, p. 11.

10. For an account of the dependence of the local official on the local gentry, see Y. K. Leong and L. K. Tao, *Village and Town Life in China*, London, 1915, pp. 33–40 and chap. iii, *passim*.

11. Wang Feng-sheng in *Mu-ling shu chi-yao*, Ch. 6, pp. 25–25b. Other handbooks make the same point. See also Yung-teh Chow, "Six Life Histories of Chinese Gentry Families," Appendix to Fei, *China's Gentry*, pp. 221–23.

12. Williams, *The Middle Kingdom*, I, 520–21. On the role of the gentry as mediators between magistrate and people, in the service of the state, see also "Lex," "The Administration of Chinese Law," *China Review*, II, 4 (1874), 235.

13. Chiang Hsing-te, *Tseng Kuo-fan ti sheng-p'ing chi ch'i shih-yeh*, pp. 181–85.

14. The compilation of the *Chung-lieh pei-k'ao*, published in 1876, illustrates the pains the government took in this respect. See also *WHTK*, pp. 8469, 8576–77; *CHTI*, Ch. 4, pp. 36–37, and Ch. 5, pp. 23–24; and edict of Sept. 8, 1868, *SL-TC*, Ch. 239, pp. 2–3.

15. See Boulais, *Code chinois*, pp. 32–48; Chang, *The Chinese Gentry*, pp .32–50.

16. Sept. 23, 1873, in *Translation of the Peking Gazette for 1873*, p. 91. A similar report from Hu Chia-yü in Chekiang is included.

17. *Ibid.*, pp. 116, 121. Reference to such cases is frequent throughout the *Peking Gazette* and the *SL*.

18. Edict of May 27, 1868, *SL-TC*, Ch. 231, pp. 10b-11.

19. Balázs, "Les Aspects significatifs de la société chinoise," *loc. cit.*, pp. 81–82.

20. On the Ch'ing acceleration of the Ming policy of cultural assimilation by extending the examination system, etc., with particular reference to Yunnan, see Li Hsieh-fei, "Ch'ing-tai ching-ying hsia ti Yün-nan," *Tung-fang tsa-chih*, XLII, 17 (1946), 43–46.

21. Sheng Lang-hsia, *Chung-kuo shu-yüan chih-tu*, Shanghai, 1934; Leong and Tao, *op. cit.*, pp. 75–78.

22. Feng, "Ch'ou p'in-min i," *CPLKI*, Ch. 1, pp. 44–45, and *Hsien-chih-t'ang kao*, Ch. 3, pp. 11–14, 30–31b.

23. *WHTK*, p. 8591; *CHTI*, Ch. 5, pp. 25–26b; *Eminent Chinese*, pp. 677–79, 722; Chin-liang, *Chin-shih jen-wu chih*, n.p., n.d., p. 72, quoting Wang K'ai-yün's diary.

24. Tso's memorial, *CHTI*, Ch. 5, pp. 12–16; Ch'in Han-ts'ai, *Tso Wen-hsiang kung tsai hsi-pei*, pp. 203–16.

25. *CHTI*, Ch. 5, pp. 27–30.

26. *Ibid.*, Ch. 3, pp. 29–30.

27. *Ibid.*, Ch. 3, pp. 17–19b.

28. Liu Ch'ang-yu, *Liu Wu-shen kung i-shu*, "Tsou-kao," Ch. 3, pp. 41–49.

29. Li T'ang-chieh, *Li Wen-ch'ing kung i-shu*, Ch. 5, pp. 7–7b, 11 ff. Li outlined Chu Hsi's reasons for beginning with the *Hsiao-ching* and argued the content of the curriculum in some detail.

30. Cheuk-woon Taam, *The Development of Chinese Libraries Under the Ch'ing Dynasty, 1644–1911*, Shanghai, 1935, pp. 41, 47, 66–67; *Eminent Chinese*, pp. 677–79, 726–27.

31. *Eminent Chinese*, pp. 753–54.

32. *CHTI*, Ch. 5, pp. 7–8b. Edict approving Ting's action, Apr. 2, 1868, *SL-TC*, Ch. 226, p. 26.

33. For examples in 1862, see *CSK*, "Pen-chi," Ch. 21, p. 6. For typical edicts on the publication of useful books, see *SL-TC*, Ch. 196, p. 15; Ch. 202, pp. 9–10b.

34. Ch'in Han-ts'ai, *op. cit.*, pp. 203–16.

35. When collating was required owing to the destruction of printing blocks in Hupeh and Hunan, Li Hung-chang farmed the work out to worthy local scholars. See his memorial of June 30, 1869, in *Li Wen-chung kung ch'üan-chi*, "Tsou-kao," Ch. 15, pp. 34–35.

36. Li T'ang-chieh wrote at length on the literati as the source of moral influence (*Li Wen-ch'ing kung i-shu*, Ch. 2, pp. 26–29, ca. 1864). For similar statements by other officials of the time, see *CSWP* and Wang Chih-p'ing, *Tseng Hu Tso ping-hsüeh kang-yao*, pp. 161–66.

37. Hsiao-t'ung Fei, *China's Gentry*, pp. 132–37, referring to studies conducted by himself and Quentin Pan (P'an Kuang-tan). Fei states that the process of "social erosion" of the countryside began at a later date.

38. The village Confucian temple, where the local literati lectured, in many respects served as the government of the village; see Y. K. Leong and L. K. Tao, *Village and Town Life in China*, London, 1915, p. 34, and chap. iii, *passim*; and Kung-ch'uan Hsiao, "Rural Control in Nineteenth Century China," *loc. cit.*, p. 177 and *passim*.

39. Leong and Tao, *op. cit.*, pp. 96–97.

40. Ting's memorial, *CHTI*, Ch. 5, pp. 7–8b. Edict of approval, Apr. 2, 1868, *SL-TC*, Ch. 226, p. 26. Proclamation, here cited, translated in *NCH*, June 27, 1868.

41. For examples, see *WHTK*, p. 8598; *SL-TC*, Ch. 196, pp. 9–9b; *NCH*, July 3, 1863; July 17, Sept. 22, 1868.

42. *SL-TC*, Ch. 196, pp. 14b–15; Ch. 205, pp. 19–21; Ch. 214, pp. 5b–6b.

43. Edict of Sept. 29, 1867, *SL-TC*, Ch. 211, pp. 3b–5.

44. Wang's memorial, *CHTI*, Ch. 1, pp. 26–31. Edict in reply, *Peking Gazette*, translated in *NCH*, Oct. 19, 1867. Wang, who won the metropolitan degree in TK-30, was a native of Changhing, Chekiang.

45. *NCH*, Oct. 19, 1867.

46. See Hsieh Hsing-yao, "Tao Hsien shih-tai pei-fang ti Huang-yai chiao," *I-ching*, No. 3 (1936), pp. 6–10; Liu Hou-tzu, "T'ung-chih wu-nien Huang-yai chiao

fei an chih i," *Shih hsüeh chi-k'an*, No. 2 (1936), pp. 195–207; Liu Hou-tzu, "Chang Shih-ch'in yü T'ai-ku hsüeh-p'ai," *Fu-jen hsüeh-chih*, VIII, 2 (1939), 81–124.

47. On relief measures and other Ch'ing policies of persuasion and nonforcible control, see Miyakawa Hisayuki (*sic*), "Shin no sembu kyūshin kōsaku," *Tōa kenkyū shohō*, No. 19 (1942), pp. 966–1064 (*FB* 3.3.3); Wang Ch'ing-yün, *Hsi-ch'ao chi cheng*, Ch. 1, pp. 3b–8b, 22–25b.

48. Memorial of the censor Wu Hung-kan, Mar. 8, 1873, *Translation of the Peking Gazette for 1873*, p. 25.

49. Prince Kung, *Lo-tao-t'ang wen-ch'ao*, Ch. 2, p. 16b; Ch. 3, pp. 4–4b; Ch. 4, pp. 15–16b.

50. *THTKTI*, Ch. 30, pp. 3–4.

51. E.g., Ting Jih-ch'ang, *CHTI*, Ch. 5, pp. 7–8b.

52. Memorial of 1861 (HF-11), *THTKTI*, Ch. 21, pp. 5–5b.

53. As late as 1915 two sociologists could write: "As far as the villages are concerned social legislation is not needed and organized relief unnecessary." The only difficulties occurred in areas where the traditional system had broken down under the impact of modernization. (Leong and Tao, *op. cit.*, p. 27.)

54. E.g., in 1862 (TC-1) the undamaged areas of Kwangtung were ordered to provide relief for wind-torn areas near Canton. In 1864 (TC-3), Tso Tsung-t'ang as governor-general was instructed to arrange relief for flooded areas near Kinhwa, Chekiang. Heavy rainfall in Chekiang continued, and neighboring provinces were ordered to provide additional relief the following year. In 1866 (TC-5), Li Hung-chang and Kuo Po-yin were ordered to provide relief for the flooded areas of Kiang-pei (*WHTK*, pp. 8408–8409). See also *THTKTI*, Ch. 33, *passim*.

55. *WHTK*, pp. 9098–99; *SL-TC*, Ch. 203, pp. 13–15; *NCH*, Oct. 25, 1867.

56. *NCH*, July 22, Oct. 19, 1867.

57. E.g., edict of June 15, 1867, *SL-TC*, Ch. 203, pp. 7b–8b.

58. Edict of June 18, 1867, *ibid.*, Ch. 203, pp. 15–16.

59. Edict of June 27, 1867, *ibid.*, Ch. 204, pp. 18b–19; edict of July 19, 1867, *ibid.*, Ch. 206, pp. 3b–4; edict of Aug. 7, 1867, *ibid.*, Ch. 207, pp. 19b–20.

60. Edict of July 26, 1867, *ibid.*, Ch. 206, pp. 19–20.

61. Edict of Oct. 6, 1867, *ibid.*, Ch. 211, p. 20b.

62. *Ibid.*, Ch. 207, pp. 6–6b; Ch. 208, pp. 3b–4; Ch. 209, p. 18b; Ch. 213, pp. 5b–6; Ch. 214, pp. 35b–36; Ch. 239, pp. 8b–9b; *CHTI*, Ch. 3, pp. 29–30. For a vivid description of poverty in the Tientsin area at this time and of relief measures, see *Ching-men tsa-chi*, Ch. 2, pp. 1–3b. See also the account by the Tientsin correspondent, *NCH*, Oct. 19, 1867.

63. Edict of Dec. 16, 1867, *SL-TC*, Ch. 217, pp. 1–1b, on the motion of Wan Ch'ing-li.

64. Memorials of Ch'ung-hou (*CHTI*, Ch. 3, pp. 23–26b) and P'eng Tsu-hsien (*ibid.*, Ch. 3, pp. 20–22b).

65. *NCH*, Mar. 14, 1868.

66. Memorials of Ch'ung-hou (*CHTI*, Ch. 3, pp. 23–26b), Liu Ch'ang-yu (*CSWP*, Ch. 90, pp. 1–1b), Li Hung-chang (*CHTI*, Ch. 8, pp. 36–37b), and P'eng Tsu-hsien (*ibid.*, Ch. 3, pp. 20–22b).

67. T'ang Ch'ing-tseng, "Tseng Kuo-fan chih ching-chi ssu-hsiang," *Ching-chi hsüeh chi-k'an*, V, 4 (1935), 53–54; Chiang Hsing-te, *Tseng Kuo-fan chih sheng-p'ing chi ch'i shih-yeh*, pp. 160–62; see also *CSWP*, Ch. 37, *passim*.

68. Gibson, Tientsin, in *China. No. 4. (1864)*, p. 39.

69. *NCH*, Mar. 1, 1862.

70. See, for example, memorial of the censor Lin Shih-kung and edict of 1866 (TC-5) *WHTK*, p. 8419.

71. *Hankow Times*, reprinted in *NCH*, Nov. 30, 1867.

72. Edict of Mar. 13, 1867, *SL-TC*, Ch. 196, pp. 20–20b. The outbreak was reported by a censor.

73. See proclamation of the Shanghai taotai in *NCH*, Mar. 28, 1868.

74. *Ibid.*, Mar. 18 and Mar. 28, 1868.

75. The most detailed factual account is to be found in Wen Chün-t'ien, *Chung-kuo pao-chia chih-tu*, Shanghai, 1935, pp. 201–54. Wen's findings, with some additional material, are usefully summarized in Robert Lee, "The Pao-chia System," *Papers on China*, III (1949), 193–224. See also Matsumoto Zenkai, "Rimpo seido: (1) Chū-goku," *Sekai rekishi jiten*, XX, 7–10; Boulais, *Code chinois*, Part III, chap. 1; Kung-ch'uan Hsiao, "Rural Control in Nineteenth Century China," *FEQ*, XII, 2 (1953), 173–81.

76. Balázs, "Les Aspects significatifs de la société chinoise," *Asiatische Studien*, No. 6, p. 86; Lei Hai-tsung, "Chung-kuo ti chia-tsu chih-tu," *She-hui k'o-hsüeh*, II, 4 (1937), 643–61.

77. Ikeda Makoto, "Hōkō hō no seiritsu to sono tenkai," *Tōyōshi kenkyū*, XII, 6 (1954), 1–32. For an interesting selection of Ming and Sung accounts, see *Ch'ien-tai yü-k'ou liang-kuei*, n.d. (ca. 1930), pp. 20–32. The volume was issued by the Kuomintang, which was seeking precedents for the reinstitution of the system.

78. Li T'ang-chieh, letter, in *Li Wen-ch'ing kung i-shu*, Ch. 1, pp. 12b–15.

79. On Tseng's views, see Wen Chün-t'ien, *op. cit.*, pp. 318–20; and Chih-ch'iang (pseud.), "T'uan-lien ch'ing-i," *Chung-ho*, II, 12 (1941), 82–87.

80. Feng, "Fu tsung-fa i," *CPLKI*, Ch. 1, pp. 10–12b; and "Fu hsiang-chih i," *ibid.*, Ch. 1, pp. 49–52.

81. For a substantial selection of representative statements, see Wang Chih-p'ing, *Tseng Hu Tso ping-hsüeh kang-yao*, pp. 327–41, and Wen Chün-t'ien, *op cit.*, pp. 273–363.

82. E.g., *SL-TC*, Ch. 205, pp. 1b–2b; *THTKTI*, pp. 3–4b.

83. *CHTI*, Ch. 1, pp. 26–31.

84. *Ibid.*, Ch. 1, pp. 20–25.

85. Ch'en Ch'i-t'ien, *Hu Tseng Tso p'ing-luan yao-chih*, pp. 95–119.

86. P. C. Hsieh's erroneous statement that the officers were elected by the people independently of the government has been given wide currency (*The Government of China, 1644–1911*, Baltimore, 1925, p. 309).

87. Wen Chün-t'ien, *op. cit.*, Ch. 1, and Conclusion, pp. 542–45; Lee, "The Pao-chia System," *loc. cit.*, pp. 208–12.

88. On this point, see Shen Yü-ch'ing, "Lun ju-chia ti fa-lü kuan," *Tung-fang tsa-chih*, XXXVIII, 5 (1941), 27–32.

89. See Jean Escarra, *Le Droit chinois*, Peking and Paris, 1936; Escarra, "La Conception chinoise du droit," *Archives de Philosophie du Droit et de Sociologie Juridique*, V, 1/2 (1935), 1–73; Escarra and Robert Germain, Introduction to Liang Ch'i-ch'ao, *La Conception de la loi et les théories des légistes a la veille des Ts'in*, Peking, 1926, pp. xxiii–xxiv; Yang Hung-lieh, *Chung-kuo fa-lü fa-ta shih*, Shanghai,

1930, Vol. II, Ch. 26; Niida Noboru, *Chūgoku hōsei shi*, Tokyo, 1952, pp. 1–61 (*FB* 3.6.1); M. J. Meijer, *The Introduction of Modern Criminal Law in China*, Batavia, 1949, p. 3; M. H. van der Valk, *Interpretations of the Supreme Court at Peking* . . . , Batavia, 1949, pp. 19–20; J. H. Wigmore, *A Panorama of the World's Legal Systems*, St. Paul, 1928, I, 153.

90. *NCH*, June 29, 1867, summarizing Alabaster's study of Chinese commercial law, prepared for the mixed court. See also M. J. Meijer, *op. cit.*, p. 4.

91. Georges Padoux (minister plenipotentiary and adviser to the Chinese government), Preface to Escarra and Germain's translation of Liang Ch'i-ch'ao, *op. cit.*, pp. ix–x.

92. Ernest Alabaster, *Notes and Commentaries on Chinese Criminal Law* . . . , *Chiefly Founded on the Writings of the Late Sir Chaloner Alabaster*, London, 1899, Introduction.

93. Ernest Alabaster, *Notes on Chinese Law and Practice Preceding Revision*, Shanghai, 1906, p. 74. For illustrations, see the sections on law of the *Handbook for Local Officials* (*Mu-ling shu chi-yao*, 1869 ed.), Chs. 7–8, *passim*.

94. Meijer, *op. cit.*, p. 6; Wigmore, *op. cit.*, I, 153; and chap. iv, *passim*, citing the *Hsing-an hui-lan*.

95. H. E. M. James, *The Long White Mountain* . . . , London, 1888, p. 155.

96. Touillier, *Droit civil français*, 1818, quoted in Roscoe Pound, *Outlines of Lectures on Jurisprudence*, Cambridge, Mass., 1943, p. 67.

97. See Roscoe Pound, "Common Law," *Encyclopaedia of the Social Sciences*, IV, 50–56.

98. G. A. Walz, "Public Law," *ibid.*, IV, 657–59.

99. See *Lü-li pien-lan (T'ung-chih); fu ch'u-fen ts'e-li t'u-yao*, 1872 (TC-11), 6 ts'e, prefaces by Chou Tsu-p'ei and others. *WHTK* notes only trivial amendments to the code during the T'ung-chih period, for example adjustments in the penalty of banishment with particular reference to its application to women, the details of military law on desertion, etc. (pp. 9958–59).

100. E.g., memorials of the censors Ma Hsiang-ju and Hu Ch'ing-yüan, *CHTI*, Ch. 8, pp. 1–3b, 8–9.

101. Two memorials by Ting Jih-ch'ang, *THTKTI*, Ch. 58, pp. 3b–4b. Other similar memorials in Ch. 58, *passim*.

102. TC-5, *WHTK*, p. 9974; see also edict of Aug. 14, 1868, *SL-TC*, Ch. 236, pp. 17–17b.

103. Memorial of Pien Pao-ti, *CHTI*, Ch. 2, pp. 1–2.

104. *NCH*, Oct. 19, 1867.

105. Translated in Meijer, *The Introduction of Modern Criminal Law in China*, p. 128.

106. *NCH*, Oct. 19, 1867, reported an illustrative case.

107. See the documents on curfew, searches, etc., for the city of Peking in the T'ung-chih period in *WHTK*, pp. 9546–47.

108. Report of the censor Hsiu-wen, Oct. 3, 1868, *SL-TC*, Ch. 241, pp. 5–5b; report of the censor Wang Tao-yung, Sept. 2, 1868, *ibid.*, Ch. 238, pp. 5–5b.

109. *NCH*, Mar. 18, 1865.

110. On the various types of flogging, exile, and capital punishment prescribed, see Boulais, *Code chinois*, Table I, pp. 1–6. See also *NCH*, Aug. 8, 1868.

111. Alabaster, *Notes on Chinese Law and Practice Preceding Revision,* p. 74. On the system of atonement for crimes, see *WHTK,* pp. 10004–5. On pardons, see pp. 10010–11.

112. E.g., the censor Hu Ch'ing-yüan reported the "sufferings" of prisoners when the fare was changed from rice to corn; an 1862 (TC-1) edict ordered that the diet be changed back to rice (*WHTK,* p. 10010).

113. Alabaster, *Notes and Commentaries on Chinese Criminal Law . . . ,* p. 5.

114. Padoux, *loc. cit.*

115. Memorial of Tso Tsung-t'ang and Hsü Tsung-kan, *CHTI,* Ch. 6, p. 38.

116. Letter of Wo-jen, *Wo Wen-tuan kung i-shu,* Ch. 8, pp. 11b–14b.

117. *CHTI,* Ch. 5, pp. 7–8b; *THTKTI,* Ch. 6, p. 6b.

118. Yen's memorial, 1865 (TC-4), *WHTK,* p. 8532.

119. Hsü Tung, compiler's preface to the *Mu-ling shu chi-yao,* reissued in 1869 in 10 ts'e, ts'e 1, p. 3.

120. Li's preface to the *Mu-ling shu chi-yao,* dated summer 1869.

121. Wo-jen, *op. cit.,* Ch. 8, pp. 11b–14b.

122. Quoted in Hu Che-fu, *Tseng Kuo-fan chih-hsüeh fang-fa,* Shanghai, 1941, pp. 95–96.

123. R. H. Cobbold, *Pictures of the Chinese,* London, 1860. Cobbold had been archdeacon of Ningpo. On the lack of standing among the people of officials who had reached office through financial subscriptions, as contrasted with the great influence of those who had advanced through the examination system, see "Lex," "The Administration of Chinese Law," *China Review,* II, 4 (1874), 235–36.

124. E.g., memorials of the governor of Hunan, Yün Shih-lin (*CHTI,* Ch. 2, pp. 16–17b), the prefect of the metropolitan prefecture, Pien Pao-ti (*ibid.,* Ch. 2, pp. 1–2), and the commissioner of the Office of Transmission, Yü Ling-ch'en (*WHTK,* pp. 8483–84).

125. Li's letter, in *Li Wen-ch'ing kung i-shu,* Ch. 1, pp. 12–15. For a similar statement by Feng Kuei-fen, see "Fu-ch'en shih-i," *CPLKI,* Ch. 1, pp. 12b–14b.

126. Edict of June 28, 1867, *SL-TC,* Ch. 204, pp. 26b–27.

127. *CHTI,* Ch. 8, pp. 10–11.

128. Edict of Feb. 15, 1868, *SL-TC,* Ch. 223, pp. 4–4b.

129. Feng Kuei-fen, *Hsien-chih-t'ang kao,* 1876, Ch. 3, pp. 30–31b.

130. Memorial of Wo-jen, presented by Li T'ang-chieh, in Li's works, *Li Wen-ch'ing kung i-shu,* Ch. 1, pp. 10–13.

131. *CHTI,* Ch. 3, pp. 7–8b.

132. *Mu-ling shu chi-yao,* 1869 ed., Ch. 1, pp. 2, 12b, and *passim;* other handbooks make the same points.

133. On the intricate structure of the office of a local official and the bureaus through which he was expected to manage the administration of justice, the collection of taxes, reports to superiors, ceremonial matters, military affairs, public works, the grain reserve, etc., see Boulais, *Code chinois,* pp. 47 ff.

134. *CHTI,* Ch. 8, pp. 14–15, and edict of Aug. 26, 1868, *SL-TC,* Ch. 237, pp. 25–25b.

135. *CHTI,* Ch. 1, pp. 17–19. Ma, a native of Lintsing, Shantung, received the metropolitan degree in 1856 (HF-6). Proposals comparable to those of Yu and Ma provide the bulk of the material in the *Peking Gazette.*

136. Edicts of June 27, 1867, *SL-TC*, Ch. 204, pp. 19–20; Oct. 3, 1868, *ibid.*, Ch. 241, pp. 5–5b.

137. On the interference of Catholic missionaries and of the French government in lawsuits involving converts, see K. S. Latourette, *A History of Christian Missions in China*, New York, 1929, pp. 309–11. According to Latourette, interference by Protestants was less frequent (*ibid.*, pp. 421–23).

138. Alabaster, *Notes and Commentaries on Chinese Criminal Law* . . . , p. 5.

139. A number of these well-known incidents are retold in Ch'iu Yü-lin, *Ch'ing-tai yi-wen*, ts'e 2, Ch. 4, pp. 19–22 and *passim*.

140. Note Governor-general Ma Hsin-i's caution to missionaries to be particularly circumspect during the forthcoming Kiangsu provincial examinations (*NCH*, July 7, 1870).

141. See annotated translation of the text of one of these proclamations with supplementary documents (*NCH*, Oct. 6, 1866). See also *NCH*, Sept. 29, 1866.

CHAPTER VIII

1. See Ma Yin-ch'u's selection of classical and other illustrations of this principle in *Tung-fang tsa-chih*, XXIV, 4 (1927), 11–19; see also Wang Hai-po, "Chung-kuo ku-tai ti ching-chi ssu-hsiang," in *Ching-chi hsüeh chi-k'an*, III, 2 (1932), 177–206. Even the reformers of the generation following the Restoration continued to hold this view. The ideas on this point of Cheng Kuang-ying, Ch'en Ts'an, Liang Ch'i-ch'ao, and K'ang Yu-wei are conveniently summarized in Chao Feng-t'ien, *Wan-Ch'ing wu-shih nien ching-chi ssu-hsiang shih*, Peiping, 1939, pp. 19–41.

2. Ch'ing writers on economics generally began with a discussion of frugality (*chien-lien*); see Wang Ch'ing-yün, *Hsi-ch'ao chi-cheng* (the standard work on Ch'ing public finance, written by a nineteenth-century official), Ch. 1, for a number of illustrations.

3. Translated by T. F. Wade in *Decree of the Emperor of China, asking for counsel, and the replies of the administration, 1850–51, with other papers*, London, 1878, p. 5.

4. Wang Ch'ing-yün, *op. cit.*, Ch. 1, pp. 8b–21b. On the reasoning behind this measure, see Yu-ch'uan Wang, "The Rise of Land Tax and the Fall of Dynasties in China," *Pacific Affairs*, IX, 2 (1936), 201–20.

5. Lo Yü-tung, *Chung-kuo li-chin shih*, Shanghai, 1936, I, 1–3; C. J. Stanley, "Chinese Finance from 1852 to 1908," *Papers on China*, III (1949), 1–23.

6. Chao Feng-t'ien, *op. cit.*, pp. 269–73.

7. Henri Maspero, "Les Régimes fonciers en Chine," *Recueils de la Société Jean Bodin*, II, "Le Servage" (1937), pp. 279–80. For a brief account of legal restrictions on merchants in Chinese history and the dependence of the merchant on official patronage, see Dawson, "Law and the Merchant in Traditional China . . . ," *Papers on China*, II (1948), 66–85. In the T'ang period a candidate in the examination system had to prove that his father was not a merchant, an artisan, or a convicted criminal (R. des Rotours, *Le Traité des examens*, Paris, 1932, p. 215). Even in the period following World War II, the Chinese merchant's security remained dependent on his personal connections with officials (Morton H. Fried, *Fabric of Chinese Society* . . . , New York, 1953, pp. 150–51).

8. E.g., Wang Ch'ing-yün, *op. cit.*, Ch. 5, pp. 24b–28.

9. Etienne Balázs, "Les Aspects significatifs de la société chinoise," *Asiatische Studien*, No. 6, p. 86.

10. Alcock, "The Chinese Empire in Its Foreign Relations," *Bombay Quarterly Review* (Apr. 1856), pp. 229–30.

11. Fei, *China's Gentry*, p. 64.

12. Maspero, *loc. cit.*, pp. 308–10.

13. The gradual decline of the Ch'ing economy prior to the Hsien-feng collapse was noted in *CSK*, "Shih-huo chih," p. 1.

14. Economic decline during the first half of the nineteenth century is outlined in Hsia Nai, "Tai-p'ing t'ien-kuo ch'ien-hou Ch'ang-chiang ko-sheng chih t'ien-fu wen-t'i," *Ch'ing-hua hsüeh-pao*, X, 2 (1935), 429–74. For a summary of the factors involved and a comparison of Ch'ing policy with the policy of the Tokugawa Shogunate, see Naitō Torajirō, *Shinchō suibō ron*, 1944, pp. 357–88 (*FB* 2.1.1). On the rising price of silver, see T'ang Hsiang-lung, "Tao-kuang shih-ch'i ti yin-kuei wen-t'i," in *She-hui k'o-hsüeh tsa-chih*, I, 3 (1930), 3–31. On the nineteenth-century rise in military appropriations and decline in appropriations for conservation as well as those for education and public welfare, see Shao-kwan Chen, *The System of Taxation in China in the Tsing Dynasty, 1644–1911*, New York, 1914, p. 33.

15. T. F. Wade in *China. No. 1. (1872)*, p. 16. Estimates of this type should merely be taken as indicating a stupendous loss of life.

16. *NCH*, Mar. 24, 1866.

17. Edict of Apr. 23, 1868, citing the memorial of the acting governor of Anhwei, Wu K'un-hsiu, *SL-TC*, Ch. 228, pp. 3b–5.

18. *NCH*, Mar. 24, 1866.

19. Wade, memorandum of Jan. 6, 1860, *Correspondence Respecting Affairs in China. 1859–1860*, pp. 14–15. Wade's memorandum was based on the *Peking Gazette* and other published Chinese sources.

20. Analysis of Chinese figures, *NCH*, July 31, 1858, reprinted in *Correspondence Respecting Affairs in China. 1859–1860*, p. 17.

21. For brief summaries of the fiscal problem confronting the Hsien-feng government, see Lo Yü-tung, *Chung-kuo li-chin shih*, I, 9–10, and Edwin G. Beal, "The Origin of *Likin*," ms. cited with author's permission, pp. 1–15 and p. 27, note 42.

22. *Correspondence Respecting Affairs in China. 1859–1860*, pp. 15–26.

23. E.g., *SL-TC*, Ch. 218, pp. 4b–5.

24. See examples cited in Ho Wei-ning, "T'ai-p'ing t'ien-kuo shih-tai Chung-kuo yen-cheng kai-kuan," *She-hui k'o-hsüeh ts'ung-k'an*, I, 2 (1934), 112.

25. T'ang Hsiang-lung, "Hsien-feng ch'ao ti huo-pi," *Chung-kuo she-hui ching-chi shih chi-k'an*, II, 1 (1933), 1–26; T'ang Ch'ing-tseng, "Tseng Kuo-fan chih ching-chi ssu-hsiang," *loc. cit.*, p. 55; Ho Wei-ning, *loc. cit.*, pp. 109–10.

26. Retrospective summary by the Board of Revenue, 1867 (TC-6), *THTKTI*, Ch. 38, pp. 10–10b; Chaoying Fang in *Eminent Chinese*, pp. 667–68; *NCH*, Mar. 31, 1860; Lien-sheng Yang, *Money and Credit in China*, Cambridge, Mass., 1952, p. 68; Chang Te-ch'ang, "Chin-tai Chung-kuo chih huo-pi," *Jen-wen k'o-hsüeh hsüeh-pao*, I, 1 (1942), 84 ff.; Morse, *Relations*, I, 204; Katō Shigeshi, *Shina keizai shi kōsho*, Tokyo, 1952–53, II, 421–47 (*FB* 9.8.8).

27. Ting Wen-chiang, "Wu-shih nien lai Chung-kuo k'uang-yeh," in Shen-pao kuan, Fiftieth Anniversary Publication, Vol. II, *Wu-shih nien lai chih Chung-kuo*, Shanghai, 1922.

28. Chia Shih-i, "Wu-shih nien lai Chung-kuo ts'ai-cheng," *ibid.*

29. On the Meiji economic program, see Thomas C. Smith, *Political Change and Industrial Development in Japan: Government Enterprise, 1868–1880,* Stanford, California, 1955.

30. T'ang Ch'ing-tseng, *loc. cit.,* pp. 52–60. T'ang notes the concentration of economic studies in Hunan in the late Ch'ing, citing among others T'ao Chu's work on the salt monopoly, Wei Yüan's studies of the grain tribute, those of Sun Ting-ch'en on currency, Kuo Sung-tao on public finance, and so forth.

31. Chao Feng-t'ien's statement to the contrary (*Wan-ch'ing wu-shih nien ching-chi ssu-hsiang shih,* Preface) is disproved by the main body of his own work.

32. *CHTI,* Ch. 3, pp. 5–8; *WHTK,* pp. 7521, 7525–26; *THTKTI,* Ch. 60, shang, pp. 16b–17.

33. *Chiang-su sheng chien-fu ch'üan-an,* 1886, Ch. 2, pp. 1–3b; *SL-TC,* Ch. 69, pp. 14b–16; *IWSM-TC,* Ch. 41, pp. 43–50.

34. *CSWP,* Ch. 16, p. 3b. On Tseng's general views on agriculture, see T'ang Ch'ing-tseng, *loc. cit.,* pp. 53–54. For a Marxist criticism of Tseng for allegedly protecting feudalism in the villages under the high-flown slogan "exalt agriculture," see Chu Ch'i-hua, *Chung-kuo chin-tai she-hui shih chieh-p'ou,* Shanghai, 1933, p. 5.

For similar statements by other officials see *CSWP,* Chs. 35–36, *passim*; Chao Feng-t'ien, *op. cit.,* pp. 19 ff.; Hsia Yen-te, *Chung-kuo chin pai-nien ching-chi ssu-hsiang,* Shanghai, 1948, pp. 16–17.

35. Prince Kung, *Lo-tao-t'ang wen-ch'ao,* Ch. 3, pp. 10 ff.

36. Letter to Tseng Chi-tse, widely reprinted, here cited from *Tseng Wen-cheng kung hsüeh-an,* Shanghai, 1925, pp. 200–201. For a study of Tseng's ideal of the poor but happy life, based on his family letters, see Ōtani Kōtarō, "Hinraku seikatsu oyobi shisō," *Tōa keizai ronsō,* II, 2 (1942) (*FB* 6.2.6).

37. Tseng, quoted in T'ang Ch'ing-tseng, *loc. cit.,* pp. 52–53.

38. Wo-jen, *Wo Wen-tuan kung i-shu,* Ch. 2, pp. 8–10.

39. E.g., *CSK,* "Pen-chi," Ch. 21, p. 2b; *CHTI,* Ch. 1, pp. 6–8b; *WHTK,* pp. 8201–2; *SL-TC,* Ch. 203, pp. 11b–13b; *THTKTI,* Ch. 2, *passim.*

40. Edict of Sept. 16, 1868, *SL-TC,* Ch. 240, pp. 1b–2b; Wu Tseng-ch'i, *Ch'ing-shih kang-yao,* Ch. 12, p. 20b; *THTKTI,* Ch. 2, pp. 13b–14.

41. Text in *CSWP,* Ch. 24, pp. 2–5.

42. *NCH,* Oct. 14, 1865.

43. "Chinese Railways" (unsigned), *China Review,* II, 5 (1874), 288.

44. Li Ta-chao, in *Hsin ch'ing-nien,* VII, 2 (1920), 47–53.

45. Williams, *The Middle Kingdom,* I, 692.

46. Note the memorials in *THTKTI,* Ch. 29.

47. Thomas W. Kingsmill, "Retrospect of Events in China and Japan During the Year 1865," *JNCBRAS,* II (1865), 134–70.

48. *NCH* Kiukiang correspondent, Sept. 1862, in *NCH,* Oct. 4, 1862; *ibid.,* summarizing communications received from Soochow, May 28, 1864.

49. Nov. 27, 1866, *IWSM-TC,* Ch. 45, pp. 44b–54b.

50. *NCH,* Sept. 21, 1867; Mar. 24, 1866.

51. E.g., Kweichow, Ling T'i-an, *Hsien T'ung Kuei-chou chün-shih shih,* Part 5, pp. 9b–16.

52. On the resettlement offices in Kweichow, see *ibid.,* Part 5, pp. 16–18; on the

Chihli regulations, see proclamation of Governor-general Liu Ch'ang-yu in his *Liu Wu-shen kung i-shu*, Ch. 24, shang, pp. 20–21.

53. Memorial of the censor Liu Ch'ing and edict, *WHTK*, p. 7519. See, for example, the report of Ying-han and Ma Hsin-i on disturbances in Anhwei attributed to immigrants who had come from Hupeh and Chekiang in response to these advertisements (edict of July 27, 1867, *SL-TC*, Ch. 206, pp. 24b–25). The point here is not the disorders but the fact that substantial numbers of people responded to the notices.

54. *NCH*, May 30, 1868. On the general post-Taiping changes in land tenure, particularly the emergence of the perpetual right to cultivate, see Amano Motonosuke, *Shina nōgyō keizai ron*, Tokyo, 1940, I, 485–88, and *passim* (*FB* 7.5.1).

55. Tseng Kuo-fan's policy proclamation in *Tseng Kuo-fan chiao-Nien shih-lu*, pp. 1–3, and *CHTI*, Ch. 3, pp. 38–40.

56. Maspero, "Les Régimes fonciers en Chine," *loc. cit.*, pp. 308–10.

57. Amano, *op. cit.*; Niida Noboru, *Chūgoku hōsei shi*, Tokyo, 1952, pp. 290–97 (*FB* 3.6.1); Morton H. Fried, *Fabric of Chinese Society . . .* , New York, 1953, pp. 11–12.

58. For a representative collection of materials, see *CSWP*, Ch. 33, *passim*. For Feng Kuei-fen's views, see *CTLT*, Ch. 3, p. 8b.

59. Edict of Jan. 27, 1868, *SL-TC*, Ch. 221, pp. 6–6b; edict of 1871 (TC-10), *WHTK*, p. 9598; both include summaries of reports.

60. T. T. Meadows to Bruce, Nov. 18, 1862, *China. No. 4. (1864)*, p. 6; biography of Jui-lin, *Ch'ing-shih lieh-chuan*, Ch. 46, pp. 36–39; edicts of 1863 (TC-2) and 1869 (TC-8), *WHTK*, pp. 7520 and 7527–28.

61. Edict of June 21, 1867, *SL-TC*, Ch. 203, pp. 23–25; edict of Sept. 10, 1867, *ibid.*, Ch. 209, pp. 29–30; edict of Aug. 3, 1868, *ibid.*, pp. 6b–7; edict of 1863 (TC-2), *WHTK*, p. 7520; edict of 1866 (TC-5), *ibid.*, p. 7524; edict of 1867 (TC-6), *ibid.*, pp. 7524–25; edict of 1868 (TC-7), *ibid.*, p. 7525.

62. *WHTK*, p. 7525.

63. Otake Fumio, *Kinsei Shina keizaishi kenkyū*, Tokyo, 1942, pp. 238–39 (*FB* 7.1.3); Shao-kwan Chen, *The System of Taxation in China in the Tsing Dynasty . . .* , pp. 49–51.

64. Feng, "Ch'ou kuo-yung i," *CPLKI*, Ch. 1, pp. 38b–40b.

65. *NCH*, Oct. 14, 1868.

66. On Tso's knowledge of and interest in agriculture, see Gideon Chen, "Tso Tsung-t'ang, the Farmer of Hsiang-shang," *loc. cit.*, p. 211 and *passim*; and Lienche Tu Fang in *Eminent Chinese*, pp. 762–67. For an encomium of Tso as a "liberal and enlightened Governor" ready to try the new for the benefit of his province, see *Foochow Advertiser* editorial on the occasion of his departure for the northwest, reprinted in *NCH*, Dec. 22, 1866.

67. *NCH*, Dec. 22, 1866.

68. E.g., *WHTK*, pp. 7525–26.

69. Memorial of the censor Juan Shou-sung, Dec. 24, 1867, *SL-TC*, Ch. 217, pp. 25b–26.

70. Ch'ung-hou's memorial (*CHTI*, Ch. 3, pp. 5–8) discusses in some detail the engineering and economic problems involved in his plan for reclaiming the entire area. On this, see also Chang Nien-tsu, *Chung-kuo li-tai shui-li shu-yao*, pp. 151–52.

71. Pien's memorial and edict of approval, 1865 (TC-4), *THTKTI*, Ch. 63, pp. 4–5b. Chang Nien-tsu, *op. cit.*, p. 152.

72. *WHTK*, p. 7613.

73. On the work of the governor of Shensi, Liu Tien, see Chang Nien-tsu, *op. cit.*, p. 160. During the Restoration Chang Yin-huan, later minister to the United States and England, did much of the work involved in Ting Pao-chen's program of river conservancy in Szechwan (Chaoying Fang in *Eminent Chinese*, pp. 60 ff.). Other examples from a variety of regions are mentioned in the memorial of the censor Chu Ch'ao, 1862 (TC-1), *THTKTI*, Ch. 28, pp. 1–2. On the importance Tseng Kuo-fan assigned to irrigation, see T'ang Ch'ing-tseng, "Tseng Kuo-fan chih ching-chi ssu-hsiang," *loc. cit.*, p. 54.

74. E.g., Ma Hsin-i's estimate of some 489,000 taels for a reservoir in Kiangsi, edict of Jan. 8, 1868, *SL-TC*, Ch. 219, pp. 7b–8.

75. See memorial of the censor Hung Ch'ang-yen, *CHTI*, Ch. 8, pp. 33–35b, and *NCH*, Mar. 25, 1865.

76. Memorial of Shen Pao-chen, summarized in edict of July 7, 1868, *SL-TC*, Ch. 234, pp. 7b–8.

77. E.g., *SL-TC*, Ch. 195, pp. 34b–35; Ch. 196, pp. 32, 38–38b; Ch. 197, pp. 3–3b; Ch. 208, pp. 1–1b, 6; Ch. 219, pp. 10b–11; Ch. 229, pp. 11–11b; Ch. 240, pp. 13–14b.

78. Chang Nien-tsu, *op. cit.*, pp. 152–53.

79. See Lin Hsiu-chu (ed.), *Li-tai chih-Huang shih*, Shantung Yellow River Bureau, preface dated 1926, Ch. 5, pp. 15b–29. Twenty-five per cent of the Ch'ing section of this compendium is devoted to the T'ung-chih reign, which in length constituted only 5 per cent of the Ch'ing period. Yellow River control during the Restoration is briefly discussed in Yin Shang-ch'ing, "Ming Ch'ing liang-tai ho-fang k'ao-lüeh," *Shih hsüeh chi-k'an*, No. 1 (1936), pp. 97–122.

A substantial selection of Restoration documents on the Yellow River is included in *CSWP*, Ch. 89–99, and *THTKTI*, Ch. 60, shang-hsia, and Ch. 61. An English translation of a long memorial on the Yellow River by Li Hung-chang, August 18, 1873, is to be found in *Translation of the Peking Gazette for 1873*, pp. 73–78.

80. See map in Lin Hsiu-chu, *op. cit.*, frontispiece.

81. On the relation of the control of the Yellow River to the navigability of the Grand Canal, see Harold C. Hinton, "Grain Transport via the Grand Canal, 1845–1901," *Papers on China*, IV (1950), 33–40. On the effect of the river's shift to the north, see Lin Hsiu-chu, *op. cit.*, Ch. 5, pp. 12–15, and *NCH*, Oct. 13, 1866.

82. For work undertaken in 1864–65, see *WHTK*, pp. 7613–14.

83. Memorial of 1864 (TC-3), *THTKTI*, Ch. 60, shang, pp. 16b–17.

84. Lin Hsiu-chu, *op. cit.*, Ch. 5, pp. 16–17. On the principle of using work to replace charity, which Yen invoked here, see Chapter VII.

85. *Ibid.*, Ch. 5, pp. 15b–29.

86. *Ibid.*, Ch. 5, p. 17.

87. *NCH*, June 29, 1867. The details of the plan are given. See also issue of Sept. 28, 1867, and Chiang Hsing-te, *Tseng Kuo-fan chih sheng-p'ing chi ch'i shih-yeh*, pp. 164–65.

88. Hoshi Ayao, "Min Shin jidai no junsō goshi ni tsuite," *Wada hakushi kan-reki kinen Tōyōshi ronsō*, Tokyo, 1951, pp. 591–606; see also Ch'ang-tu Hu, "The Yellow River Administration in the Ch'ing Dynasty," *FEQ*, XIV, 4 (1955), 505–14.

89. *WHTK*, pp. 8914–15, 1863 (TC-2).

90. *NCH*, Dec. 24, 1867; Chang Nien-tsu, *Chung-kuo li-tai shui-li shu-yao*, p. 153. Note the disjointed and unsystematic character of the reports from and the edicts to the director-general of the Yellow River, Su T'ing-k'uei, and the governors of the flooded provinces: e.g., *SL-TC*, Ch. 212, p. 3; Ch. 216, pp. 1–3; Ch. 236, pp. 15–16; Ch. 237, pp. 21–21b, 28–28b; Ch. 238, pp. 6–7, 7–8, 22–23; Ch. 239, pp. 24b–25b; Ch. 240, pp. 21b–22.

91. Memorial of Li Hung-chang, June 9, 1865, in *Li Wen-chung kung ch'üan chi,* "Tsou-kao," Ch. 8, pp. 60–64; memorial of the censor Ts'ui Mu-chih, summarized in edict of July 5, 1867, *SL-TC*, Ch. 205, pp. 4b–5b; Feng Kuei-fen in *CTLT*, Ch. 55, pp. 9b–11; memorial of Ting Pao-chen, Feb. 27, 1867, in *Ting Wen-ch'eng kung tsou-kao*, Ch. 1, pp. 51–54.

92. On these see Harold C. Hinton, "Grain Transport via the Grand Canal, 1845–1901," *Papers on China,* IV (1950), 24–57; Hinton, "The Grain Tribute System of the Ch'ing Dynasty," *FEQ*, XI, 3 (1952), 339–54; and Wang Ch'ing-yün, *Hsi-ch'ao chi-cheng*, Ch. 4, pp. 6–15.

93. Fujii Hiroshi, "Ichijōbempō no ichisokumen," in *Wada hakushi kanreki kinen Tōyōshi ronsō*, Tokyo, 1951, pp. 571–90 (*FB* 7.13.5). Fujii denies that this fusion occurred in the earlier "single-whip" tax (*i-t'iao pien-fa*) of the Ming.

94. Ling T'i-an, *Hsien T'ung Kuei-chou chün-shih shih*, Part 5, p. 18.

95. For Kweichow's chaotic temporary measures, subsequently abrogated during the Restoration, see *ibid.,* Part 5, pp. 27b–31.

96. E.g., *CSK*, "Pen-chi," Ch. 21, pp. 2b, 4, 4b, 5b, 6, 6b, 7, etc.; also *SL-TC*, Ch. 194, pp. 6, 9–9b; Ch. 196, pp. 7, 15–15b, 37b–38; Ch. 212, pp. 23–23b; Ch. 220, p. 2, etc.

97. E.g., an edict of Sept. 23, 1868, referred to general remission of back taxes throughout most of Chihli, Shantung, Honan, Anhwei, Kiangsu, and Hupeh, and invited officials from other areas to make similar requests (*SL-TC*, Ch. 240, pp. 14b–15).

98. E.g., edict of Sept. 22, 1867, *SL-TC*, Ch. 210, p. 24b.

99. For summary estimates by provinces of post-Taiping land tax reductions, see Otake Fumio, *Kinsei Shina keizaishi kenkyū*, Tokyo, 1942, pp. 212–20 (*FB* 7.1.3); and Hu Chün, *Chung-kuo ts'ai-cheng shih chiang-i*, Shanghai, 1920, pp. 332–34.

100. Described in memorial of P'an Tsu-yin, 1863, *Chiang-su sheng chien-fu ch'üan-an*, Ch. 2, p. 2b.

101. Wu Tseng-ch'i, *Ch'ing-shih kang-yao*, Ch. 12, p. 8b.

102. *WHTK*, p. 7524.

103. *Ibid.*, pp. 7521–22.

104. Edict of Mar. 18, 1867, *SL-TC*, Ch. 196, pp. 32–33.

105. E.g., *WHTK*, p. 7521, 1865 (TC-4), p. 7525, 1868 (TC-7); *NCH*, Feb. 22, Mar. 1, 1862; Mar. 4, 1865.

106. The transmission order is appended to the *SL* text, *SL-TC*, Ch. 69, p. 16. The documents in the case, *Chiang-su sheng chien-fu ch'üan-an*, 8 ts'e, were issued with prefaces by the five chief officials of the province, beginning with the acting governor-general, Li Hung-chang. The list of sponsors, from Imperial Commissioner Tseng Kuo-fan down to the magistrates of the counties involved, covers fourteen pages. The development of policy is clearly shown in the edicts, memorials, petitions,

and reports that are reproduced. There are also voluminous and detailed tables of tax rates.

107. For the figures, see Chu Ch'ing-yung, "T'ung-chih erh nien Su-Sung erh-fu chien-fu chih yüan-yin," *Cheng-chih ching-chi hsüeh-pao*, III, 3 (1935), 510–18.

108. Hsia Nai, "T'ai-p'ing t'ien-kuo ch'ien-hou Ch'ang-chiang ko-sheng chih t'ien-fu wen-t'i" *Ch'ing-hua hsüeh-pao*, X, 2 (1935), 429 ff.

109. *Chiang-su sheng chien-fu ch'üan-an*, Li Hung-chang's review of the case in his preface.

110. June 6, 1863, *ibid.*, Ch. 2, pp. 1–3b.

111. *WHTK*, pp. 7519–20; Li Hung-chang, *Li Wen-chung kung ch'üan-chi*, "Tsou-kao," Ch. 3, pp. 56–63. This memorial became famous as the classic statement of the griefs of the area, and was reissued during the Republican period by the Kun-shan County Council as an appendix to *Su Sung ts'ai-fu k'ao*, compiled by Chou Meng-yen, n.d.

112. *SL-TC*, Ch. 69, pp. 14b-16; *Chiang-su sheng chien-fu ch'üan-an*, Ch. 1, pp. 3–4.

113. Feng, "Chiang-su chien-fu chi," *Hsien-chih-t'ang kao*, Ch. 4. See also *CTLT*, Ch. 5, pp. 3–6.

114. Edict of 1865 (TC-4), *WHTK*, pp. 7523–24.

115. Ting Jih-ch'ang, *Fu-Wu kung-tu*, Ch. 22, pp. 1–2b.

116. For a brief account of the li-chia system, see Kung-ch'uan Hsiao, "Rural Control in Nineteenth Century China," *loc. cit.*, pp. 175–76. On the pao-chia system, see Chapter VII.

117. Edict of 1865 (TC-4), *WHTK*, pp. 7523–24, following a thoughtful memorial by Tso Tsung-t'ang on the dimensions of the problem and the remedies he had found effective in Fukien and Chekiang. Li Hung-chang and Tseng Kuo-fan were ordered to work out a comparable system for Kiangsu.

Censors' reports were a main source of information on collection of the land tax in excess of the quotas. See, for example, report on extralegal collection and edict of 1867 (TC-6), *WHTK*, p. 7525; report from the supervising censor Liu Ping-hou on excessive collection in Chihli and edict of 1869 (TC-8), *ibid.*, p. 7528; report of the censor Hu Chia-yü on the situation in Kiangsu, separately corroborated by Governor Liu K'un-i, and edict of 1870 (TC-9), *ibid.*, p. 7528.

118. Hsia Nai, "T'ai-p'ing t'ien-kuo ch'ien-hou Ch'ang-chiang ko-sheng chih t'ien-fu wen-t'i," *loc. cit.*, pp. 468–69.

119. On the immediate benefits from the reduction, see Chu Ch'ing-yung, *loc. cit.*, pp. 522–27. According to Hsia Nai (*loc. cit.*, p. 469), "The T'ung-chih reign has been called the T'ung-chih Restoration, and this movement for reduction of the land tax, which saved the people their hard-earned money, was its economic foundation."

120. Hsia Nai, *loc. cit.*, pp. 469–71.

121. Chu Ch'ing-yung, *loc. cit.*, p. 528.

122. Feng in *CTLT*, Ch. 5, pp. 3–6; Hart, "spectator's memorandum," *IWSM-TC*, Ch. 40, p. 19.

123. Hsia Nai, *loc. cit.*, pp. 469–73.

124. E.g., Ting Jih-ch'ang, *Fu-Wu kung-tu*, Ch. 22, pp. 1–2b. Memorial of Tso Tsung-t'ang and two edicts, *WHTK*, pp. 7523–24.

125. Feng, "Chiang-su chien-fu chi," *Hsien-chih t'ang kao*, Ch. 4, p. 12; Chu Ch'ing-yung, *loc. cit.*, pp. 528–29; Hsia Nai, *loc. cit.*, p. 472.

126. Ch'en Ts'an, *Chung-kuo shang-yeh shih*, Changsha, 1940, pp. 98–102; Lo Yü-tung, *Chung-kuo li-chin shih*, I, 10–12.

127. Lo Yü-tung, *op. cit.*, I, 173–76.

128. The standard work on the likin is Lo Yü-tung's. See also Beal, "The Origin of *Likin.*"

129. Beal, *op. cit.*, pp. 110–29, 155–64; Lo Yü-tung, *op. cit.*, I, 27–30.

130. Text of Ch'üan-ch'ing's memorial, *CHTI*, Ch. 3, pp. 35–36b. For comments, see Beal, *op. cit.*, pp. 130–31, and Lo Yü-tung, *op. cit.*, I, 37–41.

131. See summaries of the memorials of the censors Ch'en T'ing-ching and Ting Shao-chou, the Grand Secretary Wo-jen, P'an Tsu-yin, and others in Lo Yü-tung, *op. cit.*, I, 33–35.

132. *WHTK*, pp. 8042–46.

133. E.g., memorial of the censor Sun I-mou on the ease with which the branch stations became "profiteering monopolies," *CHTI*, Ch. 1, pp. 32–35; edict of Sept. 23, 1868, on motion of the censor Wu Ting-yüan, *SL-TC*, Ch. 240, pp. 16–17.

134. *WHTK*, pp. 8042–46; Liu K'un-i's account of Tseng Kuo-fan's reforms, memorial of May 29, 1866, *IWSM-TC*, Ch. 41, pp. 43–46. The fact that recorded receipts from the likin rose by 50 per cent (on the basis of Lo Yü-tung's figures, *op. cit.*, I, 173) is probably an indication of tighter official control.

135. Beal, *op. cit.*, p. 132.

136. Beal, *op. cit.*, pp. 145–50, summarizes the views of Lo, Mao, and Kuo. On Tseng's views, see T'ang Ch'ing-tseng, "Tseng Kuo-fan chih ching-chi ssu-hsiang," *loc. cit.*, pp. 56–58, and Hsia Yen-te, *Chung-kuo chin pai-nien ching-chi ssu-hsiang*, pp. 17–18. For Liu's views, see his memorial of May 28, 1866, *IWSM-TC*, Ch. 41, pp. 43–50.

137. Ho Hui-yüan, "Lun t'ien-fu fu-chia," *Tu-li p'ing-lun*, No. 89 (1934), pp. 6–9.

138. On Ch'ing commercial taxes in general, see Wang Ch'ing-yün, *Hsi-ch'ao chi-cheng*, Ch. 6, pp. 1–37. On the intricate, not readily supervised system of collecting commercial taxes through brokers in the markets (*ya-hang*), see Konuma Tadashi, "Kahoku nōson shishū no gakō ni tsuite," *Wada hakushi kanreki kinen tōyōshi ronsō*, pp. 221–36 (*FB* 7.16.5).

139. *CHTI*, Ch. 3, pp. 37–37b.

140. E.g., *China. No. 4. (1864)*, pp. 62–63, 67; *China. No. 5. (1871)*, p. 37; *NCH*, Aug. 25, Oct. 20, 1866; May 18, 1867.

141. E.g., Anking correspondent in *NCH*, No. 30, 1861; Consul Gingell, Hankow, and Consul Hughes, Kiukiang, *China. No. 4. (1864)*, pp. 41–51; Hangchow report in *NCH*, Sept. 9, 1865.

142. *NCH*, Jan. 28, 1865.

143. Such a rich assemblage of raw data as the *Ssu-ch'uan yen-fa chih* (compiled under the direction of Ting Pao-chen, 1882, 40 chüan) is scarcely usable for present purposes. The same thing is true of the tables in Wang Ch'ing-yün, *Hsi-ch'ao chi-cheng*, Ch. 5, pp. 27–66, and of the multitude of documents included in *WHTK*, pp. 7901–12, and throughout the *SL* and other general collections of Ch'ing documents.

144. The clearest general account of the system is Saeki Tomi, "Shindai ni okeru engyō shihon ni tsuite, Parts 1–2, in *Tōyōshi kenkyū*, XI, 1 (1950), 51–65; XI, 2 (1951), 38–50 (*FB* 7.8.6). See also Tseng Yang-feng, *Chung-kuo yen-cheng shih*, Shanghai, 1937, pp. 174–97. On the so-called *kang-yen* or *yin-shang* system in the

Huai area, see Wang Shu-han, "Liang Huai yen-wu yü ch'ien-chuang," *Ching-chi hsüeh chi-k'an*, II, 3 (1931), 118–19, and Hatano Yoshiro, "Shindai Ryōwai seien ni okeru seisan soshiki," *Tōyōshi kenkyū*, XI, 1 (1950), 7–31 (*FB* 7.8.7). On Kwangtung and Kwangsi, see Tsou Lin, *Tseng-ting Yüeh yen chi-shih*, Shanghai, 1927, pp. 3–6. See also note 143 above and Tso Shu-chen, "Yen-wu chi-yao li-shih kai-lun," in four parts, *Yen-cheng tsa-chih*, Nos. 16–19 (1913–15); after Part I, the title of the series was changed to "Chung-kuo yen-cheng yen-ko shih"; Tso Shu-chen, "Li-tai yen-fa t'ung-lun," *Yen-cheng tsa-chih*, Nos. 35–40 (1922–24). See also [Ch'ing] T'ao-pai, "P'iao-pen wen-t'i," *Yen-cheng tsa-chih*, No. 41 (1924); Tai I-hsüan, "Ch'ing-tai yen-cheng kuei-ting shih-yüan shih-t'an," *Hsien-tai shih-hsüeh*, I, 5 (1942), 102–6; I-chou (pseud.), "Tu-pan yen-cheng chi-lüeh," in *T'an-yen ts'ung-pao*, No. 13 (1914), 10 pp. The above have been superseded by Saeki Tomi, *Shindai ensei no kenkyū* (*The Salt Administration Under the Ch'ing Dynasty*), Kyoto, 1956.

145. Tseng Yang-feng, "Chung-kuo yen-cheng chih tung-hsiang," *Tung-fang tsa-chih*, XXXIV, 7 (1937), 73–80. The earlier Ch'ing system and the liberalizing effect of T'ao Chu's reforms are discussed in Katō Shigeshi, *Shina keizaishi kōshō*, Tokyo, 1952–53, II, 493–504 (*FB* 9.8.8).

146. Liu Chien, "Tao-kuang ch'ao fei-yin kai-p'iao shih-mo," *Chung-kuo she-hui ching-chi shih chi-k'an*, I, 2 (1933), 123–28. Hui-i (pseud.), "Huai-pei p'iao-yen yen-ko," *T'an-yen ts'ung-pao*, No. 1 (1913), 20 pp., is a careful traditional-type study of the ticket system in the Huai-pei area in the Tao-kuang period, with some attention to the post-Taiping efforts to restore it. The article was written in defense of the Ch'ing salt system against the sweeping innovations proposed by Chang Chien and others during the early years of the Republic.

On the technology of salt production, see Li Jung, "An Account of the Salt Industry at Tzu-liu-ching," translated with an introduction and notes by Lienche Tu Fang, *Isis*, XXXIX, Part 4, No. 118 (1948), pp. 228–34.

147. T. F. Wade, "The Salt Revenue of China," published as an appendix to Wade (trans.), *Decree of the Emperor of China . . .* , London, 1878, *passim*.

148. Wade, *loc. cit.*, p. 255.

149. Liang Huai salt, for example, could not pass through the Taiping territories to its licensed sales areas in Hupeh and Hunan. This affected producers as well as consumers. (Ho Wei-ning, "T'ai-p'ing t'ien-kuo shih-tai Chung-kuo yen-cheng kai-kuan," *She-hui k'o-hsüeh ts'ung-k'an*, I, 2 (1934), 111.)

150. *Ibid.*, pp. 149–51.

151. Tso Tsung-t'ang, two memorials of 1865 (TC-4), *THTKTI*, Ch. 35, chung, pp. 20–23.

152. For Restoration views of the salt question, see *CSWP*, Chs. 42–46, esp. Chs. 44–45, *passim*; *THTKTI*, Ch. 35, shang, chung, hsia, *passim*. On Tso Tsung-t'ang's views, see, in addition to reference in note 151 above, E. H. Parker's summary of Tso's "masterly state paper on the salt problem" reviewing developments since the eighteenth century, *China Review*, XII, 1 (1883), 57–58. For Hsü Chi-yü's views (apparently pre-T'ung-chih), see Hsü, *Sung-k'an hsien-sheng wen-chi*, Ch. 1, pp. 10–12b, and *Sung-k'an hsien-sheng tsou-su*, Ch. 2, pp. 40–45. For Kuo Sung-tao's analysis in terms of unified official control and diversified merchant responsibility, see his *Yang-chih shu-wu ch'üan-chi*, "Wen-chi," Ch. 28, pp. 6–11b. On the views of Tseng Kuo-fan and Feng Kuei-fen, see below.

Ting Pao-chen did not begin his reform of the Szechwan salt system until the late 1870's. He used the principle of *kuan-yün shang-hsiao* (transport by officials, sale by merchants), which he thought would provide security for the merchant, low prices for the consumer, a high volume of sales, and hence increased revenues. (See Ting's memorial of 1880 in *THTKTI*, Ch. 35, chung, pp. 1–2, and *Ssu-ch'uan yen-fa chih*, Ting's memorial preceding chüan-shou, Preface and *passim*.) For a survey of the Szechwan reforms, see Hui-min (pseud.), "Ch'uan-yen pien-fa yen-ko k'ao," in *T'an-yen ts'ung-pao*, No. 2 (1913), 10 pp., and No. 3 (1913), 10 pp.

153. Chih-kang, *Ch'u-shih t'ai-hsi chi-yao*, Ch. 1, p. 4. On Chih-kang's trip to the Occident with the Burlingame Mission, see Chapter XI.

154. Tseng Yang-feng, "Chung-kuo yen-cheng chih tung-hsiang," *loc. cit.*, pp. 77–78.

155. Three memorials by Tseng, *CHTI*, Ch. 4, pp. 23–32b; Wang Shu-han, "Liang Huai yen-wu yü ch'ien-chuang," *loc. cit.*, pp. 150–51; T'ang Ch'ing-tseng, "Tseng Kuo-fan chih ching-chi ssu-hsiang," *loc. cit.*, pp. 54–55.

156. Wang Shu-han, *loc. cit.*, pp. 150–51.

157. Feng, "Tu k'uei-k'ung i," *CPLKI*, Ch. 1, pp. 19–19b.

158. Shao-kwan Chen, *The System of Taxation in China in the Tsing Dynasty*, p. 82. For a defense of the effectiveness of the Ch'ing control of salt smuggling, without specific reference to the T'ung-chih period, see Hui-i (pseud.), "Li-tai ch'eng-chih ssu-yen fa-kuei k'uan-yen te-shih chih pi-chiao," *T'an-yen ts'ung-pao*, No. 6 (1913).

159. E.g., *SL-TC*, Ch. 197, pp. 13–14b; Ch. 204, pp. 21–22; Ch. 212, pp. 12–12b.

160. *Ibid.*, Ch. 204, pp. 21–22.

161. *NCH*, July 24, Aug. 4, 1866.

162. Exchange of notes between Alcock and Prince Kung, early October, 1869, *China. No. 1. (1870)*, pp. 18–19.

163. Tso Shu-chen, "Chung-kuo yen-cheng yen-ko shih," Part 4, *Yen-cheng tsa-chih*, No. 19 (1915), pp. 1–3; Ho Wei-ning, "T'ai-p'ing t'ien-kuo shih-tai Chung-kuo yen-cheng kai-kuan," *loc. cit.*, pp. 149–51.

164. Hsü Ta-ling, *Ch'ing-tai chüan-na chih-tu*, Peking, 1950, Preface.

165. T'ang Hsiang-lung, "Tao-kuang ch'ao chüan-chien chih t'ung-chi," *She-hui k'o-hsüeh tsa-chih*, II, 4 (1931), 434–36; Hsü Ta-ling, *op. cit.*, Chs. 1, 5; Lo Yü-tung, *Chung-kuo li-chin shih*, I, 3–9; Beal, "The Origin of *Likin*," pp. 44–47.

166. Memorial of the censor Sun I-mou, *CHTI*, Ch. 1, pp. 32–35. Memorial of the governor of Shantung, Yen Ching-ming, reviewing the whole issue and associating himself with the views expressed in previous memorials by the Grand Secretary Ch'i Chün-tsao; the supervising censor Kuo Hsiang-jui; the governor of Hunan, Yün Shih-lin; the metropolitan prefect, Chiang Ch'i-ling, and others, *CHTI*, Ch. 2, pp. 21–24.

167. Improved communications were not emphasized in general Chinese economic programs until later (Chao Feng-t'ien, *Wan-Ch'ing wu-shih nien ching-chi ssu-hsiang shih*), p. 147.

168. E.g., Gideon Chen, "Tso Tsung-t'ang, the Farmer of Hsiang-shang," *loc. cit.*, pp. 219–25.

169. *NCH*, Feb. 6, 1868.

170. Memorial of Ting Shou-ch'ang, 1863, *Chiang-su sheng chien-fu ch'üan-an*, Ch. 2, pp. 6b–7.

171. The subject is summarized in Harold C. Hinton, "Grain Transport via the

Grand Canal, 1845–1901," *Papers on China*, IV (1950), 24–57, and Hinton, "The Grain Tribute System of the Ch'ing Dynasty," *FEQ*, XI, 3 (1952), 339–54. On canal works during the Restoration, see *WHTK*, p. 7614, and Ch. 13, "T'ien-fu" 13, *passim*. Memorials of Hu Chia-yü and Li Hung-chang, *CHTI*, Ch. 8, pp. 20–32b; Li's memorial reviews the history of the issue. See also *THTKTI*, Ch. 60–62, *passim*; *SL-TC*, Ch. 200, pp. 2b–3; Ch. 228, pp. 2–3; *NCH*, Mar. 18, 1865. On the importance attached to continuing canal works in spite of the growing use of the sea route, see *WHTK*, pp. 8327–28.

172. E.g., *THTKTI*, Ch. 34, *passim*; *CSWP*, Ch. 40–41, *passim*; *CHTI*, Ch. 3, pp. 27–28.

173. E.g., *SL-TC*, Ch. 231, pp. 3b–4; Ch. 228, pp. 3–3b.

174. Edict of Jan. 3, 1868, ordering the governor-general of Kiangsu, Kiangsi, and Anhwei and the governor of Kiangsu so to instruct the taotais of the coastal areas, *SL-TC*, Ch. 218, pp. 22b–23. The sea route was referred to as tax-free because it bypassed the numerous tax posts along the land route.

175. Summarized in memorial of Li Hung-chang, 1872 (TC-11), *WHTK*, p. 11043.

176. *NCH*, Sept. 28, Dec. 14, 1867.

177. *Ibid.*, Aug. 18, 1866.

178. *Ibid.*, Sept. 28, 1867.

179. *Chefoo Daily News*, reprinted in *NCH*, Sept. 28, 1867.

180. The Chinese case was summarized in the memorial of the governor-general of Kiangsu, Kiangsi, and Anhwei, Li Tsung-hsi, 1872 (TC-11), *THTKTI*, Ch. 2, pp. 13b–14. Both Hart and Alcock agreed with the logic of the Chinese position in the existing circumstances (Supplement to *NCH*, Apr. 29, 1865; *China. No. 12. (1869)*, pp. 2–3, 5, 8).

181. *NCH*, Sept. 3, 1864; Oct. 13, 1866; Aug. 22, 1868.

182. According to the announcement of the establishment of the Shanghai Steam Navigation Company, Russell and Company dominated the enterprise, although shares were said to be popular with both Chinese and foreigners (*NCH*, Mar. 29, 1862). For a review of its history, see *ibid.*, Aug. 25, 1866. See also Kwang-ching Liu, "Financing a Steam-Navigation Company in China, 1861–62," *The Business History Review*, XXVIII, 2 (1954), 154 ff.

183. Sun Shen-ch'in, *Chao-shang chü shih-kao*, n.p., n.d. (1920's); Chu Po-k'ang, *Chung-kuo ching-chi shih-kang*, pp. 219–20; *Kuo-ying chao-shang chü ch'i-shih-wu chou-nien chi-nien k'an*, Shanghai, 1947; Miyazaki Ichisada, "Shōsho kyoku no rya-kushi . . . ," *Tōyōshi kenkyū*, XI, 2 (1951), 63–69 (*FB* 7.12.5).

184. Quoted in Paul H. Clyde, "The China Policy of J. Ross Browne, American Minister at Peking, 1868–1869," *PHR*, I, 3 (1932), 317.

185. *NCH*, Apr. 22, 1867.

186. Freeman-Mitford, *The Attaché at Peking*, pp. 231–36.

187. For Kuo Sung-tao's later views, see his *Yang-chih shu-wu ch'üan-chi*, "Wen-chi," Ch. 28, pp. 11b–15b.

188. E-Tu Zen Sun, "The Pattern of Railway Development in China," *FEQ*, XIV, 2 (1955), 179–99; comment by Moses Abramovitz, pp. 169–78.

189. *NCH*, July 15, 1865; Jan. 5, Aug. 21, 1867.

190. *WHTK*, p. 11171.

191. E.g., *SL-TC*, Ch. 225, pp. 27–27b. On the courier service, which was faster than foreigners at the time realized, see John K. Fairbank and Ssu-yü Teng, "On the Transmission of Ch'ing Documents," *HJAS*, IV, 1 (1939), 12–46.

192. *WHTK*, p. 11171.

193. Chao Feng-t'ien, *Wan-Ch'ing wu-shih nien ching-chi ssu-hsiang shih*, p. 88.

194. Matteo Ricci, *China in the 16th Century; The Journals of Matthew Ricci, 1583–1610*, New York, 1953, p. 10.

195. Alcock, "The Chinese Empire in Its Foreign Relations," *loc. cit.*, p. 238.

196. On the traditional Chinese belief in the marginal importance of foreign trade, see Otake Fumio, "Shina ni okeru bōeki no kannen," *Shina kenkyū*, 17 (1928), pp. 57–75 (*FB* 6.3.5). Otake considers that modern Chinese boycotts have in part reflected this view.

197. Memorial of May 29, 1866, *IWSM-TC*, Ch. 41, pp. 43–50.

198. *Report of Her Majesty's Consul on the Trade of Shanghai*, 1866, reprinted in *NCH*, Nov. 23, 1867; *NCH,* July 14, 1870; statement of British subjects of Chinese descent, *ibid.*, Dec. 12, 1868.

199. *NCH*, Oct. 12, 1867.

200. *Ibid.*, Mar. 22, 1862; Sept. 18, 1865; Sept. 28, 1867; Mar. 9, Oct. 31, Dec. 22, 1868. Maritime Customs statistics (reviewed in *NCH*, July 14, 1866) confirmed the impressions of observers. See also abstract of a customs report on the trade of Hankow, *The Chinese and Japanese Repository*, III, 3 (1865), 543–44; Freeman-Mitford, *The Attaché at Peking*, pp. 53–54, 98.

201. *NCH*, July 7, 1866.

202. *Ibid.*, Sept. 29, 1866.

203. Foreign Office memorandum of Feb. 17, 1870, *China. No. 3. (1870)*, No. 1.

204. "Retrospect of the Year 1862," *NCH*, Jan. 31, 1863; Alcock to Clarendon, Oct. 29, 1869, *China. No. 3 (1870)*, No. 4.

205. Ch'en Ts'an, *Chung-kuo shang-yeh shih*, pp. 108–26; S. Wells Williams, *The Chinese Commercial Guide*, Hongkong, 1863 ed., pp. 188–91; minutes of meeting of NCBRAS, Supplement to *NCH*, Apr. 29, 1865; proclamation of Li Hung-chang, Apr. 18, 1866, in *NCH*, Apr. 28, 1866.

206. Sargent, *Anglo-Chinese Commerce and Diplomacy*, Table A.

207. *NCH*, Apr. 22, 1867.

208. Col. Sykes, July 13, 1869, *Hansard*, Vol. 197, pp. 1790–94.

209. Probably more has been written in English on the Maritime Customs than on the whole of modern Chinese history. The present purpose is only to indicate the role of foreign trade in the general economic program of the Restoration. For a digest of Chinese materials on the origin of the Customs, see *WHTK*, pp. 8784–85. The chief Chinese source is *IWSM*. For a comprehensive account heavily annotated to the Western sources, see Stanley F. Wright, *Hart and the Chinese Customs*, Belfast, 1950. On the background to 1858, see Fairbank, *Trade and Diplomacy . . . ,* I, Part V.

210. E.g., Hu Sheng, *Ti-kuo chu-i yü Chung-kuo cheng-chih*, Shanghai, 1952, pp. 41–47.

211. *NCH*, Mar. 18, 1868. See also Chapter III.

212. *Ibid.*, Nov. 9, 1867, reviewing incidents cited in the memorials on treaty revision submitted by the various foreign chambers of commerce in China. See also issues of Aug. 3, Aug. 10, 1861; Jan. 24, 1868.

213. *IWSM-TC*, Ch. 30, pp. 1 ff., 12b–13b; Ch. 39, pp. 21–22b.

214. Tsungli-yamen memorial, Jan. 25, 1862; *ibid.*, Ch. 3, pp. 45b–47; edict of Feb. 7, 1862, *ibid.*, Ch. 4, pp. 1–1b. Further Tsungli-yamen memorial and edict, Feb. 19, 1862, *ibid.*, Ch. 4, pp. 9–13b.

215. Tsungli-yamen memorial, Apr. 4, 1862, *ibid.*, Ch. 5, p. 13.

216. Edicts of Mar. 27, Apr. 29, and Oct. 1, 1868, *SL-TC*, Ch. 226, pp. 11b–12; Ch. 228, pp. 25b–26b; Ch. 241, pp. 3–4b.

217. Charles J. Stanley, "Hu Kuang-yung and China's Early Foreign Loans," Harvard University Ph.D. dissertation, 1951, p. 135 and chap. vi. Ms. cited with author's permission.

218. The meager information available on a series of small, short-term loans negotiated by local authorities on the southeast coast between 1861 and 1866 is summarized in Stanley, "Hu Kuang-yung . . . ," pp. 29–41. On the failure of Hart's effort to have the Chinese government appear as the borrower, thus setting up a modern method for financing other projects, see Stanley F. Wright, *Hart and the Chinese Customs*, pp. 364–68.

219. E.g., edict refusing the governor of Fukien, Hsü Tsung-kan, permission to negotiate such loans, June 23, 1862, *IWSM-TC*, Ch. 6, pp. 50b–51b; edict of Oct. 23, 1862, *ibid.*, Ch. 10, pp. 1 ff. On a comparable issue in Chihli, see edict urging Liu Ch'ang-yu and Ch'ung-hou to be cautious, *ibid.*, Ch. 16, pp. 4b–5b. The purchase of the Lay-Osborn Flotilla raised the same issue (see Chapter IX).

220. Edict of April 29, 1867, approving Tso's request to borrow 1,200,000 teals from foreign merchants (*yang shang*) at Shanghai, *SL-TC*, Ch. 199, pp. 20–21b. On the plan for drawing drafts against funds on deposit in Yün-cheng, Shansi, see edict of May 28, 1867, *ibid.*, Ch. 201, pp. 23b–24b. Tso's memorial and edict ,Jan. 16, 1868, *IWSM-TC*, Ch. 56, pp. 8–9. The text of the edict also appears in *SL-TC*, Ch. 220, pp. 9–11. See also Stanley, "Hu Kuang-yung . . . ," pp. 46–47, and Gideon Chen, "Tso Tsung-t'ang, the Farmer of Hsiang-shang," *loc. cit.*, p. 222.

221. Edict of Jan. 22, 1868, *SL-TC*, Ch. 220, pp. 26b–28; edict of Sept. 3, 1868, *ibid.*, Ch. 238, pp. 19–20b. "Extracts from the Diary of Tseng 'Hou-Yeh,' Chinese Minister to England and France," translated by J. N. Jordan, *China Review*, XI, No. 3, pp. 135–36. Tseng Chi-tse's remarks have been effectively but improperly used in Chinese Communist attacks on Tso as the agent of foreign capitalists, e.g., Ma Hsiao-shih, *Hsi-pei Hui-tsu ko-ming chien-shih*, Shanghai, 1951, pp. 71–74.

222. Edict of Dec. 12, 1867, in reply to an Imperial Household Department memorial, *SL-TC*, Ch. 216, pp. 25–25b.

223. E.g., the Tsungli-yamen's approval of the gist of nine reports submitted by Hart containing technical suggestions for greater administrative effectiveness, *IWSM-TC*, Ch. 2, pp. 17–35. See also Chinese materials on this subject translated in *NCH*, Nov. 2, 1861.

224. *CSK*, "Shih-huo-chih," Ch. 5, pp. 15–19b. For additional examples, including some from the T'ung-chih period, see Satoi Hikoshichirō, "Shindai kōgyō shihon ni tsuite," *Tōyōshi kenkyū*, XI, 1 (1950), 32–50 (*FB* 7.9.1).

225. Chao Feng-t'ien, *Wan-Ch'ing wu-shih nien ching-chi ssu-hsiang shih*, p. 41.

226. The Chefoo correspondent of the *NCH* reported a persistent government fear that "a thirst for gold" was "likely to subvert the agricultural character of the people." (*NCH*, July 28, 1866). And in fact mining in Shantung had been suspended

in 1848, owing to clashes between the miners and the local gentry (*ibid.*, Aug. 14, 1868).

227. *THTKTI*, Ch. 12, *passim*.

228. Brief notices appeared frequently in *NCH* between July and November. See especially issues of Aug. 14 and Aug. 28, 1868. Chinese reports are summarized in a memorial of the Tsungli-yamen, Sept. 20, 1868, *IWSM-TC*, Ch. 61, pp. 5–6.

229. Memorial of the Tsungli-yamen, Nov. 8, 1868, *ibid.*, Ch. 62, pp. 9–10. A despatch of Taotai Ying (Shanghai) to foreign consuls, transmitting the Tsungli-yamen's statement on the illegality of mining by Chinese or foreigners, is translated in *NCH*, July 31, 1868. For Taotai Ying's proclamation to Chinese officials, see *NCH*, Aug. 14, 1868.

230. Memorial of the Tsungli-yamen, Oct. 30, 1868, *IWSM-TC*, Ch. 61, pp. 22–24.

231. "Return of the Import Trade at the Port of Tientsin . . . for 1862," *China. No. 4. (1864)*, pp. 38–39; *NCH*, May 30, Oct. 3, 1868. Apparently files of the vernacular edition no longer exist.

232. Feng, "Ch'ou kuo-yung i," *CPLKI*, Ch. 1, pp. 38b–40b.

233. Satoi Hikoshichirō, *loc. cit.*

234. Feng, "Chih yang-ch'i i," *CPLKI*, Ch. 2, pp. 70–74b.

235. *WHTK*, p. 8261.

236. On the structure of the Board of Revenue, see Shao-kwan Chen, *The System of Taxation in China in the Tsing Dynasty . . .*, pp. 16–19; Matsui Yoshio, *Shinchō keihi no kenkyū* (reprinted in book form), Dairen, 1935, chap. 5 (*FB* 7.13.2).

237. Board of Revenue memorial, 1869 (TC-8), *WHTK*, pp. 7525–26. On efforts to improve accounting in the reports of tax collection, see *ibid.*, pp. 7827–31.

238. E.g., *SL-TC*, Ch. 206, pp. 9b–10b; Ch. 207, pp. 2–3; Ch. 217, pp. 24b-25b. *IWSM-TC*, Ch. 3, pp. 25b–26b.

239. Chia Shih-i, "Wu-shih nien lai Chung-kuo ts'ai-cheng," in Shen-pao kuan, Fiftieth Anniversary Publication, Vol. II, *Wu-shih nien lai chih Chung-kuo*, p. 1 of the article.

240. *WHTK*, pp. 8211–12.

241. *CSWP*, Ch. 24–26; Feng, "Tu k'uei-k'ung i," *CPLKI*, Ch. 1, pp. 19–19b.

242. T'ang Ch'ing-tseng, "Tseng Kuo-fan chih ching-chi ssu-hsiang," *loc. cit.*, pp. 55–56; Feng, "Yung ch'ien pu fei yin i," *CPLKI*, Ch. 2, pp. 78b–83b; "Tu k'uei-k'ung i," *CPLKI*, Ch. 1, pp. 19–19b.

243. Edict of 1863 (TC-2), *WHTK*, pp. 7520-21; Board of Revenue memorial, 1867 (TC-6), *THTKTI*, Ch. 38, pp. 10–10b.

244. *WHTK*, Ch. 21, p. 7709; *SL-TC*, Ch. 235, pp. 14b–15b.

245. Edict of 1869 (TC-8), and other materials, *WHTK*, pp. 7709–12; edict of Apr. 12, 1868, *SL-TC*, Ch. 227, pp. 13b–14.

246. Chang Te-ch'ang, "Chin-tai Chung-kuo ti huo-pi," *loc. cit.*, p. 83.

247. Otake Fumio, *Kinsei Shina keizaishi kenkyū*, pp. 129–37 (*FB* 7.1.3); *NCH*, Mar. 16, 1867. See also Masui Tsuneo's critical review of *Yang-yin pien-cheng* (Hangchow, 1866), which reflects sharp criticism of silver forgery, in *Wada hakushi kanreki kinen Tōyōshi ronsō*, pp. 625–40 (*FB* 2.2.19).

248. Memorial of the censor Ch'en T'ing-ching, 1862 (TC-1), on the commodity operations of the native banks, and edict to the Peking gendarmerie to investigate and punish (*WHTK*, Ch. 21, "Ch'ien-pi," 3). Edict of August 21, 1868, authorizing the payment of 14 *ch'ien* (1.4 taels) of silver instead of the former 8 to a garrison at

Tsingchow, Shantung, so that an intercalary month payment in silver would buy the customary amount of rice, *SL-TC*, Ch. 237, pp. 15–15b.

249. See table in See, *The Foreign Trade of China*, Appendix II. The subsequent drop to 3/3 in 1895 began after the Restoration and was gradual. See table in Stanley, "Chinese Finance from 1852 to 1908," *loc. cit.*, p. 64.

250. Ch'en Ch'i-t'ien, *Shan-hsi p'iao-chuang k'ao-lüeh*, Shanghai, 1937; Katō Shigeshi, *Shina keizaishi kōshō*, II, 463–77 (*FB* 9.8.8); Yang, *Money and Credit in China*, pp. 81–88; Stanley, "Hu Kuang-yung . . . ," pp. 28–31. "Notes on Northern Chinese Banks," *NCH*, 1867, especially No. 15 in the series, Oct. 19, 1867. The series deals with credit, interest rates, note issues, circulation, deposits, etc.

251. Ch'en Ch'i-t'ien, *Shan-hsi p'iao-chuang k'ao-lüeh*, pp. 43–44, and Ch. 3, *passim*.

252. On the use of the Hongkong and Shanghai Bank by Chinese port merchants, see *NCH*, Aug. 25, 1866.

253. The figures are given in edict of Mar. 8, 1868, *SL-TC*, Ch. 224, pp. 47–48, summarizing Board of Revenue memorial.

254. Edict of May 8, 1868, *SL-TC*, Ch. 229, pp. 13–14b.

255. Edict of Apr. 22, 1867, *ibid.*, Ch. 199, pp. 6b–8.

256. Edict of July 6, 1867, *ibid.*, Ch. 205, pp. 10b–11.

257. On Board of Revenue advances to the governor-general of Chihli, Kuan-wen, see *ibid.*, Ch. 222, pp. 30–31b, and Ch. 238, pp. 24–25.

258. *Ibid.*, Ch. 214, pp. 3–4, 24–25; Ch. 225, pp. 21b–22; Ch. 232, pp. 23b–24b; Ch. 240, pp. 17–17b.

259. E.g., *ibid.*, Ch. 220, pp. 15b–16b; Ch. 224, pp. 19–19b.

260. E.g., *ibid.*, Ch. 210, pp. 4b–5; Ch. 212, pp. 14–14b; Ch. 213, pp. 17–18b; Ch. 221, pp. 22–23b; Ch. 231, pp. 20b–21b; Ch. 232, p. 28b; Ch. 237, pp. 1b–3; Ch. 241, pp. 12b–13b.

261. *Ibid.*, Ch. 225, pp. 33–34; see also Ch. 210, pp. 17–19; Ch. 241, pp. 1–3.

262. *Ibid.*, Ch. 202, pp. 15–16; Ch. 204, pp. 10–11b; Ch. 211, pp. 13–14, 16b–17; Ch. 218, pp. 8–8b; Ch. 221, pp. 11–12b; Ch. 224, pp. 44–45; Ch. 232, pp. 29b–31; Ch. 240, pp. 22b–23b.

263. For summaries and critiques of past estimates, see Wang Shih-ta, "Chin-tai Chung-kuo jen-k'ou ti ku-chi," *She-hui k'o-hsüeh tsa-chih*, I, 3 (1930), 32–130; I, 4 (1930), 34–105; II, 1 (1931), 51–105. Chen Ta, *Population in Modern China*, Chicago, 1946, chap. 1. A. J. Jaffe, "A Review of the Censuses and Demographic Statistics of China," *Population Studies*, I, 3 (1947), 308–28. Chen Ta, "The Need of Population Research in China," *Population Studies*, I, 4 (1948), 342–52. John K. Fairbank, *The United States and China*, Cambridge, Mass., 1948, pp. 138–43.

264. Moses Abramovitz, "Economics of Growth," with appended comment by Harold F. Williamson and Simon Kusnets, in Bernard F. Haley (ed.), *A Survey of Contemporary Economics*, Homewood, Illinois, 1952, II, 132–82.

265. *NCH*, Oct. 19, 1867. On the Yangchow salt merchants and the Shansi bankers as the two "zaibatsu" of the Ch'ing, see Saeki Tomi, "Shindai ni okeru engyō shihon ni tsuite," *loc. cit.*

266. Two articles from the *Foochow Advertiser*, reprinted in *NCH*, May 6, 1867.

267. Abramovitz, *loc. cit.*, pp. 159–60.

268. Saeki Tomi (*loc. cit.*) cites numerous illustrations from which he concludes that this was the rule and not the exception.

269. Chu Po-k'ang, *Chung-kuo ching-chi shih-kang*, pp. 217–18.

270. Yen Chung-p'ing, *Chung-kuo mien-yeh chih fa-chan*, Chungking, 1943, pp. 1–3; revised edition, Peking, 1955.

271. Chang Yüan-ch'i, "Chung-kuo t'ou-tzu wen-t'i," *Ching-chi hsüeh chi-k'an*, II, 4 (1931), 54–66.

272. Stanley, "Hu Kuang-yung . . . ," is an excellent case study. See especially pp. 4–5 and chap. 3, *passim*; see also Satoi Hikoshichirō, "Shindai kōgyō shihon ni tsuite," *loc. cit.* (FB 7.9.1), for illustrations of how these factors kept merchants from investing in mining.

273. Yen Chung-p'ing, *Chung-kuo mien-yeh chih fa-chan*, pp. 1–3.

274. Abramovitz, *loc. cit.*, p. 160.

275. On these points see Marion J. Levy, Jr., "Contrasting Factors in the Modernization of China and Japan," *Economic Development and Cultural Change*, II, 3 (1953), 161–97.

276. Yen Chung-p'ing, "Ming Ch'ing liang tai ti-fang kuan ch'ang-tao fang-chih-yeh shih-li," *Tung-fang tsa-chih*, XLII, 8 (1945), 20–26, based on a study of attempts by fifty-six local officials.

277. On the experience of wartime factories in this respect, see Kuo-heng Shih, *China Enters the Machine Age*, Cambridge, Mass., 1944.

278. For a comparison between Chinese study of Western technology during the K'ang-hsi period and in the period following the Opium War, see Naitō Torajirō, *Shinchō shi tsūron*, pp. 117–32 (FB 2.1.2).

279. *China. No. 5. (1871)*, p. 95.

280. Chang Te-ch'ang, "Chin-tai Chung-kuo ti huo-pi," *loc. cit.*, p. 85; tables in Chu Ch'i-hua, *Chung-kuo chin-tai she-hui shih chieh-p'ou*, Shanghai, 1933, pp. 12–15.

281. On the European experience on these points, see Alexander Gerschenkron, "Economic Backwardness in Historical Perspective," in Bert F. Hoselitz (ed.), *The Progress of Underdeveloped Areas*, Chicago, 1952, pp. 9, 12–13.

282. Shao-kwan Chen, *The System of Taxation in China in the Tsing Dynasty . . .*, p. 42.

283. Lo Yü-tung, "Kuang-hsü ch'ao pu-chiu ts'ai-cheng chih fang-ts'e," *Chung-kuo she-hui ching-chi shih chi-k'an*, I, 2 (1933), 189 ff.

284. Gerschenkron, *loc. cit.*; pp. 23, 25.

CHAPTER IX

1. For examples of the use of the phrase "self-strengthening" (*tzu-ch'iang*) in several contexts, see *IWSM-TC*, Ch. 43, pp. 13, 15; Ch. 46, pp. 5, 30b; Ch. 50, p. 9b; Ch. 51, p. 18b; Ch. 61, p. 28b. For typical statements on the importance of considering long-term rather than immediate effects, see Wang Chih-p'ing, *Tseng Hu Tso ping-hsüeh kang-yao*, pp. 11–20.

2. For a concise summary, with full references, of the views on these points of the three chief scholar-generals of the period, see Wang Chih-p'ing, *op. cit.*, pp. 21–30 and *passim*.

3. On the Banners of the early period, see Chaoying Fang, "A Technique for Estimating the Numerical Strength of the Early Manchu Military Forces," *HJAS*, XIII, 1/2 (1950), pp. 192–215. On the origin and development of the *lü-ying*, see Lo Erh-kang, *Lü-ying ping-chih*, Chungking, 1945, Chs. 1–3; on their decline, Ch. 4. For

further material on the decline of traditional forces, see Lo Erh-kang, "Ch'ing-chi ping wei chiang-yu-ti," *Chung-kuo she-hui ching-chi shih chi-k'an*, V, 2 (1937), 237 ff.; Naitō Torajirō, "Shinchō suibō ron," pp. 325–46, reprinted in Naitō, *Shinchō shi tsū ron*, Tokyo, 1944 (*FB* 2.1.1). For a brief summary of the general background, see Ralph L. Powell, *The Rise of Chinese Military Power, 1895–1912*, Princeton, 1955, pp. 1–31.

4. Freeman-Mitford, *The Attaché at Peking*, pp. 190–91.

5. Lo Erh-kang, *Hsiang-chün hsin-chih*, Changsha, 1939, pp. 1–15.

6. *IWSM-TC*, Ch. 40, p. 14b.

7. Lo Erh-kang, *Hsiang-chün hsin-chih*, pp. 64, 93–94, and Ch. 6, *passim*; Lo, "Ch'ing-chi ping wei chiang-yu-ti," *loc. cit.*, pp. 249 ff.; Chang Ch'i-yün, *Chung-kuo chün-shih shih-lüeh*, Shanghai, 1946, pp. 42–47, 120–23. I am indebted to Chaoying Fang for amplification of the materials referred to.

8. *NCH*, Aug. 10, 1865. For similar statements see issues of June 2, Oct. 20, 1866; Feb. 23, 1867; Mar. 28, 1868.

9. Lo Erh-kang, *Hsiang-chün hsin-chih*, p. 66.

10. Ch'en Ch'i-t'ien, *Hu Tseng Tso p'ing-luan yao-chih*, p. 14.

11. Chu Ch'i-hua, *Chung-kuo chin-tai she-hui shih chieh-p'ou*, Shanghai, 1933, pp. 123, 129.

12. Lo Erh-kang, *Hsiang-chün hsin-chih*, p. 66.

13. See the classified edition, where excerpts on a given subject are grouped together: (*Hsin-shih piao-tien*) *Tseng Kuo-fan jih-chi lei-ch'ao*, edited by Wang Ch'i-yüan, Shanghai, 1923, pp. 66–82, and Wang Chih-p'ing, *op. cit.*, pp. 1–2, 42–47, 125–34, and *passim*. Tseng Kuo-fan was the leading theoretician in the field of military reorganization, as in several spheres. For a summary of his views concerning military communications, finance, militia, training, discipline, selection of officers, strategy, modern weapons, and so forth, see Ho I-k'un, *Tseng Kuo-fan p'ing-chuan*, pp. 370–424. See particularly his letter to Tseng Kuo-ch'üan and other writings in *Tseng Wen-cheng kung hsüeh-an*, edited by Lung Meng-sun, Shanghai, 1925, pp. 314–44.

14. Lo Erh-kang, *Hsiang-chün hsin-chih*, pp. 43–44.

15. Chiang Wei-ch'iao, *Chung-kuo chin san-pai nien che-hsüeh shih*, Shanghai, 1936, pp. 41–42. On the Neo-Confucian revival, see Chapter IV.

16. Analytical table of officers of the Hsiang Army, Lo Erh-kang, *Hsiang-chün hsin-chih*, p. 64.

17. The collected biographies of the military leaders of the Restoration testify to this point. See *Chung-hsing chiang-shuai pieh-chuan*, compiled by Chu K'ung-chang, with a preface by Sun I-jang, 1897.

18. "Tientsin News," *NCH*, June 29, 1867.

19. *NCH*, Oct. 25, 1867. See also *ibid.*, July 7, 1866. On the critical importance of the governor-general, see Major General Emery Upton, *The Armies of Europe and Asia, Embracing Official Reports on the Armies of Japan, China, India, Persia, Italy, Russia, Austria, Germany, France and England*, Portsmouth, England, 1878, pp. 27–29.

20. "The Chinese Army" (unsigned), *The Times* (London), Sept. 8, 1883, p. 4.

21. *NCH*, July 28, 1866 (unsigned). On the same point, see Upton, *op. cit.*, p. 21, and *Marx on China, 1853–1860; Articles from the New York Daily Tribune*, London, 1951, p. 47.

22. Tsungli-yamen memorial, Nov. 17, 1862, *IWSM-TC*, Ch. 10, pp. 13–15;

Tsungli-yamen memorial, 1862 (TC-1), *WHTK*, p. 9742; edict of Dec. 3, 1862, *IWSM-TC*, Ch. 10, pp. 42–43; memorial of Lao Ch'ung-kuang, Feb. 12, 1863, *ibid.*, Ch. 12, pp. 55b–58b. Dec. 7, 1861, *CSK*, "Pen-chi," Ch. 21, p. 3.

23. Feng, "Chien ping-o i," *CPLKI*, Ch. 2, pp. 64–65. The point here was that the military examinations, unlike the civil, made so few demands that men of low caliber could pass (Upton, *op. cit.*, pp. 22–23). Feng chose to regard this as a recent degeneration.

24. *NCH*, July 28, 1866.

25. Edict of Feb. 15, 1868, *SL-TC*, Ch. 223, pp. 1b–2; edict of July 13, 1868, *ibid.*, Ch. 234, pp. 13–14.

26. Edict of Apr. 9, 1868, *SL-TC*, Ch. 227, pp. 5–6b.

27. See Seng-ko-lin-ch'in's memorial listing false reports by various officers, 1862 (TC-1), *WHTK*, p. 9533. Example of an edict ordering punishment for a false report, Aug. 21, 1868, *SL-TC*, Ch. 237, pp. 14–15.

28. Examples are to be found in nearly every chüan of *SL-TC*, e.g., edicts of Mar. 24, 1862, Ch. 20, pp. 19–19b; Mar. 8, 1867, Ch. 196, p. 8b; Mar. 12, 1867, Ch. 196, pp. 17b–18b; Apr. 30, 1867, Ch. 199, pp. 27b–28; June 22, 1867, Ch. 204, pp. 1b–2b; July 20, 1867, Ch. 206, pp. 7b–8b; Aug. 24, 1867, Ch. 208, pp. 14–15; Oct. 13, 1867, Ch. 212, pp. 1–1b; Oct. 23, 1867, Ch. 212, p. 16; Nov. 2, 1867, Ch. 213, pp. 12–13.

29. Placard reproduced in *NCH*, Apr. 21, 1860. Chinese text reads:

> Tsei chih, ping ho tsai
> Ping lai, tsei i k'ung
> K'o-lien, ping yü tsei
> ho jih te hsiang-feng

According to Chaoying Fang, an earlier version of the same verse was used during the White Lotus Rebellion at the beginning of the century.

30. For these and other quotations from Tseng, Tso, and Hu on this point, see Wang Chih-p'ing, *op. cit.*, pp. 133–40.

31. Edict of Sept. 23, 1867, *SL-TC*, Ch. 210, p. 29.

32. "The Shantung Rebels," *NCH*, Nov. 23, 1867.

33. Edict of July 14, 1868, *SL-TC*, Ch. 234, pp. 21–22.

34. Edict of May 3, 1867, *SL-TC*, Ch. 199, pp. 31–31b.

35. E.g., *CSK*, "Pen-chi," Ch. 21, p. 3; *SL-TC*, Ch. 209, pp. 1b–2b; Ch. 210, pp. 7b–8; Ch. 214, pp. 34–35; Ch. 216, pp. 11–12; Ch. 218, pp. 2–3; Ch. 223, pp. 18–19; Ch. 230, pp. 6b–7, 19–19b; Ch. 237, pp. 6b–7; *WHTK*, pp. 9533–44.

36. Ch'en Ch'i-t'ien, *Hu Tseng Tso p'ing-luan yao-chih*, Ch. 4. The text of the song is given (pp. 43–45) along with an account of Tseng's various measures designed to improve relations between army and people. *Tseng Kuo-fan chiao-Nien shih-lu*, pp. 25–26.

37. For a lengthy discussion of this point, see Wang Te-liang, *Tseng Kuo-fan chih min-tsu ssu-hsiang*, Shanghai, 1946, Preface and Ch. 1. The point is conceded by the opposition.

38. Lo Erh-kang, *Hsiang-chün hsin-chih*, pp. 73–74. For further material on the Hsiang Army, see Inaba Iwakichi, *Shinchō zenshi*, II, 475–81 (*FB* 2.1.4); Inaba, *Shina kinsei shi kōwa*, Tokyo, 1938, pp. 131–38 (*FB* 2.1.8); Naitō, "Shinchō suibō ron," *loc. cit.*, pp. 346–50 (*FB* 2.1.1); Negishi Tadashi, *Chūgoku shakai ni okeru shidōsō . . .* , Tokyo, 1947, pp. 185–87 (*FB* 8.3.2).

39. Ch'in Han-ts'ai, *Tso Wen-hsiang kung tsai hsi-pei*, pp. 40–47.

40. *THTKTI*, Ch. 21, pp. 11b–13b.

41. The point is ably made by Clyde Kluckhohn, "Values and Value-Orientations in the Theory of Action: An Exploration in Definition and Classification," in Talcott Parsons and Edward A. Shils (eds.), *Toward a General Theory of Action*, Cambridge, Mass., 1951, pp. 388–433.

42. Lo Erh-kang, *Lü-ying ping-chih*, p. 57.

43. Ting Pao-chen's memorials on the reform of the regular forces, autumn 1869, in *Ting Wen-ch'eng kung tsou-kao*, 1893, Ch. 7, *passim*, especially the third memorial. See also Lo Erh-kang, *Lü-ying ping-chih,* pp. 57–62; and *THTKTI*, Ch. 47, shang-hsia, *passim*.

44. Ch'en Ch'ih, *Yung shu*, Chengtu, 1893, "Nei-p'ien," Ch. 2, pp. 3–4b. It should be noted that Ch'en considered the "braves," with few exceptions, as bad as the regulars (*ibid.*, Ch. 2, pp. 5–6b).

45. Feng Kuei-fen, *CPLKI*, author's preface.

46. Edict of 1867 (TC-6), *WHTK*, p. 9597.

47. Hart, "Spectator's memorandum," *IWSM-TC*, Ch. 40, pp. 19b–20 (on the Hart memorandum, see Chapter XI); memorial of Liu K'un-i, *ibid.*, May 29, 1866, Ch. 41, pp. 43–50; Ch'ung-hou, Apr. 27, 1866, *ibid.*, Ch. 41, pp. 26b–30; Kuan-wen, May 23, 1866, *ibid.*, Ch. 41, pp. 40b–43; Chang Liang-chi, 1862 (TC-1), *WHTK*, p. 9504; Wang K'ai-t'ai, *CHTI*, Ch. 1, pp. 36–42b; *SL-TC*, Ch. 230, pp. 19–19b.

48. Table on the formation of militia units in ten provinces, Lo Erh-kang, *Hsiang-chün hsin-chih*, pp. 23–24; *WHTK*, p. 9629.

49. *Ibid.*, pp. 25–27, based on Tseng's letters.

50. E.g., edict of July 14, 1868, *SL-TC*, Ch. 234, pp. 21–22; *CSK*, "Pen-chi," Ch. 21, p. 7b, June 20, 1862.

51. Lo Erh-kang, *Hsiang-chün hsin-chih*, pp. 28–30, refutes Wang K'ai-yün's earlier interpretation point by point.

52. On the Board of War's direct control before the Hsien-feng period, see *ibid.*, pp. 222–32.

53. For a general review of the problem, see documents in *THTKTI*, Ch. 50, shang, *passim*.

54. Wang Ch'ing-yün, *Hsi-ch'ao chi-cheng*, Ch. 2, p. 39b. In all China, 7,900,000 ch'ing (not standardized, about 15 acres to one ch'ing) of land yielded a total annual land- and poll-tax revenue of 32,000,000 taels, or an average of 4 taels per ch'ing. The mou varied, but was often about 1/6 acre. A cavalryman received 2 taels per month, plus extras. In the 1930's the average family farm totaled about 21 mou, and the total area under cultivation was estimated at about twice Wang Ch'ing-yün's estimate.

55. On the crude methods of military supply, see Major General Emery Upton, *The Armies of Europe and Asia . . .* , Portsmouth, England, 1878, pp. 24–27. For accounts of the hazards in the grain transport system, see Harold C. Hinton, "Grain Transport via the Grand Canal, 1845–1901," *Papers on China*, IV (1950), 24–57; and G. M. H. Playfair, "The Grain Transport of China," *China Review*, III, 6 (1874–75), 354–64.

56. Edicts to the Grand Council, Oct. 11, 1867, and Feb. 28, 1868, *SL-TC*, Ch. 211, pp. 29b–31; Ch. 224, pp. 18–19.

57. Edicts of this type were issued nearly every day, and the casual way in which the figures were given defies tabulation.

58. *P'ing-ting Kuan-lung chi-lüeh*, compiled by Yang Ch'ang-chün, 1887, Ch. 13, pp. 1 ff.; *Huai-chün p'ing-Nien chi*, compiled by Chao Lieh-wen, Ch. 9, Part 2, pp. 14b–16. See also quotations on this point from Tseng, Hu, and Tso in Wang Chih-p'ing, *op. cit.*, pp. 31–41.

59. Feng Kuei-fen, "Chien ping-o i," *CPLKI*, Ch. 2, pp. 64–65.

60. *WHTK*, p. 9503.

61. Wu T'ing-hsieh, *Ch'ing ts'ai-cheng k'ao-lüeh*, n.p., 1914, p. 8.

62. Mar. 7, 1867, *SL-TC*, Ch. 196, pp. 4b–5; Feb. 16, 1868, *ibid.*, Ch. 223, p. 13.

63. Memorial of the Board of War and edict, *WHTK*, pp. 9597–98.

64. *CHTI*, Ch. 7, pp. 1–6. Wang Ch'ing-yün had earlier urged a plan whereby the wealthier areas would cover the military costs of the poorer areas (*Hsi-ch'ao chi-cheng*, Ch. 2, p. 39b).

65. On the growth of Chinese armies through the Tao-kuang period, and on successive efforts to limit their size, see Wang Ch'ing-yün, *op. cit.*, Ch. 2, pp. 27–45b. General Upton estimated that the official total varied between 500,000 and 1,000,000, according to internal conditions, but that the actual figure was substantially lower (*The Armies of Europe and Asia . . . ,* p. 19).

66. Memorial of 1863 (TC-2), *WHTK*, pp. 9635–42. Tso's memorial of 1866 (TC-5),*THTKTI*, Ch. 47, shang, pp. 5–6. For other documents on reduction in size of the army during the Restoration, see *ibid.*, Ch. 47, *passim*; Wang Chih-p'ing, *op. cit.*, pp. 24–30 and *passim*.

67. *IWSM-TC*, Ch. 40, pp. 19b–20.

68. Memorials of Liu K'un-i, May 29, 1866, *ibid.*, Ch. 41, pp. 43–50; Ch'ung-hou, Apr. 27, 1866, *ibid.*, Ch. 41, pp. 26b–30; Kuan–wen, May 23, 1866, *ibid.*, Ch. 41, pp. 40b–43.

69. Feng Kuei-fen, "Chien ping-o i," *CPLKI*, Ch. 2, pp. 64–65.

70. Wen-hsiang, ". . . nien-p'u," *loc. cit.*, Ch. 3, pp. 52b–54.

71. *CHTI*, Ch. 1, pp. 36–42b.

72. *WHTK*, p. 9504. According to Chaoying Fang, a portion of those discharged reappeared in the forces of Liu Ch'ang-yu in Chihli.

73. Edict of Mar. 3, 1868, *SL-TC*, Ch. 224, pp. 30b–31b.

74. Edict of Jan. 27, 1868, *ibid.*, Ch. 221, pp. 6b–7.

75. Edict of May 12, 1868, commenting on the memorial of Chu Hsüeh-ch'in, subdirector of the Court of State Ceremony, *ibid.*, Ch. 229, pp. 26–28.

76. Edict of June 13, 1868, *ibid.*, Ch. 232, pp. 19–19b.

77. *NCH*, May 13, June 17, 1865; edicts of July 19 and July 22, 1867, *SL-TC*, Ch. 206, pp. 5b–6, 13b–14.

78. For precautions taken along the Anhwei and Hunan borders and elsewhere, see edicts of Aug. 14 and Sept. 2, 1868, *ibid.*, Ch. 236, p. 18b, and Ch. 238, pp. 12–13b.

79. Edict of July 26, 1868, *ibid.*, Ch. 235, pp. 17–18b.

80. *Huai-chün p'ing-Nien chi*, Ch. 9, Part 2, pp. 17–18b.

81. Ting Pao-chen, *Ting-Wen-ch'eng kung tsou-kao*, Ch. 6, pp. 13–16b, memorial of Oct. 6, 1868.

82. Edicts on Tseng's work in disbanding troops, Oct. 5 and Oct. 8, 1868, *SL-TC*, Ch. 241, pp. 9b–10b and 16–16b. For a full translation of Tseng's proclamation and admiring editorial comment, see *NCH*, July 3, 1868. I am indebted to Chaoying Fang for supplementary material on this point.

83. *WHTK*, pp. 9827–30.

84. Early in 1862 Wen-hsiang became president of the Board of Works and concurrently director of the Gunpowder Office (Wen-hsiang, ". . . nien-p'u," *loc. cit.*, Ch. 2, p. 37).

85. Wang Hsin-chung, "Fu-chou ch'uan-ch'ang chih yen-ko," *Ch'ing-hua hsüeh-pao*, VII, 1 (1932), 4–6; Gideon Chen, *Tseng Kuo-fan*, pp. 12–13. The marked change was noted by all observers, e.g., Thomas S. Kingsmill, "Retrospect of Events in China and Japan During the Year 1865," *JNCBRAS*, II (1865), 141; "The Life and Adventures of a British Pioneer in China; Hankow in the Early Sixties," *Mesny's Chinese Miscellany*, III (1899), 140, 159–60.

86. For a summary of military industry in the T'ung-chih period, see Chang Ch'i-yün, *Chung-kuo chün-shih shih-lüeh*, Shanghai, 1946, pp. 148–49.

87. Quoted in Gideon Chen, *Tso Tsung-t'ang*, p. 76.

88. Memorials and edict of Sept. 8, 1861, *IWSM-TC*, Ch. 1, pp. 22b–27; memorial of Mar. 24, 1862, *ibid.*, Ch. 4, pp. 52b–54b; memorial of Tseng Kuo-fan, Aug. 23, 1861, quoted in Gideon Chen, *Tseng Kuo-fan*, pp. 35–36; Chiang Hsing-te, *Tseng Kuo-fan chih sheng-p'ing chi ch'i shih-yeh*, p. 163.

89. Gideon Chen, *Tseng Kuo-fan*, p. 35.

90. For documents on the development and use of naval forces during the T'ung-chih period, see *THTKTI*, Ch. 49, *passim*; *WHTK*, pp. 9709–10, 9713–15, 9721–26.

91. Edicts of June 7, 1867, *SL-TC*, Ch. 202, pp. 11–12; June 14, 1868, *ibid.*, Ch. 232, pp. 27–28; *NCH*, Jan. 12, 1867; *CSK*, "Pen-chi," Ch. 21, pp. 4b, 5b.

92. Edict of Mar. 18, 1867, *SL-TC*, Ch. 196, pp. 33–33b; June 22, 1868, *ibid.*, Ch. 233, pp. 5–7; Yin Luan-chang, *Ch'ing-chien kang-mu*, Shanghai, 1936, p. 687.

93. So Tseng reported to the Throne; account of his audience, Jan. 1869, in *Tseng Wen-cheng kung ta shih chi*, Ch. 4, pp. 6b–11b.

94. For general accounts, see Cordier, *Relations*, I, 247–57; Chang Po-ch'u, "Shang-hai ping kung-ch'ang chih shih-mo," in *Jen-wen yüeh-k'an*, V, 5 (1934), 14; Ch'üan Han-sheng, "Ch'ing-chi ti Chiang-nan chih-tsao chü," *Kuo-li chung-yang yen-chiu yüan li-shih yü-yen yen-chiu so chi-k'an*, XXIII (1951), 145–49. Kan Tso-lin, "Chiang-nan chih-tsao chü chih chien-shih," *Tung-fang tsa-chih*, XI, 5 (1914), 46–48, and XI, 6 (1914), 21–25, deals mainly with the foreigners employed at the Arsenal.

95. Tseng Chao-lun, in *Tung-fang tsa-chih*, XXXVIII, 1 (1941), 56–59.

96. Li's memorial of Oct. 2, 1863, *Li Wen-chung kung ch'üan-chi*; "Tsou-kao," Ch. 4, pp. 44–44b; Tsungli-yamen memorial, June 2, 1864, *IWSM-TC*, Ch. 25, pp. 1–11; Li's subsequent memorial, Sept. 29, 1865, *ibid.*, Ch. 35, pp. 1–6.

97. For an account of Li's trip to Shanghai for this purpose, see *Huai-chün p'ing-Nien chi*, Ch. 12, p. 11b.

98. *NCH*, June 2, 1866; Aug. 16, 1867; July 25, 1868.

99. Tseng Chao-lun, *loc. cit.* See also Gideon Chen, *Tseng Kuo-fan*, pp. 63–64.

100. *NCH*, Aug. 16, 1867.

101. Tso's two memorials and edict of Dec. 3, 1866, *IWSM-TC*, Ch. 45, pp. 56–59b; *NCH*, Nov. 24, 1866; Ch'in Han-ts'ai, *op. cit.*, p. 31.

102. *CSK*, "Hsüan-chü chih," Ch. 2, p. 2.

103. Edict of appointment, Aug. 9, 1867, *SL-TC*, Ch. 207, pp. 25–25b.

104. For documents on the accomplishments of the Foochow Shipyard, see Shen's reports in *SL-TC*, Ch. 210, pp. 35b–36; Ch. 214, pp. 5b–6b; Ch. 224, pp. 7–7b; *IWSM-TC*, Ch. 57, pp. 3b–10b; Ch. 60, pp. 33–38b; Ch. 66, pp. 6b–9; Ch. 68, pp. 41b–44; *WHTK*, pp. 9777, 9780–88; *Kuo-ch'ao jou-yüan chi*, Ch. 16, *passim*.

The standard collection of documents on the Foochow Shipyard is *Ch'uan-cheng tsou-i hui-pien*. The most informative monograph is Wang Hsin-chung, "Fu-chou ch'uan-ch'ang chih yen-ko," *Ch'ing-hua hsüeh-pao*, VII, 1 (1932), 57 pp. The most complete account in English is to be found in Gideon Chen, *Tso Tsung-t'ang*. See also Ssu-yü Teng, "Shen Pao-chen," in *Eminent Chinese*, pp. 642–44, and Prosper Giquel, *The Foochow Arsenal and Its Results, 1867–1874*, Shanghai, 1874.

105. Giquel, *The Foochow Arsenal . . .* , p. 34.

106. Robert K. Douglas, "The Progress of Science in China," *Popular Science Review*, 1873, p. 382.

107. *Ch'üan hsüeh p'ien*, "Pien fa," translated in Ssu-yü Teng and John K. Fairbank, *China's Response to the West*, Cambridge, Mass., 1954, p. 171. A metropolitan official, Sung Chin, proposed its abolition in 1872. Gideon Chen, *Tso Tsung-t'ang*, p. 84.

108. Wang Hsin-chung, *loc. cit.*, pp. 55–57.

109. *Ibid.*, pp. 49–52.

110. *Ching-men tsa-chi*, Ch. 2, pp. 18b–19b.

111. Gumpach, *The Burlingame Mission*, pp. 411–12, gives a terrified account of China's growing military power. On the Chihli arsenal, see memorials of Tsungli-yamen and Board of Revenue, 1866, *IWSM-TC*, Ch. 44, pp. 16b–18; Ch. 46, pp. 18–19b.

112. Ch'ung-hou's reports, 1862, *IWSM-TC*, Ch. 3, pp. 44–44b; Ch. 4, pp. 13b–14b, 36b–38. On training in Chihli, see also 1866–67 memorials of Liu Ch'ang-yu, *THTKTI*, Ch. 47, shang-hsia, *passim*; and Tseng Wen-cheng kung ta shih chi, Ch. 4, pp. 9b–11b.

113. Wen-hsiang, ". . . nien-p'u," *loc. cit.*, Ch. 3, pp. 44b, 45, 46b; *NCH*, Mar. 24, 1866.

114. Gideon Chen, *Tso Tsung-t'ang*, p. 65. Mesny's reminiscences of this period are to be found throughout *Mesny's Chinese Miscellany*, Shanghai, intermittently from 1895 to 1905, 4 vols.

115. *WHTK*, pp. 9505, 9742–44; *SL-TC*, Ch. 194, pp. 11b, 33–34b; Ch. 196, pp. 24–24b, 25–26b; Ch. 197, pp. 6–7, 28b–29b; Ch. 198, pp. 12–12b; Ch. 199, pp. 11–11b; Ch. 204, pp. 15–15b; Ch. 208, pp. 2b–3; Ch. 212, pp. 9–9b; Ch. 213, pp. 13–13b; Ch. 214, pp. 16b–17.

116. Oct. 13, 1862, *IWSM-TC*, Ch. 9, pp. 14–14b.

117. *SL-TC*, Ch. 17, pp. 42–42b; Ch. 19, pp. 24–24b; *IWSM-TC*, Ch. 4, pp. 25–28; Ch. 5, pp. 5b–10b; Ch. 9, pp. 9b–14; *CSK*, "Pen-chi," Ch. 21, p. 5. Mandate in praise of Ward, *Peking Gazette*, quoted in *NCH*, Oct. 4, 1862.

118. *CSK*, "Pen-chi," Ch. 21, p. 5b.

119. Tsungli-yamen memorial with enclosures, Aug. 2, 1863, *IWSM-TC*, Ch. 17, pp. 13–22. Review of the Burgevine case, *NCH*, Aug. 15, 1863. See also *ibid.*, Aug. 8, Aug. 22, and Aug. 29, 1862.

120. Edict of Dec. 14, 1863, *IWSM-TC*, Ch. 22, pp. 3b–4.

121. Bruce to Russell, Dec. 15, 1863, *China. No. 7. (1864)*, p. 1.

122. Memorial of Li Hung-chang and edict, Dec. 23, 1863, *IWSM-TC*, Ch. 22, pp. 7–11.

123. Edict of Jan. 6, 1864, *ibid.*, Ch. 22, p. 17b.

124. Edict of May 19, 1864, *ibid.*, Ch. 24, p. 29. For a review of the Li-Gordon quarrel, see *NCH*, June 18, 1864.

125. For tables identifying foreign officers and instructors in the Imperial forces and the much smaller number in the Taiping forces, see Kuo T'ing-i, *T'ai-p'ing t'ien-kuo shih-shih jih-chih*, Vol. II, Appendix VII.

126. *IWSM-TC*, Ch. 12, pp. 60b–63; Ch. 14, pp. 1–2; *CSK*, "Pen-chi," Ch. 21, p. 4b; *NCH*, May 23, 1863. For honors to Protet at the time of his death, see *CSK*, "Pen-chi," Ch. 21, p. 7, June 10, 1862; and *Peking Gazette* of June 11, 1862, as quoted in *NCH*, July 5, 1862.

127. Memorial of Tsungli-yamen and edict, May 6, 1863, *IWSM-TC*, Ch. 15, pp. 14–15; *NCH*, Mar. 7, 1863. Mesny described the star he received for his Kwei-chow campaign, 1867–69, as well as his Chinese decorations, in *Mesny's Chinese Miscellany*, III (1899), 12–13.

128. Edict of Feb. 24, 1868, *SL-TC*, Ch. 224, pp. 8b–9. Giquel served the Chinese government well until the Franco-Chinese War. He died before being able to resume his post after the war. For biographical information, see Cordier, *Relations*, I, 215–18.

129. *IWSM-TC*, Ch. 44, pp. 20–20b.

130. *NCH*, Oct. 27, 1868.

131. Alcock to Stanley, Jan. 1, 1868, *China. No. 5. (1871)*, pp. 112–16.

132. *Economist*, June 20, 1863, quoted with disapproval in *NCH*, Sept. 12, 1863.

133. *NCH*, Nov. 3, 1866. See also *ibid.*, Feb. 7, 1863.

134. Chaoying Fang has done considerable research into these interconnections.

135. Tsungli-yamen memorial, Sept. 23, 1861, *IWSM-TC*, Ch. 2, pp. 26–27; edict, Sept. 23, 1861, *SL-TC*, Ch. 3, pp. 9b–10. Report from the Imperial agent at Urga, Oct. 31, 1861, *IWSM-TC*, Ch. 2, pp. 44–45, and *SL-TC*, Ch. 8, pp. 52–52b; edict of Dec. 4, 1861, *ibid.*, Ch. 9, pp. 11b–13; Tsungli-yamen memorial, Jan. 19, 1862, *IWSM-TC*, Ch. 3, pp. 23b–26. The arrival in Peking of the second shipment of Russian arms is reported in a Tsungli-yamen memorial of Nov. 26, 1862, *ibid.*, Ch. 10, pp. 29b–30.

136. For a careful review of the episode, based on Chinese and Western sources, see John L. Rawlinson, "The Lay-Osborn Flotilla: Its Development and Significance," in *Papers on China*, IV (1950), 58–93. See also Stanley F. Wright, *Hart and the Chinese Customs*, chap. ix.

137. Edicts of Jan. 25, 1862, *SL-TC*, Ch. 14, pp. 31–32b (similar but not identical text, same date, *IWSM-TC*, Ch. 3, pp. 46b–47); Feb. 19, 1862, *SL-TC*, Ch. 17, p. 3b (this edict and preceding Tsungli-yamen memorial, *IWSM-TC*, Ch. 4, pp. 9–13b); Feb. 25, 1862, *SL-TC*, Ch. 17, pp. 42b–45b.

138. *IWSM-TC*, Ch. 4, pp. 27b–28.

139. Plan presented by the Tsungli-yamen, Nov. 20, 1862, *IWSM-TC*, Ch. 10, pp. 18b–21b; approved Feb. 6, 1863, *ibid.*, Ch. 12, pp. 35b–38.

140. July 8, 1863, *IWSM-TC*, Ch. 16, pp. 30b–33. See also Stanley F. Wright, *op. cit.*, chap. ix.

141. For the Chinese account, see *IWSM-TC*, Ch. 21, pp. 1–22, 41b.

142. Bruce to Russell, Nov. 19, 1863, *China. No. 2. (1864)*, p. 22.

143. Seward to Burlingame, Mar. 21, 1864, *U.S. Arch. China. Instructions*, I, p. 300.

144. Extensive quotations from both in F. W. Williams, "The Mid-Victorian Attitude of Foreigners in China," *Journal of Race Development*, VIII, 4 (1918), 419–22.

145. Gumpach, *The Burlingame Mission*, pp. 193–210.

146. Martin, *A Cycle of Cathay*, pp. 232–33.

147. *NCH*, Dec. 12, 1863; see also *ibid.*, Mar. 12, 1864.

148. Rawlinson, *loc. cit.*, p. 86; Stanley F. Wright (*op. cit.*, chap. ix) agrees.

149. Edicts of Jan. 26, 1862, *CSK*, "Pen-chi," Ch. 21, p. 4b; Jan. 28, 1862, *SL-TC*, Ch. 14, p. 47b; Mar. 4, 1862, *ibid.*, Ch. 18, pp. 13b–15b; Mar. 14, 1862, *ibid.*, Ch. 19, p. 10; Mar. 24, 1862, *ibid.*, Ch. 20, pp. 20–20b; Feb. 7, 1862, *IWSM-TC*, Ch. 4, pp. 1–1b; Mar. 31, 1862, *ibid.*, Ch. 5, pp. 1–1b; Feb. 25, 1862, *ibid.*, Ch. 4, pp. 26b–28; May 5, 1862, *ibid.*, Ch. 5, pp. 35–36b; May 24, 1862, *ibid.*, Ch. 5, pp. 53b–54; May 28, 1862, *ibid.*, Ch. 6, p. 3.

150. Edict of Mar. 31, 1862, *CSK*, "Pen-chi," Ch. 21, p. 5b.

151. Translated in Gideon Chen, *Tseng Kuo-fan*, pp. 69–70.

152. Memorial of Mar. 4, 1862, *IWSM-TC*, Ch. 4, pp. 28–29b.

153. June 13, 1862, *CSK*, "Pen-chi," Ch. 21, p. 7.

154. E.g., memorial of Wen-ko, acting governor of Hunan, Aug. 29, 1861, *IWSM-TC*, Ch. 1, pp. 13–14; Feng Kuei-fen, "Chien ping-o i," *CPLKI*, Ch. 2, pp. 64–65.

155. Quoted in *Kuo-ch'ao jou-yüan chi*, Ch. 16, pp. 3b–4.

156. For British accounts, with translations of Chinese materials enclosed, see *Correspondence Respecting Affairs in China. 1859–1860*, pp. 65–70, 160, 199–203. *NCH*, July 21, 1860; Mar. 29, 1862; *CSK*, "Pen-chi," Ch. 21, p. 6. Hsüeh's memorials, Jan. 26 and Feb 8, 1862, *IWSM-TC*, Ch. 3, pp. 47–49; Ch. 4, pp. 1b–2.

157. Tsungli-yamen memorial of Aug. 30, 1864, *IWSM-TC*, Ch. 27, pp. 26b–28.

158. Tung Hsün, *Huan-tu-wo-shu lao-jen tzu-ting nien-p'u*, 1892, Ch. 1, pp. 52b–53.

159. Tsungli-yamen memorial and enclosures, June 29, 1866, *IWSM-TC*, Ch. 42, pp. 25b–39.

160. Quoted in Tung Hsün, *op. cit.*, Ch. 1, pp. 52b–53.

161. Memorial of May 5, 1862, *IWSM-TC*, Ch. 5, pp. 31b–33.

162. Memorial and edict of Jan. 19, 1863, *ibid.*, Ch. 12, pp. 1–4.

163. Fan Wen-lan, *Chung-kuo chin-tai shih*, Hongkong, 1949, I, 205–7.

164. Chiang Fang-chen, "Chin wu-shih nien lai chün-shih pien-ch'ien shih," in Shen-pao kuan, Fiftieth Anniversary Publication, Vol. II, *Wu-shih nien lai chih Chung-kuo*, Shanghai, 1922, p. 1. Chiang develops an interesting theory of the patterns of interrelationship among militia, bandits, bureaucracy, and literati.

165. Prosper Giquel, *La Politique française en Chine depuis les traités de 1858 et de 1860*, Paris, 1872, pp. 47–49.

166. "The Chinese Army" (unsigned), *The Times* (London), Sept. 8, 1883, p. 4.

CHAPTER X

1. See John K. Fairbank and Ssu-yü Teng, "On the Ch'ing Tributary System," *HJAS*, VI, 2 (1941), 135–246; Fairbank, *Trade and Diplomacy* . . . , Vol. I, chap. 1; M. Frederick Nelson, *Korea and the Old Orders in Eastern Asia*, Baton Rouge, La., 1945, Part I, "The International Society of Confucian Monarchies."

2. James Legge (trans.), *Mencius*, Hongkong and London, 1861, pp. 129–30.

3. Prince Kung, *Lo-tao-t'ang wen-ch'ao*, Ch. 1, pp. 1, 2b, 17b–18b, 25.

4. On ceremonial and political relations between China and Annam, for ex-

ample, see G. Devéria, *Histoire des relations de la Chine avec l'Annam du XVI au XIX siècle, d'après des documents chinois*, Paris, 1880.

5. Materials on tributary relations are to be found throughout the general sources for the period, e.g., *SL-TC*, Ch. 4, p. 36; Ch. 5, p. 30; Ch. 14, p. 42b; Ch. 19, p. 36; Ch. 194, pp. 19b–20b; Ch. 204, pp. 13b–14; Ch. 211, p. 21; Ch. 220, pp. 28b–32b; Ch. 221, p. 10; Ch. 222, pp. 16, 32; Ch. 224, p. 50b; Ch. 229, pp. 14b–15b; Ch. 231, pp. 6, 15. *WHTK*, pp. 8189, 10711, 10729–30, 10736, 10738. *CHTI*, Ch. 6, pp. 42–42b. *NCH*, May 28 and June 11, 1864. *CSK*, "Pen-chi," Ch. 21, pp. 3b–8.

6. *NCH*, Sept. 15, 1866.

7. Translation, *ibid*., June 22, 1861.

8. E.g., *IWSM-TK*, Ch. 24, p. 36b.

9. Bruce to Malmesbury, July 13, 1859, in *Correspondence with Mr. Bruce . . .* , No. 10, pp. 21–22. See also Bruce to Russell, Apr. 7, 1860, *Correspondence Respecting Affairs in China. 1859–1860*, No. 22, pp. 37–39.

10. On Prince Kung's views at this time, see Wang Te-chao, "T'ung-chih hsin-cheng k'ao," Part I, *Wen-shih tsa-chih*, I, 4 (1945), pp. 24–29.

11. See Ssu-ming Meng, "The Organization and Function of the Tsungli-yamen," Ph.D. dissertation, Harvard University, 1949. In my opinion, Meng underestimates the importance of the yamen.

12. I am indebted for clarification of these appointments to Professor Masataka Banno of Tokyo Metropolitan University, who bases his conclusion on *IWSM-HF* and the diaries of Wen-hsiang and Weng T'ung-ho.

13. *IWSM-HF*, Ch. 71, pp. 17–19.

14. Chaoying Fang in *Eminent Chinese*, p. 381; Cordier, Relations, I, 108, 109. *IWSM-HF*, Ch. 72, pp. 27–36.

15. *IWSM-HF*, Ch. 72, p. 22.

16. Wu Ch'eng-chang, *Wai-chiao pu yen-ko chi-lüeh*, [Peking] 1913. The Tsungli-yamen made frequent references to the receipt of such material.

17. Edict of Nov. 30, 1861, *IWSM-TC*, Ch. 2, pp. 43b–44.

18. Ch'en Wen-chin, "Ch'ing-tai chih Tsung-li ya-men chi ch'i ching-fei," *Chung-kuo she-hui ching-chi shih chi-k'an*, I, 1 (1932), 51–53.

19. Wu Ch'eng-chang, *op. cit.*, pp. 3b–4b.

20. Tsungli-yamen memorial of Sept. 20, 1864, describing the growth of the yamen, the change in its function, and the need for new organizational statutes, *IWSM-TC*, Ch. 28, pp. 13–17b; *WHTK*, pp. 8778–80, 8917, 10781; Wu Ch'eng-chang, *op. cit.*, pp. 5–9b.

21. Ch'en Wen-chin, *loc. cit.*, pp. 54–57.

22. *WHTK*, p. 10781.

23. Memorial of June 13, 1862, *IWSM-TC*, Ch. 6, pp. 23b–26b.

24. Alcock to Stanley, Feb. 9, 1869, *China. No. 3. (1869)*, pp. 33–36. On the Formosan incident, see Chapter III.

25. Memorandum from Prince Kung, transmitted to Alcock, Dec. 5, 1868, *China. No. 5. (1871)*, p. 232.

26. Wang Te-chao, "T'ung-chih hsin-cheng k'ao," *loc. cit.*, Part 2, pp. 36–37. Examples of consequent failures follow on pp. 37–42.

27. On the counterparts of these men following the first treaty settlement a generation earlier, see Fairbank, *Trade and Diplomacy . . .* , I, 176–83.

28. Wen-hsiang, ". . . nien-p'u," *loc. cit.,* Ch. 3, pp. 68, 73b–74. The retrospective appraisals of Wen-hsiang and Prince Kung are from *Mesny's Chinese Miscellany,* I (1895), 292.

29. Tung Hsün, . . . *tzu-ting nien-p'u,* Ch. 1, pp. 36, 44b–45.

30. Martin, *Cycle of Cathay,* pp. 355–58. For the comment of another foreigner, see Freeman-Mitford, *The Attaché at Peking,* pp. 69–70.

31. Tung Hsün, *op. cit.,* Ch. 1, pp. 50–51b; Lienche Tu Fang in *Eminent Chinese,* p. 790, quoting Weng T'ung-ho's diary.

32. In 1855 Alcock had praised Hsü for his "great progress" as governor of Fukien and deplored his dismissal ("The Chinese Empire and Its Destinies," *Bombay Quarterly Review* (Oct. 1855), pp. 232–33). See also Lienche Tu Fang, "Hsü Chi-yü," in *Eminent Chinese,* pp. 309–10; Fairbank, *Trade and Diplomacy . . . ,* I, 281–84.

33. Tung Hsün, *op. cit.,* Ch. 1, pp. 48–48b.

34. Seward to Williams, Mar. 6, 1866, *U.S. Arch. China. Instructions,* I, 392. See also *ibid.,* I, 394–95.

35. Freeman-Mitford, *op. cit.,* pp. 69–70.

36. Seward to Williams, June 4, 1866, *U. S. Arch. China. Instructions,* I, 402; and Seward to Burlingame, Jan. 21, 1867, *ibid.,* I, 430–31.

37. Tung Hsün, *op. cit.,* Ch. 1, p. 48b.

38. Bourne, "Historical Table . . . ," *loc. cit.,* p. 323; Martin, *A Cycle of Cathay,* p. 341.

39. Tung Hsün, *op. cit.,* Ch. 1, pp. 45b–46.

40. *Ibid.,* Ch. 2, p. 8; Wu Ch'eng-chang, *Wai-chiao pu yen-ko chi-lüeh,* p. 4b.

41. Tung Hsün, *op. cit.,* Ch. 2, p. 8.

42. Bourne, "Historical Table . . . ," *loc. cit.,* pp. 314–29.

43. *NCH,* July 15, 1865; Apr. 28, Sept. 22, 1866; and June 27, 1868; Chaoying Fang in *Eminent Chinese,* pp. 721–23.

44. Bourne, "Historical Table . . . ," *loc. cit.*

45. Williams, *The Middle Kingdom,* II, 699.

46. Kuo Sung-tao, *Yang-chih shu-wu ch'üan-chi,* 1892, "Tsou-su," Ch. 12, pp. 1–3; undated, during Margary affair.

47. *Ibid.,* Ch. 12, pp. 4–12.

48. Fan Wen-lan, *Chung-kuo chin-tai shih,* Hongkong, 1949, I, 219–20.

49. Fairbank, *Trade and Diplomacy . . . ,* Vol. I, chaps. vi, vii, and xi.

50. E.g., Tsungli-yamen memorial, Dec. 24, 1862, in regard to Russian territorial claims based on previous treaties, *IWSM-TC,* Ch. 11, pp. 1–3b. Prince Kung to Bruce, June 19, 1863, *China. No. 8. (1864),* p. 4.

51. This statement is based on an examination of virtually all the documents included in *IWSM-TC.*

52. Tsungli-yamen memorial, July 18, 1866, *IWSM-TC,* Ch. 42, pp. 50b–51b.

53. Wen-hsiang ". . . nien-p'u," *loc. cit.,* Ch. 3, p. 51b.

54. Dec. 8, 1861, *IWSM-TC,* Ch. 3, pp. 2–3b.

55. Tsungli-yamen memorial, Aug. 23, 1861, *ibid.,* Ch. 1, pp. 6–6b. For further examples, see *ibid.,* Ch. 1, pp. 14–14b; Ch. 3, pp. 26–27b; Ch. 30, p. 31; Hsüeh Fu-ch'eng's essay on the principles of the treaty system in *CSWP,* Ch. 104, pp. 10b–14; Stanley F. Wright, *Hart and the Chinese Customs,* chap. iii.

56. Tsungli-yamen memorial, Mar. 18, 1867, *IWSM-TC,* Ch. 47, p. 21.

57. Edict to the Grand Council, Oct. 29, 1845, *IWSM-TK*, Ch. 74, pp. 25b–26; and *SL-TK*, Ch. 42, pp. 22b–23.

58. Memorial of the censor Ch'en Hung-i, presenting the views of Kuo Sung-tao, quoted in Liu Fa-tseng, *Ch'ing-shih tsuan-yao*, Shanghai, 1914, p. 115.

59. Edict of Jan. 4, 1862, *IWSM-TC*, Ch. 3, p. 14b; Tsungli-yamen memorial, Jan. 16, 1862, *ibid.*, Ch. 3, pp. 21b–23b; *China. No. 3. (1864), passim*; *WHTK*, pp. 10781–82.

60. Hui-i (pseud.), "Chi T'ung-chih ch'ao Ying Fa yen-cheng chiao-she an," *T'an-yen ts'ung-pao*, No. 16 (1914), 5 pp. Hui-i cites this case in refutation of Nationalist charges that the Ch'ing government was unpatriotic and treacherously ceded sovereignty to the foreigners. On the salt administration, see Chapter VIII.

61. *NCH*, Feb. 13, 1864; May 13, 1865; Jan. 6, 1866; and Nov. 24, 1868.

62. For a Chinese summary of Russian "demands" in the decade 1860–70, see Tsungli-yamen memorial, Mar. 6, 1870, *IWSM-TC*, Ch. 71, pp. 18–20.

63. On the cumbersome machinery through which Chinese-Russian affairs were handled by the two countries, as the Chinese saw it, see Tsungli-yamen memorial, Feb. 19, 1862, *IWSM-TC*, Ch. 4, pp. 20b–21b.

64. For a detailed account of the 1865 negotiations, see *IWSM-TC*, Ch. 41, pp. 1–22b.

65. On the 1869 revision, with a review of the problem since 1862, see *ibid.*, Ch. 67, pp. 23–31b. See also Cordier, *Relations*, I, 115.

66. E.g., *IWSM-TC*, Ch. 7, pp. 44–46; Ch. 15, pp. 38b–40b; Ch. 16, pp. 11–15; Ch. 18, pp. 3b–13; *SL-TC*, Ch. 4, pp. 9–9b; *CSK*, "Pen-chi," Ch. 21, pp. 6b, 7b, 8.

67. E.g., *SL-TC*, Ch. 16, pp. 13b–14b; *IWSM-TC*, Ch. 4, pp. 4–6.

68. E.g., *SL-TC*, Ch. 199, pp. 3b–4b; Ch. 203, pp. 5–5b; Ch. 232, pp. 4b–5b; Ch. 236, pp. 3b–4b.

69. Tsungli-yamen memorial with enclosures, Dec. 24, 1862, *IWSM-TC*, Ch. 11, pp. 1–9b; *ibid.*, Ch. 3, pp. 8–8b; *SL-TC*, Ch. 11, pp. 31b–33.

70. *IWSM-TC*, Ch. 19, pp. 1–11.

71. Tsungli-yamen memorial, Aug. 8, 1863, *ibid.*, Ch. 17, pp. 28–30b.

72. *Ibid.*, Ch. 18, pp. 55–62.

73. *Ibid.*, Ch. 18, pp. 50–52.

74. Text, *ibid.*, Ch. 29, pp. 28b–34b.

75. E.g., June 16, 1866, *ibid.*, Ch. 42, pp. 2–16b, 19b–22; July 3, 1866, *ibid.*, Ch. 42, pp. 39–41b; July 12, 1866, *ibid.*, Ch. 42, pp. 41b–45b; June 11, 1868, *ibid.*, Ch. 60, pp. 1–5b, and also Ch. 60, *passim*; June 13, 1868, *SL-TC*, Ch. 232, pp. 24b–25; Nov. 28, 1867, *ibid.*, Ch. 215, pp. 12–13.

76. "Final" delimitation of the northwest frontier was reported on Sept. 10, 1869 (*IWSM-TC*, Ch. 67, pp. 34b–41b).

77. On the general Ch'ing system of border administration, see *Ch'ing-tai pien-cheng k'ao-lüeh*, compiled by Pien-chiang cheng-chiao chih-tu yen-chiu hui, Nanking, 1936.

78. Memorial of Sept. 1, 1863, *IWSM-TC*, Ch. 18, pp. 43b–45b.

79. E.g., rebellion of the garrison at Bulun Tokhoi, *SL-TC*, Ch. 233, pp. 4–5, 17b–18b, 22–23b; Ch. 235, pp. 3b–6, 20b–22b; Ch. 236, pp. 22–24; Ch. 237, pp. 28b–29b; Ch. 239, pp. 19–20b.

80. E.g., *ibid.*, Ch. 196, pp. 31b–32; Ch. 198, pp. 21b–22; Ch. 199, pp. 5b–6b; Ch. 201, pp. 16–17; Ch. 203, pp. 20b–22; Ch. 215, pp. 30b–31b; Ch. 217, pp. 1b–2b.

81. *IWSM-TC*, Ch. 18, pp. 41b–43b.

82. *Ibid.*, Ch. 3, pp. 3b–8; Ch. 5, pp. 46–47b.

83. Memorial of Feb. 18, 1863, *ibid.*, Ch. 13, pp. 1–5.

84. *Ibid.*, Ch. 17, pp. 7–9, 22 ff.

85. *SL-TC*, Ch. 212, pp. 21–22.

86. *Ibid.*, Ch. 202, pp. 16–17; Ch. 203, pp. 22–22b; Ch. 204, pp. 5–6; Ch. 208, pp. 17–17b; Ch. 214, pp. 27b–29. June to November, 1867.

87. E.g., *IWSM-TC*, Ch. 5, pp. 46–46b; *ibid.*, Ch. 16, pp. 21–27b, July 2, 1863; *ibid.*, Ch. 44, pp. 3b–4b, Sept. 21, 1866; *ibid.*, Ch. 45, pp. 38b–41, Nov. 26, 1866; *ibid.*, Ch. 48, pp. 16–18b, Apr. 23, 1867.

88. *Ibid.*, Ch. 13, pp. 6b–8.

89. See note 85 above.

90. See note 86 above.

91. Edict of Jan. 30, 1863, *IWSM–TC*, Ch. 12, pp. 10b–11.

92. *CSK*, "Pen-chi," Ch. 21, p. 8.

93. E.g., memorial of the Ili Tartar General, Ch'ang-ch'ing, Mar. 7, 1863, on negotiations with the Buriats and Kazakhs, *IWSM-TC*, Ch. 13, 10b–11; two memorials of Ming-i, Apr. 16, 1863, *ibid.*, Ch. 15, pp. 27–30b; *SL-TC*, Ch. 225, pp. 21–21b; Ch. 226, pp. 33b–36; Ch. 230, pp. 16b–17.

94. *IWSM-TC*, Ch. 14, pp. 30b–36b.

95. Memorial of Ming-hsü, *et al.*, May 19, 1863, *ibid.*, Ch. 15, pp. 21b–23b. Similar materials, *ibid.*, Ch. 15, pp. 23b–29b. See also *SL-TC*, Ch. 204, pp. 5–6, June 22, 1867.

96. *IWSM-TC*, Ch. 15, pp. 41–42b, 51b–55.

97. June 19, 1863, *ibid.*, Ch. 16, pp. 17–18; Feb. 5, 1867, *SL-TC*, Ch. 194, pp. 3b–4b.

98. Tsungli-yamen memorial, enclosed correspondence with Russia, and edict, Aug. 8, 1863, *IWSM-TC*, Ch. 17, pp. 30b–48b; *ibid.*, Ch. 28, pp. 2b–4. This view is frequently expressed in the *IWSM* documents for 1865, e.g., Ch. 33, p. 35b; see also *SL-TC*, Ch. 205, p. 2b, edict of July 3, 1867, ordering the Grand Secretaries, board presidents, and Censorate to co-operate with the Tsungli-yamen in devising a policy to check Russian ambitions in Turkestan.

99. W. A. P. Martin's English preface to *Wan-kuo kung-fa* (his Chinese translation of Wheaton's *International Law*), Peking, 1864.

100. Tsungli-yamen memorial, Aug. 30, 1864, *IWSM-TC*, Ch. 27, pp. 25–26b.

101. Martin, English preface to *Wan-kuo kung-fa*; Martin, *A Cycle of Cathay*, pp. 232–34; J. Ross Browne, "Note on Chinese Matters," in Gumpach, *The Burlingame Mission*, p. 871; *The Chinese and Japanese Repository*, III (1865), 586; Freeman-Mitford, *The Attaché at Peking*, p. 86.

102. Tung Hsün, . . . *tzu-ting nien-p'u*, Ch. 1, pp. 46–46b. Martin's influence was evidently considerable. Note the number of translations included in *CSWP*, Chs. 104–6.

103. Tsungli-yamen memorial, Dec. 24, 1862, *IWSM-TC*, Ch. 11, pp. 3b–6.

104. Translated in *NCH*, Aug. 29 and Sept. 5, 1863.

105. Prince Kung to Burlingame, Mar. 16, 1864, barring the Confederate ship *Alabama* from Chinese ports, translated in *NCH*, Mar. 16, 1864; Seward to Burlingame, June 11, 1864, *U. S. Arch. China. Instructions*, I, 305.

106. Tsungli-yamen memorials of Aug. 30, 1864, *IWSM-TC*, Ch. 27, pp. 25–26b,

and of Feb. 20, 1865, *ibid.*, Ch. 31, pp. 4–5; Martin, English preface to *Wan-kuo kung-fa*. The incident is briefly treated by T. F. Tsiang, "Bismarck and the Introduction of International Law into China," *CSPSR*, XV (1931–32), 98–101.

107. Tsungli-yamen to Bellonet, Nov. 4, 1866, *IWSM-TC*, Ch. 45, pp. 14b–15. Full documentation on the Chinese handling of the Franco-Korean incident is included in an unpublished paper by the author.

108. *NCH*, June 27, 1867; May 18, Nov. 10, 1868. Examples can be multiplied.

109. Tsungli-yamen memorial, Jan. 16, 1862, *IWSM-TC*, Ch. 3, pp. 14b-16b; memorial of Nov. 14, 1861, *ibid.*, Ch. 2, pp. 19 ff.; memorial of Oct. 22, 1862, *ibid.*, Ch. 9, pp. 49–50.

110. On the *Hai-lu*, see Kenneth Ch'en, "Hai-lu—Forerunner of Chinese Travel Accounts of Western Countries," *Monumenta Serica*, VII (1942), 208–26. Of the numerous editions of the *Hai-lu*, the most convenient for general reference is the annotated *Hai-lu-chu*, Changsha, 1938. The most useful edition is that of 1842, which, in four ts'e, contains not only the *Hai-lu* itself but six additional little-known Chinese accounts of the Western world. On the editions of the *Hai-kuo t'u-chih*, see Gideon Chen, *Lin Tse-hsü*, Peiping, 1934, pp. 23–30. On the *Hai-kuo t'u-chih* and the *Ying-huan chih-lüeh*, see Fairbank, *Trade and Diplomacy . . .* , I, 178–83, 281–84.

111. On the Russian-language school, see Knight Biggerstaff, "The T'ung Wen Kuan," *CSPSR*, XVIII (1934–35), 307–12.

112. Feng, "She-li T'ung-wen kuan i," *CPLKI*, Ch. 2, pp. 99–101.

113. *IWSM-TC*, Ch. 15, pp. 31b–34b.

114. For the decision finally to send students abroad, see Tsungli-yamen memorial, Sept. 15, 1871, *IWSM-TC*, Ch. 83, pp. 1–2; memorials of Tseng Kuo-fan and Li Hung-chang, Sept. 3, 1871, and Mar. 1, 1872, *ibid.*, Ch. 82, pp. 47–52, and Ch. 85, pp. 15–18. For a traditional Chinese account, see *Kuo-ch'ao jou-yüan chi*, Ch. 17, pp. 1 ff. A modern account is Shu Hsin-ch'eng, *Chin-tai Chung-kuo liu-hsüeh shih*, Shanghai, 1927. Liang Ch'i-ch'ao criticized the Ch'ing for sending students to study technical subjects rather than Western civilization as a whole. For a defense against this charge, see Chiang Hsing-te, *Tseng Kuo-fan . . .* , pp. 157–60.

115. On Chinese translations of Western works, see E. R. Hughes, *The Invasion of China by the Western World*, New York, 1938, pp. 203–8; Tsuen-hsuin Tsien, "The Western Impact on China Through Translation," *FEQ*, XIII, 3 (1954), 305–27.

116. E.g., Jan. 28, 1864, *IWSM-TC*, Ch. 22, pp. 27b–30b; Mar. 25, 1868, *SL-TC*, Ch. 226, pp. 7b–8b.

117. Tsungli-yamen memorial, July 4, 1869, *IWSM-TC*, Ch. 66, p. 2b.

118. *NCH*, Mar. 31, 1866. See also *ibid.*, Dec. 3, 1864.

119. *Peking Gazette*, Sept. 29, 1875, translated in *China. No. 1. (1876)*, pp. 87–88.

120. Memorial of Yin Chao-yung, June 16, 1862, *IWSM-TC*, Ch. 6, pp. 31–33.

121. Jan. 4, 1862, *ibid.*, Ch. 3, pp. 14–14b.

122. Mar. 20, 1867, *ibid.*, Ch. 47, pp. 20–23.

123. W. A. P. Martin, *The Chinese: Their Education, Philosophy, and Letters*, New York, etc., 1893, pp. 35–37.

124. Letter of John, late 1869, in R. Wardlaw Thompson, *Griffith John*, London, 1906, pp. 253–54; on the missionary controversy in England, see Chapters III and XI.

125. Alcock to Clarendon, May 20, 1869, *China. No. 5. (1871)*, No. 138.

126. Alcock to Stanley, Apr. 16, 1868, *ibid.*, No. 51.

127. *NCH*, Apr. 2, 1864.

128. *Ibid.*, Jan. 5, 1867; July 31, 1868.

129. *CSK*, "Hsüan-chü chih," Ch. 2, p. 1. Modern histories of Chinese education follow this periodization.

130. For a summary of its history, see Knight Biggerstaff, "The T'ung Wen Kuan," *CSPSR*, XVIII (1934–35), 307–40.

131. Williams to Cass, Nov. 3, 1860, *U.S. Arch. China. Despatches*, No. 19.

132. Ting Chih-p'ing, *Chung-kuo chin ch'i-shih nien lai chiao-yü chi-shih*, pp. 1–2.

133. K. S. Latourette, *A History of Christian Missions in China*, New York, 1929, pp. 240, 429–33.

134. Feng, "She-li T'ung-wen kuan i," *CPLKI*, Ch. 2, pp. 99–101.

135. Translated extract from memorial of Oct. 1861, in Martin, *A Cycle of Cathay*, p. 296.

136. Tsungli-yamen memorial, Aug. 20, 1862, *IWSM-TC*, Ch. 8, pp. 29b–31b.

137. See report on the investigation of the Russian-language school, memorial of the Grand Secretary Chia Chen, Aug. 20, 1862, *ibid.*, Ch. 8, pp. 35–36; Martin, *A Cycle of Cathay*, pp. 294–96; Biggerstaff, "The T'ung Wen Kuan," *loc. cit.*, pp. 307–12.

138. Six regulations for the T'ung-wen kuan in *IWSM-TC*, Ch. 8, pp. 31–35. Tung Hsün frequently served as an examiner; see his . . . *tzu-ting nien-p'u*, Ch. 1, pp. 45, 45b, 48b; Ch. 2, pp. 2b, 5, 11b, 13b.

139. Li's memorial of Mar. 11, 1863, in *Li Wen-chung kung ch'üan-chi*, "Tsou-kao," Ch. 3, pp. 11–13. Li's memorial and following edict of Mar. 28, 1863, *IWSM-TC*, Ch. 14, pp. 2–5. Li's memorial is very similar to the earlier essay of a member of his staff, Feng Kuei-fen, "She-li T'ung-wen kuan i," *loc. cit.*

On the Canton school, see memorial of the acting governor-general of Kwang-tung and Kwangsi, Yen Tuan-shu, and the governor of Kwangtung, Huang Tsan-t'ang, June 23, 1863, *IWSM-TC*, Ch. 16, pp. 9–10; memorial of Jui-lin, Aug. 7, 1864, *ibid.*, Ch. 27, pp. 6–10.

140. See Tsungli-yamen memorials of May 6, 1863, *IWSM-TC*, Ch. 15, pp. 12b–14; Apr. 29, 1865, Ch. 32, pp. 1b–3; Dec. 22, 1865, Ch. 37, pp. 30b–35; Jan. 21, 1866, Ch. 38, pp. 17b–18; Oct. 2, 1866, Ch. 44, pp. 14–14b; and Dec. 11, 1866, Ch. 46, pp. 3–4b.

141. *Ibid.*, Ch. 46, pp. 43b–48b; English translation in *NCH*, Feb. 9, 1867.

142. *NCH*, Feb. 9, 1867.

143. Edict to the Grand Secretariat, *SL-TC*, Ch. 195, p. 11b.

144. Prince Kung "detected the face of Wo-jen behind the mask" of the censor; see Martin, *A Cycle of Cathay*, pp. 312–13. The views of the literati opposition are summarized in Wang Te-Chao, "T'ung-chih hsin-cheng k'ao," Part 2, *loc. cit.*, pp. 33–36.

145. *IWSM-TC*, Ch. 47, pp. 15–17; *SL-TC*, Ch. 195, pp. 35–35b; *CHTI*, Ch. 5, pp. 40–41.

146. Chaoying Fang in *Eminent Chinese*, p. 862.

147. Weng T'ung-ho, *Wen Wen-kung jih-chi*, facsimile ed., Shanghai, ca. 1925, ts'e 7, pp. 12–13, entries for Mar. 18, Mar. 20, 1867.

148. *IWSM-TC*, Ch. 47, pp. 24–25b; translated in Cordier, *Relations*, I, 327–29.

149. Two Tsungli-yamen memorials, Apr. 6, 1867, *IWSM-TC*, Ch. 48, pp. 1–5.

150. Wo-jen's memorial, Apr. 12, 1867, *ibid.*, Ch. 48, pp. 10b–12; Tsungli-

yamen memorial, Apr. 23, 1867, *ibid.*, Ch. 48, pp. 12b–15b; edict of Apr. 23, 1867, *SL-TC*, Ch. 199, pp. 9–9b; edict of Apr. 25, 1867, *ibid.*, Ch. 199, pp. 9b–10.

151. Edicts of Apr. 25 and Apr. 28, 1867, *SL-TC*, Ch. 199, pp. 10b, 16–17; Wo-jen's memorial of Apr. 25, 1867, *IWSM-TC*, Ch. 48, pp. 18b–19b.

152. Censorate memorial, *IWSM-TC*, Ch. 49, pp. 13–24b; edict of June 30, 1867, *SL-TC*, Ch. 204, pp. 30b–32b; edict of July 13, 1867, *ibid.*, Ch. 205, pp. 18b–19; Wu Tseng-ch'i, *Ch'ing-shih kang-yao*, Ch. 12, p. 16.

153. Censorate memorial, *IWSM-TC*, Ch. 49, pp. 13-24b.

154. Edict of June 30, 1867, *SL-TC*, Ch. 204, pp. 30b–32b; also in *IWSM-TC*, Ch. 49, pp. 24b–25b.

155. *NCH*, July 27, 1867, contains translations of memorials of Yang and Wo-jen and of edicts. See also memorial of the Imperial clansman and president of the Censorate, Ling-kuei, July 8, 1867, *IWSM-TC*, Ch. 49, pp. 31–35b.

156. Gumpach, *The Burlingame Mission*, p. 193, note, and appendix entitled "The New University of China," pp. 595–870. R. S. Gundry, *China Past and Present*, London, 1895, p. xix, also asserts erroneously that Prince Kung failed and that the Empress Dowager yielded to Wo-jen's opposition. In fact, appointments were made, courses in science were given, and examinations were taken.

157. Martin, *A Cycle of Cathay*, p. 313.

158. *London and China Express*, Nov. 26, 1867; extract in Gumpach, *The Burlingame Mission*, pp. 595–97.

159. *NCH*, Oct. 9, 1867.

160. Tsungli-yamen memorials in *IWSM-TC*, Aug. 15, 1867, Ch. 50, pp. 8b–9; Oct. 12, 1867, Ch. 50, pp. 35b–36; Jan. 18, 1868, Ch. 56, pp. 22–23b; June 26, 1868, Ch. 59, pp. 33–34b; July 2, 1868, Ch. 59, pp. 34–37; Aug. 1, 1868, Ch. 60, pp. 19b–20; memorial of Jui-lin, Dec. 1, 1868, *ibid.*, Ch. 62, pp. 19b–21b; Tsungli-yamen memorial, Apr. 6, 1869, *ibid.*, Ch. 65, pp. 12b–15b.

161. Martin, *A Cycle of Cathay*, p. 370.

162. *Ibid.*, p. 312; Tung Hsün, *op. cit.*, Ch. 2, pp. 11b, 13b.

163. *NCH*, May 9, 1868.

164. *Ibid.*, Nov. 28, 1868.

165. *Ch'üan-hsüeh p'ien*, "Pien-fa," translated in Ssu-yü Teng and John K. Fairbank, *China's Response to the West*, Cambridge, Mass., 1954, pp. 166–74; Li Yen, "Ch'ing-tai shu-hsüeh chiao-yü chih-tu," Part 1, *Hsüeh-i tsa-chih*, XIII, 4 (1934), 45–47.

166. Fan Wen-lan, *Chung-kuo chin-tai shih*, I, 202–5.

167. Memorial of Jui-lin, Feb. 29, 1872, *IWSM-TC*, Ch. 84, pp. 12b–13b.

168. Pao-yün and others, preface preceding Ch. 1, *IWSM-TC*.

169. "Situation de l'Empire," Nov. 1867, "Affaires étrangères politiques," *DD*, 1867, p. 248.

170. Parkes's letter, Shanghai, May 10, 1865, quoted in Freeman-Mitford, *The Attaché at Peking*, pp. 38–39.

CHAPTER XI

1. Reflected in the memorials of Prince Kung and others, *IWSM-HF*, Ch. 26, *passim*.

2. Alcock to Stanley, May 5, 1868, *China. No. 5. (1871)*, pp. 137–38.

3. *Ibid.*, p. 137.

4. Alcock to Stanley, Jan. 22, 1868, *ibid.*, p. 101.

5. Newspaper account of Alcock's address at Kiukiang, May 1867, reprinted *ibid.*, pp. 6–7.

6. *China. No. 10. (1870)*, p. 2.

7. Alcock to Stanley, Dec. 23, 1868, *China. No. 5. (1871)*, pp. 261 ff.

8. *China. No. 10. (1870)*, pp. 11–12.

9. For summaries of China's foreign relations during this period, see Morse, *Relations*, Vol. II; Sargent, *Anglo-Chinese Commerce and Diplomacy . . .* , chap. vi; Pelcovits, *Old China Hands and the Foreign Office*, chap. 1; Cordier, *Relations*, Vol. I, chap. xxi.

10. Chairman of the Shanghai General Chamber of Commerce to Medhurst, Feb. 1, 1869, *China. No. 12. (1869)*, pp. 5–6.

11. *NCH*, Oct. 4, 1862.

12. *Ibid.*, Oct. 12, 1867.

13. Consul Winchester, Shanghai, in *China. No. 5. (1871)*, pp. 30–32, 37.

14. On Kiukiang, see *Commercial Reports. 1862–1864*, No. 4; *NCH*, Oct. 24, 1863. On Amoy, see *China. No. 4. (1864)*, p. 67; *China. No. 4. (1870)*, pp. 17–21. On Foochow, see *ibid.*, pp. 14–16. On Ningpo, see *China. No. 5. (1871)*, pp. 154–56, and enclosure in No. 63. On Chinkiang, see *ibid.*, pp. 1–2, 4–5; *China. No. 4. (1870)*, pp. 22–26, 29–31, 34–38.

15. Wade's memorandum, Dec. 1868, *China. No. 5. (1871)*, Appendix.

16. Alcock to Clarendon, Oct. 28, 1869, *China. No. 1. (1870)*, p. 3. See also Sargent, *Anglo-Chinese Commerce and Diplomacy . . .* , pp. 158–59.

17. E.g., "Minutes of the Proceedings of the Mixed Commission, Mar. 3, 1868," *China. No. 5. (1871)*, pp. 191–92; Alcock to Medhurst, Apr. 1, 1869, *ibid.*, pp. 360–67; *NCH*, Mar. 31, Apr. 7, Apr. 21, May 5, and May 12, 1866; on Hsüeh Huan's memorial on the relation of the likin to foreign affairs, see Lo Yü-tung, *Chung-kuo li-chin shih*, I, 160–62.

18. *China. No. 5 (1871)*, p. 7.

19. Wade vouched for the accuracy of this interpretation, *ibid.*, Appendix.

20. There was, however, a division of view. See *Minutes of the Annual General Meeting of the Shanghai General Chamber of Commerce*, Aug. 23, 1865.

21. A. McPherson, Abstract of the Customs report on Hankow, *Chinese and Japanese Repository*, Nov. 1, 1865. On the interior trade, S. Wells Williams (*The Chinese Commercial Guide*, 1863 ed., p. 174) advised merchants: "This part of the trade with China must necessarily be left for the most part to the natives, who better understand the local risk, and can avoid the impositions or charges of local officials, which foreigners cannot easily arrange."

22. *China. No. 12. (1869)*, pp. 1–5; *China. No. 2. (1870)*, passim; *China. No. 8. (1870)*, passim; *Reports of Journeys in China and Japan . . .* , 1869, passim; *China. No. 5. (1871)*, pp. 33–34, 131–32, 389–90.

23. Chaoying Fang in *Eminent Chinese*, p. 380.

24. *NCH*, Feb. 16, 1861.

25. *NCH*, Mar. 21, Apr. 25, 1863.

26. Alcock to Stanley, Dec. 6, 1868, *China. No. 5. (1871)*, p. 187.

27. Alcock to Stanley, Dec. 23, 1867, *ibid.*, p. 80.

28. *Minutes of the Annual General Meeting of the Shanghai General Chamber of Commerce*, Aug. 23, 1865.

29. The Order in Council was dated March 9, and the Court was established on September 4, 1865. See review of its founding and initial cases, mainly bankruptcy, *NCH*, Sept. 14, 1865, and editorial comment, *ibid.*, Sept. 21, 1865. In 1867 an Admiralty Supreme Court in China was established to deal with maritime cases between British subjects or where the defendant was British. For its rules of procedure, see Hertslet, *Treaties*, Vol. II, No. 126.

30. See "Annual Report of the Committee of the Shanghai General Chamber of Commerce," in *NCH*, Aug. 26, 1865.

31. E.g., memorial of Lao Ch'ung-kuang, Sept. 5, 1861, *IWSM-TC*, Ch. 1, pp. 21–22b; Tsungli-yamen memorial of Apr. 30, 1866, *ibid.*, Ch. 41, pp. 36b–40.

32. See review of recent cases and translations of relevant Chinese documents, *NCH*, Sept. 23, 1865.

33. Memorial of Jardine, Matheson & Co., No. 28, 1867, *China. No. 4. (1870)*, p. 32.

34. Memorandum by Vice-consul Forrest, Nov. 1867, *China. No. 5. (1871)*, pp. 53–55.

35. Winchester to Alcock, Nov. 7, 1867, *ibid.*, pp. 34–35.

36. Memorandum by Vice-consul Forrest, *loc. cit.*

37. *NCH*, July 31, 1868.

38. Winchester to Alcock, No. 7, 1867, *China. No. 5. (1871)*, pp. 34–35.

39. *NCH*, Aug. 9, Aug. 23, 1862.

40. *Ibid.*, Mar. 19, 1864.

41. *Ibid.*, Jan. 9, 1864.

42. Text of Alcock's letter, *ibid.*, Aug. 18, 1866.

43. Elgin to Russell, Oct. 21, 1860, *Correspondence Respecting Affairs in China. 1859–1860*, p. 205; see also Bruce to Malmesbury, June 14, 1859, *Correspondence with Mr. Bruce . . .* , pp. 8–10.

44. Russell to Bruce, Jan. 9, 1861, *Correspondence Respecting Affairs in China. 1859–1860*, No. 116.

45. *NCH*, Feb. 16, 1861.

46. For general accounts of missionary affairs in the 1860's, see K. S. Latourette, *A History of Christian Missions in China*, New York, 1929, chaps. xvii–xxi, *passim*; and E. R. Hughes, *The Invasion of China by the Western World*, New York, 1938, chap. ii. The subject is also treated at some length in Morse, Cordier, and other standard works on the history of Sino-foreign relations. British documentation is to be found in the *Parliamentary Papers* (see Bibliography). Although Chinese documents on mission cases are to be found in all the chief collections, the main source is *IWSM*. A useful special collection is *Ch'ing-chi chiao-an shih-liao*, Peiping, the Palace Museum, 1937; Vol. I, pp. 1–71, deals with the T'ung-chih period. Wu Sheng-te and Ch'en Tseng-hui, *Chiao-an shih-liao pien-mu*, Peiping, 1941, is an extremely useful subject catalogue of Chinese documents from a variety of sources.

47. *China. No. 9. (1870)*, p. 70. See also Alcock, "The Chinese Empire in Its Foreign Relations," *Bombay Quarterly Review* (Apr. 1856), pp. 261–75. For Wade's views, see text of his memorandum in Méritens, *Notes upon Mr. Wade's Memorandum Regarding the Revision of the Treaty of Tientsin*, Hongkong, 1871.

48. *The North China Herald*, Sept. 29, Oct. 31, 1868, reviewed the widespread anti-Christian propaganda of the summer and autumn of 1868 and translated sample proclamations in the "paper war against missionaries."

49. The cases are briefly reviewed in Morse, *Relations*, II, 233–34.

50. Note the large number of Blue Books that relate to such incidents.

51. Clarendon to Bishop Charles R. Victoria, Dec. 13, 1869, *China. No. 9. (1870)*, No. 9.

52. For antimissionary speeches by Grey, Somerset, Clarendon, Otway, Dilke, and others, see *Hansard*, Vol. 194 (1869), pp. 933–46; Vol. 195 (1869), pp. 131 ff.; Vol. 197 (1869), p. 1797; Vol. 199 (1870), pp. 1870–72; Vol. 200 (1870), pp. 71–72; Vol. 205 (1871), pp. 562–63.

53. Jamieson to Alcock, May 21, 1868, *China. No. 3. (1869)*, p. 2. British materials on the Formosa incident are to be found in *ibid., passim*; Chinese materials are to be found in *Ch'ing-chi chiao-an shih-liao*, I, 16–26. See also Chapter III.

54. *China. No. 9. (1870)*, Nos. 2 and 4 (Mar. and July, 1869).

55. Memorandum by Wade, Dec. 1868, *China. No. 5. (1871)*, Appendix.

56. E.g., memorials of the Foochow missionaries and of the Swatow missionaries, *China. No. 4. (1870)*, pp. 16–17, 39–40; memorials of the Swatow and Ningpo missionaries, *China. No. 5. (1871)*, pp. 90–91.

57. *China. No. 9. (1870)*, pp. 10–11.

58. Alcock's notes on the missionary communication referred to above, *ibid.*, p. 29.

59. Chinese text of Hart's memorandum, *IWSM-TC*, Ch. 40, pp. 13b–22b; Chinese text of Wade's memorandum, *ibid.*, Ch. 40, pp. 24–36.

60. Memorial of Apr. 1, 1866, *IWSM-TC*, Ch. 40, p. 10b.

61. Tsungli-yamen memorial, Apr. 1, 1866, *IWSM-TC*, Ch. 40, pp. 10b–12.

62. Circular letter of the Grand Council, quoted in reply of Liu K'un-i and received by Liu on Apr. 15, 1866, *ibid.*, Ch. 41, p. 43.

63. *Ibid.*, Ch. 40, pp. 12–13b.

64. *Ibid.*, Ch. 40, pp. 36–37.

65. The summary that follows is based on the following memorials in *IWSM-TC*: the superintendent of trade for the three northern ports, Ch'ung-hou, Apr. 27, 1866, Ch. 41, pp. 26b–30; the Grand Secretary and governor-general of Hupei and Hunan, Kuan-wen, May 23, 1866, Ch. 41, pp. 40b–43; the governor of Kiangsi, Liu K'un-i, May 29, 1866, Ch. 41, pp. 43–50; the governor-general of Fukien and Chekiang, Tso Tsung-t'ang, July 14, 1866, Ch. 42, pp. 45b–48b; the governor-general of Kwangtung and Kwangsi, Jui-lin, and the governor of Kwangtung, Chiang I-li, July 30, 1866, Ch. 42, pp. 58b–65b; the governor of Chekiang, Ma Hsin-i, Nov. 27, 1866, Ch. 45, pp. 44b–54.

66. The preparations for treaty revision are summarized in Wright, *Hart and the Chinese Customs*, pp. 373–80.

67. On Alcock's tour see Michie, *The Englishman in China . . .* , Vol. II, chap. xxi.

68. This summary of the British merchants' demands is based on the following statements by merchant groups:

Addresses of the merchants of Chefoo, Kiukiang, and Chinkiang, and Alcock's replies, *China. No. 5. (1871)*, pp. 1–8.

Foochow: *China. No. 4. (1870)*, pp. 14–16; *China. No. 5. (1871)*, pp. 65–68; *NCH*, Oct. 12, 1867.

Amoy: *China. No. 4. (1870)*, pp. 17–21; *China. No. 5. (1871)*, pp. 69–73; *NCH*, Nov. 9, 1867.

Tientsin: *China. No. 4. (1870)*, pp. 34–38; *China. No. 5. (1871)*, pp. 85–90.

Ningpo: *China. No. 5. (1871)*, pp. 154–56.

Chefoo: *Ibid.*, pp. 103–5, and *NCH*, Jan. 16, 1868.

Kiukiang: *NCH*, Nov. 30, 1867.

Shanghai: *China. No. 4. (1870)*, pp. 1–10; *China. No. 5. (1871)*, pp. 17–29; *NCH*, Nov. 9, 1867, and Nov. 10, 1868; *China. No. 12. (1869)*, pp. 1–2.

Hongkong: *China. No. 4. (1870)*, pp. 22–29; *China. No. 5. (1871)*, pp. 44–51.

Jardine, Matheson and Co.: *China. No. 4 (1870)*, pp. 29–31, and *NCH*, Dec. 14, 1867.

For summary analyses of the merchants' position, see *NCH*, Jan. 16, 1868, and Alcock to Stanley, Dec. 23, 1867, *China. No. 5. (1871)*, p. 79.

69. *NCH*, Jan. 13, 1868.

70. Memorial of the Shanghai General Chamber of Commerce, *China. No. 4. (1870)*, pp. 1–4, 9–10.

71. Memorial of Jardine, Matheson, & Company, Nov. 28, 1867, *ibid.*, pp. 29–31.

72. *NCH*, June 13, 1868.

73. Alcock's circular to British consuls in China, Feb. 17, 1868, *China. No. 5. (1871)*, pp. 125–30. Text and editorial comment, *NCH*, May 4, 1868.

74. *Daily Press*, reprinted in *NCH*, July 5, 1867.

75. Stanley to Alcock, Aug. 16, 1867, *China. No. 5. (1871)*, p. 8. In this position Stanley had the support of the majority of the Derby cabinet.

76. This compilation is not included in the *IWSM*, and I have found no other reference to it.

77. Tsungli-yamen memorial, June 16, 1867, *IWSM-TC*, Ch. 49, pp. 5–7b.

78. Tsungli-yamen memorial, Oct. 12, 1867, *IWSM-TC*, Ch. 50, pp. 24–28.

79. Although the order was directed to eighteen officials, only seventeen replied, for in the interval Tseng Kuo-ch'üan took leave of absence from office. Also, Kuan-wen had replaced Liu Ch'ang-yu as governor-general of Chihli in the interval. Otherwise the list of officials ordered to comment was identical with that of those who did comment. See note 84.

The letter of the Tsungli-yamen and the replies of provincial officials are admirably summarized in Knight Biggerstaff, "The Secret Correspondence of 1867–1868: Views of Leading Chinese Statesmen Regarding the Further Opening of China to Western Influence," *Journal of Modern History*, XXII, 2 (1950), 122–36. I would modify Biggerstaff's interpretation, however. He emphasizes the "general ignorance and blindness" that characterized the thinking of these men about China's problems. If proper account is taken of the whole range of domestic and foreign problems they faced, I do not think they can be regarded as either ignorant or blind.

80. An edict of Dec. 13, 1867, repeated the order and urged haste, noting that thus far replies had been received only from Tso Tsung-t'ang, Tu-hsing-a, and Jui-lin (*SL-TC*, Ch. 216, pp. 30–30b).

81. *IWSM-TC*, Ch. 50, pp. 28–28b; *SL-TC*, Ch. 211, pp. 32b–34.

82. Text of the circular letter, *IWSM-TC*, Ch. 50, pp. 29–30b.

83. Text of the outline, *ibid.*, Ch. 50, pp. 30b–35.

84. The summaries of views of provincial officials, which follow below, are based on the following memorials in reply:

(1) The governor-general of Shensi and Kansu, Tso Tsung-t'ang, Nov. 20, 1867, *IWSM-TC*, Ch. 51, pp. 18–23b.

(2) The governor-general of Kwangtung and Kwangsi, Jui-lin, Dec. 10, 1867, *ibid.*, Ch. 52, pp. 16–21.

(3) The military governor at Mukden, Tu-hsing-a, Dec. 12, 1867, *ibid.*, Ch. 52, pp. 21–23b.

(4) The governor of Shantung, Ting Pao-chen, Dec. 14, 1867, *ibid.*, Ch. 52, pp. 25b–28b. Ting's memorial was the only one selected for inclusion in *THTKTI*, Ch. 16, pp. 1–2, dated Dec. 10, 1867 (the *IWSM* dates are, of course, the dates of presentation to the Throne, not of composition). The *THTKTI* text contains a few phrases of opinion omitted from *IWSM* text.

(5) The governor of Kiangsi, concurrently acting governor-general of Hupeh and Hunan, Li Han-chang, Dec. 16, 1867, *IWSM-TC,* Ch. 52, pp. 30b–36b.

(6) The director of the Foochow Shipyard, Shen Pao-chen, Dec. 16, 1867, *ibid.*, Ch. 53, pp. 1–7b. Second memorial of Shen, Dec. 22, 1867, *ibid.*, Ch. 54, pp. 25–26b.

(7) The governor of Kwangtung, Chiang I-li, Dec. 17, 1867, *ibid.*, Ch. 53, pp. 30–33.

(8) The governor-general of Kiangsu, Kiangsi, and Anhwei, Tseng Kuo-fan, Dec. 18, 1867, *ibid.*, Ch. 54, pp. 1–4b.

(9) The Tartar General at Foochow, Ying-kuei, Dec. 20, 1867, *ibid.*, Ch. 54, pp. 6–12b.

(10) The governor of Kiangsi, Liu K'un-i, Dec. 20, 1867, *ibid.*, Ch. 54, pp. 12b–15.

(11) The superintendent of trade for the three northern ports, Ch'ung-hou, three memorials of Dec. 21, 1867, *ibid.*, Ch. 54, pp. 15–24b.

(12) The governor-general of Fukien and Chekiang, Wu T'ang, Dec. 28, 1867, *ibid.*, Ch. 55, pp. 1–5.

(13) The governor-general of Hupeh and Hunan, Li Hung-chang, Dec. 31, 1867, *ibid.*, Ch. 55, pp. 6b–17. (Michie, *The Englishman in China* . . . , II, 185–89, contains a translation of a similar memorial, attributed to Li and dated Dec. 1, 1867.)

(14) The governor of Chekiang, Ma Hsin-i, Dec. 31, 1867, *ibid.*, Ch. 55, pp. 26–29b.

(15) The governor of Fukien, Li Fu-t'ai, two memorials and a letter of Dec. 31, 1867, *ibid.*, Ch. 55, pp. 9–16.

(16) The governor of Kwangsi, concurrently acting governor of Kiangsu, Kuo Po-yin, Dec. 31, 1867, *ibid.*, Ch. 55, pp. 37b–41b.

(17) The acting governor-general of Chihli, Kuan-wen, Jan. 16, 1868, *ibid.*, Ch. 56, pp. 9–16.

The following additional opinions on treaty revision, by officials too low in rank to memorialize independently, were forwarded to the Throne by Shen Pao-chen and Li Hung-chang:

(1) Liang Ming-ch'ien, 2d-class assistant secretary in the Board of Civil Office, *IWSM-TC*, Ch. 53, pp. 7–12.

(2) Yeh Wen-lan, Kwangtung taotai-designate, *ibid.*, Ch. 53, pp. 12–15.

(3) Huang Wei-hsüan, subprefect, *ibid.*, Ch. 53, pp. 15b–18b.

(4) Wang Pao-ch'en, holder of the provincial degree, *ibid.*, Ch. 53, pp. 19b–22.

(5) Lin Ch'üan-ch'u, holder of the preliminary degree, *ibid.*, Ch. 53, pp. 22–26.

(6) Ting Jih-ch'ang, financial commissioner of Kiangsu, *ibid.*, Ch. 55, pp. 17–26.

85. Williams to Seward, July 1868, *Foreign Relations of the United States*, 1868, Part I, pp. 516–21.

86. Edict of Oct. 3, 1868, *SL-TC*, Ch. 241, pp. 5b–6; Tsung-yamen memorial and edict, *IWSM-TC*, Ch. 61, pp. 19–19b.

87. *China. No. 5. (1871)*, pp. 13–15; *NCH*, June 13, 1868.

88. E.g., memorial of Chou Tsu-p'ei, June 23, 1858, *IWSM-HF*, Ch. 26, p. 14.

89. Tsungli-yamen memorial, Apr. 14, 1873, *IWSM-TC*, Ch. 89, pp. 25b–28, enclosing despatch from the diplomatic corps at Peking.

Further Tsungli-yamen memorial of Apr. 14, reviewing the history of the audience question, *ibid.*, Ch. 89, pp. 28–39.

Memorial of the Hanlin Academy, Apr. 15, *ibid.*, Ch. 89, pp. 41–43, opposing audience without kowtow.

Memorial of the Shantung censor Wu Hung-en, *ibid.*, Ch. 89, pp. 47–49, also opposing audience without kowtow.

Memorial of Li Hung-chang, May 1, 1873, *ibid.*, Ch. 90, pp. 1b–5b, rebutting the views of the Hanlin Academy and Wu Hung-en.

Four memorials of the Tsungli-yamen, June 14, 1873, *ibid.*, Ch. 90, pp. 19b–32b.

Memorial of the censor Wu K'o-tu, June 19, 1873, reproving courtiers who were still quibbling over the kowtow while paying no attention to the basic problems of resistance to the West (*ibid.*, Ch. 90, pp. 35–38). Wu was no radical; he shortly committed suicide in protest against the violation of the proper sequence of generations that the Kuang-hsü succession involved. But the kowtow question had become trivial.

For additional views of the audience question, see *ibid.*, Ch. 90, pp. 10b–16; Ch. 91, pp. 9–15b, 19b–22.

90. Wen-hsiang, ". . . nien-p'u," *loc. cit.*, Ch. 3, pp. 70b–71; Chin-liang, *Ch'ing-ti wai-chi*, pp. 151–52; and Tabohashi Kiyoshi, "Shin Dōji chō gaikoku kōshi no kinken," *Seikyū gakusō*, No. 6 (1931), pp. 1–31 (*FB* 2.5.6). Tabohashi's study is a detailed account of the first audience; it does not deal with the background of the audience question or its significance.

91. For Chinese views on the advantages of sending envoys abroad, see in addition to the sources in note 84 the extracts assembled in *Kuo-ch'ao jou-yüan chi*, Ch. 18, pp. 12b–14.

92. Memorial of Dec. 1, 1861, *IWSM-TC*, Ch. 3, pp. 46b–47. An edict of Dec. 3, 1861, reviewed the history of Christian missions and their legal rights and ordered the proper handling of all cases, according to treaty (*ibid.*, Ch. 3, pp. 1–1b; *SL-TC*, Ch. 9, pp. 3–3b). The governor of Kiangsi memorialized on the importance of protecting missionaries, who were described as generally peaceful people (Apr. 2, 1862, *IWSM-TC*, Ch. 5, pp. 4b–5b). A general edict of toleration, April 4, 1862, pointed out that foreign support was important; converts could be reformed later (*ibid.*, Ch. 5, pp. 11–13b).

93. *Ibid.*, Ch. 5, pp. 24b–25b; Ch. 13, p. 12b.

94. *Situation de l'Empire*, Jan. 1866, *DD*, 1866, p. 228.

95. K. S. Latourette, *A History of Christian Missions in China*, New York, 1929, p. 347.

96. E.g., *CSWP*, Ch. 112, p. 13.

97. Knight Biggerstaff's thorough study of the Burlingame Mission makes detailed treatment here unnecessary. See his "The Change in the Attitude of the Chinese Government Toward the Sending of Diplomatic Representatives, 1860–1880," Ph.D.

dissertation, Harvard University, 1934; and "The Official Chinese Attitude Toward the Burlingame Mission," *American Historical Review*, XLI (1936), 682–702. See also Tyler Dennett, *Americans in Eastern Asia*, New York, 1922, chap. xx; Telly Howard Koo, "The Life of Anson Burlingame," Ph.D. dissertation, Harvard University, 1922; Wright, *Hart and the Chinese Customs*, pp. 366–72.

The mission is ridiculed in Cordier, *Relations*, Vol. I, chap. xx, and in Gumpach, *The Burlingame Mission*.

98. Tsungli-yamen memorial of Feb. 20, 1866, *IWSM-TC*, Ch. 39, pp. 1–2b. Pin-ch'un's far from dull account of his mission was published in three separately titled ts'e, n.d.: (1) *Ch'eng-ch'a pi-chi*, 1868 preface by Hsü Chi-yü, 1869, preface by Li Shan-lan (see Chapter X); (2) *Hai-kuo sheng-yu ts'ao*, foreword by Tung Hsün, 1869; (3) *T'ien-wai kuei-fan ts'ao*. Tung Hsün mentions his preface and briefly discusses a conversation with Wen-hsiang on foreign affairs in *Huan-tu-wo-shu lao-jen tzu-ting nien-p'u*, Ch. 1, p. 52b, under an 1866 (*sic*) entry.

99. Tsungli-yamen memorial, Nov. 21, 1867, *IWSM-TC*, Ch. 51, pp. 26b–28; edict, *ibid.*, p. 29, and *SL-TC*, Ch. 214, p. 32.

100. *IWSM-TC*, Ch. 51, pp. 28b–29.

101. Tsungli-yamen memorial of Nov. 26, *ibid.*, Ch. 52, pp. 1–2; edict, *ibid.*, pp. 2–2b, and *SL-TC*, Ch. 215, pp. 1b–2. Chih-kang's *Ch'u-shih t'ai-hsi chi-yao* (1890, 4 chüan) is a straightforward factual account of the details of travel; his chief impression at the end was of the vast size of the non-Chinese world connected by modern communications. On the appointment of six additional Chinese as clerks and orderlies and of six additional Manchus from the T'ung-wen kuan as interpreters, see *IWSM-TC*, Ch. 52, pp. 6–6b.

102. For a review of contemporary gossip on the subject, and editorial comment, see *NCH*, Dec. 14, 1867; Alcock to Stanley, Dec. 31, 1867, *China. No. 5. (1871)*, pp. 107–10.

103. *China. No. 5. (1871)*, Nos. 40, 98.

104. Tsungli-yamen memorial of Mar. 21, 1868, commenting on first report from the Burlingame Mission, *IWSM-TC*, Ch. 57, pp. 25–26; memorial of Nov. 18, 1869, with attached reports from Burlingame and text of Washington Treaty, and edict appointing Tung Hsün to sign for China, *ibid.*, Ch. 69, pp. 14–21b; memorial of Nov. 28 reporting signature of the treaty by Tung Hsün and S. Wells Williams, *ibid.*, Ch. 69, pp. 38b–40b. Tung Hsün limited himself to a bare factual phrase (*op. cit.*, Ch. 2, 66. 3–3b). The *Kuo-ch'ao jou-yüan chi* notes the mission to America under the date 1868, 6th month, and mentions Chih-kang and Sun Chia-ku, but not Burlingame (Ch. 16, pp. 13b–14). I have found no discussion of the mission in the various collections of essays on public affairs.

105. Tsungli-yamen memorial and edict of May 10, 1870, reporting Burlingame's death in Russia and posthumously awarding him first rank and 10,000 taels, *IWSM-TC*, Ch. 72, pp. 8–10b.

106. Tsungli-yamen memorial of Feb. 2, 1869, reviewing chronology, *IWSM-TC*, Ch. 63, pp. 1–2; Alcock's despatch and draft proposals, *ibid.*, Ch. 63, pp. 10–20; for Alcock's account see *China. No. 5. (1871)*, Nos. 36, 40.

107. Alcock to Stanley, Jan. 22, 1868, *ibid.*, No. 36.

108. I have not been able to find out how the Tsungli-yamen got its information on Egypt. It is known, however, that they received and studied clippings from the

foreign press of Shanghai and Hongkong, and that they had translations made of many *Parliamentary Papers*. They were always particularly alert to news from countries where Western influence was growing. There was no particular incident in 1866–67 that would have captured their attention. They were presumably aware of and concerned over (1) the rapid increase in Western carpetbaggers with extraterritorial rights throughout Egypt, and (2) the foreign supervision to which the rise of Isma'il's debt to more than £15 million in 1867 had given rise. Having received only £13 million, and this with strings attached, Isma'il was obliged to direct Egypt's entire economy toward the servicing of the loan.

109. *China. No. 5. (1871)*, p. 113.

110. *Ibid.*, No. 40.

111. *Ibid.*, p. 190.

112. Minutes of the meeting of Mar. 3, 1868, *ibid.*, pp. 191–92, and Tsungli-yamen review in memorial of Feb. 2, 1869, *IWSM-TC*, Ch. 63, pp. 1–7b.

113. Alcock's instructions to the British commissioners, Apr. 26, 1868, *China. No. 5. (1871)*, p. 195.

114. British accounts of the 1868 negotiations were enclosed in Alcock to Stanley, Nov. 10 and Dec. 6, 1868, *ibid.*, pp. 177–254. On the points specifically cited here, see pp. 187, 190–213, 218–20, 222–23. Chinese accounts were attached to Tsungli-yamen memorial of Feb. 2, 1869, *IWSM-TC*, Ch. 63, pp. 1–87. The Chinese and English accounts are not identical, but there is no important discrepancy between them.

115. *China. No. 5. (1871)*, p. 222.

116. E.g., Col. Sykes's attack on the negotiations in Parliament, Apr. 23, 1868, *Hansard*, Vol. 191, pp. 1147–48.

117. Alcock to Stanley, Apr. 9 and Apr. 16, 1868, *China. No. 5. (1871)*, Nos. 50–51. This disclaimer was the subject of bitter criticism in the press. Alcock to Clarendon, Feb. 27, 1869, *ibid.*, No. 98.

118. *Ibid.*, pp. 177–81, 231–32; Nos. 74–75.

119. Alcock to Prince Kung, Dec. 7, 1868, *ibid.*, p. 238.

120. Alcock to Stanley, Jan. 12, 1869, *ibid.*, pp. 280–81.

121. Chairman of the Shanghai General Chamber of Commerce to Consul Medhurst, Feb. 1, 1869, *China. No. 12. (1869)*, p. 5.

122. Alcock to Medhurst, Mar. 23, 1869, *ibid.*, pp. 8–9.

123. Alcock to Clarendon, Feb. 27, 1869, *China. No. 5 (1871)*, No. 98.

124. *Ibid.*, Nos. 84, 103, 117, 138, and 141.

125. *IWSM-TC*, Ch. 63, pp. 1–87.

126. Text of two memorials, *ibid.*, pp. 1–7b, 7b–10.

127. The summary that follows is based on memorials of: Prince Jui (Te-ch'ang), on behalf of all Imperial princes, Feb. 9, 1869, *ibid.*, Ch. 63, pp. 91b–93b; Prince Shun, Feb. 13, 1869, *ibid.*, Ch. 64, pp. 1–8; Prince Shun, reporting on behalf of the Grand Secretaries, Feb. 17, 1869, *ibid.*, Ch. 64, pp. 8–12; Ma Hsin-i, *ibid.*, Ch. 64, pp. 26–29. On the basic and persistent conflict between Prince Shun (I-huan) and Prince Kung, see *Eminent Chinese*, pp. 384–86.

128. Tsungli-yamen memorial of Feb. 24, 1869, *ibid.*, Ch. 64, pp. 17–20.

129. Subsequent Tsungli-yamen memorial reviewing the negotiations (Feb.-Oct., 1869), Oct. 23, 1869, *ibid.*, Ch. 68, p. 12.

130. Alcock to Clarendon, Oct. 23, 1869, *China. No. 1. (1870)*, p. 3; *China. No. 5.* *(1871)*, pp. 153–54; Nos. 122 and 134.

131. *China. No. 5. (1871)*, p. 406 and Nos. 103, 138, 141. Two Tsungli-yamen memorials of Oct. 23, 1869, with attached exchange of despatches, *IWSM-TC*, Ch. 68, pp. 12–29.

132. Alcock to Clarendon, Oct. 23, 1869, *China. No. 1. (1870)*, p. 3. On Hart's "work for, and unceasing support of, the Alcock Convention (1869)—a Convention which, to her own and China's detriment, Great Britain failed to ratify," see Stanley F. Wright, *Hart and the Chinese Customs*, p. 6. The opposition agreed on Hart's importance in the negotiations (*NCH*, May 16, 1868).

133. *IWSM-TC*, Ch. 69, pp. 24–24b.

134. Wang Te-chao, "T'ung-chih hsin-cheng k'ao," *loc. cit.*, Part 1, pp. 24–29.

135. Hu Sheng, *Ti-kuo chu-i yü Chung-kuo cheng-chih*, Peking, 1952, pp. 47–49.

136. For the Chinese text, see *IWSM-TC*, Ch. 68, pp. 29–39b; English text, Hertslet, *Treaties*, Vol. I, No. 11; text of the Convention with Hart's notes, *China. No. 1. (1870)*, pp. 5–12; Wade's memorandum, *China. No. 5. (1871)*, Appendix. The references in the section that follows are to the above texts and comments unless otherwise specified. For comparison, see bilingual texts in Imperial Maritime Customs, *Treaties, Conventions, etc. Between China and Foreign States*, Shanghai, 1908, I, 212 ff. (Treaty of Tientsin); 286 ff. (Alcock Convention); 308 ff. (Chefoo Convention).

137. Inhabitants of Hongkong to Clarendon, *China. No. 6. (1870)*, No. 4. Alcock to Clarendon, Oct. 23, 1869, *China. No. 1. (1870)*, pp. 4–5.

138. Alcock to Dean of the Diplomatic Corps De Rehfues, Oct. 20, 1869, *China. No. 1. (1870)*, pp. 14–15.

139. Alcock to Clarendon, Oct. 23, 1869, *China. No. 1. (1870)*, p. 3.

140. "Letter to the Chambers of Commerce . . . Respecting the China Treaty Revision Convention," *China. No. 10. (1870)*, *passim*; Alcock to De Rehfues, *China. No. 1. (1870)*, pp. 14–15.

141. Alcock to Clarendon, Oct. 23, 1869, *China. No. 1. (1870)*, pp. 2–4.

142. Alcock to De Rehfues, Oct. 20, 1869, *ibid.*, p. 15.

143. Alcock to Clarendon, Oct. 23, 1869, *ibid.*, p. 4.

144. Not under Chinese jurisdiction as it existed, but under the jurisdiction of mixed courts to be established by China. Alcock to Stanley, Dec. 6, 1868, *China. No. 5.* *(1871)*, No. 76.

145. Alcock to Clarendon, Oct. 23, 1869, *China. No. 1. (1870)*, p. 4.

146. Memorial of the Tsungli-yamen, Oct. 23, 1869, *IWSM-TC*, Ch. 68, pp. 12–29.

147. *China. No. 1. (1870)*, p. 5.

148. Tsungli-yamen memorial, Jan. 26, 1870, *IWSM-TC*, Ch. 70, pp. 39–41; Tsungli-yamen to Alcock, Oct. 23, 1869, *China. No. 1. (1870)*, pp. 17–18.

149. E.g., memorial of the governor-general of Kiangsu, Kiangsi, and Anhwei, Ma Hsin-i, and the governor of Kiangsu, Ting Jih-ch'ang, *IWSM-TC*, Ch. 71, pp. 38–39.

150. Tsungli-yamen memorial of Jan. 26, 1870, *ibid.*, Ch. 70, pp. 39–41.

151. Texts of protests from chambers of commerce and other merchant organizations are to be found in *China. No. 4. (1870)*; *China. No. 6. (1870)*; *China. No. 5.* *(1871)*, *passim*. The main points are summarized in Wright, *Hart and the Chinese Customs*, pp. 382–83.

152. Sassoon, London, to Clarendon, Mar. 22, 1870, *China. No. 6. (1870)*, No. 5.

153. *China. No. 10. (1870)*, p. 9.

154. Alcock to Clarendon, Oct. 28, 1869, *China. No. 1. (1870)*, pp. 4–5.

155. Memorial of merchants, etc., of London following meeting of Jan. 13, 1870, *China. No. 4. (1870)*, No. 1.

156. *Ibid.*, Nos. 3, 4, 5, 6, 7, 8; *China. No. 6. (1870)*, Nos. 2, 3, 7; *NCH*, Jan. 19, July 22, 1870.

157. Alcock to De Rehfues, Oct. 20, 1869, *China. No. 1. (1870)*, p. 13.

158. De Lallemand to Alcock, Aug. 9, 1868, *China. No. 5. (1871)*, pp. 241–43; Lavalette to Lyons, June 28, 1869, *ibid.*, p. 378.

159. De Rehfues to Vlangali, Aug. 18, 1868, *China. No. 5. (1871)*, pp. 244–46; Bernstorff to Clarendon, May 3, 1869, *ibid.*, No. 97; Bismarck to Loftus, June 9, 1869, *ibid.*, pp. 370–71.

160. Vlangali to Alcock, Aug. 26, 1868, *ibid.*, pp. 249–50.

161. *China. No. 5. (1871)*, pp. 403–4, 393–94, and 405, respectively.

162. Williams to Seward, May 26, 1868, *Foreign Relations of the United States, 1868*, Part I, pp. 511 ff.; Seward to Browne, Sept. 8, 1868, *ibid.*, pp. 573–74; Williams to Alcock, Aug. 13, 1868, *China. No. 5. (1871)*, pp. 243–44; Fish to Thornton, approving Board of Trade memorandum, June 12, 1869, *ibid.*, p. 376.

163. Feb. 17, 1868, *Hansard*, Vol. 190, p. 500; Mar. 6. 1868, *ibid.*, Vol. 190, pp. 1149–50; July 13, 1869, *ibid*, Vol. 197, pp. 1779–86; Feb. 15, 1870, *ibid.*, Vol. 199, p. 330.

164. *China. No. 6. (1870)*, No. 1; *China. No. 5. (1871)*, No. 107; *Hansard*, Vol. 197, pp. 1794–96.

165. According to Granville, this was one of Clarendon's last official acts (*Hansard*, Vol. 205, p. 558).

166. Private letter to Hammond, quoted in Nathan A. Pelcovits, *Old China Hands and the Foreign Office*, New York, 1948, p. 80.

167. On this decision, see Wright, *Hart and the Chinese Customs*, pp. 383–84; Sargent, *Anglo-Chinese Commerce and Diplomacy . . .* , pp. 163–76.

168. *Hansard,* Vol. 202, p. 1624.

169. *Ibid.*, Vol. 205, p. 558.

170. Granville to Alcock, July 25, 1870, *China. No. 5. (1871)*, pp. 427–28.

171. *NCH*, Aug. 25, 1870. Italics mine.

172. Pelcovits, *op. cit.*, chap. iii.

173. E.g., Grey, Mar. 24, 1871, *Hansard*, Vol. 205, pp. 560–62.

174. Hu Sheng, *Ti-kuo chu-i yü Chung-kuo cheng-chih*, Peking, 1952, p. 57.

175. See, *The Foreign Trade of China*, p. 187, makes this claim but does not attempt to prove the point.

176. Quoted in Pelcovits, *op. cit.*, p. 104; see also memorial of Prince Shun on the failure of diplomacy to achieve any solid results after eleven years' trial, *IWSM-TC*, Ch. 79, pp. 24–27.

177. *IWSM-TC*, Ch. 79, pp. 39–42.

178. *The Journey of Augustus Raymond Margary, from Shanghai to Bhamo and Back to Maniwyne*, from his journals and letters, with a concluding chapter by Alcock, London, 1876, pp. 359, 372.

179. Text of the Convention, in Imperial Maritime Customs, *Treaties . . . ,*

1908, I, 308 ff., and *China. No. 3. (1877)*, pp. 64–67; the documents concerning its promulgation throughout China follow the latter text.

180. Wade to Derby (formerly Stanley), July 14, 1877, in a 36-page analysis of the Chefoo Convention, *China. No. 3. (1877)*, p. 147.

181. *Ibid.*, pp. 2–27.

182. Prince Kung to Elgin, Oct. 3, 1860, *Correspondence Respecting Affairs in China. 1859–1860*, p. 186.

183. Alcock to Stanley, Dec. 5, 1868, *China. No. 5. (1871)*, p. 189.

184. Alcock to De Rehfues, for the diplomatic corps, Oct. 20, 1869, *China. No. 1. (1870)*, p. 13. See also *ibid.*, p. 30, and *China. No. 5. (1871)*, pp. 243–44.

185. The sanest summary is still Morse, *Relations*, Vol. II, chap. xii. The chief Chinese documents are the memorials and other reports that constitute almost the whole of Chs. 72–76 of *IWSM-TC*. Li Hung-chang's views are to be found in *Li Wen-chung kung ch'üan-chi,* "I-shu han-kao," Ch. 1, pp. 1–9b; excerpts from Tseng Kuo-fan's reports are assembled in *THTKTI*, Ch. 18, pp. 1b–4b. For a detailed summary of events, based largely on the *IWSM*, see Nomura Masamitsu, "Tenshin kyōan ni tsuite," *Shirin*, XX, 1 (1935), 67–99 (*FB 2.5.5*). Catholic mission sources are covered in Alphonse Hubrecht, *Les Martyrs de Tientsin (21 juin 1870), d'après les documents contemporains*, Peking, imprimatur 1928; and *Le Memorandum chinois, ou violation du traité de Peking, exposé et réfutation par un missionnaire de Chine*, Rome, Imprimerie de la Propagande, 1872. French documentary sources are noted and extensively used in Cordier, *Relations*, Vol. I, chaps. xxiii–xxix.

186. W. H. Melhurst, *The Foreigner in Far Cathay*, New York, 1873, and references in Cordier, *Relations*, Vol. I, chaps. xxiii–xxvi, *passim*.

187. Hubrecht, *Les Martyrs de Tientsin . . . , passim*.

188. Memorial of Prince Shun, Feb. 17, 1869, *IWSM-TC*, Ch. 64, pp. 8–12b; memorial of the Tsungli-yamen, Feb. 24, 1869, *ibid.*, Ch. 64, pp. 17–21.

189. Tsungli-yamen memorandum to Alcock, July 18, 1869, *China. No. 9. (1870)*, p. 12; views of Wen-hsiang, June 26, 1869, *China. No. 1. (1872)*, pp. 13–14.

190. Memorial of Ch'ung-hou, June 23, 1870, reporting the massacre, and edict ordering the governor-general of Chihli, Tseng Kuo-fan, to take charge, *IWSM-TC*, Ch. 72, pp. 22–26.

191. E.g., memorial of Prince Shun on general military preparations, June 29, 1870, *ibid.*, Ch. 72, pp. 34–36; Tsungli-yamen approval of same, July 13, *ibid.*, Ch. 73, pp. 13b–15b; memorial of the Khorchin Prince Po-yen-no-mo-hu on cavalry preparations, July 27, *ibid.*, Ch. 73, pp. 37–38b; Li Hung-chang's suggestions and four edicts, Aug. 7, *ibid.*, Ch. 74, pp. 6–9b; three further edicts of Aug. 8 and 9, *ibid.*, Ch. 74, pp. 12–13b; suggestions of Ting Jih-ch'ang, three memorials and three edicts of Aug. 11, *ibid.*, Ch. 74, pp. 15b–21b; Tseng Kuo-fan recommending appointment of P'eng Yü-lin and others, Aug. 18, *ibid.*, Ch. 74, pp. 29b–32b; memorials of Li Han-chang and Kuo Po-yin, Aug. 18, *ibid.*, Ch. 74, pp. 32b–35b, pointing to the importance of distinguishing between Frenchmen and other foreigners in the coming war; suggestions of Ting Pao-chen, Aug. 18, *ibid.*, Ch. 74, pp. 36–39; Ying-han on naval defence on the Yangtze, Aug. 24, *ibid.*, Ch. 75, pp. 3b–7; Ting Jih-ch'ang's review of the occupation of Tonkin and other signs of French aggression, Aug. 25, *ibid.*, Ch. 75, pp. 9–10; suggestions of Ma Hsin-i, Aug. 28, *ibid.*, Ch. 75, pp. 25b–30b; suggestions of Ying-kuei, Aug. 31, *ibid.*, Ch. 75, pp. 35–37b; suggestions of Liu K'un-i, Aug. 31,

ibid., Ch. 75, pp. 37b–41. The number of such memorials and edicts declined sharply in September 1870, and virtually ceased in October. For detailed reports of the foreign view and translations of selected Chinese edicts and proclamations, see *NCH*, July 7, July 14, July 22, Aug. 4, Aug. 11, and Aug. 18, 1870.

192. Two memorials of Ch'ung-hou and two edicts, June 25, 1870, concerning discharge of the officials responsible, *ibid.*, Ch. 72, pp. 26–28; memorial of Ch'ung-hou requesting punishment for himself, *ibid.*, Ch. 73, pp. 2–3; memorial of Tseng Kuo-fan and Ch'ung-hou on the causes of the massacre and the persons responsible, July 23, 1870, and four edicts ordering punishments, *ibid.*, Ch. 73, pp. 23–29; edict of Aug. 16, 1870, on the discharge of officials involved, following report of judicial commissioner of Chihli, Ch'ien Ting-ming, *ibid.*, Ch. 74, pp. 29–29b (more on same, *ibid.*, Ch. 75, pp. 1–2, 3b–4b); memorial of Tseng Kuo-fan and Mao Ch'ang-hsi on the punishment of officials and edict, *ibid.*, Ch. 75, pp. 15–17. Memorial of the Peking gendarmerie on an arrest, Sept. 2, 1870, *ibid.*, Ch. 76, pp. 1–1b; memorial of Tseng Kuo-fan and others on the transfer to Peking of officials found guilty, Sept. 24, 1870, *ibid.*, Ch. 76, pp. 37–37b; further memorial of Tseng of same date reviewing the demands of the French chargé, Rochechouart, as to punishment, his own findings as to responsibility, *ibid.*, Ch. 76, pp. 35b–41b.

193. See Knight Biggerstaff, "The Ch'ung-hou Mission to France, 1870–1871," *Nankai Social and Economic Quarterly*, VIII (1935), 633–47. Tsungli-yamen memorial and edict appointing Ch'ung-hou, June 28, 1870, *IWSM-TC*, Ch. 72, pp. 28–31.

194. *IWSM-TC*, Ch. 73, pp. 8–13; Ch. 76, pp. 32b–35b; *CSWP*, Chs. 111–12, *passim*; *China. No. 3. (1871), passim.*

195. Tsungli-yamen memorial of Sept. 1, 1871, *IWSM-TC*, Ch. 82, p. 14; Chinese government circular of Feb. 9, 1871, translated in *China. No. 3. (1871)*, pp. 3–5; Wade's revised translation, *China. No. 1. (1872)*, pp. 6–7; text and comment, *Le Memorandum chinois . . .* , pp. 20–31; text and Rochechouart's reply in Prosper Giquel, *La Politique française en Chine*, Paris, 1872, pp. 51–70; extensive hostile comment in Cordier, *Relations*, Vol. I, chap. xxix, *passim*.

196. Granville to Lyons, June 27, 1871, *China. No. 1. (1872)*, p. 1; parliamentary debate of Mar. 24, 1871, *Hansard*, Vol. 205, pp. 545–53.

197. *Le Memorandum chinois . . .* , pp. 32–74.

198. *NCH*, July 22, 1870.

199. Tsungli-yamen memorial, Feb. 29, 1872, *IWSM-TC*, Ch. 85, p. 6b.

200. Williams, *The Middle Kingdom*, II, 706.

CHAPTER XII

1. Ch'en Tu-hsiu, "Hsien-fa yü K'ung-chiao," *Hsin Ch-ing-nien*, II, No. 3 (1916). The subject was discussed in virtually every issue of *Hsin Ch'ing-nien* at this period.

2. Fan Wen-lan, *Chung-kuo chin-tai shih*, Hongkong, 1949, I, 203; Fan, *Han-chien k'uai-tzu-shou Tseng Kuo-fan ti i-sheng*, n.p., Hsin-hua shu-tien, 1944; my notes on an interview with Ch'en Po-ta on this subject, Yenan, Oct. 27, 1946.

3. Fan, . . . *Tseng Kuo-fan . . .* ; P'ei-wei (pseud.), "Lun Tseng Kuo-fan," *Hsüeh-hsi* (Hankow), No. 1 (1948), pp. 4–7.

4. Author's preface, Ts'ai O, *Tseng Hu chih-ping yü-lu*, in *Ts'ai Sung-p'o hsien-sheng i-chi*, 1938; first edition 1917.

5. *Chung-kuo kuo-min-tang ti-i erh san ssu-tz'u ch'üan-kuo tai-piao ta-hui hui-k'an*, Kuomintang Information Committee, 1934, pp. 48–51.

6. Chiang briefly recalled this step in his 1932 preface to a further compilation of selections from Hu Lin-i, *(Hsin-pien) Hu Lin-i chün-cheng lu*, Nanking, n.d.; he also mentioned it in his 1935 preface to *Chiang wei-yüan chang tseng-pu Tseng Hu chih-ping yü-lu*, Nanking, third printing, 1946.

7. Wang Te-liang, *Tseng Kuo-fan chih min-tsu ssu-hsiang*, Shanghai, 1946; first edition, 1943, p. 76.

8. Chiang's 1924 preface to the Military Studies Institute edition of Ts'ai O, *Tseng Hu chih-ping yü-lu*, Nanking, 1946.

9. Tai Chi-t'ao's lecture to the Whampoa Academy, April 29, 1924, *Huang-p'u hsün-lien chi* (1924–25), n.p., n.d., II, 643–46.

10. Chiang's lectures, *ibid., passim.*

11. Kuomintang Central Political Council, Canton Branch, *Nationalist China*, Canton, May 1927, pp. 18–21.

12. *Lu-shan hsün-lien chi* (1933–34), n.p., n.d., 2 vols., *passim.* On the party's endorsement of Confucian principles as the unchanging and everlasting "basis of the people" and "basis of the state," see *Chiang-su ko-ming po-wu-kuan kuan-k'an*, reprinted in *Tang-shih shih-liao ts'ung-k'an*, No. 2 (1944), p. 1.

13. Chiang's 1924 preface to Ts'ai O, *Tseng Hu chih-ping yü-lu*.

14. Note the use of derogatory characters suggestive of pigs and dogs in references to the Taiping Rebellion in Chiang's 1932 preface to *Hu Lin-i chün-cheng lu*. Chiang went further than most of the party on this. Some party leaders went along with the new veneration for Chinese tradition but refused to condemn the Taiping (e.g., Chang Chi, *Chung-kuo kuo-min-tang shih*, Taipei, 1952, pp. 5–6; this was originally a 1943 lecture to the party's Central Training Corps). Others minimized the difficulty by downgrading the Taiping Rebellion to the "Hung Yang affair" (e.g., Lai Wei-chou's 1930 preface to *Tseng Kuo-fan chih-t'ao yao-lüeh* [Nanchang, Kiangsi Provincial Kuomintang Party Headquarters, 1930]).

15. *Lu-shan hsün-lien chi*, I, 200 and *passim.*

16. *Ibid.*, I, 212–13; see also p. 310.

17. *Chung-kuo kuo-min-tang ti-i erh san ssu-tz'u ch'üan-kuo tai-piao ta-hui hui-k'an*, pp. 48–51, 77–78, 93–95.

18. List of those recently readmitted, with their original offenses and punishments, *Kuo-wen chou-pao*, IX, No. 1 (1932).

19. Letter of T'an Yen-k'ai (Tsu-an) to T'ang Sheng-chih (Meng-hsiao), quoted in Hsü Pin, "Tseng Hu t'an-wei," Part 1, *Kuo-wen chou-pao*, VI, No. 26 (1929).

20. Chu Ch'i–hua (Hsin-fan), *I-chiu-erh-ch'i nien ti hui-i*, Shanghai, 1933, p. 63.

21. *Ibid.*, p. 45.

22. Léon Wieger, *Chine moderne*, Sienhsien, 1921–31, VII, 79.

23. *Ibid.*, VII, 67.

24. *Ibid.*, VIII, 143.

25. Chiang Kai-shek's order of May 1933 to troops in Hupeh, Hunan, and Kweichow, in *Li-tai tsun K'ung chi*, compiled by Ch'eng Yü, Shanghai, 1934, p. 50b.

26. *Tung-fang tsa-chih*, XXXI, No. 19 (1934), photographs of the ceremonies. See also Republic section of *Li-tai tsun K'ung chi*, pp. 36–51, and Yüan-chung Shao

(director of the Kuomintang Information Department), *Confucius and Present-Day China*, Peiping, 1934.

27. Ch'en Li-fu in *Tung-fang tsa-chih*, XXXII, 1 (1935), 25–29.

28. Tang-shih shih-liao pien-tsuan wei-yüan hui, *Chung-kuo kuo-min-tang shih kai-yao*, quoted in Wang Te-liang, *Tseng Kuo-fan chih min-tsu ssu-hsiang*, p. 13.

29. Chang Chi, *Chung-kuo kuo-min-tang shih*, pp. 5–6.

30. T'ao's postface, ca. 1943, to Wang Te-liang, *op. cit.*

31. T'ao, "Chung-kuo she-hui tsu-chih chien-shu," in *Chung-kuo wen-hua lun-chi*, essays in honor of Wu Chih-hui's ninetieth birthday, Taipei, 1953, p. 106.

32. Hu Shih, "Wu-shih nien lai Chung-kuo chih wen-hsüeh," in Shen-pao kuan, Fiftieth Anniversary Publication, II, *Wu-shih nien lai chih Chung-kuo*, Shanghai, 1922.

33. Hsü Pin, "Tseng Hu-t'an-wei," Part 1, *loc. cit.*, gives a number of examples. Note Chiang Kai-shek's emphasis in his 1933–34 lectures, *Lu-shan hsün-lien chi*, I, 356–57 and *passim*, and in his 1938 speech at the Nan-yo Military Council, in Wang Te-liang, *op. cit.*, p. 76.

34. Li Hsü, *Ts'ai Sung-p'o*, Models for Youth Series, compiled by order of the Generalissimo, Nanking, 1946, pp. 23, 27–29.

35. Hu Che-fu, *Tseng Kuo-fan*, Chungking, 1944, Preface.

36. Chiang based the party code of behavior on Tseng's code of behavior. Wang Te-liang, *op. cit.*, Preface and pp. 76–77.

37. Chiang Kai-shek, *China's Destiny*, authorized translation by Wang Chung-hui, New York, 1947, p. 20.

38. Ch'en Ch'ing-ch'u, *Tseng Ti-sheng chih tzu-wo chiao-yü*, Chungking, 1942, Preface.

39. Ch'en Li-fu in *Tung-fang tsa-chih*, XXXII, 1 (1935), 25–29.

40. Chiang Kai-shek in *Min-chung yün-tung fang-an fa-kuei hui-pien*, n.p., ca. 1936 (authorized by the Kuomintang as a guide to party workers in popular movements), II, Appendix, p. 6.

41. *Lu-shan hsün-lien chi*, I, 356–357 and *passim*.

42. Chiang Kai-shek, broadcast to the nation, text in *Tung-fang tsa-chih*, XXXVIII, 6 (1941), 41–44.

43. Chiang Kai-shek, "The Cause and Cure of Rural Decadence," summary of his appeal to the people of Szechwan following his June 1935 conference with the gentry and elders of the province, in Wang Ching-wei and Chiang Kai-shek, *China's Leaders and Their Policies*, Shanghai, 1935, pp. 31–36.

44. *Tung-fang tsa-chih*, XXXVI, 6 (1939), 55–56.

45. Chiang's 1932 preface to *Hu Lin-i chün-cheng lu*. Chiang stated that he had understood these truths since 1924.

46. *Ibid.*

47. See Hu Shih's detailed account of this interview with Ch'en Chi-t'ang, *Tu-li p'ing-lun*, No. 142 (1935), pp. 17–24.

48. Lai Wei-chou, Preface and Introduction to *Tseng Kuo-fan chih-t'ao yao-lüeh*. For an account of the steps taken by the Kuomintang to strengthen the upper classes and re-establish local control, see George Taylor, "Reconstruction after Revolution: Kiangsi Province and the Chinese Nation," *Pacific Affairs*, VIII, 3 (1935), 302–11.

49. Chiang Kai-shek, "The Cause and Cure of Rural Decadence," *loc. cit.*

50. Text of Chiang's telegram, Jan. 19, 1939, *Tung-fang tsa-chih*, XXXVI, 4 (1939), 61–62.

51. *Ch'ien-tai yü-k'ou liang-kuei*, published by the Kuomintang, ca. 1930, first two pages.

52. Text of the regulations in Wen Chün-t'ien, *Chung-kuo pao-chia chih-tu*, Shanghai, 1935, pp. 547–75.

53. See the review of recent government statements in Chin Ching, "Lun yung-jen," *Kuo-wen chou-pao*, XIII, 17 (1932), 7–12.

54. Ts'ai's preface to *Tseng Hu chih-ping yü-lu*.

55. See Chiang's preface of January 1929 to the combined edition of Ch'i Chi-kuang's *Chi-hsiao hsin-shu* and *Lien-ping shih-chi*. Chiang wrote that these Ming works were the most useful manuals of strategy and tactics since Sun-tzu. Since Tseng and Hu had studied them, Chiang instructed the "junior and senior officers of my whole army to do the same."

56. Lu Ti-p'ing, compiler's preface, Dec. 10, 1930, to *Tseng Kuo-fan chiao-Nien shih-lu*, n.p., n.d.

57. Ch'en Shu-hua, "Ch'ing-tai p'ing-Nien tso-chan chih chien-t'ao," *Shih-cheng chi-k'an*, published by the Ministry of National Defense, No. 1, (1948), pp. 23–25.

58. See the "Manifesto of the Ten Professors," the "Manifesto of the Eighteen Professors," and the sharp rebuttal of the liberals led by Hu Shih, *Tu-li p'ing lun*, No. 145 (1935), pp. 4–7; *I-hsüeh tsa-chih*, XIV, 1 (1935), 1–7 and XIV, 2 (1935), 39–44; *Tung-fang tsa-chih*, XXXII, 4 (1935), 81–83.

59. Passed and promulgated by the Southwestern Political Council, *Tu-li p'ing-lun*, No. 141 (1935), p. 15. For a wide sampling of views on this "Read the Classics" movement, see the special issue of *Chiao-yü tsa-chih*, XXV, No. 5 (1935).

60. E.g., *Tu-li p'ing-lun*, No. 138 (1935), pp. 18–21.

61. Hu's account, *ibid.*, No. 142 (1935), pp. 17–24.

62. *Chiao-yü tsa-chih*, XXIII, 4 (1931), 129–30; Ho Chien, *The True Spirit of China Today*, Changsha, 1936, pp. 2–3.

63. See T. F. Tsiang's answer to Ch'en Kuo-fu's proposal on education to the Kuomintang Central Executive Committee, *Tu-li p'ing-lun*, No. 4 (1932), pp. 6–8; Hu Shih, *ibid.*, No. 145 (1935), pp. 4–7, reprinted from the *Ta-kung pao*.

64. Ch'eng Yü, "Yü Chiang Chieh-shih lun chiao-yü shu," in *K'ung-chiao wai-lun*, compiled by Ch'eng Yü, Shanghai, 1934, pp. 39–40.

65. Associated Press version of Li's statement, New York, March 11, 1950, as printed in the *San Francisco Chronicle*, March 12, 1950, p. 1.

GLOSSARY OF CHARACTERS

Since characters concern specialists only, I have omitted those for (1) the names of well-known historic or contemporary figures; (2) names that appear in the Index to *Eminent Chinese of the Ch'ing Period*, edited by Arthur W. Hummel, Washington, D.C., 1943; (3) titles and institutions that appear in the Index to William Frederick Mayers, *The Chinese Government* . . . , Shanghai, etc., 1897; (4) transliterated phrases the characters for which are obvious in the context; (5) place names that appear in *The Columbia-Lippincott Gazetteer of the World*, New York, 1952, or G. M. H. Playfair, *The Cities and Towns of China*, Shanghai, etc., 1910. The spelling of place names generally follows Columbia-Lippincott, sometimes the simplified Wade-Giles romanization.

Chang Sheng-tsao......	張 盛 藻	Chou Chia-mei	周 家 楣
Chang Tsung-yü	張總禹(禹)	Chou Heng-ch'i	周 恒 祺
Ch'ang-ch'ing	常 清	Chou K'ai-hsi.........	周 開 錫
Chao Hui-fu	趙 惠 甫	Chou Tsu-p'ei	周 祖 培
chao-keng chü	招 耕 局	Chu Ch'ao	朱 潮
Ch'en Hung-i	陳 鴻 翊	Ch'uan-cheng	
Ch'en T'ing-ching	陳 廷 經	hsüeh-t'ang	船政學堂
Ch'eng-fu	成 孚	*chüan-chien*	捐 監
Ch'eng-lin	成 林	*chüan-na*	捐 納
Ch'i-hsiang	祺 祥	*chüan-shu*	捐 輸
Chiang Ch'i-ling	蔣 琦 齡	Ch'üan-ch'ing	全 慶
Chiang I-li	蔣 益 澧	*chung-hsing*	中 興
Chiang Tun-fu	蔣 敦 復	*chung-nung*	重 農
Chiao Yu-ying........	焦 祐 瀛	Chung P'ei-hsien.......	鍾 佩 賢
Chih-kang	志 剛	Feng Fang-chih........	馮 芳 植
Chih-yung Academy....	致用書院	Feng-i	風 一
Chin Chao-t'ang	金 召 棠	Ho Ching	何 璟
Ching-hsin Academy ...	經心書院	Hsia Chia-hao (Po-yin)	夏家鎬(伯音)
Ching-lien	景 廉	Hsiu-wen	秀 文
Ching-lun	景 綸	Hsü Nai-chao.........	許 乃 釗

Hsü Tung	徐　　　棟
Hu Chia-yü	胡　家　玉
Hu Ch'ing-yüan	胡　慶　源
Hu Kuang-yung	胡　光　墉
hua-ho ch'üan-ti	畫河圈地
Huang Tsan-t'ang	黃　贊　湯
Huang Ts'ung	黃　　琮
Huang-yai chiao	黃　崖　教
Hung Ch'ang-yen	洪　昌　燕
Hung Hsing	洪　　興
Jen Hua-pang (Jen Chu)	任　化　邦
Jen Wu..............	任　　武
Juan Shou-sung	阮　壽　松
Jui ch'in-wang, Te-ch'ang	
(Prince Jui)	瑞親王德昌
Jui-lin	瑞　　麟
kang-yen	綱　鹽
K'u-k'o-chi-t'ai	庫克吉泰
Kuei-hsiang	貴　　祥
K'uei-ling	魁　　齡
Kuang fang-yen kuan...	廣方言館
Kun-ko-cha-lo-ts'an	棍噶札勒參
kuo-chi min-sheng	國計民生
Kuo Hsiang-jui	郭　祥　瑞
Kuo Po-yin	郭　柏　蔭
Lan Wei-wen..........	藍　蔚　雯
Lei Cheng-kuan	雷　正　綰
Li Chao-t'ang.........	黎　兆　棠
Li Te-yüan...........	李　得　源
Li Tsung-hsi	李　宗　羲
Liang Ming-ch'ien	梁　鳴　謙
Lin Ch'üan-ch'u	林　全　初

Lin-hsing	麟　　興
Lin Shih-kung........	林　式　恭
Ling-kuei	靈　　桂
Liu Ch'ing	劉　　慶
Liu Ju-ch'iu	劉　如　璆
Liu Ping-hou	劉　秉　厚
Liu Tien.............	劉　　典
Liu Yü-nan	劉　毓　楠
Liu Yüeh-chao	劉　嶽　昭
Lo-chia-chi	羅　家　集
Lü Fan	呂　　藩
Lü Hsü-ch'eng........	呂　序　程
Ma Chan-ao	馬　占　鰲
Ma Erh	馬　　二
Ma Hsiang-ju.........	馬　相　如
Ma Hsien	馬　　先
Ma Kuei-yüan	馬　桂　源
Ma Ming-hsin	馬　明　心
Ma Te-hsing	馬　德　興
Ma Wen-lu...........	馬　文　祿
Ma Yüan-jui	馬　元　瑞
Mao Ch'ang-hsi	毛　昶　熙
Ming-hsü	明　　緒
Ming-i	明　　誼
Mu ta a-hun (Ahun Mu)	穆大阿渾
Mu-t'u-shan	穆　圖　善
nien	捻
Pai Yen-hu...........	白　彥　虎
p'iao-fan	票　　販
p'iao-yen	票　　鹽
Pien Pao-ti	卞　寶　第
Pin-ch'un	斌　　椿

ping-shang	病	商
P'ing-nan kuo.........	平 南	國
Po-yen-no-mo-hu	伯彥訥謨祜	
shih-ching chih t'u	市井之徒	
shih-tzu p'o..........	十 字	坡
Shih-wu Academy......	時務學堂	
Shun chün-wang (Prince Shun)	醇 郡	王
Su T'ing-k'uei	蘇 廷	魁
Sun Chia-ku..........	孫 家	轂
Sun I-mou	孫 翼	謀
Sun Ting-ch'en	孫 鼎	臣
Sung Chin	宋	晉
T'ang Sheng-chih	唐 生	智
Te-t'ai	德	泰
Te-ying	德	英
ti-ting yin	地 丁	銀
Ting Hsien	丁	顯
Ting Shao-chou........	丁 紹	周
Tseng Chi-feng	曾 紀	鳳
Ts'ui Mu-chih	崔 穆	之
Tu-hsing-a	都 興	阿
Tu Jui-lien	杜 瑞	聯
Tung Yüan-shun	董 元	醇
Wang Feng-sheng	王 鳳	生

Wang Hsien-ch'eng	王 憲	成
Wang Pao-ch'en	王 葆	辰
Wang Shu-jui	王 書	瑞
Wang Tao-yung	王 道	墉
Wen-ko	文	格
Wen-ming	文	明
Wu Ch'uo	吳	焯
Wu Hsün............	武	訓
Wu Hung-en	吳 鴻	恩
Wu K'un-hsiu	吳 坤	修
Wu Ting-yüan	吳 鼎	元
ya-hang	牙	行
Yang T'ing-hsi	楊 廷	熙
yeh-hu	業	戶
Yeh Wen-lan	葉 文	瀾
Yen Tuan-shu	嚴 端	書
yin-p'iao	引	票
yin-yen	引	鹽
Ying-ch'i	瑛	棨
Ying-han	英	翰
Ying-kuei	英	桂
Yü Ling-ch'en	于 凌	辰
Yüan Fang-ch'eng	袁 方	城
Yün Shih-lin	惲 世	臨

BIBLIOGRAPHY

I originally derived the major theses of this book from several years' reading in the *Shih-lu*, the *I-wu shih-mo*, the British *Parliamentary Papers* on China, and the *North China Herald*, and these have remained my most important and most frequently cited sources. As I attempted to verify the broad outlines of an emerging picture of the T'ung-chih period and to fill in some of the details, I was by degrees led to some thousand other major and minor sources of possible information; I have had occasion to refer to 662 of these in the notes. Since a long, unannotated, alphabetic bibliography of 662 Chinese, Japanese, and Western-language works cited would serve no purpose remotely commensurate with the cost of printing it, I have divided this bibliography into five parts as follows: (1) all the Chinese-language documentary sources cited in substantial evidence; (2) all the Western-language public documents cited; (3) approximately one-seventh of the 243 Chinese secondary works cited; (4) approximately one-seventh of the 244 Western secondary works cited; and (5) approximately one-ninth of the 52 Japanese works cited. The reader interested in what works I have used on any topic can consult the Index to locate the notes where the relevant references are given. The incomplete bibliography of secondary works is intended merely to make possible abridged citations in the notes.

The primacy of the *Shih-lu* as the basic source for Ch'ing history is unchallenged. Since it was reproduced by photolithography from the archives, it is entirely free of typographical errors and later editorial tampering. There is some evidence to suggest that the documents dealing with the *coup d'état* and related events immediately following the death of the Hsien-feng Emperor may have been revised before they were committed to the archives, but the *Shih-lu* has still been less subject to political editing than any other source. Its coverage of government policy is comprehensive, since it contains the full texts, day by day, of all edicts on all subjects.

I have occasionally consulted the privately compiled *Tung-hua hsü-lu* for abridgments of certain memorials that provided the occasion for edicts. Where possible, however, I have preferred the *Shih-lu* because its coverage is more comprehensive, its texts are more authentic in the event of variation, and it is easier to read.

I have made very sparing use of the Draft Dynastic History, *Ch'ing-shih kao*, because of its numerous small specific errors, and because of the storm of controversy (often ignored by Western scholars) over the principles on which it was compiled and edited.

For the study of Ch'ing foreign policy only, the *I-wu shih-mo* supersedes the *Shih-lu*, for in the former the edicts are preceded by the full texts of memorials and of such enclosed supporting evidence as correspondence with foreign envoys, reports from subordinate Chinese officials, and statements of private opinion.

For supporting materials on other aspects of state policy, I have relied in the first instance on five topically arranged general collections of documents of all types: *Huang-ch'ao cheng-tien lei-tsuan, Huang-ch'ao ching-shih wen hsü-pien, Huang-ch'ao hsü wen-hsien t'ung-k'ao, Huang-ch'ao Tao Hsien T'ung Kuang tsou-i,* and *T'ung-chih chung-hsing ching-wai tsou-i yüeh-pien.* In these collections one may locate the statements on any subject of Tseng Kuo-fan, for example, far more readily than in Tseng's voluminous works, and also statements of the greatest importance by such key figures as Shen Kuei-fen who left no collected works.

I have not been able to make use of all the writings of all the Restoration leaders. I have given greatest attention to those of Prince Kung, Wen-hsiang, Wo-jen, and Feng Kuei-fen; I have examined the others listed with some care, and cited them on particular points. For the writings of Tseng Kuo-fan and Tso Tsung-t'ang, I have been compelled to rely heavily upon classified editions and compendiums, six of which are here listed as documentary sources, nine as secondary sources.

The final group of sources in Chinese is made up of collected documents on particular events or institutions: the salt administration, the Foochow Shipyard, the various rebellions. To have investigated thoroughly all the aspects of these subjects would have been quite beyond the bounds of this book. I have listed here the collections cited in the text, even those cited only once, because in so far as they bear on the issues I have raised, they support my conclusions. They thus form a part of my basic evidence, even where their import is only *nihil obstat*. If I had failed to list the (Communist) Chinese Historical Commission's collections of documents on the rebellions, the reader might wonder whether they did not contain new evidence inconsistent with the picture I have drawn of the T'ung-chih period. They do not.

For the Chinese sources, I have used a broad definition of "documentary"; I have included not only government documents, but also the diaries, essays, and other private papers of prominent participants or eyewitnesses. I have considered the diary of the young Weng T'ung-ho a document on the Restoration because it was written at that time. I have considered that the later retrospective comment of Chang Chih-tung, although he was also a young Restoration official, was not documentary evidence; hence, although I have cited Chang's works, I have not listed them in the bibliography.

For the Western sources, it has seemed desirable to call "documents" only such writings as were actually used in government administration. Of the Western public documents cited, by far the most important are the British *Parliamentary Papers*. I have not been able to work in the Public Record Office, but fortunately the quality of the *Parliamentary Papers* reached its height in the mid-nineteenth century.[a] The evidence is that although the full record would amplify the picture of British policy in the 1860's given in the *Parliamentary Papers*, it would not substantially alter it.

The published French and American documents for the period are thin. The Department of State archives reflect the immaturity of American political reporting at that time. *Die Grosse Politik* contains no documents on the Far East earlier than 1894. Russian archival material is available only indirectly through a few books and articles, and even these have little to say about Russian policy toward China in the 1860's. Russian documents on China from the seventeenth to the early nineteenth century, and again since 1890, are relatively well known (if inadequately studied), but virtually nothing is now available on the intervening decades. The interests of Soviet scholars appear to begin with "the first steps of Russian imperialism in the Far East, 1888–1903."[b]

Throughout the book, Chinese and Japanese names usually follow the normal Sino-Japanese order—surname followed by personal name. The names of contemporary Chinese and Japanese scholars, however, follow the Western order, with two exceptions: (1) in citations of their writings in Chinese and Japanese, and (2) where the surname-first form is so well known as to make the Western order ridiculous, e.g., Hu Shih.

DOCUMENTARY SOURCES IN CHINESE

Chang kung hsiang-li chün-wu chi-lüeh 張公襄理軍務紀略, compiled by Ting Yün-shu 丁運樞 and Ch'en Shih-hsün 陳世勳, 1910, 6 chüan, 6 ts'e.

Ch'en Ts'an 陳燦, *Huan Tien ts'un-kao* 宦滇存稿, n.d., 4 chüan, 8 ts'e.

Chiang-su sheng chien-fu ch'üan-an 江蘇省減賦全案, with prefaces by the governor of Kiangsu, Li Hung-chang, the acting governor, Kuo Po-yin 郭柏蔭, and others, 1866, 8 chüan, 8 ts'e.

Chiao-p'ing Nien-fei fang-lüeh 剿平捻匪方略, compiled by an Imperial commission under the direction of Prince Kung, completed in 1872, 320 + 1 chüan.

Chiao-p'ing Yüeh-fei fang-lüeh 剿平粵匪方略, compiled by an Imperial commission under the direction of Prince Kung, completed in 1872, 420 + 2 chüan.

Ch'ien-tai yü-k'ou liang-kuei 前代禦寇良規, n.p., n.d. (ca. 1930).

Chih-kang 志剛, *Ch'u-shih T'ai-hsi chi-yao* 初使泰西紀要, 1890, 4 chüan, 2 ts'e.

Chin-tai Chung-kuo wai-chiao shih tzu-liao chi-yao 近代中國外交史資料輯要, compiled by Chiang T'ing-fu 蔣廷黻, Shanghai, 1931, 1934, Vols. I, II.

---

[a] Harold Temperley, *A Century of Diplomatic Blue Books—1814–1914*, Cambridge, England, 1938, Preface and pp. 127–33, 162–63.

[b] *Krasnyi Arkhiv*, No. 54 (1932), p. 34. The contents of the whole file support the statement.

Ching-men tsa-chi 津門雜記, compiled by Chang Tao 張燾, 1884, 3 chüan, 3 ts'e.

Ch'ing-chi chiao-an shih-liao 淸季教案史料, Peiping, the Palace Museum, 1937, Vol. I.

Ch'ing-shih ƙao (CSK) 淸史稿, revised edition, 1927–28, 529 chüan.

Ch'ing-shih lieh-chuan 淸史列傳, Shanghai, 1926, 48 chüan.

Ch'ou-pan i-wu shih-mo 籌辦夷務始末, Peiping, the Palace Museum, 1930, 100 chüan for the T'ung-chih period (*IWSM-TC*), 80 chüan for the Tao-kuang period (*IWSM-TK*), 80 chüan for the Hsien-feng period (*IWSM-HF*).

Ch'uan-cheng tsou-i hui-pien 船政奏議彙編, 1888, 24 chüan.

Chung-hsing chiang-shuai pieh-chuan 中興將帥別傳, compiled by Chu K'ung-chang 朱孔彰, 1897, 30 chüan; ... *hsü-pien* 續編, 1906, 6 chüan.

Chung-hsing ming-ch'en shih-lüeh 中興名臣事略, compiled by Chu K'ung-chang 朱孔彰, 1898, 8 ts'e.

Chung-ƙuo chin pai-nien shih tzu-liao 中國近百年史資料, compiled by Tso Shun-sheng 左舜生, Shanghai, ch'u-pien, 1926, 2 vols.; hsü-pien, 1938, 2 vols.

Chung-lieh pei-ƙ'ao 忠烈備考, compiled by Kao Te-t'ai 高德泰, 1876–80, 8 ts'e.

Feng Ching-t'ing hsing-chuang 馮景亭行狀, n.p., n.d., 1 ts'e. The full title of this memorial work on Feng Kuei-fen is 皇淸誥授通議大夫晉授榮祿大夫賜進士及第三品銜四品卿銜詹事府右春坊右中允加八級隨帶加三級顯考景亭府君行狀.

Feng Kuei-fen 馮桂芬, *Chiao-pin-lu ƙ'ang-i (CPLKI)* 校邠廬抗議, preface 1861, 2 chüan. These fifty short, important essays are arranged a little differently in each of the many editions. The 1885 edition, to which the pagination here refers unless otherwise noted, has an 1882 postface by P'eng Tsu-hsien 彭祖賢 The 1884 edition has a preface by Ch'en Pao-ch'en 陳寶琛. A later edition (Kuang-jen-t'ang chiao-pen 廣仁堂校本) includes a letter to Feng from Tseng Kuo-fan and an 1897 postface by Wang T'ao 王韜. The essays cited in the notes to this book are:

"Chieh ping O Fa i" 借兵俄法議, Ch. 2, pp. 97–98b

"Chien ping-o i" 減兵額議, Ch. 2, pp. 64–65

"Chih yang-ch'i i" 製洋器議, Ch. 2, pp. 70–74b

"Ch'ou kuo-yung i" 籌國用議, Ch. 1, pp. 38b–40b

"Ch'ung chieh-chien i" 崇節儉議, Ch. 2, pp. 60–61b

"Fu-ch'en shih-i" 復陳詩議, Ch. 1, pp. 45b–48b

"Fu hsiang-chih i" 復鄉職議, Ch. 1, pp. 10–12b

"Fu tsung-fa i" 復宗法議, Ch. 1, pp. 49–52

"Hou yang-lien i" 厚養廉議, Ch. 1, pp. 7–9

"Hsing shui-li i" 興水利議, Ch. 1, pp. 24b–26b

"I li-hsü i" 易吏胥議, Ch. 1, pp. 12b–14b

"Kai (*alt.* pien) chuan-li i" 改(變)捐例議, Ch. 1, pp. 17b–19b

"Mien hui-pi i" 免廻避議, Ch. 1, pp. 6–7

"(Shang-hai)she-li t'ung-wen kuan i" 上海設立同文館議, Ch. 2, pp. 99–101

"Sheng tse-li i" 省則例議, Ch. 1, pp. 14b–16b

"Shou p'in-min i" 收貧民議, Ch. 1, pp. 44–45

"Ts'ai hsi-hsüeh i" 采西學議, Ch. 2, pp. 67–70

"Tu ƙ'uei-ƙ'ung i" 杜虧空議, Ch. 1, pp. 19–19b

"Yung ch'ien pu fei yin i" 用錢不廢銀議, Ch. 2, pp. 78b–83b

Feng Kuei-fen, *Hsien-chih-t'ang kao* 顯志堂稿, in Feng, *Hsien-chih t'ang chi* . . . 集, 1876, 7 ts'e. "Chiang-su chien-fu chi" 江蘇減賦記 is in Ch. 4.

Hsien-feng i-lai kung-ch'en pieh-chuan 咸豐以來功臣別傳, compiled by Chu K'ung-chang 朱孔彰, 1898, 30 chüan.

Hsü Chi-yü 徐繼畬, *Sung-k'an hsien-sheng tsou-su* 松龕先生奏疏, and . . . *wen-chi* 文集, in *Sung-k'an hsien-sheng ch'üan-chi* . . . 全集, n.p., n.d., preface by Yen Hsi-shan, November 1915.

Hsüeh Fu-ch'eng 薛福成, "Chi Hsien-feng chi-nien Tsai-yüan Tuan-hua Su-shun chih fu-chu" 記咸豐季年載垣端華肅順之伏誅, reprinted in *Chung-kuo chin pai-nien shih tzu-liao*, q.v.

Hsüeh-Fu-ch'eng, *Yung an wen-pien* 庸庵文編, 4 chüan, in *Yung-an ch'üan-chi* . . . 全集, 48 ts'e, 1884–98. Ch. 2 includes "Chung-hsing hsü-lüeh" 中興敍略.

Hu Lin-i 胡林翼, (*Hsin-pien*) *Hu Lin-i chün-cheng lu* 新編胡林翼軍政錄, [Nanking] n.d., with a 1932 preface by Chiang Kai-shek.

Huai-chün p'ing-Nien chi 淮軍平捻記, compiled by Chao Lieh-wen 趙烈文, n.d., 12 chüan.

Huai-nan yen-fa chi-lüeh 淮南鹽法紀略, compiled under Imperial auspices by Fang Chün-i 方濬頤, 1873, 10 chüan.

Huang-ch'ao cheng-tien lei-tsuan (*CTLT*) 皇朝政典類纂, compiled by Lu Jun-hsiang 陸潤庠, n.d., 500 chüan, preface 1902.

Huang-ch'ao ching-shih wen hsü-pien (*CSWP*) 皇朝經世文續編, compiled by Ko Shih-chün 葛士濬, Shanghai, 1888, 120 chüan. (This collection should be distinguished from two other collections with the same title but different compilers.) Occasional reference in the notes is also made to *Huang-ch'ao ching-shih wen-pien*, compiled by Ho Ch'ang-ling 賀長齡, 1827, 120 chüan, and *Huang-ch'ao ching-shih wen hsin* 新 *pien*, 1901, 61 chüan.

Huang-(alt. *Ch'ing-*)*ch'ao hsü wen-hsien t'ung-k'ao* (*WHTK*) 皇(清)朝續文獻通考, compiled by Liu Chin-tsao 劉錦藻, Shanghai, Commercial Press edition, 1936, 400 chüan in four large volumes.

Huang-ch'ao Tao Hsien T'ung Kuang tsou-i (*THTKTI*) 皇朝道咸同光奏議, compiled by Wang Shu-min 王樹敏 and Wang Yen-hsi 王延熙, 1902, 64 chüan.

Hui-min ch'i-i 回民起義, compiled by the Chinese Historical Commission, 中國史學會, Shanghai, 1952, 4 vols.

Jou-yüan hsin-shu 柔遠新書, compiled by Chu K'o-ching 朱克敬, 1884, 4 chüan.

Kung ch'in-wang, I-hsin (Prince Kung) 恭親王奕訢, *Lo-tao-t'ang wen-ch'ao* 樂道堂文鈔, n.d., 5 chüan, author's preface 1867 (TC-6). The collection includes "Chün-tzu pien shang-hsia ting min-chih lun" 君子辨上下定民志論, "Li k'o i wei kuo lun" 禮可以爲國論, and "Wei cheng i jen-ts'ai wei hsien lun" 爲政以人才爲先論.

Kuo-ch'ao jou-yüan chi 國朝柔遠記, compiled by Wang Chih-ch'un 王之春 with the patronage of P'eng Yü-lin, 1891, 20 chüan.

Kuo Sung-tao 郭嵩燾, *Yang-chih shu-wu ch'üan-chi* 養知書屋全集, with a preface by Wang Hsien-ch'ien 王先謙, 1892, 55 chüan.

Kuo Sung-tao, Hsüeh Fu-ch'eng, and Tseng Chi-tse 曾紀澤, *San hsing-shih shu-tu* 三星使書牘, 1908, 3 chüan.

Li Hung-chang 李鴻章, *Li Wen-chung kung ch'üan-chi* 李文忠公全集, 1908, 165 chüan.

Li T'ang-chieh 李棠階, *Li Wen-ch'ing kung i-shu* 李文清公遺書, 1882, 8 chüan, 2 appendixes.

Li T'ang-chieh, *Li Wen-ch'ing kung jih-chi* 李文清公日記, facsimile edition, n.d., preface 1915, 16 chüan.

Liu Ch'ang-yu 劉長佑, *Liu Wu-shen kung i-shu* 劉武愼公遺書, 1902, 24 chüan.

Liu Yü-nan 劉毓楠, "Ch'ing Hsien-feng shih-nien yang-ping ju ching chih jih-chi i-p'ien" 清咸豐十年洋兵入京之日記一篇, edited by Meng Sen 孟森, *Shih-hsüeh chi-k'an* 史學季刊, No. 2 (1936), pp. 179–93.

Lü-li pien-lan: T'ung-chih; fu ch'u-fen tse-li t'u-yao 律例便覽同治附處分則例圖要, 1872 (TC-11), 6 ts'e. Prefaces by Chou Tsu-p'ei 周祖培 and others.

Ma Te-hsin (Fu-ch'u) 馬德新(復初), *Ho-yin Ma Fu-ch'u hsien-sheng i-shu Ta hua tsung kuei Ssu tien yao hui* 合印馬復初先生譯述大化總歸四典要會, reprinted in 1927 under the auspices of Ma Fu-hsiang 馬福祥, author's preface 1865.

Ming Ch'ing shih-liao 明清史料, three series, 30 ts'e, 1931–36.

Mu-ling shu chi-yao 牧令書輯要, compiled by Hsü Tung 徐棟 in 1838 (TK-18), revised by Ting Jih-ch'ang and issued for official use in 1869, 10 ts'e. Prefaces by Li Hung-chang, Kuo Po-yin 郭柏蔭, and others.

Nien-chün 捻軍, compiled by the Chinese Historical Commission, 中國史學會, Shanghai, 1953, 6 vols.

Pin-ch'un 斌椿, *Ch'eng-ch'a pi-chi* 乘查筆記, n.d., 1 ts'e; 1868 preface by Hsü Chi-yü; 1869 preface by Li Shan-lan 李善蘭.

Pin-ch'un, *Hai-kuo sheng-yu ts'ao* 海國勝遊草, 1869, 1 ts'e; foreword by Tung Hsün 董恂.

Pin-ch'un, *T'ien-wai kuei-fan ts'ao* 天外歸帆草, n.d., 1 ts'e.

P'ing-ting Kuan-lung chi-lüeh 平定關隴紀略, compiled by Yang Ch'ang-chün 楊昌濬, 1887, 13 chüan.

P'ing-ting Kuei-chou Miao-fei chi-lüeh 平定貴州苗匪紀略, compiled by an Imperial commission under the direction of Prince Kung, completed in 1896, 40 chüan.

P'ing-ting Shen Kan Hsin-chiang Hui-fei fang-lüeh 平定陝甘新疆回匪方略, compiled by an Imperial commission under the direction of Prince Kung, n.d., 320 chüan.

P'ing-ting Yüeh-fei chi-lüel. 平定粵匪紀略, compiled by Tu Wen-lan 杜文瀾, 1871, 22 chüan. 1865 preface by Kuan-wen 官文.

P'ing-ting Yün-nan Hui-fei fang-lüeh 平定雲南回匪方略, compiled by an Imperial commission under the direction of Prince Kung, completed in 1896, 50 chüan.

Shan-tung chün-hsing chi-lüeh 山東軍興紀略, compiled by Ching-pei ts'ao-t'ang (pseud.) 徑北草堂, 1885, 22 chüan. Postface by Chang Yao 張曜, an officer in the campaign against the Nien rebels.

Shen Kuei-fen 沈桂芬, "Shen Wen-ting Yüeh yao jih-chi" 沈文定粵輶日記, Parts 1–3, in *Chung-ho* 中和, I, 4 (1940), 95–103; I, 5 (1940), 79–84; I, 6 (1940), 92–98.

Shih-liao hsün-k'an 史料旬刊, Nos. 1–39, Peiping, the Palace Museum, 1930–31.

Ssu-ch'uan yen-fa chih 四川鹽法志, compiled under the direction of the governor-general, Ting Pao-chen, Imperial authorization for publication 1882, 40 chüan.

Ta-Ch'ing li-ch'ao shih-lu 大清歷朝實錄 photolithographically reproduced from the Mukden archives, 1938. The *Shih-lu* for the T'ung-chih reign (*SL-TC*), 334 chüan, is properly entitled *Ta-Ch'ing Mu-tsung I-huang-ti shih-lu* 大清穆宗毅皇帝實錄. In the notes occasional reference is made to the *Shih-lu* for the Hsien-feng period (*SL-HF*) and for the Tao-kuang period (*SL-TK*).

T'ai-p'ing t'ien-kuo 太平天國, compiled by the Chinese Historical Commission 中國史學會, Shanghai, 1952, 8 vols.

Ting Jih-ch'ang 丁日昌, *Fu Wu kung-tu* 撫吳公牘, preface 1877, 50 chüan.

Ting Pao-chen 丁寶楨, *Ting Wen-ch'eng kung tsou-kao* 丁文誠公奏稿, 1893, 26 chüan.

Tsei-ch'ing hui-tsuan 賊情彙纂, compiled under the auspices of Tseng Kuo-fan by a commission under the direction of Chang Te-chien 張德堅, compiler's preface 1855, 4 chüan.

Tseng Kuo-fan chiao-Nien shih-lu 曾國藩剿捻實錄, compiled by Lu Ti-p'ing 魯滌平 [Nanchang, Kiangsi Provincial Kuomintang Party Headquarters, 1930].

Tseng Kuo-fan chih-t'ao yao-lüeh 曾國藩治盜要略, compiled by Lai Wei-chou 賴維周 [*Hsin-shih piao-tien*] *Tseng Kuo-fan jih-chi lei-ch'ao* 新式標點曾國藩日記類鈔, compiled by Wang Ch'i-yüan 王啓原, Shanghai, 1923.

"Tseng Wen-cheng kung chi-wai wen" 曾文正公集外文, *Hsüeh-hai* 學海, No. 1 (1944), pp. 80–83; No. 2 (1944), pp. 81–85.

Tseng Wen-cheng kung hsüeh-an 曾文正公學案, compiled by Lung Meng-sun 龍夢蓀, Shanghai, 1925.

Tseng Wen-cheng kung ta-shih-chi 曾文正公大事記, compiled by Wang Ting-an 王定安, verified by Tseng Kuo-ch'üan and Li Hung-chang, 1876, 4 chüan, 2 ts'e.

Tung Hsün 董恂, *Huan-tu-wo-shu lao-jen tzu-ting nien-p'u* 還讀我書老人自訂年譜, 1892, 2 chüan.

Tung-hua hsü-lu: T'ung-chih ch'ao (THL) 東華續錄同治朝, compiled by Wang Hsien-ch'ien 王先謙 and Chang Shih-kung 張式恭, 1899, 100 chüan.

T'ung-chih chung-hsing ching-wai tsou-i yüeh-pien (CHTI) 同治中興京外奏議約編, compiled by Ch'en T'ao 陳弢, 1875, 8 chüan. *T'ung-chih Kuang-hsü tsou-i hsüan* 同治光緒奏議選, 1885, includes the same memorials.

Wan-Ch'ing wen-hsüan 晚清文選, compiled by Cheng Chen-to 鄭振鐸, Shanghai, 1937.

Wang Ch'ing-yün 王慶雲, *Hsi-ch'ao chi-cheng* 熙朝紀政 (alternate title: *Shih-ch'ü yü-chi* 石渠餘紀), reduced-format edition of 1898.

Wang Shih-to 汪士鐸, *Wang Mei-ts'un hsien-sheng chi* 汪梅村先生集, 1881, 12 + 1 chüan.

Wen-hsiang 文祥, "Wen Wen-chung kung tzu-ting nien-p'u" 文文忠公自訂年譜, in *Wen Wen-chung kung shih-lüeh ...* 事略, 1882, Chs. 2–3.

Wen-hsien ts'ung-pien 文獻叢編, Peiping, the Palace Museum, 1930–43, 46 ts'e.

Weng T'ung-ho 翁同龢, *Weng Wen-kung kung jih-chi* 翁文恭公日記, facsimile edition, ca. 1925, 40 ts'e.

Wo-jen 倭仁, *Wo Wen-tuan kung i-shu* 倭文端公遺書, 1875, 8 + 1 chüan.

Wu T'ing-tung (Hsing-ju) 吳廷棟 (行如), *Cho hsiu chi* 拙修集, 1871, 10 + 4 + 1 chüan.

Yü-chün chi-lüeh 豫軍紀略, compiled by Yin Keng-yün 尹耕雲 and others, 1872, 12 chüan.

DOCUMENTARY SOURCES IN WESTERN LANGUAGES

China

Imperial Maritime Customs, *Treaties, Conventions, etc. between China and Foreign States*, Shanghai, 1908, 2 vols.

Peking Gazette: Translation of the Peking Gazette for 1873, Shanghai, 1874.

Peking Gazette: Translations in the *North China Herald*, 1857–70, *passim*.

France

Ministère des Affaires Etrangères, *Documents diplomatiques (DD)*, incomplete file, 1860–69.

Great Britain

Hansard's Parliamentary Debates (third series), for the years 1857–71.

Hertslet, Godfrey E. P. (ed.), *Treaties &c., Between Great Britain and China; and Between China and Foreign Powers; . . .* , London, 1908, 2 vols.

Parliamentary Papers (Blue Books):

Correspondence Respecting Affairs in China, presented to the House of Commons following the request of Feb. 16, 1860.

Correspondence with Mr. Bruce, Her Majesty's Envoy Extraordinary and Minister Plenipotentiary in China, presented to both Houses of Parliament, January 24, 1860.

Further Correspondence with Mr. Bruce, Her Majesty's Envoy Extraordinary and Minister Plenipotentiary, 1860.

Correspondence Respecting Affairs in China. 1859–1860, presented to both Houses of Parliament, 1861.

Correspondence Respecting the Opening of the Yang-Tze-Kiang River to Foreign Trade, 1861.

China. No. 2. (1864). Correspondence Respecting the Fitting Out, Despatching to China, and Ultimate Withdrawal, of the Anglo-Chinese Fleet under the Command of Captain Sherard Osborn; and the Dismissal of Mr. Lay from the Chief Inspectorate of Customs.

China. No. 3. (1864). Papers Relating to the Affairs of China.

China. No. 4. (1864). Commercial Reports from Her Majesty's Consuls in China for the Year 1862.

China. No. 6. (1864). Extract of a Despatch from Sir F. Bruce, Respecting Maintenance of Treaty Rights in China.

China. No. 7. (1864). Correspondence Relative to Lieut.-Colonel Gordon's Position in the Chinese Service.

China. No. 8. (1864). Copy of Prince Kung's Answer to Sir Frederick Bruce's Memorandum Relative to the Affairs of China.

Reports of Journeys in China and Japan Performed by Mr. Alabaster, Mr. Oxenham, Mr. Markham, and Dr. Wills of Her Majesty's Consular Service in those Countries, 1869.

China. No. 1. (1869). Correspondence Respecting the Relations between Great Britain and China.

China. No. 2. (1869). Correspondence Respecting the Attack on British Protestant Missionaries at Yang-Chow-Foo, August, 1868.

China. No. 3. (1869). Correspondence Respecting Missionary Disturbances at Che-foo and Taiwan (Formosa).

China. No. 6. (1869). Correspondence Respecting the Outrage on British Merchants at Banca, in Formosa.

China. No. 7. (1869). Correspondence Respecting the Attack on Boats of Her Majesty's Ship "Cockchafer" by Villagers near Swatow.

China. No. 8. (1869). Correspondence with Sir Rutherford Alcock Respecting Missionaries at Hankow and the States of Affairs at Various Ports in China.

China. No. 9. (1869). Papers Respecting the Proceedings of Her Majesty's Ship "Janus" at Sharp Peak Island, near Foo-Chow-Foo.

China. No. 10. (1869). Further Correspondence Respecting the Attack on British Protestant Missionaries at Yang-Chow-Foo.

China. No. 11. (1869). Abstract of Trade and Customs Revenue Statistics from 1864 to 1868, published by the Imperial Maritime Customs.

China. No. 12. (1869). Correspondence with the Chamber of Commerce at Shanghai Respecting the Revision of the Treaty of Tientsin.

China. No. 1. (1870). Despatch from Sir Rutherford Alcock Respecting a Supplementary Convention to the Treaty of Tientsin Signed by him on October, 23, 1869.

China. No. 2. (1870). Reports by Consul Swinhoe of his Special Mission up the River Yang-Tze-Kiang.

China. No. 3. (1870). Reports on Consular Establishments in China in 1869.

China. No. 4. (1870). Memorials Respecting the China Treaty Revision Convention.

China. No. 5. (1870). Correspondence Respecting Diplomatic and Consular Expenditure in China, Japan, and Siam.

China. No. 6. (1870). Further Memorials Respecting the China Treaty Revision Convention.

China. No. 8. (1870). Report of the Delegates of the Shanghai General Chamber of Commerce on the Trade of the Upper Yang-tze River.

China. No. 9. (1870). Correspondence Respecting the Inland Residence of British Missionaries in China.

China. No. 10. (1870). Letter to the Chambers of Commerce . . . Respecting the China Treaty Revision Convention.

China. No. 11. (1870). Further Correspondence with the Chambers of Commerce . . . Respecting the China Treaty Revision Convention.

China. No. 3. (1871). Circular of the Chinese Government Communicated by the French Chargé d'Affaires.

China. No. 5. (1871). Correspondence Respecting the Revision of the Treaty of Tientsin.

China. No. 1. (1872). Correspondence Respecting the Circular of the Chinese Government of February 9, 1871, Relating to Missionaries.

China. No. 2. (1875). Correspondence Respecting the Settlement of the Difficulty between China and Japan in regard to the Island of Formosa.

China. No. 3. (1877). Further Correspondence Respecting the Attack on the Indian Expedition to Western China and the Murder of Mr. Margary.

United States

Department of State, Archives, China, *Instructions; Notes to; Despatches; Notes,* 1860–70.

Department of State, *Foreign Relations of the United States, 1862, 1863, 1868.*

PARTIAL LIST OF CHINESE SECONDARY WORKS CITED

NOTE: 208 works cited in this book, some of them of the highest quality, have been omitted here.

Ch'ai O 柴萼, *Fan-t'ien-lu ts'ung-lu* 梵天廬叢錄, Shanghai, 1936, 37 chüan, 18 ts'e.

Chang Te-ch'ang 張德昌, "Chin-tai Chung-kuo ti huo-pi ... " 近代中國的貨幣 ... , *Jen-wen k'o-hsüeh hsüeh-pao* 人文科學學報, I, 1 (1942), 72–92.

Chao Feng-t'ien 趙豐田, *Wan-Ch'ing wu-shih nien ching-chi ssu-hsiang shih* 晚清五十年經濟思想史, Peiping, 1939.

Ch'en Ch'i-t'ien 陳啓天, *Hu Tseng Tso p'ing-luan yao-chih* 胡曾左平亂要旨, Shanghai, 1932.

Ch'en Nai-ch'ien 陳乃乾, "Tseng Wen-cheng kung yü-lu" 曾文正公語錄, *Ku-chin* 古今, No. 41 (1944), pp. 27–31.

Ch'en Ts'an 陳燦, *Chung-kuo shang-yeh shih* 中國商業史, Changsha, 1940.

Chiang Hsing-te 蔣星德, *Tseng Kuo-fan chih sheng-p'ing chi ch'i shih-yeh* 曾國藩之生平及其事業, Shanghai, 1939.

Ch'ien Hung 錢宏, "Nien chün—T'ai-p'ing t'ien-kuo shih-ch'i pei-fang ti nung-min yün-tung" 捻軍　太平天國時期北方的農民運動, *Tai-p'ing t'ien-kuo ko-ming yün-tung lun-wen chi*, q.v., pp. 120–35.

Chin Chi-t'ang 金吉堂, *Chung-kuo Hui-chiao shih yen-chiu* 中國回教史研究, Peiping, n.d., preface 1936.

Ch'in Han-ts'ai 秦翰才, *Tso Wen-hsiang kung tsai hsi-pei* 左文襄公在西北, Shanghai, 1946.

Chu Ch'ing-yung 朱慶永, "T'ung-chih erh-nien Su Sung erh-fu chien-fu chih yüan-yin" 同治二年蘇松二府減賦之原因, *Cheng-chih ching-chi hsüeh-pao* 政治經濟學報, III, 3 (1935), 510–29.

Chu Po-k'ang 朱伯康 and Chu Tz'u-shou 祝慈壽, *Chung-kuo ching-chi shih-kang* 中國經濟史綱, Shanghai, 1946.

Ho Hui-ch'ing 何慧青, "Yün-nan Tu Wen-hsiu chien-kuo shih-pa nien chih shih-mo" 雲南杜文秀建國十八年之始末, 5 parts in *I-ching* 逸經 (1936) as follows: Part 1 in No. 12, pp. 9–16; Part 2 in No. 13, pp. 34–36; Part 3 in No. 14, pp. 36–39; Part 4 in No. 15, pp. 32–36; Part 5 in No. 16, pp. 29–33.

Ho I-k'un 何貽焜, *Tseng Kuo-fan p'ing-chuan* 曾國藩評傳, Shanghai, 1937.

Ho Wei-ning 何維凝, "T'ai-p'ing t'ien-kuo shih-tai Chung-kuo yen-cheng kai-kuan" 太平天國時代中國鹽政概觀, *She-hui k'o-hsüeh ts'ung-k'an* 社會科學叢刊, I, 2 (1934), 109–51.

Hsia Nai 夏鼐, "T'ai-p'ing t'ien-kuo ch'ien-hou Ch'ang-chiang ko-sheng chih t'ien-fu wen-t'i" 太平天國前後長江各省之田賦問題, *Ch'ing-hua hsüeh-pao* 清華學報, X, 2 (1935), 429–74.

Hsia Yen-te 夏炎德, *Chung-kuo chin pai-nien ching-chi ssu-hsiang* 中國近百年經濟思想, Shanghai, 1948.

Hsü Pin (Ling-hsiao-i-shih) 徐彬 (凌霄一士), "Tseng Hu t'an-wei" 曾胡譚薈, in *Kuo-wen chou-pao* 國聞週報, VI (1929), as follows: Parts 1 and 2 in Nos. 26 and 27 respectively; Parts 3–9 in Nos. 29–35 respectively; Parts 10–14 in Nos. 39–43 respectively; Part 15 in No. 45; Part 16 in No. 50. I did not use the subsequent parts of this series. There is no continuous pagination.

Hsü Ta-ling 許大齡, *Ch'ing-tai chüan-na chih-tu* 清代捐納制度, Peking, 1950.

Kuo T'ing-i 郭廷以, *T'ai-p'ing t'ien-kuo shih-shih jih-chih* 太平天國史事日誌, Shanghai, 1947, 2 vols.

Ling T'i-an 凌惕安, *Hsien T'ung Kuei-chou chün-shih shih* 咸同貴州軍事史, Shang-hai, 1932, 5 parts in 8 ts'e.

Liu Chien 劉儁, "Hsien-feng i-hou Liang Huai chih p'iao-fa" 咸豐以後兩淮之票法, in *Chung-kuo she-hui ching-chi shih chi-kan* 中國社會經濟史集刊, II, 1 (1933), 142–65.

Lo Erh-kang 羅爾綱, *Hsiang-chün hsin-chih* 湘軍新志, Changsha, 1939.

Lo Erh-kang, *Lü-ying ping chih* 綠營兵志, Chungking, 1945.

Lo Erh-kang, *Nien-chün ti yün-tung chan* 捻軍的運動戰, Changsha, 1939.

Lo Yü-tung 羅玉東, *Chung-kuo li-chin shih* 中國釐金史, Shanghai, 1936, 2 vols.

Ma Hsiao-shih 馬霄石, *Hsi-pei Hui-tsu ko-ming chien-shih* 西北回族革命簡史, Shang-hai, 1951, with a documentary appendix, "Ch'in-nan chien-wen chi" 秦難見聞記,

Pai Shou-i 白壽彝, *Hui-hui min-tsu ti hsin sheng* 回回民族底新生, Shanghai, 1951.

T'ai-p'ing t'ien-kuo ko-ming yün-tung lun-wen chi—Chin-t'ien ch'i-i i-pai chou-nien 太平天國革命運動論文集 金田起義一百週年, compiled by the North China University Historical Research Institute, 華北大學歷史研究室, Peking, 1950.

T'ang Ch'ing-tseng 唐慶增, "Tseng Kuo-fan chih ching-chi ssu-hsiang" 曾國藩之經濟思想, *Ching-chi hsüeh chi-k'an* 經濟學集刊, V, 4 (1935), 52–60.

T'ang Hsiang-lung 湯象龍, "Hsien-feng ch'ao ti huo-pi" 咸豐朝的貨幣, *Chung-kuo she-hui ching-chi shih chi-k'an* 中國社會經濟史集刊, II, 1 (1933), 1–26.

T'ang Hsiang-lung, "Tao-kuang shih-ch'i ti yin-kuei wen-t'i" 道光時期的銀貴問題, *She-hui k'o-hsüeh tsa-chih* 社會科學雜誌, I, 3 (1930), 3–31.

Wang Chih-p'ing 王之平, *Tseng Hu Tso ping-hsüeh kang-yao* 曾胡左兵學綱要, Nanking, 1935.

Wang Hsin-chung 王信忠, "Fu-chou ch'uan-ch'ang chih yen-ko" 福州船廠之沿革, *Ch'ing-hua hsüeh-pao* 清華學報, VII, 1 (1932), 57 pp.

Wang P'ei-ch'in 王佩琴, "Tu Wen-hsiu ko-ming chün ti t'uan-chieh wen-t'i" 杜文秀革命軍底團結問題, in *T'ai-p'ing t'ien-kuo ko-ming yün-tung lun-wen chi*, q.v.

Wang Te-chao 王德昭, "T'ung-chih hsin-cheng k'ao" 同治新政考, *Wen-shih tsa-chih* 文史雜誌, I, 4 (1941), 21–38; I, 5 (1941), 35–48.

Wu Tseng-ch'i 吳曾祺, *Ch'ing-shih kang-yao* 清史綱要, Shanghai, 1913, 14 chüan.

PARTIAL LIST OF WESTERN-LANGUAGE WORKS CITED

NOTE: 207 Western works cited in this book, many of them of the highest quality and of basic importance to the study of Ch'ing history, have been omitted here for technical reasons only. Although full references are given in the notes, I should like here again to acknowledge my great debt to the writings of Knight. Biggerstaff, John K. Fairbank, Chaoying Fang, Lienche Tu Fang, Franz Michael, Hellmut Wilhelm, and many others.

Alcock, [Sir] Rutherford, "The Chinese Empire and Its Destinies," *Bombay Quarterly Review*, No. 4 (1855).

———, "The Chinese Empire in Its Foreign Relations," *Bombay Quarterly Review*, No. 6 (1856).

Beal, Edwin G., "The Origin of *Likin*," unpublished ms. cited with author's permission.

Boulais, Guy, *Manuel du code chinois*, Shanghai, 1924.

Bourne, F. S. A., "Historical Table of High Officials Composing the Central and Provincial Governments of China," *China Review*, VII, 5 (1878–79), 314–29.

Chang, Chung-li, *The Chinese Gentry; Studies on Their Role in Nineteenth Century Chinese Society*, Seattle, 1955.

Chen, Agnes Fang-chih, "Chinese Frontier Diplomacy: The Eclipse of Manchuria," *Yenching Journal of Social Studies*, V, 1 (1950), 69–141.

Chen, Gideon, *Tseng Kuo-fan; Pioneer Promoter of the Steamship in China*, Peiping, 1935.

———, *Tso Tsung-t'ang; Pioneer Promoter of the Modern Dockyard and the Woollen Mill in China*, Peiping, 1938.

———, "Tso Tsung-t'ang, the Farmer of Hsiang-shang," *Yenching Journal of Social Studies*, I, 2 (1939), 211–25.

Chen, Shao-kwan, *The System of Taxation in China in the Tsing Dynasty, 1644–1911*, New York, 1914.

Chiang, Siang-tseh, *The Nien Rebellion*, Seattle, 1954.

Chu, Wen-djang, "The Policy of the Manchu Government in the Suppression of the Moslem Rebellion in Shensi, Kansu, and Sinkiang from 1862 to 1878," Ph.D. dissertation, University of Washington, 1955. Ms. cited with author's permission.

Cordier, Henri, *Histoire des relations de la Chine avec les puissances occidentales, 1860–1902*, Paris, 1901–2, 3 vols.

Costin, W. C., *Great Britain and China, 1833–1860*, Oxford, 1937.

D'Ollone, Henri Marie, *Mission d'Ollone, 1906–1909; Recherches sur les Musulmans chinois*, with notes by A. Vissière, E. Blochet, and others, Paris, 1911.

Eminent Chinese of the Ch'ing Period, edited by Arthur W. Hummel, Washington, D.C., 1943, 2 vols.

Fairbank, John King, *Trade and Diplomacy on the China Coast; The Opening of the Treaty Ports, 1842–1854*, Cambridge, Mass., 1953, 2 vols.

Fei, Hsiao-t'ung, *China's Gentry; Essays in Rural-Urban Relations*, revised and edited by Margaret Park Redfield, with six gentry life-histories by Yung-teh Chow, Chicago, 1953.

Freeman-Mitford, A. B. [Baron Redesdale], *The Attaché at Peking*, London, 1900.

Gumpach, Johannes von, *The Burlingame Mission*, Shanghai, etc., 1872.

Hsiao, Kung-ch'uan, "Rural Control in Nineteenth Century China," *Far Eastern Quarterly*, XII, 2 (1953), 173–81.

Martin, W. A. P., *A Cycle of Cathay, or China, South and North*, Edinburgh and London, 1897.

Meadows, Thomas Taylor, *The Chinese and Their Rebellions*, London, 1856.

Michie, Alexander, *The Englishman in China during the Victorian Era, as illustrated in the career of Sir Rutherford Alcock, K.C.B., D.C.L., many years consul and minister in China and Japan*, Edinburgh and London, 1900, 2 vols.

Morse, Hosea Ballou, *The International Relations of the Chinese Empire*, London, 1910–18, 3 vols.

Mutrécy, Charles de, *Journal de la campagne de Chine, 1859–1860–1861–*, Paris, 1862, 2 vols.

The North China Herald and Supreme Court and Consular Gazette (*NCH*), Shanghai, weekly, for the years 1857–70.

Rocher, Emile, *La Province chinoise du Yün-nan*, Paris, 1879–80, 2 vols.

Sargent, Arthur John, *Anglo-Chinese Commerce and Diplomacy (Mainly in the Nineteenth Century)*, Oxford, 1907.

See, Chong-su, *The Foreign Trade of China*, New York, 1919.

Stanley, Charles J., "Chinese Finance from 1852 to 1908," *Papers on China*, Harvard University China Regional Studies Program, III (1949), pp. 1–23.

———, "Hu Kuang-yung and China's Early Foreign Loans," Ph.D. dissertation, Harvard University, 1951. Ms. cited with author's permission.

Teng, Ssu-yü, "The Nien-fei and Their Guerrilla Warfare," ms. cited with author's permission.

Williams, Samuel Wells, *The Middle Kingdom*, New York, 1907, 2 vols.

Wright, Stanley F., *Hart and the Chinese Customs*, Belfast, 1950.

JAPANESE WORKS CITED

NOTE: Of the 52 Japanese books and articles cited in this book, 44 are included in John K. Fairbank and Masataka Banno, *Japanese Studies of Modern China; A Bibliographical Guide to Historical and Social Science Research on the 19th and 20th Centuries*, Rutland, Vermont, and Tokyo, 1955. The *"FB"* number of each is included in my citation. I have cited the following works beyond those in the Fairbank-Banno bibliography and in two well-known Japanese encyclopedias.

Dazai Matsusaburō 太宰松三郎, *Shina Kaikyōto no kenkyū* 支那回教徒の研究, Dairen, 1924.

Hoshi Ayao 星斌夫, "Min-Shin jidai no junsō goshi ni tsuite" 明清時代の巡漕御史について, *Wada hakushi kanreki kinen Tōyōshi ronsō*, Tokyo, 1951, pp. 591–606.

Inaba Iwakichi 稻葉岩吉, *Manshū hattatsu shi* 滿洲發達史, Tokyo, 1942.

Ikeda Makoto 池田誠, "Hokō hō no seiritsu to sono tenkai" 保甲法の成立とその展開, *Tōyōshi kenkyū* 東洋史研究, XII, 6 (1954), 1–32.

Ojima Sukema 小島祐馬, "Sō Koku-han" 曾國藩, in *Chūka rokujū meika genkō roku* 中華六十名家言行錄, edited by Yoshikawa Kōjirō 吉川幸次郎, Tokyo, 1948, pp. 276–81.

Saguchi Tōru 佐口透, "Chūgoku Isuramu no shimpi-shugi" 中國イスラムの神祕主議, *Tōhōgaku* 東方學, No. 9 (1954), pp. 75–92.

INDEX

This Index is comprehensive only for the main subject matter of this book. A great many figures of Chinese history, including a number of pre-Restoration Ch'ing figures, are referred to in the text, but in general they are not indexed, since this book is not the proper place to look them up. For the men and events of the Restoration and its direct sequels, I have attempted to include every mention that is informative and to exclude passing references that offer nothing solid.

For the major entries—e.g., Tseng Kuo-fan, Taiping Rebellion—the primary subentry is marked by some such phrase as "character and career summarized" or "cause and course." These primary subentries may profitably be (and usually should be) consulted on any aspect of the general subject, including aspects covered by other subentries.

A special problem is raised where there is an important statement by or about a man in the text, but where his name has been relegated to the Notes to place some limit upon the inevitably large number of Chinese names in the text. The exclusion of these references from the Index would be a disservice to those engaged in research in Ch'ing documents. Hence the following form: "Ma Hsin-i: on Wade-Hart memoranda, 41 (321, n 102)." This means that on page 41 at the point where note 102 is superscribed, Ma's views but not his name are given; his name appears in the note giving the source of his views, note 102 on page 321.

Abramovitz, Moses, 191
Accounting methods, Ch'ing, 185–86
Adkins, Thomas, 280
Agriculture: area under cultivation, 157–60; limits on development of, 192; Restoration's goal, 148–49; technology, 160–61
Aiguebelle, Paul d', 216
Aigun, Treaty of (1858), 35
Alcock, Sir (John) Rutherford, 25, 36, 258 n, 265, 293: on change in China, 64; on China's foreign employees, 216; on Chinese envoys, 273 n, 277, 278–79; on Chinese law, 259; on Chinese state and society, 38, 125–26, 132 n, 178, 249; criticized as pro-Chinese, 32, 39, 40, 241, 268–70; on extraterritoriality, 257, 289–90; on foreign access to interior, 257 n, 280, 283–84, 289; on Margary affair, 294; on mining, 183 n; on missionaries, 261, 262; on modernization of China, 10, 29–30, 251–52, 279, 280–81; policy toward China, 23, 28 n, 29, 41–42, 252, 295; preparations for treaty revision, 256, 268–70; on railways, 177 n; on salt reform, 173; on status of Shanghai, 260; on steam navigation on inland waters, 361 (n 180); on Suez Canal, 280; on transit tax, 255, 287, 288; on Tsungli-yamen, 241; Tsungli-yamen's attitude toward, 41, 281 n,

290; on use of force, 28, 30, 31–32, 227; on Wade-Hart proposals, 263; see also Alcock Convention (1869)
Alcock Convention (1869): Alcock on, 252–53, 280–81, 290–91; British government's views, 284; British merchants' views, 283–84, 290–92, 293; Chinese views, 284–86, 290; negotiations, 279–86; rejection of, 250, 290–95; significance of, 286–87, 293–94, 295; terms, 286–90; see also Tientsin, Treaties of
Allied forces (British and French): 1859 operations, 12; 1860 operations, 12–13, 225, 316 (n 11); withdrawal, 15, 35
Amnesty, 120–21, 215, 219
An Te-hai, 88
Anglo-Chinese War, second (Arrow War), 11, 24–25, 33
Antiforeign outbreaks: British policy on, 28, 30, 32; Burlingame on, 279 n; causes of, 30, 261–62, 276, 296; role of literati, 146–47; Anking, 32; Chinkiang, 30; Foochow, 31; Formosa, 30–31, 227; Kiukiang, 30; Yangchow, 30, 276 n, 283; see also Tientsin Massacre
Army, Chinese: cavalry, 214; discipline, 203; equipment, 210–14, 217–18; finance, 189–90, 207–8; leadership, 68–69, 80, 199–202; reforms outlined, 196; size, 208–10; training,

201, 213–14, 217–18; *see also* Banner system; Ch'u Army, Hsiang Army, Huai Army, Lü-ying; Foreign aid; Foreigners, employment of; Intervention, Western
Arrow War, 11, 24–25, 33
Artisans, Chinese, 150, 192–93
Audience, Imperial, 260–61, 273

Backhouse, (Sir) Edmund, 73
Balliuzek, Colonel L., 36, 233
Banking, 188–89, 194
Banner system, 52–54, 131, 165, 197, 204
Berthemy, Jules François Gustave, 36, 37
Bland, J. O. P., 73
Borodin, Mikhail Markovich, 302
Bourne, F. S. A., 55
Brown, John McLeavy, 278, 279
Browne, J. Ross, 36–37, 177, 292
Bruce, (Sir) Frederick W. A., 25, 36, 37, 41, 260 n: on Audience, 261; on Chinese view of foreign relations, 224; criticized by merchants, 39; on Gordon, 215; on Lay-Osborn Flotilla, 217; on Mixed Court, 258 n; on policy toward China, 26–27, 41–42; on residence in Peking, 260 n; on status of Shanghai, 29, 260; on Taiping Rebellion, 120 n; on Wen-hsiang, 71; on Yangtze regulations, 28, 256 n
Bureaucracy: disciplining of, 87–88; ethnic composition of, 55, 228–29; ideal official, 68, 91–92, 126, 145; local government, 141–45; official salaries, 90; outsiders in, 79–80, 86, 143, 145 n, 174; quality of, 69–70, 77, 79, 85 n, 94, 142; rule of avoidance, 90–91, 145 n, 267; size of, 125 n; training of, 267–68; *see also individual boards and offices*; Clerks, yamen; Corruption in government; Examination system; Foreigners, employment of; Personal aides; Rank, sale of; Recommendation, system of; Regionalism
Burgevine, Henry Andrea, 215, 237
Buriats, 236
Burlingame, Anson, 21–22, 36, 37, 39, 41, 71, 246, 256 n, 277, 279 n
Burlingame Mission, 25, 36, 39, 273 n, 277–79

Caine, Consul G. W., 30 n, 176 n
Censorate: composition of, 70; criticized by Hart, 264; functions of, 87, 89, 90 n, 140–41
Censorship. 132
Champs, Émile de, 278
Chang Chi, 304
Chang Chih-tung, 1, 81, 82, 130, 140, 213, 247–48
Chang Chih-wan, 162 n, 187
Chang Liang-chi, 80, 92, 115, 206 (369, n 47), 276 n
Chang Lo-hsing, 101, 119 n

Chang Sheng-tsao, 244
Chang T'ai-yen, 51 n, 301–2
Chang Tsung-yü, 102, 104 n, 106, 107
Chang Yin-huan, 355 (n 73)
Ch'ang-ch'ing, 236 (378, n 93)
Chao Hui-fu, 78 n
Cheeloo University, 242
Chefoo Convention (1876), 287, 293, 294
Ch'en Hung-i, 232 (377, n 58)
Ch'en Kuo-jui, 202
Ch'en Li-fu, 304
Ch'en Pao-chen, 124 (344, n 166)
Ch'en T'ao, 49
Ch'en T'ing-ching, 168 (358, n 131), 328 (n 8), 364 (n 248)
Ch'en Tu-hsiu, 3, 301
Ch'en Yü-ch'eng, 11
Cheng Tun-chin, 266–68 *passim*
Ch'eng-fu, 230
Ch'eng-lin, 230
Ch'eng-lu, 112–13, 204
Chi'i Chün-tsao, 52, 87, 89 (334, n 138), 174 (360, n 166)
Ch'i-hsiang (era name), 17–18
Ch'i-ying, 68, 231, 232
Chia Chen, 17, 380 (n 137)
Chiang Ch'i-ling, 53–54, 67, 87, 174 (360, n 166)
Chiang Chung-yüan, 305
Chiang I-li, 76–77, 80, 90, 91, 120, 164, 266–68 *passim*, 273–77 *passim*, 385–86 (n 84)
Chiang Kai-shek, 56, 300–308, 311
Chiang T'ing-fu, *see* Tsiang, T. F.
Chiang Tun-fu, 321 (n 101)
Chiao Yu-ying, 16
Ch'ien Ting-ming, 393 (n 192)
Chih-kang, 171, 278, 388 (n 101)
Chih-yung Academy, 130
Chin Chao-t'ang, 69 (328, n 9)
Chin-chih-p'u, sack of, 111–12
Chin-liang, 71
China Merchant Steam Navigation Company, 176–77
Ching-hsin Academy, 130, 131
Ching-shih, *see* Statecraft
Ching-shou, 16
Ch'ing dynasty, *see* Manchus
Chou Chia-mei, 230
Chou En-lai, 302
Chou Hsüan-wang, 46
Chou K'ai-hsi, 111, 112, 212
Chou Tsu-p'ei, 17, 273 (387, n 88)
Christianity, *see* Missionaries
Chu Ch'ao, 133, 355 (n 73)
Chu Ch'eng-lan, 137
Chu Hsüeh-ch'in, 209 (370, n 75)
Ch'u Army, 203

Ch'uan-cheng hsüeh-t'ang, 242
Ch'üan-ch'ing, 53, 168
Chuguchak, Protocol of (1864), 234
Ch'un, Prince, *see* Shun chüng-wang, I-huan
Chung P'ei-hsien, 246
Ch'ung-hou: and army, 200, 206 (369, n 47), 209, 214; on education, 131; in 1860 negotiations, 225; and foreign loans, 182 (363, n 219); on relief and reconstruction, 123, 135 (347, nn 64, 66); on salt bandits, 119, 335 (n 6); and Tientsin Massacre, 296, 297; and treaty revision, 271, 273–77 *passim*, 385–86 (n 84); on Wade-Hart proposals, 266–68 *passim*; on water control, 153, 161
Ch'ung-lun, 225, 229
Ch'ung-shih, 88 (334, n 134)
Civil Office, Board of, 87–88, 89–90, 143
Clarendon, George William Frederick Villiers, 4th earl of: and Alcock Convention, 292; and Burlingame Mission, 25; and imperial expansion, 24; on missionaries, 25; policy toward China, 25, 37 n, 41–42; on use of force, 28, 30–32 *passim*, 283
Clerks, yamen: in administration of justice, 140; character of, 91–92; in local government, 145; power of, 90; problem summarized, 93–94; in tax collection, 166
Cockchafer incident, 31
Commerce, *see* Trade
Communists, Chinese, 302–4, 307–8; *see also* Marxist interpretations
Confucianism: Han school, 59, 82 n; heterodoxy proscribed, 133; idea of change, 63–66, 267; idea of frugality, 148–49, 154–56; idea of harmony, 13–14, 18 n, 45, 100, 138, 245–46; indoctrination program, 62–63, 129–33 (*see also* Minorities); Neo-Sung revival, 2 n, 43, 59–60, 63, 72, 82 n; in twentieth century, 2, 5–6, 304; *see also* Bureaucracy; Rites, Doctrine of the
Confucian society: barriers to modernization, 9–10, 20, 21, 64, 84, 92–93, 125, 141, 190–95, 196, 201, 220–21, 248, 301; character of, 3, 61, 125–26; family, 135, 136–37; foreign relations in, 222–24; private property in, 4–5, 194
Conservatism, Chinese: contrasted with European, 1–2; limitations of, 64; principles of, 2–6, 312; *see also* Confucianism; Confucian society
Consular jurisdiction, 257–58
Coolie trade, 233, 286
Copper, 152, 184, 187–88
Corruption in government, 81, 88–90, 145, 186

Derby, Edward Geoffrey Smith Stanley, 14th earl of, 24

Derby, Edward Henry Stanley, 15th earl of, *see* Stanley
Dew, Roderick, 216
D'Ollone, *see* Ollone
Dupuis, Jean, 117 n
Dynastic cycle, 43–46

Education, 4, 129–33; in Western subjects, 212–13, 239, 243–46, 248; *see also* Examination system
Elder Brother Society, 133
Elgin, James Bruce, 8th earl of Elgin and 12th earl of Kincairdine, 11, 14–15, 16, 27, 39, 41–42, 254 n, 260 n, 261
Empress Dowager, *see* Tz'u-hsi; Tz'u-an
England: on missionary question, 298 (*see also* Antiforeign outbreaks; Missionaries, Protestant); policy toward China, 22–33, 253–63 *passim*, 265, 270; Tsungli-yamen view of, 285; *see also individual statesmen* (Alcock, Bruce, Clarendon, *et al.*) *and* Parliamentary debates on China
Entrepreneurs, Chinese, 176, 184, 191–93; *see also* Merchants, Chinese
Envoys, Chinese, 267, 273–74; *see also* Burlingame Mission
Eunuchs, 88
Ever-Victorious Army, 214
Examination system, 48, 56, 77, 79–84, 127, 142, 143–44, 267–68
Extraterritoriality, 25, 33, 254, 257–60, 274, 283–84, 289–90

Fan Wen-lan, 41, 56, 220, 226 n, 248, 324 (n 47)
Fei Hsiao-t'ung, 3, 151
Feng Fang-ch'i, 243 n
Feng Kuei-fen: on administration, 68 n; on agricultural technology, 161; on borrowing from the West, 65, 239, 243, 380 (n 139); on clerks, 93, 94; early career, 78; on education, 130; on family system, 137; on fiscal policy, 186, 187; on foreign aid, 218 (374, n 154); on industry, 184; on land system, 163 (356, n 91), 165, 166, 167; and Li Hung-chang, 76; on local government, 143; on military policy, 201, 206 (369, n 45), 207, 208; on mining, 183–84; on official salaries, 90 (334, n 143); on pao-chia system, 137; on regionalism, 57; on rule of avoidance, 91; on sale of rank, 85; on salt system, 172; on selecting from antiquity, 66; and Tseng Kuo-fan, 327 (n 90); views summarized, 66
Feng Tzu-ts'ai, 119
Feng Yü-hsiang, 311 n
Finance, public, *see* Taxes; Revenue, Board of; Army, Chinese; Corruption in government; Accounting methods, Ch'ing

Fish, Hamilton, 37 n
Fontanier, Henri, 297
Foochow Shipyard, 162, 212–13
Foreign aid, 211, 214–18: against rebellions, 101, 107, 113, 117; *see also* Foreigners, employment of; Intervention, Western
Foreigners, employment of: in army, 202, 214–17; in civil administration, 93, 181, 183, 194, 212
Foreign policy, Chinese, *see* Tributary system; Tsungli-yamen; *see also specific events and issues*
Foreign settlements in China, 29, 34, 39–40, 259–60
France: on Alcock convention, 291–92; and Indo-China, 117; intervention in Korea, 223, 238, 240; and missionary affairs, 275, 276 n, 291–92, 298 (*see also* Missionaries, Catholic; Tientsin Massacre); policy toward China, 33–34; Shanghai concession, 34, 260 n; Tsungli-yamen view of, 285; *see also* Berthemy; Gros; Tientsin, Treaties of; Peking, Conventions of
Franke, Otto, 46
Fraser, Hugh, 280

Gentry: and Ch'ing throne, 7, 52, 57–59, 117, 120–21; definitions, 127 n; frugality ideal, 154; Kuomintang use of, 308–9; Moslem, 121; privileges of, 4, 128–29; role of, 57, 119, 125–28, 199; size of, 127 n; xenophobia, 146; *see also* Literati
Gerschenkron, Alexander, 195
Gibson, Consul John, 30–31, 176 n
Giquel, Prosper, 212, 216, 220, 292 n, 296 n
Gladstone, William Ewart, 24
Gordon, Charles George, 215
Grain tribute, 149, 163
Grand Canal, 104, 105, 106, 175, 176
Granville, Granville George Leveson-Gower, 2d Earl, 292–93
Grey, Henry Grey, 3rd Earl, 24, 25, 32
Gros, Baron Jean Baptiste Louis, 15, 16, 27
Gumpach, Johannes von, 218, 247 n

Hakka, 80, 98, 119–20, 122, 124, 131
Han Kuang-wu, 46–47
Hanlin Academy, 81, 89, 246
Hart, Robert (later Sir Robert), 18, 25, 36, 180, 182, 217, 278: and Alcock Convention, 280, 285; and Burlingame Mission, 277; and Chefoo Convention, 294–95; on Chinese Army, 197, 206, 208; on Chinese idea of change, 64; criticized as pro-Chinese, 39, 181; on examination system, 84; on inland navigation, 256 n, 361 (n 180); on land tax, 166; and Li-Gordon affair, 215; on official salaries, 90; on rule of avoidance, 91, 145 n; services to China sum- marized, 181; on transit tax, 287; and trans- lation of international law, 237; Tsungli- yamen's attitude toward, 41, 277; and T'ung- wen kuan, 244; von Gumpach suit, 247, 278 n; on Wen-hsiang, 71; *see also* Wade-Hart memo- randa

Heng-ch'i, 14, 180 n, 225, 229, 233
Ho Ching, 329 (n 41)
Hongkong, Chinese consulate at, 287
Hongkong and Shanghai Banking Corporation, 188–89
Hornby, Chief Justice Sir Edmund, 33, 258
Hsia Chia-hao, 230
Hsiang Army, 52, 99, 206, 211, 220: described, 198–99; disbanded, 205; leadership, 200; morale, 203
Hsiao-chen (Dowager Empress Tz'u-an), 16, 17, 19
Hsiao-ch'in (Dowager Empress Tz'u-hsi), 7 n, 16, 17, 50, 70, 88, 199 n, 268 n
Hsien-feng Emperor (I-chu): alleged valedictory edict, 16; death of, 7, 16; flight to Jehol, 7, 12–13, 27; and Tseng Kuo-fan, 52; and "war party," 12
Hsien-feng period, decline in, 77, 89, 151–53, 197
Hsin-chiao (New Teaching), *see* Islamic doctrine in China
Hsiu-wen, 140 (349, n 108)
Hsü Chi-yü, 229–30, 244, 311 n, 359 (n 152)
Hsü Tsung-kan, 182 (363, n 219)
Hsü Tzu, 156
Hsüeh Fu-ch'eng, 45
Hsüeh Huan, 88, 219, 226, 240, 382 (n 17)
Hu Chia-yü, 79, 162, 345 (n 16), 357 (n 117), 361 (n 171)
Hu Ch'ing-yüan, 139 (349, n 100), 141 (350, n 112)
Hu Lin-i, 14 n, 70, 153, 200, 267, 300: achieve- ments, 49; on army, 202–3; in campaigns against Taiping, 11, 98; Chiang Kai-shek on, 302–3, 307–8, 311; K'ang Yu-wei on, 207; Kuomintang on, 303, 305; on Kweichow, 118; and land tax reduction, 69, 154, 164; on moral training, 126; philosophic training of, 60; role summarized, 76; and selection of officials, 77; Ts'ai O on, 302, 310
Hu-pu, *see* Revenue, Board of
Hu Sheng, 41, 286
Hu Shih, 308, 310–11
Hua-chung University, 242
Huai Army, 104, 199 n, 200, 209
Huai River, 162, 163
Huang Tsan-t'ang, 380 (n 139)
Huang Ts'ung, 114
Huang Wei-hsüan, 386 (n 84)
Huang-yai chiao, 133

Hughes, Consul P. J., 39
Hung Ch'ang-yen, 161 (355, n 75)
Hung Hsiu-ch'üan, 301, 302
Hunter, William, 246 n

I-chu, *see* Hsien-feng Emperor
I-hsin, *see* Kung ch'in-wang, I-hsin
I-huan, *see* Shun chün-wang, I-huan
Ignatiev, Major General Nikolai Pavlovich, 35
Imperialism in China, 8, 21; *see also* England;
  France; Russia; United States
Imperial Maritime Customs, 93, 181–83, 226,
  258, 277
Inaba Iwakichi, 56, 90 n
Indemnities, 242
Industry, cottage, 150, 151, 193; *see also* Tech-
  nology, Chinese
Industry, modern, 156, 184; *see also* Technology,
  Western
Inflation, 153
Interior, foreign access to: under Alcock Conven-
  tion, 289; British views, 25–26, 255–57; Chi-
  nese views, 274, 289; French rights, 283–84;
  problems of, 257 n; Russian rights, 283–84;
  see also Railways; Steam navigation
Intervention, Western: Alcock's views, 30 n;
  change in Western policy, 27, 31; Chinese
  views, 218–20; in Korea, 223, 238, 240; in
  Taiping Rebellion, 22, 101; Wade's views, 264;
  see also Allied forces; Foreign aid
Investment, Chinese, 176, 184, 191–92
International law, *see* Law, international
Islamic doctrine in China: Ma Te-hsin's teaching,
  115; New Teaching, 97, 107–12 *passim*, 115,
  116; Old Teaching, 108; *see also under* Moslem . . .
Isma'il, Khedive of Egypt, 280

Japan, 65, 232, 239; *see also* Meiji Restoration
Jardine, Matheson, and Co., 269
Jen Chu (Jen Hua-pang), 102, 104 n
John, Griffith, 64, 241 (379, n 124)
Johnson, Andrew, 36
Juan Shou-sung, 161 (354, n 69)
Jui ch'in-wang, Te-ch'ang (Prince Jui), 284–85
  (389, n 127)
Jui-lin: on colonization of Jehol, 160; on co-operation with British, 31; on importance of men,
  328 (n 8); on land tax, 164; and Liang Kuang
  administration, 80; on local government, 143;
  on official salaries, 90; on rule of avoidance, 91;
  on treaty revision, 273 – 77 *passim,* 385 – 86
  (n 84); on Wade-Hart proposals, 266–68 *passim;* on Western learning, 242, 248, 380
  (n 139)
Jung Hung (Yung Wing), 239
Justice, *see* Law, Chinese

K'ang Yu-wei, 51 n, 53, 60, 94, 205 n, 206, 207,
  306 n
Kazakhs, 235–36
Keppel, Vice Admiral Sir Henry, 31
Kiangnan Arsenal, 211–12, 239
Kiangsu Provincial Library, 131
Ko-lao hui, 133
Korea: and England, 232; and France, 223, 238,
  240; and Japan, 232
Kowtow, 260–61, 273
Kuan-wen, 18, 77: on army, 206 (369, n 47),
  209; in campaign against Nien-fei, 106; demo-
  tion and reinstatement, 89–90; on treaty re-
  vision, 273–77 *passim,* 385–86 (n 84); on
  Wade-Hart proposals, 266–68 *passim*
Kuang fang-yen kuan, 242
K'uang Yüan, 16
Kuei-hsiang, 155
Kuei-liang, 225–26
Kuei Wen-ts'an, 82
Kun-ko-cha-lo-ts'an, 236 n
Kunming, siege of, 116
Kung ch'in-wang, I-hsin (Prince Kung), 7 n, 40,
  71, 258 n, 300, 311: An Te-hai case, 88; attempted bribery of, 89 n; in campaign against
  Nien-fei, 106; on civil government, 68 (327,
  n 2); demotion of, 70; in 1860 negotiations,
  14, 224, 225; on foreign policy, 222–23, 227,
  232 (376, n 50), 249, 286; on frugality, 154;
  and Ignatiev, 35; on importing salt, 173; Marxist criticism of, 220; on modern arms, 210;
  praised by Western powers, 15, 16 n, 19, 30,
  36; on railways, 177 n; rise to power, 13, 17,
  72; role in domestic politics, 50; social and
  political philosophy of, 61–62, 133; on Treaty
  of Tientsin, 256, 295; and Tseng Kuo-fan, 53;
  in Tsungli-yamen, 225, 228, 273 n; and Wo-
  jen, 244; writings characterized, 70
Kuo-chi min-sheng, 153, 154
Kuo Hsiang-jui, 86, 174 (360, n 166)
Kuo Po-yin, 134 (347, n 54), 162 n, 273–77
  passim, 385–86 (n 84), 392 (n 191)
Kuo Sung-lin, 104
Kuo Sung-tao: criticized by literati, 147, 228; on
  education, 131; on foreign policy, 230–31; on
  Marxist appraisal of, 286; on poetry, 50; on
  public finance, 169, 353 (n 30), 359 (n 152);
  on railways, 177; role summarized, 76; on
  selection of officials, 78; on Treaty of Tientsin,
  232 (377, n 58); on Wade-Hart proposals,
  266–68 *passim*
Kuomintang, 300–312 *passim; see also* Nationalist
  interpretations
Kweichow uprisings, 80, 97, 118, 122

Labor force, Chinese, 193
Lai Wen-kuang, 102, 104 n, 106

Lan Wei-wen, 225
Land ownership, 122, 124, 129, 151, 159, 166–67
Land tax, 69, 149, 154, 155–56, 163–67
Lao Ch'ung-kuang, 116, 117, 201 (368, n 22), 258 (383, n 31)
Law, Chinese, 17, 61, 63, 138–41, 194, 257, 259, 289–90; *see also* Extraterritoriality
Law, international, 32–33, 237–38, 247 n
Lay, Horatio Nelson, 32, 217, 218
Lay-Osborn Flotilla, 211, 217
Le Brethon de Caligny, A. E., 216
Lei I-hsien, 53, 167
Levenson, Joseph, 5
Li Chao-t'ang, 230
Li Chen-ling, 159 n
Li-chia system, 165 n, 166
Li-chiao, *see* Rites, Doctrine of the
Li-fan yüan, 225
Li Feng-pao, 230
Li Fu-t'ai, 273–77 *passim*, 385–86 (n 84)
Li Han-chang, 188 n, 273–77 *passim*, 385–86 (n 84), 392 (n 91)
Li Ho-nien, 105, 106, 107
Li Hsiu-ch'eng, 11, 99, 211, 302
Li Hung-chang, 14, 70, 71, 73, 75, 88, 153, 181, 200, 207, 225, 230, 246, 248, 294: and agrarian resettlement, 159; on amnesty, 120 n; on audience, 387 (n 89); and Burgevine, 215, 237; in campaigns against rebels, 100–111 *passim*, 201, 209; character summarized, 76; and examination system, 81; on extraterritoriality, 260 n; on foreign trade, 180 (362, n 205); and Gordon, 215; and land tax reform, 163 (356, n 91), 165, 357; on local government, 142; Marxist comment on, 41, 220; on mining, 183, 275; on modern arms, 211, 212; on public works, 135 (347, n 66); on railways, 177; and regionalism, 198; relations with Ch'ing, 72; relations with foreigners, 216, 241; on relief, 134 (347, n 54); on salt system, 172; on schools, 130; on steamers, 176 (361, n 175); on Tientsin Massacre, 392 (n 191); on traditional learning, 132 (346, n 35); on treaty revision, 271, 273–77 *passim*, 385–86 (n 84); on Wade-Hart proposals, 266–68 *passim*; on water routes, 361 (n 171); on Western learning, 239, 242, 243
Li Hung-tsao, 89 (334, n 138)
Li-pu, *see* Civil Office, Board of, *or* Rites, Board of
Li Shan-lan, 78, 247, 321 (n 101)
Li Shu-ch'ang, 67 (327, n 96)
Li Ta-chao, 157
Li T'ang-chieh, 70, 71: career summarized, 72; on clerks, 94; on education, 131; on local government, 67 (327, n 96), 143; on pao-chia system, 136; on role of literati, 132 (346, n 36)

Li Tsung-hsi, 49, 156, 176 (361, n 180)
Li Tsung-jen, 311
Li Tz'u-ming, 174 n
Liang Ch'i-ch'ao, 60, 71, 307 n
Liang Ming-ch'ien, 386 (n 84)
Likin, 53, 93, 167–68, 185, 287
Lin Ch'üan-ch'u, 386 (n 84)
Lin-hsing, 234, 235
Lin Shih-kung, 135 (348, n 70)
Lin Tse-hsü, 78
Ling-kuei, 246 (381, n 155)
Linton, Ralph, 8–9
Literati: antiforeignism of, 147, 228, 250–51, 276, 295; and Ch'ing throne, 57–58, 62, 120–21, 199; and commerce, 149; and Foochow Arsenal, 213; and modern education, 244, 247–48; resistance to reform, 84, 147, 245; role of, 3, 128, 132; statistics on, 127 n; Taiping alienation of, 99; *see also* Gentry
Literature and arts, 49–50, 132
Liu Ch'ang-yu: on agrarian resettlement, 353–54 (n 52); on education, 131 (346, n 28); and foreign loans, 182 (363, n 219); on public works, 135 (347, n 66); on selection of officials, 331 (n 72); on status of Bannermen, 54; on Western military training, 214 (372, n 112)
Liu Chin-t'ang, 111, 112
Liu Ch'ing, 159 (354, n 53)
Liu Ju-ch'iu, 67
Liu K'un-i: on clerks, 140; on examination system, 84; on foreign trade, 179; on land tax, 357 (n 117); on likin, 169; on militia system, 206 (369, n 47); on missionaries, 277 n; on rule of avoidance, 91; on Tientsin Massacre, 392 (n 191); on treaty revision, 273–77 *passim*, 385–86 (n 84); on Wade-Hart proposals, 266–68 *passim*
Liu Ping-hou, 357 (n 117)
Liu Sung-shan, 111, 200
Liu Tien, 111, 355 (n 73)
Liu Yü-nan, 86, 316 (n 11)
Liu Yüeh-chao, 116, 117
Liu Yung-fu, 119
Lo Erh-kang, 199, 206
Lo Ping-chang, 53, 76, 91, 92, 116, 168, 169, 267
Lo Tse-nan, 60
Loans, foreign, 182, 280
Lü Hsu-ch'eng, 187
Lü-ying, 54, 197, 204–5
Lung-men Academy, 130

Ma Chan-ao, 110, 112, 121
Ma Erh, 109
Ma Fu-ch'u, *see* Ma Te-hsin
Ma Hsiang-ju, 139 (349, n 100)

Ma Hsien, *see* Ma Ju-lung
Ma Hsin-i, 188 n, 207: and Alcock Convention, 290 (390, n 149); career, 76; on land tax, 164; on missionary question, 351 (n 140); on reconstruction, 158, 354 (n 53); on restoration, 49; and Tientsin Massacre, 392 (n 191); on treaty revision, 273–77 *passim*, 385–86 (n 84); on Wade-Hart memoranda, 41 (321, n 102), 266–68 *passim*; on water control, 355 (n 74)
Ma Hua-lung, 109–14 *passim*
Ma Ju-lung (Ma Hsien), 114–17 *passim*, 121
Ma Kuei-yüan, 110, 112
Ma Ming-hsin, 108
Ma Te-hsin (Ma Fu-ch'u, Ma Te-hsing, Ma To-sin), 114, 115, 116, 121
Ma Wen-lu, 110, 112
Ma Yüan-jui, 67 (327, n 96), 144
Macartney, Samuel Halliday (later Sir Halliday), 75, 216
Manchuria: administration, 52; colonization of, 52, 160; disturbances in, 119, 209; reconstruction, 124
Manchus: and land confiscation, 151 n; role in bureaucracy, 228–29; Sinicization of, 51–56, 129; *see also* Banner system
Manufacturing, *see* Industry
Mao Ch'ang-hsi, 168, 230, 393 (n 192)
Mao Hung-pin, 169, 181 n
Margary, Augustus Raymond, 294
Maritime Customs, *see* Imperial Maritime Customs
Markets, 150, 193–94
Martin, W. A. P.: criticized allies in 1859, 241; and introduction of international law, 237; on Lay-Osborn Flotilla, 218; Marxist comment on, 276 n; on Tung Hsün, 229; on T'ung-wen kuan, 247; on Wen-hsiang, 71
Marx, Karl, 24–25
Marxist interpretations of: Alcock Convention, 286; antiforeign outbreaks, 276 n; British policy, 293; Ch'ing alienation of people, 204 n; Co-operative Policy, 41; Doctrine of the Rites, 301; Feng Kuei-fen, 327 (n 90); foreign aid to Ch'ing, 219–20; gentry, 127–28; Hsiang Army, 199; imperialism in China, 21, 51; Kuomintang, 303–4; Li Hung-chang, 73, 248; Maritime Customs, 181; Nien-fei Rebellion, 102; pao-chia system, 137 n; role of Manchus, 51, 56, 324 (n 47); Taiping Rebellion, 99; Tientsin Massacre, 299 n; Tseng Kuo-fan, 73, 199, 301, 330 (n 46), 353 (n 34); Tso Tsung-t'ang, 73, 363 (n 221); Tsungli-yamen, 226 n, 231; T'ung-chih Restoration, 70, 99, 301; T'ung-wen kuan, 248
Meadows, Thomas Taylor, 148 n
Medhurst, Consul W. H., 30
Mei Tseng-liang, 43

Meiji Restoration, 45 n, 131, 150, 153, 191, 193
Merchants, Chinese: as compradors, 243; in foreign trade, 8, 179–80; interests and aims of, 127, 191–92; as officials, 80, 86; restrictions on, 149–50
Merchants, Western: on Alcock Convention, 283–84, 290–92, 293; attitude toward China, 16, 19–20, 27–28, 29, 37–38; on British policy, 27–30; interests summarized, 253–61 *passim*; on Treaty of Tientsin, 251; on treaty revision, 241, 268–70; on Tsungli-yamen, 233
Méritens, Baron de, 266
Mesny, William, 214
Metropolitan Field Force (Shen-chi-ying), 103, 106, 200, 214
Miao, 122, 124, 131
Miao P'ei-lin, 101, 121
Militia system, 137, 205–6
Ming-hsü, 236 (378, n 95)
Ming-i, 235, 236 (378, n 93)
Mining, 113–14, 150, 183–84, 275
Minorities: indoctrination of, 123–24, 130–31; Russian influence on, 234–36; *see also* Hakka; Manchus; Miao; Moslems
Missionaries, Catholic: in education, 242; French protection of, 34, 291–92; rights in interior, 262; on Tsungli-yamen, 298; *see also* Tientsin Massacre
Missionaries, Chinese views of, 30, 146–47, 261, 266, 275–77, 296, 298
Missionaries, Protestant: British government's policy on, 25, 32, 261–63; in education, 242; views and interests of, 28, 253, 262–63; *see also* Antiforeign outbreaks
Mixed Court, Shanghai, 258–59
Modernization of China, *see* Confucianism; Confucian society; Reform; Western influence
Money, 153, 186–88, 194
Mongolia, 160, 234–36
Moslem Rebellion, Northwestern: amnesty, 121; attitude of people, 203–4; cause and course, 107–13; destruction, 122; reconstruction, 123, 130, 203–4; relations with other rebellions, 97, 109; Russian interference, 219, 235
Moslem Rebellion, Southwestern: cause and course, 113–17; destruction, 122; reconstruction, 124
Moslems in China: customs, 107–8; official Ch'ing policy toward, 107, 110, 116, 117; *see also* Islamic doctrine in China
Most-favored-nation principle, 287
Mu, Ahun (Imām), 109
Mu-yin, 15, 16
Mu-yu, 92–93
Muraviev, Count Nikolai Nikolaevich, 35

Nationalism, Chinese, 2, 301–2, 307, 312

Nationalist interpretations of: Hsiang Army, 199; imperialism, 21, 51; likin, 53; role of Manchus, 51, 56; *see also* Kuomintang

Navy, Chinese, *see* Yangtze Navy; Foochow Shipyard

New Teaching, *see* Islamic doctrine in China

Nien-fei Rebellion: amnesty, 121; cause and course, 101–7; causes, 208; Kuomintang study of, 310; leadership, 96–97; popular support, 203; reasons for failure, 310; reconstruction, 123, 209–10; recruitment, 119; relations with clerks, 145 n; relations with other rebellions, 97; Western arms, 107, 219

Ollone, Henri Marie Gustave, vicomte d', 115

Opium, 289

Osborn, Captain Sherard, 217, 218

Pai Yen-hu, 109, 111, 113

Palmerston, Henry John Temple, 3d Viscount, 24, 33

P'an To, 116

P'an Tsu-yin, 164 (356, n 100), 165, 168 (358, n 131)

Panthay Rebellion, *see* Moslem Rebellion, Southwestern

Pao Ch'ao, 209

Pao-chia system, 136–38, 308–9

Pao-yün, 82, 229, 248

Parkes, Harry S. (later Sir Harry), 14, 229 n, 249

Parliamentary debates on China, 24–26, 32–33, 181, 254 n, 262, 292, 293

Peasants: indoctrination of, 62–63, 125–26, 129–30, 132; role in society, 3–4, 62, 126; as soldiers, 201, 214; values of, 127, 154, 193

Peking, Conventions of (1860), 15, 35

Peking, right of residence in, 260–61

Pelcovits, Nathan A., 23 n

P'eng Tsu-hsien, 135 (347, nn 64, 66)

P'eng Yü-lin, 58–59, 169 n, 211, 392 (n 191)

Personal aides (*mu-yu*), 92–93

Pien Pao-ti, 140 (349, n 103), 143 (350, n 124), 161

Pin-ch'un, 277

Ping-pu, *see* War, Board of

Po Chü-i, 48

Po-chün, 81

Po-yen-no-mo-hu, 392 (n 91)

Poutiatine, *see* Putiatin

Prices, 134–35, 149–50

Property, private, 2, 4–5, 194

Protet, Admiral August Léopold, 216

Prussia, 238, 291–92

Public opinion, Chinese, 4, 86, 125–26, 133, 147, 202–4, 267, 274

Public opinion on China, European, 26, 216

Public works, 135, 153, 161–63, 176

Publishing, 131–32, 239

Putiatin, Admiral Count Efimii, 35

Railways: Chinese views, 175, 177–78, 266, 274; Western views, 26, 175, 177

Rank, sale of, 85–87, 88–89, 173–74

Rebellions, *see* Taiping Rebellion; Nien-fei Rebellion; Moslem Rebellion, Northwestern; Moslem Rebellion, Southwestern

Rebellions, local, 97, 118–20

Recommendation, system of, 77–79

Reconstruction, *see individual rebellions*; *see also* Agriculture; Public works; Social welfare

Reform: Chinese views, 266–68 (*see also* Confucianism, Confucian society, Western influence); Western views, *see* Alcock; Wade-Hart proposals; Western influence

Regina v. Reynolds and Holt, 33

Regionalism, 57–59, 70, 71, 72, 90–91, 197–99, 206–7, 220–21

Regular forces, *see* Lü-ying

Relief, 133–36

Religion, popular, 133

Restoration (*chung-hsing*): defined, 18, 44–45; historic usage, 46–48; *see also* T'ung-chih Restoration

Revenue, Board of, 85–86, 93–94, 149, 158, 185, 189–90, 207–8

Rites, Board of, 15, 225, 238

Rites, Doctrine of the: Ch'en Tu-hsiu on, 301; defined, 2–3, 60–63; Kuomintang on, 306–7; Li Tsung-jen on, 311

Russell, (Lord) John Russell, 1st Earl, 27, 41–42

Russia: on Alcock Convention, 291–92; border relations, 232, 234; exchange of books, 239–40; influence on minorities, 234–36; military aid, 217, 219; overland trade, 233, 283–84; policy toward China, 34–36, 320 (n 68); Tsungli-yamen view of, 285

Russian-language school, Peking, 239, 243

Salt: bandits, 118; import of foreign, 173, 233, 275; riots, 173; smuggling, 172

Salt monopoly, 93, 170–73

Sandford, U.S. Consul at Chefoo, 36

Sassoon and Company, 290

Seng-ko-lin-ch'in, Prince: ability of, 200; British view of, 15; in campaign against Nien-fei, 101, 103; in 1859 campaign, 12; in 1860 campaign, 7, 12, 14; on false military reports, 202 (368, n 27); foreign policy of, 14 n; on local government, 67 (327, n 96), 143

Seward, William Henry, 36, 230, 246 n, 260 n

Shanghai, status of, 29, 260

Shanghai Chambers of Commerce, views of, 28, 40, 255 n, 268–70

Shanghai Steam Navigation Company, 176
Shen-chi-ying, *see* Metropolitan Field Force
Shen Kuei-fen, 58, 70, 71–72, 230, 331–32 (n 84)
Shen Pao-chen: and Foochow Shipyard, 212, 213; and foreign loans, 182; on land tax, 154; on mining, 275; on railways, 177; relations with foreigners, 216; on sale of rank, 86; on treaty revision, 273–77 *passim*, 385–86 (n 84)
Sheng-pao, 17, 110, 121
Shih Ta-k'ai, 74, 97, 302
Shipping, 175–76, 274, 283, 289
Shun chün-wang, I-huan (Prince Shun), 284–85 (389, n 127), 285 n, 296, 391 (n 176), 392 (n 191)
Silk, 150, 161, 289
Silver-copper ratio, 151–52, 186–88
Sinclair, Consul Charles, 31
Sinkiang, 160, 219, 235
Social welfare, 133–36
Soochow, recapture of, 100, 120 n, 215, 241
Social usage, principles of, *see* Rites, Doctrine of the
Solun, 235
Somerset, Edward Adolphus, 12th duke of, 25, 32
Stanley, Edward Henry (from 1869, 15th earl of Derby), 41–42, 270, 283
Statecraft (*ching-shih*), 59 n, 63, 304–5
Steam navigation: coastal waters, 175–76; inland waters, 176, 274, 283, 289; views of Tso Tsung-t'ang, 266; *see also* Foochow Shipyard; Yangtze Navy
Suchow, recapture of, 112–13
Su-shun, 12, 16, 17, 52
Su T'ing-k'uei, 153, 356 (n 90)
Suez Canal, 280
Suleiman, Sultan, *see* Tu Wen-hsiu
Sun Chia-kan, 43 (320, n 1)
Sun Chia-ku, 278
Sun I-jang, 131
Sun I-mou, 168 (358, n 133), 174 (360, n 166)
Sun Ting-ch'en, 353 (n 30)
Sun Yat-sen, 56, 154 n, 267 n, 301, 304, 306 n
Sung Chin, 372 (n 107)
Supreme Court for China and Japan, H.B.M. (at Shanghai), 33, 247 n

T'a-ch'i-pu, 323 (n 38)
Tai Chi-t'ao, 303, 304
Taiping Rebellion: causes and course summarized, 98–101; Chiang Kai-shek on, 302–3; destruction, 7, 122, 152, 158, 171; foreign aid to Ch'ing, 218–19; foreign policy of, 223; funds for suppression, 167; ideology, 56, 62, 97, 128, 203; Kuomintang interpretation of, 304, 394 (n 14); leadership, 119, 120; outbreak and rise, 11, 315 (n 1); reconstruction, 158–59,

161, 210; relations with other rebellions, 97, 109, 110, 119
T'an Ssu-t'ung, 60
T'an T'ing-hsiang, 162, 230
T'ang Sheng-chih, 303
T'ang Su-tsung, 47–48
Tali, sack of, 117
T'ao Chu, 171
T'ao Hsi-sheng, 304–5
Taxes, 149, 152: collection of, 145, 185–86; receipts summarized, 195; remission of, 123, 152, 164; types of, 169, 184–85, 254–55; *see also* Imperial Maritime Customs; Land tax; Likin; Salt monopoly; Silver-copper ratio; Transit tax
Te-t'ai, 155
Technology, Chinese, 3, 150–51, 160–61, 194, 345 (n 8)
Technology, Western (Chinese views on), 210–11, 266–67; *see also* Foochow Shipyard; Kiangnan Arsenal; Yangtze Navy
Telegraphs, Chinese attitudes toward, 178, 266, 274
Tenantry, *see* Land ownership
Tientsin, Treaties of (1858): attitudes of Western merchants, 251, 253–61 *passim*; British government on revision, 253–63 *passim*; Chinese attitude toward, 251, 295; Chinese views of revision, 253–54, 271–77; missionaries on revision, 253; missionaries' rights under French treaty, 34; problems of ratification, 11–12, 15, 22, 27, 35; Western merchants on revision, 268–70; *see also* Alcock Convention
Tientsin Massacre, 32, 74, 250, 271, 293; summarized, 295–99
Ting Hsien, 162
Ting Jih-ch'ang: on administration of justice, 140 (349, n 101); as administrator, 140; on Alcock Convention, 290 (390, n 149); on censorship, 132; and examination system, 83–84; in foreign affairs, 230; on French policy, 392 (n 191); on land tax, 166; on local government, 141; on publication, 131; on public opinion, 133 (347, n 51); on sale of rank, 86–87; and schools, 130; on treaty revision, 386 (n 84)
Ting Pao-chen: achievements summarized, 77; An Te-hai case, 88; in campaign against Nien-fei, 105; on examination system, 81; and land tax, 163 (356, n 91); on military reform, 205 (369, n 43); on relief and reconstruction, 123; resettlement of troops, 209–10; on salt system, 359–60 (n 152); on selection of officials, 78; on treaty revision, 273–77 *passim*, 385–86 (n 84); on water control, 162, 355 (n 73)
Ting Ping, 131
Ting Shao-chou, 168 (358, n 131)

Ting Shen, 131
Ting Shou-ch'ang, 164 n, 165, 175 (360, n 170)
To-lung-a, 110, 200
Trade, domestic, 156, 167, 169–70; *see also* Likin; Merchants, Chinese; Taxes; Transit tax
Trade, foreign, 150, 151, 156, 178–81, 182–83, 191; *see also* Imperial Maritime Customs; Likin; Merchants, Western; Transit tax
Transit tax, 254–55, 282, 287–88
Translations from foreign works, 194, 212, 239
Treaties, Chinese attitude toward, 231–34, 236
Tributary system, 222–24
Tsai-ch'un, *see* T'ung-chih Emperor
Tsai-yüan, 12–17 *passim*
Ts'ai O (Ts'ai Sung-p'o), 302, 303, 305, 309–10
Tsatlee, 241
Ts'en Yü-ying, 116, 117
Tseng Chi-feng, 124 (344, n 165)
Tseng Chi-tse, 147, 363 (n 221)
Tseng Kuo-ch'üan, 100
Tseng Kuo-fan, 2 n, 14, 40, 70, 71, 72, 101, 114, 116, 153, 199 n, 200, 221, 246, 300: on amnesty for rebels, 120 n; Anking printing office, 131; in campaign against Nien-fei, 103, 104, 105, 107, 310; in campaign against Taiping, 11, 99, 100, 203; character and career summarized, 63, 66, 73–75; and Chiang Kai-shek, 302–3, 306, 307, 311; on Chinese envoys, 274; and Ch'ing throne, 52, 53, 57–58, 72, 198; death of, 7 n; on disbandment of troops, 205, 210; on earlier restorations, 49; on education, 130, 131; and examination system, 80, 84, 332 (n 107); family letters, 150; and Feng Kuei-fen, 327 (n 90); Feng Yü-hsiang on, 311 n; on foreign military aid, 218, 219; on granaries, 135; and Hu Lin-i, 76; ideal of austerity, 154–55; on indoctrination of troops, 203; on investigating officials, 87; Kuomintang cult of, 305, 308, 310; on land tax, 165, 357 (n 117); and Li Hung-chang, 76; on likin, 169; on local government, 142; on "loving the people," 133, 203; Marxist criticisms of, 41, 73, 199, 220, 286, 301, 330 (n 46), 353 (n 34); on military finance, 208; on military leadership, 199–200; on militia, 137, 206; on mining, 183, 275; on missionaries, 277; on modern arms, 210, 211; on navy, 211; on pacification of southwest, 113; on pao-chia system, 136–37; on popular support of army, 202; on primacy of agriculture, 154; on provincial boundaries, 69; on relation between foreign and domestic policy, 249; on role of gentry, 128; on salt system, 172; and selection of officials, 77, 78; on silver-copper ratio, 186–87; T'ao Hsi-sheng on, 304; and Tientsin Massacre, 298, 392 (n 191); and treaty revision, 271–77; Ts'ai O on, 302, 310; and T'ung-ch'eng school, 60; on Wade-Hart proposals, 266–68 *passim*;

on water control, 162–63; on Western learning, 239, 245
Tseng Pi-kuang, 118
Tsiang, T. F. (Chiang T'ing-fu), 35 n, 244 n, 310–11, 320 (n 68)
Tso Hsiung, 91
Tso Tsung-t'ang, 14, 70, 71, 73, 153, 190 n, 200, 207, 300, 302: on agriculture and forestry, 161; on audience, 273; in campaign against Nien-fei, 105, 106, 107; in campaign against Northwestern Moslem Rebellion, 109–13 *passim*, 120, 188; in campaign against Taiping, 11, 100; character and career summarized, 75–76; on Ch'eng-lu, 204; on Chinese envoys, 274; on civil government, 43, 68; on the Classics, 131–32; compared to Chou restoration leaders, 48–49; distrust of Cantonese, 274; on education of minorities, 130; on examinations, 80; and Foochow Shipyard, 212, 242; and foreign loans, 182; Kuomintang on, 305; on land tax, 69, 164, 357 (n 117); on local government, 141; as a military leader, 203–4; on mining and industry, 184 n; on modern arms, 210, 212, 213; philosophic training of, 60; preference for French, 266 n; on relation between foreign and domestic policy, 249; relations with Ch'ing, 52; relations with foreigners, 216; on relief and reconstruction, 123, 134 (347, n 54); in resettlement program, 159; on rule of avoidance, 90 n; on sale of rank, 86; on salt system, 171, 172; on selection of officials, 77, 78, 79; served as personal aide, 92; on size of army, 208; on strategy of pacification, 98; on treaty revision, 273–77 *passim*, 385–86 (n 84) *passim*; on Wade-Hart proposals, 266–68 *passim*
Ts'ui Mu-chih, 163 (356, n 91)
Tsungli-yamen: achievements summarized, 8; on Alcock Convention, 284, 285, 290, 293–94; attitude toward foreign officials, 41, 226, 277; composition of, 228–31; on England, 285; on foreign aid, 219; on France, 285; knowledge of West, 238–39, 267 n, 388–89 (n 108); on missionary question, 275–77, 298; on Russia, 234, 285; on sanctity of treaties, 231–32; structure and functioning of, 224–28; on treaty revision, 271–76; on United States, 278, 285; on Wade-Hart proposals, 265–68; on Western learning, 239–40, 243–44, 245–46
Tu Han, 16
Tu-hsing-a, 119, 200, 211, 273–77 *passim*, 385–86 (n 84)
Tu Jui-lien, 54, 66–67, 131
Tu Wen-hsiu (Sultan Suleiman), 96, 113–17 *passim*
Tuan-hua, 12, 16, 17
Tung Fu-hsiang, 111, 114, 121
Tung Hsün, 13, 219, 229, 230, 237, 241, 277

Tung Yüan-shun, 17
T'ung-ch'eng school, 59–60
T'ung-chih Emperor (Tsai-ch'un), 16, 49, 50
T'ung-chih Restoration: achievements summarized, 7–8, 312; aims of, 65–66, 68; Chiang Kai-shek on, 302–3; compared to earlier restorations, 48–49; dates of, 7 n; diplomatic achievements summarized, 248–49; economic achievements summarized, 157; end of, 299; general program of, 66–67; influence on Kuomintang, 300–312 *passim*; Marxist interpretation of, 301; meaning of era name, 18 n, 45, 49; military reforms summarized, 196, 214, 220–21; pacification program summarized, 96–97; reasons for failure, 9–10, 72, 94–95, 146–47, 166–67, 195, 196, 201, 220–21, 250, 301, 312; regionalism in, 59; role of Western powers, 20; significance of, 8–10
T'ung-wen kuan, 147, 241–48
Tz'u-an Dowager Empress (Hsiao-chen), 16, 19
Tz'u-hsi Dowager Empress (Hsiao-ch'in), 7 n, 16, 17, 50, 70, 88, 199 n, 268 n

United States: on Alcock Convention, 291–92; on Lay-Osborn Flotilla, 217; on missionary question, 298; principles of China policy, 36–37 (*see also* Burlingame; Seward; *et al.*); sends books, 240; Tsungli-yamen view of, 278, 285; on T'ung-wen kuan, 246
Uriankhai, 235, 236

Vlangali, General A., 36, 233

Wade, Thomas Francis (later Sir Francis), 36, 219, 258 n, 294, 298; attitude of Tsungli-yamen, 41; basic policy toward China, 41–42, 265; on Chinese idea of change, 64; criticized as pro-Chinese, 39, 40; on rejection of Alcock Convention, 293; and Tientsin Massacre, 298; on T'ung-wen kuan, 243
Wade-Hart proposals, 41, 263–68
Wan Ch'ing-li, 134 (347, n 63)
Wang Ch'ing-yün, 149
Wang Fu, 47
Wang Hsien-ch'eng, 169
Wang K'ai-t'ai: founds schools, 130; on militia system, 206 (369, n 47); on official salaries, 90 (334, n 143); on sale of rank, 86; on size of army, 209; on system of recommendations, 79 (331, n 80); views summarized, 67
Wang K'ai-yün, 77
Wang K'ang-nien, 93
Wang Pao-ch'en, 386 (n 84)
Wang Shu-jui, 133, 137
Wang Tao-yung, 67 (327, n 96), 80 (331, n 83), 140 (349, n 108), 143–44, 164 n
Wang T'ao, 321 (n 101)
Wang Te-chao, 286

War, Board of, 198, 205, 206, 207
Ward, Frederick Townsend, 214
Ward, John Elliot, 13
Washington, Treaty of (1868), 278–79
Water control, 161–63
Wellington, Arthur Wellesley, 1st duke of, 24
Wen-hsiang, 14, 72, 259 n, 294, 371 (n 84): and Alcock Convention, 285, 293; on allied occupation of Peking (1860), 12–13; on amnesty, 120 n; audience of 1873, 273; Chinese opinions of, 71; death of, 7 n; foreigners' opinions of, 36, 71, 228: on foreign military aid, 219; on foreign policy, 253; on foreign trade, 180–81; and international law, 237; in Manchurian campaign, 119, 209, 232; as military leader, 200; and missionary question, 296 (392) n 189); on modern arms, 210; negotiations with Russia, 234; on Nien-fei Rebellion, 106; on size of army, 208–9; on Taiping Rebellion, 315 (n 1); in Tsungli-yamen, 225, 228; and Wo-jen, 244; writings characterized, 70–71
Wen-ko, 218 (374, n 154)
Wen-lan ko, 131
Wen-ming, 88 (334, n 135)
Weng T'ung-ho, 71, 229
Western influence, 9, 65, 126, 157: on army (*see* Army, Chinese; Foreign aid; Foreigners, employment of; Intervention, Western); on economy, 151–52, 156; on examination system, 84; on ideas, 2, 212, 237–38, 239, 241–48 (*see also* Education; Feng Kuei-fen, Hsü Chi-yü, Li Shan-lan, Tseng Kuo-fan, Tung Hsün, Wen-hsiang, *et al.;* Hart, Wade, Martin, Williams, *et al.*); on local control, 146–47
Whampoa Academy, 302, 303
Wheaton's *International Law,* 237–38
Williams, Samuel Wells: on Chinese statistics, 148 n; criticized as pro-Chinese, 39; on Hsü Chi-yü, 229–30; Marxist comment on, 276 n; on modern education, 242; on new Chinese diplomacy, 230; on reconstruction, 158; on Tientsin Massacre, 298; on Wen-hsiang, 71
Winchester, Consul Charles A., 40
Wittfogel, Karl August, 51, 54–55, 324 (n 47)
Wo-jen: on Alcock Convention, 285 n; career summarized, 244; on civil government, 68 (327, n 2); on education, 131; on frugality, 155; influence of, 72; on likin, 168 (358, n 131); on local government, 141, 142, 143; on missionaries, 296; on moral training, 89 (334, n 138); philosophic views, 43; on primacy of moral worth, 68; on T'ung-wen kuan, 244–45
Wu Ch'uo, 82
Wu Hsing-ju, *see* Wu T'ing-tung
Wu Hsün, 127–28
Wu Hung-en, 387 (n 89)
Wu Hung-kan, 133 (347, n 48), 323 (n 26)

Wu K'o-tu, 204, 387 (n 89)
Wu K'un-hsiu, 152 (352, n 17)
Wu T'ang, 77, 130, 273–77 *passim*, 385–86 (n 84)
Wu Ting-yüan, 168 (358, n 133)
Wu T'ing-tung (Wu Hsing-ju), 72, 325 (n 68)

Yamen clerks, *see* Clerks, yamen
Yang T'ing-hsi, 246
Yangtze Navy, 210, 211
Yangtze river, foreign trade on, 28, 256
Yano, Jin'ichi, 50 n
Yeh Ch'u-ts'ang, 304
Yeh Wen-lan, 386 (n 84)
Yellow river, control of, 153, 162–63, 176
Yen Ching-ming, 86, 141, 162, 164, 174 (360, n 166)

Yen Fu, 60, 213
Yen Hsi-shan, 311 n
Yen Tuan-shu, 380 (n 139)
Yin Chao-yung, 240 (379, n 120)
Ying-ch'i, 110
Ying-han, 354 (n 53), 392 (n 191)
Ying-kuei, 209, 273–77 *passim*, 385–86 (n 84), 392 (n 191)
Yu Pai-ch'uan, 67 (327, n 96), 144, 145 n
Yü Ling-ch'en, 87, 143 (350, n 124)
Yüan Chen, 48
Yüan Chia-san, 218
Yüan Fang-ch'eng, 87, 145 n
Yüan Shih-k'ai, 302
Yün Shih-lin, 87, 143 (350, n 124), 174 (360, n 166)
Yung Wing (Jung Hung), 239